Islamic Theological Themes

Islamic Theological Themes

A PRIMARY SOURCE READER

EDITED BY

John Renard

UNIVERSITY OF CALIFORNIA PRESS

University of California Press, one of the most distinguished university presses in the United States, enriches lives around the world by advancing scholarship in the humanities, social sciences, and natural sciences. Its activities are supported by the UC Press Foundation and by philanthropic contributions from individuals and institutions. For more information, visit www.ucpress.edu.

University of California Press
Oakland, California

For acknowledgments of permissions and credits, please see page 435.

Library of Congress Cataloging-in-Publication Data

Islamic theological themes: a primary source reader / edited by John Renard.
pages cm
Includes bibliographical references and index.
ISBN 978-0-520-28188-2 (hardback)
ISBN 978-0-520-28189-9 (paper)
ISBN 978-0-520-95771-8 (e-book)
1. Islam—Doctrines. I. Renard, John, 1944–
BP166.I85 2014
297.2—dc23

2014005897

Manufactured in the United States of America

23 22 21 20 19 18 17 16 15 14
10 9 8 7 6 5 4 3 2 1

In keeping with a commitment to support environmentally responsible and sustainable printing practices, UC Press has printed this book on Natures Natural, a fiber that contains 30% post-consumer waste and meets the minimum requirements of ANSI/NISO Z39.48–1992 (R 1997) (*Permanence of Paper*).

CONTENTS

Preface xi
Acknowledgments xvii

PART ONE
THE SCIENCE OF INTERPRETATION:
READING THE SACRED SOURCES 1

1 · Qurʾān and Hadith 3
Theological Themes in the Qurʾān 3
Transcendence: Divine Throne and Footstool 4
Immanence: The Verse of Light and God's Anthropomorphic Features 5
Revelation in Creation and through Prophets 7
Divine Freedom and Human Responsibility 9

Theological Themes in the Hadith 12
Exegetical Hadiths 24
Hermeneutical Hints in the Hadith 25

2 · Interpreting the Sacred Sources 27
Varieties of Exegesis (Tafsīr) on the Throne Verse 27
Interpreting the Verse of Light 32
Avicenna on Metaphorical Meanings of the Verse of Light 32
Ghazālī on the Similitudes in the Verse of Light 34
Ṭabrisī on the Verse of Light 37
Abū ʾl-ʿAlā al-Mawdūdī on the Verse of Light 41

Theological Principles in Hermeneutics 46
Ibn al-Jawzī on Exegetical Method 47

Suyuṭī on the Occasions of Revelation 51
ʿAbd al-Jabbār on Rational Interpretation of Scripture 58
Shāh Walī Allāh on the Causes of Abrogation 65
Ayatollah Khuʾī on the Divine Miracle of the Qurʾān 68

PART TWO
THE SCIENCE OF COMMUNITY: MAPPING THE BOUNDARIES OF TRUE BELIEF 75

3 · Muslim Awareness of Other Religious Communities 77
Identifying and Evaluating the Beliefs of Others 78
ʿAlī ibn Rabbān aṭ-Ṭabarī on Interpreting the Stories of Other Faiths 78
Shahrastānī's Heresiography on Non-Muslim Communities 85
Ibn al-Jawzī on the Devil's Deception of Jews and Christians 92
Ibn Taymīya on Christian Alteration of Scripture 96

4 · Creed and Polemic 103
Creeds 103
Ḥanbalī Traditionalist Creed 104
Ghazālī's Ashʿarī Creed 109
Nasafī's Māturīdī Creed 113
Ḥillī's Twelver Shīʿī/Muʿtazilī Creed 116
Sayyid Aḥmad Khān's Modern Sunnī Creed 120

Intra-Muslim Polemics in Practice 126
ʿAlī ibn Abī Ṭālib on Heresy 126
Ibāḍī Views on Associating with Muslims of Deficient Faith 128

PART THREE
THE SCIENCE OF DIVINE UNITY: SCHOOLS AND THEMES IN SYSTEMATIC THEOLOGY 135

5 · Theological Schools and Principles 137
Divergent Schools of Thought 137
Shahrastānī's Doxography of Muslim Schools 137
Sālim ibn Dhakwān on the Murjiʾa 146

Methodological Overviews 151
Al-Ashʿarī's Vindication of *Kalām* 151

ʿAbd al-Jabbār's Muʿtazilī *Five Principles* 160

Theology's Foundation: Prophetic Revelation 164
Avicenna on Assessing Claims to Prophetic Revelation 164
Bāqillānī on Prophetic Miracle and Veracity 167
Ṭūsī's Ismāʿīlī Views on Postprophetic Authority 175

6 · Major Themes in Systematic Theology 181
God Creating: Transcendent Unity, Ongoing Involvement with Creation 181
Ibn al-ʿArabī on Divine Majesty and Beauty 181
Ibn Taymīya on God's Perpetual Creativity 186
Javanese *Admonitions of Seh Bari* on God's Perpetual Creativity 192

God Revealing 195
Ibn Qudāma on the Divine Voice 195
Jāmī on God's Voice 201
Mullā Ṣadrā on Divine Speech and Attributes 205

Experiencing God Hereafter 209
Bāqillānī on the Vision of God in the Next Life 209
ʿAlī on the Vision of God 211
ʿAbd al-Jabbār on God and Humanity in the Hereafter 211

Theological Bookends: Cosmogony and Eschatology 214
Wang Daiyu on Translating *Tawḥīd* into Chinese Traditional Terms 214
Nuʿmānī on the Greater Occultation of the Twelfth Imam 226

PART FOUR
THE SCIENCE OF HEARTS:
SPIRITUALITY AND LITERATURE 233

7 · Knowledge and the Spiritual Quest 235
Ways of Knowing: Acquired and Experiential 235
ʿAlī on Knowledge and the Spiritual Life 235
Hujwīrī on Experiential Knowledge 238

Theological Dimensions of the Spiritual Quest 250
Ibn al-ʿArabī on What Is Indispensable for the Spiritual Seeker 250
Naṣīr ad-Dīn Ṭūsī on the Spiritual Quest 259
Kemas Fakhr ad-Dīn on the Quest for Self and God's Oneness 264

8 · Poetic, Pastoral, and Narrative Theology 269
Poetic Theology and Theological Poetry 270
Sanāʾī on God's Attributes, Unity, and Anthropomorphisms 270
ʿAṭṭār on the Valley of Experiential Knowledge 276
Muḥammad Iqbal on "Secrets of the Self" 278

Pastoral Theology: Talking and Teaching about God 287
Rūmī on the Many Languages of God Talk 287
Ibn ʿAbbād on Relating to God's Attributes and Names 292

Narrative Approaches to Major Theological Themes 296
Ibn Ṭufayl on Acquiring Knowledge of Divine Names and Attributes 297
Najm ad-Dīn Dāya Rāzī on Muḥammad's Spiritual Finality 303
A Shīʿī Narrative on the Spiritual Status of Fāṭima az-Zahrāʾ 309

PART FIVE
THE SCIENCE OF CHARACTER AND COMPORTMENT: ETHICS AND GOVERNANCE 315

9 · Ethics in Theory 317
Divine Omnipotence, Human Freedom 317
Ḥasan al-Baṣrī on Moral Responsibility 317
Shaykh al-Mufīd on Divine Predetermination and the Battle of Ṣiffīn 325

Theories of Moral Capacity and Responsibility 326
Bāqillānī's Ashʿarī Perspective on Human Acquisition of Divinely Created Acts 326
Bazdawī's Māturīdī Perspective on Moral Capacity 332
Brethren of Purity on Divine Initiative, Human Responsibility, and Law 339
ʿAbd al-Jabbār's Muʿtazilī View of Ethical Principles and Theodicy 342

Classical and Modern Views of the Devil, Destiny, and Fate 350
Ibn Qayyim al-Jawzīya on God's Wisdom in Creating Iblīs 350
ʿAbduh and Afghānī on Destiny and Fate 358

10 · Ethics in Practice 368
The Foundation of Ethics in Practice 369
Juwaynī on Commanding the Good and Forbidding the Reprehensible 369

Theologies of History: Contending Narratives of Early Muslim Governance 371
Nawbakhtī on Divergent Views of the Imamate 371
Bāqillānī on Rightly Guided Caliphs and the Imamate 375

Theologies of Governance: Holding Up a Mirror to Kings and Sultans 380
Ghazālī on the Larger Context of Islamic Governance 380
Muḥammad Bāqir Najm-i Thānī on Justice and Discipline 382

Social and Personal Ethical Guidance 384
Ibn Ḥazm on Anxiety, Self-Knowledge, and Virtue 385
Ghazālī on Contentment with Divine Destiny 389
Shāh Walī Allāh on the Ranks of Sin 392
Mullā Ṣadrā on Forgiveness 395

Notes 401
Appendix: Synoptic/Comparative Table of Texts 423
Acknowledgments of Permissions and Credits 435
Index of Names of Persons 445
General Index 450
Index of Qur'anic Citations 457

PREFACE

SCOPE AND ORIENTATION

Islamic Theological Themes: A Primary Source Reader has five specific purposes. First, it offers a wide variety of primary sources as introductions to Islamic religious texts as well as Islamic theology and relational/comparative theology, especially for students who have some familiarity with the Islamic tradition and for readers with special interest in Islamic thought. Second, it broadens conceptions of Islamic theological literature beyond the confines of traditional "philosophical theology" (*kalām*), locating the latter within a spectrum of literature: *kalām* is thus presented as a particular *method* within the larger *field of inquiry* called *theology*. Third, it foregrounds the theological implications of a broad range of textual sources, from "pretheological" material on the scriptural-exegetical end of the spectrum, to the more practical and humanistic material at the other. Fourth, the collection exemplifies a rich diversity of views on a wide spectrum of topics, questions, themes, and contested issues, underscoring the problem so often posed by attempts to make sweeping generalizations about "what Muslims believe." Finally, it situates Islamic theological literature within the context of the emerging subdiscipline of relational/comparative theology. Some texts included here are new translations of works, either never before translated into English or available only in now-antiquated or less than reliable versions; some reprint existing translations never before widely available; all are freshly situated and introduced with a view to opening doors into the larger world of Islamic life, belief, and culture.

STRUCTURE AND CONTENTS

Islamic Theological Themes: A Primary Source Reader organizes the material into five major parts according to genre and theme. Text selection resulted from a number of considerations. First, I wanted to provide examples across a broad chronological and geographic spectrum, with attention to as many major figures, schools, literary genres, and theological themes as possible in a single volume. Second, a broad search gathered prospective texts already available in reliable translations, but published in older or less accessible journals or in anthologies of a much broader purview and not suitable for use in courses dedicated to theological themes. Third, in view of the resulting underrepresentation of major figures, schools, or crucial themes, I solicited previously unpublished translations from scholars specializing in those topics, or I contributed my own renderings.

Selection of material—given size limitations, availability and cost of texts previously published, and a host of other practical considerations—has required a number of difficult editorial choices. Paramount in determining the ultimate arrangement and contents has been the concern to provide as broadly representative a selection as possible, including some less celebrated, as well as better-known, figures, works, and schools across a broad chronological and geographic spectrum. The overall genre/theme arrangement is designed to facilitate maximum pedagogical utility. Some overlap from one organizational segment to another is naturally unavoidable.

I have adopted an overall organizational structure based on an adaptation of five traditional Islamic intellectual disciplines or sciences (*ʿulūm,* plural of *ʿilm,* "knowledge"): the science of interpretation (*tafsīr*), the science of history (*taʾrīkh*)—which I call here the science of community—the science of divine unity (*tawḥīd*), the science of hearts (*qulūb*), and the science of character (*akhlāq*). (Readers interested in making cross-traditional connections with Christian theology that build on this kind of structural approach might want to look, for example, at Bernard Lonergan, SJ's eight "functional specializations" in *Method in Theology,* University of Toronto Press, 1971.) A general developmental principle assumes the priority of selected foundational themes in scripture and tradition (Qurʾān and Hadith) and interpretation thereof (part 1). Part 2 moves to genres designed to delineate divergent views both within and beyond early Muslim communities, including perceptions of pre- and non-Islamic traditions as well as intra-Islamic articulations of the faith. Relevant material here includes heresiography, creedal formulations, and polemic. In part 3, the focus shifts to texts dealing with principles, methodologies, and foundational themes associated with various "schools" of systematic theology. Diverse theological dimensions associated with "spirituality" and communicated through several literary genres occupy part 4. Finally, theoretical and functional aspects of theological ethics form the substance of part 5.

A note on optimal pedagogical utility of the text: Differing approaches might occasionally suggest reordering chapters or even whole parts. For example, though scriptural (Qur'ān) and traditional texts (Hadith) and exegesis thereof are situated first, some might want to have students read chapters 3 and 4 first and then return to the foundational texts after providing some specific context in advance.

STYLE AND PRESENTATION

Practical editorial concerns have led to specific choices in respect to transliteration, general presentation, style, and annotation. I address the ever-vexing matter of transliteration as follows: I include macrons (long vowels), along with the Unicode-supplied ayn, hamza, and sublinear Arabic diacritical devices. Another aid to optimal pronunciation is the use of elision in the case of Arabic compounds where "sun letters" are involved (dropping the *l* in the definite article *al-* and in effect doubling the initial consonant of the following word, such as Jalāl ad-Dīn rather than Jalāl al-Dīn). As for dating conventions, I have opted to supply solar dates only rather than including Islamic "lunar" or Hijrī dates. I have generally left out the initial definite article (*al-*) before often-used proper names, such as Ḥasan, after first use in a text.

With respect to reproducing texts previously published many years ago, I have taken the liberty of freshening up the diction by replacing archaisms (such as, *thee, thou, dost, wherein, yea verily,* etc.) with more current usage, and I have inserted gender-inclusive equivalents where appropriate. I have also changed British spellings to American (e.g., honour to honor, etc.).

In order to standardize treatment of in-text apparatus, I have used the following conventions: *Parentheses* are used for (1) Qur'ān citations (sūra:verse), (2) glosses (either from English to language of origin or vice-versa), and (3) dates of major figures mentioned, including those mentioned in primary texts. *Brackets* indicate insertions into primary texts (other than parenthetical insertions just listed) that are implied but not explicitly included in original text, for example, "And he [Muḥammad] said . . . ," or portions of names added for the purpose of clearer identification, for example, Ḥasan [al-Baṣrī].

To render the reading of difficult texts as smooth as possible, I have deleted honorific and devotional interjections common to traditional Islamic texts (e.g., "Muḥammad, may God bless him and give him peace," and other such items associated with major figures such as pre-Islamic prophets, Companions of Muḥammad, and deceased individuals of high reputation). Readers familiar with traditional Islamic written discourse will be aware of what is missing, and teachers can easily inform students accordingly.

Concern for maximum pedagogical utility has in many instances led to modifications in the annotation provided in the original versions of texts reproduced here. I have exercised editorial license in deleting or abbreviating identifying notes originally included with previously published translations in cases where the item glossed has been so noted earlier in the volume, or when the note would have been of use to specialists only. I have also minimized notes dedicated to text-critical questions or extended discussions of related scholarship, and I have deleted notes clarifying technical terms where those terms have been explained earlier in the anthology or glossed parenthetically in the text. In general, other "identifying notes" are provided only on first appearance of a crucial name or technical term. I have also sparingly retained in-text parenthetical provision of Arabic or other original language terms, occasionally deleting from translators' versions.

In some instances the translators whose contributions are the substance of this volume have included parenthetical reference to the pagination or other text locator (e.g., paragraph or item number) in the original; to simplify reading I have taken the liberty of removing these references as well. And in the interest of optimal coverage of important texts on key themes representing major schools and figures, I have occasionally opted to abbreviate some texts, leaving out segments less pedagogically critical, as indicated by an ellipsis at the end of a paragraph or by bracketed explanations as to what has been left out.

Finally, readers will notice that in some instances a given Qur'ānic quotation may appear in slightly different renderings. I have not tried to standardize these translations, first, because they represent legitimate alternatives by serious scholars, and second, because the variation is in itself a useful reminder that translation of such ancient texts can never be presumed final and definitive.

. . .

A note about the appended Synoptic/Comparative Table of Texts: It provides essential data on texts in order of their appearance in the collection, with quick reference to the scope and variety of major figures, schools, themes, and literary genres and a few hints of the many religious and intellectual associations in the background of the authors. Like other condensed schematic devices of its kind, its drawback is the oversimplification that inevitably attends attempts at compact characterization of such complex and expansive realities as this volume embraces. In particular, the data supplied in the last column, on "affiliations," is occasionally based on inference and does not account for the fact that many important figures maintained "hybrid" allegiances, especially in law (i.e., the various *madhhabs*).

ACKNOWLEDGMENTS

I acknowledge first my great debt to the several dozen scholars both living and deceased without whose translations this volume would have been impossible. I am particularly grateful to David Vishanoff of Oklahoma University for his ongoing interest in this project, as well as for his several contributed translations. David provided invaluable advice on various aspects of the work based on his considerable experience in teaching related university courses. Likewise, I am indebted to David Thomas, of the University of Birmingham in the United Kingdom, for his interest in the project, his contribution of two important fresh translations, and his generosity with numerous ad hoc "consultations." I thank also my dear friend Ahmet T. Karamustafa of the University of Maryland for his sage reflections on presenting and organizing the material in early stages of development. I am grateful to Mohammed Rustom for suggestions in early stages of development concerning desirable content and also to reader/referees for their helpful observations.

I thank also Jacob Van Sickle of Saint Louis University for his extensive logistical support over two years in preparing editable text from previously published material, developing indexing lists, securing permissions, and offering detailed and perceptive suggestions in various stages of editing. His assistance in juggling the numerous components and shaping the parameters of the final text has been invaluable. To Kyle Schenkewitz of Saint Louis University I am grateful for assistance in editing the final manuscript and in completing preliminary index lists. Timely completion of this project would not have been possible without a Summer Research Award in the Humanities from Saint Louis University, which included significant support for the cost of permissions for a number of the texts included here; for this I thank Dr. Ray Tait and the staff of the Office of Research Development and Services, especially Carole Knight.

Special thanks to the staff of the University of California Press, Stacy Eisenstark, and especially to long-time Religious Studies Editor Reed Malcolm: it has been my good fortune to collaborate happily with Reed on half a dozen large projects over nearly twenty years. I thank also project manager Rachel Berchten for seeing through its final phases this our third collaboration on a UC Press volume; and Julie Van Pelt for her preternaturally keen-sighted copyediting. Thanks too to Jeff Masamori for the cover design and to the University of California design team for the interior design.

This collection would not have been possible were it not for the dedication of colleagues and the generosity and cooperation of various providers. I begin with colleagues who provided new translations for this collection: Omid Ghaemmaghami, Valerie J. Hoffman, Sachiko Murata, David Thomas, and David Vishanoff. I also express my thanks to the following for their assistance at various stages of the project: Omar Ali-de-Unzaga, Lenn Evan Goodman, Ralph Lerner, Ellie Bush, Robin Bligh, James Morris, and Walid Hamamsy. And I thank Elaine Wright and Frances Narkiewicz of the Chester Beatty Library of Dublin for making the splendid cover image available.

Finally, as always I am ever grateful to Mary Pat for her loving, gracious good humor and unfailing support through the long process of bringing this large project to completion.

PART ONE

The Science of Interpretation

READING THE SACRED SOURCES

ISLAM'S FOUNDATIONAL SACRED TEXTS are not theological manuals or treatises, but they are in essential and too seldom acknowledged ways the inspirational wellsprings of theological themes in works of all subsequent generations of Muslims. Part 1 explores several large aspects of this substrate of Islamic theological discourse traditionally known as the science of interpretation (*ʿilm at-tafsīr*). First, a small selection of many possible Qurʾānic texts about divine transcendence, immanence, and revelation in creation and through prophets sets the overall scene. Second, anecdotal gems from the treasuries of Hadith and Sacred Hadith add further detail, color, and affect to the picture, particularly with respect to important nuances in the emphasis on divine foreordainment of human events and on various specific ways of responding to divine initiative expected of Muslims. Third (in chapter 2), a vast library of scriptural exegesis provides deeper insight into the ways Muslims have understood the theological imagery of the Qurʾān. Here the texts selected feature commentary on Qurʾānic images of God. Fourth, many Muslim scholars have analyzed key theologically based hermeneutical principles. I include here samples of classic explorations of exegetical method, the problem of "ambiguous" texts, study of the contexts of individual revelations, and the notion of "abrogation." Finally, a contemporary Shīʿī text discusses the "miraculous" nature of the Qurʾān.

ONE

Qurʾān and Hadith

EVERY VOLUME IN THE VAST LIBRARY of Islamic religious literature owes its inspiration, thematic content, and "technical" vocabulary in some measure to the Qurʾān and Hadith and to the countless scholars who dedicated their life's work to elucidating those sources. Knowledge of key themes in the Qurʾān and Hadith, and of the hermeneutical questions they raise, is essential to a fuller appreciation of the distinctly theological import of Islam's immense Prophetic legacy. The present chapter supplies the fundamentals of that knowledge.

THEOLOGICAL THEMES IN THE QURʾĀN

A good deal of the Qurʾānic text is of genuinely theological significance, whether inherently or by implication. The overall *concept* of divine revelation comprises the single largest theological category. At its broadest, it embraces not only a host of self-referential observations on the nature of the revealed text itself but a large number of narrative texts on some two-dozen prophets, ranging in length from a few lines to the whole of sūra 12 with its literarily unified story of Joseph. Numerous brief texts allude to the Qurʾān's divine origin, purity, clarity, veracity, and undeniability (e.g., 2:2, 10:1–2, 15:1, 24:1, and *passim*). References to Muḥammad's role over some twenty-two years form the single largest subset of prophetic texts. Perhaps the second-most numerous category of theological texts consists of scores of often brief allusions to God's nature and relationship to His creation. References to a variety of specific "doctrinal" matters, from the nature of faith to eschatological themes, comprise a third major theological category.

Among the more important specific theological themes suggested in the Qurʾān are divine transcendence and immanence; revelation in creation and through prophets; and the question of human responsibility even in the face of God's perfect knowledge, freedom, and power. The first two themes, divine transcendence and immanence, bookend what is arguably the most fundamental of theological paradoxes—God's complete otherness melded with intense divine involvement with created realities. These two concepts, *tanzīh* (difference) and *tashbīh* (similarity), overlap in such a way that the distinction employed in this chapter is a matter of emphasis rather than an absolute dichotomy—a "coincidence of opposites." The second pair, modes of divine disclosure, illustrates the pervasive nature of God's communication. And the last two concepts, divine omnipotence in tandem with human moral accountability, represent one of the most contentious of conundrums. All of these themes eventually became grist for the theological mill of subsequent generations of Muslims, some generating veritable storms of controversy. They represent a very small sample of the full array of theologically charged texts in this scripture. Here are some of the numerous, typically brief, passages that illustrate these themes.

Transcendence: Divine Throne and Footstool

God's transcendence and unlikeness to all that is not God (*tanzīh*) is fundamental to any understanding of Islamic theology. Countless short scriptural texts advert to the perfect divine transcendent unity (*tawḥīd*), including several, like the celebrated Throne Verse, that incorporate important metaphors. Beginning with that text, here is a sample of key passages.

Texts

God—there is no deity but He; the Living, the Everlasting. Neither slumber nor sleep overcomes Him. To Him belong all that heavens and earth encompass. Who can intercede with Him, except by his leave? He knows all that surrounds [created beings], when they can grasp nothing of what He knows, except as He chooses. His Throne stretches across heaven and earth; sovereignty over them tires Him not, for He is the Exalted, the Magnificent. (2:255)

It is God who elevated the heavens without visible supporting pillars, then established Himself on the Throne, and made the sun and moon His subjects. Each [natural feature] moves along for a designated term, all matters under [divine] administration and [nature's] signs meticulously detailed so that perhaps you will believe in [your future] encounter with your Lord. (13:2)

It is God who fashioned the heavens and the earth and all that is between in six days, then established [Himself, or "sat"] upon the Throne. Apart from Him you have no protecting patron or intercessor. Will you not therefore be mindful? (32:4)

They do not measure accurately God's true sovereignty: on Resurrection Day the entire earth will be [no more than] one handful [lit., a grasping], and the heavens will be enclosed in His right hand. Glory to Him who far transcends what the [idolators] associate with Him. (39:67)

Blessed be the one who owns dominion, whose power is all-pervasive. It is He who created death and life, to discern who among you were loftiest in action. He is the mighty, the forgiving. He spread out the seven heavens, and the merciful Lord's work leaves nothing lacking. Examine it as you like, you will discover no blemish. (67:1–3; see also 57:1–6)

Worship the one who oversees all things. No [human] vision can encompass Him; rather it is He who encompasses all vision, and He is aware [of all things] in minutest detail. (6:102–3)

. . .

In addition, a number of texts beautifully combine divine transcendence and immanence, thus providing a transition to a clearer articulation of immanence. Here is one such text: "Who responds to the one who calls out to Him in dire straits? And who removes evil [from you] and makes you [pl.] vicegerents of the earth? Is there [another deity] beside God? How little attention you pay. And who leads you in profound darkness on land and sea? And who dispatches, from the [depths of] His mercy, the winds with good news? Is there [another deity] beside God? God far transcends anything [idolaters] equate with Him" (27:62–63).

Immanence: The Verse of Light and God's Anthropomorphic Features

Often less appreciated by non-Muslims are the numerous allusions to God's accessibility and affinity with His creation (*tashbīh*). Here the images of pervasive light and references to God's face, eyes, and hands offer a sense of this dimension of the divine being. On the other hand, texts describe human beings as capable of surprisingly intimate connection with the Creator.

Texts

God is the light of heaven and earth. Picture His light as a niche within which there is a lamp, and the lamp is within a glass. And it is as though the glass were a glittering star lit from a sacred olive tree neither of east nor west, whose oil would fairly radiate even without the touch of fire. Light upon light, and God guides to His light whom He will. (24:35)

To God belong the east and the west and no matter where you turn, there is the face of God. Truly God is all-suffusing. . . . (2:115)

I am truly near; I answer the prayer of the petitioner who beseeches me. Therefore let them respond to me and have faith in me, that they might receive guidance. (2:186)

Everything on earth perishes; but the face of your Lord remains, majestic and most revered. (55:26–27)

We created the human being and are aware of his most intimate thoughts; we are nearer to the individual than the jugular vein. Indeed, to his right and his left sit two [angels] intent on [his thoughts]; no expression of his eludes an attentive guardian. (50:16–18)

Your Lord knows what is concealed in the [idolaters'] inmost beings, and what they disclose. (28:69)

[God explains to Moses how He saved the prophet as an infant, telling his mother to cast the baby into the river, which would then deposit the vessel on the bank:] I surrounded you with my love so that you would be nurtured under my eye. (20:39)

The Jews say, "The hand of God is shackled." May their hands be shackled, and cursed may they be for what they assert! On the contrary, His two hands are expansive in their reach [so that God] lays out resources as He wishes. (5:64; see also 51:47)

God's hand rests on the hands of [those who pledged themselves to Muḥammad at Ḥudaybīya]. (48:10)

Know that God intervenes between the human being and his heart. (8:24)

There is no living being that God does not grasp by the forelock. (11:56)

It was He who fashioned the heavens and the earth in six days, and then sat upon the Throne. He knows what goes into the earth and what emerges from it, what descends from heaven and what ascends to it. He is with you wherever you may be, and God's vision (*baṣīr*) includes all you do. (57:4)

Do you not see that God knows what is in the heavens and what is on earth? Never will three converse privately but that He is the fourth; nor five, but that He is the sixth—nor among fewer or more, but He is with them wherever they may be. (58:7)

Whether you conceal what is in your inmost being or divulge it, God knows it. (3:7)

When my servants ask you [Muḥammad] about Me, I am indeed near; I respond to the invocation of every petitioner who calls out to Me. (2:186)

On that Day, faces [of some will be] radiant as they gaze upon [or: toward] their Lord. (75:22–23)

Revelation in Creation and through Prophets

God's commissioning of an unbroken line of prophetic emissaries beginning with Adam forms the most evident theological medium of revelation in the formal sense. But the Qur'ān's consistent use of the striking imagery of signs (*āyāt*) on the horizons and within the individual person expands the concept of revelation considerably. One of the most evocative scriptural verses (*āyāt*) in this context even suggests that one could think of the earth herself as God's "first prophet." Referring to apocalyptic signs that the end has come, the text says, "On that day, she [earth] will publish her news, for your Lord will have revealed [that] to her" (99:4–5). The term translated here as "revealed" is from a root otherwise used almost exclusively to denote revelation to prophets (*awḥā*)—apart from the human prophets, God has communicated thus only with the earth and, curiously, the bee. I begin here with a sample of the many self-referential texts in which the Qur'ān describes its own revelatory credibility and a longer text on the specific issue of the scripture's "inimitability" (a hermeneutical theme to be addressed more fully in the next chapter) in the context of the public's demand for "miracles" from Muḥammad.

Texts

Truly this is a sending-down of the Lord of the Universe, with which there also descended to your heart the Trustworthy Spirit [i.e., Gabriel], so that you might be among those who give warning, in a pellucid Arabic tongue. (26:192–96)

[This is] a Book sent down to you [Muḥammad]—and let there be no constriction in the core of your being (*ṣadr*) because of it—so that through it you might warn the believers and bring them to mindfulness. [Addressed now to the people:] Adhere to what has been sent down to you [pl.] and do not pursue protecting friends other than Him. How fleeting is your mindfulness. (7:2–3)

[This is] a Book whose signs/verses are unambiguous, then laid out in detail by the One who is Wise, Aware. [Its message is that] you must not serve any but God. [Say, Muḥammad:] Truly to you [pl.] I have been sent from Him as a warner and a herald. (11:1–2)

These are the signs/verses of the clear Book. We have sent it down as an Arabic recitation [Qurʾān], so that perhaps you will understand. (12:1–2)

These are the signs/verses of the Book, and what has been sent down to you from your Lord is the perfect truth, though most human beings do not believe. (13:1)

[This is] a Book that We have sent down to you [Muḥammad], so that you might bring humankind out of darkness into the light, by permission of their Lord, to the Path of the One Almighty and Praiseworthy. (14:1)

When We substitute one sign/verse in place of another, and God knows best what He sends down [progressively], they say [to Muḥammad] "You are nothing but a charlatan [or: forger]," but most of them do not understand. Say: the Sanctified Spirit [Gabriel] has brought it down from our Lord in truth, in order to affirm those who believe and as a guidance and good news for those who surrender [to God]. Truly We know that they say, "A mere mortal instructs him." The language to which they allude cynically is patently foreign, whereas this is a pellucid Arabic tongue. (16:101–3)

Say [Muḥammad:] Were all of humankind and the Jinn to assemble for the purpose of bringing the likes of this Qurʾān, they would not bring forth its counterpart, even if they colluded intently. And in this Qurʾān, we have truly explicated for humankind all manner of similitude. Still, the majority of humankind receives it ungratefully at best. They say, "We will not believe you [Muḥammad] until you bring forth a spring welling up from the earth for us; or [until] you own a garden of date palms and grapes, and make the rivers within them flow freely and copiously; or [until] you make the firmament fall, as you claim it will to put us to shame; or [until] you bring God and the angels forth; or [until] you own an ornate palace, or ascend into the heavens. No, indeed, even if you ascend, we will not believe until you send down to us a book that we can read." Say [to them]: "Glory to my Lord! Am I anything other than a mortal man and a messenger?" (17:88–93)

Behold, in the heavens and the earth are signs for those who believe. And in your creation, and all the wild creatures He has scattered over the earth, are signs for a people of firm faith. And the alternation of night and day, and the sustenance that God sends down from the sky, to revive the earth after its death, and the shifting of the winds—these are signs for a people who understand. . . . Here is vision for humankind, guidance and mercy. . . . (45:3–5, 20)

Among His signs are night and day, sun and moon. Do not bow to sun and moon in worship; worship instead the God who created them, if indeed you are among His servants. And even though human beings are [too] haughty, some in God's presence never tire of prostrating themselves before Him night and day. (41:37–38)

And in the creation of the heavens and the earth, and the variety of your languages and ethnicities, are signs of God for every living being. In the quotidian pattern of repose in sleep, too, and in your drive to gather good things are signs for those who are attentive. And in the lightning whose appearance engenders apprehension and longing in you, and in the resuscitating rain falling from the firmament are signs for those who seek understanding. . . . We have sent messengers before you [Muḥammad], each bringing to a people manifest proofs of their mission. . . . It is not you [Muḥammad] who make the dead attentive, or alert the deaf to the message if they stubbornly reject it. It is not you who lead the blind forth from their intransigence. You can nudge to attentiveness only those who give credence to Our signs and who have [already] surrendered to God. (30:22–23, 47–53 intermittently)

We believe in God and what has been revealed to us and what was revealed to Abraham and Ismāʿīl and Isaac and Jacob and the tribes, and what was given to Moses and Jesus and what was given to the prophets from their Lord. We make no distinction among them and to Him do we surrender gratefully [lit., we are *muslims* to Him]. (2:136; see also 29:46)

[God speaking to Muḥammad:] It is not fitting that God should speak to a human being except by inspiration [*waḥy,* a technical term indicating revelation given to a prophet], or from behind a veil, or in commissioning a messenger that he might deliver a revelation by God's leave. . . . So by our command we have revealed to you spiritually. You knew neither the scripture nor the faith, but we have made of it [the Qurʾān] a light by which we guide whomever we choose among our servants. And it is you who guide to the Straight Path, the Path of God to whom belong what is in the heavens and what is on earth. Do not all things move toward God? (42:51–53)

Divine Freedom and Human Responsibility

Many brief Qurʾānic texts not only emphasize God's absolute control but also suggest an almost capricious freedom in determining the ethical course of individual people. Given the larger context, however, these paeans to God's untrammeled supremacy are far more about who God *is* than what human beings are *not*. The Qur'ān frequently underscores the divine prerogative by declaring in numerous general comments that God "guides whom He will and leads astray whom He will" (14:4), occasionally offering a brief further specification of the theme, as, for example: "One whom God guides is thus guided, but for one whom God leads astray you will encounter no patron who can suggest a course correction" (18:17). As we shall see, texts such as the following would become pivotal to later discussions of theological ethics.

Texts

To every people We sent a messenger [to say] "Serve God and repudiate evil." Among them were some whom God guided, while for others wandering in error was inevitable. Therefore make your way across the earth and observe the outcome of those who rejected [the message]. If their guidance is a concern to you, indeed God does not guide those He causes to wander in error, and they have none to assist them. (16:36–37)

Indeed, you [Muḥammad] will not provide guidance to those you love, but God does guide whom He will and knows best those who benefit from guidance. (28:56)

Do you see one who chooses mere whim as his deity? Because God knows [this condition], He has sealed that person's hearing and heart and placed blinders on him. Who [under these circumstances] can guide such a person after God [has ceased to guide]? (45:23)

Here is a reminder: Let whoever so wishes pursue a path to his Lord. But you have no power of will apart from what God wills. Indeed God is knowing and wise. (76:29–30)

. . .

Other texts, however, present a more nuanced picture, hinting at some measure of self-direction.

Texts

[To those who are convinced their deeds will entail no recompense:] On the contrary, those who choose wickedness and surround themselves in sinfulness will be the denizens of the Fire [of Hell] where they will reside eternally;

while people of faith and good deeds will inhabit the Garden [of Paradise] forever. (2:81–82)

God tasks no soul beyond its capacity. To each redound both the benefits and the liabilities of its choices. [One ought to pray:] "O our Lord, do not dismiss us if we succumb to forgetfulness or sin. Our Lord, do not burden as you did our forebears. Our Lord, do not encumber us beyond our capability." (2:286; also 6:152, 7:42, 65:7)

God has promised people of faith and good deeds forgiveness and abundant reward, but those who refuse to believe and call Our signs lies will abide in Hell. (5:9–10)

God does not change a people's state till they change their own soul's thoughts. (13:11)

We will assuredly reward those who endure in patience with recompense commensurate with the comeliness of their deeds. Every believer, male or female, who does righteous deeds We will enliven with a good life and will indeed bestow [on them] a reward proportionate to the goodness of the preponderance of their actions. (16:96–97)

Anyone who performs upright deeds [does so to the good] of his soul, and anyone who does evil [does so to] its detriment; and your Lord does no injustice to [His] servants. (41:46)

• • •

All things considered, the added ingredient in the Qurʾān's consistent language of accountability for one's actions at judgment and the certainty of reward or punishment seems to suggest something of an ethical balance: God indeed possesses all power to dispose, but human beings are not simply constrained to one course or another. If not for that sliver of responsibility, divine justice would be merely a cruel hoax. As for references to specific kinds of actions that will have an effect on one's prospects for salvation, the Qurʾān does offer concrete options. In earlier texts especially, it seems to emphasize aspects of social justice, as in the following text.

Text

What will convey to you what the Steep Ascent is? It means freeing a slave, and feeding in time of hunger an orphan of your extended family, or a poor person on hard times [lit., in the dust], and to be among people of faith who encourage each other to patience and urge each other to deeds of compassion. Such as these will have a place on the right, while those who reject our signs will find themselves on the left, around whom there will be a wall of fire. (90:12–19)

. . .

Many other texts of the Qur'ān consistently require Muslims to share their resources with the needy (e.g.,, 3:134, 51:19, 76:8–9) as an essential ingredient in the ethical life. During the Medinan period (622–32) the Muslim community grew from minority to majority status. Behavioral requirements increasingly came to include actions more formally "religious," as suggested by countless texts that emphasize the centrality of performing ritual prayer, almsgiving, profession of faith, and fasting. Other texts, however, place greater stress on inward transformation, as in sūra 49.

Text

The Bedouin say, "We believe." Respond [to them]: "You are not [truly] believers; say [instead], 'We have surrendered [lit., we are *muslims*],' for faith (*īmān*) has not entered your hearts. If you obey God and His Messenger, He will by no means minimize your actions. Indeed, Allāh is the Forgiving, the Merciful." Believers are those who put faith in God and His Messenger and have had no doubts thereafter, and have exerted themselves through their outward possessions and inner selves in the Way of God. It is these who manifest authenticity [in faith].... They insist they have given you [Muḥammad] a gift by surrendering. Tell them, "Do not consider your *islām* as a gift to me. On the contrary, Allāh has given you [all] the gift of guiding you to the faith, if indeed you behave authentically." (49:14–15, 17)

THEOLOGICAL THEMES IN THE HADITH

Hidden amid the ore of traditions attributed to Muḥammad and his Companions are dozens of theologically sparkling gems.[1] Long-standing Muslim tradition teaches that the Hadith, like the Qur'ān, communicate a divinely revealed message, but, unlike the scripture, the articulation of the content is that of Muḥammad himself. From a theological perspective, the most telling texts are those that deal explicitly with a variety of attitudes and values underlying the countless rituals and other practices with which many thousands of Hadiths deal. Sections in the major Hadith collections most likely to contain such themes are those on God's transcendent unity (*tawḥīd*); faith (*īmān*); the virtues or excellent qualities (*faḍāʾil*) of Muḥammad and his Companions and of the Qurʾān; virtuous behavior (*adab*); God's dominion over human affairs (*qadr*); the active remembrance of God (*dhikr*); piety/asceticism and the "softening of hearts" (*zuhd, ar-raqāʾiq*); repentance (*tawba*); and eschatology (*al-qiyāma,* "resurrection"; *al-janna,* "garden"; *an-nār,* "fire"; *al-fitan,* "end-time strife"; *as-sāʿah,* "the Hour").

Here we have space to deal with only a limited selection of these theologically relevant traditions. A signature Hadith, one that opens the first section of Muslim's collection in the *Book of Faith,* sets the overall context for theological themes. Known as the Hadith of Gabriel, the extended anecdote recounts a gathering at which a number of Muḥammad's Companions had joined him. Note the revealing angel's "Socratic method" as he draws responses from the Prophet.

Text

God's Messenger said [to the Companions], "Ask me [about matters of religious import]," but out of reverence for him they declined to question him. Then a man arrived, sat knee to knee [with the Prophet], and said, "Messenger of God, what is *islām?*" [Muḥammad] replied, "Not associating anything with God, and performing the ritual prayer, and giving alms, and fasting during Ramaḍān." [The man] responded, "You are correct. Messenger of God, what is *īmān?*" [Muḥammad] said, "Believing in God, and His angels, and His Book, and [eventually] meeting Him, and His messengers; and believing without reservation in the divine destiny." [The man] said, "You are correct. Messenger of God, what is *iḥsān?*" He replied, "Fearing God as though you saw Him, for even if you don't, He surely sees you." [The man] said, "You are correct. Messenger of God, when will the Hour arrive?" He answered, "The one you have asked knows no more about that than the questioner. But I will inform you about its characteristics. When you see the indentured woman giving birth to her master, that is one of its signs. And when you see those who are barefoot, unclothed, deaf and mute rulers of the earth, that will be one of its signs. And when you see herders of black camels living luxuriously in buildings, that will be one of its signs. [The Hour] is among the five things so mysterious none but God knows." Then he recited, "Indeed, God alone has knowledge of the Hour, and it is He who sends down the rain and knows what is in the wombs. No individual knows what he may gain tomorrow, and no one knows in what land he will die. Indeed, [it is] God who is knowing and aware" (21:34). [Abū Hurayra, the narrator (d. 678)] went on: Then the man stood [and left]. So God's Messenger said, "Bring him back to me." So they searched for him but did not find him. God's Messenger then said, "This was Gabriel wanting to teach you, when you declined to ask."[2]

. . .

Many of the Hadiths bearing on human freedom and responsibility seem to tip the balance decidedly toward predetermination of human acts, one of the ingredients of *īmān* in the Hadith of Gabriel. Witness, for example, a text that states quite starkly the dilemma of predestination.

Text

[It may be that] one of you behaves like the inhabitants of Paradise until he is barely an arm's length from it, when his recorded destiny overtakes him so that he [suddenly] behaves like the people of Hell-fire and therefore enters it [instead]; [conversely] one of you [might] behave like the denizens of Hell-fire until he is barely an arm's length from it, when his recorded destiny overtakes him so that he [suddenly] behaves like the people of Paradise and thus he enters it.[3]

. . .

Note the striking implication that no matter how one leads one's life, a power far greater than individual choice is at work. As parts 2 and 3 or this volume discuss further, this thorny matter would become a major point of debate among systematic theologians during the third and fourth centuries after Muḥammad's death. Not surprisingly, traditions that feature this theme appear in sections of Hadith collections called the Book of Divine Foreordainment (*kitāb al-qadr*).

Texts

A man asked [Muḥammad], "O messenger of God, can one distinguish the People of the Garden from the People of the Fire?" He replied, "Yes." Then [the questioner] asked, "Then why do [people bother to] do [good] deeds?" [He replied,] "All individuals will [be inclined to] do what they were made for or what is easy for them."[4]

Someone asked God's Messenger about the children of unbelievers, and he said, "God knows what they are inclined to do." ... [Muḥammad also] said, "Every child is born with the disposition to Islam (*fiṭra*), then his parents turn him into a Jew or a Christian, much as when you assist birthing of beasts. Will you find any [of those offspring] mutilated before you yourself make a brand on them?" They replied, "O Messenger of God, What is your view of those who die young?" He replied, "God knows what they would have done [had they survived]."[5]

ʿĀʾisha asked God's Messenger about the plague. He replied, "It was a punishment that God inflicted upon whomever He so chose. For believers, however, He made it a mercy: any servant living in a region (*balad*) afflicted by it, who stays there and does not leave the region, exercising long-suffering and counting on [God's mercy], knows that he will not suffer harm except insofar as God has ordained it [lit., written for him] and would [in any case] receive a reward equal to that of a martyr."[6]

God's Messenger said, "Indeed, the hearts of all the children of Adam are between two of the fingers of the Merciful, as if [they were] a single heart that He orients as He wishes." Then God's Messenger said, "O God, turner of hearts, orient our hearts toward obedience to You."[7]

. . .

One intriguing Hadith combines two important theological themes: God's control of all human dispositions and an aspect of the interrelationships among the great prophets.

Text

According to Abū Hurayra, the Messenger of God said: Adam and Moses had an argument in the presence of their Lord, and Adam got the better of Moses. Moses said, "Are you the Adam whom God fashioned with His hand and into whom He breathed some of His spirit, and to whom He caused the angels to prostrate themselves, and whom He settled comfortably in the Garden? [And was it you who] then bound humankind to the earth as a result of your fault?" Adam replied, "Are you the Moses whom God chose for delivering his message and to converse with Him, and to whom He entrusted the tablets containing clear explanation of all things, and whom He brought near in intimate conversation? How long before I was created do you think God wrote the Torah?" Moses replied, "Forty years." Said Adam, "And did you see there the words, 'Adam rebelled against his Lord, and was misled'" (20:121)? [Moses] said, "Yes." [Adam] went on, "And [yet] you condemn me for performing an act that God had written, forty years before I was created, that I would do?" God's Messenger added, "Thus did Adam get the better of Moses."[8]

. . .

On the other hand, a minor subgenre within the corpus of Hadith are sayings emphasizing the priority of God's mercy, even for individuals whose record of detrimental choices in life has destined them for Hell in the hereafter. Unlike the first selection of Hadiths above, many of which occur in sections of major collections dedicated to the theme of divine foreordainment (*qadr*), more hopeful Hadiths appear in sections on faith (*īmān*) and repentance (*tawba*). One intriguing Hadith combines a variety of eschatological themes with a narrative that underscores God's susceptibility to the entreaties of human beings so desirous of a heavenly reward that they persist in badgering God regardless of the limits He has imposed on them.

The Hadith opens with people asking Muḥammad whether they would "see" God at resurrection—an issue that arises both in the creeds (see part 2) and the works of systematic theology (see part 3). Muḥammad asks whether the questioners would have any difficulty seeing the full moon, or the sun on a cloudless day. Just so, he explains, they would see God, and He would explain that all people follow what they worship, whether the moon, the sun, or demons. God would appear among the Muslim community in "a form not His own" and announce "I am your Lord," to test them. True believers would "take refuge in God" from what must surely be a deception and insist on staying put until their Lord came in a form they would recognize as God. Then God would appear "in His own form," and after the believers acknowledged that this was indeed their Lord, they would follow him on a tour of the infernal realm. God would then ask angels to bring out of Hell those who had clearly never worshipped any but God, as evidenced by the traces of prostration on their foreheads, marks that God had commanded the Fire to refrain from effacing. At length the final man to emerge from Hell stands before God to plead for his release, but continues to stand facing Hell. Here we pick up the text of this lengthy narrative as the man entreats God insistently, much as Abraham refused to give up when seeking the salvation of the just at Sodom and Gomorrah.

Text

"O Lord, avert my face from the Fire, whose fumes have poisoned me and whose flames have scorched me." Then he will implore God as God wishes him to supplicate. God the Blessed and Exalted will say, "Were I to do [as you request], you might just ask for more." Then [the man] will say, "I won't ask for more," and will provide his Lord such covenants and assurances as God desires. Then God will avert [the man's] face from the Fire. When [the man] turns to the Garden and beholds it, he will cease to speak as long as God desires his silence. Then [the man] will say, "O Lord, advance me to the gate of the Garden." And God will say to him, "Did you not agree and assure me that you would not ask for more than I have granted you? Woe to you, most deceitful Son of Adam!" And [the man] will say, "O my Lord," and will go on supplicating God until He replies, "If I accede to that request of yours, perhaps you will ask for more." Then [the man] will say, "No, by your might," and will provide his Lord agreements and assurances. And [God] will bring him to the gate of the Garden. And as the man stands at the gate of the Garden, the Garden will spread wide before him and he will see the good things and evil in it. He will hold his peace so long as God wishes him to do so, then he will say, "O my Lord, grant me entry into the Garden." And God the Blessed and Exalted will say to him, "Did you not make a solemn pact that you would not ask for more than you have been given? Woe to you, most deceitful Son of Adam!" Then [the man] will say, "O my Lord, let me not be the most unfortunate of your creatures, and he will go on entreating God until God, the blessed and exalted, laughs at him. Then God will laugh at him, and say, "Enter the Garden." And when [the man] has entered, God will say to him, "Make your request," and he will ask his Lord for what he desires, until God reminds him of this and that [which the man will have left out]. And when [the man] has run out of things to ask for, God the exalted will say, "[All] that is for you, and that much again."[9]

. . .

Many Hadiths make it clear that people's actions toward others influence how they can expect God to act toward them when they are called to account at judgment.

Text

According to Abū Hurayra, the Prophet said, "Once there was a man who loaned money to people, and who used to say to his assistant, 'When you encounter a person going through hard times, go easy on him, and perhaps God will go easy on us.' And [Muḥammad went on] when he came to meet God, God went easy on him."[10]

. . .

Some Hadiths emphasize that regardless of an individual's sinfulness, in the end, attitude trumps actions.

Text

Abū 'd-Dardā' (d. 652) reported that he heard the Prophet delivering a sermon from the *minbar,* saying, "Anyone who fears being in the presence of his Lord will receive two Gardens." [Abū 'd-Dardā'] asked, "Even after fornicating and stealing, Messenger of God?" Then [the Prophet] repeated, "Anyone who fears being in the presence of his Lord will receive two Gardens." [Abū 'd-Dardā'] asked again, "Even after fornicating and stealing, Messenger of God?" Again [the Prophet] repeated, "Anyone who fears being in the presence of his Lord will receive two Gardens." A third time, [Abū 'd-Dardā'] asked, "Even after fornicating and stealing, Messenger of God?" And [Muḥammad] replied, "Even in spite of Abū 'd-Dardā'."[11]

. . .

The question of prophetic *intercession,* and intercession in general, has been a much-discussed theme in Islamic theological texts. Numerous Hadiths on the subject lean decidedly toward Muḥammad's intercessory prerogative, describing his superiority over the previous prophets in this respect. An important narrative form of this theme opens with a setting in which Muḥammad and a group of Muslims are discussing the subject of the Day of Resurrection, and the Prophet asserts that he will lead all humankind on that day. The narrative then unfolds with a description of how people in great travail and anguish on the Day will cast about for an intercessor and progress from Adam through a succession of major prophets until at length they discover that only Muḥammad can fulfill their need. The following version foregrounds the theme of Muḥammad's insistence on effecting maximum assistance for believers residing in Hell, until He secures God's assurance that even a virtually imperceptible quantity of faith will suffice.

Text

[The famous traditionist Anas ibn Mālik (d. ca. 710) recounted the Hadith of Intercession, reporting the words of Muḥammad as follows:] On the Day of Resurrection, people will encounter one another in agitation [lit., heaving like waves]. They will come to Adam, saying, "Intercede for your descendants." He will reply, "That is not for me to do. You must approach Abraham, for he is God's Intimate Friend (*khalīl*)." So they will go to Abraham, but he will say, "That is not for me to do. You must go to Moses, for he held direct conversation with God (*kalīm*)." So they will approach Moses, but he will reply, "That is not for me to do. You need to approach Jesus, for he is the Spirit and Word of God." So to Jesus they will go, but he will say, "That is not for me to do. You need to see Muḥammad about this. So they will come to me, and I will say, "That is my prerogative, and I will hasten to seek permission of my Lord, and he will allow it. Then I will stand in His presence, and laud Him with praises the likes of which I am now unable [to express], but with which God will inspire me. I will then fall prostrate, and [He will say] to me, 'O Muḥammad, lift your head; proclaim and you will be heard; ask and it will be granted; make intercession and intercession will be made.' Then I will say, 'My Lord, my community! My community!' And the reply will come, 'Go forth, and bring out whoever has faith in his heart the weight of a grain of wheat or barley seed,' and I will hasten to do so. Then I will return to my Lord and laud Him with that praise [that He will teach me then], and I will fall prostrate before him. Then the words will be said, 'O Muḥammad, lift your head; proclaim and you will be heard; ask and it will be granted; make intercession and intercession will be made.' Then I will say, 'My Lord, my community! My community!' And the reply will come, 'Go forth, and bring out whoever has faith in his heart the weight of a mustard seed,' and I will hasten to do so. Then I will go back to my Lord and laud Him with that praise [that He will teach me then], and I will fall prostrate before him. Then the words will be said, 'O Muḥammad, lift your head; proclaim and you will be heard; ask and it will be granted; make intercession and intercession will be made.' And I will say 'My Lord, my community! My community!' And the reply will come, 'Go forth, and bring out whoever has faith in his heart the minutest fraction of a miniscule grain of mustard seed,' and I will hasten to do so."[12]

. . .

Some Hadiths comment on specific texts of the Qur'ān and function as examples of ad hoc exegesis. In this tradition, for example, Companion Ibn

ʿAbbās (d. ca. 687), also among the earliest authors of a formal exegetical commentary, reports on the meaning of one such scriptural verse.

Text

When the following verse was revealed, "Whether you divulge what is within your mind, or keep it hidden, God will hold you responsible for it" (2:284), something penetrated their hearts the likes of which had never before penetrated their hearts. The Prophet said, "Proclaim: We have heard and obeyed and surrendered." [Ibn ʿAbbās] went on: Then God introduced faith into their hearts and God most high revealed [the verse], "God tasks no soul beyond its capacity. To each redound both the benefits and the liabilities of its choices (2:286). [One ought to pray:] "O our Lord, do not dismiss us if we succumb to forgetfulness or sin." [The Lord] said, "So I acted accordingly." [Prayer continues:] "Our Lord, do not burden us as you did our forebears. . . . And forgive us and be merciful to us, [for] you are our protector" (2:286). [The Lord] said, "So I acted accordingly."[13]

• • •

It is hard to imagine how anyone could read chapters on "repentance" in the Hadith collections and conclude that the God to whom Muslims pray is cold and capricious and that human choice and moral responsibility are a sham. Many Hadiths on the subject of repentance turn on the conviction that God so intensely desires repentance as a reason for forgiving humankind that if His creatures did not sin, He would arrange a pretext for forgiving.

Text

God's Messenger said, "By the One who holds my life, if you did not commit sin, God would surely dispense with you and would replace you with a people who would sin. They would then ask God's forgiveness and He would grant his pardon."[14]

• • •

Some traditions emphasize that God's mercy can counterbalance even the most desperate human attempts to circumvent the divine justice, as in the following remarkable narrative of a man who was convinced that God could not possibly forgive the depth of his sinfulness.

Text

A man who had done absolutely nothing good for his family said [as a last will and testament]: "When [my body] is dead, burn it. Then scatter half of it on land and half at sea." He swore that if God got hold of him He would punish him as He had never punished anyone in the two worlds. And when the man died, they did as he had stipulated. But then God ordered the land to gather what [had been scattered] over it, and commanded the sea to bring together what [had been scattered] over it. Then [God] asked [the man], "Why did you do this?" He replied, "Out of [fear of] your reckoning, O Lord, but you know [that]." So God forgave him.[15]

• • •

Muslim tradition presents the unmistakable underlying conviction that "God's mercy outweighs His wrath."[16] In fact, one Hadith insists that God in effect "foreordained" that orientation for Himself, "writing it in His Book" at the very moment He created the world while sitting on His Throne.[17] Forgiveness is one of God's favorite pastimes, as in this brief Hadith: "Each night, during the third watch, God descends to the lowest heaven and asks, 'Is there anyone who calls me that I might answer? Who makes a request of me that I might grant it? Who seeks my forgiveness that I might forgive?'"[18] Indeed virtually all of creation is composed of divine mercy, even with God holding ninety-nine percent of the total in reserve for Resurrection Day.

Text

On the day He created the heavens and the earth, God fashioned a hundred mercies, every one of which could span the distance between heaven and earth. One of these mercies he planted in the earth, and by means of it the mother expresses affection toward her child, and the wild beasts and birds show tenderness to one another. So on the Day of Resurrection, He will complete those [ninety-nine] mercies with this [earthly] mercy [i.e., He will apply the whole of His storehouse of mercy].[19]

• • •

Many other Hadiths highlight God's forbearance and mercy, as well as a strong sense of the individual's moral responsibility in choosing his or her course of action. Here there is no question but that in God's eyes the benefit of even the intent to do good far exceeds the damage done by an evil deed contemplated and consummated.

Text

God's Messenger said that God said: "When a servant of mine takes a notion to do good, but does not do it, I record a good deed for him; but if he does it, I record from ten to seven hundred goods to his credit. And if he considers doing evil but does not do it, I do not record it against him; but if he does the evil deed, I record him [as responsible for] one evil deed."[20]

. . .

The prior Hadith begins to reveal an important level of historical and theological complexity in the literature, suggesting important but too little appreciated facets of the divine interest in human welfare. Many other Hadiths offer a sense of God's irresistibility and attractiveness, as in the refreshingly direct, "God is beautiful and He loves Beauty."[21] But there is yet another dimension of the literature that underscores the divine accessibility in a way that deserves special attention. Tucked away among some of the sayings attributed to the Prophet are sayings in which Muḥammad reports striking revelations not considered part of the Qur'ān. Quoting God, as it were, Muḥammad discloses arresting insights into the Creator's complex relationships with His creation at every level. As in the prior Hadith about the centrality of moral intention, these Sacred Hadiths typically emphasize God's mercy, immanence, and affection for humankind and a willingness to meet human beings more than halfway. Here are several Hadiths that describe God's intimate relation to creation and to humankind, concluding with one that reprises the essential connection between many Hadiths and the sacred scripture.

Texts

I am in the midst of my servant's thoughts of me [or perhaps: I conform to my servant's image of me], and I am with him when he brings me to mind. Should he remember me privately, I remember him in private; and if he recalls me in public, I bring him to mind in public in a still better way.[22]

My servant comes ever closer to me through works of devotion [i.e., other than those prescribed as religious duties]. When anyone comes toward me a hand's breadth, I approach a forearm's length; if anyone comes toward me a forearm's length, I approach by the space of outstretched arms; if anyone comes toward me walking, I will come running. Then I love that person so that I become the eye with which he sees, the ear with which he hears, the hand with which he takes hold. And should that person bring to me sins the size of the earth, my forgiveness will be a match for them.[23]

Abū Dharr (d. 652) reported: God's Messenger recounted that God the Exalted says, "My servants, apart from those I have guided, you are all wandering in error; but if you petition Me, I will show you the way. Except for those I have enriched, you are all impoverished; but if you petition Me, I will provide you sustenance. Except for those I have kept [from sinning], you are all sinners; but if anyone aware of my power to forgive asks my forgiveness, I will forgive that person without question. If all of you from first to last, living or dead, young or old, were as pure in heart as my most pure-hearted servants, it would not amplify my sovereignty by even a gnat's wing. If all of you from first to last, living or dead, young or old, were as false-hearted as the most false-hearted of my servants, it would not detract from my sovereignty by even a gnat's wing. If all of you from first to last, living or dead, young or old, assembled in an open plain, and every one pleaded for everything his hopes could embrace, and I responded with all that every person had requested, my sovereignty would no more diminish than would the sea if one of you walked by, dipped a needle in and withdrew it. For I am beneficent and exalted, and I do whatever I will. My very speech brings about both reward and punishment. When I desire something, I need only say 'Be' and it comes to be."[24]

[A Hadith that enshrines direct citation of God:] According to Abū Hurayra (d. 678), God's Messenger said: "Whoever prays the ritual prayer without reciting as part of it the 'Mother of the Qur'ān' [i.e., Sūrat al-Fātiḥa], then [that prayer] is defective [he said this three times] and incomplete." So someone said to Abū Hurayra, "But we are behind [i.e., following the lead of] the imam." So he replied, "Recite it to yourself, for I have heard God's Messenger say, 'God Most High has said, "I have divided the ritual prayer in two parts between Me and my servant, and my servant will get what he asks for. So when the servant says, 'Praise to God, Lord of the Universe,' God Most High says, 'My servant has praised Me.' And when [the servant] says, 'The Compassionate, the Merciful,' God Most High says, 'My servant has extolled me.' And when he says, 'Master of the Day of Judgment,' [God] says, 'My servant has given me glory,' or sometimes 'My servant has given his life over to me.' Then when [the servant] says, 'It is You we serve and from You we ask assistance,' [God] replies, 'This is between me and my servant, and my servant will get what he asks for.' And when [the servant] says, 'Guide us along the straight path, the path of those to whom you have been gracious, not of those who have incurred your anger or of those who wander in error,' [God] says, 'This is for my servant, and my servant will get what he asks for.'"[25]

EXEGETICAL HADITHS

As the prior Ḥadīth Qudsī suggests, some of the earliest commentaries on individual texts of the Qur'ān are those enshrined in sections of the great Hadith collections called the *Book of Exegetical Commentary* (*Kitāb at-tafsīr*) and the typically shorter *Book of the Excellent Qualities of the Qur'ān* (*Kitāb faḍā'il al-Qur'ān*). I will later comment further on theological resonances relating to the latter. Bukhārī's edition of the Hadith includes one of the larger assortments (more than 350) of exegetical comments in the genre. Most of the relevant traditions offer information as to early views on the "circumstances of the revelations" (*asbāb an-nuzūl*) with short anecdotes describing the context in the life of the Prophet or one of the Companions.[26] Here are examples of Hadiths on the theme of the power and excellence of the Qur'ān.

Texts

The Prophet of God said to his Companions, "Do any of you experience difficulty in reciting a third of the Qur'ān in a single night?" That [question] was hard for them, and they replied, "O Messenger of God, which of us can do that?" So he said [alluding to key terms opening sūra 112], "God the One, the besought of all . . . " amounts to a third of the Qur'ān.[27]

Abū Hurayra said, "God's Messenger delegated me to look after the alms donated during Ramaḍān. Then someone came and began to purloin the [donated] food supplies. I got hold of him and said, 'I'm taking you to God's Messenger!' . . . He said to me [attempting to offer me a reason for not doing so], 'When you retire to your bed, you should recite the "Throne Verse" (2:255) so that a protector will descend to you from God, and Satan will not come near you till you awake.' Then the Prophet said, 'He was telling you the truth, even though he is a liar—that was Satan.'"[28]

Usayd ibn Ḥuḍayr recounted that as he recited Sūrat al-Baqara (sūra 2) one night, while he had his horse tethered nearby, the horse became agitated. When [Usayd] stopped, the horse calmed down, and when he resumed reciting, the horse was again agitated. So he stopped again, and again the horse became calm. [Usayd] resumed reciting again, and once more the horse became riled and distressed. So he ceased [reciting] again, for his son Yaḥyā was nearby and he was concerned that [the horse] would step on him. When he removed the boy [from danger] he lifted his head toward the heavens, but could not see them. When he awoke, he related [this story] to the Prophet, who said, "Recite, Ibn Ḥuḍayr; recite, Ibn Ḥuḍayr!" Ibn Ḥuḍayr replied, "Messenger of God, I was concerned [the horse] would trample my son, Yaḥyā, who was nearby. I looked up as I turned to him. When I lifted my head toward the sky, [I saw] something like clouds in which there appeared to be lanterns, so I departed to prevent myself from seeing that." [The Prophet] asked, "Do you understand what that was?" [Ibn Ḥuḍayr] answered, "No." [The Prophet] said, "That [cloud] was angels attracted to your voice. Had you continued reciting, it would have remained till dawn so that people would have observed it because it would not have disappeared from [their sight]."[29]

HERMENEUTICAL HINTS IN THE HADITH

Chapter 2 features primary texts of various scholars explicitly concerned with a range of hermeneutical issues adumbrated in the Qurʾān and Hadith. Here are two examples of how a number of Hadiths raise these questions in a nontheoretical way.

In addition to the many Hadiths that offer commentary on various verses of the Qurʾān, others provide insight into important and sometimes contested matters of how the sacred text was revealed. One such point of interest has to do with Muḥammad's manner of responding to texts as they were being revealed and another with the so-called seven readings of the Qurʾān. The first Hadith turns around Ibn ʿAbbās's commentary on the Qurʾānic verse in which God instructs Muḥammad, "Do not move your tongue [in the recitation] in an attempt to hasten the process" (75:16; see also 20:114).

Texts

[Ibn ʿAbbās commented]: Whenever Gabriel came down to him with the revelation, he would move his tongue and lips, and it was a struggle for him and one could tell accordingly [that God was communicating with him]. So God sent down the verse [in the sūra] that begins, "I swear by the Day of Resurrection" (75:1), "Do not move your tongue [in the recitation] in an attempt to hasten the process, for We will see to gathering it [in your memory] and the recitation of it" (75:16–17). In other words, it is up to Us to assemble [the message] in the core of your being and [make it possible for you] to recite it. "So when We have recited it, follow its recitation" (75:18) [means] "So when We have sent it down, listen attentively." Then, "It is up to Us to clarify it" (75:19) [means] "It is up to Us to articulate it with your tongue." Therefore, when Gabriel came to him, he would bow his head in silence, and when [Gabriel] departed, he would recite as God had promised him.[30]

ʿUmar ibn al-Khaṭṭāb (d. 644) said, "I heard Hishām ibn Ḥakīm ibn Ḥizām reciting Sūrat al-Furqān when God's Messenger was still living. I listened carefully to his recitation, and [noticed that] he recited it with many vocalizations (*ḥurūf*) with which God's Messenger had not accustomed me to recite. I nearly set upon him during the ritual prayer, but held off for him to complete it. I then confronted him and said, 'Who taught you to recite this sūra as I heard you reciting it?' He replied, 'God's Messenger taught me to recite it.' So I said, 'You're lying, by God! God's Messenger [definitely] taught me to recite this sūra I heard you reciting.' So I hustled him off to God's Messenger, and I said, 'O Messenger of God, I heard this man reciting Sūrat al-Furqān with vocalizations you did not teach me to recite, and it was indeed you who taught me to recite Sūrat al-Furqān.' So he said, 'Recite it, Hishām.' Then he recited it as I had heard him recite it [earlier]. God's Messenger then said, 'It was sent down that way.' Then he said [to me], 'Recite, ʿUmar.' So I recited it as he had taught me to recite it, and God's Messenger said, 'It was sent down that way.' God's Messenger went on, 'In truth the Qurʾān was sent down in seven vocalizations, so recite [pl.] in the manner that is easiest for you.'"[31]

TWO

Interpreting the Sacred Sources

CHAPTER 1 BEGAN TO SUGGEST the emergence of "exegesis" as a mode of thinking nestled in the Hadith corpus and noted the kernel of several hermeneutical issues latent in key Qurʾānic texts. Here the focus shifts to two large varieties of theological writing dedicated to exegesis and hermeneutical considerations. First come samples of how major exegetes, both classical and modern, Sunnī and Shīʿī, have found a striking range of meanings in the sacred text. Then a selection of short topical or thematic pieces offers insights into the most pressing methodological questions in interpretation.

VARIETIES OF EXEGESIS (*TAFSĪR*) ON THE THRONE VERSE

Muslim exegetical literature, beginning in the late seventh century at least, could fill the shelves in a theological library, yet it is relatively seldom mined for its theological insight. Here are five texts commenting on two of the most oft-repeated and inscribed Qurʾānic verses. First is a selection by Mahmoud Ayoub in which he collates and summarizes an instructive array of exegetical perspectives on the Throne Verse (2:255). Though the nature of the pastiche Ayoub has produced does not offer a concrete sense of the original "tone" of the major exegetes whose views he presents, it does provide a very useful sense of thematic breadth and of the specific concerns that shape the approaches of commentators of varying "schools" of thought.[1] He begins with the Throne Verse itself.

Text

> God! There is no god but He, the Everliving, the Eternal Sovereign. Neither slumber nor sleep seizes Him. To Him belongs all that is in the heavens and in the earth. Who is there that shall intercede with Him, save by His leave? He knows all that is present with them and that which is to come upon them, but they comprehend nothing of His knowledge save what He wills. His Throne encompasses the heavens and the earth, and the preservation of them does not burden Him. He is the Most High, the Most Great. (2:255)

This verse, known as the Throne Verse (*Āyat al-Kursī*), is regarded by Muslims as one of the most excellent verses of the Qur'ān. It has therefore played a very important role in Muslim piety. Moreover, because of its imagery, the verse has been the subject of a great deal of theological and exegetical controversy. It has as well evoked much mystical thought and feeling through the lyrical beauty of its language. These qualities have no doubt given it the prominent place it occupies in the intellectual and pietistic life of Muslim society.

Qurṭubī (d. 1272) relates that the Throne Verse was revealed at night and that the Prophet immediately sent for Zayd ibn Thābit to write it down. He relates further on the authority of Muḥammad ibn al-Ḥanafīya, "When the Throne Verse was revealed, every idol and king in the world fell prostrate and the crowns of kings fell off their heads. Satans fled, colliding with one another in confusion until they came to Iblīs [their chief]. . . . He sent them to find out what happened, and when they came to Medina they were told that the Throne Verse had been sent down." . . .

Like the *Fātiḥa,* and especially the *basmallah,* the Throne Verse is said to possess powers of protection for human beings against evil or malevolent spirits. It is related that [the second caliph] ʿUmar ibn al-Khaṭṭāb (d. 644) one day wrestled with a creature of the *jinn,* whom he vanquished. The *jinnī* said, "Let me go and I will teach you that which would protect you from us." Having been released, he continued, "You may be protected from us by the Throne Verse."

Commentators have differed with regard to the meaning of the word *kursī.* (I [Ayoub] have rendered this word "throne" in accordance with the dominant view of commentators, as well as the accepted usage of Western scholarship.) In some traditions, the *kursī* is depicted as an actual object containing the heavens and the earth and as independent of the Throne (*ʿarsh*). In other traditions, it is identified with it. Ṭabarī (d. 923) reports a number of traditions from the Companions dealing with the identity and location of the *kursī.* He relates on the authority of Abū Mūsā al-Ashʿarī (d. ca. 662), "The *kursī* is the place of the two feet [footstool of God]. It has a squeaking sound like that of a new saddle." According to as-Suddī (d. ca. 745) and aḍ-Ḍaḥḥāk (d. 723), "The heavens and the earth are inside the *kursī* and the *kursī* is before the Throne. It is His footstool." Ar-Rabīʿ reported that the Companions of the Prophet said to him when this verse was revealed, "O Apostle of God, if this *kursī* encompasses the heavens and the earth, how big then is the Throne?" Ibn Zayd reported that the Apostle of God said, "The seven heavens are contained in the *kursī* just as seven coins placed in a shield." Abū Dharr (d. 653) said, "I heard the Apostle of God say, 'The *kursī* is in the Throne; it is no more than an iron ring placed in a large empty space in the earth.'"

According to aḍ-Ḍaḥḥāk and Ḥasan al-Baṣrī (d. 728), the *kursī* is the Throne. It is related that a woman came to the Prophet and asked that he pray God to make her enter Paradise. In the course of his supplications, the Prophet said, "Surely His *kursī* encompasses the heavens and the earth. He sits upon it, and not even the span of four fingers of it remains unoccupied. . . . It has a squeaking sound like that of a new saddle when ridden by a heavy person."

Saʿīd ibn Jubayr (d. 714) related on the authority of Ibn ʿAbbās (d. 687) that the *kursī* here means God's knowledge. [Ibn Jarīr aṭ-]Ṭabarī accepts this view and comments, "This may be proved by His saying, 'And the preservation of them does not burden Him,' which means that He is not burdened by the preservation of that which His knowledge encompasses, which is all that is in the heavens and the earth. God also said of His angels that they say in their prayers, 'Our Lord, You encompass all things in mercy and knowledge'" (40:7).

Shīʿī tradition reflects similar popular ideas regarding the *kursī*. Ṭabarsī (d. 1154) relates that the fifth imam was asked whether the *kursī* or the heavens and the earth are larger. He answered, "No, it is the *kursī* which contains the heavens and the earth, and everything which God created is contained in the *kursī*." ʿAlī (d. 661), the first imam, was asked about the meaning of the phrase, "His throne encompasses the heavens and the earth." He said, "The heavens and earth and all the creatures therein are contained in the *kursī*. Four angels bear it by God's leave. The first angel has a human image; it is the noblest image before God. He invokes God continuously and intercedes for human beings, praying for their sustenance. The second angel is in the image of a bull who invokes God continuously, interceding for all domestic animals and praying for their sustenance. The third angel is in the image of an eagle which is the lord of all birds. He invokes God and intercedes for all birds and prays for their sustenance. The fourth is in the image of a lion which is the king of beasts. In his devotion to God he intercedes and prays for the sustenance of all wild beasts. The most beautiful of all these was the image of the bull; it was of the best stature. When, however, the people of the Children of Israel took the calf for a god which they worshiped with devotion instead of God, the angel . . . bowed his head in shame before God because man had worshiped something resembling him. He feared lest he be afflicted with punishment." Ṭabarsī further reports that the fifth imam said, "Whoever recites the Verse of the Throne once, God shall spare him a thousand afflictions in this world and a thousand in the world to come; the lightest of those [afflictions] in this world is poverty, and in the next the punishment of the grave."

[Muḥyī 'd-Dīn] Ibn al-ʿArabī (d. 1240) declares the Throne Verse to be the greatest in the Qurʾān because of its profundity. He agrees with those commentators who interpret the word *kursī* to mean knowledge. He goes further, however, and asserts, "The *kursī* is the locus of knowledge as the heart is the locus of knowledge. Abū Yazīd al-Bisṭāmī (d. 875) said, 'Were the world and all that is in it to fall a thousand thousand times into a corner of the heart of the *ʿārif* ["knower" of God], he would not feel it because of the spaciousness of his heart.' For this reason Ḥasan al-Baṣrī said, 'The [concept] *kursī* of His throne is taken from the Prophet's saying, "The heart of the man of faith is of the throne of God."' The word *kursī* denotes a small footstool which cannot be separated from the seat of the Throne. It is like the heart both as imagined and portrayed in its greatness and magnitude. But as for the greatest and most glorious Throne, it is the first spirit and its image. Their ideal form is present in the eighth and greatest sphere, which encompasses the seven heavens and all that is in them."

Ibn al-ʿArabī interprets the phrase, "the preservation of them does not burden Him," to mean "their preservation does not burden Him because they have no existence without Him so that their preservation may be a burden on Him. Rather the realm of the ideal form is His inner dimension and the realm of forms is His outer dimension. They have no existence except in Him. Nor are they other than He. He is the Most High, higher than whom is nothing—He is above everything. He dominates everything within the great annihilation. His greatness is beyond imagination, and the greatness of anything that can be imagined is no more than a drop of His greatness. Absolute greatness belongs to Him alone and to no one else."

Zamakhsharī [a Muʿtazilite, d. 1144] declares with regard to the *kursī,* "It is no more than an image expressing God's greatness. In reality, there is neither *kursī,* an act of sitting, nor one who sits." Zamakhsharī sees the entire verse as an affirmation of God's oneness. He thus argues, "The *sūra* of Sincere Faith [*Al-Ikhlāṣ*] is declared to be excellent because of what it contains concerning God's unity, His exaltation and glorification and His great attributes. For there is no one more worthy of mention than the Lord of Majesty. Thus whatever may be said in remembrance of Him is greater than all remembrances. This means that the highest and noblest of all branches is the knowledge of the people of justice and divine unity [i.e., the Muʿtazila]. Let not the multiplicity of their foes tempt you away from it."

Other commentators have been critical of anthropomorphic interpretations of the verse under discussion. [Fakhr ad-Dīn ar-]Rāzī (d. 1209), after reviewing various interpretations, cites the famous exegete al-Qaffāl with approval, "The words, 'His Throne encompasses the heavens and the earth,' are meant to describe God's greatness and exaltation through images. This means that God addressed His creatures in ways familiar to them through their own kings in order that He might make known His essence and attributes to them. He therefore made the Kaʿba a house for Himself, and people circumambulate it as they do the houses of their kings. It is also said that the Black Stone is the right hand of God on this earth; thus He made it an object of reverent kissing, as men would kiss the hands of their kings. Hence by analogy He declared a throne for Himself through His saying, 'The All-merciful sat upon the Throne' (20:5). . . . Likewise, He declared a *kursī* for Himself in His saying, 'His throne encompasses the heavens and the earth.'"

Sayyid Quṭb (d. 1966) agrees with Rāzī and Zamakhsharī in taking the phrase, "His throne encompasses the heavens and the earth," metaphorically. He writes, "Expression by means of concrete imagery is used here in place of absolute freedom from anthropomorphism, in the usual manner of Qurʾānic expression through images. This is because the picture here employed gives the reality, which is metaphorically presented to the heart with power, depth, and firmness. Thus the word *kursī* is normally used to refer to dominion. Therefore, 'His throne encompasses the heavens and the earth' means that His authority encompasses them. This is reality from the intellectual point of view, but the picture which is impressed on the mind through the use of concrete imagery is stronger and firmer. Likewise, the expression, 'And the preservation of them does not burden Him,' is a metaphor for absolute power. It is presented, however, as concrete imagery; the imagery of the total absence of effort and fatigue. This is because the trend in the Qurʾānic expression is toward painting a picture of the actual meaning to the mind so as to be more immediate, deeper, and more powerfully felt. There is therefore no need for all the debate that has raged around such expressions in the Qur'ān, if we understand the way in which the Qur'ān uses symbols and metaphors, and if we do not borrow the foreign and strange philosophical ideas which have distorted for us much of the simplicity and clarity of the Qur'ān. It is well that I note here the fact that I have not come across any sound *hadith* concerning the *kursī* and Throne which would explain and determine what is actually intended in the Qur'ān by such words. For this reason I prefer not to enter into greater detail than is here given."

INTERPRETING THE VERSE OF LIGHT

Of at least equal theological importance to the Throne Verse is the Verse of Light (24:35). We begin with the intriguing views of Avicenna (Ibn Sīnā), arguably among the "most theological" of the great philosophers, follow up with discussions by major medieval Sunnī and Shī'ī theologians (Ghazālī and Ṭabrisī), and conclude with a modern South Asian Sunnī author, Mawdūdī.

Avicenna on the Metaphorical Meanings of the Verse of Light

Translated by Michael E. Marmura

By way of contrast, here is a sample of how Avicenna (Ibn Sīnā, d. 1037), an early philosopher whose views were highly influential in theological circles, explains the "symbols and metaphors" of the Verse of Light.[2] Avicenna's epistemological analysis of the use of language provides important context for theological themes articulated in subsequent texts here. Note how he draws parallels between the individual elements of the extended image and epistemological concepts, likening the niche to the material intellect/rational soul; the lamp to the acquired/actualized intellect; and the kindling from an olive tree to the cogitative power, for example.

Text

It has been said that a condition the prophet must adhere to is that his words should be symbols and his expressions hints. Or, as Plato states in the *Laws:* whoever does not understand the apostles' symbols will not attain the Divine Kingdom.[3] Moreover, the foremost Greek philosophers and prophets made use in their books of symbols and signs in which they hid their secret doctrine—men like Pythagoras, Socrates, and Plato. As for Plato, he had blamed Aristotle for divulging wisdom and making knowledge manifest so that Aristotle had to reply: "Even though I had done this, I have still left in my books many a pitfall which only the initiate among the wise and learned can understand."[4] Moreover, how could the prophet Muḥammad bring knowledge to the uncouth nomad, not to say to the whole human race considering that he was sent a messenger to all? Political guidance, on the other hand, comes easily to prophets; also the imposition of obligations on people. [Here he comments on several "symbolic texts," including only his line-by-line observations on 24:35.]

I say: *light* is an equivocal term partaking of two meanings, one essential, the other metaphorical. The essential stands for the perfection of the transparent inasmuch as it is transparent, as Aristotle said [in *De anima*]. The metaphorical meaning is to be understood in two ways: either as the good, or as the cause that leads to the good. Here, the sense is the metaphorical one in both meanings. I mean that God, the Exalted, is in Himself the good and the cause of everything good. The same judgment applies to the essential and to the nonessential. *The heavens and the earth* stands for the "whole." The *niche* stands for the material intellect and the rational soul. For the walls of a niche are close to each other and it is thus excellently predisposed to be illuminated since the closer the walls of a place are to each other, the greater the reflection and the light it holds. And just as the actualized intellect is likened to light, its recipient is likened to the recipient of light, which is the transparent. The best of transparent things is air and the best [transparent] air is in the niche. Thus what is symbolized by the niche is the material intellect, which is to the acquired intellect as the niche is to the light. The *lamp* stands for the acquired actualized intellect. For light, as the philosophers defined it, is the perfection of the transparent and that which moves it from potentiality to actuality. The acquired intellect is to the material intellect as the lamp is to the niche.

The expression *in a glass* is used because between the material and the acquired intellects there exists another [intermediate] level or place that is related to these two as that which intervenes between what is transparent and the lamp is related to the latter two. Here, in visual sight, the lamp does not reach [and hence could not be seen through] the transparent [air] without a medium. This is the oil vessel with the wick from which the glass protrudes. For glass is one of the transparent things receptive of light. Hence the subsequent utterance, *is as it were a brilliant star,* is given to convey that it is pure transparent glass, not opaque colored glass, since nothing colored is transparent. By *kindled from a blessed tree, an olive,* is meant the cogitative power, which stands as subject and material for the intellectual acts in the same way that oil stands as subject and material for the lamp.

Neither from the east nor from the west is explained as follows: "East" lexically derives from the place whence light emanates and "west" where it is quenched; and *east* is used metaphorically for the place where there is light and *west* for the place where there is no light. (Notice how the rules of simile are adhered to: *light* was made the basis of the statement and the simile constructed thereon; *light* was conjoined with the apparatus and materials that produce it.) Thus what is symbolized by the expression, *neither from the east nor from the west,* is as follows: the cogitative power, in the absolute sense, is not one of the pure rational powers where light emanates without restriction. This is the meaning of the saying, *a . . . tree . . . neither from the east.* Nor is it one of the animal powers where light is utterly lost. This is the meaning of *nor from the west.*

The saying, *its oil almost shines even if no fire touched it,* is in praise of the cogitative power. In this expression, *even if no fire touched it,* the word *touch* stands for connection and emanation. The saying *fire* is explained as follows: when the similarity between metaphorical *light* and real light and between the instruments and the consequences of the former and those of the latter was drawn, the essential subject that causes a thing to be in another was likened to what is customarily considered a subject, that is to say, fire. For although in reality fire is colorless, custom takes it to be luminous. (Observe how the rules of simile are adhered to!) Moreover, since fire surrounds the elements (*ummahāt*), that which surrounds the world, not in the spatial sense, but in a verbal metaphorical sense, is likened to fire. This is the universal intellect. This intellect, however, is not as Alexander of Aphrodisias believed—attributing the belief to Aristotle—the true God, the First. For, although in one respect this first intellect is one, it is multiple inasmuch as it consists of the forms of numerous universals. It is thus one, not essentially, but accidentally, acquiring its oneness from Him who is essentially one, the one God.

Ghazālī on the Similitudes in the Verse of Light

Translated by David Buchman

It has become unfortunately common to assume that because Abū Ḥāmid al-Ghazālī (d. 1111) wrote *The Incoherence of the Philosophers,* he must surely be out to cast aspersions on all manner of intellectual inquiry—or at least to discredit Avicenna, the chief object of his critique in that volume. A closer look at Ghazālī's systematic writings, however, provides sufficient evidence to call that assessment into question. The following short summary of Ghazālī's reading of the Verse of Light, juxtaposed here with Ibn Sīnā's views of the same text, make an arresting case in point. In his *Niche of Lights,* Ghazālī associates the main elements of the extended Qurʾānic simile to epistemological categories that he calls "spirits"—the sensible, imaginal, rational, reflective, and prophetic.[5]

Text

Know that drawing a parallel between these five spirits and niche, the glass, the lamp, the tree, and the olive can be a long discussion. But I will be brief and confine it to calling attention to the path of drawing parallels. I say:

As for the sensible spirit, when you consider its specific characteristic, you find that its lights come out of numerous holes, like the two eyes, the two ears, the two nostrils, and so forth. Hence, the most suitable similitude for this spirit in the visible world is the niche.

As for the imaginal spirit, we find that it has three characteristics: First is that it derives from the clay of the dense low world, because the imaginalized thing possesses measure [and] shape, [has] specified and confined directions, and is near or far relative to the one who does the imagining. A characteristic of a dense thing that is described by the attributes of bodies is that it veils the pure rational lights, which are incomparable with being described in terms of directions, measures, nearness, and farness.

The second characteristic is that when this dense imagination is purified, refined, polished, and organized, it becomes parallel to the rational meanings and points toward their lights. It does not obstruct the light that radiates from the meanings.

The third characteristic is that, at the beginning, imagination is much needed, because through it one can organize rational knowledge so that knowledge will not be agitated, shaken up, and scattered with a scattering that eliminates the organization. What a wonderful help are the imaginal similitudes for rational knowledge!

We find these three characteristics in relation to the seen lights of the visible world only in glass. Originally, glass is a dense substance, but once it is purified and made clear, it does not veil the light of the lamp. Rather, it conveys the light in a proper manner. Furthermore, it protects the light from being extinguished by violent winds and rough movements. Glass, therefore, is the first similitude for the imaginal spirit.

As for the third spirit—the rational spirit through which perception of noble, divine knowledge takes place—the manner of using the lamp as a similitude for it is not hidden from you. You came to know this in the earlier clarification of the fact that the prophets are light-giving lamps.

As for the fourth spirit—the reflective spirit—one of its specific characteristics is that it begins with a single root and then branches off from it into two branches. Then from each branch grow two branches, and so on until the branches of rational divisions become many. Then, at last, it reaches conclusions that are its fruits. These fruits then go back and become seeds for similar fruits, because some of them can fertilize others so that they continue to bear fruits beyond them. This is similar to what we mentioned in the book *The Just Balance.* Hence, it is most appropriate that in this world the similitude of the reflective spirit be the tree.

Since the fruits of the reflective spirit are a matter within which the lights of knowledge may be augmented, fixed, and given subsistence, it is appropriate that the likeness that is used not be the quince, apple, pomegranate, or other [kinds of] trees. But, among all the trees, the olive tree specifically is used, because the quintessence of its fruit is olive oil, which is the matter for lamps. Out of all oils, olive oil is singled out for the specific characteristic of having a great deal of radiance with little smoke.

If cattle and trees that have many offspring and much fruit are called "blessed," then it is even more worthy to call that tree whose fruit does not end at a defined limit a "blessed tree" (24:35).

If the branches of pure rational thoughts cannot be ascribed to directions [or to] nearness and farness, then it is appropriate that the tree be "neither of the East nor the West" (24:35).

The fifth spirit is the holy prophetic spirit ascribed to the friends of God when it is in the utmost degree of purity and nobility.

The reflective spirit is divided into [two kinds:] a sort that needs instruction, awakening, and help from the outside so that it may continue partaking of many types of knowledge; and another sort that has such intense purity that it is, as it were, awakened by itself without help from the outside. It is most appropriate that the one that is pure and has reached full preparedness be referred to by the words, "Its oil would well-nigh but shine, even if no fire touched it" (24:35), since among the friends of God are those whose light would all but shine so that they could all but dispense with the help of the prophets. And among the prophets are those who could all but dispense with the help of the angels. This similitude is suitable for this kind.

When these lights are ranked in levels, one on top of the other, then the sensory spirit is the first. It is like the preparation and introduction to the imaginal spirit, since the imaginal cannot be conceived of as being placed in its situation except after the sensory. The reflective and rational spirits come after these two. Hence, it is most appropriate that the glass be like the locus for the lamp and the niche like the locus for the glass. Hence, the lamp is in a glass and the glass is in a niche. Since all of them are lights, one above the other, it is appropriate that they be "light upon light" (24:35).

This similitude becomes clear only to the hearts of those who have faith or to the hearts of the prophets and the friends of God, not to the hearts of the unbelievers. After all, by "guidance" is meant light. That which is kept away from the path of guidance is falsehood and darkness—or, rather, it is more intense than darkness, because darkness does not guide to falsehood any more than it guides to truth.

Ṭabrisī on the Verse of Light

Translated by Feras Hamza and Sajjad Rizvi

Ṭabrisī's (d. 1154) commentary on theVerse of Light is a representative example of his comprehensive style of exegesis.[6] He includes the usual discussions of variant readings, grammar, and poetical citations to underpin the traditional understanding of the verse. He attempts to cover the divergent opinions on the verse's meaning and what exactly the phrase "the likeness of His light" refers to. In affirmation of his Shīʿī affiliation, Ṭabrisī (also known as Ṭabarsī) cites a version of the tradition from the eighth imam, ʿAlī ar-Riḍā (d. 818) that extols the virtues of the imams. Ṭabrisī concludes with a summary of the special qualities of the oil extracted from olives and the blessed status of the olive tree, and he draws an interesting comparison between the blessed tree and the believer.

Text

There is divergence as regards the meaning of *God is the Light of the heavens and the earth.* Some say that it means: (1) God guides the inhabitants of the heavens and the earth to that which is beneficial for them in it, as reported by Ibn ʿAbbās; (2) God is the One who lights up the heavens and the earth with the sun, moon and stars, as reported by al-Ḥasan [al-Baṣrī], Abū 'l-ʿĀliya and aḍ-Ḍaḥḥāk; (3) [God is the One who] decorates the heavens with angels and the earth with prophets and *ʿulamāʾ*, as reported by Ubayy ibn Kaʿb (d. 639 or 649). "Light" (*nūr*) is used to describe God, may He be exalted, because every benefit, good deed and blessing is from Him, like when one says someone is a *raḥma* (mercy) or an *ʿadhāb* (torture), if such acts are frequently observed in him. For this reason God referred to him [the Prophet] as *sirājan munīran* (an illuminating torch, cf. 33:46).

The likeness of His light is interpreted variously: (1) [His light is] that which God has guided the believers with: the belief in their hearts, as reported by Ubayy ibn Kaʿb and aḍ-Ḍaḥḥāk; Ubayy used to read *the likeness of His light is the one who believes in Him;* (2) it is the Qurʾān in the heart, as reported by Ibn ʿAbbās, Ḥasan [al-Baṣrī] and Zayd ibn Aslam (d. 753); (3) it is Muḥammad, whom He has added to Himself as a way of honoring him, as reported by Kaʿb and Saʿīd ibn Jubayr; (4) it is the proof which points to His unity and justice, which are apparent to see like light, as reported by Abū Muslim (d. 755); (5) it is obedience to God in the heart of the believer, as reported by Ibn ʿAbbās in another transmission.

As a niche wherein is a lamp: a *mishkāt* is a niche in a wall in which a glass is placed with the lamp behind it, but with another access to the lamp, being the place from where the lamp is inserted. It is said that a *mishkāt* is the pole of the lantern, into which the wick is placed, and that it is like a niche; *almiṣbāḥ* is a *sirāj* (torch), and the *mishkāt* is a *qindīl* (lantern), [although] according to [early exegete] Mujāhid (d. ca. 720), *miṣbāḥ* is the actual wick. *Al-miṣbāḥu fī zujāja* (*The lamp in a glass*): glass is used in this description because it is the clearest of substances and allows light [in it] for greater glow. *Az-zujāja kaʾannahā kawkabun durrīyun* (*The glass as though it were a glittering star*) means that the glass is like a great star that shines like pearls in its clarity, light and purity.

Kindled from a blessed tree: that is, the lamp is lit from the oil of a tree that is blessed. *An olive tree:* he identifies the blessed tree as that of the olive, because it has an array of benefits: oil from it is burnt to give light; it is used as a tanner; firewood and residues from it can be burnt; dye, silk is washed with its ash; and one needs not crush it to extract its oil. It is said that He singled out the olive tree because its oil is purer and gives off better light [when lit] and, it is said, because it was the first tree to grow from the earth after the Flood, and its natural growing area is the homeland of prophets;[7] it is also said that through it He made seventy prophets prosper (*bāraka fīhā*), including Abraham, and that is why it is "blessed" (*mubāraka*).

Neither of the east nor the west: it is not covered by shade either from the east or the west, always sunlit, and not obscured by any mountain, tree or cave, and its oil is yellow, as reported by [seventh-century exegetes] Ibn ʿAbbās, al-Kalbī (d. 763), ʿIkrima (d. ca. 723) and Qatāda (d. 736). Hence, the meaning is that it is not of the east, so the sun does not shine on it when it sets, and not of the west, so the sun does not shine on it when it rises, but it is of east and west, taking its share of both. It is said: it means that it does not belong among the trees of this world, for it to be either of the east or west, as reported by Ḥasan [al-Baṣrī]. It is also said: it is not in an enclosure such that sunlight cannot reach it, nor is it exposed such that there is no shade for it, but it receives sunlight and shade alike, as reported by Suddī. It is also said: it is neither of trees [that grow] in the east nor of trees [that grow] in the west, since the tree that belongs in only one of the two directions [produces] less oil and [its oil] does not burn as brightly; it is instead of the trees of Syria (*ash-Shām*), which is in between east and west, as reported by Ibn Zayd (d. 798).

Whose oil well-nigh would shine, on account of its purity and the extent of its brilliance [when lit]; *even if no fire touched it,* that is, before fire were to light it and consume it. Opinions differ with regard to the person to which this simile refers:

(1) It is an allegory which God offers to His Prophet Muḥammad [according to which] the "niche" is his chest, the "glass" is his heart, and the "lamp" therein is his prophethood, neither of the east nor of the west, i.e., neither Jewish nor Christian, *kindled from a blessed tree,* i.e., the tree of prophethood, which is Abraham; the "light" of Muḥammad, is almost apparent to people even if he did not speak with it, just as that oil would shine even if no fire touched it, as reported by Kaʿb and some commentators.

(2) It is also said that the "niche" represents Abraham, the "glass" Ishmael, and the "lamp" Muḥammad, since [the latter] is called a "torch" in another instance (cf. 33:46). *From a blessed tree,* i.e., [from] Abraham, since most of the prophets are descended from his loins; *neither of the east nor of the west,* i.e., neither Christian nor Jewish, since Christians pray to the east, while the Jews pray to the west. *Its oil well-nigh would shine,* that is, the good qualities of Muḥammad were on the verge of being apparent before revelation was given to him. *Light upon light,* that is, one prophet descended from another, as reported by Muḥammad ibn Kaʿb.

(3) It is also said that the "niche" is [Muḥammad's grandfather] ʿAbd al-Muṭṭalib, the "glass" ʿAbd Allāh, and the "lamp" Muḥammad; [they are] *neither of the east nor of the west* but Meccan; since Mecca is the center of the world, as reported by aḍ-Ḍaḥḥāk.

(4) It has been reported from [ʿAlī] ar-Riḍā that he said: we [Shīʿī imams] are in the "niche" and the "lamp" is Muḥammad, God guides to our friendship whomever He likes.

(5) In the *Kitāb at-Tawḥīd* (*Book of Divine Unity*) of Abū Jaʿfar ibn Bābawayh (d. 991), through the chain of transmission ʿĪsā ibn Rāshid [from] Abū Jaʿfar al-Bāqir concerning His saying *as a niche wherein is a lamp,* he said: the light of knowledge is in the chest of the Prophet. *The lamp in a glass,* the glass is the chest of ʿAlī, the knowledge of the Prophet reached the chest of ʿAlī; *kindled from a blessed tree,* the Prophet taught ʿAlī the light of knowledge; *neither of the east nor of the west,* neither Jewish nor Christian. As regards its *oil well-nigh would shine,* he said: the person of knowledge from among the family of Muḥammad would impart knowledge before he was asked; *light upon light,* that is, each imam in turn from the family of Muḥammad is fortified by the light of knowledge and wisdom, from the time of Adam until the arrival of the Hour. These are the trustees whom God has made vice-regents on His earth and His proofs against His creation; the earth will have one of these in every age.

An analysis of this statement suggests that the "blessed tree" mentioned in this verse must be the principal tree of devoutness and [divine] satisfaction, of guidance and belief, its trunk being prophethood, its bough the imamate, its branches the revelation, its leaves interpretation (*taʾwīl*), and its two guardians are Gabriel and Michael.

A second opinion is that this [verse] is an allegory that God gave to the believer: the "niche" is the [believer] himself, the "glass" his chest, the "lamp" belief, and the Qurʾān in his heart is *kindled from a blessed tree,* which is sincere devotion to God alone who has no partner. The tree, therefore, is green and delicate, surrounded by other trees so that no sunlight ever reaches it, neither when [the sun] rises nor when it sets: such too is the believer, who has guarded himself from any weakness, since he is between four pillars that keep him secure: (1) if he is granted something, he is thankful; (2) if he is tested, he is patient; (3) if he judges, he is just; (4) if he speaks, he does so truthfully, and so he is a living person amidst people, walking amid graves, light upon light. His speech is "light," his knowledge is "light," his entrance is "light," his exit is "light," and his way to Paradise is "light" on the Day of Resurrection, as reported by Ubayy ibn Kaʿb.

The third opinion is that this [verse] is a simile of the Qurʾān the heart of the believer: it is like a "lamp" that never decreases in light. Such too is the Qurʾān, with which one seeks guidance and in accordance with which one conducts oneself. The "lamp" is the Qurʾān, the "glass" is the believer's heart and the "niche" is his tongue and mouth; the "blessed tree" is that of inspiration, *whose oil well-nigh would shine,* i.e., the proofs of the Qurʾān would make themselves known, even if they were not read. It is also said that the proofs of God against His creation "would well-nigh shine" for those who ponder them and reflect upon them, even if the Qurʾān had not been sent down. *Light upon light:* the Qurʾān is "light" and all the proofs (*adilla*) that preceded have acquired, through [the Qurʾān], more "light," "light upon light," as reported by Ḥasan [al-Baṣrī] and Ibn Zayd. According to this last [interpretation], it is possible that the main point [of the verse] has to do with order of proofs, since proofs can follow one another in [logical] order, and a person of reason can profit from these only through following such an order—the one who neglects this order cannot profit at all. Mujāhid said: the glow of the light from the lamp is above the light of the oil, which is above the light of the glass. *God guides to His light whom He will:* that is, God guides to His religion and belief in Him whom He will by bestowing upon him a grace (*luṭf*), which, once he is aware of it, leads him to choose on account of belief. It is also said that it means that God guides to prophethood and His friendship whom He will from among those He knows to be fit for such matters. *And God strikes similitudes for humankind,* as a way of making [things] easier [for them] to understand and [for them] to realize their needs. *And God has knowledge of everything,* and so He gives everything its proper place.

Abū 'l-ʿAlā al-Mawdūdī on the Verse of Light

Translated by Feras Hamza and Sajjad Rizvi

Another sample of exegesis of the Verse of Light is that of contemporary Sunnī author Abū 'l-ʿAlā al-Mawdūdī (d. 1979).[8] Mawdūdī's commentary on this celebrated verse displays two key characteristics of modernist, Muslim reformist thinking and exegesis. First, it stresses the evident nature of divine guidance (the light) and the obligation for total submission to it in all spheres of one's life; hence, the attack upon hypocrisy. Second, it attempts to familiarize the divine text by appealing to the reader's association with literary forms. When techniques of literary analysis are applied to the Qurʾānic text, the metaphor of light is shown to express a tropic formulation akin to other tropes in literature. Furthermore, literary devices used in the Qurʾān are assimilative but do not actually provide "real comparisons." To detail this, and stress divine alterity (another major feature of his thought), Mawdūdī makes a distinction between humans making sense of a word or phrase (its "basic sense") and an "absolute, God's point-of-view sense," thus articulating a relative theory of meaning in which signification is one thing when applied to humankind and quite another when applied to God. This allows for a critique of literal anthropomorphism while retaining a somewhat traditional Sunnī Ashʿarī reluctance to engage in extensive metaphorical analysis and advocating a Traditionalist agnosticism about those anthropomorphisms (the *balkafa* in classical *kalām*).[9] Thus to say "God is light" has meaning for us as a metaphor but the absolute sense, or one might say the mode in which He is light, is not available to us. (Note how Mawdūdī simply proceeds by listing individual words and phrases from the scripture and expands upon each in turn.)

Text

God: [A continuation of a critique of hypocrites] . . . These hypocrites had become totally myopic because of their excessive worldliness. Despite their profession of faith, they were totally devoid of the light which, thanks to the Qurʾān and the Prophet, had begun to radiate all around. At this point, without directly addressing [the hypocrites], the observations made about them here have three aims. First, to admonish them; for, it is the foremost requirement of God's mercy and lordship that if a person falls into error and is straying, then notwithstanding all his mischievous and ugly deeds, every effort should be made, to the last moment, to make him understand [the truth and mend his ways]. Second, to lay bare the distinction between faith and hypocrisy in unambiguous terms so that it is not difficult for even an average person to differentiate between the believing and the hypocritical individuals in Muslim societies. If, despite all the clarification, someone lets himself get caught in the noose of the hypocrites, or seeks to be a partisan of the hypocrites, then they are to be held responsible for this act. Third, to clearly warn the hypocrites that God's promises are meant only for the believers who are sincere in their faith and fulfill its requirements. These promises are not meant for nominal believers, for those whose identification with Islam is no more than their registration as Muslims in official records. Hypocrites and those who willfully transgress the commands of God should not expect that God's promise be fulfilled for them.

Light of the heavens and the earth: In Qur'ānic usage, the expression "the heavens and the earth" is generally used in the sense of "the universe." An alternative rendering of the verse, therefore, could be "God is the Light of the whole Universe."

By "light" is meant that thing which makes other things visible. That is to say, [light is] what is apparent in and of itself and which causes other objects to become apparent. This is the general perception, in the human mind, of light and illumination. The state of total non-comprehension has been called "darkness" and "obscurity" by man. By contrast, when everything becomes comprehensible and all things are apparent, then man says that there is light. It is according to this fundamental understanding of the word "light" that it is used for God, exalted be He. It is not to be taken literally to mean that God is some ray of light, which travels at the speed of 186,000 miles per second and reaches the retina of our eyes and ultimately affects the center of vision in the brain. This particular attribute is not a part of the essential meaning for which the human mind invented the word. Rather that attribute is used for those types of illuminations that enter our experiences in the material world.

Whatever phrases human language utilizes for God are spoken with regard to their fundamental aspects and not with regard to their material examples. For example, we say of God that He sees. Now this does not mean that God sees by means of a physical organ called an eye, in the manner of animals and human beings. Likewise, we say that God hears. This does not mean that, like us, God hears by means of ears. Likewise, we are told that God seizes. Again, this is not in the sense of God seizing by means of an instrument, namely the hand, in the manner that humans and animals seize.

All such statements have an absolute meaning. Hence, it is people of very limited understanding who believe that there can be no other form of seeing, hearing and seizing except in the specific limited form with which we are familiar through our own experience. In the same way, in connection with "light," to imagine that its significance may be manifested/perceived only in the form of a ray that emanates from some shining object and falls upon the retina of the eye, is sheer narrow-mindedness. God is light, not in this limited sense but rather in an absolute sense; in other words, in this existence God alone is selfapparent; all else is nothing other than mere darkness. Any other thing that emits light is luminous and illuminating only because God has invested it with light, otherwise they have nothing innate whereby they could perform this miracle [of being luminous and illuminating].

The word "light" is also used to mean "knowledge," and its antonym—ignorance—is described by "darkness." In this sense, too, God is the light of the universe, for the knowledge of realities and of the right way [that human beings should tread] can only be gained from God. Without receiving of God's abundance, it is impossible to do away with ignorance and its consequences of error and sinfulness.

A blessed tree, an olive: "blessed" meaning of many beneficial uses, bearing very many advantages.

Neither of the east nor of the west: That is, the tree is situated on an open site or at a height so that it is constantly exposed to the sun. It is not behind anything, for if it were, it would receive sunlight either only in the forenoon or only in the afternoon. Now the oil of such an olive tree is more subtle and produces a stronger light. A tree that faces only eastward or westward produces a relatively thicker oil, the light of which is weaker in a lamp.

Light upon light: In this parable, the lamp is an allegory of God Himself while the niche is a symbol of creation; and what is intended by the lamp is that veil behind which He the Truth, exalted be He, has kept Himself hidden from the eyes of creatures. However, the veil in reality is not one of concealment but rather one of intensity of visibility.

Thus, the inability of creatures to behold God is not because of some dark curtain between them [and God]. Rather, the real reason is that in-between there is a diaphanous veil; and the light that passes and comes through this diaphanous veil is so intense, clear and all-encompassing that physical constitutions of limited power [i.e., humans with limited faculties] are too weak to perceive it.[10] These weak constitutions can perceive only those limited lights that contain within themselves a vacillation, and which sometimes cease [to be seen] and sometimes appear; and in contrast to which a darkness may appear—it is in the face of their opposites that such lights are understood. As for absolute light [sc. that of God] which has no contrast or rival, which never ceases, which always shines in every direction with a constant splendor—the perception of this light is beyond the capacity of those weak creatures.

The statement: "the lamp is illuminated by the oil of such an olive tree as is neither eastern nor western," is made purely for the sake of presenting an image of the light's perfection and intensity. In past times, the most light was obtained from lamps lit by olive oil. Among such lamps, the most brightly burning ones were those which were lit with oil derived from a tree situated in an open and elevated place.

The purpose of this comparison is not to say that God derives energy from something other [than Himself], like the lamp to which the comparison has been made. Rather the intention is that, in the similitude, we should picture not an ordinary lamp but the brightest one that we have ever witnessed, [and we should understand that] even as such a lamp lights up the whole house, even so God bestows illumination upon the whole of creation.

Similarly, the intention of the statement that *whose oil well-nigh would shine even if no fire would touch it* is to present an image of how the light of the lamp is exceedingly intense. In other words [it is as though we are being told]: [when contemplating] the similitude imagine that lamp whose luminosity is the ultimate in brightness, containing as it does such fine and incandescent oil. These three things, namely the olive tree, its being neither of the east nor the west, and its oil which shines forth of its own without being lit by fire, are not independent elements of the parable. Rather, they are contained within the first element of the parable, namely the lamp. There are three essential elements of the parable: namely, the lamp, the niche and the transparent glass.

The phrase in the verse "*the likeness of His light is as . . .* " likewise eliminates the [possible] misunderstanding, which might have arisen regarding the statement *God is the Light of the heavens and the earth.* From [the phrase "the likeness of His light is as . . . "], it is understood that the intention in saying of God that He is "light" is not to say that His [essential] reality is nothing but light. In His reality He is one perfect essence Who, along with being possessor of knowledge, of power, of wisdom, etc., is also the possessor of light. However, He Himself has been called purely Light because of the perfection of His luminosity—just as, to describe someone's state of perfect generosity they are said to be generosity itself; or as, to describe someone's perfect good looks, they are declared to be beauty itself.

God guides to His light whom He will. Although God's absolute light illuminates the whole universe, not everyone has the fortune to perceive it. The blessing of having the [God-given] success to perceive [the divine light] and to draw benefit from its superabundant emanation (*fayḍ*), is granted by God alone to whom He wills. Otherwise, as in the case of the blind man who cannot differentiate between day and night, for a seeing person the light of lightening—the sun, the moon and the stars—is indeed light but they fail to discern the light that comes from God. From this point of view, for such an unfortunate person there is only darkness on darkness, on every side in the universe. A physically blind person cannot see even what lies next to him, so much so that it is only when he bumps into it and feels the hurt that he realizes that thing was present in that place. In the same manner, a man without perceptive vision cannot see even those realities which are directly in front of him, radiant with the light of God. Such a person realizes their existence only when he has stumbled against them and has been seized by his perdition.

And God strikes similitudes for humankind and God has knowledge of everything. This statement has two meanings. The first is that God knows very well which realities may be explained by which similitudes in the best possible way. The second [meaning] is that God knows best who is entitled to this blessing and who is not. God has no need to forcibly show the light of [God] the Truth to that person who is not in search of it, and who is engrossed always in their worldly ambitions, and the pursuit of material comforts and mundane benefits. It is only those whom God knows to be seekers, and sincere seekers, of it, who are entitled to this gift [of the light of God the Truth].

THEOLOGICAL PRINCIPLES IN HERMENEUTICS

No study of Qurʾānic hermeneutics can begin without some reference to texts of the scripture itself that comment on the nature of the revealed message and the underlying challenge of interpreting it. The signature text in this respect is 3:7:

> It is He who sent the book down to you [Muḥammad]. Some of its signs/verses are incontrovertible in meaning (*muḥkamāt*), and they are the Mother of the Book. Others are of debatable interpretation (*mutashābihāt*). So those of divergent heart seek out the debatable [verses] from [the scripture] in a desire for dissension and seeking its inward meaning. But none knows its hidden meaning, except God. Those firmly rooted in knowledge say, "We believe in it, all of it from our Lord." None will reflect deeply [on it] except possessors of deep understanding.

An important and contentious variant reading of this text turns on simply altered punctuation, changing a period to a comma following "God," as follows: "But none knows its hidden meaning, except God, and those firmly rooted in knowledge. They say, 'We believe in it. . . . '" The seemingly minor change opens the door for the inclusion of the pursuit of "hidden meaning" (*taʾwīl*) within the orbit of acceptable exegetical methodology.

Numerous exegetical concerns such as those hinted at in these last selections have prompted important Muslim authors to produce works both short and expansive on methodological issues with significant theological resonances. Questions about the "uncreated" (and therefore divine) nature of the Qur'ān form the most fundamental theme of the kind, and specific texts laying out the terms of the debate appear in later sections of this volume. Several other topics approach its centrality but come to the fore more clearly in the present context. We begin with a remarkable overview of Qur'ānic hermeneutics by Ibn al-Jawzī, a propaedeutic "full-scale exegetical typology" on the subject of *tafsīr*. In addition, from the earliest days Muslim exegetes developed an intense interest in the "circumstances of revealed messages" (*asbāb an-nuzūl*) into an essential hermeneutical tool, a discussion represented here by the views of Suyūṭī. Theologians have long discussed a question raised in Qur'ān 3:7 about levels of interpretation, as in the selection here on *mutashābih,* with the use of the term *ta'wīl.*[11] Here 'Abd al-Jabbār discusses the role of reason in exegesis. Another essential theme is the underlying principle of *naskh* (abrogation). Since God tailors revelatory communication to humanity's limited capacity to receive ultimate truth, He therefore reserves the right to "abrogate" earlier messages in favor of refinements needed to move the community of believers further toward full understanding. Shāh Walī Allāh's early modern interpretation of abrogation describes the nature of this concept. Finally, Ayatollah Khū'ī offers a contemporary Shī'ī approach to the miraculous inimitability of the sacred text.

Ibn al-Jawzī on Exegetical Method

Translated by Jane Dammen McAuliffe

In the introduction to his scriptural commentary, *Provisions for the Journey on the Science of Exegesis* (*Zād al-maṣīr fī 'ilm at-tafsīr*), Ibn al-Jawzī (1116–200) offers a précis of his hermeneutical method. This very prolific scholar thereby sets the table for further individual considerations of specific topics that are the constituent features of the religious discipline known as the Qur'ānic sciences (*'ulūm al-Qur'ān*). That the entire work was large enough to fill ten volumes in its modern edition did not prevent its author from recommending that readers memorize all of it. Since the Qur'ān is the most important possible object of understanding, Ibn al-Jawzī insists that its exegesis is the highest intellectual activity.[12]

Text

INTRODUCTION TO PROVISIONS FOR THE JOURNEY IN THE SCIENCE OF EXEGESIS

In the name of God, the merciful, the compassionate, praise be to God who has honored us over other peoples with the illustrious Qurʾān and has called us, by granting us sound judgment, to a rightly-guided state of life. By it He has set our souls firmly between promise and threat and He has protected it from change made by the ignorant and alternation by the obdurate: "Falsehood cannot enter it from before or behind, a sending down from a wise, a praiseworthy One" (41:43).

I praise Him for making the highest praise possible and thank Him for actualizing the affirmation of divine unity. I bear witness that there is no god but God alone, who has no complement—an act of witness whose stored treasure is continuously reinforced—and that Muḥammad is His servant and His messenger, sent to those both near and far, a herald to created beings and a warner, a lamp in the cosmos shining. From His abundance He gave him much bounty and set him ahead of all others, making him great, with no human his equal. Yet he forbade anyone to pray in his name as a way of glorifying and honoring him. God sent down on him a spoken revelation and confirmed the authenticity of His word by challenging to the production of its equivalent: "Say, in truth, if humans and jinn agree to produce the equivalent of this Qurʾān, they will not be able to do so, even if they were to back each other up" (17:88). . . .

Since the mighty Qurʾān is the noblest fund of knowledge, understanding its ideas is the most perfect form of understanding. This is because the degree of eminence of the act of knowing lies in the eminence of that which is known. Yet I have carefully examined a whole range of commentaries and have found them either so vast as to induce despair in the [would-be] memorizer or so short as to preclude the full attainment of one's purpose. Those of average size, too, are of little benefit, being poorly arranged and sometimes neglecting the problematic while explaining the obvious. Therefore I offer you this simple compendium, containing knowledge in plenty, and have designated it "Provisions for the Journey on the Science of Exegesis." I have striven to keep it short so try, to the extent of your God-given capacity, to memorize it. God it is who aids in its realization, for He has never ceased generously to offer success.

Abū ʿAbd ar-Raḥmān as-Sulamī (d. 1021) reported on the authority of Ibn Masʿūd: "We would learn from the Messenger of God ten verses of the Qurʾān and would not go on to the next ten until we knew what they contained in the way of knowledge and action." Qatāda reported that al-Ḥasan [al-Baṣrī] said: "God has sent down no verse for which I would not want to know why it was sent and what was intended by it." Īyās ibn Muʿāwiya said: "The situation of one who can recite the Qurʾān and who knows how to interpret it [as opposed to not so knowing] is like that of a group to whom there comes at night a written message from one of their comrades, but who are without a lamp. With the message's arrival, fear at not knowing what is in it overcomes them. But when the lamp is brought to them they [immediately] recognize what is in it."

Those educated in the religious sciences have held various views on whether the terms *at-tafsīr* and *at-taʾwīl* have the same meaning or two different meanings. A group whose proclivities were linguistic held the view that the two meant the same thing. This is the opinion of the generality of earlier exegetes. A group with primarily legal interests was persuaded that the two terms differed in meaning. They defined *tafsīr* as "moving something out of concealment into full view" and *taʾwīl* as "shifting discourse from its conventional signification to some allusion which may even neglect the literal sense of the utterance." Lexically, the term *taʾwīl* is derived from the stem *ʾWL* in a sense synonymous with the stem *SWR*, i.e., "to lead to," "to arrive at."

ON THE DURATION OF THE QURʾĀN'S DESCENT

ʿIkrima (d. 723) reported from Ibn ʿAbbās saying, "On the Night of Power the Qurʾān was sent down from the Preserved Tablet to the House of Splendor as a single unit. After that it was sent down over a period of twenty years." Ash-Shaʿbī (d. 725) said "God divided up the Qurʾān's revelation so that there were twenty years between the beginning and the end of it." Ḥasan said: "Someone told us that between the beginning and end of it were eighteen years, eight of those elapsing in Mecca."

There has been a difference of opinion about what part of the Qurʾān came down first. The traditional view affirms that the first part to come down was: "Recite in the name of your Lord" (96:1). ʿUrwa (d. ca. 713) reported this on the authority of ʿĀʾisha. Both Qatāda and Abū Ṣaliḥ (d. 738) held the same view. It has been reported from Jābir ibn ʿAbd Allāh that the first thing that came down was "O, you who are encloaked" (74:1). The right view is that when "Recite in the name of your Lord" came down on him [Muḥammad], he went back and wrapped himself in a cloak. Then "O, you who are encloaked" came down. This is also suggested by the argument in the two *Ṣaḥīḥs* [of Muslim and Bukhārī] from the *ḥadīth* of Jābir who said: "I heard the Prophet speak about the period of revelation, and in talking about it he said: 'While I was walking along I heard a sound from the heavens, so I raised my head. Lo and behold! The angel who had come to me on Mt. Ḥirā' was sitting on a throne between heaven and earth. I was torn apart with fear (*juthithtu minhu ruʿban*). I went home and said: 'Keep close to me, keep close to me.' So they covered me with a cloak. Then God sent down 'O, you who are encloaked.'" (The sense of *juthithtu* [I was uprooted, i.e., terrified] is *furriqtu* [I went to pieces, came apart—out of fear]. One can say a man is *majʾūth* or *majthūth*.) Some professional transmitters have distorted it and said "I shrank back (*jabuntu*), from cowardice (*jubn*)." But the first reading is the valid one. It has been reported from Ḥasan and ʿIkrima that the first part to come down was "In the name of God, the merciful, the compassionate."

There have been different views expressed about the last [part of the Qurʾān] to come down. Bukhārī relates, in his section [of the *Ṣaḥīḥ*] on those *hadīth* with a single attestation, one such from Ibn ʿAbbās who said: "The last verse to be sent down on the Prophet was the verse about usury." In the uniquely attested hadiths from Muslim's collection there is one, also from Ibn ʿAbbās, which states: "The last sūra to come down in its entirety was [the one that begins] 'When the help of God comes and the victory'" (110:1). Ḍaḥḥāk, also reporting on the authority of Ibn ʿAbbās, said: "The last verse which was sent down was 'Beware the day in which you will be returned to God'" (2:281). This is also the view of Saʿīd ibn Jubayr and Abū Ṣāliḥ. On the authority of al-Barāʾ, Abū Isḥāq said: "The last verse sent down was 'They will seek legal judgments from you; say: God will decide for you about those who die without heirs'" (4:176). The last sūra to be sent down was *al-barāʾa.* It has been related from Ubayy ibn Kaʿb that the last verse to come down was "Indeed there has come to you a messenger from among yourselves" (9:128).

Whereas I have seen most of the exegetes' works, scarcely a single one discloses the purport in a manner properly aspired to, so that one must study an individual verse in multiple sources. Many a *tafsīr* fails to provide full, or even partial, knowledge of the abrogating and abrogated verses. Again, if that is to be found therein, then information is lacking about all or most of the situations which occasioned revelation. If these latter are present, then a clear distinction as between which verses were revealed in Mecca, and which in Medina, is absent. If that clarification is to be found, then allusion to the prescriptive implication of the verse is missing. If such is there, then there is no attempt to deal with any ambiguity which occurs in the verse. All this is to say nothing of the various other areas of highly prized knowledge.

In this book, I have included of the subjects mentioned above (together with others not mentioned, but indispensable to exegesis) such matters as I hope will make this book sufficiently useful to avoid the need for most others of its sort. I have been very careful to repeat any elucidation of a previously-mentioned word only by brief allusion. Yet I have not omitted exegetical opinions with which I am well acquainted, except those of [sufficiently doubtful] validity to accord uneasily with thoroughgoing brevity. Whenever you see in the whole range of verses something whose elucidation is not mentioned, its absence will be due to one of two reasons. Either it has already been presented or it is so clear that there is no need for elucidation. This book of ours has selected the choicest works of *tafsīr* and taken from them what is most sound, most fitting, and best preserved, and arranged it in concise form. This is the moment to enter upon what we have already undertaken, but God is the one who guarantees success.

Suyūṭī on the Occasions of Revelation

Translated by David R. Vishanoff

In chapter 9 of his *Mastery of the Qurʾānic Sciences,* Jalāl ad-Dīn as-Suyūṭī (1445–505) addresses the theologically significant theme of "knowledge of the occasions of revelation" (*asbāb an-nuzūl*). It is of crucial importance that Muslim exegetes developed a sense of historical context as an essential ingredient in scriptural interpretation, and here a major fifteenth-century scholar of Mamluk Egypt offers a clear, cogent overview of the issue. His broad historical perspective includes reference to many other influential theologians and exegetes.[13]

Text

A number of scholars have composed works dedicated to this topic. The earliest of them was ʿAlī ibn al-Madīnī (d. 849), the teacher of al-Bukhārī (d. 870). One of the most famous works, in spite of its deficiencies, is the book by [Abū ʾl-Ḥasan ʿAlī ibn Aḥmad] al-Wāḥidī (d. 1075). It was summarized by [Burhān ad-Dīn Ibrāhīm ibn ʿUmar] al-Jaʿbarī (d. 1331–2), who omitted its chains of transmitters but added nothing to it. Shaykh al-Islām Abū ʾl-Faḍl Ibn Ḥajar [al-ʿAsqalānī] (d. 1449) wrote a book on this subject, but he died leaving only a draft, and it is not known to us in its entirety. I have myself composed a bountiful, succinct, carefully edited book, the like of which has never been written on this subject, which I called *Lubab an-nuqūl fī asbāb an-nuzūl* (*The Best of Treats Concerning the Occasions of Revelation*).

Al-Jaʿbarī said: "The revelation of the Qurʾān consists of two parts: a part that was revealed unprompted, and a part that was revealed following an event or a question." Concerning the latter there are several matters to discuss.

[BENEFITS OF KNOWING THE OCCASIONS OF REVELATION]

The first is the claim that someone made that this study [of the occasions in response to which individual verses of the Qurʾān were revealed] is useless because it is nothing but history. He is wrong about this; on the contrary, it has several benefits. One of these is to understand the wise reason that impelled God to impose a given rule of law. Another is using one's knowledge of the occasion of revelation to narrow the range of cases to which a legal rule applies—at least according to those scholars who say the import of a revelation is limited by the specific situation in which it was revealed. Yet another is that when an expression [in revelation] appears generally applicable, but some other evidence indicates that it should not apply to all cases, then if one knows the occasion of revelation, one knows not to exclude cases that resemble the original occasion. We know for certain that the expression does apply to cases like the original occasion, so excluding them by one's own interpretive reasoning is forbidden. That is the consensus opinion reported by Judge Abū Bakr [al-Bāqillānī] (d. 1013) in his [book on legal theory titled] *Al-Taqrīb* [*wa-l-irshād,* the Book of Clarification and Guidance], though he also held it permissible to side with those who disagree.[14]

Yet another benefit of knowing the occasions of revelation is their usefulness in figuring out the meanings of revelations and resolving interpretive puzzles. Al-Wāḥidī said: "It is impossible to discover the meaning of a verse without finding out its story and the circumstances of its revelation." Ibn Daqīq al-Īd (d. 1302/3) said: "Uncovering the occasion of revelation is a powerful means toward understanding the meanings of the Qurʾān." Ibn Taymīya (d. 1328) said: "Knowing the occasion of revelation directs one to a comprehension of the verse; knowing the occasion leads to knowing what is occasioned."

Marwān ibn al-Ḥakam (d. ca. 685) was puzzled about the meaning of the Qur'ānic verse "Think not that those who exult in what they have given [and love to be praised for what they have not done—think not that they have found refuge from punishment; a painful punishment is theirs]" (3:188). He said, "If everyone who exults in what is given and loves to be praised for what he has not done is to be punished, then surely we will all be punished." Then Ibn 'Abbās explained to him that the verse came down concerning the People of the Book [i.e., Jews and Christians], when the Prophet asked them about something and they concealed it from him and told him something different, and made him think that they had told him what he had asked about, and then sought his commendation for it. (This report was published by the two *shaykhs* [the Hadith compilers Bukhārī and Muslim].)

It is recounted that 'Uthmān ibn Maẓ'ūn and 'Amr ibn Ma'dī Karab used to say that wine is permitted, appealing to the Qur'ānic verse "Those who believe and do good works are not blamed for what they eat . . . " (5:93). They would not have said this if they had known the occasion when this verse was revealed. When wine was made forbidden some people said, "What of those who fought and died in the way of God, and who used to drink wine when it was merely unclean [and not yet forbidden]?" Then this verse was revealed. (This report was published by Aḥmad [ibn Ḥanbal] [d. 855], Nasā'ī [d. 915], and others.)

[There follow three more examples of Qur'ānic verses whose meanings were clarified by the occasions of their revelation.]

Another benefit of knowing the occasion of revelation is dispelling the misimpression that a verse has enumerated something completely. [Muḥammad ibn Idrīs] ash-Shāfi'ī (d. 820) explained the significance of the occasion of revelation of the verse "Say 'I do not find in what has been revealed to me anything forbidden [for people to eat except carrion, flowing blood, pork (which is unclean), or a sinful sacrifice over which a name other than God's has been invoked]'" (6:145). When the disbelievers forbade what God had allowed and allowed what God had forbidden, and were being contrary and antagonistic, this verse opposed their desire. It was as if God had said "Nothing is allowed except what you forbid, and nothing is forbidden but what you allow." It is like when someone says "Do not eat sweets today" and you answer "I will eat nothing but sweets today": the point is to be contrary, not actually to assert or deny anything [about what you will do]. So it is as if God had said "Nothing is forbidden except the very things that you allow—carrion, blood, pork, and sacrifices over which a name other than God's has been invoked," not intending thereby to permit other things, because his intent was to declare certain things forbidden, not declare anything allowed. Imam al-Ḥaramayn [al-Juwaynī] (d. 1085) said: "This is an excellent point, and if Shāfiʿī had not come up with this, we would not think it permissible to disagree with Mālik [ibn Anas] (d. 795) about limiting forbidden foods to those mentioned in this verse."

Other benefits of knowing the occasion of revelation include knowing the name of the person about whom a verse was revealed, and identifying the referents of pronouns and other things that are not explicitly named. Marwān used to say that the verse "The one who said 'fie on you!' to his parents . . . " (46:17) had been revealed concerning ʿAbd ar-Raḥmān ibn Abī Bakr, but then ʿĀʾisha corrected him and explained to him the real occasion for the verse's revelation.

[THE IMPORT OF REVELATION IS DETERMINED BY THE GENERALITY OF ITS VERBAL FORM, NOT THE PARTICULARITY OF ITS OCCASION OF REVELATION]

The second matter for discussion is this: specialists in the theory of law disagree as to whether the import of a revelation is determined by the generality of its verbal form, or by the particularity of its occasion of revelation. The most correct view, according to us, is the first. There are verses that were revealed on specific occasions but that everyone agrees should be applied to other situations as well. Examples include the verse about *ẓihār*[15] which was revealed concerning Salama ibn Ṣakhr, the verse about *liʿān*[16] which was revealed concerning the matter of Hilāl ibn Umayya, and the punishment for slander (cf. 24:4) which was revealed for those who accused ʿĀʾisha (d. 678) but was then extended to others. Those who do not consider the generality of the verbal form to be determinative say that this verse and others like it extend beyond the occasion of revelation because of some other evidence, just as there are verses that everyone agrees apply only to their original occasion because of some evidence to that effect.

Zamakhsharī said that the Qurʾānic chapter "The Backbiter" (104) might well be occasioned by a particular backbiter, yet still serve as an implicit general threat against everyone who engages in that kind of evil.

One argument for considering the generality of the verbal form to be determinative is the common and widespread practice of the Prophet's

Companions, and of others as well, who adjudicated situations that arose by appealing to the general meanings of verses that had been revealed on particular occasions.

Ibn Jarīr [aṭ-Ṭabarī] said: "Muḥammad ibn Abī Maʿshar told me: Abū Maʿshar Najīʿ informed us: I heard Saʿīd al-Maqbarī admonishing Muḥammad ibn Kaʿb al-Quraẓī (d. ca. 737). Saʿīd said: 'It is said in one of God's revealed books that some of God's servants have tongues sweeter than honey and hearts more bitter than aloe; their clothes are of wool (like those of ascetics) yet supple as a shorn lamb, and they fleece the world by their religion.' Muḥammad ibn Kaʿb shot back: 'Well, in the Qurʾān it is said that "among the people there is one whose words about this present life bedazzle you, [and who calls God as witness of his sincerity, yet he is an obstinate quarreler]"' (2:204). Saʿīd responded: '[Come now,] you know very well concerning whom this verse was revealed.' Muḥammad ibn Kaʿb answered: 'A verse may be sent down concerning a specific person, but then it applies generally to others.'"

Now you might object that Ibn ʿAbbās did not attach importance to the generality of God's words "think not that those who exult . . . " (3:188); instead he applied this verse only to the incident mentioned above involving the People of the Book, which was the occasion of its revelation. My answer to that objection is that Ibn ʿAbbās was not unaware that the verbal form of this verse was more general than the occasion of its revelation; he merely explained that it was only intended to apply to that particular case. A similar example is the Prophet's interpretation of "wrongdoing" in God's words ["Those who have believed,] and have not cloaked their faith in wrongdoing, [they are the secure and rightly guided ones]" (6:82). The Prophet's Companions understood this to apply generally to any kind of wrongdoing, but the Prophet took it to mean only idolatry, on the basis of God's words "truly idolatry is great wrongdoing" (31:13). Besides, we have a report from Ibn ʿAbbās that indicates the meaning of an expression is determined by the generality of its verbal form. That was his view of the verse about theft (5:38), even though it came down concerning a specific woman who had stolen something. Ibn Abī Ḥātim (d. ca. 938) said: ʿAlī ibn al-Ḥusayn told us that Muḥammad ibn Abī Ḥammād informed us that Abū Thumayla ibn ʿAbd al-Muʾmin told us that Najda al-Ḥanafī said: "I asked Ibn ʿAbbās whether the Qurʾānic verse 'Cut off the hands of the male thief and the female thief' (5:38) was particular or general, and he said it was general."

Ibn Taymīya (d. 1328) said: "You often hear it said on this topic that 'this verse was revealed concerning such and such,' most often concerning a person. For example, people say that the verse on *ẓihār* was revealed about the wife of Thābit ibn Qays, that the verse on *kalāla*[17] was revealed concerning Jābir ibn ʿAbd Allāh, that the verse 'Judge between them, [O Prophet, according to what God has revealed, and do not follow their wishes]' (5:49) was revealed regarding the Jewish tribes of Banū Qurayẓa and Naḍīr, and that other such verses were revealed regarding certain idolaters in Mecca, or certain Jews and Christians, or certain believers. Those who say this do not mean that what the verse teaches is applicable to those particular individuals exclusively. There is not a single Muslim, nor a single rational person, who would say that. People debate whether the import of a general expression revealed on a specific occasion is limited by the particularity of that occasion, but no one claims that the general expressions in the Qurʾān and the Sunna apply only to specific individuals. The most that anyone claims is that a general expression applies only to the kind of person concerning whom it was revealed, and applies to those who resemble that person, rather than to all those encompassed by the expression's general verbal form. If a verse revealed on a specific occasion is a command or a prohibition, it applies to that person and to anyone else in his position; if it is a statement of praise or blame, it applies to that person and to anyone in his position."

Now you will have noticed from what has been said so far that this whole discussion presupposes a general verbal form. A verse that was revealed concerning something or someone specific, but whose verbal form is not general, is unquestionably restricted to that individual. An example is the verse "The most pious one (*al-atqā*) will be spared from [the Fire], the one who gives his wealth in self-purification" (92:17–18), which everyone agrees was revealed concerning Abū Bakr aṣ-Ṣiddīq. Imam Fakhr ad-Dīn ar-Rāzī (d. 1210) used this verse, along with the verse "The most noble of you in God's eyes is the most pious" (49:13), to prove that Abū Bakr was the best of people after the Prophet of God.[18] Whoever thinks that this verse applies generally to everyone who does the things Abū Bakr did, following the principle [that the import of a verse is determined by the generality of its verbal form rather than by the particularity of its occasion of revelation], is mistaken. That is an error. There is no general verbal form in this verse, because *al-* ("the," as in *al-atqā,* "the most pious one") only implies generality if it marks a relative clause,[19] a definite plural noun,[20] or, some people add, a singular noun [referring to a whole class of things] rather than to a particular thing that has already been identified.[21] But *al-* in *al-atqā* does not mark a relative clause, because everyone agrees that a word in that superlative form cannot serve as a relative clause; and *al-atqā* is not plural but singular, and what it refers to has already been identified—as is clear especially from the fact that a superlative serves precisely to distinguish and set apart the thing it describes. So the claim of generality is false, and it is indubitably clear that this verse is particular and applies only to the one concerning whom it was revealed—Abū Bakr.

[CONTEXT WITHIN THE QUR'ĀN ALSO HELPS DETERMINE THE MEANING OF GENERAL EXPRESSIONS]

The third matter for discussion is this. We have already seen that a general verse applies [not only to its original occasion of revelation but also,] at the very least, to situations that resemble its occasion of revelation. Now such a verse can be revealed on a particular occasion and then be placed in the Qur'ān alongside a second general verse with related content, for the sake of order and continuity. In that case the first verse functions almost like an occasion of revelation for the second verse: we can be sure that the second verse applies at the very least to all situations that resemble the situations to which the first verse applies.

[Tāj ad-Dīn] as-Subkī (d. 1370) said that [general verses of this type, whose context within the Qur'ān helps us to determine what situations they apply to,] represent an intermediate type of verse: they are [harder to interpret than verses for which we know] the occasion of revelation, but [easier to interpret than verses] with no relevant context at all.

One example is the verse "Do you not see that those who have been given a portion of scripture believe in [the idols] Jibṭ and Ṭāghūt [and say that the disbelievers are more rightly guided than the believers]?" (4:51). This refers to Ka'b ibn al-Ashraf and other Jewish scholars like him. When they went to Mecca and saw those who had been killed at the Battle of Badr, they incited the idolaters to avenge them and to wage war against the Prophet. The Meccans asked them "Who is more rightly guided, Muḥammad and his companions, or we?" They answered "You are," even though they were aware of the accurate description of the Prophet that was in their own scripture, and even though they were bound by covenant not to conceal that description. This description was something they held in binding trust, but they did not fulfill that trust, since, out of envy toward the Prophet, they told the disbelievers that they were the more rightly guided ones. Now this passage contains not only the words they spoke [in favor of the disbelievers in 4:51], but also a threat [of severe punishment for those words, which is spelled out in the following verses,] and this in turn implies a command for them to do the opposite of what they did—that is, at the very least, to fulfill their trust by making known the description of the Prophet and telling people that he is the one described in their scripture. Now this implicit command is related in content to the next verse, "God commands you to return things you hold in trust to their rightful owners" (4:58). This second verse is general, encompassing all trusts, whereas the first verse is particular to the description of the Prophet that was entrusted to the Jews, according to the principle enunciated earlier [about general verses applying to situations like their occasion of revelation]. The general verse is written down following the particular one, and was revealed after it. Since they are related in content, the meaning of the particular verse must be included in the meaning of the general verse. That is why [Muḥammad ibn ʿAbd Allāh Abū Bakr] Ibn al-ʿArabī (d. 1148) said in his commentary "The way this passage is ordered is that first God tells how the People of the Book concealed the description of the Prophet and said the idolaters were more rightly guided, which was a breach of trust on their part, and this leads to mentioning trusts in general." Someone else has pointed out that it cannot be objected that the verse about trusts in general was revealed some six years after the verses preceding it, because agreement in time is only required for a verse and its occasion of revelation, not for verses related in content. The point of relatedness is just that verses are put in places that suit their content. Each verse was revealed on its own occasion, and the Prophet used to direct that each one be set down in the place in the Qurʾān where God had told him it belonged.

ʿAbd al-Jabbār on Rational Interpretation of Scripture

Translated by David R. Vishanoff

ʿAbd al-Jabbār ibn Aḥmad al-Hamadhānī (d. 1025) was a major exponent of the Muʿtazilī school of systematic theology. Sometimes referred to as paragons of a "rationalist" approach, the Muʿtazilites argued that the Qurʾān represents the created word of God, against the "Traditionalist" views of Ibn Ḥanbal and his intellectual descendants that the Qurʾān is the *un*created word. ʿAbd al-Jabbār addresses here the exegetically contentious matter of how to interpret the Qurʾān's apparent "anthropomorphic" references to the revealing deity.[22]

Text

In the name of God, the Merciful, the Compassionate. May his prayers be upon his Prophet.

HOW THE QUR'ĀN CAN BE USED AS A PROOF FOR THAT WHICH IT PROVES

[In this section ʿAbd al-Jabbār argues that the Qurʾān—which he regards as God's created speech and thus as one of God's acts—cannot indicate (serve as evidence or proof of) God's being or attributes, because these must already be known from natural evidence (the senses and reason) before one can rely upon the Qurʾān as evidence.]

With some kinds of actions, we must know what the agent [the one who performs the act] is like before we can determine whether the action constitutes a valid proof or evidence of anything, and if so, what it proves and how it proves it. Such an act cannot be used as evidence of the agent's being or attributes; it can only be used as evidence of other kinds of facts. For if such an act could serve as evidence of what the agent is like, even though we don't know that it constitutes valid evidence until we know the agent himself, this would entail that the act can only serve as evidence about the agent after we already know the agent. But once we know a thing, we no longer need any evidence for it!

This point can also be demonstrated as follows. [If such an act could serve as evidence of what the agent is like, even though we don't know that it constitutes valid evidence until we know the agent himself,] this would entail [a paradox regarding the Qurʾān]: we cannot know that the Qurʾān constitutes valid evidence of anything until we know God himself, yet we cannot know God himself until we know the Qurʾān [since we are assuming that the Qurʾān serves as our evidence about God]. This requires that the Qurʾān and God each serve as evidence about the other, and [indirectly] about itself, [which is circular reasoning].

Someone might object: Why do you claim that the Qurʾān's validity as a piece of evidence is known only once one knows God?

To this one should reply: Because a statement [such as those contained in the Qurʾān] is not known to be truthful or false from its wording alone, even if one knows about the thing the statement describes. For it is obvious that we cannot have prior knowledge about the things God informs us of in the Qurʾān [for if we did God would not be informing us of them], whereas it is possible for us to have prior knowledge about the speaker himself, so it must be that we only know the Qurʾān's statements are truthful once we know what the speaker is like, and that he is wise. The same is true of commands and prohibitions: [we only know that they truthfully indicate what is good and bad once we know that the speaker is wise].

Someone might object: Why do you claim that what the Qurʾān proves and how it proves it is known only once one knows God?

To this one should reply: Because the Qurʾān only indicates what it indicates by virtue of the fact that it is spoken by one who is wise and cannot choose to lie or to command evil. If the agent of the Qurʾānic act were not so, one would not know what the Qurʾān indicates or how it indicates it. So one must first know that God is wise and does not choose evil, before one can use the Qurʾān as evidence for that which it indicates. This means that the Qurʾān cannot be used as evidence for God's being or his wisdom [since one must already know these things, and one does not need evidence for what one already knows].

Furthermore, if someone disagrees about this, he must either say that the Qurʾān's statements can indicate something even if one is uncertain whether they are true, or he must say that they only indicate something if they are known to be true. The first option is obviously false, because a statement that [may be] false does not indicate anything about the thing it describes. If that is so, then a statement must be known to be true [before it can be used as evidence]. Now in order to know that a statement is true, one must rely on either (1) the statement itself, or (2) another statement, or (3) the natural evidence of the senses and reason. But one cannot know that the statement is true by relying on the statement itself (1), because a statement only indicates facts about other things, not about itself. And if one knows the statement to be true by relying on another statement (2), that other statement must come either from God or from someone else. One may not rely on someone else's statement [to prove the truth of God's statements]. If, however, one relies on another of God's own statements, without yet knowing that he is wise, one is presuming that God's other statements are true; but if we allow that God's other statements might possibly be false, then the Qurʾānic statement whose truth we are trying to prove might also be false and therefore is not binding. [So the only option left is (3): we can only know that God's statements are true by relying on natural evidence, which is what proves that God is wise and does not do evil.]

That is why we say that the Ashʿarites,[23] who allow the possibility that God might do evil, have no way to know that God is truthful—neither through reason nor through revelation!

The upshot of all this is that we must rest our confidence in the evidentiary value of the Qurʾān on our prior knowledge, from natural evidence, that God is, that he is wise, and that he does not choose to do evil, in order that we might be able to use the Qurʾān as evidence for that which it indicates.

Someone might object: If one may use God's other actions [such as creation] as evidence about him, without having any prior knowledge of him, why may one not use the Qurʾān as evidence about him without having prior knowledge of him?

To this one should reply: We have already explained that speech does not indicate what it indicates because of anything pertaining to the speech itself; it only indicates what it indicates because the speaker is wise. For the same reason, the speech of the Prophet cannot function as evidence for the rules of law until one knows that he is the messenger of someone wise who would not manifest miracles through him if he were not truthful in all the messages he transmits. Such is not the case with an action's being evidence of its agent's ability to act, because an action indicates the agent's power to act solely because of something pertaining to the act itself, independent of [the agent's] choices. That something [by virtue of which an action indicates its agent's ability to act] is the fact that if an action is possible for one agent but impossible for another similar agent, then the first agent must have some distinguishing characteristic [such as the power to act] that makes the action possible for him. This fact about actions holds true regardless of [the agent's] choices. That is why the occurrence of things that physical beings could not possibly bring about can properly be used as evidence of God and of his power and knowledge [which are the distinguishing characteristics that enable him to do such things]. The Qurʾān is different [because its statements only indicate what they indicate because God does not choose to lie].

This is also evident from the obvious fact that even before any miracles had been manifested through the Prophet, the Prophet's actions proved that he had the power and knowledge [that those acts required], but that did not mean his words likewise functioned as proofs for the rules of law. That required that miracles be manifested through him, and that one know the qualities and wisdom of the [God] who sent him. This is just like what we have been saying [about the Qurʾān].

Someone might object: If that is so, then all the statements in the Qurʾān that point to God and his wisdom must be useless and of no value whatsoever, because they cannot be used as evidence, but are known to constitute valid evidence only after one already knows God and his oneness and justice.

To this one should reply: God did not utter those statements [to serve as evidence in their own right]. He uttered them in order to prompt seekers to pursue a rational line of inquiry, and to reason from the evidence God made available through their natural human faculties. Or he may have uttered them because he knew that those creatures whom he required to know and obey him would be more likely to reason from [natural] evidence to a knowledge of God if they heard these statements and reflected on them than if they never heard them at all. Since it has these benefits, God's speech cannot be called pointless.

To make this point even clearer, consider those of us who act as missionaries, inviting people to acknowledge God. When a missionary approaches someone who does not know God, inviting him and showing him the way to know God and his unity and justice, the missionary's proselytizing cannot be considered pointless, even though the person he invites cannot know God by means of the preaching alone, without also engaging in rational inquiry and reflection. The same is true of God's speech, especially considering that some people already believe that the Qurʾān is God's speech and that God cannot lie. They believe this simply by accepting what they have been told, and without having come to know God for themselves. For such a person, the Qurʾān is a stronger inducement to rational inquiry than the words of a missionary would be, since he would not believe such great things about a missionary. The prophets [understood that the most their words could do was encourage people to reason from natural evidence], and that is why, when their people asked them about God, they were content to mention God's works of creation: the heavens, the realms of earth, and other things.

Someone might object: If that is so, then one cannot learn from the Qurʾān what is allowed and what is forbidden, unless one follows this same method [of first engaging in rational inquiry]!

To this one should reply: Precisely. One cannot learn from the Qurʾān what is allowed and what is forbidden until one knows that the one who speaks through the Qurʾān is wise, that his statements cannot be false, and that he cannot obfuscate, command what is evil, or forbid what is good. One does not need prior knowledge [of the law itself] in order to learn the rules of law from the Qurʾān, as long as one has prior knowledge of God. But one does need prior knowledge of [theological truths such as] God's not being a physical body before one can infer [theological truths such as] the fact that

God does not resemble [created] things from his words "there is nothing like him" (42:11). That is because of what we said earlier: one cannot know an agent and his wisdom from one of his actions if we have to know what the agent is like before we can know whether the action constitutes a valid proof, what it proves, and how it proves it.

For this same reason—and given that miracles are like statements in that they can only be known to constitute valid evidence if one already knows what the one who performs them is like and that he is wise—we assert that anyone [such as an Ashʿarite theologian] who allows that God might possibly do evil cannot use miracles as evidence that the prophets were true prophets. Indeed, such a person cannot even be sure that God does not bestow miracles on [false prophets] who call people to error and wickedness and bar people from guidance and uprightness!

[THE PRIORITY OF NATURAL EVIDENCE AND CLEAR VERSES OVER AMBIGUOUS VERSES]

[In this section ʿAbd al-Jabbār uses the Qurʾānic distinction between clear and ambiguous verses to argue that some things the Qurʾān appears to say must be reinterpreted in light of the natural evidence of the senses and reason, and of other verses that accord with that natural evidence. This sets up the rest of his book *Ambiguous Verses of the Qurʾān,* in which he explains how to interpret Qurʾānic verses so that they support his Muʿtazilite rational theology.]

Someone might object: Do you hold that the clear verses (*muḥkam*) in the Qurʾān constitute stronger evidence than the ambiguous verses (*mutashābih*), or not? If you say they are alike, you go against the consensus of the Muslim community, which holds that the clear verses are more fundamental than the ambiguous verses, and are endowed with something that the ambiguous verses lack. The Qurʾān says this explicitly: "It is God who has revealed the book to you; some of its verses are clear, and they are the heart of the book; [others are ambiguous]" (3:7). On the other hand, if you say that the clear verses constitute evidence in a way that the ambiguous ones do not, then you contradict the principle that you have just put forward, because you have said that all of God's speech is alike in that it only serves as evidence once one knows about God and his wisdom. If that is so, then what is the point of distinguishing between the clear and the ambiguous? Does this not prove to you that your claim is false?

To this one should reply: What we say on this matter does not contradict the principle we have put forward, nor does it deviate from the consensus of the Muslim community, nor from the Qurʾān. What we say is this: the clear verses are like the ambiguous verses in one respect, while they differ in another respect.

They are alike in the way that we have already explained: neither can be used as evidence until one knows that the agent [who uttered the Qurʾān] is wise and cannot choose to do evil. Our rationale for this claim applies to both clear and ambiguous verses without distinction. The clear and ambiguous parts of the Prophet's speech are also equivalent in this respect, since the only way to know that either one constitutes valid evidence is [for God to perform] a miracle [that confirms the Prophet's truthfulness].

They differ, however, in this respect: a clear verse has only a single possible meaning, either because the Arabic language only assigns it one meaning, or because some accompanying evidence specifies its meaning. So when a person who knows how to speak the language and is aware of the accompanying evidence hears the clear verse, he is immediately able to use it as evidence for whatever it indicates. Ambiguous verses are different, for even someone who knows the language and is aware of the accompanying evidence must think from scratch and inquire afresh when he hears an ambiguous verse, so that he might interpret it in a way that agrees with clear verses or natural evidence. This is clearly correct, because God declared the clear verses to be the foundation upon which the ambiguous ones rest, and for that to be true one's knowledge of the clear verses must precede one's knowledge of the unclear verses. The only way to fulfill that requirement is the way we have set forth: [by interpreting the ambiguous verses in accordance with the clear verses].

Verses that speak of God's unity and justice, however, whether they are clear or unclear, must all be interpreted in accordance with natural evidence, because someone who does not already know that God is one, is wise, and does not choose to do evil, cannot use God's speech as evidence that he has these attributes. In this matter [of God's unity and justice], clear verses are just like ambiguous ones. They differ only in this other sense, that we can refer to clear verses as proofs against those [Muslim theologians] who disagree with us about the doctrines of God's unity and justice. We can use clear verses to show them that they are out of accord with something that in principle they accept as valid evidence. It is difficult, however, [to pin them down in that way] using ambiguous verses. That is why we find the writings of our Muʿtazilite forebears to be full of such references. These are intended to show that our opponents have strayed not only from the path of reason, but also from the Qur'ān. On the other hand, when we are speaking to someone who does not know God or his wisdom at all, and demonstrating that God does not choose to do evil and does not resemble physical bodies or their properties, we cannot use either the clear or the ambiguous verses of the Qur'ān, as we have already explained.

For this reason, the clear and the ambiguous verses of the Qur'ān must be sorted out based on the natural evidence of the senses and reason. Verses whose only possible meaning is precisely what reason requires must be called clear, and verses that can mean either that or something else must be called ambiguous. Natural evidence is the surest ground for determining which verses are clear and which are ambiguous. Sometimes this can be determined just as well from another verse that precedes or follows an ambiguous verse, but even then it is only thanks to reason that we know the ambiguous verse must mean what the clearer verse requires.

To see this more clearly, consider how the [Arabic] language is set up. Of all the words to which the language has assigned a meaning, there is not a single one that does not sometimes mean something besides the meaning it was originally assigned. [Since all words, then, have multiple possible meanings,] there would be no way to distinguish clear words from ambiguous ones if we could not refer to some completely unambiguous criterion—[namely, the natural evidence of the senses and reason].

Shāh Walī Allāh on the Causes of Abrogation

Translated by Marcia Hermansen

One of the many hermeneutical questions that have occupied the thoughts of exegetes for centuries is the principle of abrogation (*naskh*), according to which God revealed the Qur'ān in a progressive manner lest human beings be unable to absorb the full impact at a stroke.[24] Some texts of the scripture are, therefore, thought to supersede others, though scholars have been by no means of one mind as to the all-important specifics in identifying which texts are "abrogating" and which "abrogated." Here an influential Indian theologian, Shāh Walī Allāh (1703–62) of Delhi, weighs in on this contentious question.[25]

Text

The basis of this is God's saying, "We do not abrogate any verse or cause it to be forgotten unless we bring one better than it" (2:106).

Know that abrogation is composed of two categories.

One of them is that whereby the Prophet examined the supports of civilization or the aspects of acts of obedience, and then fixed them with different types of regulation consistent with the ordinances of the divine legislation, and this is the independent reasoning (*ijtihād*) of the Prophet. Therefore God did not determine this for him, but rather revealed to him what He had decreed upon the ruling in this issue, either

(a) through a Qurʾānic revelation in agreement with it or
(b) by a change in his independent reasoning in this, and his decision on this.

An example of the first case is the Prophet's command to face Jerusalem [during the prayers]; the Qurʾān was later revealed abrogating this (2:142–45). An example of the second is that he had forbidden the people from making *nabīdh*[26] except in animal skins, then he allowed them to make *nabīdh* in any container saying, "Don't drink anything intoxicating." This is because he saw that the intoxicating property was a hidden thing, and he established for it an overt anticipated source which was the making of *nabīdh* in vessels which were not porous such as ones made of clay, wood, or gourds, for these hastened the intoxicating properties of the *nabīdh* made in them. Therefore he established making *nabīdh* in a water skin as an anticipated source of something in which intoxicating properties would not be present for up to three days. Then he changed his independent reasoning to base the ruling on the intoxicating property because the intoxicating properties of something can be recognized by its bubbling and emitting froth. Therefore he established whatever had in it the properties of intoxication, or the attributes of an intoxicating thing, as being a more appropriate anticipated source than assigning something which was extraneous to it. According to another interpretation, we may say that the Prophet [at first] saw that the people were enamored of intoxicants, and that if he were to forbid these to them, there would be a loophole for someone to drink it [an intoxicating thing] and make the excuse that he had thought that it was not intoxicating or that the indications of its being an intoxicant were not clear to him, or that the vessels had become contaminated with some intoxicating thing, so that the intoxicating quality emerged more rapidly in whatever was brewed in ones like them. Then when Islam became strong and they were content to abandon intoxicants, and those vessels had gone out of usage, the order was made to apply to the intoxication itself, according to this interpretation. This is an example of the varying of the ruling according to the variation of the anticipated sources.

Concerning this division of abrogation there is the Prophet's saying, "My speech does not abrogate the speech of God; but the speech of God abrogates my speech, and the speech of God can abrogate a previously delivered speech of God."

The second category of abrogation is that whenever a thing is thought to be conducive to good or to harm, it is ruled on in accordance therewith, then a time comes in which it is no longer an anticipated source for this and thus the rule will be changed. An example of this is that when the Prophet emigrated to Medina and help for them from their blood relatives was cut off, and there only existed brotherhood aid,[27] which the Prophet made a means for the necessary beneficial purpose—the Qurʾān was revealed basing inheritance on a relationship of "brotherhood." God explained the benefit of this when He said, "If you don't do it there will be sedition on the earth and a great evil" (8:73). Then when Islam became strong, and the immigrants were reunited with those related to them, the command was revoked in favor of the previous inheritance by kinship. Or it may be that a thing did not have a beneficial purpose in the prophetic mission which had not included the Caliphate as was the condition before the Prophet and as was the case in his time before the emigration to Medina; although the beneficial purpose came to be found in the Prophetic mission including the Caliphate. An example is that God did not make taking booty lawful to those before us, but permitted it to us, and this is justified in the hadith reports from two aspects: the first is that God saw our weakness and permitted us booty, and the second is due to God's esteeming our Prophet above the rest of the prophets and his community above other communities.

The explanation of these two aspects is that prophets before the Prophet were sent to their particular nations, and these people were of limited numbers. Sometimes the duration of the Jihād among them was a year or two and so on, and their peoples were strong and able to combine the Jihād with trades such as agriculture and commerce so that they did not have a need for booty. God wanted that a worldly intention should not be mixed with their actions so that the people would get the fullest rewards for them. He sent our Prophet, however, to all people, and they are uncountable and the duration of the Jihād against them is not limited. The Muslims were not able to combine the Jihād with occupations such as agriculture and trade, so they had a need for the permission to take booty. The Prophet's community, due to the universality of his call, included people of weak intentions, and concerning them is reported in the hadith, "Indeed God will support this religion even by a profligate man." These people would only fight for a worldly goal, and God's mercy in the matter of the Jihād encompassed them mightily, and God's anger was directed against their enemies most strongly. This is the Prophet's saying, "God looked at the people of the earth, and loathed the Arabs and the non-Arabs among them." This required the termination of the safeguarding of their property and lives in the most complete way, and the galling of their hearts by the disposal of their wealth as when the Prophet of God bestowed upon the Sacred Precincts [to be sacrificed] the camel of Abū Jahl[28] with a silver ring in its nose, so that this galled the unbelievers, and when he ordered the cutting down of the date palms and burning them, this galled their owners.[29] Therefore the Qur'ān revealed the permissibility of booty for this community.

Another example is that fighting the unbelievers was not forbidden to this community at first, but at that time there was no army, neither was there a Caliphate. Then when the Prophet emigrated, and the Muslims collected and the Caliphate [i.e., Prophetic rule] appeared, and the Jihād with the enemies of God became possible, God revealed, "Permission is given to those who fought because they have been wronged; and Allāh is able to give them victory" (22:39). About this division [of abrogation] is God's saying, "We do not abrogate any verse or make it forgotten, but that we bring a better one or one like it" (2:106). His saying, "A better one" refers to the Prophetic mission containing the Caliphate and His saying, "or one like it," refers to the changing of the ruling according to the variation of the anticipated sources, and God knows better.

Ayatollah Khu'ī on the Divine Miracle of the Qur'ān

Translated by Abdulaziz A. Sachedina

Another major hermeneutical theme concerns the "inimitability" of the Qur'ān or, put another way, its "miraculous" quality. Numerous theologically astute authorities—Sunnī and Shī'ī alike—have written eloquently on the subject for well over a millennium. Among the more recent Shī'ī treatments of the topic is that of contemporary Twelver Iranian Ayatollah Sayyid Abū al-Qāsim al-Mūsawī al-Khū'ī (d. 1992) in his *Prolegomena to the Qur'ān.*[30]

Text

Every intelligent person to whom the call of Islam has reached knows that Muḥammad announced to all mankind the call to accept Islam, and through the Qurʾān, established for them the proof [of the claim to prophethood] and challenged them, with [the Qurʾān's] inimitability, to produce its like, even by helping each other in so doing. Then he lowered this and challenged them to produce ten sūras [like those in the Qurʾān]. And, finally, he challenged them to produce only one sūra like it.[31]

Had that been possible, it would have behooved the Arabs—especially those among them who excelled in eloquence—to take up the Prophet's challenge and invalidate his proof by matching it. Indeed, it would have behooved them to counter one sūra of the Qurʾān and match it in eloquence so as to invalidate the proof of this claimant who was challenging them in their most outstanding skill and their most notable distinction. They would thus have gained a manifest victory, endless renown, and eminence in honor and position. A contest like this would have spared them wars, great expenses, separation from their homeland, and the suffering of hardship and affliction.

But the Arabs reflected on the eloquence of the Qurʾān and conceded its inimitability, for they knew that they would be defeated trying to match it. Hence, some of them believed the caller to the truth and submitted to the call of the Qurʾān and attained the honor of Islam. Others took the course of obduracy and chose to counter with swords rather than words, and preferred a contest of lances to a contest of eloquence. This incapacity and opposition were the ample proof that the Qurʾān was a divine revelation beyond human capability.

Some ignorant non-Muslims have claimed that the Arabs matched the Qurʾān and countered it with this proof, and that this contest has been forgotten because of the passage of time. The response to such a view is that this encounter, had it taken place, would have been made known by the Arabs in their gatherings and publicized at their annual fairs and markets. The enemies of Islam would have taken it for [use as] a ballad, chanting it in every gathering, repeating it on every occasion, passing it on to posterity, and guarding it as a litigant would guard his evidence. This would have been more satisfying to them than preserving the history of their ancestors. Yet, although pre-Islamic poetry has filled the books of history and the compendiums of literature, we do not see any trace of this encounter, nor do we hear any mention of it. This is in spite of the fact that the Qurʾān challenges all humans—rather, all the jinn and humans—without limiting the challenge to any particular group. This is what God the Almighty says to those [who do not believe in the divine origin of the Qurʾān]:

> Say: "Verily though mankind and the jinn should assemble to produce the like of this Qurʾān, they should not produce the like thereof, though they were helpers one of another." (17:88)

Moreover, we see the Christians and the enemies of Islam spending enormous amounts of money to detract from the prestige of this religion and derogate its great Prophet and holy Book. They do this every year, rather, every month. Had they been able to counter the Qurʾān, even by matching one sūra of it, that would have served as a greater proof for them and a better means of accomplishing their aim; and they would not have needed to spend all this money and exert themselves.

> Fain would they put out the light of God with their mouths, but God will perfect His light however much the rejecters of faith are averse (61:8).

On the other hand, a person who deals regularly and deeply with an eloquent text, would, with time, be expected to acquire the ability of matching its style, or coming close to it. This can be observed in everyday life, but does not apply to the Qurʾān, for, despite frequent perusal and prolonged study, no one has been able to imitate it to any extent. This proves to us that the Qurʾān has a style beyond teaching or learning. Moreover, had the Qurʾān been the Prophet's own words and composition, we would have found passages in the Prophet's orations and sayings that resemble it in style and equal it in eloquence. However, the sayings of the Prophet and his orations that have been preserved in writing are characterized by a different style. Had there been among his sayings anything that resembles the Qurʾān, it would have been widely transmitted and recorded, especially by his enemies, who wanted to harm Islam by whatever means and device. One more point to add is that customary eloquence has limits which it rarely exceeds. Wellversed Arab poets and prose writers specialize in one genre or even two and three. One may excel in *ḥamāsa* (heroic) poetry, for example, but not in love poetry. The Qurʾān, by contrast, dwells on numerous subjects and applies many forms of style, and in all this has excelled other writings. This versatility is impossible for human beings.

THE QURʾĀN: AN ETERNAL MIRACLE

We have seen that belief in prophethood and faith in it are only through the miracles the prophet performs as a proof of his claim. Since the prophecies of earlier prophets were limited to their own times, divine wisdom dictated that their miracles be of short duration, for they were proofs for prophecies that were to serve for a limited time. Therefore, some contemporaries of these prophets were eyewitnesses to these miracles and, hence, these miracles served as evidence for them. Others learned about these miracles by means of eyewitness accounts related without any break in transmission (*tawātur*); hence, the miracle served as evidence for these as well.

However, in the case of the eternal Sharia (sacred law of Islam), the miracle that attests to its truthfulness must be timeless, because if the miracle were limited and of short duration, it would not be observed by those far away. Consequently, if the transmission and reports regarding it were to be disrupted, those living far away would not be able to ascertain its truthfulness. Hence, if God were to impose on such persons the obligation to believe in this miracle, He would be imposing on them an impossible obligation. Imposing an impossible obligation is inadmissible of God. Hence, the final and lasting prophethood inevitably requires a lasting miracle. It is for this reason that God sent down the Qurʾān as a lasting miracle so that it would be a proof of the truthfulness of the final and lasting prophethood. It would, as well, be a proof to posterity as it was a proof for those who preceded them. We can conclude two points from what we have said so far.

First, [there is] the superiority of the Qurʾān over all other miracles which were accomplished by the past prophets, and over the other miracles which were accomplished by our Prophet, Muḥammad, because the Qurʾān is lasting and timeless, and its inimitability is continuous, to be heard by all generations and to serve as proof through the centuries.

Second, the earlier sacred laws are temporary. What points to the fact that their viability has ended is that the proofs and evidence serving them have ended with the passing of the miracles which confirmed their truthfulness.

Moreover, the Qurʾān has another unique characteristic that makes it superior to all the miracles performed by earlier prophets. This characteristic is that the Qurʾān is responsible for the guidance of mankind[32] and for leading them to their ultimate perfection. The Qurʾān is the guide that enlightened the uncouth and oppressive Arabs—they who had embraced the worst habits and worshiped the idols, and who were preoccupied with tribal warfare and the vainglorious boasting of the pre-Islamic age,[33] instead of pursuing knowledge and rectifying their souls. With the Qurʾān as a guide, they became, in a very short time, a community significant in its learning and history, and superior in its customs. Whoever studies the history of

Islam and probes into the biographies of the Prophet's Companions, who met their martyrdom in his presence, would realize the greatness of the Qur'ān in the effectiveness of its guidance and the extensiveness of its influence. Indeed, it was the Qur'ān that pulled them out of the abyss of the age of ignorance (*jāhilīya,* the pre-Islamic age) [and brought them] to the heights of knowledge and perfection, and made them be devoted to the cause of invigorating the Sharia, with no regret about wealth, children, and wives they left behind.

The words of al-Miqdād to the Messenger of God, when the Messenger consulted the believers about setting out for Badr, are a fair corroboration of what we have said [quoting Ibn Jarīr aṭ-Ṭabarī as follows]:

> O Prophet of God, carry out what God has commanded you to do, for we are with you. By God, we shall not say what the Children of Israel said to Moses: "Go, you and your Lord, and fight. We are slackers here" (5:24). But we say: "Go, you and your Lord, and fight. Indeed, we are with you as fighters. I swear by the One who has sent you with the truth, if you march us toward Birk al-Ghimād [across the sea]"—by which Miqdād meant the capital of Abyssynia—"we shall endure it with you until you attain it." The Prophet of God said kind words to him and prayed for him.

Miqdād was only one of the Muslims to express his belief and determination, and to dedicate himself with heart and soul in order to vitalize the truth and destroy associationism (*shirk*). Many Muslims were of this faith, overflowing with sincerity.

Undoubtedly, it was the Qur'ān that enlightened the hearts of those who had been devoted to the idols and who had engaged in tribal warfare and pre-Islamic vainglory. It made them hard on the rejecters of faith and merciful to each other, each of them valuing his companion's life over his own. Hence, by virtue of Islam, the Muslims conquered, in eighty years, more than others conquered in eight hundred. Whoever compares the lives of the Prophet's Companions with those of earlier prophets would realize that therein lies a divine mystery, and that the beginning of this mystery is the Book of God, which shone on the souls and cleansed the hearts and the spirits with a lofty faith and a steadfast doctrine.

Look at the history of the disciples of Jesus, and at the history of other companions of the prophets, and you will see what their ways were. They abandoned their prophets under adversity and betrayed them for fear of destruction! As a result, those earlier prophets had no power over the oppressors of their time, but used to hide from them in caves and ravines. This is the second attribute that gives the Qurʾān merit over all other miracles.

Having learned from the preceding that the Qurʾān is a divine miracle of eloquence and style, it should be added that its inimitability is not confined to that. Rather, it is a miracle pertaining to the Lord and a manifold proof of the prophethood of the one to whom it was revealed. It is appropriate for us at this point to present some of these aspects [of the Qurʾān's inimitability], however briefly.

PART TWO

The Science of Community

MAPPING THE BOUNDARIES OF TRUE BELIEF

CHAPTER 1 BEGAN BY SAMPLING from the most important theological themes—about God, revelation, and questions of freedom and responsibility—mentioned in the Qur'ān and Hadiths. Close attention to the implications of those themes led (in chapter 2) to exegetical commentary as well as to more theoretical discussions of hermeneutical principles (such as potential ambiguities, abrogation, the circumstances of revelation, and the Qur'ān's inimitability) central to the development of the science and practice of *tafsīr*. In part 2, new theological themes and questions go hand in hand with an expanding repertoire of descriptive genres marshaled in service of sorting out believers from unbelievers. Tools for historical inquiry originally developed in service of gathering and authenticating Prophetic traditions gradually expanded beyond "prosopography" (the study of individual personalities) into properly "historiographical" methods designed to discern broader patterns in the story, not only of Islam, but of "universal history."

Two overarching themes here are the description and evaluation of the beliefs of non-Muslim communities; and the discernment, definition, and evaluation of an emerging diversity of views within the early communities of people who identified themselves as Muslims. Within a century of Muḥammad's death, a growing and geographically expanding Muslim community had already experienced significant internal fragmentation in a series of dissensions (*fitna*) concerning the criteria for legitimate leadership of, and authentic membership in, the community of believers. Early religious scholars began to deal with problems of internal pluralism, and the serious threat to Muslim unity that it represented, by articulating "correct" positions on the various emerging disputes. Most articles of the earliest "creedal" statements were directed at fine-tuning the wayward interpretations of individuals and groups not yet judged to have gone irretrievably beyond the pale. Here increasingly pressing questions about the nature of faith and about what constitutes a sin sufficiently grave to separate an individual from the community are especially important. Some formulations also addressed, however cryptically, views ascribed to groups increasingly identified definitively as "non-Muslim."

Moving beyond the typically rather brief formulaic descriptions of the creeds, scholars began to develop other ways of cataloging and responding to theologically unacceptable views. Heresiographical texts sought to define specific communities of erroneous thought and detailed their signature positions on points of major disagreement. During the tenth and eleventh centuries, a number of influential Muslim scholars painted their pictures of the religious world on the still broader canvas of a genre known as the "universal history." Such works contribute to the traditional Islamic "discipline of history" (*ʿilm at-taʾrīkh*). Their individual programs varied, of course, but many of these authors shared the grand purpose of depicting the corrective role and ultimate superiority of Islam within the larger scheme of global religious history. From the perspective of literary genres, these two chapters sample how Muslim authors from the tenth through the fourteenth centuries devised a language and modes of argumentation ideally suited both to contesting the claims of non-Muslim faith traditions (polemics) and to defending the internal cohesiveness and cogency of Islamic teachings (apologetics).

THREE

Muslim Awareness of Other Religious Communities

SAVVY MUSLIM OBSERVERS of the human condition began to offer their reflections on religion and society well over a millennium ago in a wide range of literary genres. Their purview reached far beyond the predominantly Muslim communities in which they lived, embracing not only the other Abrahamic faiths but also the exotic traditions and history of Hinduism, Buddhism, and Confucianism. While some accounts of the broader religious scene were naturally polemical in tone and intent, others approached the expansive subject out of a desire to chronicle the story of humankind more impartially—though with the occasional hint of fronting for a patron's political agenda. Beneath the latter approach one can occasionally discern a fascinating, but too seldom acknowledged, willingness to ask probing questions about the nature of faith and the role of absolute truth claims in the wider scenario of human religiosity.

A major social critic and literary figure of tenth-century Baghdad named Abū Ḥayyān at-Tawḥīdī (c. 930–1023) showcased this kind of critical thinking through a fictional dialogue featuring his mentor in skepticism, a certain Abū Sulaymān. A minister of the ruling Būyid family asked Abū Sulaymān why he continued to espouse Islam even though he publicly contended that no one faith could argue its claims with unassailable cogency. Abū Sulaymān replied that the foundation of his adherence to Islam was, frankly, that he had been born into a Muslim family in a society suffused with Islamic tradition. He went on to fashion a remarkable metaphor about the dynamics of belief under such conditions:

> I am in the situation of a man who has entered the courtyard of a caravansary by day to seek a moment's shade, at a time when the sky was cloudless. The

keeper of the caravansary brought him to an apartment without asking about his condition or health. In this situation he suddenly found that a cloud had blown up and released a downpour. The apartment leaked, so the occupant looked at the other apartments in the inn, and saw that they too were leaking. He saw mud in the courtyard of the building, and considered staying where he was and not moving to another apartment; [for, by remaining,] he could enjoy his ease and avoid getting his legs splattered by the thick mud and slime of the courtyard. [So] he was inclined to wait patiently in his apartment and stay in the situation in which he found himself. This man is like me: at the time of my birth I could not reason; then my parents brought me into this religion without my prior experience of it. Then, when I examined it closely, I found its ways to be like the ways of other religions. [However] I considered my staying in it patiently to be a more inviting course than my abandoning it, since I could leave it and become inclined to another [religion] only if I had some clear preference of choice for that [religion], and predilection for it over [my present religion]. Yet I have not found any proof in its favor without finding a like proof of another religion against it.[1]

Not all classical Muslim thinkers, needless to say, have adopted such a remarkably open mode of critical thinking about religion and the nature of belief. We have, nevertheless, a striking profusion of Islamic literature that bespeaks an important awareness of the "theological other." Though classical descriptions of the other are often riddled with what we would call factual inaccuracies (a fault from which few even today are entirely innocent), texts evidence a quest for overriding principles by which Muslim authors might characterize the claims of others in relation to their own religious convictions. Here are four views of the larger theological and religious environs of which important Muslim authors were keenly aware. In these examples, as in so much of this rich, varied segment of Islamic religious literature, the line between chronicle and critique, and between apologetic and polemic, is often blurred.

IDENTIFYING AND EVALUATING THE BELIEFS OF OTHERS

ʿAlī ibn Rabbān aṭ-Ṭabarī on Interpreting the Stories of Other Faiths

Translated by David Thomas

ʿAlī ibn Rabbān aṭ-Ṭabarī (c. 838–70) is said to have been a Christian convert to Islam, giving him a particular perspective on both traditions. Around 855 he composed *The Book of Religion and Empire* for the purpose of demonstrating the superiority of Islam over other faiths and featuring large sections on Muḥammad's laws, miracles, prophecies, the signal miracle of the Qur'an, and the Prophet's ultimate victory over the "pagan" enemies of his day. Ṭabarī begins with a kind of hermeneutical preface explaining his principles for interpreting and judging the veracity of the narratives of non-Muslim communities. Here he sets the context and offers an unusual reflection on the nature of contending religious narratives against which to propose his "Directions for the Verification of Stories." His overriding concern is to show how Islam is predicted in the biblical "reports" and should thus be accepted as the last revealed teaching.[2]

Text

I have discovered that all those who oppose Islam do so for four reasons. Firstly, out of doubt over the report of the Prophet, while the second is disdain and loftiness, the third adherence to tradition and custom, and the fourth stupidity and foolishness. But if they only examined the report closely and understood it, they would accept it and not reject it. But since they inquire into what is of God in violation of the command of God, we are bound to try to substantiate the report they possess,[3] to remove doubt from them and to explain to them the primary and secondary elements of the reports, their causes and outcome, the ways in which the truth in them can be known from their error, and the reasons why the nations accept their prophets and obey their preachers. Then we will compare our reports with theirs and those who delivered them to us with those who delivered them to them, and if our evidence and their evidence about their trust in the prophets they trust is identical, then they have no pretext before God or themselves to maintain their denial of our master [Muḥammad] and trust in their masters [Jesus and the Hebrew prophets]. For if two opponents produce identical evidence about any claim and they both alike accept it, what applies to one about it must undeniably apply to the other.

[Here ʿAlī describes at some length a variety of types of accounts and the kinds of claims they make for the veracity of specific religious communities, especially in regard to claims of Prophetic revelation. He resumes now with more specific description of the content of those accounts, with a focus on Manichaean, Zoroastrian, Jewish, and Christian claims in relation to those of Islamic sources.]

We have seen that nations great in number, mighty in extent and epitomized by people of understanding and discrimination bear witness to numerous lying deceivers in all that they claim, such as the Manicheans and Zoroastrians, either through keeping to tradition and custom, as we have shown, through ignorance and quarrelsomeness, or through compulsion and force. This was the case with Zarādusht the false prophet of the Zoroastrians, for he kept on trying to get to king Bishtāṣaf until he managed to enter his presence and sowed his insinuations in his heart. Then he went on wiping away from him the remembrance of God and prayer to him, and twisting over and under until he twisted him from his religion and bent him to his own view. Then he revealed to him the dualism that he was keeping hidden, and painted for him a picture of intercourse with mothers and daughters and of eating rotten, putrid filth. After this it was the king who forced the people of his realm to follow his religion.[4]

Mānī did something similar to this. He appeared at a time when for the most part there were two religions, Christianity and Zoroastrianism. He misled the Christians by telling them that he was the apostle of Christ, and he beguiled the Zoroastrians by agreeing with them on the two principles.[5]

When we find a consensus of this kind, and we find one such as Islam, we come to know that to accept every consensus is discord, to reject every consensus is error, and consensus alone is not sufficient to confirm prophetic status without the testimonies and marks of truth which God almighty has brought together for the Prophet. So, one who wishes to know the truth in reports such as these and to discriminate between them must understand the report that he receives and must consider its intention and shortcomings. If he discovers anything in it that contradicts it, or anything accompanying it that falsifies it, he has no need of proof other than this. This is like the report of Musaylima the liar:[6] when he claimed to be a prophet he was asked about the Prophet and he said that he was truthful and he expressed belief in his prophetic status. And the Prophet was asked about him, and he said he was a liar. So in Musaylima's acknowledgment of truthfulness to the one who said he was a liar is his own acknowledgement of being a liar about his own self, and evidence of his self-contradictoriness and foolishness. For this reason scholars have said that if some false person makes a claim to be a prophet, God will not be slow to make contradiction pass over his tongue to be used against those who say he is truthful, as God caused to pass over the tongues of Zarādusht and Mānī and those like them. For they were inconsistent, they lied, and they wavered.

Zarādusht said that Hurmiz[7]—this is the name of the one they worshipped—was eternal, compassionate and perfect in knowledge and power, but then he soon described him in the way that feeble-minded and ignorant people are described, saying that Satan was begotten from his thought and that God was too weak to destroy him. Mānī did the same thing in saying that God was eternal, mighty and there was nothing like him, and then saying that darkness is eternal and that God is overcome and his supporters are overcome and made captive. Whoever believes in someone who contradicts himself commits a most singular error.

The Christians are like this. When they say at the beginning of the law of their faith, "We believe in God, Creator of all that is visible and invisible," and then follow this statement of theirs with "Christ is Creator not created," contradiction appears in what they say. If we refer to the books of their religion, we find that they are different from their belief, for all of them confirm that God is the Maker and everything apart from him is made. I have set this out in the part that follows this, and have explained there what is related to each of the denominations of the Christians and have presented a hundred and thirty arguments against them from the books of the prophets, together with demonstrative arguments, apposite parables and splendid analogies. In this my intention has been to give them clarity of sight, guidance and the fulfillment of the love and compassion that God enjoins on one part of humanity towards another.

Concerning what pertains to the Jews and others beside them, in the fourth part I have set out teaching about it briefly but without any omission.

The detailed point and concise rebuttal, simple and uncomplicated refutation, is that if a man of intelligence and understanding receives any report, he will consider it readily, and will scrutinize it outside and in. And if he discovers something in it that falsifies it and with it that contradicts it, or if he discovers that it differs from the books of people's religion, he will have no need of anything else to show it is lying and to reveal its defectiveness and imperfection. To find the truth speedily is healing for the mind. It is like what [Umayyad caliph] Muʿāwiya (d. 680) did with a man from the people of Basra who asked him for two thousand tree trunks to build his house. Muʿāwiya said to him, "How big is your house?" He said, "Two parasangs by two parasangs," to which he replied, "Is it in Basra or is Basra in it?" He said, "It is indeed in Basra," to which Muʿāwiya said, "But the whole of Basra is smaller than two parasangs." His very report itself contained what shows its falsehood.

It is like a man in Iraq who, we heard, said, "We have an orchard in Qūmis[8] three hundred parasangs to the west of the town." The person who was told this said, "If the report is right then we are now in the middle of this orchard, because it is less than this between Qūmis and Iraq."

It is similar to the words of al-Fākhir in his book in which he prefers Qaḥṭān to ʿAdnān.[9] For he refers to a son of ʿAdī ibn Ḥātim,[10] and says, "Where will you have one like him? His father ordered him to chase people away from his feast, but the boy refused and said, 'My father, order someone else to do this, not me.'" Al-Fākhir said, "This is a generous son of a generous son, one stamped with the character of a son stamped with the character of a son stamped with character." I find that this very report proves his statement wrong for the reason that the boy's father ordered him to chase the people from his meal, and this is what the boy found objectionable and asked to be excused from doing. So he was the generous son of a miser, and someone stamped with character, the son of one with no character.

Anyone who wishes to clarify and distinguish the reports of the prophets should do the same. He might inquire into the testimonies to truth and normative arguments for the Prophet, which I have found are numerous and can be brought together according to ten characteristics, the like of which cannot be brought together for anyone at all except Christ. I will interpret this and disclose it with clarity so that anyone inquiring into it will know that the one who has these qualities in his possession must have prophetic status, and the one who disbelieves in him is faced with a serious plea before God.

The first of these is his praying to the unique, everlasting, all-knowing and just One who is not overcome or wronged, and his conformity to all the prophets in this.

The second is what he possessed of piety, asceticism and sincerity, and the praiseworthiness of his ways and his laws.

The third is that he manifested clear signs that only the prophets and chosen ones of God produce.

The fourth is that he foretold things that were hidden from him but were fulfilled in his time.

The fifth is that he predicted numerous events happening in the world and its empires that were fulfilled after him.

The sixth is that the book which he delivered is by necessity and undeniable arguments a sign of prophetic status.

The seventh is that his victory over the nations is by necessity and undeniable arguments a clear sign.

The eighth is that his missionaries who conveyed his reports were the first and most godly of people, to whose like lies and untruth could not be imputed.

The ninth is that he was the Seal of the Prophets (33:40), and that if he had not been sent the prophecies of the prophets about him and Ishmael would have proved false.

The tenth is that the prophets had prophesied about him a long time before his appearance, describing his sending, his homeland and his course, and the submission of communities to him and of kings to his community.

These are luminous qualities and sufficient testimonies, that whoever exhibits them and they refer to him his arrow will achieve its goal, his truth will succeed, and belief in him will be indispensable. Whoever rejects them and repudiates them will have his course run out, and his existence here and in the hereafter lost. I will present the nub of this point by point, and will cite the witnesses of the prophets about it. I will not limit myself in this to a single prophet but to a number, nor to a single prophecy but to sixty or more prophecies. My foremost desire is that God will make it conducive and censuring, and a way out of blindness for anyone who is not proud or haughty, not misguided or malicious.

But if we ask the Christians in particular what is their reason for denying the Prophet, they say, "This is for three reasons: the first is that we have not found that any of the prophets prophesied about him before his coming; the second is that we have not found in the Qurʾān mention of a miracle or of a prophecy of the one who delivered it; and the third is that Christ informed us that there would be no prophets after him (see, e.g., Matthew 24:24). These are the strongest arguments they have for this, and with the help of God I will undo it. For if I can establish before them that the situation is contrary to what they say and that there is no need of what they say in order to believe the prophets, no excuse will be left to them in what is between God and themselves, and the one who keeps on using these pretexts and clutching to them will be on the path to conflict and ruin.

The response to their statement that no prophet has prophesized about him is that if the prophetic status of the prophets is only to be confirmed and can only be accepted by previous prophesies about it, so that whoever believed in any prophet who was not preceded by the prophecy of a prophet about him would be in error and conflict, then let them tell us about the person of the prophet Moses, who was it prophesied about him, or about David, Isaiah or Jeremiah? In their eyes they are among the supreme prophets, although there was no previous prophecy about them. So whoever believes in them has abandoned truth for falsehood by his acceptance of them and has drawn upon himself the wrath of the Lord of the worlds.

An answer to what they say that there is no mention in the Qurʾān of a miracle of the Prophet, and that one who does not have in his book any mention of a miracle or prophecy should not be trusted, then let them tell us about the miracle belonging to the prophet David in his Psalms. If they cannot provide this for us, then why and on what pretext do they call him a prophet when no prophet before him foretold him and there is no mention of a miracle in his book?

It must be clear from what I have explained that in the verification of the report about prophets there is no need for a preceding prophecy about them, or in order to prove them for there to be mention set down in their books of their miracles or signs. Among the prophets there have been those with a sign mentioned and prophecy expressed in their books although no prophet before them has foretold them, as we have made clear above, and this has not been a reason to set aside the truth about them. Such are Moses, Daniel, Isaiah and the like. Among them are those for whom God joined everything together, such as Christ, for he performed dazzling miracles and foretold hidden and concealed matters, and prophecies about him were manifested before his appearance. Among them were those who possessed a miracle, but there was no prophecy of theirs mentioned in their book, such as Elisha: he revived two dead people (2 Kings 4:18–37, 2 Kings 13:20–21), but he made no prophetic utterance of a direct kind. Among them were such as Ezekiel the prophet, Hosea and the like of them, who did not possess any miracle but did possess prophecy, although their prophecy which they uttered was only fulfilled after a long interval, there thus being no proof about him in it for those who actually saw him, and among those who were before him no evidence to prove him trustworthy for them without a miracle which he could perform for the people of his time. Among them were those who possessed neither miracle nor prophecy, nor convincing reports in his book, although they are numbered among the company of prophets, such as Malachi, Haggai and Nahum, whose prophetic books are only three or four pages. Among them are the prophetess Miriam, sister of Moses (Exodus 15:20–21), and the prophetess Hannah,[11] neither of whom in particular possessed a book, prophecy, miracle or sign, although they have included them among the prophets.

My dear cousins, why and on what evidence have you called these prophets, if this is their status, and why do you disbelieve in the prophetic status of the Prophet, who had all these enumerated qualities, some of them eternally fixed in the Qurʾān, and some in the traditions which are equivalent to the Qurʾān, although the ones that are in the Qurʾān are more certain as evidence, are clearer for the formulation of proof, and are more trustworthy as prophecy? How can it be, when there are the prophecies and indications of the godly prophets about him that I am going to make clear, with the majority of them to his prophetic status and his time? So if you say, "We dissociate ourselves from the Prophet and will have nothing to do with him, because there is no prophet after Christ," I will make clear to you from your books that the one who breathed this into your ears and caused it to come from your tongues was not being sincere to you but deceitful, not reliable but dubious.

This kind of thing is what is written in the Book of the Acts, which is the letters of the Apostles, in chapter 11: "In those days prophets came from Jerusalem, and one of them who was named Agabus stood up and prophesied to them saying, 'In this country there will be a famine and severe drought'" (Acts 11:27–28). It says in this chapter that in the church of Antioch there were prophets and wise men, among them Barnabas, Simon and Lucius of the town of Cyrene, and Manael and Saul.[12] These five were among the prophets in Antioch, according to what is related. Prophetesses are also mentioned: in chapter 19 of this book it says, "Philip the interpreter had four daughters who were prophetesses."[13] And in the Book of the Acts, Luke (see Acts 1:1, and cf. Luke 1:1) says that the group making their way to Antioch arrived at the house of Judas and Silas because they too were prophets.[14] So this point has no force, talk about it is quite nonsensical, and the arguments in their favor are slack and without conviction. For it is clear that after Christ there were people whom they called apostles and prophets, such as Paul himself.

Shahrastānī's Heresiography on Non-Muslim Communities

Translated by W. Montgomery Watt

Muḥammad ibn ʿAbd al-Karīm ash-Shahrastānī (d. 1153) was among the more important authors of heresiographical texts. His *Book of Religious and Philosophical Sects* offers his characterizations of a range of non-Muslim religious traditions, as well as of major Muslim theological views (to which we will return in chapter 4). Here are his summaries of central doctrines of Christians generally and of several specific positions generally regarded as early Christian heresies.[15] Not unlike ʿAlī ibn Rabbān aṭ-Ṭabarī, Shahrastānī exhibits a keen interest in and awareness of religious communities well outside of his own, in a way one rarely finds in Christian authors of his day.

Text

THE CHRISTIANS [IN GENERAL]

[They are] the community of the Christ, Jesus son of Mary. He it is who was truly sent [as prophet] after Moses, and who was announced in the Torah. To him were [granted] manifest signs and notable evidences, such as the reviving of the dead and the cure of the blind and the leper. His very nature and innate disposition are a perfect sign of his truthfulness; that is, his coming without previous seed and his speaking without prior teaching. For all the [other] prophets the arrival of their revelation was at [the age of] forty years, but revelation came to him when he was made to speak in the cradle, and revelation came to him when he conveyed [the divine message] at [the age of] thirty. The duration of his [prophetic] mission was three years and three months and three days.[16]

When he was raised up to heaven, the disciples and others differed in respect of him. Their differences go back to only two things. One was the manner of his coming down and his connection with his mother and the incarnation of the Word; and the second was the manner of his ascension and his connection with the angels and the unity of the Word. As for the first [point] they assert the incarnation of the Word, but there is discussion about the manner of the union and the incarnation.[17] Some of them say that there was a shining on the body like the shining of light on a transparent substance. Some say [something] was stamped on it [the body] as a design is stamped on wax. Some say it was manifested in it [the body] as the spiritual is manifested in the corporeal. Some say the divinity clothed itself with the humanity. Some say that the word was mingled with the body as milk is mingled with water.

They affirmed that God has three hypostases (*aqānīm*). They said that the Creator is one substance (*jawhar*), meaning by this what is self-subsistent (*al-qāʾim bi ʾn-nafs*), not [what is characterized by] spatial location (*taḥayyuz*) and physical magnitude (*ḥajmīya*); and he is one in substantiality, three in hypostaticity (*uqnūmīya*). By the hypostases they mean the attributes (*ṣifāt*), such as existence, life and knowledge, and the father, the son and the holy spirit (*rūḥ al-qudus*). The [hypostasis of] knowledge clothed itself and was incarnated, but not the other hypostases.

In respect of the ascension they said that he was killed and crucified. The Jews killed him because of wrongful envy and because they rejected his prophethood and his rank. The killing did not affect the divine part but only the human part. They also said that the perfection of the human person (*ash-shakhṣ al-insānī*) was in three things: prophethood, leadership (*imāma*)[18] and kingship (*malaka*). While other prophets were characterized by these three properties or by some of them, the Christ had a rank higher than that, because he was the unique son without peer and beyond comparison with any other prophet. It is through him that the fault of Adam was pardoned; and it is he who [on the Last Day] will call the creatures to reckoning.

In respect of the [second] coming down there are differences. Some of them say he will come down before the Day of Resurrection, just as the people of Islam say. Some of them say he will not come down except *on* the Day of Reckoning (*ḥisāb*). As for him, after he was killed and crucified he came down, and Simon Peter saw his person, and [Jesus] addressed him and made him legatee; then he left the world and ascended to heaven. Simon Peter was his legatee (*waṣī*),[19] being the best of his disciples in knowledge, asceticism and conduct (*adab*).

Paul, however, disordered his affair, made himself [Peter's] partner, altered the bases of his knowledge, and mixed it with the arguments of the philosophers and the [evil] suggestions of his heart. I have seen a letter by Paul which he wrote to the Greeks [in which he said]: "You think that the position of Jesus is like the position of the other prophets, but it is not so; rather is his likeness the likeness of Melchizedek, who is king of peace, to whom Abraham was giving tithes, and who was blessing Abraham and anointing his head." Now [this] is surprising; it is reported in the Gospels that the Lord said, "You are the unique son"; but how can he who is unique be like one of the human race?[20]

Then four of the disciples came to an agreement, and each of them made a collection of [material for] the Gospel. They are Matthew, Luke, Mark and John. The conclusion of the Gospel of Matthew is that [Jesus] said: "I send you to the nations *(umam)* as my father sent me to you; go and summon the nations in the name of the Lord and of the Son and of the Holy Spirit." The opening of the Gospel of John [is]: "From all eternity there had been the Word, and that Word was with God, and God indeed was the Word, and all was [or came into being] by his hand" (cf. Matthew 29:19, John 1:1–3).

Then the Christians divided into seventy-two sects [according to a Hadith]. The greatest of their sects were three, the Melkites, the Nestorians and the Jacobites. From these there split off the Julianists, the Apollinarians, the Macedonians, the Sabellians, the Photinians, the Paulicians and various others.

THE MELKITES

[These are] the associates of Malkā, who triumphed over the Byzantines (Rūm) and mastered them.[21] The majority of the Byzantines are Melkites. They say that the Word was united with the body of the Christ and clothed itself with his humanity. By the Word they mean the hypostasis of knowledge, and by the Holy Spirit they mean the hypostasis of life. They do not call the knowledge "the Son" before it clothes itself with [humanity], but the Christ, along with what clothed itself with him [it], is Son. Some said that the Word mingled with the body of the Christ as wine with milk or water with milk.

The Melkites explain that the substance is other than the hypostases. That is like [the relation of] the thing-described (*mawṣūf*) and the description [or attribute] (*ṣifa*); and from this they explained the affirmation of the Trinity (*ithbāt at-tathlīth*). The Qur'ān reported of them: "disbelieved have those who say God is the third of three" (5:73).

The Melkites say that the Christ is humanity entirely, not partially, and that he is eternal (*qadīm azalī*) from eternal. Mary gave birth to him as eternal deity (*ilāh azalī*). The killing and the crucifying happened to [both] the humanity and the divinity. They apply the expression of fatherhood and sonship [respectively] to God and to the Christ because of what they found in the Gospel where [God] said, "You are the unique son", and where Simon Peter said, "You are truly the Son of God." Perhaps that is a linguistic metaphor, as when one says of the seekers of [this] world "sons of the world" and of the seekers of the world-to-come "sons of the world-to-come."

The Christ said to his disciples: "I say to you, love your enemies, bless those who curse you, do good to those who hate you, and pray for those who harm you, so that you may be sons of your father who is in heaven, who makes his sun shine on the upright and the wicked, and sends down his rain on the just and the unjust; and be perfect as your father who is in heaven is perfect." He also said: "Look to your alms and do not give before people to dissemble with them, for then there will be no reward for you with your father who is in heaven." At the time when he was crucified he said: "I go to my father and your father."[22]

When Arius said, "the eternal is God, and the Christ is created," the patriarchs, metropolitans and bishops met in the city of Constantinople in the presence of their king; they were 313 men.[23] They agreed on this word as creed and proclamation, namely; "We believe in the one God (*Allāh al-wāḥid*), ruler of everything and maker of what is seen and what is unseen; and in the one Son, Jesus the Christ, son of the one God [or the one son of God], first-born before all the creatures and not made; true deity from true deity, from the substance of his father; by his hand the worlds and all things were formed aright; for our sake and for the sake of our salvation (*khalāṣ*) he came down from heaven, and became incarnate through the Holy Spirit, and was born of Mary the Virgin; he was crucified in the days of Pilate and was buried; then he rose on the third day, and ascended into heaven and took his seat on the right hand of his father; and he is ready to come a second time for the judgment of the dead and the living. We believe in the one Holy Spirit, the spirit of truth, who proceeds from his father; and in one baptism for the forgiveness of sins; and in one holy Christian catholic community (*jamāʿa . . . jāthilīqīya*); and in the rising of our bodies and the life forever and ever."

This is the first agreement in these words. In it is a reference to the assembling of the bodies [on the Last Day]; but among the Christians there are some who say there is an assembling of spirits [only], not of bodies, and say [further] that the recompense of the wicked in the resurrection is grief and sorrow and ignorance, and the recompense of the good is pleasure and joy and knowledge. They deny that in paradise there will be marriage and eating and drinking.

One of them, Mār Isḥāq,[24] said that God promised [good] to the obedient and threatened [evil] to the disobedient, and that he may not act contrary to his promise, for that does not befit the honorable, though he may act contrary to his threat by not punishing the sinners and may [thus] bring back the creation to pleasure and happiness; and he made this common for all, since [to inflict] eternal punishment does not befit the Generous and True.

THE NESTORIANS

[These are] the associates of Nestorius, the philosopher, who appeared in the time of al-Maʾmūn.[25] He treated the Gospels in accordance with his [own] view. His relation to them [other Christians] was the relation of the Muʿtazila to this [Islamic] Sharia.[26] He said that God is one but has three hypostases, existence, knowledge and life, and that these hypostases are not additional to his essence, and are not he. The Word is united with the body of Jesus, not by way of mingling as the Melkites said, and not by way of manifestation as the Jacobites said, but like the shining of the sun in a small aperture or a crystal or like the appearance of the design on the seal. The doctrine of Nestorius about the hypostases resembles most closely that of Abū Hāshim of the Muʿtazila for he affirmed different properties [existing] in one thing; and he [Nestorius] means by saying [God] is one in substance that he is not composed of genus [and differentia], but is simple, one. He means by life and knowledge two hypostases, two substances, that is, two roots or principles for the world [or for the knower]. Then he interpreted knowledge as speech and word. In the end his teaching amounts to [God's] being existent, living and speaking, as the philosophers say in the definition of man, except that these "forms" differ from one another in the case of a human being because he is composite, whereas [God] is a simple substance, not composite.

Some of them affirm that God has other attributes, such as power, will and the like; but they do not make hypostases of these as they make hypostases of life and knowledge. Some of them express the view that each of the three hypostases is a living speaking deity. The remainder of them consider that the name of "deity" is not applied to each of the hypostases. They consider that the Son is everlastingly begotten from the Father, but was only incarnated and united with the body of the Christ at the time he was born. Temporal occurrence relates to the body and the humanity. He is deity and man in union; and these are two substances, two hypostases, two natures, an eternal substance and a temporal substance, a complete deity and a complete man. The union was not destroyed by the eternity of the eternal or the temporality of the temporal, but the two became one Christ and one will. Sometimes they change the term and instead of "substance" use "nature" and instead of "hypostasis" use "person."

Their view about the killing and the crucifying differs from that of the Melkites and Jacobites. They say that the killing befell the Christ in respect of his humanity, not in respect of his divinity, because pains do not inhere in the deity.

Photinus and Paul of Samosata said that God [or the deity] is one, and that the Christ began from Mary, and that he was a good man (*ʿabd*) and was created, but that God honored and dignified him because of his obedience and called him "son" by adoption (*tabannī*), not by birth and union.

Among the Nestorians was a group called the Worshippers. They held the same view about the Christ as Nestorius, except that they said that, when an individual makes special efforts in worship and in giving up eating flesh and fat and in denying sensual animal desires, his substance becomes pure until he reaches heaven and sees God openly; there is [then] disclosed to him what is in the unseen, so that nothing in heaven or earth is hidden from him.

Among the Nestorians [too] are some who deny anthropomorphism and affirm the doctrine that the determination of good and bad is from humanity [not God], as the Qadarīya held.

THE JACOBITES

[These are] the associates of Jacob. They hold that there are three hypostases, as we mentioned, but they said that the Word was transformed into flesh and blood and became the deity which is the Christ; he is manifest in his body, but he is he. About these the Noble Qurʾān informed us: "Disbelieved have those who say God is the Christ, the son of Mary" (5:17, 72).

Some of them said that the Christ is God. Some of them said that the divinity manifested itself in the humanity, so that the humanity of the Christ became the place-of-manifestation of the Truth [that is, God], not by way of the inherence of a part in it and not by way of the union of the Word which has the status of an attribute; but he became he [God]. This is like saying "The angel was manifest in the form of a man" and "Satan was manifest in the form of an animal" and, as the revelation reported of Gabriel, "he took for her the form of a handsome man" (19:17).

Most of the Jacobites consider that the Christ is one substance, one hypostasis, but that he is [formed] out of two substances. Sometimes they say "one nature [formed] out of two natures." The eternal substance of the deity and the temporal substance of the man are compounded as [in human beings] soul and body are compounded. Thus they two become one substance, one hypostasis; and he is man all of him, deity all of him. One says that the man became deity but not the reverse; that is, one does not say that the deity became man. [It is] as when charcoal is thrown into the fire; one says the charcoal became fire but one does not say the fire became charcoal; in reality it is neither fire absolutely nor charcoal absolutely but an ember or live coal. They consider that the World was united with the partial, not the entire man. Sometimes they speak of the "union" as "mingling" or "being clothed" or "inherence" like the inherence of the form of a man in a polished mirror.

All the Trinitarians (*aṣḥāb at-tathlīth*) agree that the eternal may not be united with the temporal, except that the hypostasis which is the Word is [so] united, not the other hypostases. They agree that the Christ is the child of Mary, and was killed and crucified. Then they differ with regard to the manner of that. The Melkites and Jacobites say that that which Mary bore was the deity. The Melkites, since they believe that the Christ is universal eternal humanity, say that Mary is a partial human-being and that the partial cannot give birth to the universal, so that it was only the eternal hypostasis that gave birth to him. The Jacobites [on the other hand], since they believe that the Christ is a substance [formed] out of two substances and is [also] a deity and what was born, say that Mary gave birth to a deity. Similarly they say in respect of the killing that it happened to the substance which was [formed] out of two substances; they say that, if it happened to [only] one of them, then there is no union.

Some of them took the view: "we affirm two aspects to the eternal substance, and the Christ is eternal in one aspect and temporal in [another] aspect. Some of the Jacobites considered that the Word did not take anything from Mary, but passed through her like water in a pipe; and what was manifested visually of the person of the Christ was like the shape and image in the mirror. Otherwise he was not really a solid material body. Similarly the killing and the crucifying happened only by way of conjecture and fantasy. These were called the Julianists, and they were a community in Syria, the Yemen and Armenia. They said also "the deity was crucified only for our sake that he might save us." Some of them supposed that the Word entered the body of the Christ [only] sometimes, and then there proceeded from him the signs of reviving the dead and healing the blind and the leper; and it separated from him at other times and there came upon him pains and sufferings.

Ibn al-Jawzī on the Devil's Deception of Jews and Christians

Translated by D. S. Margoliouth

Chapter 2 introduced the work of the renowned Ḥanbalī Traditionalist thinker and preacher Ibn al-Jawzī in the context of Qur'ānic hermeneutics. Ibn al-Jawzī (d. 1200) was a prolific author of works in a wide variety genres and themes, including one of the more unusual and imaginative polemical works, *The Devil's Delusion* (*Talbīs Iblīs*). Here is a selection from Ibn al-Jawzī's no-holds-barred views on the ultimate reason for the wayward thinking of Jews, Christians, and (on a lesser scale) various other non-Muslim communities. He describes briefly at the outset how his sense of responsibility to warn against Satanic stratagems prompted him to compose this large work. He aligns himself with a Companion of the Prophet named Ḥudhayfa, chosen by Muḥammad as the community's expert on hypocrisy. He cites Ḥudhayfa's comment that whereas most people asked the Prophet about "the good," Ḥudhayfa preferred to ask about "the evil," for fear that it might otherwise blindside him.[27]

Text

ACCOUNT OF THE WAY IN WHICH HE DELUDES THE JEWS

He has indeed deluded them in numerous matters of which we will mention a selection which will serve as a guide to the rest. Among them is their assimilating the Creator to the creature; were such assimilation correct, He would be liable to what they are liable to [i.e., human frailty]; our colleague [the Ḥanbalī] Abū ʿAbd Allāh ibn Ḥāmid records how the Jews maintain that God who is to be worshipped is a man of light on a throne of light, having on His head a crown of light and having the same members as a human being. Another is their assertion that ʿUzayr [Ezra] is the son of God; had they understood that filiation belongs to division, and that God is not divisible, since He is not composite, they would not have asserted such filiation. Further, a son is of the same category as his father, and ʿUzayr must have been maintained by food, whereas God is the maintainer of things, not maintained by them. Now what suggested this to them together with their ignorance of reality, was that they saw him come back after death and recite the Torah from memory; and they talked about this with erroneous fancies. And what shows that these people were far from intelligent is that, having seen the effect of the divine power in the dividing of the sea, then, coming across idols, they demanded the like, saying "Make unto us gods even as they have gods" (7:138). And when Moses rebuked them for this, still the idea remained in their minds, and that which was hidden came to light when they worshipped the calf, a course to which they were impelled by two things; one, their ignorance of the Creator, and the second their wanting something which would appeal to the sense, so dominant was sensation with them, and so far removed were they from reason. Had they not been so ignorant of the object of worship, they would not have dared to use improper expressions concerning Him, saying "Truly God is poor and we are rich" and "The hand of God is fettered" (3:181, 5:64). God is high above all that!

Among the delusions that the devil inflicted on them is their assertion that there is no abrogation of the codes. They were aware that the system of Adam permitted marriage with sisters and other prohibited degrees, and working on the Sabbath day; then this was abrogated by the code of Moses. They say: If God enjoins anything, that is wisdom, and it may not be altered. I reply: At certain times alteration may be wisdom; the change in the human being from health to disease and from disease to death is wisdom, all of it. He has forbidden you to work on the Sabbath day, and permitted you to work on the Sunday: and this belongs to the category of what you disapprove. Further God commanded Ibrāhīm to sacrifice his son, and then forbade him to do so.

Another delusion which he inflicted on them is their saying "The fire shall not touch us save for a certain number of days" (2:80) these being the days wherein they worshipped the calf. Indeed their atrocities are numerous, and then the devil induced them to practice pure contumacy, so that they rejected the description of our Prophet which was in their books and altered it. They had been ordered to believe in him; but they were content to be damned. Their learned ones were contumacious, and the ignorant among them followed their lead. It is indeed a marvel that they should have altered and mutilated what had been prescribed to them, and made what they wanted their religion. What place has service with one who neglects the command and acts according to his lust? Further they contradicted Moses and found fault with him, declaring that he had a personal defect and charging him with the murder of Aaron; just as they charged David with seizing Uriah's wife (2 Samuel 11).

The following was told us by Muḥammad ʿAbd al-Bāqī al-Bazzāz, with a chain of authorities going back to Abū Hurayra (d. ca. 677). He said: The Prophet went to the school of the Jews, and said: Bring out to me the most learned among you. There came out ʿAbd Allāh ibn Sūriya, and they had a private interview. The Prophet adjured him by his religion and God's bounty in feeding them with manna and quails, and causing the cloud to overshadow them, to answer the question: Do you know that I am God's Apostle? He replied: Yes, by God! And indeed the people know what I know, and that your description and characteristics are clear in the Torah; only they are envious of you. The Prophet said: Then what hinders you yourself? He said: I am unwilling to go against my people; possibly they may follow you and accept Islam, in which case I shall do the like. . . .

ACCOUNT OF THE WAY IN WHICH HE DELUDES THE CHRISTIANS

This is of many kinds, one of them being that the devil makes them fancy that the blessed Creator is a substance. The Jacobites, followers of Jacob, the Melkites, followers of the imperial religion, and the Nestorians, followers of Nestorius, maintain that God is a single substance, self-maintained, being one in substantiality, three in personality; one of the persons according to them is the Father, another the Son, and another the Holy Ghost. Some of them say that the Persons are properties, others that they are qualities; others that they are individuals. These persons forget that if God were a substance, He would be liable to those things to which substances are liable, limitation in space, motion and rest, and colors. Then the devil suggested to some of them that Christ is God; Abū Muḥammad an-Nawbakhtī (d. ca. 920) says: The Melkites and Jacobites maintain that the person born by Mary is God. To some of them Satan suggested that Christ is the son of God; some of them hold that Christ is two substances, one of them ancient and the other modem. In spite of their saying this concerning Christ they admit that he needed food, neither differing on that point nor on the fact that he was crucified, and was unable to protect himself. They say that this was done only with the humanity; why then did not the divinity in him protect the humanity?

Further he deluded them with regard to our Prophet, so that they rejected him after he had been mentioned in the Gospel. Some of the "People of the Book" admit that he was a prophet, only sent exclusively to the Arabs. This is one of the devil's delusions, wherein he has got them off their guard. For if it be certain that he was a prophet, then a prophet cannot lie; and the Prophet said "I am sent unto all humankind"; and he wrote letters to Caesar, Khosroes, and the rest of the foreign kings.

ACCOUNT OF THE WAY IN WHICH HE DELUDES BOTH JEWS AND CHRISTIANS

An example is their saying God will not punish us for the sake of our ancestors, since of us [i.e., among our ancestors] are the saints and prophets. God tells us about this saying of theirs "We are the sons of God and His beloved" (5:18), i.e., being His sons ʿUzayr and ʿĪsā. The dispelling of this illusion is that every individual is answerable for God's claims upon him, which no relative can avert; and if love of an individual could be transferred to another in virtue of relationship, hatred also would be transferable. Our Prophet said to his daughter Fāṭima, "I cannot avail you at all against God."[28] The advantage of the loved one is by reason of his piety, and whoever lacks this, lacks the divine love. Further God's love of a creature is no passion like that of one human being for another; were it indeed like that, then transference would be admissible. . . .

[Here Ibn al-Jawzī continues with sections on how Iblīs deludes the Sabians and Mazdians.]

Ibn Taymīya on Christian Alteration of Scripture

Translated by Thomas Michel, SJ

Sooner or later, all theological issues come back around to sacred scripture. This is so in the context of Muslim understandings of the "other" as in Islamic literature focused only on the Qur'ān, perhaps doubly so because of the inherent multivalent connections among the Abrahamic scriptures. A foundational concept in Muslim polemic is the conviction that discrepancies between the Bible and the Qur'ān are traceable to Christian (and Jewish) tampering with the sacred text. Ibn Taymīya's (d. 1328) elaborate response to Christian claims to definitive scriptural revelation includes a classic formulation of the problem of alteration (*taḥrīf*) in a section entitled "The Extent of the Corruption in the Bible." Note how the author develops specific features of the classic Muslim concepts of divine revelation and absolute veracity of Islam's sacred scripture.[29]

Text

[The Christians] state: We are amazed at these people, that with all their knowledge, intelligence, and learning, they can make a claim like this against us. It is just as if we were to bring a similar charge against them: "They have changed and corrupted the Book which they possess at this time, and have written in it whatever they wanted and felt like." Would they approve of our saying this?

But I [Ibn Taymīya] say: This is something that is not possible for anyone to claim—the changing or substitution of even one word is impossible.

[Christians say:] Praise to the great God! If it is impossible for their Book which is in one language to have undergone the change or substitution of even a word, then how could the alteration of our books which are written in 72 languages have occurred? In each of those languages there are so many thousands of copies. Our books lasted over 700 years before the coming of Muḥammad, and came to be used by peoples who read them in different languages in far distant countries. Who has ever spoken 72 languages or governed the whole world, with its kings, priests, and scholars so that he gained control over all copies of our Books in all areas of the earth, collected them from the world's four corners so that he could change them?

It would not even have been possible for him to have changed some copies and omitted others, because all copies of our Books have one wording, one expression in all languages. Thus no one can ever make such a charge as theirs.

[Ibn Taymīya:] The analogy of their books to the Qurʾān—that just as no claim of *tabdīl* (substitution) is heard concerning it, so should it be with their books—is a false analogy in its meaning and expression. As for the meaning: everything in their religion on which Muslims agree by a well-known, openly manifested consensus is transmitted from the Messenger by successive transmission, and even known by necessity to be from his religion. The five prayers, the poor tax, the fasting during the month of Ramaḍān, the pilgrimage to the Kaʿba, the necessity of justice and honesty, the prohibition of shirk, impurities, and wrongdoing, even the prohibition of wine, gambling, and interest-taking, and still other things—all these are successively transmitted from the Prophet, just like the transmission of the texts of the Qurʾān which indicate them.

In this category is the universality of the prophetic mission of Muḥammad, and his being sent to all humanity—People of the Book as well as others, even to all humankind and jinn. It is similarly known that he accused those Jews and Christians who did not follow what God revealed through him of unbelief, just as he accused others than them of unbelief who refused to believe the message; he waged jihād against them and commanded his followers to also wage jihād against them.

Muslims know three matters as handed down by successive transmission from their prophet: the text of the Qurʾān, its interpretations on which Muslims find consenṣus, and the successively transmitted *sunna,* which is the "Wisdom" (*ḥikma*) which God handed down outside the Qurʾān (2:151, 2:231, 4:113, 33:34). Moreover the Muslims preserve the Qurʾān by memory in their hearts, thus dispensing with the printed text. This is proven by the sound hadith from the prophet reported by Muslim:

The Lord said to me, "I am handing down to you a Book which is not washed by water, which you can read waking and sleeping."

What He is saying is that even if the text were washed off the printed copies by water, it would not be washed off people's hearts. By contrast, the preceding Books, if their printed copies were lacking, there would not be found anyone who could transmit them successively by preserving them in their hearts.

The Qur'ān is still preserved in human hearts by successive transmission, so that if someone should want to change a thing in a printed copy, and that were presented for inspection to Muslim youths, they would know that he had changed a copy because of their memorization of the Qur'ān. Rather than accepting the printed copy, they would reject it.

Among the People of the Book, however, some one of them could transcribe many copies of the Torah and the Gospel and change some of them and present them to their scholars, who would not know what he had changed if they did not have their own copies at hand. Thus, were those copies which had been changed to circulate among groups of Christians, they would not have been aware of the alteration.

Moreover, Muslims have chains of reliable, trustworthy authorities connected to one another on the authority of reliable men whom one can trust in the minutiae of religion just like the generality of Muslims have transmitted its main tenets. The People of the Book have nothing like this.

It is not possible for anyone to alter the Qur'ān, since it is preserved in human hearts and handed down by consecutive transmission. We do not bear witness, nevertheless, that every one of the copies are in agreement. An error may occur in one of the handwritten copies which will be recognized by those who have memorized the Qur'ān; they have no need to refer to another copy.

Their books are not memorized, nor is there a group of transmitters who can act as a reference for their copies. In the time when the prophets were present among men, they acted as the competent authority for people, on whom others could depend if some among them had changed something in the books. But when prophecy was interrupted, some people were quick to make changes in the books.

Many Christians replaced much in the religion of Christ only a short time after the ascension of Christ. They began replacing one thing after another, although there remained a group among them who held fast to the true religion until God sent Muḥammad.

The religion on which Muslims have agreed by a clear and well-known agreement has been handed down from their prophet by successive transmission.

They transmitted the Qurʾān as well as the *sunna,* which explains and clarifies the Qurʾān (16:44). The wording and the meaning of what God revealed is clear. The meanings of the Qurʾān which Muslims have agreed upon by evident consensus are among what the community has inherited from their prophet, just as they have inherited from him the texts of the Qurʾān. And since, thank God, the community has never agreed on any altered or corrupted interpretation, how could it have done so for the texts of those meanings?

The transmission of the texts and the consensus upon them was even clearer in the case of the wording than it was on the interpretations. Thus the religion manifested among Muslims is that upon which they have agreed, whose text and interpretation is among what they have transmitted from their prophet. There was no *taḥrīf* or *tabdīl* in it, neither in wording nor in meaning.

In contrast to this, in the Torah and the Gospel are found texts on whose meaning and legal judgments Jews, Christians, or both have done evident substitution. This is well known among the generality of their people. For example, the Jews changed what was found in the earlier books by way of prophecies of Christ and Muḥammad, laws in the Torah, and His command in some of its information. Christians similarly replaced much in the reports and laws in the Torah and the prophetic books which Christ had not changed. However, Christ must be followed in what God abrogated of the Torah through his preaching.

As for what they replaced after Christ, like permitting the eating of pork, and their changing what God had forbidden and Christ had not permitted, like the omission of circumcision, prayer to the east, the lengthened period of fasting and changing it from one time to another, the use of pictures in churches, glorifying the cross, establishing monasticism—none of these practices were legislated by Christ or any other prophet. By these things they followed what God had not commanded through the preaching of any prophet in opposition to what God had commanded and sent through His prophets.

The Qurʾān has been established by successive transmission, and it is known by necessity to those who agree with or oppose Muḥammad that he claimed the Qurʾān to be the speech of God—not his own speech—and that it reached him from God. He used to distinguish between the Qurʾān and what he spoke from the *sunna,* even though the latter was among that which had to be followed by acceptance and deed.

God handed down the Book and the Wisdom, and taught the Book and the Wisdom to his community, as He himself has said (2:231, 3:164, 4:113,

33:34). God spoke thusly about Abraham and his son Ismāʿīl (2:128–29). The Prophet said: "I was given the Book, and along with it what is similar to it." He was teaching his community the Book which is the beloved Qurʾān, and he informed them that it is the speech of God, not his own speech. The Qurʾān is that about the excellence of which God spoke (17:88).

It is that which he commanded his community to recite in their prayer, so that the prayer is not correct without it. In addition to this Book he also taught them the Wisdom which God handed down; he distinguished between it and the Qurʾān in various ways:

(1) The Qurʾān is miraculous.
(2) The Qurʾān is that which is read at prayer without the *sunna*.
(3) The Arabic text of the Qurʾān has been handed down according to the exact wording of its verses, and no one may change them in the Arabic language by the agreement of Muslims. It is possible, however, to explain them in Arabic or to translate them in other languages than Arabic. Their formal recitation in Arabic with other than their proper wording is not permissible by the agreement of Muslims. This is in contrast to the Wisdom he taught them, for there is no judgment made on its wording as there is on the wording of the Qurʾān.
(4) The Qurʾān is that which "None touches but the purified" (56:79). One in a state of ritual impurity may not read it, as his *sunna* has indicated according to the majority of the community. This is in contrast to anything else than the Qurʾān.

The community received the Qurʾān from him by memory during his lifetime; more than one of the Companions memorized the whole Qurʾān during his lifetime, and all of the Companions memorized some of it. Some of them memorized what others had not memorized. Thus all of it is handed down from him by hearing in successive transmission, and he claimed that it reached him from God, that it was the speech of God, not his own speech.

In the Qurʾān there are many texts which show it to be the speech of God. Those who saw Muḥammad and transmitted his miracles, his deeds, and his Law, which they saw with their own eyes, and the Qurʾān and hadith which they heard, were thousands taken from more than a hundred thousand who saw and believed in him.

But the Gospels which the Christians possess are four—that of Matthew, Mark, Luke, and John. Christians agree that Luke and Mark had never seen

Christ, but only Matthew and John saw him. These four writings which they call the Gospel, and they may call each one of them a gospel, were only written after the assumption of Jesus. It is not stated in them that they are the speech of God, nor that Christ received them from God; rather they transmit some things from the speech of Christ and some things from his deeds and miracles. They state that they have not handed on all that they saw and heard from him. They are therefore of the same nature as the sayings and deeds of the Prophet related about him by the hadith-collectors, the biographers, and the narrators of his campaigns. But these latter are not a Qurʾān.

The gospels which they possess are similar to the biography, the books of hadith, and books like these. If most of it is true and what Christ actually said, it has come to him from God and one should confirm its message and obey its command, just as the Messenger said about the *sunna.* It resembles what the Messenger said about the *sunna,* for there is found in it what the Messenger states to be the word of God, as when he says God says: "Whoever treats a friend of Mine as an enemy, I permit [My friend] to war against him."

In the *sunna* there is also that which he [Muḥammad] says, but this also is among what God revealed to him. Whoever obeys the Messenger has obeyed God. So it is with what is handed down in the Gospel, for it is of this type. If it is a command from Christ, then the command of Christ is the command of God. Whoever obeys Christ has obeyed God. Whatever Christ reported about the unknown, God has informed him of it, for he is preserved from error in the message he brings.

If the Gospel is similar to the transmitted *sunna,* error mars it in some of its expressions, just as occurs in the biography, or the books of sound hadiths by Abū Dāwūd (d. 889), At-Tirmidhī (d. 892), and Ibn Māja (d. 886). These books have been spread and circulated widely among Muslims; consequently it is not possible for anyone, after their dissemination and the proliferation of their copies, to change all of them.

Nevertheless in some of their expressions error occurred before they were widely disseminated. The narrator, although he was honest, may have erred. However, the information which Muslims have accepted by assent, confirmation, and action is firmly claimed by Muslims to be truly from their prophet.

The books handed down through the prophets were of the same type as the book handed down through Muḥammad, but there was no successive transmission of them, nor was there the confirmation of the fallible as a proof, nor was there among them means for distinguishing between what is truthful and what is false as there is among Muslims. For this reason the gospels which the Christians possess are of this type; they contain many of the sayings, deeds, and miracles of Christ, but also contain what is undoubtedly in error against him and against that which he wrote in them in the beginning. Even if there is no one who has accused them of intentionally lying, still one, two, three, or four persons do not prevent the occurrence of error or omission in the books.

There is especially much error in what someone has heard or seen and then reports many years later. Moreover there was no inerrant community at the time to receive those reports by giving assent and confirmation which would necessitate knowledge in these matters, for the inerrant community could not agree on an error. But the apostles were only twelve men.

The story of the crucifixion is a case in which doubtfulness occurred, and an argument has been established to show that the one crucified was not Christ, "but it was made to appear so." They thought that it was Christ, although not one of the apostles had seen Christ crucified, but it was only reported to them by some Jews who had witnessed it.

Some people hold that they intentionally lied, but the majority hold that they were uncertain about the matter. The majority of Muslims have held that the words in God's saying "But it was made to appear so to them" refer to the hearers of their report. It is possible that they erred in this report, and they were not inerrant in transmitting it. Therefore it is possible that they erred in some of what they reported about Christ. This is not anything that maligns the messengership of Christ, nor is it included in what religious tradition has successively transmitted about him which says that he is messenger of God and must be followed whether he was crucified or not. What is successively transmitted about him demands faith in him whether or not he was crucified.

The apostles believed what they were handing on about Christ, and are not charged with intentionally lying about him, but there is nothing to prevent some of them from having erred in what they reported about him; that is, we do not know otherwise, especially when the error of that on which they were mistaken is clearly shown in other places.

Christians themselves have differed concerning the generality of that in which error occurred, even to the matter of the crucifixion. Some of them hold that the one crucified was not Christ, but someone similar, as Muslims say. Some Christians hold for his being the servant of God, and deny any indwelling or union, like the Arians. Others, like the Nestorians, deny the union but profess the divine indwelling.

FOUR

Creed and Polemic

TWO LARGE, MULTIFACETED GENRES of theological literature emerged fairly early in Islamic history, evolved somewhat over centuries, and continued to be written well into modern times. One could argue that creedal formulations are an extension of early doxographical texts, with their descriptions of the beliefs, correct and unacceptable alike, of the various subcommunities who identified themselves as "Muslims." Overtly polemical texts also became an important tool by which Muslims of one persuasion underscored their disagreement with fellow Muslims, even to the point of dismissing them from the fold.[1]

CREEDS

Known as both *shahāda* (testimony) and *kalima* (word, articulation), the statement "I testify that there is no deity but God and that Muḥammad is the Messenger of God" is Islam's earliest and most fundamental profession of faith. Muslim authors began forging more detailed creedal statements as early as the eighth century and generated them in considerable profusion during the subsequent two to three centuries. Many of the early jurists and theologians have had their names attached to these *ʿaqāʾid* (pl. of *ʿaqīda,* lit. "binding," hence article of faith or "creed").

Here are excerpts from creedal formulations that exemplify a range of approaches to divine acts and attributes, representing characteristic views of Ḥanbalī, Ashʿarī-Shāfiʿī, Māturīdī-Ḥanafī, and Shīʿī perspectives (the last of the four excerpts translated by W. Montgomery Watt also shares important features with Muʿtazilī theology). This section concludes with a popular creed of a major early modern South Asian theologian, Sayyid Aḥmad Khān.

Ḥanbalī Traditionalist Creed

Translated by W. Montgomery Watt

From a "school" of jurisprudence and theology named after Aḥmad ibn Ḥanbal (d. 855) comes the following extended "Traditionalist" treatment of central themes and questions. Thoroughly consistent with Ibn Ḥanbal's thought, the "anonymous" creed may well reproduce the master's own formulation, at least in part. Note the prominence of eschatological themes, the distinctively Ḥanbalī emphasis on the waxing and waning of "faith," and the frequent reference to various "sectarian" schools.[2]

Text

Faith is speech, action [or works] and intention, and holding to the *Sunna*. Faith increases and decreases. It is [right] to express uncertainty in respect of faith, but the expression of uncertainty is not [actual] doubt; it is only an old custom among scholars. If a man is asked, "Are you a believer?" he says, "I am a believer, if God wills," or, "I am a believer, I hope," or, "I believe in God, His angels, His books and His messengers." He who supposes that faith is speech without works is a Murjiʾite. He who supposes that faith is [only] speech and that works are legal matters is a Murjiʾite. He who supposes that faith increases but does not decrease has adopted the view of the Murjiʾites. He who does not recognize the expression of uncertainty in respect of faith is a Murjiʾite. He who supposes that his faith is like the faith of Gabriel, Michael and the angels is a Murjiʾite. He who supposes that knowledge [or religious truth] in the heart is beneficial, but does not speak of it [profess it openly], is a Murjiʾite.

The predetermination of everything [is from God], [both] of the good and the evil, of the little and the much, of what is outward and what is inward, of what is sweet and what is bitter, of what is liked and what is disliked, of what is fine and what is bad, of what is first and what is last. [It is] a decree He has decreed and a predetermination He has predetermined for [human beings]. Not one of them opposes God's will or does other than His decree, but all of them come to what He has created them for and fulfill what He has predetermined for them to do. This is justice on His part. Adultery, theft, wine-drinking, homicide, consuming unlawful wealth, idolatry and all sins [come about] by God's decree and predetermination, without any of the creatures having an argument against God, although He has a conclusive argument against His creatures. He is not questioned about what He does, but they are questioned. The knowledge of God is efficacious in respect of His creatures by a volition from Him. He has known the sin of Satan and the others who sin against Him—and He is being sinned against until the coming of the Hour—and He has created them for that. He knows the obedience of the people of obedience and has created them for that. Everyone does what he was created to do, and comes to what was decreed for him and known about him. Not one of them opposes God's predetermination and His will. God is the doer of what He decides on and the accomplisher of what He wills. If anyone supposes that for His servants who sin against Him God wills good and obedience, and that the human beings will for themselves evil and sin and carry out what they have willed, then [that person] has supposed that the will of human beings is more effective than the will of God. And what is a greater lie against God than this?

If anyone supposes that adultery is not by predetermination, he is asked, "Do you see this woman, pregnant as a result of adultery and producing a child?—did God will that He should create this child, or was it established in His previous knowledge?" If he says, "No," he has supposed that along with God there is [another] creator, and this is pure idolatry.

If anyone supposes that stealing, wine-drinking and consuming unlawful wealth are not by [God's] decree and predetermination, he is supposing that this person is powerful enough to be able to consume the sustenance of another [person], and this is pure Magian doctrine. On the contrary, a [person] eats his [own] sustenance, and God has decreed that he should eat it in the way in which he eats [sc. lawful or unlawful].

If anyone supposes that killing a person is not by [God's] will in His creating [of those involved], he is supposing that the one killed died at other than his appointed term, and what unbelief is clearer than this? On the contrary, that [event] was by God's decree and by His will in respect of His creatures and by His arranging for them, and [was] of what came about by His previous knowledge about them. He is justice and truth, and He does what He wills. He who asserts God's knowledge must assert His predetermination and His will [even] of the small and the paltry.

We do not bear witness of any of the People of the Qibla that he is in Hell for an evil he has done or a great sin he has committed, unless there is a

how can people be punished for doing God's will?!

hadith about that.... We do not bear witness of any of the People of the Qibla that he is in Paradise for something noble and good he has done unless there is a hadith about that....

The caliphate is in Quraysh [i.e., the office will be held by a member of the Quraysh tribe] so long as two people remain [alive]. It is not [right] for any of the people to contend with them about it, nor to rebel against them. We do not acknowledge the caliphate of any other than [Quraysh] until the coming of the Hour. The Jihād is valid along with the imams, whether they act uprightly or sinfully; it is not invalidated either by the evil of the evildoer or by the justice of the just. The Friday worship, the [celebration of the] two feasts and the pilgrimage [are to be observed] with the rulers, even if these are not upright, just and pious. [Various taxes], the legal alms, the land-tax, the tithes and the [proportion of the] booty and spoils are to be paid to the commanders, whether they have dealt justly or evilly in respect of them. Him to whom God has entrusted your affairs is to be followed, and you are not to withdraw your hand from obeying him nor to rebel against him with the sword, until God makes for you an opening and an exit. Do not rebel against the authority, but listen and obey, and do not break your oath of allegiance. He who does that is an innovator, opposing and separating himself from the community. If the authority commands you to do what is a sin against God, you must certainly not obey him, but it is not for you to rebel against him or to deny him his right. Keeping apart [from both sides] in civil strife is an ancient *Sunna* whose observance is obligatory. If you are made to suffer, set your self [life] before your religion. In civil strife, do not give your assistance by hand or tongue, but withhold your hand, your tongue and your sympathy; and God is the Helper.

[It is obligatory] to hold back from the People of the Qibla and not declare any of them an unbeliever on account of sin, or exclude him from Islam for some act [of his]; but [it is not so] if there is a hadith about that [point] and the hadith has been related as it came [to you] and you count it true and accept it as it was related, and know that it was as it was related. [This applies in cases of] the omission of formal worship, the drinking of wine and similar things, or where there is an innovation such that the person holding it is assigned to unbelief and exclusion from Islam. Then you follow the report in respect of that and do not go against it.

(a) The one-eyed Dajjāl will undoubtedly appear; he is the greatest of liars.

(b) The punishment of the tomb is a reality; a person will be questioned about his religion and his Lord, and about Paradise and Hell. Munkar and Nakīr are a reality; they are the two interrogators of the tomb. We ask God for steadfastness.

(c) The Basin of Muḥammad is a reality; his community will go to drink there; there are vessels with which they will drink from it.

(d) The Bridge is a reality. It is set stretching over Gehenna. People pass over it and Paradise is beyond it. We ask God for safety [in crossing].

(e) The Balance is a reality. In it are weighed good deeds and evil deeds, as God wills they should be weighed.

(f) The Trumpet is a reality. Isrāfīl blows on it and created beings die. Then he blows on it a second blast and they are raised before the Lord of the Worlds for the reckoning and the decree, and reward and punishment, and Paradise and Hell.

(g) The Preserved Table [is a reality]. From it the works of human beings are copied [or given their form] because of the determinations and the decree already contained in it.

(h) The Pen is a reality. With it God wrote the determinations of everything and mentioned each explicitly.

Intercession on the day of resurrection is a reality. People will intercede for other people so that they do not enter Hell; and people will be taken out of Hell by the intercession of the intercessors. People will be taken out of Hell after entering it and spending in it what [time] God willed; they are then taken out of Hell. [Other] people will be in it everlastingly and forever. These are the people of idolatry and counting false and denial and unbelief in God. Death will be done away with on the day of resurrection between Paradise and Hell.

Paradise and what is in it have already been created, and also Hell and what is in it. God created them and the created beings for them. They will never come to an end, nor what is in them.

If an innovator or a dualist tries to prove [the opposite] by God's word, "Everything is perishing except His face" (28:88) and similar ambiguous [passages] of the Qur'ān, the [reply] to him is: everything for which God wrote [sc. predetermined] coming to an end and perishing will perish; but Paradise and Hell were created to be eternal, not to come to an end and perish. They belong to the world to come, not to this present world. The black-eyed maidens do not die at the coming of the Hour or at the trumpet-blast or at any time, because God created them for eternity, not to come to an end, and He did not write [predetermine] death for them. Whoever holds a contrary view is an innovator who has deviated from the true path.

[God] created seven heavens one above another, and seven earths one below another. Between the highest earth and the lowest heaven was a distance of 500 years, and between any two heavens was a distance of 500 years. There was water above the highest heaven; and the Throne of the Merciful was above the water, and God was on the Throne; and the Sedile was the place of His feet. He knows what is in the seven heavens and earths and what is between them and what is under the ground and what is in the depths of the seas. [He knows] the sprouting of every plant and tree, of every grain and vegetable, and the falling of every leaf. [He knows] the number of every word, the number of every pebble and grain of sand and of dust, and the weights of the mountains, and the works of human beings and their reports and their breathing. He knows everything, and nothing is hidden from Him. He is on the Throne above the seventh heaven, and beneath Him are veils of light and fire and darkness and what He best knows.

If any innovator and opponent tries to prove [the opposite] by God's words, "We are nearer to him than his neck vein" (50:16), and "He is with you wherever you are" (57:4), and "There is no meeting of three except where He is the fourth . . . and He is with them wherever they are" (58:7), and similar ambiguous [passages] of the Qur'ān, then say [in reply to him] that these mean [God's] knowledge; for God is on the Throne above the seventh and highest heaven, and separate from the creatures, but there is no place to which His knowledge does not reach.

God has a Throne, and the Throne has bearers carrying it. God is on the Throne, to which there is no limit; God knows best about its limit.

God is hearing undoubtedly, and seeing undoubtedly. He is knowing and not ignorant, generous and not mean, forbearing and not hasty, remembering and not forgetting, awake and not sleeping, near [with His favor] and not neglectful. He moves and speaks and considers [or observes]; He sees and laughs; He rejoices and loves and dislikes; He shows loathing and good pleasure; He is angry and displeased; He is merciful and pardons; He impoverishes and enriches and is inaccessible. He descends every night to the lowest heaven as He wills. "There is nothing like Him, and He is the hearing and seeing [one]" (42:11). The hearts of human beings are between two of the fingers of the Merciful; He turns them as He wills, and bestows on [or holds back from] them what He wants. He created Adam by His hand in His image. The heavens and the earth on the day of resurrection are in His hand.

He places His foot in Hell and it shrinks, and by His hand He takes from Hell a group of people. The people of Paradise look on His face and see Him; thus He honors them. He appears in glory to them, and makes gifts to them. Human beings appear before Him on the day of resurrection, and He Himself administers the reckoning; none other than He administers that.

The Qur'ān is the Speech of God by which He speaks. It is not created. If anyone supposes the Qur'ān to be created, he is a Jahmite, an unbeliever. If anyone supposes that the Qur'ān is the Speech of God, but suspends judgment and does not say it is uncreated, this is worse than the view of the previous [person]. If anyone supposes that our utterance of [the Qur'ān] or our reciting [or reading] of it is created, while the Qur'ān is the Speech of God, he is a Jahmite. He who does not declare all these people unbelievers is in a similar [position] to them.

Ghazālī's Ashʿarī Creed

Translated by W. Montgomery Watt

Abū Ḥāmid al-Ghazālī (d. 1111), a prime exponent of Abū 'l-Ḥasan al-Ashʿarī's (d. 935) theological views, incorporated this creedal summary into the second of the forty "books" in his masterwork, *The Revitalization of the Religious Disciplines.*[3]

Text

An exposition of the creed of the People of the *Sunna* [contained] in the two words of the Shahāda, which is one of the pillars of Islam.

Praise belongs to God. . . .

God is the witness who makes known to [His chosen people] that in His essence He is one, without partner, alone and without any like, enduring and without opposite, unique and without equal. He is one, pre-eternal with no first [state], from eternity without beginning, continuing in existence with no end [state], remaining to eternity without termination, stable and not cut short, lasting without being interrupted. He has not ceased, and will not cease, to be characterized by qualities (*nuʿūt*) of majesty. He is unaffected by passing away and separation through the interruption of enduring [states] and the elapsing of appointed terms. Rather, He is the first and the last, the external and the internal, and He is knowing about everything.

God is not a body shaped nor a substance delimited and determinate. He does not resemble bodies either in being determinate or in being susceptible of division. He is not a substance, and substances do not inhere in Him; and He is not an accident, and accidents do not inhere in Him. He does not resemble any existing thing, and no existing thing resembles Him. Nothing is like Him, and He is not like anything. Measure does not limit Him, and boundaries do not contain Him.

God is seated on the Throne in the manner He stated, and with the meaning He willed for "sitting." He is not to be described as touching [it] or as being settled [on it] or being placed or inhering or moving away [from it]. The Throne does not bear Him, but the Throne and its bearers are borne by the grace of His power and subdued by His handgrasp. He is above the Throne and the heaven and everything to the bounds of the earth, and He is above in a way that does not bring Him nearer to the Throne and the heaven, as it does not take Him further from the earth and the ground. Rather, He is exalted by degrees from the Throne and the heaven, just as He is exalted by degrees from the earth and the ground. Despite that, He is near to every existent thing, and He is nearer to a human being than his neck vein (see 5:16). Over everything He is a witness, since His nearness does not resemble the nearness of bodies, just as His essence does not resemble the essence of bodies.

God does not inhere in anything, and nothing inheres in Him. He is exalted above being contained by space, and too holy to be bounded by time; on the contrary, He existed before He created time and space. He now has [the attributes] by which He was [previously characterized], and is distinguished from His creatures by His attributes. There is not in His essence what is other than He, nor in what is other than He is there [anything of] His essence. He is exalted above change [of state] and movement. Originated things do not inhere [or subsist] in Him, and accidental [events] do not befall Him. Rather, He does not cease; through the qualities of His majesty He is beyond cessation, and through the attributes of His perfection He is independent of [or does not require] any further increase of perfection.

God in His essence is known by reason to exist. His essence is seen by the eyes in the enduring abode, as a favor from Him and a grace to the upright; and He completes His favor by [giving] sight of His noble countenance.

God is living, powerful, compelling, constraining. Shortcoming and impotence do not befall Him. Slumber and sleep do not take hold of Him. Passing away and death do not happen to Him. He is king of the worlds, the visible and the invisible, possessor of strength and might. He has authority and sovereignty. His it is to create and to command. The heavens are folded in His right hand, and created things are securely held in His grasp. He is alone in creating and producing; He is unique in bringing into existence and innovating. He created the creatures and their works, and determined their sustenance and their appointed terms. Nothing determined escapes His grasp. The changes of things are not beyond His power. The things that He has determined cannot be numbered, and the things that He knows are infinite.

God is knowing of all objects of knowledge, and comprehending of all that happens from the bounds of earth to the highest heaven. He is knowing [in such a way] that not the weight of an atom in heaven or earth is beyond His knowledge. Indeed, He knows the creeping of the black ant on the hard rock in a dark night, He perceives the movement of the mote in the air, He knows what is secret and what is concealed, and is aware of the suggestions of the minds, the movements of the thoughts, and what is hidden in the hearts; and [He does this] by a knowledge pre-eternal and without beginning, with which He has not ceased to be characterized from the ages of ages, not by a knowledge that is originated, renewed and produced in His essence by inherence and change.

God is willing existent things and arranging originated things. In the visible and invisible worlds there is nothing little or much, small or great, good or bad, helpful or harmful, faith or unbelief, knowledge or ignorance, increase or decrease, obedience or disobedience, except by His decree and predetermination, His wisdom and His will. What He wills comes about, and what He does not will does not come about. Not the glance of an eye nor a sudden thought goes beyond His will. He is the one who begins [things] and restores, the one effecting what He wills. None opposes His command, and none repeats His decree. The human being cannot escape disobeying Him except by His succor and His mercy, and has no power to obey Him except by His will and His volition. If humankind, the jinn, the angels and the demons united to cause a single atom in the world to move, or to cause it to rest, apart from His volition and will, they would be unable for that. His will subsists in His essence beside all His attributes, and thus He has not ceased to be characterized as willing from all eternity the existence of things at the time He determined for them. They come into existence at their [proper] times as He willed from all eternity, neither too early nor too late. They occur in accordance with His knowledge and His will without change or alteration. He orders the affairs, but not [as human beings do] by arranging thoughts and awaiting a time, and so one matter does not keep Him from [doing] another.

God is hearing and seeing. He hears and sees, and nothing audible is beyond His hearing, even if it is hidden, and nothing visible is absent from His sight even if it is very small. Distance does not veil His hearing, and darkness does not repel His sight. He sees without eyeball or eyelid, and hears without earhole or ears, just as He knows without a heart, overwhelms without a limb and creates without an instrument. [This is] because His attributes do not resemble the attributes of created beings, just as His essence does not resemble the essence of created beings.

God is speaking, [and in His speech] He commands, forbids, promises and threatens. He does this by speech which is pre-eternal and from eternity, subsisting in His essence. The speech of created beings does not resemble it. It is not a sound produced by the emission of air or the closing of the throat; and it is not letters made distinct by joining the lips or moving the tongue. The Qurʾān, the Torah, the Gospel and the Psalms are God's books sent down to His messengers. The Qurʾān is recited by the tongues, written in the copies, and remembered in the hearts, but despite this it is from eternity subsisting in God's essence, and it does not suffer division and separation by being transferred to the hearts and pages. Moses heard the speech of God without sound or letter, just as the upright see the essence of God in the world to come without substance or accident.

Since God has these attributes, He is living, knowing, powerful, willing, hearing, seeing, speaking; [and He is such] by having Life, Knowledge, Power, Will, Hearing, Sight and Speech, not by His mere essence [apart from these attributes].

There is no existent apart from God except what is originated by His act and proceeds from His justice; [and that] is the finest, most perfect, most complete and most just of manners. He is wise in His acts and just in His decrees. His justice is not analogous to the justice of human beings, since wrong doing is conceivable for the human being when he is dealing with the property of others; but wrongdoing from God is inconceivable, since He does not encounter property belonging to another, such that His dealing with it would be wrongdoing. What is apart from God—human beings, jinn, angels, demons, the heaven and the earth, animals, plants and inanimate objects, substance and accident, what is perceived and what is sensed—all this is originated. By His power, God brought it into being after its non-existence, and made it something after it had been nothing, since from eternity He alone was existent and there was nothing along with Him. After that, He originated creation as a manifestation of His power and a realization of what He had previously willed, and of what from eternity had been truly His word. [He did this] not because of any lack of it or need for it.

God showed favor [to His creatures] by creating them, bringing them into being and imposing laws on them, though there was no necessity [to do this]; and He showed generosity by doing good to them and helping them, though He was not obliged [to do so]. His it is to favor, to benefit, to be gracious, to bestow gifts, since He has power to inflict various kinds of punishment on human beings, and to try them with various forms of pain and illness. If He did that, it would be justice on His part, and it would not be something foul or wrong. He rewards His servants, the believers, for their acts of obedience; [and He does so] in accordance with His kindness and His promise, not on the basis of their rights [or deserts] or of an obligation to them. No act on behalf of anyone is obligatory for Him, and wrongdoing on His part is inconceivable, while no one has any binding right against Him.

God's right to acts of obedience is an obligation for created beings, because He made it so by the tongues of His prophets and by pure reason. Moreover, in sending prophets He showed their truthfulness by clear evidentiary miracles; and they communicated His commands, prohibitions, promises and threats. It is obligatory for human beings to count true what they brought.

Nasafī's Māturīdī Creed

Translated by W. Montgomery Watt

Nearly two centuries after Abū Manṣūr al-Māturīdī (d. 944), a preeminent exponent of the "school" that bears his name penned one of several important creedal formulations. Najm ad-Dīn Abū Ḥafṣ an-Nasafī (1068–142), from Samarkand (present-day Uzbekistan), provides this representative summary.[4]

Text

The People of Truth say that the real natures of things are established [or fixed], and that knowledge of them is really [knowledge]. [This is] contrary to the view of the Sophists.

The causes of knowledge for created beings are three: the sound senses, true report and reason. The senses are five: hearing, sight, smell, taste and touch; by each sense, information is given about [the class of objects] for which it is appointed. True report is of two kinds. One of these is the widely-transmitted report, that is, a report established by the tongues of [many] people, whose agreement on a falsehood is inconceivable. This is bound to give a necessary knowledge, such as the knowledge of former kings in past times and of distant lands. The second kind is the report of the messenger [who has been] attested by an evidentiary miracle [about what has come to him by revelation]. This is bound to give deductive knowledge. The knowledge established by [such a report] resembles in certainty and fixity knowledge necessarily established [such as sense knowledge and that from widely transmitted reports]. Reason, again, is also a cause of knowledge. What is established by immediate intuition is necessary, such as the knowledge that every thing is greater than its part. What is established by inference is acquired knowledge. Inspiration is not one of the causes of the knowing of the soundness [or truth] of a thing in the view of the People of Truth.

The world with all its parts is originated, since it [consists of] substances [or individuals] and accidents. Substances are what is self-subsistent. A substance is either composite, that is, a body, or non-composite, such as the atom, which is the part that cannot be further divided. The accident is what is not self-subsistent but is originated in the bodies and atoms, such as colors, physical states, tastes and smells.

The Originator of the world is God. He is the One, the Pre-eternal, the Living, the Powerful, the Knowing, the Wishing, the Willing. He is neither accident nor body nor atom. He is neither formed nor limited nor multiple. He has neither portions nor parts, and He is not composite. He is not finite. He is not characterized by quiddity nor by quality. He is not located in a place, nor does time pass over [or affect] Him. Nothing resembles Him. Nothing is beyond His knowledge and power.

God has pre-eternal attributes subsisting in His essence. They are not He and not other than He. They are: Knowledge, Power, Life, Strength, Hearing, Sight, Will, Volition, Activity, Creativity, Provision of sustenance [for creatures] and Speech.

God is speaking with a Speech that is a pre-eternal attribute for Him, and which is not of the class of letters and sounds. It is an attribute that excludes silence and defect. God speaks with this [attribute], commanding, prohibiting and making statements [or reporting].

The Qurʾān is the Speech of God, uncreated. It is written in the copies, remembered in the hearts, recited by the tongues, heard by the ears; but it does not inhere in these.

Causing-to-be is a pre-eternal attribute of God. It is His causing-to-be of the world and all its parts, not from eternity but at the time of its coming into existence in accordance with His knowledge and His will. [The attribute of causing-to-be] is other than what has been caused to be in our view.

Will is a pre-eternal attribute of God subsisting in His essence.

By reason, the vision of God [in Paradise] is possible; and by transmitted [reports] it is necessary that He should be seen. A proof based on oral [material] has been handed down showing that it is necessary that the believers should see God in the world to come. He is not seen in a place, nor in any direction from [the person] facing Him, nor by the coming together of light rays, nor with a fixed distance between the person seeing and God.

God is the creator of all the acts of human beings, whether [acts] of unbelief or faith, of obedience or disobedience. All these acts are by His will and volition, by His judgment, His decreeing and His determining. Human beings [perform] acts of choice for which they are rewarded or punished. The good in them is with God's good pleasure, and the bad in them is not with His good pleasure.

The acting-power [in people] exists along with the act [not before it]. It is the reality of the power by which the act comes to be. This name [acting-power] is used where the causes, instruments and limbs [involved in the act] are sound. [A person's] being genuinely liable [to obey the law] depends on this acting-power; a person is not liable for [carrying out] what is not within his capacity.

The pain existing in a [person] beaten as a result of human beating, and the broken [condition] of a glass after a human [act of] breaking, and similar things, are all created by God. The person has no function in the creating of these.

The one killed dies at his appointed term. The appointed term is one.

Unlawful [food] is [nevertheless] sustenance from God. Everyone receives in full his own sustenance, whether lawful or unlawful. It is inconceivable that a person should not eat his sustenance or that his sustenance should be eaten by someone else.

God leads astray whom He wills, and guides whom He wills. It is not obligatory for God to do the best for a human being.

The punishment in the tomb for unbelievers and for some sinful believers, and the bliss in the tomb of the obedient people, are in accordance with God's knowledge and will. The interrogation by Munkar and Nakīr is established by proofs based on oral [reports]. The raising of the dead is a reality. The

Balance is a reality. The Book [recording a person's deeds] is a reality. The interrogation [by God] is a reality. The Basin is a reality. The Bridge is a reality. Paradise is a reality, and Hell is a reality, and they are [already] created and existent. They are everlasting and will not pass away, and their people will not pass away.

A great sin does not exclude the believing person from faith and place him in unbelief [i.e., does not make him an unbeliever]. God does not forgive one who assigns partners to Him, but He forgives to whom He wills what is less than that of small and great sins. The punishing of a small sin is possible [for God] and also the forgiving of a great sin, provided this is not the considering lawful [of what is forbidden], for such considering lawful is unbelief.

The intercession of the messengers and of the elite is established for the case of those committing great sins. Those believers who commit great sins do not remain everlastingly in Hell.

Faith is the counting true of what [a messenger] has brought from God [as revelation] and the confessing of it. Works increase in themselves, but faith neither increases nor decreases. Faith and Islam are one [or the same]. Where a person counts true and confesses, it is proper for him to say "I am truly a believer," and he does not have to say "I am a believer if God wills."

The happy one sometimes becomes miserable and the miserable one happy, but the change is in [the human experience] of happiness and misery, not in the making happy and the making miserable, for these are attributes of God, and there is no change in God or in His attributes.

Ḥillī's Twelver Shīʿī/Muʿtazilī Creed

Translated by W. Montgomery Watt

One of the most influential late medieval exponents of Twelver Shiʿism is the celebrated Iraqi scholar known widely as ʿAllāma al-Ḥillī (the Teacher from Ḥilla, 1250–325). The views expressed here evidence important correspondences with various Muʿtazilī understandings of God's attributes and names.[5]

Text

WHAT IS NECESSARY FOR ALL MATURE BELIEVERS REGARDING KNOWLEDGE OF THE PRINCIPLES OF RELIGION

The scholars all agree in considering obligatory the knowledge of God, of His positive and negative attributes, of what is essential to Him and of what is impossible for Him; and [also the knowledge] of prophethood, of the imamate and of the Return. All this is [known] by proof, not by following an authority. There must be mention of those things of which it is not possible for any Muslim to be ignorant, since whoever is ignorant of any of them is outside the circle of believers and worthy of eternal punishment.

GOD'S POSITIVE ATTRIBUTES, WHICH ARE EIGHT

God is powerful and freely-acting. The world is originated, because it is a body, and every body is inseparable from originated [things], namely, movement and rest. Both these are originated, because both require something preceding them. What is inseparable from originated [things] must itself be originated. It follows [from the world's being originated] that it has a mover, namely God, the powerful and freely-acting. If the cause [of the world] was a [mechanical] cause [and not freely acting], then necessarily its effect would not continue [to exist] after it [had ceased]. That would imply either that the world was eternal [like its cause], or that God [its cause] was originated; and both [these conclusions] are false. God's power is connected with all objects of power. What makes them need His power is [their] possibility. The relation of His essence to all things is equal, and so His power is universal.

God is knowing, since His acts are well-ordered and perfect, and everyone who so acts must be knowing. His knowledge is connected with every object of knowledge, because all objects of knowledge are equally related to Him. He is also living, and all living things truly know their objects of knowledge. Thus he must have knowledge, since otherwise He would be lacking something.

God is living. Because He is powerful and knowing, he must also be living.

God is willing [one who wills] and rejecting [one who wills something should not be]. [This is] because the particularizing of an act to come about at one time and not another requires a particularizing [agency], and that is the will; and also because God gives commands and prohibitions, and these require will for them or against them.

God is perceiving, because He is living and therefore truly perceives. This is proved in the Qurʾān, and so it must be asserted that [perception] belongs to Him.

God is pre-eternal and existent from eternity, and also everlasting and existent to eternity. [This is] because He is the necessarily existent. Nonexistence, whether prior to existence or following upon existence, is impossible for Him.

God is speaking, as all agree. By speech is meant letters and sound which are audible and possess order, and [so] for God to be speaking means that He brings speech into existence in some body. The account given by the Ashʿarites is contrary to reason.

God is truthful. A lie is necessarily evil, and God is far removed from evil, because it is impossible for him to have any imperfection.

GOD'S NEGATIVE ATTRIBUTES, WHICH ARE SEVEN

God is not composite. If he were, he would be in need of parts, and what is in need is [only] possible.

He is not a body nor an accident nor an atom, because, if He were, He would need a place [i.e.,, would be lacking something]; and also because, since a body cannot be separated from originated things, He would be an originated thing, and that is impossible. He cannot be in a place, for then He would be in need of it; nor in a direction, for then He would be in need of it. Likewise, pleasure and pain are not ascribed to Him, because He cannot have a [bodily] constitution. He does not unite with what is other than Himself, because uniting is altogether impossible for Him.

God is not a locus for originated things [sc. accidents], because he cannot be acted upon by anything other and cannot have any imperfection.

The vision [or seeing] of God is impossible. [This is] because everything that is seen is in a direction [from the viewer]; it is either opposite to him or in a comparable relation. If God were seen, He would be a body, which is impossible. In God's word to Moses, "You shall not see Me" (7:143), the negative (*lan*) is eternal.

God has no partner. [This is] because of tradition, and [also] because [if there were a partner], the two would be in conflict with one another, and the orderly existence [of the created world] would be destroyed. [It is also] because He would then have to be composite, since two beings sharing necessary existence would [each] require something to distinguish them.

God has no forms or states. [This is because] if His being powerful were due to His power, and His being knowing were due to His knowledge, and so on, He would have need of that form [power, etc.] among His attributes, and His existence would only be possible.

God is independent and not in need. [This is] because His being necessarily existent apart from anything else requires His having no need of anything else, whereas all other things are in need of Him.

God's Justice

Reason necessarily judges what actions are good, such as returning something entrusted [to one], treating kindly, and truthfulness which is profitable, and also [judges] what actions are bad, such as injustice and a harmful lie. Those who deny all systems of revelation, like the Malāḥida [one of many terms roughly equivalent to "heretic"] and the philosophers of India, judge good and bad in this way [by reason]. Moreover, if [good and evil] are not affirmed by reason, they would be denied by tradition, because the evil of lying would not be affirmed in the case of the author of revelation.

We act by choice. This must be so because (1) there is a necessary difference between a person falling from a roof and going down from it by a ladder; otherwise the imposing of duties on us would be impossible and[stet] here [stet] would be no sin. [It must also be so] because (2) of the evil of God's creating an act in us and then punishing us for it; and (3) because of tradition.

It is impossible that God should do evil, because the knowledge he has of evil holds Him back from it. Also He has no motive for doing evil, since the motive would be either need, which is [something] He cannot have, or else the wisdom [of the evil act] which does not exist. Moreover, if it were possible for evil to proceed from God, the proof of revelation to prophets would be impossible. [It may also be said that] the will to do evil is impossible for God, because [such a will] is itself evil.

God acts with an aim. [This is because] the Qur'ān teaches this, and also because to deny this would imply [that the act] is vain; and that is evil. The aim of God is not to harm the person but to benefit him. For this [reason] there must be an imposition of duties; and this is the commissioning by God, obliging [persons] to engage firstly and knowingly in [acts] involving labor. [If there were no imposition of duties] God would be inciting to evil by creating [in people] the passions and the desire for evil and hatred of good; [to counter these] there must be a restraint, and that is the imposition of duties. Knowledge [of blame and praise] is not sufficient because it is easy [to bear] the blame [incurred] in attaining a desired object. The imposition of duties is good, because it makes [people] aware of reward, which is deserved benefit joined with being honored and respected. This [reward] is impossible without a previous [imposition of duties].

Kindness is incumbent on God. Kindness [or favor] is what leads the creature towards obedience and keeps him from disobedience. It is not an aspect of empowering [him] and does not go so far as compelling [him]. The aim [of God] in imposing duties is based on [kindness]. If God, in willing an act from [a person], knows that he will not do it without the help of an act which [He], the Willer, can perform easily, then, if God does not perform it, He would be contradicting His own aim; and reason declares this to be evil.

An act compensating for the sufferings which come to a person from God is incumbent on Him. A compensatory [act] is a deserved benefit, but without [the person] being honored and respected [as is the case with reward]; otherwise it would be unjust, and God is exalted above that. The compensation must also be in excess of the suffering, since otherwise it would be in vain.

Sayyid Aḥmad Khān's Modern Sunnī Creed

Translated by Christian Troll, SJ

Though new formulations have not been nearly as common in modern times as in classical and medieval centuries, we have a number of important nineteenth- and twentieth-century texts. Among the most theologically prolific modern thinkers of the "modernist" persuasion, Sir Sayyid Aḥmad Khān (d. 1898) represents South Asian Muslim communities quite prominently. He penned several *ʿaqāʾid* in the latter nineteenth century, in Urdu, the "national" language of what would become Pakistan in 1947, occasionally interspersing Persian texts as well. Here (from 1872) is one of his more famous creedal statements.[6]

Text

[GOD THE CREATOR, THE CAUSE OF CAUSES]

Someone or other is the Creator of or the Final Cause of or the Cause of causes of all existing things. Allāh is His name.

The foremost belief of the religion of Islam is that there is a Creator of all beings. All that exists and all that we can, in some way, understand or imagine is linked by a connecting chain so that the existence of one [thing] depends on a second and the second on a third. Thus, by necessity, this chain ends up in a final being or cause or reason. That at which it ends up is the Creator and God and the Lord of the worlds.

It cannot be believed with certainty that the totality of that which exists should itself be the final cause of its own existence. If it was not a fact that every thing from among the existing things needs in its existence some other existence, or if one existence was not the effect of a second existence, we might perhaps be then entitled to believe thus [i.e., that the totality of what exists should itself be the final cause of its own existence]. But since we find every single thing to be caused by a cause how can we fail to consider the sum of these very things to be caused by some Cause of causes?

[ETERNITY OF MATTER AND THE EXISTENCE OF A CREATOR]

All things that exist truly are neither impossible nor capable of non-existence. If they were impossible then why should they exist and if they were capable of non-existence then they at some time would also be non-existent.

We see that no truly existing thing can ever fall into nonexistence; only a constant change of accidents or forms goes on. Water becomes air and air becomes water. There are many things that become clay and again from clay are born the most wondrous of things. In short, nothing becomes non-existent; only the change of accidents and forms goes on constantly. So if the specific and the individual accidents of all existing things fall into non-existence, then what remains will be imperishable. God says:

> Everyone that is thereon will pass away; There remains but the Countenance of thy Lord of Might and Glory. (55:26–27)

No doubt, it cannot be definitively decided what this imperishable existence that remains after the perishing of the specific and individual accidents of all the existing things is, and whether it [i.e., the remaining imperishable existence] will be one or many. But the existence of a Creator cannot be denied because of the impossibility of that decision, since the existence or non-existence of the Creator has nothing to do with either the fact of this imperishable existence or with [the problem of] its unity or plurality.

If they [i.e., the imperishable existence, taken here as a plurality] are multiple, one will, of course, then have to ask whether the power to "receive" the accidents resides in themselves or comes to them from other existing things. That it [i.e., this power to "receive"] should be in them themselves we cannot accept, since we see all existing things with their specific and individual accidents "helping one another." Imagine that the specific and individual accidents of all existing things were non-existent; so what remains of the multiple imperishable existences will likewise most certainly be "helping one another" and there is no other cause for them to do so [i.e., to "help one another"] but a common cause. Thus there remains no doubt that the cause of their "helping one another" is some existence and this existence we call Allāh.

And if the imperishable existence is one then the question will arise, does the power to "receive" the accidents reside in it or is some other existence its cause? If in itself, then its name is God and if a second existence is its cause then the name of this Cause of causes is Allāh.

[THE DOCTRINE OF *WAḤDAT AL-WUJŪD* AND OF *WAḤDAT ASH-SHUHŪD*]

On this matter the opinion of the great men of Islam has remained divided. Most of them say that in this imperishable existence there are two potencies, the *potentia activa* and the *potentia passiva,* the latter being understood as the potency to "receive" accidents. For this reason these people hold the theory of Unity of Being (*waḥdat al-wujūd*) and speak thus:

> He Himself is the earthen pot, He himself is the potter, He Himself is the clay of the pot. He Himself came to the market as customer. He broke it into pieces and went off. [Per.]

And some say that the cause of this *potentia passiva* is another existence and for this reason they hold [the theory of] Unity of Appearance (*waḥdat ash-shuhūd*). But basically the following is true:

> Oh You who are higher than thought and analogy, than imagination and guess, who are higher than all we have been told and we have heard and read of. [Per.]

In any case, whichever of the two propositions is true, it does not in any way affect the Islamic doctrine that there is One Creator of all beings.

People have considered the doctrine of Unity of Appearance to be unbelief. They [i.e., those who follow this teaching] have fallen into the error of holding this imperishable existence, for which we have to postulate a second being as the cause for its [functioning as] *potentia passiva,* as being equally eternal, without beginning and end, which is outright associationism. Or their religion is to hold God and matter to be two separate eternal entitles, without beginning nor end, and some express the same reality by [the terms of] darkness and light. But this is a mistake in the understanding of these people because the existence of an effect, by necessity, is linked with the existence of a cause and since the effect exists because of the existence of the cause then where is there any trace of *shirk?* The effect of an eternal cause without beginning and end is itself, also, eternal without beginning and end. If you are eternal without beginning and end, then we too are eternal without beginning and end.

> We became creatures and walked with the Creator. Where God was there we were, too. [Per.]

So from the existence of the existing things alone we come to the firm belief in a Creator.

[GOD—MERE IDEA OR REALITY?]

Against this may be said that [all] this, after all, is not certain but [merely] an idea of which there has been no experience. The concept of idea implies two possibilities—one that it be "after experience" according to fact; the other, that it be not according to fact. Since we have no experience of this idea, how can we be sure that it is in accordance with fact?

This objection is sound, yet our ideas are of two kinds. First, those which our nature itself creates or which come about in us from non-verified, merely fanciful causes. Undoubtedly the concept of such an idea implies the possibility of its being "after experience" according to fact. But the ideas of the second kind, that is those that neither our nature produces spontaneously nor are born in us by the [merely] ideal, unauthenticated cause, rather which other authenticated realities have brought forth—these are enduring and are "after experience," totally in accordance with fact.

Whenever we hear a voice or see smoke we think that over there is someone who produces the voice, or, over there is a fire. Our thinking is a [mere] idea, yet not of the kind that comes about in our nature spontaneously or which, unauthenticated, merely ideal causes create in us. Rather it is an idea that is brought forth by other authenticated truths. Such an idea of ours is always correct and "after experience," in full accordance with fact, provided we ourselves make not a mistake concerning the thing that brings about in us such an idea. Whenever we find several things in one place, arranged in order and adorned beautifully we are certain that there is someone responsible for doing this. Accordingly when we see all the existing things in such wonderful order, made by such wisdom and molded in such beauty, then we can believe with certainty that there is an Arranger and a Maker. If it is true that whenever we see a stone on the road we conclude that somebody exists who put it there, then why should we not believe with certainty that a great and wise Maker has made all the things that transcend the nature of humanity and that it is this Maker that we call God.

Our idea of God's existence has been brought forth by things that are a reality, that are, in other words, authenticated truths. Ideas of this kind are always found to be correct and, "after experience," in conformity with fact. Therefore we, too, believe firmly in this idea and maintain that since and insofar as it is "after experience," our idea will be fully according to fact and for this reason we do not call it an "idea," but rather a certain fact.

[BELIEF IN THE CREATOR AND REASON: THE EVIDENCE OF THE QUR᾿ĀN]

Thus all these existing things are a good guide to the common human reason that there exists a Creator of them. Therefore the faith in the existence of a Creator is a doctrine that the common human reason can well understand and so human beings have been obligated to believe in Him. If this doctrine had not been fit to enter human reason or, say, to be understood by human beings then he could never have been obligated to it. As God says, "Allāh tasks not a soul beyond its scope" (2:286).

It is not the object of the Founder of Islam that humankind should make its own, without understanding it, the doctrine of the existence of a Maker. Nor does He want that humankind should accept it for the [sole] reason that the prophets have commanded it. Rather, the Founder of Islam has quite clearly ordered humankind to believe in the existence of a Maker on the basis of arguments from these existing things and after he himself had pointed out and shown again and again in detail the wonders of *nature,* that is *qudrat* and *fiṭrat.*

In what lovely and true words he has said:

> It is one of His signs that He has created you from dust and that now you, man, are spread from place to place. It is one of His signs that He has created a companion for you in your very likeness so that from her your heart might find rest and a wondrous love and He has put into you the madness of heart—

for those who understand there are in this many signs. It is one of His signs to have created heaven and earth and a multitude of languages and complexions. In this there are signs for the people of all the world. It is one of His signs that He has created the night for your rest in sleep and the day for procuring bread. One of His signs is also the lightning and the longing for rain because from rain the dead soil becomes alive again. It is one of His signs that heaven and earth are supported by His order alone (cf. 30:20–25).

> It is one of His signs that cool wind announces the good news of coming rain (cf. 30:46). The same God alone moves the wind. Then He drives the clouds by it. Then He spreads them over the whole heaven as He likes it. Then He makes them fold up. Then you see raindrops issuing from them (cf. 30:48). From heaven He sends down rain in measure. Then He gives it lodging in the earth. Then He produces for you [therewith] gardens wherein there is much fruit and dates and grapes for you to eat. From the mountain he makes sprout a tree that grows oil. For you there is also a great lesson in animals. Whatever comes from their udders you drink and you derive much use from it. Some animals can be eaten by you. Animals carry you and take you around, and ships, too, take you around (cf. 23:18–22).

> In what wisdom has He made the mountains on the earth so that it may remain in balance. Thus He has made mountain passes so that there will be no difficulty in walking on the roads (cf. 21:31).

> He alone has made day and night, sun and moon that run their course (cf. 39:5).

> Why don't you regard the camel how wondrous it is made and the heaven how high He has made it and the mountains how firmly they are fixed and the earth how it is spread (cf. 88:17–20).[7]

In short, in this way, again and again in the Holy Qurʾān the Founder of Islam has shown by arguments from the existing things that we see, [the necessity] to believe in the existence of a Maker. In no place has He said: believe in God without understanding. In one place He has said:

> When you ask even from unbelievers: Who has made heaven and earth and moon and sun, who has made them obedient: They will answer Allāh (cf. 29:61). And when you ask from them: Who has made it rain from heaven by which He has made alive again the dead soil, then they will say: Allāh (cf. 29:63).

[UNIVERSAL CLAIM OF THE TRUTH OF ISLAM]

Therefore, how true is the [basic] doctrine of the religion of Islam—for all men, whether they inhabit jungles or mountains or cities or the countryside, whether they are educated or not, whether the message of some prophet has reached them or not, whether a religion has been given to them or not, they all by duty are bound to believe in the fact that there is a Maker of all existing things, and He is God, be He exalted and glorified!

INTRA-MUSLIM POLEMICS IN PRACTICE

ʿAlī ibn Abī Ṭālib on Heresy

Translated by I. K. A. Howard

As always, ʿAlī is the standard for traditional Shīʿī theological views. Among sayings attributed to him are several brief but instructive observations on the nature of creedal divergence. Historian Shaykh al-Mufīd's (d. 1022) compendium of the sayings and thoughts of ʿAlī and his successor imams is a most important source for understanding the history of Shīʿī thought.[8]

Text

Among his speeches concerning heretics and those who speak of religion in terms of their own opinion while opposing the way of true believers through what they say, is [the speech] reported by sound traditionists of the non-Shīʿa and the Shīʿa. The speech opens with the praising of God and blessings on His Prophet [and then goes on]: "My responsibility for what I say is guaranteed and I am answerable for it. It will not wither the cornseeds that human beings have sown, nor will roots be parched as a result of it. All goodness is within a person who knows his own ability. Not knowing one's own ability is sufficient ignorance for humankind. A creature who is most hateful to God is [someone] whom God, the Exalted, has left to himself, [a person] who is deviating from the true path, [someone] enamored of words of heresy. [In this heresy, the misguided person] has become addicted to fasting and prayer. Yet he is a seduction to those who are seduced by him, himself going astray from the guidance of those who came before him, and leading into error those who follow him. Thus he bears [responsibility] for the sins of others, being [himself] settled in his own sinfulness. [Such a one] has picked up the refuse of ignorance amid ignorant people without guidance. Unaware of the intense darkness of rebellion, he is blind to guidance. Yet people like himself call him knowledgeable while he is not constant in following it even for one complete day. He goes out early and seeks to make much of what is little [regarding it as] better than what is [truly] much, so that when he has quenched his thirst on polluted water and sought to increase [his knowledge] from what is vile, he sits as a judge responsible for the clarification of what is obscure to everyone else. He fears that those who came before him were without his wisdom and that the action of those who come after him will be like the action of those who came before him. If an obscure matter is brought before him, he gives an irrelevant comment on it according to his own opinion and then asserts [that] categorically. Thus he is enmeshed in doubts as if in the spider's web, not knowing whether he is right or wrong. He does not see that what is beyond [him] is within the reach [of others]. If he made an analogy of one thing with another, he would never regard his opinion as being wrong. If a matter is obscure to him, he conceals it because he knows his own ignorance, deficiency, and the necessity [of hiding it] in order that it cannot be said that he does not know. Therefore he puts himself forward without knowledge. He is one who wanders aimlessly like riders without direction amid the uncertainties of unknown tracts of desert. Never does he excuse himself for what he does not know. Thus he gives a decision without ever having bitten into knowledge with a tooth that can bite. He scatters the traditions like the wind scatters sand. Inheritances [wrongly distributed] weep because of him, blood cries out for vengeance because of him. By his judgments he makes lawful the forbidden parts and forbids those that are allowed. He is invalid when he issues [judgments on cases] that come before him and he does not regret his inadequacy.

"People, it is required of you to obey and to know the one whom there is no excuse to be ignorant of. The knowledge with which Adam descended, and everything with which the prophets were favored down to your Prophet, the seal of the prophets, is in the offspring of your Prophet, Muḥammad. Where has it brought you? Or rather where are you going, you who are descended from the loins of the people who were on the Ark? This [offspring of the Prophet] is like [the Ark of Noah]. Therefore [adhere to them as] you would board it. Just as those who were in it were saved, so those who enter into [association with this family] will be saved through them. I guarantee that by a true oath and I am not one of those who make false claims. Woe on those who hold back, woe again on those who hold back. Haven't you been aware of what your Prophet said among you, when he said in the Farewell Pilgrimage: 'I leave behind me among you two important things which, if you cleave to them, you will never go astray—that is the Book of God and the offspring from my family. They will never scatter from you until they lead you to me at the [sacred] waters [of Heaven]. Now take care how you oppose me with regard to these two [things]. Otherwise there will be dread punishment.

Indeed this [agreement with the Book and the family] is a sweet pleasant drink, so drink. But that [opposition] is salty and brackish, so avoid it.'"

Ibāḍī Views on Associating with Muslims of Deficient Faith

Translated by Valerie J. Hoffman

Very early in the history of the Muslim community, a faction that parted company with ʿAlī over his conduct of war with the Umayyads at the Battle of Ṣiffīn in 657 came to be known as the Khārijites (those who secede, *khawārij*). Originally part of ʿAlī's army and general support group, they disagreed with his recourse to human arbitration, arguing that only God could decide their next course of action. Not unlike the early Christian faction called the Donatists, the Khārijites developed a highly restrictive notion of what it meant to be a "true Muslim" and in effect refused to accept anyone whose outward sin (they argued) was a clear indication of defective faith. ʿAlī became the prime exemplar of such an unworthy person whom all true Muslims must shun. Now the dominant *madhhab* (school of thought, jurisprudence) in Oman, Ibāḍīs are often identified (by outsiders) as "moderate Khārijites," largely because although they do delineate their religious views sharply from those of outsiders, they have long since repudiated the tendency of less tolerant Khārijites to deal very harshly with outsiders.

This excerpt from a nineteenth-century Ibāḍī text, by Nāṣir ibn Sālim ibn ʿUdayyam ar-Rawāḥī (d. 1920), is a fine example of the principles that ought to guide the way they regard and deal with individuals who disagree with them. Lessons 1 through 3 of the text explain in detail the specifics of both affiliation and dissociation and make it clear that it is incumbent on true Muslims to practice clearly one mode of relationship or the other in most instances. In lesson 4 of chapter 5 of *The Creed of Wahb* (the first Ibāḍī imam), the student (S) asks the teacher (T) about circumstances under which one may, or must, suspend judgment as to either affiliation or dissociation.[9]

Text

LESSON 4: SUSPENDING JUDGMENT AND ITS REGULATIONS

S: Is suspending judgment from someone with whom neither affiliation nor dissociation is permissible a religious obligation in the same way that affiliation and dissociation are when they are appropriate?

T: It is obligatory for a person who is accountable before God to suspend judgment when appropriate, just as it is obligatory to affiliate or dissociate when appropriate.

S: When is suspending judgment appropriate, and what makes it obligatory?

T: It is appropriate and obligatory when you do not know whether something someone has done requires affiliation or dissociation, or if there are two opinions on it, or if there are two contradictory obligations in which one does not overrule the other. In the case of such ignorance you must dissociate from him until you know the rule for that deed, whether it requires affiliation or dissociation.

S: What is the basis for the obligation to suspend judgment?

T: It is based on the Book and the *Sunna*. From the Book are the words of the Most High, "Do not form an opinion on something of which you have no knowledge" (17:36), and "My Lord has forbidden indecencies, whether evident or hidden, and sin and unjust oppression, and that you associate with God others to whom He has not given authority, or that you say about God what you do not know" (7:33). And in the *Sunna* are the Messenger's words, "Suspend judgment concerning what you do not know."

S: If two men curse each other or fight each other and I do not know which of them is right and who is wrong, what should I do?

T: Leave each of them in the condition they already were with you, whether in affiliation, dissociation, or suspending judgment. That is with regard to their status with you. As for what they are doing, suspend judgment and do not decide that it is right or wrong. If it becomes clear to you which of them started the cursing or fighting, you must dissociate from him; at that point you may not suspend judgment concerning what he did, because you know that it is something that requires dissociation.

S: If I see someone do something and I don't know the rules for that act, and I know that I have kept the one who did it in the condition he was before [affiliation, dissociation, or suspending judgment], and I am suspending judgment concerning what he did, as to whether it was right or wrong, am I required to ask about the judgment of the Law on that act?

T: You are not required to ask about the judgment on that act, although some claim that you are. But if you wish to ask, do so without naming the person who did the act; just ask as if you were wishing to learn the rule regarding that act, without attributing it to a specific person. For example, you could say, "What is the rule concerning someone who does such-and-such?" or "What is the rule concerning an affiliate who does such-and-such?" Because if you identify the one who did the deed and, for example, it is polytheism or adultery, whoever hears what you say must dissociate from you unless you bring three witnesses in a case of adultery, in which you are the fourth witness, and they confirm your testimony, and you say before you report the matter, "These three say the same as I," or in a case of polytheism if there is a second person who gives the same testimony as you. If one of them is not a valid witness, or if you do not say "They say the same as I," the one who hears your allegation must dissociate from you as well as from the three who confirm your testimony in a matter of adultery, or the single person who confirms what you say on a matter of polytheism, if you do not say "They say the same as I" or "This one says the same as I," because your testimony would then be null and void. They must also say the same thing, if their testimony is valid. If you identify the accused, and the sin is a grave sin that falls short of polytheism or adultery and the accused is an affiliate, your accusation would be a sin that would require dissociation from you, unless you have someone else with you who gives the same testimony and you are both valid witnesses and you say "This person says the same as I" before you give your report.

S: If the person I am asking says, "The person who did this is an infidel," should I dissociate from him?

T: No, why would you do that? His infidelity is based only on a description, not on the testimony of an eyewitness. And you must say "I am asking," lest you become obligated to dissociate from the person you are asking by not dissociating from the person who committed the grave sin. That is what the scholars say, and the *Quṭb* ["Axis," religious leader] said:

> This is so you explicitly tell him that you are not dissociating from the perpetrator although you know that the deed is a grave sin, or so it is clear to the person you are asking that you are an affiliate of the perpetrator or that you are suspending judgment regarding him, although you know that the deed is a grave sin. It is not required for you to say "I am asking," as some have said. You should then ask a second scholar, and if they issue a joint opinion that the deed is a grave sin, then you must dissociate from him.

S: What is the status of someone who affiliates with someone because of a deed the rule for which he does not know and it is a grave sin, and of someone who for the same reason abandons affiliation or dissociation, and of someone who dissociates from him because of that deed?

T: His correct status is hypocrisy. Some say he has disobeyed God, and others say he has committed an error that does not lead to perdition—there are different opinions.

S: If the deed is permitted or disapproved or is a minor sin, and on the basis of that someone affiliates, dissociates or suspends judgment, what is his status?

T: His status is the infidelity of hypocrisy, unless he believes it to be permitted or reprehensible or prohibited; in that case, his status is the infidelity of unbelief. Likewise, if he believed a minor sin to be unbelief, or if he believed it to be the beginning of unbelief, his status is the infidelity of hypocrisy.

S: If someone applies one of the three judgments to all people, what is his status?

T: He is an unbeliever (*mushrik*).[10]

S: Is the one who hears him do this excused?

T: Some say he is excused if he does not dissociate from him regarding his affiliation with all people, but not if he does not dissociate from him regarding his suspension of judgment concerning all people or dissociation from all people. So they say, but the *Quṭb* says:

> The most obvious interpretation is that either he must be excused for all the stances the other person takes, or he must be subjected to dissociation for all of them. What is required is that one dissociate from him in all these cases. The argument that the speaker applied the same judgment to all but only meant some, and that since he is a monotheist the one who heard him do this must be excused in all cases, although they did not excuse him in all cases, is unsound.

S: Why did Imam Aflaḥ ibn ʿAbd al-Wahhāb[11] say, "Do not dissociate from a believer until he is present and can defend himself"?

T: The Imam was truthful and righteous, may God be pleased with him! He said this because of the hadith in which Abū Dharr did something reprehensible, and the people said, "Messenger of God, Abū Dharr is an unbeliever (*ashrak*)!" This is how it appeared to them, and they were wondering about it. He replied, "Abū Dharr is not an unbeliever," meaning that he would wait until he came to say, "My heart is not at peace with the faith," at which point he could judge him to be an unbeliever. God forbid that Abū Dharr would ever commit sedition or fall into temptation! He had said something the people found repugnant, but his heart was at peace with the faith. And the words of the Messenger, God's blessings and peace on him, "Abū Dharr is not an unbeliever" is an assurance that Abū Dharr is happy [in the afterlife]. So the hadith is a proof for the Imam.

S: If someone dies as an affiliate, should testimony that he was an infidel be accepted?

T: There are two opinions on this, but the witnesses against him are not subject to dissociation.

S: Why are the witnesses not subject to dissociation?

T: How can they be subject to dissociation, when they are one of the proofs of God? Those who feel that one should dissociate from the person against whom they are testifying do so because proof has been given against him, and since he has passed on to his Lord, one cannot wait for him to defend himself. The Messenger of God said concerning the dead, "They have passed on to their Lord."

S: If someone says to someone else, "You adulterer!" or "You unbeliever!," and the second replies, "You are the adulterer," or "You are the unbeliever," what should I do with them?

T: Dissociate from both of them in God, though some say you should not dissociate from the one who replied to the person who called him this. Anyone who calls a monotheist an unbeliever is himself an unbeliever, so if the second person replies, "You are the unbeliever," he would be telling the truth and one should not dissociate from him for telling the truth. In my opinion it is correct to deem an unbeliever anyone who calls a monotheist an unbeliever, if the judgment is based only on his theology, not like those who deem disobedient members of the people of the *qibla* to be unbelievers. If a person says to an affiliate, "You infidel (*yā kāfir*)!" and he replies, "You are the infidel!" there is no harm on the one who replied, because he is telling the truth. The Messenger of God said, "If a man says to his companion, 'You infidel!' one of the two is an infidel, and the one who said it first is more unjust." He spoke of them collectively when he said, "One of the two is an infidel," and then he made a distinction between them by saying, "The one who said it first is more unjust." What he meant by "more unjust" is "unjust," because one cannot think that the person who replies is unjust, only the one who declared the other to be an infidel.

S: If an affiliate says to another, "One of us is an infidel," what should I do with him?

T: Dissociate from him in God, because he is either declaring that he is an infidel, or he is accusing his affiliate of being an infidel, and both cases require dissociation.

S: What if he says to a group of people who are in a state of affiliation, "One of you—or one of them—is an infidel"?

T: Dissociate from him for saying this.

S: What if an affiliate of mine directs a word of general infidelity such as "infidel" or "profligate" or "deviant" at a person who is in an affiliated group, and the person who is in the affiliated group responds in kind, what do I do with the one who responds?

T: Do not dissociate from the person who responds, because he is defending himself and proof does not stand on the testimony of a single individual. If two or more affiliates say "You infidel" or something like that, you must dissociate from the person who is in the affiliated group, even if he does not respond. If he is accused of something specific, such as "You thief" or "You drinker of wine," dissociate from him if he responds.

S: If two affiliates, and one says to the other during the quarrel in front of an arbiter, for example, "You have wronged me," or if he makes this accusation after the quarrel, or if the second says, "You accused me of being unfair" or "a liar" or "unjust," or if he says to witnesses something like "You have testified that I acted unjustly," or if he says to the arbiter, "You have judged me to have acted unjustly," as if he is asking for his proof and it has not yet been given, what should I do with them?

T: Keep them both in affiliation. There is nothing in this that requires dissociation from them, for such a case does not constitute slander; it is only self-defense and a request for proof. The Messenger of God said, "A truthful person has the right to speak." Some say one should dissociate from a person who says this, and the *Quṭb* said, "and that is better," and God knows best.

S: What if they go beyond proper bounds in their allegations and say something that requires dissociation, what should be done with them?

T: Dissociate from the one who went beyond proper bounds and said something requiring dissociation, and the judge and witnesses should dissociate from them if the litigants accuse them of injustice or unfairness, if the judge and witnesses have been wrongly accused.

S: What if I dissociate from someone who commits a grave sin, because of it, and then he commits another, must I renew my dissociation, or does it remain as it is?

T: You do not need to renew your dissociation unless you have forgotten the first one or have forgotten that he is in a state of dissociation, even if the second sin is polytheism. If you forget why you dissociated from him, retain him in dissociation, and you are pardoned what you forgot. If you forget from whom it is you dissociated, you are not pardoned, according to the authoritative opinion. The *Quṭb* says, "Really, he should be pardoned. One scholar said this, and it is related that he retracted his opinion and was treated roughly for his retraction."

PART THREE

The Science of Divine Unity

SCHOOLS AND THEMES IN SYSTEMATIC THEOLOGY

AT THE HEART OF ALL Islamic theological reflection and debate is an intense interest in articulating the manifold mystery of God's perfect transcendent oneness. It is the pivot around which all other questions about God's being, attributes, and acts turn. Many of the problems and concerns that appear in creedal formulations derive from this focus and have been the subjects of much more extended and detailed discussion in the various "schools" of systematic or speculative theology, the best known of which employ the dialectical method of *kalām* (discourse). Chapter 5 includes primary texts that identify and describe several of those schools, and it addresses some of the core methodological principles elaborated by major *mutakallimūn* as well as by systematic theologians of various other methodological persuasions. Among those schools of thought are some that went on to become major contributors to the ongoing development of Islamic theological thinking, as well as others now long "dormant," even if the questions that originally gave them their reason for being have continued to be debated. The chapter includes the foundational theme of prophetic revelation and authority in order to establish an essential methodological context. In chapter 6, the focus shifts to large theological themes, especially questions relating to divine attributes and key modalities of divine creativity and disclosure, such as God's "voice" and what it means to assert that believers will "see" God in the afterlife.

FIVE

Theological Schools and Principles

WE BEGIN WITH AN ACCOUNT by Shahrastānī, a noted medieval historian of Islamic thought, describing the key actors in the dramatic unfolding of Islamic systematic theology. This sets the stage for more detailed presentations of specific methodological concerns of the schools most influential in the ongoing development of the kind of systematic theological thinking often referred to as *kalām*. Discussion of the broad variety of views espoused by the schools and sects of the kind sampled here led to the evolution of a theological vocabulary that reflected a general spectrum of theological or confessional deficiency.[1]

DIVERGENT SCHOOLS OF THOUGHT

Shahrastānī's Doxography of Muslim Schools

Translated by Michael A. Sells

Muslim scholars began very early identifying and debating the merits and liabilities of various schools of thought. Heresiographers produced extensive treatments of belief systems generally agreed to be beyond the pale of "authentic" Islamic creedal formulations. But in addition, matters of "doxography" also occupied apologists among the early historians of Islamic thought. As samples of creedal statements in part 2 suggest, more than a few articulations of the faith qualified as not quite "heretical," but were nonetheless cause for scrutiny in the evolving discourse of "Islamic" theology.

Shahrastānī's (d. 1153) *Book of Religious and Philosophical Sects* includes what amounts to a brief overview of several of the principal schools of thought engaged in articulating central theological themes.[2] A critical term in the discussion is *qadar*, from a root whose first meaning is "to decree or decide"; but because its secondary meaning is "to have power, strength, capability," the term *qadar* has been applied somewhat confusingly to both *divine* decree and power, on the one hand, and to the *human* power to choose (with concomitant ethical responsibility), on the other. Shahrastānī begins by seeking to sort out the ambiguities of the terminology, dividing his overview into three main groups: the Muʿtazila, the Compulsionists, and the Attributionists.

Text

I. THE MUʿTAZILA

The Muʿtazila were called the people of justice and unity (*tawḥīd*). They were also given the name "the Qadarites" (al-Qadarīya, the determinists). However, they themselves claim that the term Qadarites would in that case be ambiguous. They maintain that the term should be applied to those who maintain that the determination (*qadar*) of things—both for good and evil—is from God. They are wary of the disgrace implied by the name due to the low esteem it has received from the saying of the Prophet: "The Qadarites are the Magians of the community." The Attributionists opposed the attempt of the Qadarites to disclaim the term "Qadarite." The Attributionists appealed to the general usage in which the Jabrites (compulsionists) and the Qadarites are opposites. How then, could one term [Qadarite] be applied to its opposite [Jabrites: those who affirm divine compulsion or predetermination]?

The Prophet said that the Qadarites were the opponents of Allāh in predetermination (*qadar*). Opposition in divine predetermination and the dividing of good and evil between the act of Allāh and the act of the servant are inconceivable in the school of those who affirm submission, trust in God, and the procession of all states according to the determination sealed and the decree ordained.

The belief that unites all Muʿtazila as a single group is the claim that Allāh Most High is eternal and that eternity is the unique characteristic of his essence (*dhāt*).[3] They completely deny the [divine] attributes, saying that God is knowing through his essence, powerful through his essence, living through his essence, not through knowledge, power, and life, which would be eternal attributes and meanings subsisting in him. If the attributes shared in his eternity, which is his unique characteristic, then they would share in his divinity.

They are agreed that his words are originated [as opposed to eternal], created in a substratum that consists of letter and sound, the likenesses of which are composed in books as stories from him. Whatever exists in a substratum is only an accident that passes away. They are agreed that will, hearing, and seeing are not meanings that subsist in his essence, but they disagree on the manner of their existence and the loci of their meanings—as will be seen.

They are agreed in denying any perceptual vision of Allāh in the final abode, and denying any likeness of him in terms of directions, place, form, body, position, motion, coming to an end, change, or passibility. They demand a figurative interpretation (*taʾwīl*) of any anthropomorphic verses and they call this mode of interpretation "*tawḥīd*."

They are agreed that the servant is powerful, creator of his own acts, both good and evil, and deserving of the reward and punishment he receives in the after abode. They agree further that the lord Most High is exalted beyond any attribution to the lord of evil, oppression, or any act of unbelief or disobedience, because if he created oppression he would be oppressive, in the same way that if he creates justice he is just. [The Muʿtazila] agree that the All-Wise does only what is beneficial and good. He *must* act, in accordance with his wisdom, in the interest of his servants. They disagree, however, on the necessity of his acting in the best interest of his servants and with special grace. They call this mode of interpretation justice.

They agree that the believer, when he leaves the world in a state of obedience and repentance, deserves reward and requital, while special favor is something other, beyond due reward. When he departs without repentance for major sins he has committed, he merits an eternity in the fire. His punishment is less severe than the punishment of the unbeliever. They call this mode of interpretation the promise and threat.

[The Muʿtazila] agree that the principles of intuition (*maʿrifa*) and the gratitude for well-being are necessary even before the reception of revelation. They also agree that a rational intuition of what is right and wrong, as well as the embracing of the right and avoiding of the wrong, is also necessary before revelation. The reception of divine ordinances is a special favor of the creator, Most High, sent to servants through the intermediary of the prophets as a test and a forewarning, "so that one who perishes, perishes after a clear sign, and one who lives, lives after a clear sign" (8:42).

They disagree on the Imamate [leadership of the Islamic community], and upon its being founded upon special designation or upon choice, as will be shown in the discussion of each individual group. Now we will specify, group by group, what distinguishes the followers of each group [of Muʿtazila].

The Wāṣilīya. The Wāṣilīya are the disciples of Abū Ḥudhayfa Wāṣil ibn ʿAṭāʾ al-Ghazzāl (d. 748). He was a student of Ḥasan of Basra. He studied religious sciences and traditions with Ḥasan. The two lived in the time of [the Umayyad caliphs] ʿAbd al-Mālik and Hishām ibn ʿAbd al-Mālik. There is still a small party of the Wāṣilīya in the West, in the province of Idrīs ibn ʿAbd Allāh al-Ḥasanī, who led a rebellion in the West in the period of Abū Jaʿfar al-Manṣūr. So they are called the Wāṣilīya.

The Wāṣilīya are said to have four basic doctrines.

The first doctrine consists of the denial of the attributes of the creator, Most High, such as knowledge, power, will, and life. This position was at first undeveloped. Wāṣil ibn ʿAṭāʾ formulated it in popular terms as an affirmation of the impossibility of the existence of two pre-eternal and everlasting deities. He said: Whoever affirms an eternal mode (*maʿnā*) or attribute is affirming two deities.[4]

However, after the circulation of the books of the philosophers,[5] Wāṣil's students reformulated the position and ended up affirming the view that reduced all attributes to the deity's being "knowing" and "powerful," with the provision that these two attributes were essential and were attributes of the eternal essence. This was the position of Al-Jubbāʾi (d. 915), whereas [his son] Abū Hāshim (d. 933) considered these two [i.e., the qualities of being "knowing" and "powerful"] as two states. Abū 'l-Ḥusayn of Basra inclined toward reducing them to a single attribute, that of knowingness, which is exactly the position of the philosophers. We will give the details of this position later. The Traditionalists opposed the Wāṣilīya in this [denial of the attributes] on the grounds that the attributes are mentioned in the Book [the Qurʿān] and the tradition.[6]

The second doctrine [of the Wāṣilīya] is the affirmation of free will [*qadar*, the word that means "predeterminism" but that comes to mean, confusingly, its opposite, "free will"]. In this they followed the line of Maʿbad al-Juhanī (d. 699) and Ghaylān of Damascus (d. ca. 735). Wāṣil ibn ʿAṭāʾ insisted upon this doctrine even more than he had insisted upon the doctrine of attributes. He said: The creator, Most High, is all-wise and just. Evil and oppression cannot be properly attributed to him, nor is it possible for him to will for his servants what is in disagreement with his command—to control their action and then punish them for what they did. The servant himself is the actor of good and evil, faith and disbelief, obedience and disobedience, and he is requited according to his actions. The lord Most High gives him the power to do all that. The acts of godservants are confined to motion and rest, applications, speculation, and knowledge. He said that it is impossible that God should enjoin action upon his servant without the servant being able to act and sensing that the ability and the act resided within himself. Whoever denies this denies the necessary truth. Wāṣil would appeal to various verses of the Qur'ān in his discussion.

I [Shahrastānī] saw a letter that Ḥasan of Basra is said to have written to ʿAbd al-Malik ibn Marwān (d. 705), who had asked him about the affirmation of *qadar* (free will) and *jabr* (compulsion).[7] Ḥasan's reply was in agreement with the school of free will (*qadarīya*), and appealed to verses from the Book and to logical proofs. However, perhaps the letter was really by Wāṣil ibn ʿAṭā', since Ḥasan was not one to oppose the position of the Traditionalists, who were in complete consensus that all determination (*qadar*), for good and for evil, was from God Most High.

It is remarkable that with this issue they [the Wāṣilīya] applied the relevant expression [on divine predetermination] from the tradition to suffering and well-being, difficult times and times of ease, sickness and health, death and life, and other such acts of Allāh Most High, but not to good and evil, acts of charity and acts of wickedness originating in the acquisition of servants. Thus in the issues examined in this treatise, the entire party of the Muʿtazila has based themselves on the position of this group [the Wāṣilīya].[8]

The third doctrine is the affirmation of the mean between two extremes. The source of this position is as follows: Someone paid a visit to Ḥasan of Basra and said:

> O Imam of the faith, in our time there are those who dispute the affirmation of the reality of capital sins. For this group, a capital sin does not take away from one's faith. According to them, action is not a pillar of faith. Disobedience does not mar one's faith and obedience is of no use if one lacks faith. These are the *murji'a* of the community. What is your judgment of what should be believed in this matter?

Ḥasan began to think over the question, but before he could respond, Wāṣil ibn ʿAṭā' said: "I maintain that one who commits capital sins is neither an absolute believer nor an absolute unbeliever. Rather, he is in a position between the two extremes, neither believer nor unbeliever." Then he rose and went off to another pillar in the mosque, repeating [to the new group] what he had said to Ḥasan's group. Ḥasan said: "Wāṣil has gone off (*i'tazala*) from us." Thus he and his followers came to be called the Mu'tazila [i.e., those who cut themselves off or go off by themselves].

The point of his position is the claim that faith is a manifestation of virtuous characteristics. When they are brought together, a person is said to be a believer, and that is a name of praise. The ethically corrupt does not bring together the traits of the good, does not merit a name of praise, and therefore is not a believer. However, he is not an unbeliever, either, because the Testimony of belief (*shahāda*) and the other good acts exist in him and there is no point in denying them. However, when he departs from this world with a capital sin and without repentance, he is condemned eternally to the fire, since in the afterworld there are only two groups, one group in the garden and one in the blaze. However, his torment will be lighter and his level higher than that of the unbelievers. Wāṣil was followed in this view by 'Amr ibn 'Abīd, who also agreed with him on the issue of *qadar* and on denying the attributes. . . .[9]

II. THE COMPULSIONISTS (JABRĪYA)

Jabr (compulsion) is the denial that any act can be attributed to the servant. Instead, the act is attributed to the lord Most High. There are different kinds of Jabrites (compulsionists). The pure Jabrites refuse to attribute to the servant any act or power (*qudra*) to act whatsoever. Moderate Jabrites attribute to the servant a power, but a power that is not in any way effective. If anyone attributes to that originated power any effect upon the human act and calls such an effect "acquisition" (*kasb*)—such a person is not a Jabrite.[10]

A. The Jahmīya. The "Jahmites" are the followers of Jahm ibn Ṣafwān (d. 746), who was a pure compulsionist. His innovation first appeared in the city of Tirmidh. He was executed at the command of Sālim ibn Aḥwaz al-Māzinī in Marw at the end of the Umayyad dynasty.

Jahm agreed with the Mu'tazila in denying the eternal attributes, but went beyond them in certain respects. First, he claimed that one cannot attribute to the creator, Most High, attributes that are attributed to creatures, because that would be a form of *tashbīya* (the "likening" of the deity to the creature). Therefore he denied that the creator was living and knowing, but affirmed that he was powerful, acting, and creating, because to none of his creatures can be attributed power, act, and creation.

Second, he claimed that cognitions belonging to the creator, Most High, are originated, and have no substratum. He said that it is not possible that the creator would know a thing before he creates it, because if he knew it and then created it, either his knowledge would remain as it was or it would not. If it remained as it was, then it would be ignorance, for the knowledge that he was about to create is not the same as the knowledge that he had created. If it did not remain, then it would change, but what changes is what is created, not the eternal. In this position, he was in agreement with the school of Hishām ibn al-Ḥakam (d. 796).... [Ellipsis in original translation.]

He said, further, that once the originated nature of such cognition is acknowledged, then there are the following possibilities. If it is originated in his essence, Most High, that would entail change in his essence and make his essence a substratum for new occurrences. If it occurs in a substratum, then it would be an attribute of the substratum, not the creator, Most High. Thus it can be seen that divine cognition can have no substratum. For Jahm, then, there are as many originated cognitions as there are existent objects of knowledge.

Third, Jahm claimed concerning the originated power that the human being has no power over anything, cannot be attributed capability, and is compelled in his acts. He has no power or will or choice of his own. God Most High creates the acts in him just as he creates them in all the inanimate objects. Acts are ascribed to the human being figuratively, in the same way they are ascribed to inanimate objects, as when a tree is said to bear fruit, water to run, a rock to move, the sun to rise and set, the sky to cloud over and rain, the earth to quake and to sprout, and the like. Just as the acts are compelled, so are reward and punishment compulsory. Once compulsion is affirmed, then *taklīf* (the imposition of particular obligations upon the human) is also compelled.[11]

Fourth, Jahm maintained that the movements of the people of the two eternal afterworlds come to an end. The garden and the fire will pass away after the people enter them, after the people of the garden enjoy its bliss and the people of the fire suffer its burning. We cannot conceive of motions that have no end, any more than we can conceive of motions that have no beginning. [God's] words "eternal in it" (11:107), should be taken as hyperbole and emphasis, not as literally true in reference to eternity. We say, for example, "May God make so-and-so's dominion eternal." Jahm also cited in full his saying Most High, "Eternal in it as long as the heavens and earth endure, except by the will of your lord" (11: 107). The verse contains a condition and an exception, but eternity and everlastingness are unconditioned and accept no exception.

Fifth, he maintained that one who achieves *maʿrifa* and then verbally abjures the faith is not an infidel because of his abjuration. Knowledge and *maʿrifa* do not come to an end with an abjuration, so that he is still a believer. He said faith is not divisible into parts. It cannot be divided up into contract, word, and act. People cannot be placed in different degrees of faith, for the faith of the prophets and the faith of the community are of the same kind, because religious understandings (*maʿārif*) cannot be put one above the other. The upholders of the old tradition refuted him vehemently and accused him of *taʿṭīl* (stripping the deity of its attributes). Jahm also agreed with the Muʿtazila in denying the final vision, in affirming the createdness of the words [of the Qurʾān], and in maintaining the necessity of rational, religious understandings for the acceptance of audition [of revelation].

B. The Najjārīya. The Najjārīya were the followers of Ḥusayn ibn Muḥammad an-Najjār (d. ca. 836). Most of the Muʿtazila in Rayy and its environs are of this school. Even though they might differ in some areas (dividing into the schools of the Barghuthīya, Ẓaʿafranīya, and Mustadrika), they do not disagree on the basic issues discussed here.

They agree with the Muʿtazila in denying the attributes of knowledge, power, will, life, hearing, and sight, but they agree with the Attributionists in affirming that actions are created. The Najjārīya affirm that the creator, Most High, is a willer-for-himself (*murīd li nafsihi*) just as he is a knower-for-himself. Najjār extracted the necessary conclusions, and was in turn compelled by them to admit that the Most High was a willer of good and evil, benefit and harm. Najjār also said that the meaning of God's being a willer is that he is not subject to coercion or oppression. He also maintained that he [the deity] creates of the deeds of servants, both good and evil, praiseworthy and blameworthy, and that the servant acquires the deeds. He thus affirmed an influence on the part of the created power and called it "acquisition" (*kasb*) in accord with what Ashʿarī maintained. He also agreed with Ashʿarī in affirming a capacity with the act.

In regard to the question of the vision [by the human of the deity], he denied the possibility of a vision of Allāh Most High through any perceptive faculty, although he granted that Allāh Most High could transform the power of knowing (*maʿrifa*) within the heart to a kind of eye with which Allāh could be seen, and that would be a kind of vision. . . .

III. THE ATTRIBUTIONISTS (*ṢIFĀTĪYA*)

Know that most of the Traditionalists affirmed that Allāh Most High has eternal attributes of knowledge, power, will, hearing, seeing, speech, beauty, munificence, generosity, bestowal, glory, and majesty. They did not distinguish between attributes of essence and attributes of act, but spoke in the same way of them all. They also affirmed the "announced" (*khabarī*) attributes, such as "the two hands" and "the face," and did not interpret them figuratively. Instead they said: "These attributes have come to us in the divine ordinance (*sharʿ*), so we call them announced attributes."

Because the Muʿtazila denied the attributes and the Traditionalists affirmed them, the Traditionalists were named "attributionists" (*ṣifātīya*) and the Muʿtazila were named "vacators" (*muʿaṭṭila*) [for vacating the deity of its attributes]. In their affirmation of the attributes, some of the Traditionalists crossed the boundary into "likening" (*tashbīh*), by applying to the deity attributes of creatures. Others limited themselves to attributes implied by the acts [of the divine] and those that were announced. They divided further into two camps. One camp would employ a moderate contextual interpretation. The other stopped short of interpretation, saying: "We know through the dictates of reason that concerning Allāh 'there is nothing like his like,' that he is like no creature and no creature is like him. Of that we are certain."

Then a later group went beyond what the Traditionalists had said and maintained that such expressions must be taken literally and should be explained [through *tafsīr*] as they appear without *taʾwīl*. However, they did not stop at the literal meaning, but fell into pure anthropomorphism (*tashbīh*), which was contrary to the belief of the Traditionalists.

A very pure form of anthropomorphism existed among the Jews, not all of them, but among the Qaraites who found in the Torah many expressions suggesting anthropomorphism. Then the Shīʿa in our religion [i.e., Islam] fell into either *ghuluw* or *taqṣīr*. *Ghuluw* is the likening *(tashbīh)* of the Imams to the deity and the affirming of their transcendence. *Taqṣīr* (lit. "abbreviation") is the likening of the deity to one of the creatures.

With the appearance of the Muʿtazila and the Mutakallimūn among the Traditionalists, some of the Shīʿa went back on their *ghulūw* and *taqṣīr* and fell into the Mu'tazilite belief. At the same time, a group of the Traditionalists went beyond literal explanation and fell into anthropomorphism.

Among the Traditionalists who neither accepted *ta'wīl* nor fell into anthropomorphism was Mālik ibn Anas (d. 795). He affirmed that the "settling" [upon the throne] is known but "how" it occurred is unknown, that faith in it is incumbent, but the asking about it is innovation. Others include Aḥmad ibn Ḥanbal, Sufyān, Dāwūd al-Iṣfahānī, and their followers, and more recently, 'Abd Allāh ibn Sa'īd al-Kilānī, Abū 'Abbās al-Qalānisī, and Ḥārith ibn Asad al-Muḥāsibī (d. 857). These latter were of the Traditionalists, except that they propagated scholastic theology and supported the dogmas of the Traditionalists with scholastic proofs and basic arguments. Some wrote and some taught, until a debate took place between Abū 'l-Ḥasan al-Ash'arī (d. 935) and his teacher over a question concerning interest and best interest (*ṣalāḥ* and *aṣlaḥ*). They disagreed and Ash'arī went over to the Traditionalists. Ash'arī supported their positions with scholastic methods, and that became a school for the people of *sunna* (tradition) and *jamā'a* (community). Thus the name "Attributionists" came to be applied to the followers of Ash'arī. Inasmuch as the anthropomorphists and the Karramites also affirm the attributes, we have numbered them as two groups within the larger category of "Attributionists."

Sālim ibn Dhakwān on the Murji'a

Translated by Patricia Crone and Fritz Zimmermann

An important group not described in Shahrastānī's text above are the Murji'a. They raised critical questions about a number of key theological issues, as suggested in the following overview. Traditional accounts have in effect made the notion of "postponing" judgment as to another's spiritual status a kind of signature doctrine, as suggested by the root of the name *murji'a—raja'a,* "to hold out hope" of salvation. Mistakenly attributed to a Sālim ibn Dhakwān, this eighth-century "pulpit manifesto" describes the theological positions of the Murji'a (and other early sectarian movements) from an Ibāḍī perspective. The Ibāḍīs were at least distantly related to the original Khārijī "seceders" who parted company with 'Alī and the Shī'a in the mid-seventh century (see chapter 4 for a related text). Classic Ibāḍī theology affirms (like the Mu'tazila) the created nature of the Qur'ān, and in matters legal the Ibāḍīs most resemble the Sunnī Mālikī *madhhab.* It is important to read the text's views of the Murji'a with its unique sectarian bias in mind.[12]

Text

Then others, who had no predecessors whose path they followed or authorities on whose guidance they modeled themselves, propounded the doctrine of suspended judgment. They said, "We will pronounce on the recent schism, having seen it and been there; but we suspend judgment on the first schism"—for they were not there, it happened before their time. This is what they claim. They hold that whoever accuses someone of error on the basis of the testimony of the Muslims concerning something he was not there to see, or that happened before his time, he is himself in error. This, they claim, is God's religion.

But if that doctrine of theirs is right, then all the participants in the first schism were infidels. For when ʿAlī went out to the Kufans and called upon them to separate from ʿUthmān (d. 656), to disown him, and to fight those seeking vengeance for his death, they responded without having been there to see ʿUthmān's behavior and on the sole strength of the testimony of the Muslims who told them [about it]. And when Ṭalḥa and az-Zubayr went out to the Baṣrans and called upon them to declare for ʿUthmān and seek vengeance for him by fighting ʿAlī and his party, they responded even though they had not been there to see any of what they disagreed about. So if it is right to suspend judgment, [it follows that] the people of Kūfa and Baṣra were guilty of unbelief when they responded to [calls to take sides over] something that had happened in their absence and on which they accepted the testimony of people they regarded as Muslims. [It also follows] that ʿAlī, Zubayr, and Ṭalḥa fell into unbelief when they called upon people to [take sides over] events that these people had not been there to see, but over which they nonetheless deemed it lawful to shed Muslim blood and to disown those who failed to respond; for they acted contrary to [the principle of] suspension of judgment [which would be wrong] if the latter is indeed God's religion regarding cases where one was absent from an event or lived after it happened. And [it also follows that] the Murjiʾites are themselves guilty of unbelief when they suspend judgment on people who acted contrary to their religion.

If, as they say, it is wrong to charge a user of the *qibla* with error when that person lived before one's time, then they profess a doctrine that they violate in practice: for they call on the younger generation of their *qawm* to separate from Muʿāwiya and to disown him. If it is wrong for a Muslim to accuse someone who lived before his time on the basis of the testimony of the Muslims [at large], then they are wrong in calling [people] to a cause that it would be wrong for them to join; and if it is right for a Muslim to accuse someone who lived before his time on the basis of the testimony of the Muslims [at large], then they are wrong in pronouncing it wrong.

From all this, God be praised, they have no way out. If they say that Muʿāwiya is not like the people of the first schism, who were companions of the Messenger of God—if that is what they say, [we answer that] Muʿāwiya was a relative by marriage and a secretary of the Messenger of God, and that ʿUmar ibn al-Khaṭṭāb only appointed him governor of the Syrians because he so liked and admired him.

If they say that they have conflicting testimony from the people of the *qibla* regarding the participants in the first schism [but not about Muʿāwiya, we reply that] on Muʿāwiya too there is conflicting testimony from the people of the *qibla* [i.e., literally those who face Mecca in prayer]. Some approve and some disapprove of him. If they say that these days no one disagrees with them about Muʿāwiya unless he is himself astray, then [they admit that] it is not for us to reject the testimony of the Muslims [at large] on account of what is said by those who are astray: God has commanded us to believe the believers and forbidden us to believe those who are astray by saying, addressing His Messenger, "He believes in God and believes the believers" (9:61). And, addressing others, "Do not make excuses, we will not believe you; God has told us tidings of you" (9:94).

If they argue that the younger generation whom they call upon to separate from Muʿāwiya and to disown him can tell that he was wrong from the reports of his [conduct] still current in their time, then [we reply that just so] we, thank God, can tell today the error of those who were wrong in the first schism from the reports still current in our time, and from the fact that the Muslims [at large] disown them.

How, moreover, do they know that Abū Bakr and ʿUmar were right when they claim not to be able to tell who was wrong from who was right among the participants in the first schism, who were later than those two? If they say that the people of the *qibla* are unanimous in proclaiming Abū Bakr and ʿUmar right, and that this is why they affiliate to them, whereas the people of the *qibla* disagree about the participants in the first schism, and that this is why they suspend judgment on them—if this is what they argue, then [we reply that] on Abū Bakr and ʿUmar too the testimony of the people of the *qibla* is contradictory. Many of the Sabaʾīya dissociate from them. If they reply that they can tell the mendacity and injustice of the Sabaʾīya regarding Abū Bakr and ʿUmar from the errors they observe in them today, then let them [likewise] tell the mendacity or truthfulness of those who affiliate to the misguided participants in the first schism on the basis of the error or right guidance that they can observe in them [today]. If they ask, "how can we reject the testimony of people who profess our creed, use our *qibla,* and believe in our Prophet?" then how do they reject the testimony of the Sabaʾīya regarding Abū Bakr and ʿUmar, when they too profess their creed, use their *qibla,* and believe in their Prophet? And how do they reject what the Azāriqa [Khārijīs], who also use the *qibla,* say about stoning?

They claim that the kings of their *qawm* (tribe, faction) are believers and Muslims but that God has made it lawful to separate from them and to disown them, and unlawful to associate with them and to ask for forgiveness for them. But if they are indeed believers and Muslims, they are wrong in deeming it unlawful to associate with them and to pray for forgiveness for them, given God's words "The believers, the men and women, are friends of one another" (9:71), and "Ask forgiveness for your sin, and for the believers, men and women" (47:19). And if God has made it unlawful to associate with them and to pray for forgiveness for them, then they are wrong in calling them believers.

They claim that they [the kings] are believers who have gone astray, that their faith does not preserve them from error and that [conversely] their error does not necessarily make them infidels or exclude them from faith. But everyone is either a believer or an infidel. For God, whose promise will come about without fail (cf. 22:47, 30:6), has decreed that He will "guide those who believe to a straight path" (22:54) and that He will "confirm those who believe with the firm words in this life and the next" (14:27). If the kings are believers, the Murjiʾites are wrong in saying that they have gone astray, given that God has told them that He will "guide those who believe to a straight path" (22:54); for one whom He has guided to a straight path cannot be astray. And if the kings are astray, the Murjiʾites are wrong in declaring them believers.

Some of them profess that the kings are infidels devoid of faith and claim to know this from the Qurʾān. For all that, they associate with those Murjiʾites who profess that the kings are believers devoid of unbelief. If the kings are infidels, as they say they are, devoid of faith, then those who declare infidels to be believers devoid of unbelief have gone astray, and those who associate with them despite their profession have gone astray as well.

The Murjiʾite cause has thus [split up], but the error that unites them is that they base their doctrine on their own opinion, decide their stance for themselves, oppose the way of those whom God has guided before their time and reject the testimony of the Muslims for the testimony of people who have gone astray.

They claim that it is wrong to admit the testimony of the Muslims on events that happened before one's time. But if that doctrine of theirs is right, they are wrong in calling the younger generation of their *qawm* to separate from people who lived before their time. [Further,] if the kings of their *qawm* are believers, they are wrong in forbidding association with them, in disowning them and separating from them outright, and in omitting to ask for forgiveness for them; and if they are not believers, they are wrong in calling them believers, and in associating with those who claim that believers they are. [Further,] they are wrong in associating with people to whom they will respond when [they call for] separation from their enemy, but with whom they will not associate as long as they are not disowning them.[13] They are wrong in the discrepancy between their declarations and their conduct.

They are wrong in interpreting the Book of God in a sense different from that with which God sent it down. For they interpret as references to suspension of judgment the words of God, "That is a nation that has passed away; there awaits them that they have earned, and there awaits you that you have earned; you shall not be questioned concerning the things they did" (2:134, 141); and Pharaoh's question to Moses about the former generations (20: 51) to which "he replied, 'The knowledge of them is with my Lord, in a book; my Lord goes not astray, nor forgets'" (20:52).

By the life of God, if we place the people of the *qibla* involved in the [first] schism in the same category as the nation here described by God as having passed away, then we classify them as chosen, excellent (38:47) messengers of God. This verse has nothing to do with suspension of judgment. The nation referred to here is the one regarding which God told the people of the Book who disagreed about it, "Or do you say Abraham, Ishmael, Isaac, and Jacob, and the tribes—they were Jews or Christians? Say: have you then greater knowledge, or God? And God is not heedless of the things you do. That is a nation that has passed away; there awaits them that they have earned, and there awaits you that you have earned; you shall not be questioned concerning the things they did" (2:140–41). We, for our part, thank God, do not propose to suspend judgment on God's messengers. Rather, we profess that they are distinguished by degrees (cf. 2:253), and we affiliate to them and testify that they are free from all doubt and blemish. If we compare [the participants in] the first schism to *them,* there can be no occasion for doubt or suspension of judgment about them.

As for Pharaoh's question to Moses about the former generations, God sent Noah, Hūd, Sāliḥ, Abraham, and Lot before Moses: they and their followers and foes are the former generations. Do the Murji'ites think that Moses put them [all] in a single category? He did not. Rather, he affiliated to his brethren and disowned their enemies. The Murji'ites are mistaken, praise be to God. They argue without proof (cf. 2:111, etc.) and distort the Qur'ān by quoting it out of context. They take religion to mean communal unity (*al-jamā'a*). By God, if [all] the servants of God involved in the first schism were unbelievers, the Murji'ites would not recognize their unbelief; and if they were separated by guidance and error, the Murji'ites would not throw in their lot with either side.

METHODOLOGICAL OVERVIEWS

Al-Ash'arī's Vindication of Kalām

Translated by Richard McCarthy, SJ

A *Treatise in Defense of Kalām,* attributed to Abū 'l-Ḥasan al-Ash'arī (d. 935) and handed down by generations of his intellectual descendants, lays out this major theologian's views on the foundations of "speculative or dialectical" theology in scripture and tradition. Beginning with a widespread critique of systematic theological reflection, the text responds from several perspectives to "objections" posed by opponents of *kalām,* offering a concise summary of one major systematic theological method.[14]

Text

A certain group of people [Ḥanbalites?] have made ignorance their capital. Finding reasoning and inquiry into religious belief too burdensome, they incline towards the easy way of servile sectarianism. They calumniate him who scrutinizes the basic dogmas of religion and accuse him of deviation. It is innovation and deviation, they claim, to engage in *kalām* about motion and rest, body and accident, accidental modes and states, the atom and the leap, and the attributes of the Creator.

They assert that if that were a matter of guidance and rectitude, the Prophet and his Caliphs and his Companions would have discussed it. For, they say, the Prophet did not die until he had discussed and amply explained all needful religious matters. He left nothing to be said by anyone about the affairs of their religion needful to Muslims, and what brings them near to God and removes them far from His anger.

Since no *kalām* on any of the subjects that we have mentioned has been related from the Prophet, we know that such *kalām* is an innovation and such inquiry a deviation. For if it were good, the Prophet and his Companions would not have failed to discuss it. For the absence of such *kalām* on the part of the Prophet and his Companions can be explained in only two ways: either they knew it and were silent about it; or they did not know it, nay, were ignorant of it. Now if they knew it and did not discuss it, then we also may be silent about it, as they were, and we may abstain from plunging into it, as they abstained. For if it were a part of religion, they could not have been silent about it. On the other hand, if they did not know it, then we may have the same ignorance of it. For if it were a part of religion, they would not have been ignorant of it. So according to both explanations such *kalām* is an innovation (*bidʿa*) and plunging into it is a deviation (*ḍalāla*).

This is the summary of their argument for abstaining from reasoning about the basic dogmas of religion.

FIRST ANSWER

There are three ways of answering that argument. The first is to turn the question against them by saying: It is also true that the Prophet never said: "If anyone should inquire into that and discuss it, regard him as a deviating innovator." So you are constrained to regard yourselves as deviating innovators, since you have discussed something that the Prophet did not discuss, and you have accused of deviation him whom the Prophet did not so accuse.

SECOND ANSWER

The second answer is to say to them: Actually the Prophet was not ignorant of any item of the *kalām* that you have mentioned concerning body and accident, motion and rest, atom and leap. It is true that he did not discuss every one of these points specifically; and the same is true of those with deep insight and learned men among the Companions. Nevertheless, the basic principles of these things that you have mentioned specifically are present in the Qurʾān and the *Sunna* in general terms, not in detail.

Take motion and rest and the *kalām* about them. Their basic principle is present in the Qurʾān, where they prove the affirmation of God's oneness; and so for union and separateness. In relating what His friend Abraham said in the story of the setting of the star and the sun and the moon and their being moved from place to place, God said what proves that his [Abraham's] Lord cannot be subject to any of that, and that one who is subject to setting and translation from place to place is not a divinity (6:75–79).

The *kalām* on the basic principles of the profession of God's oneness is also taken from the Book. God said: "Were there divinities other than God in them, the heavens and the earth would be in disorder" (21:22). This *kalām* is a brief reminder of the proof that God is unique and peerless, and the *kalām* of the *mutakallimūn,* in which they argue to the divine unicity from mutual hindrance and contention, simply goes back to this verse. God also said: "God has taken for Himself no son, and there is no other divinity with Him—else each divinity would have taken away what he had created, and some would have been superior to others" (23:91). And so on until He said: "Or have they appointed for God partners who have created even as He has, so that creation is a puzzle to them?" (13:16). The *kalām* of the *mutakallimūn,* in which they argue to the unicity of God, simply goes back to these verses that we have mentioned. And similarly, all the *kalām* that treats in detail of the questions deriving from the basic dogmas of God's oneness and justice is simply taken from the Qur'ān.

Such is also the case with the *kalām* on the possibility and the impossibility of the resurrection [of the body]. This question had been disputed by intelligent Arabs and by others before them until they were amazed at the possibility of that and said: "What! When we have died and become dust? That is an incredible return!" (50:3); and: "Never, never a hope of what you are promised!" (23:36); and: "Who will quicken bones when they have decayed?" (36:78); and God's words: "Does he promise you that when you shall have died and become dust and bones you will be brought forth?" (23:35). Apropos of such *kalām* of theirs God put into the Qur'ān argument designed to confirm, from the viewpoint of reason, the possibility of the resurrection after death. Moreover, He taught and instructed His Prophet how to argue against their denial of the resurrection in two ways, according to the two groups of adversaries. For one group admitted the first creation, but denied the second, while the other group denied both [first and second creations] on the ground that the world is eternal.

So against him who admitted the first creation God argued by saying: "Answer: He will quicken them who produced them a first time" (36:79), and by saying: "It is He who gives life by a first creation, then restores it; and it is very easy for Him" (30:27), and by His words: "As He first made you, you will return" (7:29). By these verses He called their attention to the fact that he who is able to effect something without reference to a preexisting exemplar is all the more able to effect something which has already been produced. Indeed, the latter is easier for him, as you know from your own experience. But in the case of the Creator, it is not "easier" for Him to create one thing than to create another.

It has been said that the objective pronominal suffix in *ʿalayhi* (for *him*) is an allusion to the capacity of creatures, the meaning being: It is easier and lighter for one of you to be raised and restored than to be created the first time. For his initial creation is always associated with parturition, rearing, severance of the umbilical cord, swaddling clothes, cutting the teeth, and other painful and distressing signs, whereas his restoration takes only a single instant in which there is none of that. Hence his restoration is easier on him than his initial creation. This, then, was the argument that God [or Muḥammad?] adduced against the group that admitted creation.

As for the group that denied both the first creation and the second, and maintained the eternity of the world, a doubt entered their minds simply because they said: "It is our experience that life is wet and hot, and death is cold and dry, akin to the nature of earth. How, then, can there be any amalgamation of life and earth and decayed bones, resulting in a sound creation, since two contraries do not combine?" For this reason, then, they denied the resurrection.

It is certainly true that two contraries do not combine in one substrate, or in one direction, or in what exists [already] in the substrate. But they can exist in two substrates by way of propinquity. So God argued against them by saying: "He who makes fire for you from the green tree—for behold! you kindle fire from it" (36:80). In saying that, God referred them to their own knowledge and experience of the emergence of fire from green trees, notwithstanding the heat and dryness of the former and the coldness and wetness of the latter. Again, God made the possibility of the first production a proof of the possibility of the last production, because it is a proof of the possibility of the propinquity of life to earth and decayed bones and of making it a sound creation—for He said: "Just as we created the human being a first time, so we shall restore him" (21:104).

As for the discussion of the *mutakallimūn* involving [the principle] that [the series of] things that begin to exist has a first member, and their refutation of the Materialists who hold that there is no motion not preceded by a motion, and no day not preceded by a day, and the *kalām* against him who holds that there is no atom that cannot be halved ad infinitum—we find the basis of that in the *Sunna* of God's Apostle. On a certain occasion he said: "There is no contagious disease and no bad omen." And a Bedouin said: "Then what is the matter with camels, flawless as gazelles, that mingle with scabby camels and become scabby?" And the Prophet said: "And who infected the first?" And the Bedouin was silent because of what he had made him understand by that rational argument. Likewise we say to him who claims that there is no motion not preceded by a motion: If that were the case, then not a single motion would ever have begun to be, because the [antecedently] limitless cannot begin to be.

Similarly, when a certain man said: "O Prophet of God! My wife has borne a black male child"—and he hinted that he would repudiate it—the Prophet said: "Have you any camels?" He replied: "Yes." The Prophet said: "What color are they?" He said: "Red." And the Apostle of God said: "Is there an ash-colored one among them?" He said: "Yes, there is an ash-colored one among them." The Prophet said: "And whence came that?" He said: "Perhaps a sweat spoiled it." And the Prophet said: "And perhaps a sweat spoiled your son." This, then, is the way in which God taught His Prophet to refer a thing to its kind and like, and it is our basis in all the judgments we make regarding the similar and the like.

We use that argument against him who holds that God resembles creatures and is a body by saying to him: If God resembled anything, He would have to resemble it either in all of its respects or in one of its respects. Now if He resembled it in all of its respects, He would of necessity be produced in all of His respects. And if He resembled it in one of its respects, He would of necessity be produced, like it, in that respect in which He resembled it. For every two like things are judged the same regarding that in which they are alike. But it is impossible for the produced to be eternal, and for the eternal to be produced. Indeed God has said: "There is nothing like Him" (42:11), and He has said: "There is no one equal to Him" (112:4).

The basis for declaring that the body has a limit, and that the atom cannot be divided (*ad infinitum*), is the statement of God: "And everything has been numbered by us in a clear archetype" (36:12). Now one cannot number what has no limit, and the single thing cannot be divided [ad infinitum]. For this would necessitate that they [endlessly] be two things—and God has declared that numbering applies to them both.

The basis for declaring that the act must be effected for the Producer of the world as He intends and chooses, and in the absence of any aversion for it on His part, is the utterance of God: "Do you not then see what you eject? Is it you who create it? Or are we the creators?" (56:58–59). And they could not affirm with proof that they created [it]. Despite their desire to have a child, he would not come if God was unwilling that he should. Thus God called their attention to the fact the Creator is He from whom creatures proceed according to His intention.

The basis of our rational refutation of our adversary is taken from the *Sunna* of our Master, Muḥammad. I refer to the teaching he received from God when he met the fat rabbi and said to him: "I conjure you by God, do you find in what God has revealed of the Torah that God detests the fat rabbi?" And the rabbi became angry at being thus reproached, and he said: "God has not sent down anything to a human being!" (6:91). Then God said: "Say: Who sent down the Book that Moses brought as light and guidance for humankind? etc." (6:91). So he quickly refuted him, because the Torah is a thing, and Moses a human being, and the rabbi admitted that God had sent down the Torah to Moses. And in a similar way he refuted the people who claimed that God had enjoined upon them that they should not believe an apostle until he should come to them with a sacrifice that fire would consume (3:183). For God said: "Say: Apostles before me have already brought you evidences, and the very thing you have mentioned. Why, then, did you kill them, if you are truthful?" (3:183). And by means of that he refuted them and argued against them.

Our basis in correcting the sophistry of our adversaries is taken from the words of God: "You and what you worship, apart from God, will be fuel for Gehenna. You are drawing near to it! If these false gods had been divinities, they would not have arrived at [Gehenna]. All will be there eternally. There they will send forth groans, but they will not be heard" (21:98). For when this verse came down, word of it reached ʿAbd Allāh ibn az-Zibaʿrā—a disputatious and contentious man—and he said: "I have as good as triumphed over Muḥammad and the Lord of the Kaʿba!" Then the Apostle of God came to him, and ʿAbd Allāh said: "O Muḥammad, do you not claim that Jesus and ʿUzayr and the angels were worshiped?" And the Prophet was silent,[15] not from confusion or the lack of anything to say, but from astonishment at ʿAbd Allāh's ignorance, because there is nothing in the verse that necessitates the entrance into it of Jesus and ʿUzayr and the angels. For God said: "and what you worship"; but He did not say: "and everything that you worship, apart from God." But Ibn az-Zibaʿrā simply wanted to argue speciously against the Prophet, in order to make his people think that he had argued against

Muḥammad successfully. So God sent down the verse: "Those, indeed, who have already received from us the best [reward]"—i.e. those of them who are worshiped—"are far removed from it [Gehenna]!" (21:101). The Prophet then recited that verse, and thereupon they raised a great outcry to mask their confusion and their error, and they said: "Are our divinities better, or is he?"—i.e. Jesus. So God sent down the verses: "When the Son of Mary is proposed as an example, see how your people turn away from him. They ask: 'Are our divinities better, or is he?' They have proposed this example to you only out of disputatiousness. Truly they are a contentious people" (43:57–58).

All the verses that we have mentioned, as well as many that we have not mentioned, are a basis and argument for us in our *kalām* on what we mention in detail. It is true that no question was particularized in the Book and the *Sunna*. But that was because the particularization of questions involving rational principles did not take place in the days of the Prophet. However, [he and] the Companions did engage in *kalām* of the sort that we have mentioned.

THIRD ANSWER

The third answer is that the Apostle of God did know these questions about which they have asked, and he was not ignorant of any detail involved in them. However, they did not occur in his time in such specific form that he should have, or should not have, discussed them—even though their basic principles were present in the Qur'an and the *Sunna*. But whenever a question arose that was related to religion from the standpoint of the Law, people discussed it, and inquired into it, and disputed about it, and debated and argued. Such, for example, were the questions concerning the fraction of the inheritance to which grandmothers are entitled—which is one of the questions involving obligations—and other questions touching on legal determinations. Such, too, were the questions pertaining to what is unlawful, and to the effects of irrevocable divorce, and to "*ḥabluki ʿalā ghāribiki,*"[16] and the questions concerning *ḥadd*-punishments [determined by Qur'anic law] and divorce. These questions, too numerous to mention, arose in their days, and in the case of each one of them there had come no explicit determination from the Prophet. For if he had given explicit instructions concerning all that, they would not have differed over those questions, and the difference would not have lasted until now.

But even though there was no explicit instruction of the Apostle of God regarding each one of these questions they referred and likened each to something that had been determined explicitly by the Book of God, and the *Sunna,* and their own *ijtihād* (independent investigation). Such questions, then, which involved judgments on unprecedented secondary cases, they referred to those determinations of the Law that are derivative and which are to be sought only along the line of revelation and apostolic tradition. But when new and specific questions pertaining to the basic dogmas arise, every intelligent Muslim ought to refer judgment on them to the sum of principles accepted on the grounds of reason, sense experience, intuition, etc. For judgment on legal questions that belong to the category of the traditional is to be based on reference to legal principles that likewise belong to the category of the traditional. And judgment on questions involving the data of reason and the senses should be a matter of referring every such instance to [something within] its own category, without confounding the rational with the traditional, or the traditional with the rational. So if *kalām* on the creation of the Qurʾān and on the atom and the leap, in these precise terms, had originated in the Prophet's time, he would have discussed and explained it just as he explained and discussed all the specific questions that did originate in his time.

Then one should say: There is no sound tradition from the Prophet to the effect that the Qurʾān is uncreated or created. Why, then, do you hold that it is uncreated? They may say: Some [or: one] of the Companions and the Followers held that. One should say to them: The Companion, or the Follower, is subject to the same constraint as you are, namely, that he is a deviating innovator for saying what the Apostle did not say. And another may say: I suspend my judgment on that, and I do not say created, nor do I say uncreated. To him one should say: Then you, in suspending your judgment on that, are a deviating innovator. For the Prophet did not say: "If this question should arise after my death, suspend your judgment on it, and say nothing." Nor did he say: "Regard as deviating and unbelieving him who affirms that it is created, or, him who denies that it is created."

Furthermore, tell us: If one were to say that God's knowledge is created, would you suspend your judgment on that, or not? If they say no, then say to them: Neither the Prophet nor his Companions said a word about that. And likewise, if someone were to say: Is this Lord of yours surfeited with food, or with drink, or is He clothed, or naked, or cold, or bilious, or damp, or a body, or an accident, or does He smell odors, or not smell them, or has He a nose, and a heart, and a liver, and a spleen, and does He make the pilgrimage every year, and does He ride horseback, or not, and is He grieved, or not—and other questions of that sort—you would have to refuse to answer him. For neither the Apostle of God nor his Companions ever discussed a single one of those points. Or you would not remain silent, and would explain by your *kalām* that none of those things can be predicated of God, etc. etc., because of this argument, and that, etc.

Someone may say: I should be silent and answer him not a word, or, I should shun him, or, I should leave him, or, I should not greet him, or, I should not visit him if he fell sick, or, I should show no respect to his corpse if he died. To him one should say: Then you would be bound to be, in all these ways that you have mentioned, a deviating innovator. For the Apostle of God never said: "If anyone should ask about any of those things, refuse to answer him, or, do not greet him, or, leave him." Since he said nothing of the sort, you would be innovators if you did that.

Moreover, why have you not refused to answer him who says that the Qurʾān is created? And why have you accused him of unbelief? There is no sound tradition from the Prophet on denying its creation and accusing of unbelief him who says that it is created. They may say: Because Aḥmad ibn Ḥanbal denied that it is created and held that he who says that it is created should be accused of unbelief. One should say to them: And why did not Ahmad keep silent about that instead of discussing it? They may say: Because ʿAbbās al-ʿAnbarī, and Wakīʿ, and ʿAbd al-Raḥmān ibn Mahdī, and so-and-so, and so-and-so, said that the Qurʾān is uncreated, and that he who says that it is created is an unbeliever. One should say to them: And why did not they keep silent about what Muḥammad had not discussed? They may say: Because ʿAmr ibn Dīnār, and Sufyān ibn ʿUyayna, and Jaʿfar ibn Muḥammad, and so-and-so, and so-and-so, said that it is neither creating nor created. One should say to them: And why did not they refrain from saying this, since the Apostle of God did not say it?

And if they refer that back to the Companions, this is sheer obstinacy. For one may say to them: And why did not they refrain from saying that, since the Prophet did not discuss it, and did not say: "Call him who says it an unbeliever." They may say: The *ʿulamāʾ* simply must engage in *kalām* on a new question, so that the ignorant may know how to judge the matter. One should say: This is the admission that we wanted you to make! Why, then, do you hinder [people from engaging in] *kalām?* You use it yourselves when you want to; but when you are silenced [in a discussion], you say: We are forbidden to engage in *kalām*. And when you want to, you blindly and unquestioningly follow your predecessors, without argument or explanation. This is willfulness and capriciousness!

Then one should say to them: The Prophet did not discuss vows and testamentary injunctions, or manumission, or the manner of reckoning the uninterrupted transmission of estates, nor did he compose a book about those things, as did Mālik [ibn Anas] (d. 795), and [Sufyān] ath-Thawrī (d. 778), and ash-Shāfiʿī (d. 820), and Abū Ḥanīfa (d. 767).[17] Hence you are forced to admit that they were deviating innovators, since they did what the Prophet had not done, and said what he had not said explicitly, and composed what the Prophet had not composed, and said that those who maintain that the Qurʾān is created are to be called unbelievers, though the Prophet had not said that.

ʿAbd al-Jabbār's Muʿtazilī Five Principles

Translated by Richard Martin

In another distinctive "vindication of *kalām*," major Muʿtazilī theologian ʿAbd al-Jabbār (d. 1025) prefaces his seminal *Book of the Five Principles* with the following précis of his school's methodological foundations. Not unlike the Ashʿarī text above, this text also sets forth a series of questions and follows up with specific rejoinders according to the Muʿtazilī theological method.[18]

Text

If someone asks: What is the first duty that God imposes upon you? *Respond*: Speculative reasoning that leads to knowledge of God, because He is not known intuitively nor by the senses. Thus, He must be known by reflection and speculation.

Then if someone asks: Why do you say that is obligatory? *Respond:* Because we fear that if we do not come to know Him we will disobey Him and thus we will perish. Therefore, it is obligatory for us to know Him in order to avoid disobedience and to perform obedient acts.

Then if someone asks: Why did speculative reasoning become the first of the duties? *Respond:* Because the rest of the stipulates of revelation (*sharāʾiʿ*, pl. of *sharīʿa*) concerning what [we should] say and do are no good until after there is knowledge of God. Do you not see that it is no good for us to pray without knowing to whom we are to pray?

Then if someone asks: What is the first grace bestowed upon you by God? *Respond:* That is something that I cannot account for. In general, however, He created me a living [being], and provided me with power and physical means. And He perfected my nature and gave me passions and enabled me to enjoy a variety of pleasurable things. Then, He issued me commands and prohibitions so that I could attain the [requisite] level of reward and enter the Heavens. Therefore, it is incumbent on me to establish His existence and to know Him so that I can worship Him, give Him thanks and do what satisfies Him and avoid disobedience toward Him.

Then if someone asks: If reasoning speculatively on the knowledge of God is incumbent then on what do you speculate? *Respond:* On evidentiary proofs.

Then if someone asks: What are the proofs? *Respond:* There are four: rational argument, scripture, the example [of the Prophet] (*Sunna*), and the consensus [of the community]. Knowledge of God can only be gained by speculating with rational argument, because if we do not [first] know that He is truthful we will not know the authenticity of the Book, the *Sunna* and the communal consensus.

Then if someone asks: What is the proof by which speculative reason leads to the knowledge of God? *Respond:* My own being [or: self] and what I observe about [physical] bodies.

Then if someone asks: How can your own being be evidence of God? *Respond:* Because I find my own being in a state of perfection, and it is impossible for me to create something like myself or some parts of myself. Thus, *a fortiori,* as I am unable in my original state of being a drop of sperm to create myself, I know that I have a creator and designer who is good, and who is other than me, and He is God.

Then if someone asks: How does this give proof of God? *Respond:* Because I know that bodies must have motion, rest, contiguity and separation, and these things are contingent. Thus, bodies must be contingent since transitory things are not eternal.

Then if someone says: Tell me all that is necessary for one to know about the fundamentals of religion. *Respond:* There are five fundamentals of religion: unicity; justice; the promise and the threat; the intermediate position; and commanding the good and prohibiting evil. These are the fundamentals on which religion is based. Anyone who opposes them is in great error and may commit unbelief or grave sin because of that. But if you know these fundamentals, it follows that you will have to know about jurisprudence (*fiqh*) and divine legislation (*sharʿīyāt*).

Then if someone asks: What is [God's] unicity? *Respond:* It is the knowledge that God, being unique, has attributes that no creature shares with Him. This is explained by the fact that [a] you know that the world has a creator who created it and that [b] He existed eternally in the past and He cannot perish, while we exist after being non-existent, and we can perish. [c] And you know that He was and is eternally all-powerful and that impotence is not possible for Him. [d] And you know that He is omniscient of the past and present and that ignorance is not possible for Him. [e] And you know that He knows everything that was, everything that is, and how things that are not would be if they were. [f] And you know that He is eternally in the past and future living, and that calamities and pain are not possible for Him. [g] And you know that He sees visible things, and perceives perceptibles, and that He does not have need of sense organs. [h] And you know that He is eternally past and in future sufficient and it is not possible for Him to be in need. [i] And you know that He is not like [physical] bodies, and that it is not possible for Him to get up or down, move about, change, be composite, have a form . . . [ellipsis in original translation] limbs and body members. [j] And you know that He is not like the accidents of motion, rest, color, food or smells. [k] And you know that He is One throughout eternity and there is no second beside Him, and that everything other than He is contingent, made, dependent, structured, and governed [by someone/thing else]. Thus, if you know all of that you know [God's] unicity.

Then if someone says: Tell me about [divine] justice; what is it? *Respond:* It is the knowledge that God is removed from all that is morally wrong and that all His acts are morally good. This is explained by the fact that you know [a] that all human acts of injustice, transgression, and the like cannot be of His creation. Whoever attributes that to Him has ascribed to Him injustice and insolence and thus strays from the doctrine of justice. [b] And you know that God does not impose faith upon the unbeliever without giving him the power for it, nor does He impose upon a human what he is unable to do, but He only gives to the unbeliever to choose unbelief on his own part, not on the part of God. [c] And you know that God does not will, desire or want disobedience. Rather, He loathes and despises it and only wills obedience, which He wants and chooses and loves. [d] And you know that He does not punish the children of polytheists in Hellfire because of their fathers' sin, for He has said: "Each soul earns but its own due" (6:164); and He does not punish anyone for someone else's sin because that would be morally wrong, [and] God is far removed from such. [e] And you know that He does not transgress His rule and ... [ellipsis in original translation] that He only causes sickness and illness in order to turn them to advantage. Whoever says otherwise has allowed that God is iniquitous and has imputed insolence to Him. [f] And you know that, for their sakes, He does the best for all of His creatures, upon whom He imposes [moral and religious] obligations, and that He has indicated to them what He has imposed upon them and clarified the path of truth so that we could pursue it, and He has clarified the path of falsehood so that we could avoid it. So, whoever perishes does so only after [all this has been made] clear. [g] And you know that every benefit we have is from God; as He has said: "And you have no good thing that is not from Allāh" (16:53); it either comes to us from Him or from elsewhere. [h] Thus, when you know [all of] this you become knowledgeable about [God's] justice.

Then if someone says: Tell me about the promise and the threat; what are they? *Respond:* They are the knowledge that God promises recompense to those who obey Him and He threatens punishment to those who disobey Him. He will not go back on His word, nor can He act contrary to His promise and threat nor lie in what He reports, in contrast to what the Postponers (*Murji'a*) hold.

Then if someone says: Tell me about the intermediate position; what is it? *Respond:* It is the knowledge that whoever murders, or fornicates, or commits serious sins is a grave sinner and not a believer, nor is his case the same as that of believers with respect to praise and attributing greatness, since he is [to be] cursed and disregarded. Nonetheless, he is not an unbeliever who can't be buried in our [Muslim] cemetery, or be prayed for, or marry [a Muslim]. Rather, he has an intermediate position, in contrast to the Seceders (*Khawārij*) who say that he is an unbeliever, or the *Murji'a* who say that he is a believer.

Then if someone says: Tell me about commanding the good and prohibiting evil; what are they? *Respond:* Commanding the good is of two types. One of them is obligatory, which is commanding religious duties when someone neglects them, and the other is supererogatory, which is commanding supererogatory [acts of devotion] when someone omits to do them. As for prohibiting evil, all of it is obligatory because all evil is ethically wrong. It is necessary, if possible, to reach a point where evil does not occur in the easiest of circumstances or lead to something worse, for the goal is for evil simply not to happen. And, if it is possible to reach the point where good occurs in the easiest of circumstances, then preferring the difficult [circumstances] would be impermissible. Similarly, God has said: "If two parties among the believers fall into a quarrel, make peace between them; but if one of them transgresses beyond bounds against the other, then fight against the one who transgresses until he complies with the command of Allāh; [then, if he complies, make peace between them with justice, and be fair: for Allāh loves those who act fairly]" (49:9). Thus, prohibiting evil is obligatory only if the view does not prevail that [prohibiting a particular evil] would lead to an increase in disobedience, and [if] a preference for what was harmful were [not] predominant. If such a view does prevail, [prohibiting evil] would not be obligatory, and avoiding it would be more appropriate.

THEOLOGY'S FOUNDATION: PROPHETIC REVELATION

An essential theological theme is that of God's revelation through prophetic messengers. Here we illustrate several aspects of the topic: First, the belief in God's self-disclosure is the bedrock and fundamental "presupposition" of any "theological" activity, as indicated in chapter 1's Qurʾānic texts on the subject. We begin here with the views of a very influential classical philosopher, Avicenna (Ibn Sīnā). Second, evidence of the *truthfulness* of those to whom God first delivered His message is critical to any further argument. Hence the important theme of the prophetic miracle, seen here from an Ashʿarite perspective. Finally, Shīʿī theologians have developed distinctive models for describing how divine communication with humanity has continued in the postprophetic age, as exemplified in the thought of a major Ismāʿīlī thinker.

Avicenna on Assessing Claims to Prophetic Revelation

Translated by Michael E. Marmura

Responding to a request from a friend who expressed misgivings about accepting claims as to the truth of prophetic revelation, the great philosopher-theologian Avicenna (Ibn Sīnā, d. 1037) addresses two large questions. Are such claims logically possible but simply assumed and not adequately proven? Or are they impossible assertions, similar to fairy tales, and therefore not subject to proof by any means?[19]

Text

Anything that inheres in another essentially, exists in it in actuality as long as the latter exists; and anything that inheres in another accidentally, exists in it potentially at one time and actually at another time. Whatever has this essential inherence is always actual and is itself the thing that changes whatever is potential into actuality, mediately or without mediation. An example of this is light, which is the visible in essence and the cause that changes whatever is potentially visible into actuality; and fire, which is the hot in essence and which heats other things, either mediately—as, for example, when it heats water through the mediation of the copper pot—or without mediation—as when it heats the copper pot by itself, I mean by direct contact. Many examples could be given of this. Moreover, if anything is composed of two things, if one of the two can be found without the other, the other can be found without the first. An example of this is oxymel, which is composed of vinegar and honey: if vinegar can be found without honey, honey can be found without vinegar. Another example is the formed statue composed of bronze and the human form: if bronze can be found without the human form, the human form can be found without the bronze. This can be found by induction and has many examples.

I now say: there exists in human beings a faculty by which he is differentiated from the rest of animals and other things. This is called the rational soul. It is found in all persons without exception, but not in all its particulars since its powers vary among people. Thus there is a first power ready to become informed with the universal forms abstracted from matter, which in itself has no form. For this reason it is called the material intellect by analogy with prime matter. It is an intellect in potentiality in the same way that fire in potentiality is a cold thing, not in the sense in which fire is said to have the potentiality to burn. Then there is a second power, which has the capability and the positive disposition to conceive the universal forms because it contains the generally accepted opinions. It also is an intellect in potentiality, but in the sense in which we say that fire has the potentiality to burn. There is, besides these two, a third power that is actually informed with the forms of the universal intelligibles of which the other two form a part when these have become actualized. This third power is called the acquired intellect. It does not exist actually in the material intellect and thus does not exist in it essentially. Hence the existence of the acquired intellect in the material intellect is due to something in which it exists essentially and that causes existence; through it, what was potential becomes actual. This is called the universal intellect, the universal soul, and the world soul.

The reception of whatever possesses essentially the power of being received occurs in two ways, directly and indirectly. The reception from the universal active intellect occurs, similarly, in two ways, either directly—like the reception of the common opinions and the self-evident truths[20]—or indirectly—like the reception of the second intelligibles through the mediation of the first, and of the intelligibles acquired through the mediation of organs and materials such as the external sense, the common sense, the estimative faculty, and the cogitative faculty. Now the rational soul, as we have shown, receives at times directly and at others indirectly; hence the capacity to receive directly does not belong to it essentially but accidentally. This capacity, therefore, must exist essentially in something else whence the rational soul acquires it. This is the angelic intellect, which receives essentially without mediation and by its very reception causes the powers of the soul to receive. (The property peculiar to the first intelligibles that allows their reception without mediation is due only to two factors: briefly, it is because these intelligibles in themselves are easily receivable, or because the recipient can receive without mediation only that which is easily receivable.)

We have also seen that there are different degrees of strength and weakness, ease and difficulty, in that which receives and that which is received. Now, it is impossible for the capacity to receive to be infinite. For there is finitude in the direction of weakness, which consists of the inability of the power to receive even one intelligible, directly or indirectly, and there is finitude in the direction of strength, which consists in the ability of the power to receive directly. [Hence, the affirmation that the capacity to receive is infinite would involve our saying that] it is both finite and infinite in both directions, and this is an impossible contradiction. Moreover, it has been shown that in the case of that which is composed of two things, if one of them can be found without the other, the other can be found without the one. We have also seen that some things receive at one time directly and at other times indirectly. Moreover, we have found that there are things that cannot receive emanations from the [active] Intellect without mediation, while there are other things that receive all the intellectual emanations without mediation; also that when the capacity to receive is finite in the direction of weakness, it is also necessarily finite in the direction of strength. Now the degrees of excellence among the causes run along the lines I say: some individual essences are self-subsisting while others are not, and the first are better. The self-subsisting are either immaterial, essential forms or forms that are in matter, and the first are better. Let us proceed and subdivide the latter group since here lies what we seek: the forms and materials that constitute bodies are either organic [lit., growing] or inorganic, and the first are better. The organic are either animals or not animals, and the first are better. The animals, in turn, are either rational or irrational, and the first are better. The rational either possess reason by positive disposition or do not, and the first are better. That which is rational by positive disposition either becomes completely actual or does not, and the first is better. That which becomes completely actual does so without mediation or through mediation, and the first is better. This is the one called prophet and in him the degrees of excellence in the realm of material forms culminate. Now, if that which is best stands above and rules the inferior, then the prophet stands above and rules all the genera above which he excels.

Revelation is the emanation and the angel is the received emanating power that descends on the prophets as if it were an emanation continuous with the universal intellect. It is rendered particular not essentially, but accidentally, by reason of the particularity of the recipient. Thus the angels have been given different names because [they are associated with] different notions; nevertheless, they form a single totality, which is particularized, not essentially, but accidentally, because of the particularity of the recipient. The message, therefore, is that part of the emanation termed "revelation" that has been received and couched in whatever mode of expression is deemed best for furthering man's good in both the eternal and the corruptible worlds as regards knowledge and political governance, respectively. The messenger is the one who conveys what he acquires of the emanation termed "revelation," again in whatever mode of expression is deemed best for achieving through his opinions the good of the sensory world by political governance and of the intellectual world by knowledge.

This, then, is the summary of the discourse concerning the affirmation of prophecy, the showing of its essence, and the statements made about revelation, the angel, and the thing revealed. As for the validity of the prophethood of our prophet, of Muḥammad, it becomes evident to the reasonable person once he compares him with the other prophets.

Bāqillānī on Prophetic Miracle and Veracity

Translated by Richard J. McCarthy, SJ

A key element in the theology of prophetic authority is God's provision of "evidentiary miracles" in proof of His messengers' authenticity. Many

Muslim theologians have authored studies dedicated to the question of the prophetic miracle (*muʿjiz*). One of the major works on the theme is by an important, and too little-studied, tenth-century theologian of the Ashʿarī school, al-Bāqillānī (d. 1013). Here is a selection from his treatise *Explaining the Distinction between (Prophetic) Miracles and (Saintly) Marvels, Trickery, Soothsaying, and Magic,* introducing Bāqillānī's underlying views on the *muʿjiz,* the highest kind of "miraculous" feat granted only to God's prophets and messengers.[21]

Text

[The] *muʿjiz* is of two kinds. One kind is that over which God alone has power: e.g. the creation of bodies, the quickening of the dead, the healing of the born blind and the leprous, the changing of inert matter into animals, and such things; and this is regarded by the majority of people as the more important and higher type of *muʿjiz.* But the *muʿjiz* may also include that, the like of which and what belongs to its genus can fall within the scope of the powers of creatures: e.g. eloquence in the composition of speech, leaping over seas, carrying the firm-fixed mountains, and such things. This second kind takes place in two ways: one that is little and usual; and the other that is much and unusual, and takes place in a way that is quite opposed to the little. Thus the latter becomes in itself a proof of the veracity of the Apostles when it takes place in that way. It is not that its very genus is a proof in favor of the one claiming the office of [divine] messenger, but its abundance and its taking place in a special way is what proves his veracity against his adversaries. And the like of this is not forbidden in setting forth proofs. Do you not see that a few well-wrought works, and a little movement, and the proffering of a word, and the writing of a letter or two do not prove the knowledge and intention of the agent, but that a great deal of that, taking place in a well-ordered and coherent manner, does prove knowledge and intention and surpasses the little that does not prove that?

Therefore, also, we do not deny that producing a word or two, or a verse or part of a verse, does not prove that such a production is a miracle, although the composition of the like of the Sūra of the Heifer (2) or the Sūra of ʿImrān's Family (3) does prove that such a composition is a miracle violating custom. Similarly, one need not conclude that jumping over rivers and leaping from east to west and mounting into the heavens do not prove the veracity of him at whose hand that appears simply because jumping a span or two or a cubit or two does not prove that. Again, one need not conclude that the carrying off of mountains does not prove the veracity of him who carries them just because the carrying off of a *mithqāl* [tiny bit] or two or of a *raṭl* [equivalent to several pounds] or two does not prove that. For when a great deal of that takes place, it attains to the degree of the violation of custom and is quite different from the occurrence of a small amount. *Mutatis mutandis,* it is the same as the difference between a little done well and a great deal done well in the matter of proving the knowledge of the agent.

Hence one should pay no attention to whether the genus of the miracle falls within the scope of the powers of creatures or does not fall within the scope of their powers, but one must attend only to the particular way in which it takes place. Even if that [be attributable] to superior reasoning and reflection on the difference between the two ways, that is still not like the creation of bodies and quickening the dead, for doubt concerning that is dispelled, and desire to be able to do it vanishes. Since that is so, no one has the right to impugn the miraculousness of the Qurʾān in its eloquent composition and its beauty of form and coherence that surpass all the rhetorical patterns and compositions of the Arabs, simply because people admit that a human being may produce the like of a letter or two, or a word or two, or a verse or part of a verse. For the production of a great deal of that is to be judged quite differently from the production of a little.

If the matter were as they maintain, the outstanding poet and brilliant orator and eloquent letter writer could not be superior to the illiterate and the incorrect speaker and the stammerer and all who could produce a bit of prose. Thus they would be unable to compose a hemistich or a verse of poetry simply because the incorrect speaker of Arabic and the stammerer can produce a word or two and a letter or two and can do a bit of prose discourse. Now this is something on the falsity of which there is general agreement. Moreover it is also agreed that the classes of people versed in all the measures of eloquence are superior to those not so versed, although the non-eloquent person may be able to compose a bit of what the eloquent individual is capable of in prose or some other form. If that be so, it is also false to reject on this score and to impugn the miraculousness of the Qurʾān thereby.

It is also possible to maintain that the miraculousness in the composition and eloquence of the Qurʾān is more important in its kind and greater than the healing of the born blind and the leprous and the quickening of the dead and changing the rod into a snake and similar miracles. For the Brahmins and many other people believe that such things are accomplished simply by means of tricks and manipulations and devices by means of which one may succeed in deception therein. Thus, one may believe that someone who quickened a dead person did not really quicken him after he had died, but that he simply dazed and stupefied him with various kinds of drugs and poisons, so that his movements ceased and he seemed to be dead. Subsequently the period of his stupefaction passed, and the effect of that drug wore off, and perhaps the person gave him something to drink or injected into him something that counteracted the effect of that stupefying drug, and then the individual again began to move and speak, and the onlookers supposed that the individual had quickened the dead man, although that was not the case at all.

The same may be said of the case of raising up a paralytic. For it is not impossible for a man to suppose that there is a medicine that raises up paralytics and that the paralytic rose because of protracted treatment. Similarly, some have believed that there is a remedy that does away with leprosy or checks it if the treatment be prolonged. So it cannot be denied that one may suppose that a person who does away with leprosy in a brief time has come to know a remedy with the property of doing away with that in the twinkling of an eye. The same may also be maintained about mounting into the heavens and leaping over seas, for a person may imagine that that is accomplished in virtue of a trick, just as sleeping on water and swimming in bonds are accomplished by the skillful swimmer in virtue of his knowledge of swimming and subtle cleverness that are lacking in others.

In all this doubts can occur, but there can be no doubt about the eloquence of the Qurʾān. For eloquence is natural and not something that can be acquired; it is based on factors that exist in the soul and are known by the eloquent. Now the Prophet was sent among a people who were the most eloquent of all the Arabs and the greatest and most skillful in the exercise of the arts of speech. These he challenged to produce the like of the Qurʾān, or the like of a single Sūra, and they were absolutely unable to do it. Instead they summoned men to fight and contend with him, things that could not prove that he was lying. For he had not said to them: "The proof that I am lying is that I shall not be fought or overcome or slain"; but he said simply: "The proof that I am lying, if, as you claim, I am lying, will be your producing the like of the Qurʾān or of a single Sūra of it." But instead of the proof that he had proposed they undertook what would not be a proof that he was lying, that is, fighting him. Even if they had overcome him and slain him, that action of theirs would not have proved him a liar; but if they had produced the like of a single Sūra of the Qurʾān, they would have thwarted him and branded him as a liar.

Hence their turning away from the endeavor to produce a Sūra like it to coming forth and fighting against him was a turning away from the stipulated proof and the clearest of proofs that they were unable to produce its like or what would approach and come near it in eloquence. Moreover, had the like of Qurʾānic eloquence been in their power, fighting would not have diverted them from it, just as it did not keep them from composing speeches and verses and *qaṣīdas* (odes) on the very field of battle. For their ability to give expression to such things was not impeded by fighting. So if their ability had included the power to produce the like of the Qurʾān, they would have done so in addition to fighting and giving battle.

Similarly, had they had it in their power to produce what would come near and approach the Qurʾān, they would certainly have turned their minds to it and been most zealous to do it. For the production of what approaches it is very like the production of what exactly rivals it, that being the way it is with eloquence. They knew very well that their eloquent men surpassed one another in eloquence, and that what approaches some specimen of eloquence is virtually equivalent to it, and that the work of the most eloquent is not necessarily a miracle if it be a little superior to the work of those inferior to him. It is the same with the exponents of any art. Some surpass others therein and others are inferior in skill and accomplishment. But no miracle is therefore ascribed to the most skillful, because others are able to produce what approaches and comes near his work.

So if they had been able to produce what would approach the Qurʾān in eloquence, they would have rivaled it and said to him: "This approaches and resembles what you have produced, even though it is a little inferior to it. The slight superiority of your eloquence is not a miracle on your part, but is rather of the same sort as the superiority of Imruʾ al-Qays (6th c.) and his likes over inferior poets, and the superiority of Ziyād and al-Ḥajjāj and their likes over inferior orators. But that is no miracle on their part, for it is well known that people surpass one another in eloquence." Similarly, then, if those people had produced something approaching the Qurʾān in eloquence they would have excluded it thereby from being a miracle of the Apostle. So their turning away from that and busying themselves in fighting him is a proof of the cutting off of their hopes of producing the like of the Qurʾān or something approaching it, and of their consciousness of their personal inability to do that, i.e. the impossibility of doing it.

Another proof that they were powerless to produce anything approaching the composition of the Qurʾān in eloquence is found in this. Had they been able to do that they would have done it straightaway and thereby given rise to doubt and scattered Muḥammad's following. For when something approaches and comes near to another thing it is a difficult and doubtful matter to distinguish and separate it from the other, and it is possible that some will believe that the one is the exact equivalent of the other. If, therefore, he knew that, one able to produce eloquence approaching the composition of the Qurʾān would certainly have produced that eloquence straightaway. For he would have known that it would certainly give rise to disagreement among people, and that many of them would suppose that his production was of equal rank with the Qurʾān in rhetorical perfection and eloquence. Thus that would have been a means of counteracting the Apostle's argument and detaching people from his allegiance. Hence their refraining entirely from that and their refusal to exert themselves to rival little or much of the Qurʾān is the clearest proof that they were unable to produce its like or anything approaching it.

Since that is so, and since eloquence was something natural to them, they could have had no doubt that the eloquence brought by Muḥammad was not something that could be achieved by any artifice whatsoever, like the achievement by tricks of what we have mentioned previously. For they knew that eloquence is something natural and innate, not to be accomplished by artifices and manipulations, just as the poet cannot succeed in being a poet by some sort of artifice and deceit. Hence it must be maintained that the Prophet's sign in the eloquence of the Qurʾān is greater and more effective than all the signs of the Apostles. For some have imagined that what happened to the rod of Moses was accomplished by some sort of artifice, and, similarly, that the quickening of the dead man and the healing of the man born blind and the leper were accomplished by means of artifice and superior knowledge. But eloquence is not something that can be achieved by any sort of artifice, being rather something natural and created. So the eloquence of the Qurʾān, surpassing all the examples of Arab eloquence to such a marked and evident degree, is the most obvious proof that it comes from God!

In the miracle of the Qurʾān there is another outstanding feature not present in any other of the miracles of the Apostles. This is its remaining a perpetual challenge to the adversaries of Muḥammad's prophetic mission to bring its like and their inability to do that. Thus it is a perduring sign, ever present, with no need, for the knowledge of its existence, to be related and handed on by people who might possibly be supposed to be guilty of lying and collusion and conspiracy and the forging of traditions without foundation.

Perhaps, even, many people would [not] believe their report, even though they constituted the strongest kind of tradition well known to be sound by proof, in view of the fact that proofs can be subject to doubt and error. But the ever present existence of the Qurʾān makes it unnecessary to have recourse to transmission and proof of the same. Hence this too is one of its most glorious merits and a reason for its being preferred to other signs and a proof of the error of him who claims that the preceding signs of the Apostles were more noteworthy than the Qurʾān.

Yet a certain theologian has maintained the last mentioned opinion. He justified it by claiming that the reason for the magnitude of those signs is not that preceding Apostles were superior to our Prophet. Rather it is to be ascribed to the excessive ignorance and extreme error of their peoples, and the fact that some of them worshipped Pharaoh for a long time, although he was a man [like other human beings] eating food and walking in the open air markets, and the fact of Christians' worship of the Messiah and their belief that he was a Lord. This was extraordinary ignorance and could only be dispelled by an extraordinary and indubitable contravention of custom.

This same theologian maintained that the minds of these people were not equal to the effort of reasoning about the difference between examples of eloquent speech and the subtler kinds of signs. But the members of Quraysh, among whom the Apostle was sent, had keen minds and sound qualities and excellent understandings, and they were also acquainted with monotheism and the confession of the Creator, Mighty and Glorious, notwithstanding their denial of the resurrection. And "they are a contentious folk" (43:58), as God Himself described them. Hence their intellects and minds had no need of such signs as were required by the worshippers of the Messiah and of Pharaoh and his likes. This theologian also maintained that if anyone had claimed divinity among the Quraysh, they would have made light of his ravings and mocked him and met him with sharp wit and scorn. He maintained that this, then, was the reason why they had no need of such [miracles] as the creation of bodies and the quickening of the lifeless and what was even more contrary to custom and opposed to the natural order.

We have already explained that, in describing and defining the *muʿjiz,* it is better to maintain that it belongs of its essence to the objects of the power of the Lord of the Worlds, Glorious and Mighty, and is not something falling within the scope of any creature's powers. Accordingly, the composition of speech surpassing all other patterns, and movements in the direction of the heavens, and leaping from east to west, and moving freely in the air with no support, and other such things, the genus of which falls within the scope of the powers of creatures, are not [of themselves] miracles. But the miraculousness is to be found in the violation of custom present in empowering them to produce a considerable amount of such things and to acquire it in a way in which it is not customary for them to be so empowered. So the miraculousness consists in their being empowered to produce a quantity that is contrary to custom.

Similarly, if the Apostle challenged his opponents to rise from their places and move their limbs and use their tongues, and they were hindered from doing so while he was empowered to do so, the miraculousness would consist in the violation of what they were accustomed to by the creation in them of impotence and inability to do what they had been challenged to produce of what they were accustomed to be empowered to produce when they wished and desired it. In this case, then, the miraculousness is not to be found in the speech of the Prophet and his rising from his place, but in their being prevented from doing the same, which is a violation of their custom. This opinion is further strengthened and supported by the agreement of the whole community and of all those who follow other religions that it is God Who proves the veracity of His Apostles and distinguishes them from the lying and undertakes to manifest miraculous signs and overwhelming proofs at their hands, and that no one of them can by his own action prove his own veracity.

Since that is so, therefore, the genus of the Prophet's mounting into the heavens and his moving about in the air as freely as a bird and his leaping from east to west cannot be a sign for him. For if he be empowered and enabled to do that, the mounting and leaping are of his own action and belong to the objects of his power. But he cannot prove his veracity by any of his own acts. If he could do that, doubt would ensue, the proof would be vitiated, and we could not be sure but that he had succeeded in effecting this act belonging to the objects of his power by some subtle knowledge and artifice.

If that be impossible, we know that the miraculousness consists simply in God's empowering them to do what He empowers them to do of these things and hindering others from it and violating custom by empowering them to do a great amount of these things in a way in which they are not accustomed to be empowered to do the like. Thus the miracle belongs properly to the objects of the Eternal's power which are peculiar to Him alone, doubt is dispelled, and there is no place for the questions which would arise if the miracle included what falls within the scope of men's powers. For [otherwise] how could you deny that the manifestation of a great deal of what human beings can do was achieved merely by some kind of artifice and subtlety which they had attained by some refinement of thought, although it had escaped others able to produce its like and genus? So this answer that we have described is better and more to the point.

Ṭūsī's Ismāʿīlī Views on Postprophetic Authority

Translated by S. J. Badakhchani

For Shīʿī Muslims, formal teaching authority does not end with the last Prophet. It continues in a succession of spiritual descendants of Muḥammad known as *imāms,* understood in a precise technical sense rather than in the more general sense of "leader." Naṣīr ad-Dīn Ṭūsī (d. 1274) was a major historian and theorist of Shīʿī theology whose view of the relationship between prophets and postprophetic authority provides insights into his community's distinctive views on the subject. Note the underlying historical pattern that pairs each prophet with both a spokesperson (or legatee) and an implacable archetypal enemy.[22]

Text

Concerning the cycles of the six Prophets with authority, from Adam to Muḥammad and the truthful Imams—and the appearance of the mission of the Resurrector, and the proclamation of the mission of Resurrection.

Every Prophet has had a legatee (*waṣī*) in whom the light of the Imamate has been firmly set and established with surety, and to whom the knowledge of prophecy has been temporarily entrusted through trusteeship (*istīdāʿ*). The reason for this legacy is that during the period of each Prophet, the truthful Imams perceived it to be in the best interests of the people to manifest themselves as legatees of that Prophet. Adam's *waṣī* was Seth (*Shīth*), who has been called the son of Adam. The vestiges of knowledge in which Adam was instructed by God and the illumination of those words, by means of which Adam's repentance was accepted [by God], were exclusively his. From the time of Adam that legacy has continued in the progeny of Seth, "offspring, one of another" (3:34), and will continue to the end of the life of the world.

The *waṣī* of Noah (Nūḥ) was Sām (Shem), who has been called the son of Noah.

The *waṣī* of Abraham (Ibrāhīm) was Malik as-Salām, who has been called the son of Abraham.[23]

The *waṣī* of Moses (Mūsā) was Dhū 'l-Qarnayn,[24] who was called Aaron (Hārūn), being more celebrated by that name. Since Aaron was destined to be the *waṣī* of Moses, but he died during Moses' lifetime, and since Moses had to entrust the legacy to the sons of Aaron, and Aaron's two boys were infants, [Moses] charged Joshua (Yūshaʿ bin Nūn) with that legacy and appointed him temporarily with keeping the mysteries of the guardianship, so he might hand that legacy over to Aaron's sons. The wisdom in that was to make clear the benefit of making such an appointment, which is necessary for the succession to continue.

The *waṣī* of Jesus was Maʿadd[25] who is also called Simon of the Rock (Shamʿūn-i Ṣafā', i.e., Simon Peter), being more celebrated by that name.

The *waṣī* of Muḥammad the Chosen was our master ʿAlī.

It is said that after Abraham [the functions of] royalty, prophethood, and religion and the Imamate continued in two lineages. One was the exoteric lineage [through] the progeny of Isaac (Isḥāq), and the other was the esoteric lineage [through] the progeny of Ishmael (Ismāʿīl). While the signs of royalty and prophethood continued to be passed down in the lineage of Isaac, the lights of religion and the Imamate continued in the lineage of our lord Ishmael. Jesus represented the last of those signs that had passed down the lineage of Isaac, and he also attained to the commencement of the divine illuminations that had graced the progeny of our lord Ishmael. Muḥammad the Chosen was a grand spiritual compendium, unifying in himself both the terminus of those signs and the commencement of those illuminations. He was thus unique, without peer in authority, prophethood, majesty and statesmanship, preeminent both in the spirituality of his words and his physical conduct.

Now, every one of the prophets was each pitted against various adversaries and pharaohs, some visible and others hidden. It is well-known among the common folk that Adam's adversary was Iblīs, Noah's adversary was [the idol] Nasr, Abraham's adversary was Nimrūd, Moses's adversary was Pharaoh (Firʿawn), Jesus's adversary was Judas (Yahūdā), and Muḥammad's adversary was Abū Lahab.

The conservation of religious prescriptions of the Prophets was committed into the hands of the real Imams. However, because of the benefits they saw therein, and the divine wisdom they understood therein, they have sometimes effected this conservation through their own sacred selves, and have at other times entrusted it to their vicegerents and other people. Had they always effected this conservation themselves, the spirituality of these religious laws would have always remained firm and all the disagreements [there have been] would never have occurred. But since God has made these disagreements a cause for concord, as Muḥammad has said, "Differences amongst my community are a mercy," they have done whatever they deemed advisable for mankind at that time, and in like manner they have made the continuance of these rules an obligation.

The true Imams have sometimes been called the "son of Adam" or the "son of Noah" or the "son of Abraham." They have maintained this on account of the benefits and relations they have seen to be proper. But in reality, they were neither of the lineage of these Prophets, nor of the progeny of philosophers, nor of the offspring of kings, nor of any other lineage except their own blessed and sacred one.

Since Muḥammad was the Seal of [all the previous] cycles of legislative religions, and the one who began the cycle of the Resurrection, and all religious laws and religions reached their perfection in his religious law and religion, he is likened to the day Friday, which subsumes the five previous days and joins them to Saturday, namely to the Resurrector. In this respect, Saturday or Sabbath serves to symbolize that Resurrector, who is that which is symbolized.

He [the Prophet] has been called the "Seal of the Prophets" because [as has been said], "God, the Blessed, the Exalted, has based His religion on the likeness of His creation, so that they might find His creation a sign indicating His religion, and His religion a sign indicating His unicity."

By the same measure, the pattern of the creation of the divine religious prescriptions corresponds to the pattern of the physical creation. For example, the physical creation of human beings is in six stages: semen, sperm, coagulated blood, the embryo, bone and the whole human form. The creation of the prescriptions of religion likewise was accomplished by six Prophets endowed with revelations: Adam, Noah, Abraham, Moses, Jesus and Muḥammad. From this perspective, the mission of Adam is like the semen, the mission of Noah like the sperm, the mission of Abraham like clotted blood, the mission of Moses like the embryo, the mission of Jesus like flesh and bones, and the mission of Muḥammad like the perfect human form.

Since the creation of legislative religion was thus perfected with Muḥammad and no further perfection was required, he is called the "Seal of the Prophets." There is a full explanation of why he is the "Seal of the Prophets," and that is that every Prophet who preceded him indicated that another Prophet would come after him, declaring that his religious law would reach perfection in that of the next Prophet, but Muḥammad said: "After me will come the Resurrector, and my religious law will reach perfection in his resurrection."

He [Muḥammad] warned mankind and conveyed the glad tidings about the Resurrector who would bring about the Resurrection, and since he was the last herald and conveyor of the glad tidings of the Resurrection, he said: "The Hour and I were sent together, like these two forefingers," meaning that "Both the Resurrector and I have come together like two forefingers that are stretched out beside each other, but I came a little in advance." Since it was intended that there be no further religious law after Muḥammad, and since the mission and religious laws of all previous Prophets were to be terminated by means of his own mission [in summoning people to] the Resurrection, he was thus the Seal of all the Prophets and their various legal codes.

The legal statutes of each Prophet who succeeded the Prophet who preceded him were all aimed at perfecting those previous laws, not their abrogation. But that perfection has, from the exoteric and formal point of view, appeared like abrogation not perfection, because until something is changed from one state to another it cannot be given the form which is the aim of the perfection of that thing. For example, until the sperm changes its state through alteration and modifications, it will not move on from the form in which it is and pass through the stages of coagulated blood, embryo, flesh and bone—in attaining to each of which it moves closer to the soul—and so it will not attain the completeness of the human form.

One must understand the process of perfecting and abrogating (*iṭṭāl*) religious laws in the same manner. If, [for instance], a religious statute instituted by one Prophet remains unchanged and is not followed by another edict instituted by the Prophet who succeeds him, then in the end, the lord of the Resurrection will be unable to exercise his [proper] spiritual authority, and consequently, those who are subject to this [outdated] religious edict will never be able to progress from the way to the aim, from the letter to the spirit, from deceptive similitudes to what is distinctly clear, from relativity to reality, and from legalistic religion to the Resurrection.

The exponents of spiritual exegesis (*aṣḥāb-i taʾwīl*) have said that [the meaning of] those six days mentioned in the Qurʾān (7:54) during which the heavens and the earth were created, refer to the six cycles of the six Prophets with their respective revelations, each cycle corresponding to one day, and every day to one thousand years: "A day of your Lord is as a thousand years of your reckoning" (22:47).

By "heaven" they allude symbolically to exoteric religious commandments pertaining to the body, and by "earth" they allude to esoteric spiritual rules. In other words, the exoteric physical commandments and the esoteric spiritual commandments achieved their completion during the six cycles of the six apostolic Prophets. They also declare that Adam was distinguished by [being taught] the Names, Noah was distinguished by [knowing] their hidden meanings, and Abraham was distinguished by integrating both of these. [Likewise, they say] that Moses was distinguished by [preaching] the exoteric revelation (*tanzīl*), Jesus was distinguished by [his knowledge of] spiritual exegesis (*taʾwīl*), and Muḥammad by his integration of both within himself.

Now, the cycle of Muḥammad was the beginning of the cycle of the Resurrection, and the resurrection is particular to the Imam who is the lord of the Resurrection. Despite the fact that all the Prophets have, from the time of Adam [to Muḥammad], made direct or indirect allusions to the Imam of their time, no Prophet ever announced the sublimity and majesty of the Imam more openly than the Seal of the Prophets. [Among the things he has said is]: "If the earth were devoid of an Imam even for a moment, it would perish with all its inhabitants." In another place, he has said: "He who dies without knowing the Imam of his time, dies the death of an ignoramus."

Throughout the course of the religious mission of the Prophet there are three clear and evident mandates. One pertains to the initial period, during which the truthful master is recognized by means of the divine truth. Another kind of mandate applies to the intermediary period, during which one recognizes the divine truth through the truthful master, and the truthful master through the divine truth. Finally, there is the mandate proper to the final period in which one recognizes the divine truth through the truthful master. [As the Prophet has said], "Recognize the truth and you shall recognize the one who possesses it. ʿAlī is with the truth and truth is with him. May the truth follow him wheresoever he turns." [Thus is summed up] the origin, the intermediate and the final periods.

He [the Prophet also] said, "I was a Prophet when Adam was still between water and clay." This statement has the same meaning alluded by the maxim, "First comes thought, then action," that whatever is initially intended to happen, it being the ultimate purpose and perfection, will in the end become manifest. By the same token, although Muḥammad was chronologically later than all the previous Prophets from Adam to Jesus yet he was the ultimate perfection of all their religious laws, being preeminent and superior in the ranks of nobility over all of them.

It is for this reason that he said, "I have been sent with the comprehensive revelation," that is to say, "All words are comprehended in what I have brought"; and, "I have been sent for your welfare in this world and your salvation in the Hereafter"; and, "I know not what will be done with me or you" (46:9), meaning, "I know not what will be done with me and you until the Resurrection."

When the divine designation and indication of the investiture (*waṣāyat*) of our lord ʿAlī was revealed in the verse, "O Prophet, convey the message that has been sent down to you from your Lord, and if you do not, you will not have delivered the message" (5:70), meaning, "Convey that message for which We sent you and if you do not do, you will not be a Prophet," he immediately entrusted his prophethood to [ʿAlī's] Imamate, thus uniting the religion of law with the [religion of] Resurrection. He announced: "ʿAlī is the lord of all those for whom I am their lord. O God, love him who loves ʿAlī and hate him who hates ʿAlī, support him who supports ʿAlī, and abandon him who abandons ʿAlī, and may the truth follow him wheresoever he turns."

The Prophet established the foundation of his community on seven pillars of religious law.[26] As was explained earlier, since his religious mission was the beginning of the [religion of] Resurrection, it was all [expressed in the form of] creaturely realities consisting of divine mandates, physical substances made from spiritual substances, practical activities based on intellectual realities and relative affairs referring to divine realities. Exponents of spiritual exegesis have assigned a spiritual meaning and truth to each of these pillars [of religion], providing both an abbreviated and detailed explanation of them.

The summary explanation [of these pillars] is that ritual ablutions means to dissociate oneself from previous religious customs and traditions; the confession of faith is to know God through Himself; ritual prayer means to be always speaking with the knowledge of God [in mind]; fasting means to speak with the followers of falsehood with precautionary prudence, and to maintain such fasting continually; alms-giving is to render unto your other brothers in religion that which God Almighty has given you; pilgrimage means to abandon this temporal world and seek the eternal abode; holy war means to annihilate oneself in the Essence of God Almighty.

SIX

Major Themes in Systematic Theology

FOLLOWING UP ON THE THEME of divine disclosure in scripture, and the attendant themes of the need for prophets and proof of their reliability, Muslim systematic theologians have discussed at considerable length and depth questions about who God is and how God "works" in and beyond the world of human experience. Such questions include matters of God's transcendent unity (*tawḥīd*) interpreted as a blend of beauty and majesty; the nature of God's relationship to His creation; what human beings can know about God; the nature and very essence of the divine communication; and the ways believers will experience God hereafter. A look at the distinctively Shīʿī concept of Greater Occultation, and a major Chinese Muslim scholar's pioneering work to translate Islamic themes into Chinese terms complete the chapter.

GOD CREATING: TRANSCENDENT UNITY, ONGOING INVOLVEMENT WITH CREATION

Ibn al-ʿArabī on Divine Majesty and Beauty

Translated by Tosun Bayrak and Rabia T. Harris

Since the beginning of chapter 1, the concept of *tawḥīd,* the affirmation of God's perfect transcendent unity, has been a central theme viewed in some of its many facets from a variety of perspectives. Perhaps it is counterintuitive to begin this chapter with an author whose views have often been rallying points for theological contentiousness. But, love him or hate him, Muḥyī 'd-Dīn ibn al-ʿArabī (d. 1240) has unquestionably kept the larger Islamic discussion about God and divine engagement with the world simmering, occasionally at a rolling boil.[1] His central theme is that "unacceptable behavior in the divine presence is the cause of alienation and expulsion."

According to the Qur'ān, the one unforgivable sin in the eyes of Allāh is *shirk,* the assignment of partners to Him. For Sufis, the crux of *shirk* is an innate tendency to set *oneself* up as of comparable importance to God. The price of *shirk* is thus the loss of unity, since self-absorption in God is impossible. Allāh's majesty in itself prevents self-absorption, for the manifestation of grandeur instantly destroys all pretense. A danger inherent in the nature of human apprehension of beauty is that the moment one sees oneself in Him, rather than ourselves in Him, we have committed the very act that cuts the link. Becoming the object of one's own delight means loss of the beloved. Only *awe* can mitigate the danger of self-glorification, for awe means an authentic awareness of holiness.

Text

Praise belongs to Allāh the Great; His Majesty is part of the manifestation of His Beauty. In His proximity He is the Near; in His loftiness, the Observer. Power, splendor, grandeur, and magnificence are His—He whose essence is great beyond any resemblance to other essences.

His essence is exalted above all motions and stillnesses, all bewilderment and mindfulness. It is too high to be overtaken by any explanation, express or implied, just as it is too great to be limited and described.

It is beyond any physical descent or ascent, any tangible enthronement upon any throne, any haste to seek an object, and—when an object is gained—any satisfaction at reuniting with something that had been missed.

Just so, it is too great to be described in detail or in summary, to be the basis for creeds, to alter with the differences among creeds; to find pleasure or pain in action, or to be qualified with anything but eternity.

It is too great:

- to draw together or be divided,
- for anything that refers to bodies to refer to it,
- for understanding to encompass the core of its reality,
- to be as imagination would describe it,
- to be as wakefulness or dream would seek to perceive it.

It is too great for times and places to hold it, for the permanence of its being to be measured with the passing of months and years, for above and below, right and left, behind and before.

It is too great for denial or confusion to hinder its majesty.

It is too great to be comprehended by intellectual reflection, by the spiritual practices of the masters of illumination, by the knowers' secrets, by the majestic range of leaders' visions—for it is too great to be confined behind veils and curtains and so cannot be comprehended by anything but its own light.

It is too great:

- either to exist in the shape of a human being or to lose anything by the existence of particular essences;
- either to accept an alien condition belonging to the entities it has created or to be defined by negative conditions (though it is confirmed by faith);
- either to be the place of manifestations or to be known as past, present, or future time.

It is too great for the senses to rest upon, for doubt and confusion to affect, for likeness and analogy to comprehend, for material classification, or for the intimacy of the man of knowledge.

It is too great to be the third of three in company.

It is great beyond spouse and parents, beyond there being "a single thing like unto it" (112:4), beyond anything preceding its existence, beyond being attributed limbs, hands, fingers, feet, beyond anything else being with it in eternity.

It is great beyond the laughter and joy promised for the repentance of servants, beyond wrath, beyond habitual wonder, beyond transformation as it is among humankind.

So glory be to Him, mighty in His magnificence, grand in His splendor.

"There is nothing like unto Him, and He is the Hearing, the Seeing" (14:11).

To proceed:

The matter of *jalāl* and *jamāl,* the Divine Majesty and the Divine Beauty, has attracted the attention of the witnesses of truth, the knowers of Allāh among the Sufis. Each of them has spoken of these as was appropriate to his own state. Most, however, have connected the condition of intimacy with

Beauty and the condition of awe with Majesty, and things are not as they have said.

Or rather, to a certain extent, things are just as they have said—that is, Majesty and Beauty are indeed two attributes of Allāh, and awe and intimacy two attributes of human beings. And when the souls of the Knowers witness Majesty they feel awe and diminution; while when they witness Beauty they feel intimacy and elation. Because this is so, the Knowers have equated Majesty with Allāh's overpowering force and Beauty with His mercy; they came to this decision because of what they experienced in themselves.

I wish, if Allāh so wills, to clarify the realities of the two to the extent that Allāh enables me to explain them.

I say, first, that Allāh's Majesty is a relation[2] referring back from Him to Himself, that prevents us from knowing Him. Beauty, though, is a relation referring back from Him to us, and it is this that grants us any knowledge we possess of Him, as well as all revelations, contemplations, and spiritual states. Among us, it has two modalities: awe and intimacy. That is because this Beauty has an exalted aspect and a related aspect. The exalted aspect is called "the Majesty of Beauty," and it is this of which the Knowers speak and which appears to them, though they believe that they are speaking of the first Majesty we mentioned.

For us, this Majesty of Beauty has been linked to the state of intimacy, and the closer, related aspect of Beauty has been linked to the state of awe.

When the Majesty of Beauty manifests to us, we are drawn intimately close. Were it not for this, we would be destroyed, for nothing can continue to exist in the face of Majesty and awe together. Thus Majesty in Him is countered by intimacy in us so that we may keep our balance in contemplation and maintain a mental awareness of what we see, rather than falling into distracted terror.

When Beauty manifests to us here—and Beauty is the welcoming openness of the Truth towards us, while Majesty is its unattainable exaltation over us—then His expansiveness in His Beauty is countered by our state of awe. For, were one expansiveness to be met with another, it would lead to unacceptable behavior, and unacceptable behavior in the divine presence is the cause of expulsion and alienation. On account of this, one of the witnesses of truth who knew its importance said, "Seat yourself upon the prayer-mat (*bisāṭ*) and beware of presumption (*inbisāṭ*)."

Allāh's Majesty acting upon us prevents us from unacceptable behavior in the divine presence, as likewise does our awe at His Beauty and expansiveness toward us.

Therefore, what has been spiritually disclosed to our colleagues is correct. It is their judgment—that Majesty in itself closes and diminishes them and that Beauty in itself opens and expands them—that is in error. So long as the divine disclosure is sound the rest is inconsequential, but Majesty and Beauty, in their essences, are as we have described them.

Know that the Qur'ān encompasses Beauty and the Majesty of Beauty. As for Absolute Majesty, no created being possesses any means of entering into it or bearing witness to it. The Truth has singled it out for Himself. It is the presence in which the Truth sees Himself as He is. Were we to have a means of entering into this, we would possess a comprehensive knowledge of Allāh and all that is with Him, and that is impossible.

And know, brother, that since Allāh Most High possesses two realities and has described Himself with two hands and knows us as two "handfuls," the whole of existence has carried out this rule: there is nothing in existence that does not contain its compensatory opposite (cf. 5:64, 38:75).[3]

Out of all this counterposition, we are here especially concerned with what pertains to the Divine Majesty and the Divine Beauty (and I mean by "Majesty" here the Majesty of Beauty, as mentioned above).

No divine saying related through transmitters from Allāh Most High contains anything indicative of Majesty without its being accompanied by something of Beauty to counter it. It is the same way in all revealed scriptures and in everything.

For example, whenever there is a verse in the Qur'ān that speaks of mercy, it has a sister that speaks of retribution to balance it. Thus His calling Himself "Forgiver of sins, Accepter of repentance" is countered by His calling Himself "Terrible in retribution" (40:3). His saying "Inform My servants that I am All-Forgiving, Most Merciful . . . " is countered by " . . . and that My punishment is the painful punishment" (15:49–50). His saying, "The Companions of the Right, how happy are the Companions of the Right! Amid thornless lote-trees . . . " (56:27–28), is countered by "The Companions of the Left, how wretched are the Companions of the Left! In hot wind and boiling water . . . " (56:41–42). "Faces that day will be radiant" (75:22) is balanced by "Faces that day will be gloomy" (75:24). "On the day when (some) faces will turn white" is balanced by " . . . and (some) faces will turn black" (3:106). "(Some) faces that day will be downcast, laboring, toiling" (88:2–3) is balanced by "(Some) faces that day will be happy and well-pleased because of their striving" (88:8–9). "(Many) faces that day will be bright, laughing, joyous" (80:38–39) is balanced by "(Many) faces that day will have dust upon them, darkness will cover them" (80:40–41).

If you follow this strand through the Qur'ān you will find that all the verses of this type follow this pattern. And it is all for the sake of the two divine watchers [the recording angels of good and bad deeds; see 50:17–18] mentioned in His sayings: "All do We aid, those [who seek this world] as well as these [who seek the eternal] . . . " (17:20); and: "He reveals to it its way of evil and its way of good" (91:8); and His saying about the truthful giver: "We facilitate for him the way to ease" (92:7), which He balances with His saying about the lying miser: "We facilitate for him the way to distress" (92:10).

Ibn Taymīya on God's Perpetual Creativity

Translated by Jon Hoover

Among the more intriguing views of the nature of divine creativity is Ibn Taymīya's (d. 1328) argument that God's interaction with creation is not, as it were, a one-off affair. On the contrary, the Creator continues to be active in maintaining the "universe" in being in most remarkable ways. Here the great Ḥanbalī theologian reflects on the various interpretations of a seminal Hadith on this large question, offering a superb example of theological interrogation of a text of Prophetic Tradition. Note the importance of divine attributes—particularly God's speech—in Ibn Taymīya's discussion. After a typical prefatory prayer, Ibn Taymīya cites Bukhārī's version of the Hadith of ʿImrān ibn Ḥusayn and analyzes its implications with special reference to the views of Fakhr ad-Dīn ar-Rāzī (d. 1209).[4]

Text

[Muḥammad said:] "O People of [the tribe of] Tamīm! Accept the glad tidings!" They said, "You have proclaimed glad tidings to us. Now give us [something]!" He turned to the People of Yemen and said, "O People of Yemen! Accept the glad tidings since the People of Tamīm did not accept them!" They said, "We have accepted [them], O Messenger of God." They said, "We have come to you in order to gain understanding of religion and to ask you about the beginning of this matter." He said, "God was, and there was nothing before Him"—and in one wording, "with Him," and in another wording, "other than Him"—"And His Throne was on the water. And He wrote everything in the Reminder. And He created the heavens and the earth"—and in another wording, "Then, He created the heavens and the earth." Then a man came to me [ʿImrān ibn Ḥusayn] and said, "Catch your camel!" for it had gone away. [So, I started off]; suddenly, the mirage cut in this side of it. "By God, I wish I had left it and not got up."

His statement, "He wrote everything in the Reminder" refers to the Preserved Tablet, as when [God] said, "Indeed, we have written in the Psalms, after the Reminder" (21:105), that is, after the Preserved Tablet. What is written in the Reminder is called a reminder just as that in which [something] is written is called a book, as in His statement, "This is indeed a noble Qurʾān in a hidden book" (56:77–78).

[TWO COMPETING INTERPRETATIONS OF THE HADITH: (I) GOD'S ACTIVITY HAD A BEGINNING AND (II) GOD CREATED THIS WORLD AFTER THE THRONE]

People are of two views concerning this hadith. [I] Some of them have said that what the hadith intends to inform about is that God was existent alone and then He started originating all originating events, as well as to inform about [the following]: that the genus of originating events has a start and that their concrete entities are preceded by nonexistence; that the genus of time has originated outside time and the genus of movements and moved things has originated [in time]; and that God became an agent after not having done anything from pre-eternity until the time at which He started to act, acting not having been possible [before].

Then these are of two views. [Ia] Some of them say that in the same way He began to speak after not having said anything. Speech (*kalām*) was not even possible for Him. [Ib] Others say that speech is something by which He is qualified in a way that He is able to do it, [but] not that He speaks by His will and His power. Rather, [speech] is something necessary with His essence, apart from His power and His will.

[Ib1] Then some of these say that [His speech] is the meaning, apart from the recited words, and He expressed it by each of [the following]: the Torah, the Gospel, the Psalms, and the Furqān ("criterion" i.e. Qurʾān). [Ib2] Others say that, on the contrary, it is letters and sounds, that are necessary with His essence from eternity to eternity, all the words of the Books that He sent down, and other than that.

[II] The second view concerning the meaning of the hadith is that this was not the Messenger's intent. Rather, the hadith contradicts this. His intent was to inform about the creation of this visible world that God created in six days, after which He sat on the Throne, just as the great Qurʾān informs about this in more than one place (see 7:54, 10:3, 25:59). He [also] said, "He it is who created the heavens and the earth in six days, and His Throne was on the water" (11:7).

It has been established in the *Ṣaḥīḥ* of Muslim, from ʿAbd Allāh ibn ʿAmr [ibn al-ʿĀṣ], from the Prophet, that he said, "God determined the determinations of created things fifty thousand years before He created the heavens and the earth, and His Throne was on the water." [The Prophet] informed of the determination [fifty thousand years earlier] of the creation of this created world in six days, and that at that time His Throne was on the water. So too, the Qurʾān and the previous hadith that Bukhārī transmitted in his *Ṣaḥīḥ* from ʿImrān have informed about this.

Pertaining to this is the hadith that Abū Dāwūd, Tirmidhī, and others have transmitted from ʿUbāda ibn aṣ-Ṣāmit, from the Prophet, that he said, "The first thing God created was the Pen. He said to it, 'Write!' It said, 'What shall I write?' He said, 'What will be until the Day of the Resurrection.'" He created this Pen when He commanded it the written determination fifty thousand years before the creation of the heavens and the earth. It was created before the creation of the heavens and the earth; it was the first thing created of this world; and its creation was after the Throne, as the texts indicate. This is the view of the majority of the *salaf* [i.e., the early Muslims]. I have mentioned the views of the *salaf* in another place. The point here is to clarify what the texts of the Book and the *Sunna* indicate.

[PROOF FOR THE SECOND INTERPRETATION: GOD CREATED THIS WORLD AFTER THE THRONE]

[Aspect 13: Some like Fakhr ad-Dīn ar-Rāzī got confused between the irrational views of the philosophers and the *kalām* theologians. Contrary to the philosophers, reason dictates that originated things come into existence in time after not existing, and, contrary to the *kalām* theologians, reason dictates that God could not have become an agent after not having been one without a cause. The rational view is that God in His perfection has been perpetually creating individual things, each of which is originated and preceded by nonexistence. The philosophers, by conjoining enacted things to God eternally, strip God of His activity.]

The thirteenth aspect is that error concerning the meaning of this hadith [derives] from not knowing the texts of the Book and the *Sunna,* and moreover, what has been reasoned clearly. This has made many thinkers and their followers fall into confusion and go astray. They knew of only two views: the view of the eternalist [philosophers] speaking of the eternity [of the world] and the view of the Jahmī [*kalām* theologians] who say that He had been stripped (*muʿaṭṭal*) [of His ability] to act or speak by His power and His will from eternity. They saw that the necessary concomitants of either view entailed its corruption and its contradiction. So, they remained confused, doubting, and ignorant. This was the state of an uncountable number of them. Some of them even clearly stated this about themselves. For example, [Fakhr ad-Dīn] ar-Rāzī and others stated it clearly.

Among the greatest reasons for this is that they looked into the reality of what the philosophers were saying and found that the concretized, enacted thing had been conjoined with the Agent pre-eternally and post-eternally. Clear reason requires, [however], that the Agent must inevitably precede His act. Positing something enacted by the Agent together with positing that it has been conjoined with Him from eternity [in such a way that] the Agent did not precede it—rather, it is with Him pre-eternally and post-eternally—is a matter contradicting clear reason. It has been firmly established in [our] natural constitutions that for something enacted to be a created thing requires that it be after it was not. Therefore, what God informed of in His Book, namely, that He created the heavens and the earth, is among the things that make all creatures understand that [the heavens and the earth] originated after they were not. As for positing their being with Him from eternity, despite their being created by Him, [our] natural constitutions deny this. And no one has said this except a very small group of eternalists such as Ibn Sīnā and those like him. As for the great majority of the eternalist philosophers, such as Aristotle and his followers, they did not say that the [celestial] spheres were caused by an efficient cause, as [Ibn Sīnā and those like him] say. Moreover, even though the view of [Aristotle and his followers] was more corrupt than the view of those who came later, they did not oppose clear reason on this point—which [the later ones] opposed—although they opposed it from other angles.

And [then those like Rāzī who got confused] looked into the reality of what the Jahmī and Qadarī *Kalām* theologians and those who followed them were saying, found that the Agent became an agent after He was not an agent, without anything originating to necessitate His being an agent, and saw that clear reason requires that since He became an agent after He was not an agent, something must inevitably have originated. [They also saw] that it is impossible in reason that [being an agent] became possible after it was impossible without origination, that no cause necessitates the occurrence of a time of origination at the time of origination, and that origination of the genus of time is impossible.

So, they came to suppose that if they synthesized [the *kalām* theologians with the philosophers], synthesis of the two contradictories would follow necessarily, namely, [I] that the Agent is before the act and [II] that it is impossible for Him to become an agent after He was not [one], in which case the act is with Him, so that the act is [at once] [II] conjoined and [I] not conjoined—that is, being after it was not, originating [in time], preceded by nonexistence. It is impossible from this perspective [II] that the act of the Agent be preceded by nonexistence. [On the contrary] it is necessary in the first perspective [I] that the act of the Agent be preceded by nonexistence. So, they found their intellects unable to cope with what the latter affirmation [I] makes necessary and what the former negation [II] makes necessary. The synthesis of two contradictories was impossible, and so this made them fall into confusion and doubt.

One of the causes of this is that they did not know the reality of tradition and reason. They did not know what the Book and the *Sunna* indicated, and concerning the intelligibles, they did not distinguish between ambiguous things. That is to say, reason differentiates between the Speaker speaking one thing after another perpetually and the Agent doing one thing after another perpetually and the units of act and speech. So, [reason] says that every one of His acts must inevitably be preceded by the Agent and be preceded by nonexistence. It is impossible that the concretized act should be with the Agent pre-eternally and post-eternally. As for the Agent having committed one act after another from eternity, this is part of the perfection of the Agent.

Since the Agent is living, and [since] it is said that life makes acting and movement follow necessarily—as the imams of the Hadith experts such as Bukhārī, Dārimī and others have said, and [since, moreover, it is said] that He has been speaking when He wills and what He wills and such like from eternity—as Ibn al-Mubārak, Aḥmad [ibn Ḥanbal] and other imams of the experts of Hadith and *Sunna* have said—then His being speaking or acting is among the necessary concomitants of His life. Now His life is a necessary concomitant of Him; so, He has been speaking and acting from eternity. Together with [this, however, goes] the knowledge that the Living speaks and acts by His will and His power and that this necessitates the existence of one word after another and of one act after another. The Agent precedes every one of His acts, and this necessitates that everything other than Him be originated and created. We do not say that He was at any moment without power until He created. Whoever does not have power is [indeed] impotent. We say, rather, that God has been knowing, powerful, and sovereign from eternity, without anything being similar to Him, and without [defining] any modality. With God none of the things He does are eternal with Him. No, on the contrary, He is Creator of everything; everything other than Him is a creation of His, and every created thing is originated, being after it was not, even if it is assumed that He has been creating and acting from eternity.

As it is said that creating is an attribute of perfection (*ṣifāt kamāl*) because of His statement, "Is He who creates like one who does not create?" (16:17), is it not possible that His creativity is perpetual (*khāliqīyatuhu dā'iman*), everything created by Him is originated and preceded by nonexistence, and nothing eternal is with God? This is more profoundly perfect than being stripped [of attributes and] unable to act, and then becoming powerful such that acting [becomes] possible for Him without a cause.

As for making the concretized, enacted thing conjoined with Him pre-eternally and post-eternally, this is in reality stripping away His creating and His acting. For the Agent's being conjoined with the thing He does pre-eternally and post-eternally conflicts with clear reason. Even if these eternalist philosophers claim that they establish the perpetuity of agency (*dawām al-fā'ilīya*), they are, in reality, stripping away the agency, even though it is the attribute that is the most obvious of the Lord's attributes and therefore, information about it comes in the first of what He sent down to the Messenger.

Indeed, the first thing [He revealed] is: "Recite! In the name of your Lord who created, created the human being from a blood-clot. Recite! And your Lord is the most generous, who taught by the Pen, taught the human being what he did not know" (96:1–5). He spoke of creation in the absolute, and then He spoke in particular of the human being. He spoke of teaching in the absolute, and then He spoke in particular of teaching by the Pen. Creation includes what He does, and teaching includes what He says. For He teaches by His speaking, and His speaking is by revelation, by speaking from behind a veil, and by sending a Messenger who by His authorization reveals what He wills (cf. 42:51). He said, "He taught you that which you did not know" (4:113). He said, "And whoever disputes with you concerning Him after the knowledge that has come to you" (3:61). He said, "Do not be in haste with the Qur'ān before its revelation to you is completed, and say, "My Lord! Increase me in knowledge!" (20:114). He said, "The All-Merciful, He taught the Qur'ān. He created the human being. He taught him the Explanation. The sun and the moon follow a computation" (55:1–5).

What these philosophers say implies in reality that He did not create and did not teach. What they do establish with respect to creation and teaching indeed implies only stripping away [His attributes] (*taʿṭīl*). According to what they say, the [celestial] sphere has been conjoined to Him pre-eternally and post-eternally. Thus, it is then impossible that it be something enacted by Him, since the Agent must inevitably precede His act. For them, He knows none of the particulars of knowledge. Now, teaching is a branch of knowledge, and it is impossible for someone who does not know particulars to teach them to someone else. Moreover, every existent is particular, not universal. Similarly, the existence of universals is only in minds, not in concrete things. If He knows none of the particulars, He knows none of the existents. So, it is impossible that He teach someone else any knowledge of concretized existents. The view of those of them who said that He knows neither the universal nor the particular is viler.

As for those who said that He knows the established universals (*al-kullīyāt ath-thābita*) but not the mutable things (*al-mutaghayyira*)—for them, He does not know any of the originating events, and He does not teach them to any of His creatures, just as what they said requires that He did not create them. According to their view, therefore, He did not create and He did not teach. This is the reality of what their leader Aristotle said. For he did not establish that the Lord is Originator (*mubdiʾ*) of the world, and he did not make Him an efficient cause (*ʿilla fāʿila*). Instead, what he established was that He is a final cause (*ʿilla ghāʾīya*): the [celestial] sphere moves in order to assimilate itself to Him, like a beloved moving a lover. He plainly stated that He does not know things. So, for him, He did not create or teach. However, the first thing God sent down to his Prophet Muḥammad was, "Recite! In the name of your Lord who created, created the human being from a blood-clot. Recite! And your Lord is the most generous, who taught by the Pen, taught the human being what he did not know" (96:1–5).

Javanese Admonitions of Seh Bari *on God's Perpetual Creativity*

Translated by G. W. J. Drewes

Three hundred years later and thousands of miles east, an intriguing Javanese text offers a very different approach to the question of the nature of divine creativity. The main character in this unusual literary conceit, Seh (Shaykh) Bari, is a teacher in a noted Indonesian school of mystical tradition. Seh Bari describes how he took three Sufi teachers suspected of incorrect views on God's creativity to see the great eleventh-century Baghdadi Sufi and theologian Ghazālī (d. 1111) in hopes of setting them straight. In this fanciful dialogue within a dialogue, Seh Bari's disciples ask him questions, and he responds by offering his recollections of Ghazālī's interaction with the wayward Sufis. Tradition then adds a third layer of credibility by suggesting that Seh Bari's disciple who wrote down the whole exchange was none other than Sunan Bonan (d. 1525), one of the "Nine Friends of God" credited with Islamizing the Indonesian archipelago—never mind the multiple chronological discrepancies. We begin here with Ghazālī's interrogation of the first of the three errant Sufis as to their views that *there was a time when God did not create.* Note the importance of the divine names in the discussion.[5]

Text

Shaykh Ṣūfī answered: Imam Ghazālī! It is not my opinion that my words: The Lord did not create, should be taken at their face-value. They should be interpreted as being the utterance of the mystic whose being, sight and speech are submerged by the Being of Allāh, and therefore I say: Allāh the most high did not create.

Imam Ghazālī said: Shaykh Ṣūfī! You are an infidel according to the four [Sunnī legal] schools, because your doctrine detracts from the attributes of the Lord. Because you attribute non-existence to or minimize the attributes of the Lord your words have been branded as heretical. You will have it that they are to be interpreted as a mystic utterance, but the mystic would not speak in this vein. For with the mystic it is as expressed in the words, "He does not know of his servantship, does not see it or have remembrance of it." In other words, the mystic is unconscious of his own being, oblivious of his own speech and sight and has no knowledge of the Lord [as a separate being]. This is the meaning of the words: realized, overpowered, replaced, blotted out as regards existence, speech and sight, as it is only by the mercy and the grace of the Lord that one is granted annihilation. That is what the mystic is like, and not what you said, detracting from the attributes of the Lord because you are tainted by the heresy of the Muʿtazila.

Imam Ghazālī asked further: Shaykh al-Jaddī, what are the contents of your doctrine?

Shaykh al-Jaddi answered: Imam Ghazālī! My doctrine that Allāh the most high did not create, applies to Him *before* He created the Apostle [Muḥammad] or anything else. Tablet and Pen, Throne and Seat, Heaven and Hell and the atmosphere did not exist, and after all these things have vanished this condition will continue itself [i.e., God will not create further]. There will only be the Lord alone without anything beside Him, and not creating. This is the phase of the Absolute Essence, Nothingness itself. This is what is meant by He alone, the Ruler in His Realm, the Exalted One in His exaltedness. Then, manifesting Himself in the being of Muḥammad He willed His works and became manifest in the universe.

Then Imam Ghazālī—to whom was granted deep wisdom and who while still in his mother's womb was shown the preserved Tablet and was authorized to draw up the principles of mysticism—said: Shaykh al-Jaddī! You are an infidel according to the four schools, because to the Being of Allāh the most high who is willing and creating from all eternity you apply the epithet "dull" and call him idle, not yet willing or active. So you attribute a temporal character to the attributes of the Lord; that is your unbelief. Should it rest with me to kill you, I would hang you upside down and kill you by the sword. Your words are thoughtless to the extreme, for the attributes of the Lord are far exalted above your teachings.

Allāh and all his attributes are from all eternity. Before this universe came into existence there was only the Being of Allāh, prior, everlasting and transcendent, with all His attributes. He is without equal, prior, immaterial, loving, eternally creative; without beginning, end or change. The attributes of the Lord being subtle, everlasting and exalted, the Being of Him who is possessed of these eternal attributes cannot be said to have not yet or already created the universe.

This Being, immaterial and willing, is eternally creative, as His attributes are that He is *ʿālimu 'l-maʿlūm* (omniscient); *khāliqu 'l-makhlūq* (the creator of creation); *qāhiru 'l-maqhūr* (almighty); *qādir al-māqdūr* (the author of all things subject to this power); *kun fa-yakūnu* (Be, and it is). How could there be question of after or before He created, as His Being is possessed of eternal attributes; exalted in His exaltedness; ruling in His realm; one in His unity and praised by Himself. And after the Universe has come into existence He is still the same; His Being is not different after and before the creation of the world; it remained His Being that is prior and everlasting, immutable, transcendent, ruling without change or alteration.

Thereupon Imam Ghazālī said to Shaykh Nūrī: Shaykh Nūrī! What is the meaning of your doctrine that there was a time when the Lord had not [yet] created?

Shaykh Nūrī said: Imam Ghazālī! What I mean is that the universe was not created by the names but by the works.

Imam Ghazālī answered: Shaykh Nūrī! Your opinion is unbelief. For would names and attributes pertain to two different entities? The Being of the Lord is eternally creative; all His attributes are creative, as they are not different from His Being. All that exists is in conformity with its [archetypal] idea in God's knowledge, and the reverse. So how could there be room [for plurality], as Being as such is one and not two, His attributes are the attributes of the Essence, His works are the works of the Essence? Actually names are of two categories: the names of the attributes and the names of the Essence, on the understanding that all His distinct attributes are not different from His Essence. As to Creator and creation, these are certainly two undifferentiated entities.

Imam Ghazālī said further: Shaykh Ṣūfī, Shaykh al-Jaddī and Shaykh Nūrī! Your opinion is wrong. You are unbelievers according to the four schools.

Then the three teachers requested that Imam Ghazālī make them repent of their errors, but Imam Ghazālī answered: I cannot make saints repent of their errors. You had better repent personally to the Lord and abandon your heretical views. Should you not do that, then may the Lord depose you from your saintly rank. May all your relatives renew their faith and their marriages; make them see the error of their ways.

I heard the prophet of Allāh saying while addressing me: Imam Ghazālī! Should anybody speak as follows: "The Being of Allāh knows no love and does not love, and neither He nor His names are creative," then he denies the mercy of the Lord and confuses His distinct attributes. But, Imam Ghazālī, do not hesitate to brand as an infidel anybody who attributes God's attributes to something different from Him or detracts from these. Such a man is outside the fold of Islām. Allāh orders him to look for another Lord and a guide other than the prophet Muḥammad, if he does not abandon and repent of his heretical doctrine. This is to make you of the right opinion.

My friends! These were the words Imam Ghazālī spoke to me and the three teachers.

GOD REVEALING

Ibn Qudāma on the Divine Voice

Translated by George Makdisi

Among the various divine attributes and acts about which theologians and philosophers contended, one of the most important in this context has been the need to understand what it means to claim that God "speaks" in the first place. As the following "Traditionalist" approach to the question indicates, a prime concern about the nature of the language used to describe the deity is that of asserting a truth about God without descending into simple anthropomorphism, on the one hand, or reducing divine elocutions to "mere metaphor," on the other.

Major contributions to classic Islamic theological literature take their stand by explicitly disputing the methods and conclusions of the proponents of a host of systematic positions. One such work is that of Ḥanbalī thinker Muwaffaq ad-Dīn ibn Qudāma (1146–223). Born near Jerusalem, Ibn Qudāma received most of his education in Baghdad. After several teaching stints in Damascus and a military enlistment during the second Crusade, he died in Damascus. Among his major extant works is the *Refutation of Ibn ʿAqīl,* composed in Damascus to set the record straight as to the errors in the early Muʿtazilite-influenced work of Ibn ʿAqīl (1040–119), even though Ibn ʿAqīl had recanted in 1072 and thereafter became an exponent of Ḥanbalī thought. In the following excerpt, Ibn Qudāma analyzes Ibn ʿAqīl's excesses in his original denial that God "speaks" in revealing the Qurʾān—an important aspect of the theological theme of divine attributes and acts.[6] Ibn Qudāma's preface includes the disclaimer that he critiques the *repudiated* views of a fellow Muslim out of an abundance of caution, since in fact some of his contemporaries have come under the influence of Ibn ʿAqīl's pre-recantation views and need to be disabused of those notions. Ibn ʿAqīl thus stands as a salutary example of how the wiles of the Muʿtazilites can catch an otherwise sincere Muslim unawares.

Text

Our answer to this denial is as follows: It has been established that Moses heard the words of God from God Himself without any intermediary. Indeed, if he had heard it from a tree or a stone or an angel, then the Israelites would have been superior to him in this regard; for they had heard it from Moses, the Prophet of God, and Moses is superior to the tree and the stone. Why then was Moses given the epithet of "he who is spoken to by God?" And why did God say: "O Moses! I have chosen you above the people with My messages and My speaking to you?" (7:144) and again: "When he came to it, he was called to: 'Moses! I am your Lord'" (20:12). Now no one would say this to him except God.

Since this is certain, then the divine voice is that which was heard, and of which the audibility is feasible. Furthermore, reference to the divine voice has been explicitly made in the traditions that have come to us. ʿAbd Allāh (d. 903), son of the Imam Aḥmad [Ibn Ḥanbal], has said: "I once said to my father: 'Father, the Jahmīya claim that God does not speak by uttering a voice.' He replied: 'They lie; they simply occupy themselves with the science of divesting God of His attributes.' Then he said: 'I heard ʿAbd ar-Raḥmān ibn Muḥammad al-Muḥāribī (d. 810), who had it on the authority of Sulaymān ibn Mihrān al-Aʿmash (d. 765), on the authority of Abū 'ḍ-Ḍuḥā, on the authority of Masrūq (d. 682), on the authority of ʿAbd Allāh, say: 'When God gives utterance to revelation, the people of heaven hear His voice.'" Sijzī has said: Among the relators of this tradition there is not a single Imam who is not approved; and it has been related with a chain of transmitters going back to the Apostle of God.

In the tradition transmitted by ʿAbd Allāh ibn Anīs (al-Juhanī, d. 673), it is related that God will call to the people on the Day of Resurrection with a voice that will be heard by him who is far as well as by him who is near: "I am the King! I am the Requiter!" This is a well-known tradition. It is also related in the traditions that Moses, when called to by his Lord (e.g., 79:16), "O Moses!" answered quickly, rejoicing in the divine voice, and saying: "At your service! At your service! Where are You? I hear your voice, but I see not where You are." God replied: "O Moses! I am above you, and to your right, and to your left, and to the front of you and to the back of you." Then, knowing that this attribute cannot belong except to God, he answered: "So are You, O my Lord!" It is also related that Moses, upon hearing thereafter the words of humans, loathed them, so great was the impression remaining in his ears at hearing the words of God.

[Ibn ʿAqīl's] statement that "the divine voice is a burst or a crack in the air," is sheer raving, and an empty assertion, the soundness of which is not attested by any prophetic tradition; nor has he any tradition from the Companions concerning it; nor has he furnished an argument for it; nor is he on the right track with regard to it. Suppose now that he were to be told, "we do not concede that it is so," what then would his argument be? Were he to say, "This is the terminology of us speculative theologians," we would reply: "This is very far from what is right and much closer to what is wrong. For you people have cast away the Book and the *Sunna,* and have become aloof from God and His Apostle; you are in nowise assisted by God towards the right, nor directed towards the truth; what you say is not accepted, nor is your terminology heeded." Should he then say, "This is a definition, and definitions cannot be denied," we would answer: "Why not? Have you ever heard of an assertion that constrains the adversary's submission to the bare mention of it, without manifestation of its soundness, or furnishing evidence in its support?" Should he reply, "It is impossible to furnish evidence in support of it," our retort would be: "This, then, is an admission of inability to furnish its proof, and of ignorance of its soundness. If you do not know its proof, by what means then did you recognize its soundness?" He who admits ignorance of the soundness of what he says, spares others the trouble of determining it, and admits to them his ignorance and the falsity of his assertion. Now how can an assertion be referred to that cannot be known to be sound or false? How will his adversary submit to him regarding that in which he admits blindness of mind and ignorance?

It is strange that these speculative theologians—may God blind their faculties of understanding more so than He has already done!—claim that they are not satisfied except by decisive proofs and convincing arguments, and judge that the traditions—which they assert to be traditions transmitted by a single traditionist—do not convey certain knowledge; then they adduce arguments such as this that does not prove anything at all, neither manifestly nor by way of certainty. On the contrary, it is but sheer blindness and raving that he fabricates from his own mind and brings forth from the scum of his stomach. When he is denied it and asked to prove its soundness, he has nothing with which to prove it except, "We have already adopted as a rule that definitions cannot be denied." Now do you think that since God has blinded their eyes and the perceptive faculties of their mind, that they suppose we will accept from them their bare assertion and follow them in their blindness? Their case is simply that of a blind man who is urinating on a roof, facing the people with his pudendum, and supposing that no one sees him, since he himself is incapable of seeing his own person.

We say further: On the contrary, the voice is that of which the audibility is feasible. This is the sound definition attested by experience. For the voice has always been qualified by audibility; and the relation of audibility to the voice is the same as that of visibility to things visible. Moreover, the adjoining of the voice to God has been firmly established by sound prophetic tradition, and the Prophet knows more about God and is more truthful than the speculative theologians who have neither knowledge, nor religion, nor the blessings of the present world nor of the world to come. They are simply the worst of mankind, of whom *zandaqa* (free-thinking) is the predominant quality. God has inspired the hearts of his servants with repugnance towards them, rendering them an object of hatred to them.

Moreover, even if it should be established with certainty that the voice in the case of things perceived by the senses, be the result of the clicking movements of the throat, why should it be thus in the case of the attributes of God? Their assertion is: "That which can be established with certainty with regard to ourselves, can be established in like manner with regard to that which is *absent.*" And our answer is: "You are wrong for three reasons."

First: Your calling of God by the name of *Absent,* though the names of God and His attributes are only known by means of the Law. But you—may God remove you far from prosperity!—could not find for God a single name, among ninety-nine names, with which you could call Him, so that you had to invent a name for Him on your own authority! Besides, God has denied this attribute of Himself, for He has said: " . . . and We were not absent" (7:7).

Second: You have reverted to *tashbīh*-anthropomorphism, the rejection of which is your main support in refuting the Book of God and the *Sunna* of His Apostle; and you have caused God to follow the analogy of His servants, and be comparable to them in His attributes and names. Now this is the very essence of *tashbīh*-anthropomorphism!—May God curse you!

Third: This anthropomorphism is false as regards the rest of the attributes of God that you have conceded, namely, hearing, sight, knowledge and life. These attributes cannot exist in our case except in consequence of certain instruments. Thus hearing exists because of a perforation; sight, because of an iris; knowledge, because of a mind; and life exists in a body. Moreover, all of the attributes cannot exist except in a body; therefore, if you say that it is the same in the case of the Creator, you are guilty of *tajsīm* (embodiment)- and *tashbīh* (imputed likeness)-anthropomorphism, and have become unbelievers. On the other hand, if you should say, "the divine attributes do not require a body," then why were they required in the present case?

However, that which has been firmly established by the Book and the *Sunna* cannot be put aside by the sheer raving of your spokesman (*mutakallim*), nor shall we desert the doctrines of the Apostle of God for those of a meddlesome heretical innovator. We will not accept their doctrines [i.e., those of the *mutakallimūn*] in matters that find no support in revealed scripture or in prophetic tradition. In our eyes, they have neither honor nor dignity. How are we to consent to the nullification of the Book and the refutation of the *Sunna* despite our clinging to them, our adhering to them, our holding fast to them, and the eagerness of our desire for them, in the manner of him who is persuaded that salvation consists in adhering to them, perdition in abandoning them, transgression and the lack of divine preservation in opposing them?—We beseech God to grant us that we keep steadfastly to them during our life, and after our death, until the day when we shall meet Him, so that He may recompense us for our steadfastness and place us in the company of the Prophet who announced them.

He argues falsely when he asserts that the following statement [from Abū Dāwūd's Hadith] constitutes *tashbīh*-anthropomorphism; namely, that when God speaks, there is a sound in the heavens "similar to the sound that results from dragging a chain on smooth rocks." Such an assertion constitutes an objection against the Master of Apostles, Muḥammad, the truthful and trustworthy Apostle of God, as well as an accusation of *tamthīl*- and *tajsīm*-anthropomorphism leveled against him. Whoever does this has deserted the orthodox faith. But the matter is not as this faithless forger of false accusations asserts it to be; he has but simply been deceived by the evilness of his purpose and the paucity of his understanding.

How many persons have censured a valid statement,
Whose censure was the result of meager understanding!

Now the above comparison has nothing to do with the thing heard. It is simply the comparison of one hearing with another hearing; that is to say that our hearing of the sound of a chain over smooth rocks would be like our hearing of the divine voice. This comparison is akin to the one that the Prophet made in this other tradition: "Truly, you shall see your Lord as you see the full moon, you shall not gather together in order to see Him"; that is to say that your seeing of your Lord is like your seeing of the full moon, in that the full moon is such that it can be seen by all, not by some to the exclusion of others. This now is the case of one who is about to break his fast; in order to do so, he does not need to join ranks with other fasters in order to see the full moon, as is the case in the seeing of the crescent, at which time they gather together so that he who sees it points it out to him who does not. But the seeing of the full moon is not done in this manner. For this reason, the tradition has been related with the two variants of *you will not be harmed,* from the root *DYM,* and *you will not gather together,* from the root *DMM.* Now the present case likewise involves a comparison of one hearing with another hearing, and not of one thing heard with another thing heard.

He who seeks the truth, God will direct him to that which is right, and wisdom and useful knowledge will accrue to him as a result of the words of God and those of His Apostle. But he who seeks other than the truth, God will cause him to be blind to the right direction, and the Qur᾿ān and *Sunna* will then become, for him, false arguments by means of which he will go astray. God has said: "We send down, through the Qur᾿ān, that which is healing and mercy to the believers and which only adds to the perdition of the unjust" (17:82). Similar to this is the sun's light that brightens the way for him who has good sight; but he whose sight is weak, and his eye diseased, will be increased in weak-sightedness by its light and caused to become blind. The poet has said:

Knowledge, for the sensible person, is an enhancement,
But for the weak-minded fool, a defect;
Just as daylight to the perception of humankind
Adds brightness, and blinds the eyesight of bats.

Jāmī on God's Voice

Translated by Nicholas L. Heer

Three and a half centuries later, a prominent member of the Naqshbandī Sufi order named ʿAbd ar-Raḥmān Jāmī (1414–92) took up the theme of the "divine voice" from a different perspective. Better known for his exquisite Persian mystical poetry and a widely popular hagiographical anthology, Jāmī had a solid grounding in classical religious studies. After he had penned his greatest literary/mystical works, an Ottoman sultan asked him to put the theological views of important Sufis into broader intellectual perspective by comparing them to the positions of major theologians and philosophers. Jāmī's response was his Arabic *Precious Pearl* (*Ad-Durrat al-fākhira*). Here he examines key issues concerning God's "voice." Jāmī includes substantial quotations from Ghazālī, Muḥyī 'd-Dīn ibn al-ʿArabī, and the latter's most renowned student, Ṣadr ad-Dīn al-Qūnawī (d. 1274).[7]

Text

ON HIS SPEECH (*KALĀM*)

The proof that He is a speaker (*mutakallim*) is the consensus of the prophets concerning that. It is related about them by *tawātur*[8] that they used to affirm speech of Him and to say that God commanded such and such, prohibited such and such and narrated such and such, and that all that is among the divisions of speech.

It should be known that two incompatible syllogisms are involved here. The first is that God's speech is one of His attributes, that all of His attributes are eternal, and that consequently God's speech is eternal. The second is that His speech is composed of parts consecutively ordered in existence, that everything that is like that is originated, and that therefore God's speech is originated. The Muslims thus divided into four groups. Two of these groups accepted the validity of the first syllogism, one of them rejecting the minor premise of the second syllogism, and the other rejecting the major premise. The other two groups accepted the validity of the second syllogism, each group rejecting one of the two premises of the first syllogism in the manner mentioned above.

As for the people of truth, some of them accepted the validity of the first syllogism and rejected the minor premise of the second syllogism saying that His speech is not of the genus of sounds and letters but, on the contrary, is an eternal attribute, subsisting in God's essence, by which He commands, prohibits, and narrates, and so forth, and that is indicated by [verbal] expression, writing, or sign. Thus if this attribute is expressed in Arabic, it is the Qurʾān, if in Syriac the *Injīl,* and if in Hebrew the *Tawrāt.* The difference lies in the expressions rather than in the thing named.

By way of elaboration at this point [it may be said] that if God narrates something, commands it, or prohibits it, and so forth, and if the prophets relay this to their nations by means of expressions signifying it, then without doubt three things are involved: meanings known [to God], expressions signifying them, also known [to God], and an attribute by which God is able to make those meanings manifest through these expressions for the purpose of instructing those persons addressed. There is no doubt as to the eternity of this attribute with respect to God, nor as to the eternity of the form through which these meanings and expressions are known to God. If, therefore, His speech is equivalent to this attribute, then there is no doubt as to its eternity. If it is equivalent to those meanings and expressions, however, then there is no doubt that they too, with respect to their being known to God, are eternal. However, this eternity is not restricted to them alone but applies [not only to them] but also to all the other expressions and significations of created beings, for all of these are known to God eternally and everlastingly. On the other hand, if [His speech] is equivalent to something beyond these three things, then there is no proof to establish this that rests on a leg.

As for the speech of the mind affirmed by the theologians, if it is equivalent to this attribute, then its nature is obvious. If, however, it is equivalent to those meanings and expressions known [to God], then there is no doubt that their subsisting in God is only in consideration of the form through which they are known, and that therefore it is not an attribute in itself but rather one of the particulars of [His] knowledge. As for the object of [His] knowledge, whether it be the expressions or their significations, it does not subsist in Him. The expressions in their basic existence[9] come under the category of successive accidents.[10] As for their significations, some of them are of the class of substances and others of the class of successive accidents; so how can they subsist in Him!

At this point let us mention what the Sufis have to say, so that, God willing, the truth may become evident. Al-Imam Ḥujjat al-Islām [al-Ghazālī] said: "Speech is of two sorts, one of which is attributed to the Creator and the other to human beings. As for the speech that is attributed to the Creator, it is one of His attributes of lordship. There is, however, no similarity between the attributes of the Creator and the attributes of human beings, for the attributes of human beings are superadded to their essences, so that, through these attributes, their unity becomes multiple, their individual existence is constituted, and their definitions and descriptions are determined. . . . God's attributes, however, do not define His essence nor do they describe Him, and consequently they are not things superadded to [His] knowledge, which is the reality of His ipseity.

"Whoever wishes to enumerate the attributes of the Creator is in error. . . . It is incumbent upon the rational person to reflect and to realize that the attributes of the Creator are not multiple, nor can they be separated one from the other except with respect to the levels of expression and the sources of allusion. Thus, if His knowledge is related to listening to the prayer of those in need, He is said to be a hearer. If it is related to seeing into the hearts of created beings, He is said to be a seer. . . . If from the mysteries of His knowledge He pours forth upon someone's heart the divine secrets and the subtleties of the power of His lordship, then He is said to be a speaker. It is not [true], then, that some part of Him is the instrument of hearing, and another part the instrument of sight, and yet another instrument of speech. . . . Thus, the Creator's speech is none other than His relating the mysteries of His knowledge to whomever He wishes to honor. As God said: 'And when Moses came to Our appointed tryst and His lord had spoken unto him' (7:143). God honored him with His nearness, and drew him near with His holiness, and seated him on the carpet of His intimacy, and addressed him with the most majestic of His attributes and spoke to him with the knowledge of His essence. As He wished He spoke, and as He willed He heard."[11]

In *Al-Futūḥāt al-Makkīya* (*Meccan Revelations*), [Ibn al-ʿArabī] says that with respect to the Qurʾān's being letters "two things can be understood. The first is what is called discourse, speech, or utterance, and the second is what is called writing, script or calligraphy. Since the Qurʾān is written, it consists of written letters, and since it is also pronounced, it consists of spoken letters. From what, then, does its being spoken letters derive? Is it from the speech of God, which is one of His attributes, or is it from what is interpreted from it? It should be known that God has informed us through His prophet that He will manifest Himself in various forms at the resurrection, and that He will be both recognized and denied. Anyone whose reality can accept this manifestation [of God] will not think it improbable that speech in [the form of] spoken letters and called the speech of God should be attributed to one of these forms [of manifestation] in a manner befitting His majesty. Just as we say that He has manifested Himself in a form befitting His majesty, so also we say that He spoke with letters and sounds as befits His majesty." Then, after a lengthy discussion, he stated: "If you examine what we have asserted, you will see clearly that the speech of God is that which is recited, heard, and pronounced and is called *Qurʾān, Tawrāt, Zabūr,* and *Injīl.*"

[Disciple of Ibn al-ʿArabī] Shaykh Ṣadr ad-Dīn al-Qūnawī (d. 1274) said in exegesis of the *Fātiḥa* [sūra 1]: "Among the sum of things that God granted to His servant," by which he meant himself, "was that He revealed to him some of the secrets of His Noble Book, which contains every important science, and showed him that it emerged from an otherworldly conflict occurring between the two attributes of power and will, dyed with the nature of that which [God's] knowledge encompassed at the plane linking the invisible and visible worlds but in accordance with the requirements of place and station. He assigned to him the nature of a person addressed [by God] as well as such a person's condition and time as a necessary consequence.

What is apparent from the statements of these eminent [Sufis] is that the speech that is an attribute of God is none other than His relating and pouring forth the mysteries of His knowledge upon whomever He wishes to honor. Moreover, the books sent down composed of letters and words, such as the Qurʾān and similar books, are also His speech, although they are only some of the forms of that relating and pouring forth which have appeared through the mediacy of [God's] knowledge, will and power in the intermediate world linking the invisible and visible worlds, that is, the world of similitude, from some of His formal and similative places of manifestation in a manner befitting Him.

Thus the two syllogisms mentioned at the beginning of this discussion are not in reality incompatible, since what is meant by speech in the first syllogism is the attribute subsisting in God's essence, whereas in the second it is what has appeared in the intermediate world (*al-barzakh*) from some of the divine places of manifestation. The disagreement occurring between the various groups of Muslims is due to the failure to distinguish between these two [kinds of] speech. God, may He be glorified, knows best.

Concerning God's statement: "And when your Lord said unto the angels: Lo! I am about to place a viceroy in the earth" (2:30), a certain person[12] said: "Know that this discourse varies in accordance with the different worlds in which the conversation occurs. If it occurs in the similative world, it is similar to sensible speech in that the Truth manifests Himself to the angels similatively, just as He manifests Himself in various forms to the people of the Hereafter as stated in the tradition of the transformation. If the conversation occurs in the world of spirit, in view of their immateriality, then it is like the speech of the mind, and God's speaking to the angels is His injecting the intended meaning into their hearts." From this the intelligent person becomes aware of what God's speech is as well as its various levels. Thus, at one level it is identical with the Speaker, and at another it is a meaning subsisting in Him like the speech of the mind. Finally, in both the world of similitude and that of sense, and in accordance with them, it is composed of letters and expressed by them.

Mullā Ṣadrā on Divine Speech and Attributes

Translated by James W. Morris

One of the most creative and influential late medieval/early modern Shīʿī thinkers is Ṣadr ad-Dīn ash-Shīrāzī (1571–640), more popularly known as Mullā Ṣadrā. Known especially for his development of the concept of "transcendental wisdom," Mullā Ṣadrā's intellectual ancestry includes Ibn Sīnā (especially his metaphysics), important *mutakallimūn* and Ismāʿīlī thinkers, Ibn al-ʿArabī, and the "illuminationist" school of Iṣfahān. Here is an excerpt from his Arabic *Wisdom of the Throne* (*Al-Ḥikmat al-ʿarshīya*).[13]

Text

PRINCIPLE [CRITICIZING MISTAKEN VIEWS OF GOD'S KNOWLEDGE OF PARTICULAR THINGS]

His knowledge of contingent things is not of forms inscribed in His Essence—as is the well-known position of the Master of the philosophers [Aristotle] and the Peripatetics, and of their followers Al-Fārābī (d. 950), Avicenna, and the rest. Nor is His knowledge of contingent things the same as the essences of externally existing contingent things, which was the view of the "Stoics" and their followers such as Suhrawardī, aṭ-Ṭūsī, and the more recent thinkers. This is impossible because His Knowledge is eternal, while those contingent things occur in time.

The position of the Muʿtazilites is also mistaken, because non-existent things (a "square circle" and the like, which they considered actually to subsist in God's Knowledge) do not exist at all [in the way they had posited]. The Ashʿarites, too, were wrong in imagining that His Knowledge is eternal, and yet only comes into connection with the contingent thing at the moment it originates in time.

The view that has been ascribed to Plato is likewise false in holding that His Knowledge consists in self-subsistent essences and forms that are separate both from Him and from matter. Nor [can we accept] what has been attributed to Porphyry [which speaks] of His "unification" with the intelligibles, at least if "unification" is understood in the way that most people do [i.e., in the sense of conjoining two originally *separate* entities].

Nor can God's Knowledge [of particulars] be encompassed simply in a general, summary form, as some more recent thinkers rashly tried to argue [since general knowledge in no way implies knowledge of all individual instances]. Rather, the truth [about the relation of general and particular knowledge] is as we have indicated and confirmed in a solid manner that is set forth in our more lengthy books.

But the most foolish theory of all is proposed by those who maintain that these very material forms—despite their being submerged in matter and mixed with all the privations and veils and shadows that necessarily follow from being in specific times, places, and positions—are [nevertheless] forms of knowledge present in Him as His Knowledge. For it has been proven that this mode of shadowy and material being is veiled from itself by itself. So with regard to this [material] mode [of being], the presence [of a material thing] is precisely the same as its absence from itself; its coherence is the same as its separability; its unity is the same as its potential multiplicity; and its conjunction is the same as its divisibility. So tell me, then, you "man of knowledge": if this material being, *qua* being, is by essence known to the Creator, present with Him in this form submerged in matter and spatial location—although this [material] form cannot even be grasped by sensation, not to mention imagination or intellection, then how can the intelligible [form], insofar as it is actually intelligible, still be a material form and therefore susceptible of division into quantities and location in space?! For intellective [or noetic] being is a mode of being separate and different from spatial [material] being. Therefore it is impossible that the act of intelligence should be corporeal, or that the corporeal thing should be an intelligible.

So do not pay any attention to the words of whoever says that these generated, corporeal beings, although within their own limits corporeal and constantly changing, are nevertheless [eternally] fixed and unchanging intelligibles in relation to what is above them, that is, to the First Principle and the world of His Kingdom. This is [impossible] because the mode of something's being in itself does not change through a relation [that it may have to something else]. The fact that something is material is an expression for the [essential] characteristics of its being, and the materiality of a thing and its separation from matter are not two attributes external to the essence of that thing. Similarly, the substantiality of a substance and its particular being are a single thing, and the accidentality of an accident and its [particular] being are likewise [a single different thing]. So just as a single being cannot be both a substance and an accident, [simply] according to two points of view, neither can it be both material and separate from matter [simply] from two points of view.

However, if you were to say that these material forms are present in Him through their Forms which are separate [and immaterial] by essence, and that in consequence of those Forms, these [material] things are also known in an accidental manner, then that view would be justified. For it has already been mentioned that "What is with God" (2:89, etc.) are the primordial essential Realities of [all contingent] things, and that those things are related to "What is with God" as a shadow is related to its source.

PRINCIPLE, CONCERNING HIS SPEECH

[God's] Speech is not, as the Ashʿarites have said, an "attribute of [His] Soul" and the eternal meanings subsisting in His Essence that they called the "speech of the soul." For His Speech is something other than a [pure] intelligible, or it would be Knowledge and not Speech. But neither is His Speech [as the Muʿtazilites have argued] [merely] an expression for the creation of sounds and words signifying meanings, since in that case all speech would be God's Speech. Nor does it help [as some Muʿtazilites have attempted] to restrict God's Speech to [that which is spoken] "in the intention of informing another on the part of God" or "with the intention of their presentation on His behalf," since everything is from Him. And if [by these restrictions] they were intending a speech without any [human] intermediary, this would also be impossible, since in such a case there would be no sounds or words at all. No, God's "Speech" is an expression for His establishment of Perfect Words and the "sending down of definite Signs—They are the Mother of the Book—and others that are similitudes" (3:7), in the clothing of words and expressions. Hence His Speech is *"Qurʾān"* (that is, "joining," or the noetic Unity of Being) from one point of view and *"Furqān"* (that is, "separate," manifest reality) from another point of view.

[As *Qurʾān,* or the inner noetic reality of Being and the "Mother of the Book,"] God's Speech is different from the "Book," because the "Book" belongs to the world of [manifest] Creation: "You [Muḥammad] did not recite any book before this, nor did you write one with your right hand, for else those who would oppose [you] might have doubted [your purely divine inspiration]" (29:48). For His Speech belongs to the World of the Command [i.e., the noetic modality of Being], and Its dwelling is the hearts and breasts [of humankind], as in His saying: "The Faithful Spirit brought it down upon your heart, with God's permission" (conflating 26:193–94 and 97:4), and His saying: "Verily It is clear Signs in the breasts of those who have been given knowledge" (29:49). The "Book" [of manifest, contingent beings] can be perceived by everyone: "And We wrote down for him [Moses] upon the tablets the counsel to be drawn from every thing" (7:145). But God's Speech [i.e., noetic Being] is "[a hidden Book] that can only be touched by those purified (cf. 56:78–79) from the pollution of the world of man's mortal [animal] nature.

The Qurʾān was [God's] creation of the Prophet [perhaps as the noetic pleroma or "Adam," the "Complete Human Being"] before the "Book" [of contingent being]. The difference between the Qurʾān and the "Book" is like that between Adam and Jesus. [Both were alike to the extent that] "the likeness of Jesus is with God as is the likeness of Adam: He created him from dust; then he said to him 'Be!' and he comes to be" (3:59). But Adam is the Book of God, "written with the two Hands" (38:75) of His Power:

You (O Adam) are the "Clear Book" (5:15, etc.)
Through Whose letters what was hidden appears.

Jesus [on the other hand] was His Saying, resulting from His Command [*Kun!* "Be!"] and "His Word that He conveyed to Mary, and a spirit from Him" (4:171). That which was created by God's "two Hands" (38:75) is not to be likened in nobility of rank to that which came to exist through two letters [*k-n* of the divine command "Be!"]. So whoever maintains the opposite of this is mistaken.

PRINCIPLE [DERIVING FROM] THE SOURCE OF ILLUMINATION [CONCERNING THE UNION OF GOD AND HIS SPEECH IN ALL BEINGS: THE "BREATH OF THE MERCIFUL"]

The speaker is he through whom speech subsists. The writer is he who causes speech—that is, the book—to exist. And each of these has several levels. Every book is speech in some respect, and every speech is also a book in some respect, since every speaker is a writer in some way, and every writer is in some way also a speaker. A visible image of that is the following: when you witness a man speaking, the form of letters and the shapes of speech arise from his breath in his chest, throat, and the other places that produce the sounds and letters; and his breath is from the one who causes the speech to be. So he "writes" with the "pen" of his power on the "tablet" of his breath, and ultimately on the places that produce the various sounds. He is the same individual through whom the speech subsists, so he becomes the speaker.

Now take this as an analogy for What is above it [i.e., the eternal creative self-manifestation or the "Breath of the Merciful"], and be among "those who speak wisely" (28:20, etc.) and do good, not among "those who quarrel among themselves" (50:28, etc.)!

EXPERIENCING GOD HEREAFTER

Bāqillānī on the Vision of God in the Next Life

Translated by Richard J. McCarthy, SJ

From "hearing" God's voice in this life we move to classical *kalām*'s questions as to whether and how believers will "see God" in the next life. Debate turns around how human beings, even given the concept of the resurrection of the body, could experience "ocular vision" of God who is the ultimate spiritual reality. Ash'arite theologian Bāqillānī (d. 1013) deals with the problem as members of his school typically handle such conundrums: by declining to examine them too closely, that is, by not "asking how" an apparently contradictory notion might be.[14]

Text

You must also know that the vision of God is possible from the standpoint of reason, and that it is absolutely certain for believers in the next life, as a mark of honor and benevolence, because God has promised it to them. The proof of the possibility of seeing God, from the standpoint of reason, is the request made by Moses when he said: "My Lord! Show me [Yourself], that I may gaze upon You" (7:143). Now it is impossible that one of the Prophets, in view of his eminent worth and lofty station, should ask God for something impossible respecting Him. So if Moses had not believed that it was possible to see God, he would not have made that request. Moreover, God Himself made the vision [of Himself] dependent on the immobility of the mountain [a thing possible]. The possibility of the vision of God is also proved by the fact that God exists; for what exists can be seen.

The certainty of the vision from the standpoint of Book and *Sunna* is proved by God's words: "Their salutation on the day when they shall meet Him will be: Peace" (33:44; cf. 10:10, 14:28); for when meeting is conjoined with salutation it can mean only seeing. God has also said: "For those who do good is the best [reward] and more [thereto]" (10:27). Abū Bakr said that the "more" is looking at His noble countenance, and the same has been related from the Apostle himself. And God has said: "That day will faces be resplendent, looking toward their Lord" (75:22–23). The meaning of *nāḍira* is *mushriqa* (shining), and *ilā rabbihā nāẓiratan* means that they will see their Lord. For when *an-naẓar* is used with *ilā* it must have the explicit meaning of "seeing," as in God's words: "Just look at your food and drink" (2:259); and: "Will they not regard the camels, how they are created?" (88:17). And Ibn 'Abbās was asked about God's saying "more" (10:27), and he replied: "it is looking at the face of God, without asking how."

Moreover, when the Companions asked Muḥammad: "Shall we see our Lord?" he replied: "You shall see your Lord clearly, as you see the moon on the night of full moon, without being harmed by seeing Him"—and another version has: "without being damaged by seeing Him"—and another: "and no harm or damage will overtake you in seeing Him." That means that he likened seeing to seeing, and that, just as the seer who sees the moon on the night of full moon, i.e. the night of the fourteenth, does not doubt that what he sees is the moon, so the one who looks at God in the Garden will not doubt that the One he sees is God Most High, without inquiry or likening or defining. This is like one's saying: "I know your veracity as I know the day," and: "I saw Zayd as I saw the sun." It is also proved by Muḥammad's saying that God will show Himself to creatures in general and to Abū Bakr in particular.

ʿAlī on the Vision of God

Translated by I. K. A. Howard

An interesting contrast is evident in the following brief excerpt from Shaykh al-Mufīd's (d. 1022) *Book of Guidance,* with its distinctively Shīʿī interpretation of "vision of God."[15] ʿAlī, the first Shīʿī imam, is the main figure here.

Text

The historians report that a man came to the Commander of the faithful and asked: "Commander of the faithful, tell me about God, the Exalted. Did you see Him when you worshipped Him?"

"I am not one who worships someone whom I have not seen," he answered.

"Then how did you find Him when you saw Him?" he asked.

"Woe upon you," he said, "the eyes do not see Him in terms of human eye-sight. Rather the hearts see Him through the inner realities of faith. [He can be] known through evidence and can be characterized by signs, which cannot be compared to people nor attained through sense perception."

The man went away saying: "Indeed, God knows well how He should deliver His message."

In this account there is evidence that [the Commander of the faithful] denied the possibility of direct vision of God, the Mighty and High.

ʿAbd al-Jabbār on God and Humanity in the Hereafter

Translated by Richard Martin

An important related eschatological theme has generated complex discussion in the history of Islamic thought: how does God deal with sinners after death? Muʿtazilite theologians developed their own distinctive approach to this and a variety of eschatological problems. Here is a sample of that method.

From ʿAbd al-Jabbār's (d. 1025) "Five Principles," here are several important matters as to what awaits after death.[16]

Text

If someone asks: Are you saying that God has threatened grave sinners with Hellfire? *Respond:* Yes, because God said: "Those who unjustly consume the property of orphans, shall consume a fire into their own bodies: they will soon be enduring a blazing fire" (4:10). And He said: "Consume not your property among yourselves in vanities; but let there be amongst you trade by mutual good will: Nor kill yourselves: for verily Allāh has been to you Most Merciful! If any do that in rancor and injustice, soon shall we cast them into the Hellfire: And easy it is for God" (4:29–30). And He said: "If any does turn his back to them on such a day unless it be in a stratagem of war, or to retreat to a troop [of his own]—draws on himself the wrath of God, and his abode is Hell—an evil refuge [indeed]" (8:16)! These passages indicate that those who commit sins of great magnitude will be the People of Hell.

Then if someone asks: Are you saying that those [who commit grave sins] will be in Hellfire eternally and they will remain there forever, or will they be let out? *Respond:* Indeed, they will be there eternally according to what Allāh informs us in His Book: "But those who disobey Allāh and His messenger and transgress His limits will be admitted to a fire, to abide therein eternally" (4:14)! And He said: "If a man kills a believer intentionally, his recompense is the Hellfire, to abide therein [forever]: and the wrath of Allāh is upon him" (4:93). And He said: "And the wicked—they will be in the Hellfire, which they will enter on the Day of Judgment, and they will not be able to keep away therefrom" (82:14–16). This clarifies the fact that they will not be absent from the Hellfire.

Then if someone asks: It is narrated from the Prophet in several reports that a group of people will leave the Hellfire. *Respond:* There cannot occur on the basis of reports attested unilaterally (*akhbār aḥadīya*) . . . [ellipsis in original translation] reports that contradict their claim. When they are contradicted we should refer to the Book of God, and we have just explained passages that indicate the eternity [of the Hellfire].

Then if someone asks: But God said: "Those who are wretched shall be in the Hellfire: There will be for them therein [nothing but] the heaving of sighs and sobs. They will dwell therein for all the time that the Heavens and the Earth endure, except as your Lord wishes" (11:106–7). This indicates that they will not abide there forever. *Respond:* If this indicated what you said, the following saying of His would so indicate: "As for those who are gladdened on the Last Day, they shall be in Paradise [eternally so long as the Heavens and the Earth endure, except as God wills, a gift that can't be cut off]" (11:108). If that is not an indication concerning the People of Paradise, similarly neither is what you said. God intended only to make remote their departure from the Hellfire by correlating it with the duration of the Heavens and the Earth because that is remote, according the lexicographers. As the poet has said:

When crow's feathers turn gray,
I shall go back to my family
And tar has turned into a pure milk.

Then if someone asks: What does His saying mean: "Allāh forgives not that partners should be set up with Him; but He forgives anything else, to whom He pleases" (4:48)? *Respond:* It means that God does not forgive polytheism, but that nonetheless He forgives what He wishes to, if it is among the lesser sins. God has explained: "If you avoid the gravest sins that you are forbidden to do, we shall expiate your misdeeds from you" (4:31).

Then if someone asks: Has God not said: "Say: O my servants who in their prodigality have harmed themselves! Despair not of the mercy of God, who forgives all sins" (39:53). What does that mean? *Respond:* Its meaning is that you should not despair of God's mercy when there is repentance. To this He said: "Turn to your Lord in repentance and submit to Him before the punishment comes on you" (39:54).

Then if someone asks: Are you claiming that there is intercession and do you believe in it? *Respond:* Yes, but it is for the believers, not for grave sinners, because God has reported that He will cast the grave sinner into eternal Hellfire. He says: "The wrongdoers have no close friend and no intercessor who will be obeyed" (40:18), and He says: "The wrongdoers have no helpers" (2:270). And He says: "And they offer no intercession except for those who are acceptable" (21:27). All of that indicates that the grave sinner has no intercession, and that the Prophet intercedes on behalf of believers.

Then if someone asks: What is the use of his intercession on behalf of the believers if they are the People of Paradise? *Respond:* by his intercession for them, God will increase their level and stature in Paradise, and that is in honor of the Messenger of God, thus this is a great benefit.

Then if someone says: Intercession is only for those who are being harmed or are in prison, thus one intercedes in order to end those things. Why then do you say: "There is no intercession for grave sinners?" *Respond:* Intercession in the visible world might concern the increase of stature and merit, just as one of us petitions someone else and thereby requests an increase in his rank and stature.

Then if someone asks: The Prophet said "My intercession is for the serious sinners in my community." Why don't you say that? *Respond:* It is not possible to substitute for what is manifest in the Book of God a report whose validity cannot be decided. If [the report] were valid, it would mean that one who commits serious sins and then repents would be among the people [for whom there] was intercession, so that no one would presume that the intercession is only for those who always obeyed God, and from whom there was never any great or small disobedience.

THEOLOGICAL BOOKENDS: COSMOGONY AND ESCHATOLOGY

In addition to the many theological articulations of the questions and themes that comprise the majority of the material in chapters 5 and 6, Muslim theologians have also delved into other, yet more specialized and recondite topics. Seventeenth-century Chinese convert to Islam Wang Daiyu here paints on one of the broadest of all theological canvases, that of "cosmogony"—how the "ten thousand things" came to be and the relationships were established between "created" reality and the Creator. From the perspective of the other end of the span of created time, Twelver Shīʿa theologian Nuʿmānī outlines the essentials of a Shīʿī "theology of history," with its "millennialist" expectation of the twelfth imam's emergence from the Greater Occultation.

Wang Daiyu on Translating Tawḥīd *into Chinese Traditional Terms*

Translated by Sachiko Murata

Islam arrived in China more than a millennium ago and remains an important presence in several regions of the country. But *The Real Commentary on the True Teaching* (*Zhengjiao zhenquan* 正教眞詮), the first book in Chinese on Islam written by a Muslim, did not appear until 1642. Chinese Muslims consider the author, Wang Daiyu 王岱輿 (d. 1657/58) the father of Chinese-language Islam. Wang tells us in the introduction to the book that his ancestor had come to China three hundred years earlier from the Islamic world to serve the Chinese emperor as an astronomer. Wang himself studied Arabic and Persian as a youth, but he did not begin studying literary Chinese until he was in his twenties. He wrote the book mainly with the aim of presenting authentic Islam to those Muslims who did not know the languages of their own heritage. Thoroughly familiar with the Chinese classics, Wang freely employs terminology drawn from Confucianism, Daoism, and Buddhism. So, for example, he refers to the angels as the "heavenly immortals" and the creatures of the world as the "ten thousand things." He presents Islam's essential teachings as harmonious with the teachings of the Chinese traditions, though at times he is also critical of specific beliefs and practices of these traditions. Wang devotes the first of the book's two parts mainly to theological principles, such as the divine attributes, predestination, creation, and human nature. The second part focuses more on spiritual attitudes, ethics, and various commandments of Islamic law. Here Wang reprises many of the themes represented earlier in this anthology concerning the divine attributes, acts, and relationships with humankind and all of creation.[17]

Text

1. THE REAL ONE

Only the Real Lord is one, and nothing can be compared to Him. He is the Original Being without beginning, the Being that does not receive the mandate.[18] Even if you try, it is impossible to attain the details of the Real One's original Being with the words and sentences of those who have received being. Why? Because the Root Suchness of the Real One never begets, nor was it ever begotten. Nothing whatsoever is similar to it. It has no going or coming, no beginning or ending. It has no place of abiding or time, no rising or falling, no opening or closing. It relies on nothing and depends on nothing. It has no vital-energy and stuff. Nothing encloses it and nothing is together with it. The wakeful awareness of wisdom and intelligence and the comparisons of sounds and colors are all unable to act in its regard.

Know that the Real One is the single, Unique One, not the Numerical One. The Numerical One is not the Unique One. When it is said, "The Great Ultimate begets the two wings, the two wings beget the four images" [Yijing], this is the Numerical One. When it is said, "One root with ten thousand variations" or "ten thousand dharmas going home to the one" [Buddhism], this also is the Numerical One. When it is said, "The nameless is the beginning of heaven and earth, the named the mother of the ten thousand things" [Laozi], this also is the Numerical One. From this standpoint, each of these so-called ones is the one seed of heaven, earth, and the ten thousand things. Each is the Numerical One. The Real One is the lord of the Numerical One. Only the Real is the Unique One.

The Dao accords with the Real, so it cannot alter or change. Its principle is one from beginning to end. If the Real One is not attained, then the taproot will not be deep. If the taproot is not deep, the Dao will not be firm. If the Dao is not firm, faith will not be sincere. Not one, not deep, not sincere—how can this be the eternal Dao?

Thus the True Teaching honors only the Real One. The Real One is together with the Numerical One, and the Numerical One is together with the ten thousand beings. Were It not with the ten thousand beings, the ten thousand beings would be destroyed. Were It together with the ten thousand beings, It would be enclosed by all ten thousand. Here, however, being "together" means that at once It is together and not together, at once It is and is not. This is not like the things' being together with the I's.

Were the Real One together with the ten thousand things, then the Original Being and the newly born would not be distinct. For example, the nature of the spiritual in the head and the nature of awareness in the heart come together in one body.[19] If someone encounters calamity and harm, the nature of the spiritual in the head will be unsettled and the nature of awareness in the heart will also be disordered, for one of them cannot be governed when the other is disordered. Man's perplexity and disorder, however, can certainly not interfere with the firm settledness of the Real Lord. The Real Lord's purity and cleanness will never be tainted by the darkness and obscurity of the human heart. This is enough to see that the Real One by Itself has nothing to do with the ten thousand kinds.

The nature of awareness in the heart is rooted in the bodily form and completed at its boundary. The nature of the spiritual in the head begins in the Former Heaven and later comes down to the bodily ground. After heaven and earth are established, it gradually becomes manifest. It waits for the time to issue forth, like flowers and fruit. It is completed when a man reaches the age of twenty-eight. It matures as he reaches the perfection of old age.[20]

At root people's deception and mistakes nowadays have no cause other than their inability to discriminate why things are so. Inwardly things are so because of yin and yang and the four agents. Outwardly things are so because of the making of the Master Workman.

The ways in which things are together are of more than one kind. Sometimes a thing is inside something else, like a person inside a room. Sometimes a thing is in a body, like the body's four limbs. Sometimes that which is reliant and dependent is together with that which stands by itself, like the spots of a leopard or saltiness in water.

Sometimes one thing and another thing have the same reason for why they are so, like the sun's light interwoven with the brightness of a moon or a lamp, which are undifferentiated and appear as one body. If you differentiate them, their principles are different, but they do not hinder or obstruct each other. The root bodies and root natures of these things do not blend together or taint each other, for each of them has its own place. Thus water moves bamboo's shadow, but these two bodies do not interfere with each other. Wind plays with the flowers' fragrance, but the two do not have a common [nature].

When the commonality of these principles is examined, there are differentiations of pure and turbid, inside and outside, as well as discriminations of far and near, large and small. The turbid is near and small; it connects the outside with the inside. The pure is far and large; it does not have an outward and inward. Thus water is purer than soil, wind is purer than water, light is purer than wind. Those who travel on land travel a hundred *li* and those on water travel a thousand *li*. The wind travels a thousand thousand *li*, and light travels beyond measure. Water enwraps soil, wind enwraps water, fire enwraps air—all because of the self-suchness of the principles.

Although sun and moon are bright and illuminate all places, they cannot penetrate a dark room. The light of a candle fills the room, but it cannot advance outside to heaven and earth. Hence far and near, inside and outside, all belong to place. They pertain to the existence of the newborn, not to being together with the Original Being. If the Original Being were together with the newborn, there would be none of the pure and turbid, the inside and outside, which bring about stagnation and obstacles.

If we talk about It as together, this has nothing to do with the ten thousand things. If It is together, It cannot be together everlastingly. If we say that It is not together, how will It encompass and penetrate the ten thousand things? Even if It is not together, It cannot not be together everlastingly.

Know that before there was heaven and earth, and after heaven and earth have come to be, the Original Being is single, unique, and always one. I have depicted many things, but if you want to determine how things are together with the Most Great, that was only one ten-thousandth of it. Even in the case of tiny things, like crickets and ants, human beings cannot entirely know their natures—how much more so in the case of the most honored and most mysterious Real Lord! Only the principles that are of the utmost refinement are clear in themselves. The man of knowledge will transmit the Dao, but if there is no such person, the Dao will reach no one.

The principles, however, are mysterious and hard to clarify; the meanings are deep and difficult to realize fully. When you know them, it is difficult to speak, though you cannot not know them. All who examine them have the evidence of clarity in their own bodies. The Classic says, "When someone attains recognition of his own self, only then will he attain recognition of the Real Lord who created and transformed the self."[21] Certainly those who can thoroughly penetrate into this principle will be superior to the most talented people under Heaven, far beyond ignorant and stupid men. Hence the Sage said that whoever attains recognition of his own Real Lord can speak as a matter of course. But, he also said that whoever attains recognition of his own Real Lord will of course not speak.

"He will not speak" means that he cannot speak about the subtleness of the Root Suchness, because It is pure and clean, without taint. It is the ultimately honored and the ultimately noble, the utmost subtle and the utmost mysterious. It does not fall into sounds and colors, so no one can deliberate upon It or consider It. The heart cannot think of It, the eyes cannot see It, the ears cannot hear It, and the mouth cannot speak It.

"He can speak" means that he will be able to speak about the mysterious secret of movement and stillness and the subtleness of judgment.

You should know that in regard to the Root Suchness movement and stillness are like cold and heat in regard to winter and summer. Cold and heat should not be taken as winter and summer, but without winter and summer is neither cold nor heat.

That which has not yet issued forth is called "stillness," and that which has already issued forth is called "movement." Stillness is the Root Substance, and movement is the work and function. The moment between that which has issued forth and that which has not issued forth is called "movement-stillness."[22] Even if we talk about its stillness, the mysterious, hidden secret has already been disclosed. Even if we talk about movement, the trace has not yet been seen. Only when these two are designated as substance and function will the principles be proper. As soon as movement-stillness becomes manifest, the honorable names are displayed. Then the Lord's honorable designations issue forth in words and sentences.

Movement-stillness is included in the meaning of the principles. If we talk about the two as united, they are varied; if we talk about them as differentiated, they are not different. You must know this.

As a whole, movement-stillness is of two types, but there are three levels of making judgments about it. The two types are the movement-stillness of the Root Suchness and the movement-stillness of sustaining.[23] The movement-stillness of the Root Suchness is like the original knowledge and the original life, the root looking and the root listening. Self-power and self-standing are of this kind.

Know that the Real Lord's original knowledge is that He knows without the heart,[24] so all of Him knows and there is nothing that He does not know. His original life is that He lives without life, so all of Him is alive and there is nothing in which He does not live. His root looking is that He looks without eyes, so all of Him looks and there is nothing at which He does not look. His root hearing is that He hears without ears, so all of Him hears and there is nothing that He does not hear. His self-power is without hands, so all of Him is powerful and there is nothing over which He is not powerful. His self-standing is without feet, so all of Him is standing and there is nothing in which He does not stand.

By itself this movement-stillness has nothing to do with the ten thousand kinds and is unlike that of humanity and spirits, which relies on the assistance of eyes, ears, nose, tongue, body, and heart.

As for the movement-stillness of sustaining, it has the power, for example, to cause man's birth and death, his nobility and meanness, his seeing and hearing, his knowledge and awareness. The creation and transformation of heaven and earth is of this kind.

If the movement-stillness of the Root Suchness is taken as the movement-stillness of sustaining, or the movement-stillness of sustaining is taken as the movement-stillness of the Root Suchness, this is all outside the Dao. Why? Because the movement-stillness of the Root Suchness is within itself, a firmness and stillness that does not shift, alike in being and nonbeing. The movement-stillness of sustaining makes things; it becomes manifest when functioning and stays hidden when not functioning. Since these two are different and distinct, how can they be talked about as the same?

The three levels of making judgments are judgment by the ten thousand things, by this very body, and by the Teaching and the Dao.

Judgment by the ten thousand things is like heaven's height and earth's solidity, fire's heat and water's cold, wind's movement and soil's firmness, the ascending and descending of sun and moon, the darkness and brightness of day and night, the going and coming of cold and heat, the waxing and waning of the four seasons, the highness and lowness of flyers and divers, the prosperity and decay of grass and trees, and the alteration and transformation of metal and stone. Were it not for the Real Lord's creation and transformation, how could anything have these powers? Were any of these lacking, the world would not come to be. Anything that rebels against its own creation and transformation will of course never be at ease or settled.

Judgment by this very body is like the four limbs and the hundred bodily members, the five viscera and the six entrails, seeing and hearing, listening and speaking, knowledge and awareness, the spiritual and the living, the hand's grasping and the foot's walking. Its principle is united with heaven and earth, surpasses and excels the ten thousand kinds, and goes through and penetrates being and nonbeing. Were it not for the Real Lord's great power, how could anything be like this? Were any of these lacking, the corporeal body would not come to be. Anything that rebels against this great power will not be worth looking at.

Judgment by the Teaching and the Dao is that you must comply with the clear mandate in all things like recognizing the Lord and recognizing oneself, bearing witness to the Sage, going home to the Real, the five human relationships, and the one hundred actions. Were this not so, how could one cultivate the body, conduct oneself in society, regulate the family, and govern the country?[25] Were it not for the Real Lord's mysterious directives, how could anyone be like this? Were any of these lacking, the Teaching and the Dao would not come to be. Anyone who rebels against His pointing and showing will of course be perplexed and disordered.

This explanation of the Root Suchness of the Real Lord and His movement-stillness, however, is only a bit helpful, for it is sketched roughly, like dust motes gathered in the great earth, or drops of water following the vast ocean.

It may be that a wise and profound person will attempt to seek out the utmost Dao. He will seem to be on the true path, but he does not know the great learning of going home to the Real. He is like a blind person who chooses a road and is annoyed at where it goes. His great pains over his lifetime will certainly turn absurd.

Furthermore, our fathers and mothers bestowed on us the corporeal body, hair and skin, so we should show filial piety and respect. The ruler confers on us field and village and enjoyable tasks, so we should be fully loyal. Much more so is the case for the Real Lord of all the fathers and all the rulers, who creates and transforms heaven, earth, and the ten thousand things, mandates man's birth and death, causes his nobility and meanness, and confers on him clothing and wages. How can it be possible not to recognize Him but to pay attention instead to ghosts and specters? A poet said,

> The Non-Ultimate and the Great Ultimate
> are the taproot of heaven and earth, being and nonbeing.
> They are suited to be the seed of the ten thousand things,
> but not of this Human who planted the taproot.[26]
> You cannot but know this.

Someone said: When we rely on the principles and infer the details, then the Non-Ultimate is the Great Ultimate, which is the Lord of *yin* and *yang*, the five agents, and the ten thousand things.

I said: The utmost principle of the Pure and Real is not apart from this very body. If we speak about the principle as apart from this very body, that would be absurd and without evidence. Why? Because the root human nature has the pattern of the Non-Ultimate, and the root stuff of this body is clear proof of the Great Ultimate. The head is round in the image of heaven, and that which is light and pure ascends above and belongs to *yang*. The foot is square in the image of earth, and that which is heavy and turbid descends down and belongs to *yin*. The five viscera correspond to the five agents, and the body as a whole is like the ten thousand things.

Acting and stopping as well as knowledge and awareness depend on the nature and spiritual of the Non-Ultimate, but the one hundred bones certainly emerge from the root stuff of the Great Ultimate. Nonetheless, life and death, success and failure, safety and danger, gain and loss, are not within the ability of one's own root nature and root substance. Thus we come to know that the Non-Ultimate receives the Real Lord's mandate to act as His representative in heaven, earth, and the ten thousand things, but the authority to decide life and death, nobility and meanness, certainly does not rely on the independent ability of the Non-Ultimate and the Great Ultimate. This is the utmost great affair amidst heaven and earth. How can the foundation of the True Dao let people conjecture without restraint?

2. THE ORIGINAL BEGINNING

The people of the world do not comprehend the original beginning of creation and transformation. Some confusedly argue about principle and vital-energy and some discuss empty nonbeing and silent annihilation, but all are guesses and suppositions in the dark without any real evidence.[27] The True Teaching, having obtained the clear mandate of the Real Lord and the real transmission of the Utmost Sage, understood these fully without any double-mindedness. I wish to clarify this according to what has been transmitted by the Classics and the Histories, but there are meanings that cannot be conveyed with today's words and sentences or described with similes and comparisons. It is difficult to speak of this, but I will do the best I can.

The Classic says that when the Real Lord first began to create and transform, the subtle clarity of the human being had the utmost perfection and complete uprightness. Later He made it descend to the lowest of the low.[28] This indicates that huamity is the ultimate level, the highest and the lowest, totally enwrapping the ten thousand images. It means that the Real Lord is the Original Being with no beginning, and the Human Ultimate is the original ancestor that has a beginning.

Only the Lord is without beginning and end, singularly distinct and uniquely one. He is honorable and great, pure and clean, equipped with all in Himself, borrowing nothing from outside. If there were no heaven, earth, and the ten thousand things, He would not decrease, and even though there are heaven, earth, and the ten thousand things, He has not increased.

Beyond this, man, spirits, and heavenly immortals all have beginnings, but they do not have the power to create their beginnings by themselves. Only the Real Lord has the power to create them, and His power is the complete power. Hence He is all-powerful, and everything made is based totally on His power. His power brings all things into being, no matter how large or tiny, how many or few. It has no need for creative activity, does not wait for time, nor does it differentiate between difficult and easy. When He wishes being, there it is. When He wishes nonbeing, nothing is there.

Thus, before the appearance of things, the Real Lord wished to create heavenly immortals, spirits and demons, heaven and earth, and the ten thousand things. From the surplus light of the Only One, He made manifest the original chief of the ten thousand sages, Muhammad, who is the root origin of the Non-Ultimate and the beginning of all the subtle clarities.

The meaning of the surplus light is connected to the Real Lord's Being, which has the two levels of Original Being and Powerful Being. The Original Being has nothing to do with the ten thousand things. In contrast, the Powerful Being protects and nourishes the ten thousand things, and this is the meaning of the surplus light.

For example, holding and grasping, or taking and granting, belong to the Original Being, but good writing and good drawing belong to the Powerful Being. If someone is good at taking and granting but has no ability to write and draw, this does not harm the root substance of taking and granting. Without the root power of taking and granting, however, there is certainly no power to practice writing and drawing. If you were to say that holding and grasping are writing and drawing, you would fail to differentiate between the root and the practice. Even if you say that writing and drawing are not holding and grasping, writing and drawing cannot by itself come to be without holding and grasping. But this example can barely illustrate one of ten thousand similarities between the two levels.

Then the Real Lord illuminated the root origin of the Utmost Sage with His original good pleasure. At this very moment, a fountainhead of shame issued forth, like the moment when one faces the emperor and sweat runs down the back. It issued forth from a place awareness does not reach. This was the first beginning of spiritual awareness. From the subtleness of this fountainhead of the mandate, He then made fully manifest the surplus light of spiritual awareness and completed the creation and transformation of the ordinary sages' origin. From the ordinary sages' origin, He completed the creation and transformation of the worthies' origin. From the worthies' origin He completed the creation and transformation of good people's origin. From good people's origin He completed the creation and transformation of common people's origin. From common people's origin He completed the creation and transformation of perplexed people's origin. From the origin of the various kinds of people He completed the creation and transformation of the origin of all the heavenly immortals. From the various heavenly immortals' origin He completed the creation and transformation of spirits and demons' origin. From the surplus of all the various things He completed the creation and transformation of the origin of all things in water and land, all who fly and walk.[29]

The difference in kind of the various levels is like many kinds and degrees of sugar created by someone from the white center of sugar cane. That which floats up the first time becomes crystal-sugar, followed by rock-sugar, then white sugar, then yellow sugar, then red sugar. What is left after this is the dregs of the juice. Although there are several kinds of sugar, both the high and low grades come to be by themselves, without anyone's deliberate intention to make them the former and the latter, the better and the worse. In the end, however, nothing emerges without the prearrangement of the master.

Someone said: In the midst of the Only One's light, something like various levels of good and evil, high and low, are originally either nonbeing or being. If we say they are being, then the light of the Only One will not be perfect. If we say they are nonbeing, whence does the origin of the Utmost Sage come to be?

I said: Since the origin of the Utmost Sage has a beginning, it receives the movement-stillness of the newly born, but in the midst of the Only One's light, it is originally nonbeing. Here there are two reasons: First is that anything that has an arising and a beginning will certainly have the blackness and darkness of birth in the midst of its being. That which does not have an arising and a beginning is the light and clarity of the Original Being in the state of its undifferentiated suchness.

The second reason is that the Real Lord has the movement-stillness of both mercy and severity, and these two are not the same. As for the light and clarity in the midst of the human spiritual awareness, that is the surplus light of the movement-stillness of the Real Lord's mercy and compassion. The blackness and darkness in their spiritual awareness is the surplus light of the movement-stillness of severity and majesty.

Afterwards, from the principle of the fountainhead of wisdom, He made fully manifest the surplus light of nature and principle. He finished creating and transforming the origin of all those without spiritual awareness, that is, the origins of the various heavenly worlds, the sun and the moon, the stars and the constellations; soil, water, fire, and wind; grass and wood, metal and stone. The origins of the ten thousand things and these various levels of subtle clarity were completed in less than an instant. The saying that creative activity has no time nor any difficult and easy points precisely to this.

What is preserved here is the turbid in the midst of the pure. This is the Great Ultimate. Depending on the illumination and shining of both kindness and compassion and the severity and majesty of the Real Lord, water and fire were transformed, thus storing dust in water and air in fire. When these encroached on each other, fire surpassed water, and foam issued forth inside water. The lightweight and pure ascended upwards and were transformed to become the corporeal form of heaven. The heavy and turbid descended downwards and were transformed to become the corporeal form of the earth.

Thus the Non-Ultimate is the beginning of not having the form of heaven, earth, and the ten thousand things, and the Great Ultimate is the beginning of having the form of heaven, earth, and the ten thousand things. If we talk about them as differentiated, they are being and nonbeing; if we talk about them as united, they are not two substances. When you observe the concealed and refined details, how is it possible not to distinguish between the two levels of origin and power? Without the real transmission of the True Teaching, how could you know for sure even one affair of the utmost principle of the Former Heaven and the great origin of creation and transformation? A human being is not able to suppose and guess the sequential order of humans and things from the time of the opening up and cleaving [of heaven and earth]. You must base yourself on the proclamations of the Real Lord as recorded in the Classics and the Histories so that you do not make the smallest mistake.

Let me provide an example of the sequential order of humans and things after the first differentiation of the Chaos [*hundun* 混沌]. On the Day of the Portent, first heaven and earth were created and transformed. This Day of the Portent existed right between [the realms of] color and subtlety, attached to neither position, so it was not an ordinary day.

Heaven is the largest of things without spiritual awareness. Its form is perfectly spherical, its substance solid, clear, and transparent. It is not similar to other things, which can be altered and spoiled. Altogether it is one heaven, but it has seven layers that are able to rotate and revolve. Above the seven layers are two more layers of ultimate clarity and ultimate greatness that never turn and move. These are called "the heavens of stillness." In their midst are all the great sages and great worthies, with the heavenly immortals serving nearby, and beyond them is no place to go, for it does not belong to creation and transformation. They are enduring, secluded, clear, and silent, without smell or sound. No one can go beyond their limit, though not because the place is prohibited. Rather, this is like things on land that cannot walk in water, or things in water that cannot travel on land—all of these are so in their self-suchness. Only the Utmost Sage can go there.

Earth is a name for the unification of water and soil. Although its form is round, its principle is square. This means that it has come to a stop and does not travel. The substance of earth is heavy and turbid and goes down to the ultimate lowness. When it takes up its dwelling in the midst of heaven, it settles down and becomes secure and does not go farther down.

Earth is like one spot in the midst of heaven, so it does not have much substance, though it is deep. At the outset of its creation, water covered the soil completely. After it was created, the Real Lord issued the mandate for the water to retreat so as to make the oceans, without allowing it to go beyond its root boundaries. Then the earth began to appear and became uncovered so it could carry things.

Except for the two uppermost levels, all else was perfected during the Day of the Portent. On the first day the mountains and rivers were created and transformed, on the second day grass and trees, and on the third day hatred and dislike, which became darkness, fogginess, obscurity, and disturbance in heaven and earth, and calamity, misfortune, and sickness in humans and things. On the fourth day, the sun, moon, stars, and constellations were created and transformed; on the fifth day the things that fly and walk. There is nothing of this that was not provided for the sake of human use. This principle is in reality not apart from this very body.

Nuʿmānī on the Greater Occultation of the Twelfth Imam

Translated by Omid Ghaemmaghami

A distinctive feature of Twelver Shīʿī eschatology is the concept of an unbroken series of *imāms,* spiritual leaders descended from Muḥammad, each designated by his predecessor. According to this "theology of history," after the eleventh imam (Ḥasan ibn ʿAlī al-ʿAskarī, d. 874), his designee entered into a state called "concealment" without ever assuming "ordinary" direct leadership of the community. Shīʿī tradition by then included the belief that an awaited eschatological figure called the Mahdī (Rightly Guided One). According to the group that came to be known as the Twelver Shīʿa, the Mahdī was none other than the son of Ḥasan al-ʿAskarī. The Twelver Shīʿa held that the young son of Ḥasan al-ʿAskarī went into concealment (*ghayba*) and was available very rarely, and only to a select group of representatives for a period of approximately sixty-seven years. After the fourth deputy died (in 941) without having designated a successor, the twelfth imam entered into the "greater concealment." That state will come to an end only when the twelfth imam returns to usher in an age of justice. Ibn Abī Zaynab an-Nuʿmānī (d. 956/71) is one of the earliest and most important sources on Twelver eschatology and theology of history.

Ibn Abī Zaynab an-Nuʿmānī was an itinerant scholar of Shīʿī Hadith, whose quest for traditions of the imams took him to Shiraz, Baghdad, Damascus, and Aleppo. He was a student of the famous Shīʿī traditionist Muḥammad ibn Yaʿqūb al-Kulaynī (d. ca. 940) and is commonly referred to by the agnomen *al-kātib* (the scribe) because he personally copied the latter's *Al-Kāfī.* However, unlike his teacher, who is believed to have died before the end of the period that is commonly known as the first or Lesser Occultation (*al-ghayba aṣ-ṣughrā*) of the twelfth imam, Nuʿmānī lived and wrote into the early years of the Greater Occultation (*al-ghayba al-kubrā*) as well.[30]

Nuʿmānī's *Book of Occultation* (*Kitāb al-ghayba,* completed in Dhū al-Ḥijja [Month of Ḥajj, April–May] 954),[31] is the earliest extant defense of the *ghayba* of the twelfth imam written after the start of the Greater Occultation. It is difficult to overestimate its importance as a window into the Shīʿī community of the period of heightened *ḥayra* (confusion, helplessness, and loss) that characterizes the period that immediately followed the plenipotentiaries, or representatives (*sufarāʾ*, pl. of *safīr*) of the hidden twelfth imam. This was especially so in light of the fact that unlike Kulaynī's *Al-Kāfī,* which is a catalog of Shīʿī traditions with few comments from its compiler, Nuʿmānī offers valuable observations about the state of the fledgling Twelver Shīʿī community of his time and on rarer occasions, his own interpretation of the traditions he cites.

In the work's introduction, Nuʿmānī bemoans the fact that the Shīʿa have split into numerous branches. Those who believe in the line of the imams either do not know who the Hidden Imam is, dispute his existence, or are so pusillanimous as to allow themselves to be overcome with doubt about the *ghayba.*[32] He has therefore taken matters into his own hands and decided to write a formal defense of the *ghayba* from the attacks of "those who oppose the tiny group [of believers] who steadfastly follow" the hidden twelfth imam. It is clear from the work's prologue that at the time in which Nuʿmānī is writing (some twelve years after the death of the last representative of the Hidden Imam), the Shīʿa who upheld the *ghayba* of the twelfth imam were barely a visible minority. Nuʿmānī refers to his fellow believers as "the small band" (*al-ʿiṣāba al-qalīla*) and "tiny group who stand apart from the great majority who claim to be Shīʿa but who have split into different factions (*firaq*) as a result of their corrupt and selfish inclinations." These he accuses of stubbornly refusing to patiently endure the loss (*fiqdān*) of the imam and the length of his *ghayba* despite repeated warnings from the (previous) imams to remain steadfast, for example, "Be not distressed at the small number of those who tread the path of guidance."

The *Kitāb al-ghayba* is the first Shīʿī work in which the distinguishing features of the two *ghaybas* are delineated: "As for the first *ghayba,* it was when there were representatives (*as-sufarāʾ*) between the Imām and the people who had been appointed (*manṣūbīn*) [by the imam]." It is noteworthy that Nuʿmānī neither identifies these representatives nor for that matter suggests that they were only four in number as codified a century later by the famous Shīʿī scholar and Qur'ān commentator Muḥammad aṭ-Ṭūsī (d. 1066/7), known as Shaykh aṭ-Ṭā'ifa (the Elder [spiritual leader] of the Group). He says only that they were "prominent people who were visible and well-known to the believers." These representatives served as messengers between the imam and the faithful, providing answers to all manner of abstruse questions and problems posed by the believers to their imam. However, Nuʿmānī adds, "This was the short *ghayba* (*al-ghayba al-qaṣīra*) whose days have come to an end and whose time has now passed. The second *ghayba* (*al-ghayba ath-thānīya*) is the one during which the representatives (*as-sufarā'*) and the intermediaries (*al-wasā'iṭ*)[33] have been removed for a purpose intended by God." Nuʿmānī declares that this "second *ghayba*," a time in which the believers are tested, thrown into confusion (*al-balbala*), sifted (*al-gharbala*), and purified (*at-taṣfiyya*), "is now upon us."[34] Yet according to him, the traditions of the Prophet and previous imams predicted both the *ghayba* of the twelfth imam (referred to inter alia as the "the master of truth"—*ṣāḥib al-ḥaqq*) and the *ghayba* of "the means [of reaching the imam]" (*as-sabab*), that is, the imam's representatives and intermediaries who constituted the support (*as-sanād*) whom the Shīʿa relied on. The moment this support was removed, they became like goats without a shepherd and the upheaval (*fitna*) of the second occultation commenced. For as long as they had intermediaries (*al-wasā'iṭ*) between themselves and the Hidden Imam, there was a means to communicate (*balāgh*) with him and receive guidance (*hudā*). God then decreed "the removal [of] such means" (*rafʿ al-asbāb*) during the second *ghayba* in order to further test the Shīʿa.

What follows is an abridged translation of the final section of Nuʿmānī's introduction, in which he lays out the contents of his *Kitāb al-ghayba,* summarizing his main themes and the traditional sources upon which he relies.[35]

Text

In this book, I have compiled the Traditions that have narrated by our masters on the authority of the Commander of the Faithful (Imam ʿAlī) and the [other] truthful Imams about the *ghayba* and other matters related to it. Time has not permitted me to mention everything nor has everything which has been narrated about the *ghayba* reached me or been mentioned by me due to distance and the fact that I am unable to remember every Tradition I heard. Indeed, what others have narrated about this matter is greater in number than what I have in my possession.

In what follows, I have arranged the Traditions in chapters beginning with:

1. [The Hadiths] that have been narrated concerning the need to protect the secret of the Family of Muḥammad (i.e., Fāṭima and the Imāms) from those who do not have the capacity [to understand it] and to comport oneself with the conduct of the Friends of God in concealing what they were commanded (by God) to conceal from the enemies of religion, those who harbor enmity [toward the imams] and oppose [them], and other groups such as those who create heretical innovations, those who doubt, and the Muʿtazilites who reject the excellence of the Commander of the Faithful, who allow those who must follow an Imam to take precedence over the Imam, and who permit the one who is deficient to precede he who is perfect. In this manner, they have opposed God who said: "Which is worthier to be followed—He who guides to the truth, or he who guides not unless he is guided? What then ails you, how you judge?" (10:35) . . . They reject the excellence of the pure Imams and the station of Imamate even after God established the proof through His words, "And hold you fast to God's bond, together, and do not scatter" (3:103), and His Messenger fulfilled the evidence by proclaiming that his family are the source of guidance, the ark of salvation, and one of the two weighty testimonies that he taught us to cling to when he said [in a Hadith], "I leave among you my twin weighty testimonies: the Book of God and my family, the people of my house. They are an extended cord between you and God. One end of this cord is in God's hands and the other end in yours. As long as you cling to it, you will never go astray."

Then we will mention the following:

2. The Cord of God which He has commanded us to cling to through His words, "Cling fast one and all to the cord of God and do not divide into factions" (3:103).
3. [The Hadiths] that have been narrated about the Imamate, that it is from God and by His choice just as He has said, "and your Lord creates whatsoever He will and He chooses; they have not the choice" (28:68). The Imamate is a covenant and trust from God that is passed on from one Imam to the next.
4. [The Hadiths] that have been narrated about Imams being twelve in number. Here, we will include passages from the Qurʾān, the Torah, and the Gospel that establish this fact after narrating Traditions that have been narrated by Sunnīs regarding the twelve Imams.
5. Those Traditions that have been narrated about those who claim the Imamate or falsely claim to be an Imam, and that the owner of any flag

raised before the rise of the Qāʾim (the One who will arise) is an evil enchanter.

6. [Other] Traditions that have been narrated by Sunnīs.
7. What has been narrated about those who have entertained doubts about one of the Imams, spent a night not knowing their Imam or worshipped God without [knowing] the Imam.
8. What has been narrated about the fact that God never leaves the earth bereft of a proof.[36]
9. What has been narrated concerning the fact that if only two people were left on earth, one of them must be the proof.
10. What has been narrated about the *ghayba* of the Imam, what the Commander of the Faithful and the Imams after him have mentioned about this matter, [and especially] the warnings they have provided.
11. What has been narrated about the fact that the Shīʿa have been ordered to be patient, forbearing, and eagerly await [the appearance of the Imam] during the *ghayba*.
12. What has been narrated about the fact that the Shīʿa will be tested and split into numerous groups during the *ghayba* such that only a few will remain believing in the truth of this matter.
13. What has been narrated about the times of adversity that will come to pass before the rise of the Qāʾim.
14. What has been narrated about [the Qāʾim's] characteristics and life.
15. What has been revealed in the Qurʾān about [the Qāʾim].
16. What has narrated about the portents that will occur before his appearance and which will point to his rise and the fact that his cause (*amr*) is close.[37]
17. What has been narrated about the prohibition of setting a time [for his appearance] or mentioning the name of the lord of the cause.
18. What has been narrated about [the affliction] that has befallen the Qāʾim since he [first] appeared and that he will continue to suffer at the hands of the ignorant.
19. What has been narrated about the army of wrath who are the companions of the Qāʾim and their number.
20. What has been narrated about as-Sufyānī, that his *amr* is definite and he [will appear] before rise of the Qāʾim.[38]

21. What has been narrated about the banner of the Messenger of God, its features, and that no one but the Qāʾim will unfurl it again after the Day of the Camel.[39]
22. What has been narrated about the state of the Shīʿa before, during, and after the Qāʾim's revolt.
23. What has been narrated about the fact that the Qāʾim will renew Islam, that Islam began as a strange thing and will once again become a strange thing as it was in the beginning.
24. What has been narrated about the length of time during which the Qāʾim will rule after he appears.
25. What has been narrated about Ismāʿīl ibn ʿAlī ʿAbd Allāh[40] and the falsehoods spread by those who are in error and who remain bereft of ears with which to listen and learn.
26. What has been narrated concerning the fact that whosoever knows his Imam will never be harmed if this cause is delayed or comes soon.

We beseech God by His noble countenance and great station to bless the chosen elect from his creation, His strong chord and most firm handle which "can never break" (2:256): Muḥammad and his pure family. We pray that he confirm us "with the firm word, in the present life and in the world to come." We ask Him for all this alone—nothing more, nothing less. Truly, He is the All-Beneficent, the Ever-Generous.[41]

PART FOUR

The Science of Hearts

SPIRITUALITY AND LITERATURE

MUSLIM AUTHORS HAVE VENTURED WELL beyond the more "technical" theological genres of part 3 in their quest to communicate the riches of their tradition. Much of the content there leans toward slightly more "theoretical" dimensions of Islamic belief, the "science of divine transcendent unity" (*'ilm at-tawḥīd*). Part 4 now tilts toward the more practical or experiential implications of that content, or what ancient Muslim tradition names the "science of hearts" (*'ilm al-qulūb*). Here we highlight two large clusters of themes with far-reaching, but too seldom acknowledged, theological implications: knowledge and spiritual quest (chapter 7) and literary/narrative theological pedagogy (chapter 8). In addition to providing a new angle on theological content, Islam's treasures of "spiritual" or mystical literature also embrace a wide range of literary forms and religious functions. Part 4 therefore samples a variety of genres in both prose and poetry. Prose texts include the genres of letter, short treatise, and narrative with theological import. Poetic works in the "spiritual couplets" (*mathnawī*) literary form communicate in a distinctively "didactic" manner. Chief functions include both the *pastoral* (such as a letter from a spiritual guide to a seeker eager for advice on various theologically important topics) and the more narrowly *pedagogical* (as in several short treatises). As for theological themes, examples emphasize the metaphor of spiritual journey as well as the qualities and demands of intimate or experiential knowledge (*ma'rifa*) of God.

SEVEN

Knowledge and the Spiritual Quest

MANY THEOLOGICAL TREATISES, AS WELL as a number of traditional creedal formulations, begin with a discussion of the critical role of knowledge in Islamic tradition. In most instances those texts are talking about traditional or "acquired" knowledge, or *ʿilm,* the focal point of the work of Muslim religious scholars, whose designation *ʿulamāʾ* shares the same verbal root. But there is more to the theological significance of knowledge as manifest in a whole other "category," another mode by which human beings can know God. A central theme in an important genre of Sufi literature is the nature and significance of intimate, experiential, or "infused" knowledge—*maʿrifa.*

WAYS OF KNOWING: ACQUIRED AND EXPERIENTIAL

ʿAlī on Knowledge and the Spiritual Life

Translated by I. K. A. Howard

Both early Shīʿī tradition and centuries of Sufi teaching emphasize spiritual wisdom as a blend of "traditional" acquired or discursive knowledge (*ʿilm*) and experiential knowledge (*maʿrifa*). Here we have sayings attributed to ʿAlī (d. 661), providing insight into classic Shīʿī emphasis on the importance of *ʿilm,* as recorded in the so-called Hadith of Kumayl.[1]

Text

[This is a selection of] some of the words of [the Commander of the faithful] in praise of [traditional] knowledge (*ʿilm*), about the categories of people, the merit of [traditional] knowledge, and about acquiring it and wisdom.

The traditionists (*ahl an-naql*) have reported on the authority of Kumayl ibn Ziyād, that he said: One day the Commander of the faithful took me by the hand in the mosque and led me out of it. When he had gone out into the desert, he breathed a deep sigh and said: "Kumayl, these hearts are containers [of knowledge]; the best of them are those that best preserve [the knowledge]. Therefore preserve what I say to you. There are three kinds of people: one who knows the Lord [for His own sake], one who acquires knowledge as a means of salvation and low class rabble, followers of every crower, who bend with every breeze. These people do not seek to be illuminated by the light of learning, nor do they resort to any sure authority (*rukn*).

"Kumayl, knowledge is better than wealth. Knowledge guards you while you guard wealth. Wealth is diminished by expenditure while knowledge is increased even by giving it away.

"Kumayl, the love of knowledge is a [kind of] religion that is professed [by a human being] and through which he perfects his obedience [to God] during his life and acquires a noble reputation after his death. Knowledge is a judge and wealth is something that is judged.

"Kumayl, those who amass wealth die even as they live while those who possess knowledge will continue to exist for as long as time lasts. Their individual entities will disappear but their images will remain in the hearts [of human beings].

"Here, indeed is much knowledge," and he pointed to his breast. "If I could come upon people who would carry it (*ḥamala*).... Indeed I came upon such as took it too quickly and [thus] did not protect it. Such a person would use the tools of religion for [success in] the world. He would seek to use the proofs of God and His favors as a means of dominating His friends and His Book. Or [there was the sort of person] who submitted to the wisdom [of God's knowledge] without having true vision of his own [need for] humility. At the first appearance of any problem, doubt would eat into his heart. Neither this individual nor that one [was appropriate]. [As each] eagerly sought pleasures and was easily dominated by passions or enamored of amassing and hoarding wealth, they were not of the kind who would be shepherds of religion. They were both much more like cattle wandering without restraint in search of fodder. Thus in the [living] death of such carriers of knowledge would knowledge itself die.

"O God, indeed the earth will never be without [someone who is] a proof [*ḥujja,* i.e., an imam] of You to Your Creation, whether [he acts] openly in the public eye or secretly out of fear. [In this way] the proofs of God and His signs will not be brought to naught. Where are those people? They are individuals who are least in number yet greatest in God's esteem. Through them God preserves His proofs [to the world] until they hand them as a trust to their equals and sow them as seeds in the hearts of those like themselves. Through them knowledge has broken into the inner realities of faith and they have found the spirit of certainty to be something gentle and comforting. They have found easy what those who love the easy life have found to be hard and difficult. They are familiar with things that the ignorant distrust. They have travelled through this world with their bodies while their souls have been [always] associated with the Highest Abode. These are the representatives (*khulafāʾ*) of God on His earth and those who summon His worshippers to His [true] religion.

Then he breathed a deep sigh and said: "Oh, how I long to see them." He took his hand from mine and said to me: "Go now, if you wish."

Among the words of [the Commander of the faithful] urging people to knowledge (*maʿrifa*), explaining its merit, and the qualities of those who possess knowledge (*ʿulamāʾ*), and [describing] how those who seek knowledge should be, is [this report] of a speech that scholars have handed down in [their] accounts. However, we have omitted the beginning of it, [starting at] his words:

"Praise be to God, Who has guided us from error, Who has given us vision [and kept us away] from blindness, Who has [bestowed] on us the religion of Islam. [It is He] Who has caused prophethood to have been among us and Who has made us good people. He has made our ultimate pinnacle the ultimate pinnacle of prophets. He has made us the best community which has come for humankind. We enjoin the good and forbid the evil. We worship God and we do not associate anything with Him, nor do we take any master (*walī*) apart from Him. We are witnesses of God and the Apostle was our witness [of Him]. We seek intercession and are given intercession along with those with whom we sought intercession from Him. We ask and our request is granted. He forgives the sins of those whom we pray for. God has elected us. We do not call on any master apart from Him.

"People, help one another to [acts of] good faith and piety. But do not help one another to sin and aggression. Fear God. Indeed God is severe in [His] punishment.

"People, I [ʿAlī] am the cousin of your Prophet and the closest of you to God and His Apostle. Therefore question me, question me. It is as if knowledge (*ʿilm*) has already wasted away among you. When anyone who possesses knowledge perishes, then part of his knowledge perishes with him. Those among the people who possess knowledge (*ʿulamāʾ*) are like the full-moon in the sky whose light illuminates the rest of the constellations. Take hold of whatever knowledge appears to you. Beware of seeking it for four reasons: that through it you may vie with [other] possessors of knowledge; or that by it you may quarrel with the ignorant; or that as a result of it you act hypocritically in discussions; or that through it you may disregard the leaders of the people in favor of yourselves becoming leaders. Those who do [good] acts and those who do not will not receive equal punishment from God. May God benefit both us and you by what He has taught us. May [a person who has knowledge] use it only for the sake of God. Indeed He is One Who hears, One Who answers."

Among his statements about the description of the one who possesses knowledge (*ʿālim*) and the training of one who seeks to possess knowledge is what is reported by al-Ḥārith al-Aʿwar (d. 684). He said: I heard the Commander of the faithful say, "It is the right of the one who possesses knowledge that he should not be questioned too much, nor be required to answer. Nor should he be troubled when he is tired, nor caught hold of by the sleeves when he rises [to leave]. No [finger] should be pointed at him with regard to anything which is needed, nor should any secret of his be divulged. No one should speak slander in his presence. He should be given great respect in as much as he has preserved the command of God. The student should only sit in front of him and should not expose him to too much of his company. If a student [seeking] knowledge, or anyone else, comes to him while he is in a group, he should make a general greeting to them all and give particular good wishes to him.

"Let him be respected whether he is present or absent. Let his right be known. Indeed the person who possesses knowledge receives greater reward than the one who fasts, the one who undertakes [other religious duties], [or] the one who strives along the path of God. When the one who possesses knowledge dies, a breach is made in Islam which can only be filled by his successor and the one who seeks after knowledge. The angels ask for forgiveness for him and those in heaven and on earth pray for him."

Hujwīrī on Experiential Knowledge

Translated by John Renard

In *Revelation of Realities Veiled* (*Kashf al-maḥjūb*), the first major Sufi work in Persian, Hujwīrī (d. 1072) sets his whole discussion of the spiritual life on the foundation of discursive or acquired knowledge (*ʿilm*). Then, as he maps out the path toward the upper reaches of mystical attainment, he discusses *maʿrifa,* in his chapter 15, as the first of a series of veils to be lifted for the seeker. Hujwīrī often quotes the Arabic of famous authorities and then glosses in Persian: I have indicated those texts with an astrisk (*) but have not included a translation of his gloss except when it amounts to significantly more than a simple, literal rendering of the Arabic original.[2]

Text

CHAPTER 15. DRAWING BACK THE FIRST VEIL: EXPERIENTIAL KNOWLEDGE OF GOD

God has said, "And they do not measure God's expansiveness accurately" (6:91). The Prophet said, "If you knew God experientially, you would walk on the seas, and mountains would disappear at your bidding." *Maʿrifa* of God is of two kinds: one is discursive (*ʿilmī*) and the other affective (*ḥālī*). Discursive *maʿrifa* is the basis of every good thing in this world and the next: knowledge of God is the most important condition in all spiritual moments and states. God has said, "I did not create jinns and human beings except to serve Me" (51:56), that is, so that they would know Me experientially.* Most people, however, ignore this state of affairs, except those whom God has chosen and led forth from the darkness of this world, and whose hearts He himself has brought to life with His own presence, according to the word of the Most High, "He made for him a light by which he might walk among the people" (6:122)—alluding to a life "like one in profound darkness" (6:122 cont.), by which he meant Abū Jahl.[3]

Maʿrifa is the life of the heart through God, and the innermost being's refusal to attend to anything but God. Each individual's value is in experiential knowledge, and whoever lacks experiential knowledge is worthless. Religious scholars and jurists and others call sound conceptual knowledge (*ṣiḥḥat-i ʿilm*) of God *maʿrifa*, but the Sufi shaykhs use the term *maʿrifa* to mean sound spiritual/emotional state (*ṣiḥḥat-i ḥāl*). They therefore consider *maʿrifa* superior to *ʿilm*, since sound spiritual/emotional state presupposes sound conceptual knowledge, and the two are quite distinct. In other words, one cannot possess experiential knowledge without conceptual knowledge of God, but one can possess conceptual knowledge without possessing experiential knowledge. Members of these two groups who have been unaware of the aforementioned two types of "knowledge" have become embroiled in unprofitable debate, one faction repudiating the views of the other.

Let me now unveil the mystery of this situation in a way that both factions, God willing, might find helpful.

Understand that there is considerable divergence of views concerning the experiential knowledge of God and sound traditional knowledge of Him. The Muʿtazila claim that *maʿrifa* of God is intellectual and that it is proper only to a rational individual. Such a claim is flimsy, given that insane persons within the Abode of Islam are judged to possess *maʿrifa,* and that children who have not attained the age of reason are judged to possess faith. If, therefore, *maʿrifa* were an intellectual quality, people like these could not be judged to possess *maʿrifa* since they lack rationality, nor could unbelievers be judged guilty of unbelief if they possessed reason. If rationality were the cause of *maʿrifa,* one would have to conclude that every rational person possessed *maʿrifa* and that everyone lacking rationality was ignorant of God, but that is clearly absurd.

One faction claims that the cause of *maʿrifa* of God is demonstrative argument, and that only those who engage in deductive reasoning attain *maʿrifa.* This argument's weakness is that Iblīs witnessed many divine signs, including heaven and hell, and the divine Throne and Footstool, but these did not bring about *maʿrifa* in him. As the Most High said, "Even if We were to send them angels and the dead were to speak to them, and We were to bring together all things before them, they would not believe except as God willed" (6:111).* If the vision of divine signs and demonstrative proof of them were the cause of *maʿrifa,* then, in the above scriptural verse, God would have pointed to that, rather than to His own will, as the cause of *maʿrifa.*

Sunnī Muslims regard soundness of intellect and the vision of divine signs as a means to *maʿrifa,* but not its cause; that cause is none other than God's favor, kindness, and will. Lacking the divine favor, the intellect is blind, for by itself intellect is ignorant even of itself and cannot know the reality of other intellects. Since it does not know even itself, how can it know something other than itself? Without divine favor demonstrative proof and reflection on the vision of divine signs are all inaccurate, for whimsical people and sundry heretical factions rely on demonstrative proof but most of them do not possess *maʿrifa.*

As for those privy to the divine favor, however, all their spiritual movements are indications of *maʿrifa.* When they pursue demonstrative proof, they are searching, and when they leave demonstrative proof aside, they are surrendering to God. But with respect to sound *maʿrifa,* surrender to God does not take precedence over searching. Abandoning the quest is not an acceptable principle, and surrender to God is a principle in which no anxiety is appropriate, but the spiritual reality of these two is not *maʿrifa*. Understand that in the final analysis there is no heart-expanding[4] guide for the individual except God in the face of all that the wrongdoers say. Neither intellect nor rational proofs are capable of guiding the individual, and there is no demonstrative proof clearer than the fact that God has said, "For if they were brought back, they would surely revert to what had been forbidden them" (6:28). That is,* if the unbelievers were brought back into this world, they would still act on the basis of their infidelity.

When someone asked ʿAlī, Commander of the Faithful, about experiential knowledge, he replied, "I gained experiential knowledge of God through God, and of that which is other than God through the light of God."* God fashioned the body and entrusted its life to the soul; He fashioned the heart and entrusted its life to Himself. Therefore, since neither intellect nor human judgment have the power to give life to the body, neither can they give life to the heart, as God has said, "or one who was dead and whom We brought back to life . . . " (6:122). He has thus entrusted all life to Himself, as when He continued in the same verse, "and for whom We have made a light by which he might walk among humankind." In other words, "I am the creator of the light that illumines the faithful one." He also said, "What of the one whose spiritual center God has expanded toward surrender and so toward receiving light from his Lord . . . ?" (39:22). He has taken charge of the unfolding of the heart Himself, and its closure as well, as He has said, "God seals their hearts and their hearing" (2:7), and, again, "Pay no heed to any person whose heart we have allowed to stint in remembering Us" (18:28).

It follows, thus, that since it is He who contracts and expands, seals and amplifies the heart, it would be impossible for the heart to recognize any other guide than Him. For all that is not God is a cause or a means, and anything that proceeds from cause and means cannot show the way apart from the providence of the One who creates the means—without God's favor it is a veil and a highway robber rather than a guide.[5] The Most High has said, "But God has made the faith dear to you and has made it attractive to your hearts" (49:7). He has thus associated beautification and endearment with Himself, and the requirement of the reverential fear that is essential to intimate knowledge is from Him. They who are so obliged, since they are under the obligation, cannot choose [either] to reject it or undertake it. As a result, in the absence of God's tutelage, human beings' share of *maʿrifa* of Him will be none other than their incapacity to know Him.

Abū 'l-Ḥasan Nūrī (d. 907) says, "There is no guide to God apart from Him, for one seeks knowledge in the performance of service."* Apart from God, hearts have no guide to *maʿrifa;* let them seek knowledge to render service, not the soundness of *maʿrifa.* No creature has the capability of taking anyone else to God. People who use demonstrative proofs are no more rational than Abū Ṭālib,[6] nor was there a guide greater than Muḥammad. Even so, since it was the foreordained lot of Abū Ṭālib to come to an unfortunate end, Muḥammad's guidance was of no use to him.

In demonstrative proof, one first turns away from God, since demonstrative proof requires one to focus on something else; but the essence of intimate knowledge is turning away from all that is not God. Ordinarily one searches for objects of knowledge through demonstrative proof, but intimate knowledge of God goes against the grain. As a result, intimate knowledge of God is impossible apart from endless intellectual perplexity. One does not receive the divine favor by a process of human acquisition. Without God's graces and kindnesses the individual has no guidance—that comes from revelations to hearts and from the treasuries of the unseen realms. Everything other than God is created in time. It stands to reason that while a contingent being might come to its own kind, it cannot arrive at the ontological status of its own Creator. For a being that "acquires" another must be of a higher order than the one acquired, so that the one acquired is overcome. The marvel here is not that evidence of an act leads the intellect to affirm the existence of the agent, but that by the light of God the heart denies its own existence. In the former instance, the resulting realization is discursive, in the latter, affective.

The faction that considers intellect to be the cause of *maʿrifa* should ask themselves what aspect of *maʿrifa* it is that reason establishes in the heart, since whatever reason affirms, *maʿrifa* can only deny. In other words, God is the opposite of whatever image of Him reason constructs in the heart. And if the image of God that reason fashions is different from God's reality, how can intellect attain *maʿrifa* through demonstrative proof? Since reason and imagination are of the same genus, and since the affirmation of genus negates *maʿrifa,* any affirmation [of the existence of God] from demonstrative proof amounts to anthropomorphism and any denial of God amounts to a denial of divine attributes. It is impossible for intellect to transcend these two opposite principles, both of which are sheer ignorance from the perspective of *maʿrifa,* since those who adhere to both views do not proclaim God's transcendent unity.

Once intellect has reached its limit, and the hearts of God's Friends have no remedy other than their quest, they take repose in the courtyard of helplessness, bereft of resources. But they become restless in their repose, raising their hands in a plea for help as they seek a balm for their hearts. When they have exhausted their own power to continue the quest, the power of God becomes their power. In other words, they find the way from Him to Him, experience relief from the anguish of separation, and find rest in the garden of intimacy, nestled in perfect refreshment and joy. When intellect saw that the hearts had achieved their desire, it searched in vain for mastery and did not find it. Intellect was left behind and became perplexed, and in its perplexity and agitation it lost its power to act. At that point God clothed the intellect in the garb of service and said to it, "When you relied on your own resources, your attempts to do so kept you behind a veil; but when your resources vanished, you were left behind, and in your being left behind you arrived at the goal."

Nearness to God is therefore the heart's portion, while that of intellect is service. God supplies the individual infused knowledge of God by His tutelage and instruction, so that the individual knows God through Him rather than as a result of human faculties. This is a knowledge in which the existence of the human being is merely borrowed, so that for the existence of one endowed with intimate knowledge, narcissism is a betrayal, and the individual's remembrance of God is incessant, his labor unstinting, and his experiential knowledge becomes a spiritual condition rather than a mere claim.

Yet another faction claims that *maʿrifa* is a matter of inspiration. Again, this is not possible because experiential knowledge is based on the ability to distinguish falsehood from truth, whereas those who appeal to inspiration do not provide a sound criterion for distinguishing wrong from right. Suppose one person claimed, "I know by inspiration that God does not occupy a place," while another argued, "Inspiration tells me that God does have a place." One of these two contradictory claims must be true and the other false, but both appeal to inspiration. One needs to distinguish between truth and falsehood with respect to these two claims, and that requires evidence. Thus, the argument for inspiration is folly. This is a view espoused by Brahmins and inspirationists, and I have known some people who have taken the position to extremes while associating their work with the views of religious people. These people, however, are entirely in error and their opinions are at odds with [all] rational people, unbelievers and Muslims alike. As a result, if ten proponents of inspiration put forth ten contradictory opinions concerning the same issue, all are equally mistaken and not one gets it right. If someone were to say that anything at odds with the Revealed Law is not inspiration, I would respond that the view was inherently mistaken and ill-conceived. For if one evaluates and affirms inspiration in relation to Revealed Law, then intimate knowledge derives from the Revealed Law, prophethood, and divine guidance rather than from inspiration. Consequently, the issue of inspiration in relation to *maʿrifa* is moot.

Another group has claimed that *maʿrifa* of God is necessary. That, too, is impossible, for it would imply that rational human beings would have to be in agreement on what they know. But we observe that certain reasonable people willfully deny and disavow the truth by holding teachings of anthropomorphism or denial of divine attributes, proving that intimate knowledge is not innate. In addition, if intimate knowledge of God were innate, the concept of religious duty would be meaningless. For obligation in *maʿrifa* in relation to things known as necessary, such as the self, the heavens and the earth, day and night, pain and pleasure and the like, is an absurdity: no rational person can doubt these things, for there is great need to know them, and even one who preferred not to know them would be incapable of doing so. There is, however, a faction of would-be Sufis who, reflecting on the soundness of their certitude, claim, "We know God innately." Since they have not the slightest doubt in their hearts, they call their certitude necessity. They are not mistaken about the meaning of their claim, but their mode of expression is faulty. Knowledge of that which is necessary cannot be the sole possession of an elite, but belongs to all rational beings. Moreover, innate knowledge would be evident in the hearts of lovers without a secondary cause, while discursive knowledge of God, as well as intimate knowledge of Him, must be a result of some cause.

However, the master Abū ʿAlī Daqqāq[7] and Shaykh Abū Sahl [Suʿlūkī] (d. 980) and his father, who was an authoritative teacher at Nīshāpūr, hold that the inception of *maʿrifa* is based on demonstrative proof but that its end is intuitive, just as one initially acquires a knowledge of devotional actions, a knowledge that eventually becomes necessary. Some Sunnī Muslims put it this way: "Don't you see that in paradise knowledge of God becomes necessary, so that what is necessary there should be necessary here as well? In this world, too, when the prophets were in the spiritual state in which they heard God's word, whether directly or when an angel mediated the revelation, they knew necessarily." To that I respond that those who dwell in Paradise know God necessarily because no religious duty applies in Paradise, and the prophets are preserved from punishment and safe from separation. The one who has necessary knowledge about Him has no fear of being cut off. The superiority of faith and experiential knowledge is in their hiddenness, for when these things become visible, faith becomes common knowledge; and when something becomes visible, free choice departs and the roots of Revealed Law are disturbed. Even the law of apostasy becomes pointless, so that Balʿam[8] or Barṣīṣa[9] or Iblīs[10] are not precisely guilty of unbelief, since it is agreed that they had experiential knowledge of God. Regarding Iblīs, for example, God has informed us about the situation of his banishment and reproach, with the words spoken by Iblīs, "Then, by Your might, I will lead them all astray" (38:82). Indeed, his saying "by your might," and his hearing God's response implies a degree of experiential knowledge.

One who possesses experiential knowledge, while he remains in that condition, is safe from being separated from God. Separation results from the cessation of *maʿrifa,* whereas one cannot conceive of the loss of necessary *ʿilm.* For the majority of people this question is fraught with difficulty. The crux of the matter is that if one is to steer clear of the danger, one must understand that, apart from God's ceaseless informing and guidance, human beings have no *ʿilm* or *maʿrifa* of Him. It is appropriate that individuals' certitude in experiential knowledge may wax and wane, but the principle of experiential knowledge itself is not subject to increase or diminishment, for a change in either direction would amount to a diminishment.

Uncritical acceptance of authority must not characterize one's knowledge of God. One must know God through the attributes of His perfection, a knowledge incomplete except by the goodness of God's providence and the assurance of His favor. For the guidance of minds belongs entirely to God and they are wholly under His disposition. As God chooses, He can either make one of His deeds a source of guidance with which to point the way to Himself, or use the same deed as a veil that thwarts access to Him. Jesus, for example, was a source of guidance to some people through *maʿrifa,* while for others he was a hindrance to intimate knowledge: the first said, "He is God's servant," and the second, "He is God's son." Some people, similarly, have taken idols and moon and sun as guides to God, while for others these proved to be false leads.[11]

If sources of guidance such as these were the cause of intimate knowledge, it would follow that every one guided by them would possess intimate knowledge, but that is clearly not the case. God chooses individuals and transforms things into their guides so that by means of those things people come to Him and know Him. But a source of guidance is a means only and not a cause, and no one means has any priority over another with respect to God who brings all means into existence. Those who possess intimate knowledge, who swear by a particular means are guilty of dualistic thinking. Acknowledgment of anything other than the object of intimate knowledge is idolatry, [according to the divine words], "Those whom God leads astray have none to guide them" (7:186). If according to the Preserved Tablet, indeed, according to God's preference and foreknowledge, an individual is destined to misery, how can any evidence or demonstrative proof provide guidance? According to an Arabic saying, "The *maʿrifa* of one who turns to attend to what is other than God is dualism." Such an individual is annihilated and overwhelmed in the wrathful power of God, so how can anything other than God be His witness?

Ordinarily one apprehends proof more readily, and marvels are more apparent, by day. But if evidence were the cause of intimate knowledge of God, and evidences are more easily apprehended and wonders more accessible by day, how is it that when Abraham emerged from the cave by day, he saw nothing, but when he came out at night, "He beheld a star" (6:76)? Therefore, God shows the way to whatever servant He chooses and in whatever way He chooses, and opens for him the door of experiential knowledge. The servant thus arrives at a level in which the essence of *maʿrifa* seems alien and its qualities become harmful to him. *Maʿrifa* itself becomes a veil over the One Known and turns into a vain pretense. Dhū 'n-Nūn of Egypt says, "Be careful not to make a pretense of experiential knowledge." An unidentified poetic verse says:

Mystics make a pretense of experiential knowledge.
I sidle up to ignorance—that is my experiential knowledge.

Take care, therefore, not to make a pretense of experiential knowledge, or you will be destroyed. Adhere instead to the meaning of *maʿrifa* so that you will find salvation. When an individual is ennobled by a revelation of God's grandeur, his very being becomes a burden and all his personal characteristics become occasions of misfortune.

An individual who is God's, and to whom God belongs, remains unassociated with any thing in creation and the two worlds. The central reality of experiential knowledge is understanding that dominion belongs to God. Once an individual realizes that God has disposition of all possessions, why would he continue dealing with creatures to the point where he becomes veiled by them or by himself? Veils result from ignorance, so that, when ignorance vanishes, veils are obliterated, and experiential knowledge sees life here in terms of the life to come. And God knows best.

Shaykhs have made many veiled references to the meaning of *maʿrifa,* and, God willing, I will mention some of those for the reader's benefit. ʿAbd Allāh Mubārak (d. ca. 797) says, "*Maʿrifa* means not being astonished at anything."* The object of astonishment is a deed that exceeds the capability of the agent, but the Most High and Most Holy One [the agent] is omnipotent, so the one who possesses experiential knowledge cannot be astonished at what God does. If astonishment were to occur, it should be at the fact that God so elevates a handful of dust that it is capable of receiving His commandments, and so ennobles a drop of blood that it speaks of intimate friendship and experiential knowledge of God, seeks the vision of God, and becomes intent on nearness and union with Him. Dhū 'n-Nūn the Egyptian (d. 869) says, "The inner reality of *maʿrifa* is human access to mysteries through the imparting of the subtlest of lights."* In other words, by His light, God adorns the servant's heart with favor, and removes all troubles from it, to the point that in the servant's heart created earthly beings are of less weight than a mustard seed. The contemplation of mysteries, whether hidden or manifest, does not overpower him; and once God has brought this about, the merest glance becomes a contemplation.

Shiblī (d. 945) says, "*Maʿrifa* is ceaseless perplexity." There are two kinds of perplexity: one at God's existence and the other at God's attribute. Perplexity over God's existence is idolatry and unbelief, while perplexity over God's attribute is experiential knowledge: one who possesses experiential knowledge can have no shred of doubt about God's existence, while God's qualities elude the intellect altogether. What remains here is certitude concerning the being of God and perplexity concerning His manner of being, about which someone said, "O Guide of the perplexed, increase my perplexity." On the one hand, he affirmed experiential knowledge of the divine existence and the perfection of the divine attributes, while acknowledging that God is the desire of creation and the one who answers their prayers and gives perplexity to the perplexed. On the other, he asked for greater perplexity, thereby acknowledging that with respect to the object of its quest, the intellect is stymied between confusion and idolatry.

This is a subtle observation, recognizing, as it does, the possibility that experiential knowledge of God's existence necessitates confusion about one's own existence: a human being who knows God recognizes that he is wholly in thrall to God's power. Since both his being and non-being arise from God, and both his rest and movement depend on God's power, he becomes astonished, saying, "If all that I am rests with God, who am I and for what purpose do I exist?" It was in reference to this that the Prophet said, "An individual endowed with intimate self-knowledge knows his Lord intimately."* One who understands his own annihilation understands God's perdurance. As a result of annihilation, intellect and human attributes vanish. And if the intellect cannot comprehend the essence of a thing, it cannot arrive at experiential knowledge of it except through perplexity.

Abū Yazīd [al-Bisṭāmī] (d. 875) said, "*Maʿrifa* means understanding that both the motion and repose of human beings depend on God."* And no one exercises control over God's dominion without God's permission: an essence is an essence through Him; an effect is an effect through Him; an attribute is an attribute through Him; and it is He who gives motion and repose. None has the capability of motion or repose, or can perform any action unless God creates their possibility and instills in the human heart the desire. Human acts are unreal; only God's actions are real. Describing the person endowed with experiential knowledge, Muḥammad ibn Wāsiʿ says, "One who knows God intimately says little and is ceaselessly astonished."* For only that which falls within the limits and principles of human expression can be expressed, and expression is fundamentally limited. Since, in this case, that which one would like to talk about is unlimited and cannot be confined within the boundaries of human language, how can one affirm it? If, therefore, there is no way to express it in human language, what option remains for the servant other than ceaseless astonishment?

Shiblī says, "The essence of experiential knowledge is the inability to attain it," that is, apart from the very incapacity to know the central reality of a thing, the servant has no inkling. It follows, therefore, that once a servant arrives at experiential knowledge, claiming personal credit would be inappropriate. Incapacity implies ongoing quest, but as long as the seeker continues to depend on his own resources and qualities, "incapacity" does not aptly describe him. When these resources and qualities leave the servant, then his condition is annihilation rather than incapacity. A faction of charlatans who affirm human qualities and the ongoing responsibility for sound judgment, as well as God's eternal standard of proof, nevertheless identify *maʿrifa* entirely with powerlessness, claiming that human beings lack the capacity to achieve anything. This view is erroneous and harmful. I say to them, "In quest of what object have you become incapacitated? You manifest neither of the two indicators of powerlessness, namely, the annihilation of the means of seeking, and the appearance of the divine manifestation of transcendence." Where human faculties are annihilated, expression fails. Verbal expression ceases in its inability to speak of incapacity, for speaking about incapacity is not incapacity. And where the manifestation of divine transcendence occurs, there is no indication and powers of discrimination are out of the question.

Since that is the case, the incapacitated individual is unaware, either of being incapacitated, or that one would call his condition helplessness. Helplessness is other than God, and affirming *maʿrifa* of what is other than God is not *maʿrifa*. As long as the heart has room for anything other than God, and as long as the would-be possessor of experiential knowledge talks about other than God, that person does not yet truly possess experiential knowledge. Abū Ḥafṣ Ḥaddād (d. ca. 878) says, "Since I gained experiential knowledge of God, neither truth nor falsehood has entered my heart."* When desire and passion arise in the heart, the individual turns to the heart, so that the heart can offer guidance to the ego-soul, where falsehood resides. But when a person discovers evidence of experiential knowledge, he likewise has recourse to the heart so that it can guide him to the spirit, the wellspring of truth and spiritual reality.

When the heart is occupied by anything other than God, and the one who seeks experiential knowledge has recourse to the heart, that individual ends up in ignorance of God. Every human being seeks evidence of experiential knowledge from the heart, and they seek passion and desire from the heart as well; that is why they do not attain what they desire. Apart from God there is no repose so long as they go on seeking the truth from the heart. When an indication of evidence is required, they must return to God: this is the difference between a servant who has recourse to the heart and one who has recourse to God. Abū Bakr Wāsiṭī (d. ca. 932) says, "One endowed with experiential knowledge of God is isolated, in fact, he is mute and totally subdued."* And the Prophet said, "I cannot praise you adequately." While he was in a state of absence from God, the Prophet was the most eloquent among Arabs and non-Arabs alike. When he was taken from absence to presence, he said, "My tongue is incapable of praising You adequately, for I have gone from speech to speechlessness, from a spiritual state to being without a spiritual state. You are the one who is You. My speech is either from me or from You. If I spoke on my own, I would be veiled by my own speech. If I spoke through You, the apparent accomplishment of realizing proximity to You would in reality be a flaw. So I won't speak." Came the reply [to the first saying],

"O Muḥammad, if you do not speak, We will speak. By your life (15:72), if you do not speak in praise of Me, then all of you will be My praise. Since you do not consider yourself among those who praise Us, We have made every part of the universe your representative, so that they praise Me in your stead." And in God is success; God is our portion and the best of Friends.

THEOLOGICAL DIMENSIONS OF THE SPIRITUAL QUEST

Ibn al-ʿArabī on What Is Indispensable for the Spiritual Seeker

Translated by James W. Morris

Few Muslim authors have left a more enduring, and often controversial, legacy than Muḥyī 'd-Dīn ibn al-ʿArabī (d. 1240). The scope of his work—from the astonishing variety of literary genres to the range of theological and mystical themes to the sheer reach of his intellectual power, imagination, and creativity—is vast. A relatively small coterie of dedicated religious studies scholars have been responsible for making Ibn al-ʿArabī's thought accessible, though it is always challenging. Here is one of his more "pastoral" approaches to plumbing the theological depths of the spiritual life.[12]

Text

You asked, O seeker, about the quintessence of what the seeker must do, so I have answered you in these pages. And God is the One Who brings fulfillment, there is no *rabb*[13] but He!

Know, O seeker—may God bring you and us to the fulfillment of freely obeying Him, and may He cause us and you to know what pleases Him!—that [our] closeness to God is only known through His informing us of that.[14] Now He has already done that through His sending the Messengers and sending down the Scriptures and making clear the Paths leading to the eternal happiness. So once we have faith and hold [all that] to be true, there only remains putting into practice in their proper place those [prescribed] actions set down by the revelation in which we have faith and which have become established in the souls of those who have faith.

Next it is incumbent on you, O seeker, to realize the Unicity (*tawḥīd*) of your Creator and His Transcendence and what is befitting of Him!

As for realizing His Unicity, if there were a second god alongside God it would be impossible for any action to occur from those two gods, because of the difference between their acts of Will, both in being and actual determination. So the order [of all being] would be destroyed, as in His saying: "If there were among them [the heavens and earth] gods other than God, both of them would have been destroyed" (21:22). And don't argue, O my brother, with anyone who associates [other creatures with God], nor do you need to establish any proof of [the divine] Oneness and Unicity. For the associator has already joined you in affirming the existence of the Truly Real, while he is the one who goes beyond you in adding an "associate [god]": so he is the one who needs to give a proof for what he has added. This is enough for you concerning the realization of [His] Unicity, since time is scarce and the connection [you have with God] is sound—while there is really nothing underlying [the claims of] the [associator] who disagrees with you, thank God.

As for realizing His transcendence [of any likeness to creation], which is urgent for you because of the literalist (*ẓāhirī*) anthropomorphists and "corporealists" in this age, just hold to His saying: "There is no thing like Him/like His Likeness" (42:11), and that is sufficient for you: whatever description [of God] contradicts this verse is to be rejected, and do not add to or go beyond this "homeland." This is why it has come down in the tradition [of the Prophet, his saying]: "God was, and there was no thing with Him"—may God be far exalted above what the wrongdoers/darkeners say! So every [scriptural] verse or hadith which makes us imagine a likening [of God to the creatures], whether that expression has come in the language of the Arabs, or in the language of anyone else upon whom God has sent down some revelation or information, you must simply have faith in it to the extent of what *God* has taught and sent down through that—but not like those who falsely imagine something [about God] and then ascribe their "knowledge" of that [imagination] to God. Nothing is beyond "There is no thing like Him/His Likeness," and there is no one who can better affirm His Transcendence, since He Himself has already affirmed His own Transcendence, and that is the most fitting expression of His Transcendence!

Then after that, O seeker, you should have faith in the Messengers and in what they have brought and what they have informed us about Him: that He is far greater and more exalted than anything you have either known or been unaware of!

Next, you should love absolutely *all* the Companions. There is no way at all that they could be charged with any offense or criticized, and no one of them should be raised in excellence above the others, except as his Lord has established that excellence in His Noble Book or through the words of His Prophet. And you should respect and esteem whomever God and His Messenger have respected and esteemed.

Next, you should accept and acknowledge the people of this Path, with regard to all the stories that are recounted about them, and also with regard to everything you *see* from them that the [ordinary] mind and [worldly] knowledge cannot encompass.

In general, you should hold a good opinion of everyone, and your heart should be at peace with them. You should pray specially, in secret, to/for the people of faith.[15] And you should serve the poor, recognizing their excellence and nobility in that they are content with letting you serve them, and in their bearing patiently with their burdens, troubles and difficulties.

Among what is indispensable for the seeker is keeping silent, except for "mentioning" God, reciting the Noble Qurʾān, guiding in the right way someone who has gone astray, exhorting to do what is right and forbidding what is wrong, reconciling those who have broken up, and strongly encouraging acts of voluntary charity—indeed every form of good.

Among what is indispensable for the seeker is searching for someone who is in harmony with your essential nature, in accord with what you are aiming for and the way leading there. For so much comes to the person of faith from his brother.[16] And watch out for the company of the person who is fundamentally opposed [to your quest].

Among what is indispensable for the seeker is an actively guiding spiritual master (*shaykh murshid*). [With regard to finding such a guide], pure inner sincerity of intention (*ṣidq*) is the essential watchword of the spiritual seeker, because if the seeker is truly sincere with God, He will turn every [outward] "devil" for that person into an angel rightly guiding them to the Good, and He will inspire in that [sincere seeker the awareness of] what is good. For inner sincerity is the Greatest Elixir,[17] which can only be applied to the heart of our essential being (*qalb al-ʿayn*).

Among what is indispensable for the seeker is seeking out the [spiritually licit] source of support,[18] since the very foundation of this Path is the licit livelihood. The supporting Pillar of this Path rests on that foundation [of right livelihood]: do not be a burden to anyone, and do not accept [inappropriately] from anyone. Always earn your own living and be spiritually conscientious about what you acquire, and about what you say, look at, listen to—indeed in all of your actions. Do not be excessive in your clothing or housing, or in what you eat, for what is spiritually appropriate (*ḥalāl*) is very little, without allowing for any excess. Know that once human beings have planted [animal] desires in their carnal selves, it is very hard to uproot them after that. There is no need for wealth and abundance in any of this.

Among what is indispensable for the seeker is eating little. For hunger brings about an increase in [spiritual] energy for obeying God, while it takes away [spiritual] laziness.

You should properly cultivate and make fruitful[19] the moments of the night and the day: As for those hours to which the revelation (*shar*ʿ) has called you, for standing before your Sustainer/Teacher, those are the five moments [of ritual prayer] that are obligatory for you. As for the rest of the moments lying between those [five obligatory prayers], if you have a trade, then strive to work in that time [enough to earn your living] for several days, like the son of [the ʿAbbāsid caliph] Hārūn ar-Rashīd. And do not leave your place of prayer after the pre-dawn prayer until the sun actually rises, nor between the afternoon prayer and sunset, [filling that special period] with remembrance of God and humility and submission. Nor should you let pass the period between the noon and afternoon [prayers] and between the evening and final night [prayers] without standing in prayer for twenty [extra] prostrations. Remember to keep the four [supplementary cycles of] prostrations at the beginning of the day, before noon, and before the afternoon [prayer]. And make your concluding night prayer (*wiṭr*) another thirteen prostrations, nor should you finish those until you are overcome [by sleep].[20]

And you shouldn't eat except when you really need to, nor should you wear anything but what you need to protect you from the heat and cold, or to cover your nakedness and avoid any discomfort that would keep you from worshipping your Sustainer/Teacher.

And if you are among those who are literate, then impose on yourself reading a section (*wird*) of the Qurʾān from the written text. [While you are] in your place of retreat, pick up the Qurʾānic text, placing your left hand under the book, while your right hand follows the letters as you are looking at them, raising your voice enough so you hear yourself while you are reciting the Qurʾān.

Ask and inquire [of God], with regard to each Sūra, what it is you ought to ask about regarding that. Try to figure out for every verse its special relevance and lesson for you.[21] Meditate and put into practice, for each verse, what is its relevance and connection [to your situation], and what those qualities and attributes[22] are indicating [that you should now learn or do]. Reflect on those qualities and attributes you have and on those that you are missing. Then give Him thanks for those that you have and those that you haven't [yet] attained! And when you read a description of [the contrasting attributes of] the hypocrites and those who ungratefully reject [God], then reflect as to whether there is not also something of those attributes in you.

Among what is indispensable for the seeker is that you should observe and take account of your animal self (*muḥāsabat an-nafs*) and pay close attention to your inner thoughts and impulses (*khawāṭir*) at every moment. Then you will feel a shame in your heart that comes directly from God.[23] For if you are ashamed before God, then He will prevent your heart from experiencing any thought or impulse that is contrary to the revelation or keep you from carrying out an action that is not pleasing to the Real (*al-Ḥaqq*). Indeed we once had a master who would record his actions [during the day] in a notebook, and then when night came he would set them out before him and take an account of his animal self according to what was noted there. And I added to my master's practice by recording my inner thoughts and impulses as well.

Among what is indispensable for the seeker is to constantly be aware of [the correspondence between your] inner thoughts and impulses and the [spiritual demands of] every moment. That is, you should reflect on the moment you are in and consider what it is that the revelation has said to you that you should do, and then you should do that. So if you are in the moment of a prescribed duty, then you should carry that out—or else regret [your having missed] it and then hurry to make it up. But if you are a time that is "open,"[24] then busy yourself with performing all the different kinds of good that the Real has assigned to you. But if you start to do a prescribed action that bestows closeness [to God], don't tell yourself that you will be alive after that to do another action. Instead, make that your last action in this world, the one in which you will encounter your Sustainer/Teacher. For if you do that, you will be released [or: finished], and with that release comes [God's] acceptance.

Among what is indispensable for the seeker is that you should always sit down in a state of Purity. So whenever you become impure, purify yourself;[25] and once you have completed your ablutions, pray two [cycles of] prostrations—unless it is one of those three disapproved moments when you are forbidden to do the ritual prayer: at sunrise until exactly at noon, except on Fridays, and after the evening prayer until sundown.

Among what is indispensable for the seeker is striving for the noble virtues of character[26] and actually carrying them out in the specific situations calling for them—and likewise avoiding all the bad traits of character. For know that whoever abandons a noble virtue of character [already] possesses a vice of character through abandoning [that corresponding virtue]. And know that the virtues of character are of different kinds, just as there are different sorts of creatures. So it is indispensable for you to know which virtuous trait you should employ [in each specific situation], and which virtue[s] extend to most of the other kinds, in order to bring relief (*rāḥa*) to the creatures and keep harm away from them. But [all this must also be only] for the Contentment of God!

So know that the [human] creatures are [God's] servants, constrained and compelled in their actions and their destinies by the hand of what [or Who] moves them. So the Prophet brought us all relief in respect to this condition, when he said: "I have been sent to complete the noble virtues of character." For in every situation about which the revelation has said that if you want, you can carry it out, and if you want, you can leave it alone [not do it], choose *not* to do it. Or if [the revelation] has said to you that if you want, you can exact a compensating [punishment, fine, etc.], and if you want, you can pardon [the offense], then prefer the side of pardon and forgiveness, and your "reward is with God" (42:40). And beware of seeking revenge for your [carnal] self against whoever has done evil to you, for God has called all of that "evil,"[27] even including the evil done by the person exacting their revenge.

But in every situation where the revelation has told you to be angry, then if you fail to be angry, that is not a praiseworthy character trait, because anger for God's sake is among the noble virtues of character, for God. So blessed are those who proceed in that way and keep company with [those divine principles], for they hear God saying: "Certainly you have an extraordinary character!" (68:4)

Among what is indispensable for the seeker is to stay away from those who are "opponents" [of God] and those who are not of your [spiritual] kind—but without your believing them to be evil, or even ever having such a thought occur to you! Instead, [what is truly essential is] having your intention (*nīya*) on keeping company with the Truly Real and His people, and preferring Him to them [i.e., His opponents].

Likewise you should treat these animals with tender sympathy and compassion (*raḥma*) for them, because they are among those whom God has caused to be of service [or "subjugated": *taskhīr*) to you. So don't impose on them [work] that is beyond their capacity,[28] and do not heedlessly ride [or: load] those of them you ride/load.

And act likewise with regard to whatever slaves your right hand possesses, because they are your brothers and God has only given you possession of their bodies so that He can see how you treat them.[29] For *you* are *His* servant, so whatever way you love for Him to act toward you, then you should act precisely like that with your own male and female servants. Indeed God is requiting you [accordingly]. And whatever evil and ugly deeds you would love to have Him avert from you, then act precisely that same way with regard to them. For all [of those creatures] are *God's* family, and you are [a member] of that Family.

If you have a child, then teach them the Qurʾān—but not for any purpose in this lower world! And oblige them to observe the appropriate behavior of the revealed Path (*ādāb ash-sharīʿa*) and the virtuous character traits of true Religion (*dīn*). Induce them to kindness and empathy, and non-attachment [to this world: *zuhd*] from infancy onward, so that they become habituated to those qualities. Don't encourage desires and cravings in their heart, but rather diminish the attractions of the life of this lower world. And [impress upon them] the lack of any share in the next life that is the ultimate outcome for the person who possesses this lower world, and the endless Bounty and Grace in the next life that is the outcome for the person who abandons [attachment to this lower world]. But don't do any of that out of stinginess with your money or property!

Among what is indispensable for the seeker is that you shouldn't even come near the gates of the powers-that-be (*as-sulṭān*), nor should you keep company with those who are competing for this lower world, since they will take your heart from God. But if something should oblige you to keep their company, then behave toward them with frank good counsel (*nasīḥa*), and don't try to fool them [by pretending to agree with them]. For [in reality] you are interacting with the Real, and whatever you do, they will be made to be of service to you through [their impact on] your wider spiritual situation. Therefore always keep your intention directed toward God [asking that] *He* deliver you from the situation you are in, through the means that are best for you with regard to your true Religion (*dīn*).

Among what is indispensable for the seeker is always to be present with God, in all of your actions and all your states of rest.

Among what is indispensable for the seeker is always to be giving, whether you have much or little, whether you are in straightened circumstances or at ease. For that is a sign of your heart's solid confidence in what is with God. . . .

You must restrain your anger. For that is a sign of the openness of your heart (*ṣadr*). Now when you restrain your anger, you please the All-Compassionate (*ar-Raḥmān*). And [at the same time] you outrage the devil,[30] since you have tamed your animal self and subdued it, so that the devil cannot conquer it. You have also brought delight to the heart of the person from whom you have restrained your anger, by not requiting them in kind for their [offending] action. And that can be a cause of their returning to the Real and His just action, and for their recognizing their own unjust and offensive treatment of you. Indeed they may even regret and repent for what happened because of their misconduct.

So you must know the right ways to receive [offense and hostility], and strive to take on that character trait. Then the greatest result and the highest merit, if you restrain your anger against the person who has given rise to that anger, is that God will reward you for your [good] action. And what result could be more perfect than your pardoning your brother and bearing with his harming you, while restraining your anger? And what the Real wants you to do toward [another] servant, He also wants to do precisely that toward you! So struggle and strive (*ijtihād*) to take on these qualities [of mercifulness and compassion], since they give rise to love and affection in people's hearts. Thus the Prophet already ordered us to practice mutual affection and to love one another. And this [restraining one's anger] is one of the highest causes that lead to mutual love.

You must practice *iḥsān* [doing what is good and beautiful], for that is a sign of your shame [or "conscience," *hayā'*] before God, and of the glorification of God in the heart of the person who is *muḥsin*. For Gabriel [asked, in the Hadith]: "What is *iḥsān?*" And the Prophet replied: "It is that you should worship/serve God as though you see Him. For even if you don't see Him, He sees you!" And the Prophet said [in another Hadith]: "Shame/conscience is part of true faith, and it is entirely Good." So ultimately it is impossible for the person of true faith to do harm (*sharr*).

You must practice *dhikr* [remembering God] and asking His Forgiveness. For [asking His forgiveness] after you've sinned effaces and removes the sin, while doing so after you've been willingly obedient and have done good (*iḥsān*) brings "light upon light" and joy upon joy. As for *dhikr,* that unifies the [scattered] heart and purifies your inner thoughts and intentions. But if you should tire [of performing *dhikr*], then turn to reciting the book of God, reciting it deliberately and reflectively, glorifying and exalting God. [Recite the Qur'ān] while asking and imploring [God], if it is a verse of imploring;

or with awe and humility, if it is a verse [suggesting] fear and a threat and a warning and lesson. As for the Qurʾān, the one who recites it never tires of it, because of the [constantly changing] diversity of meanings within it.

You must strive to loosen the knot of persistence and stubborn insistence [on sinning] in your heart. . . .

You must remain cautiously conscious of God (*taqwā*), both with regard to your inner life and outwardly. For the meaning of *taqwā* is to take precautions to avoid His punishment. So the person who is afraid of His punishment will hasten to do what pleases God. As God says: "And God warns you all to be cautious regarding Himself" (3:27). And He said: "And know that God knows what is in all your souls, so be cautious regarding Him" (2:235). Thus [the word] *taqwā* is derived from *wiqāya* [taking protection]. So be cautiously aware of God regarding God's actions, as [the Prophet, in praying] said: "I take refuge with You from You!" Therefore whatever it is that you fear and dread, avoid the way leading to that. For sinful-disobedience (*maʿṣīya*) is the way leading to misery and distress, while willing obedience (*ṭāʿa*) is the way leading to [eternal] happiness.

You must avoid spiritual self-deception (*ightirār*), which is when your animal self deludes you concerning God's graciousness and forbearance, while you continue to persist in your sinful-disobedience. So Iblīs deludes you by saying to you: "If it weren't for your sinning and your opposition [to God], how could His Grace and Compassion and Forgiveness even appear?" Now that is the ultimate form of [spiritual] ignorance in whoever says such a thing. . . .

You must practice spiritual conscientiousness (*waraʿ*), which is an intuitive avoiding [of something wrong, illicit] that comes to you in your heart. The Prophet said: "Abandon what disturbs you for what does not disturb you." So even if you are in need of that [which disturbs you] and you can't find anything to replace it, then leave that [need] to God: He will provide you in exchange with what is better than that. So don't be hasty[31] [in rushing to do what you feel is not right]. For this conscientiousness (*waraʿ*) is the very foundation of true Religion (*asās ad-dīn*). So as you begin to apply it in practice, your actions will become purified, your conditions [inner and outer] will become successful, your speaking will become perfected, blessings of divine grace (*karamāt*) will rush toward you, and you will be protected and preserved by a divine protection in everything you do, without a doubt. By God, by God, o my brother—[practice] conscientiousness, conscientiousness!

And you must practice non-attachment (*zuhd*) regarding this lower world and reducing your desire for it—indeed removing that love for it from your heart completely. But if you can't help seeking [something from it], then restrict yourself to seeking from it your sustenance [acquired] in the [properly licit] way.

Nor should you compete with any of those who are devoted to it, for [this lower world] is spoiled "merchandise" (4:94) that does not remain. The person desiring this lower world will never attain their goal, since God only gives each person what He has apportioned to them. So the person desiring this lower world will be continually saddened by it, and disgusting in God's sight. Indeed the likeness of the person seeking it is like the person who drinks sea water: the more they drink, the thirstier they become! It should suffice you to take note of the Prophet's likening [this lower world] to a dead corpse and a dunghill: only dogs gather around those two things.

God said [in a "divine saying"]: "O child of Adam, if you are content with what I have apportioned to you, then your heart and your body will be at peace; your daily bread will come to you and you will be worthy of [God's] praise. But if you are not content with what I have apportioned to you, your heart and body will both be wearied as you chase after [this world] like wild beasts racing in the desert. By My Glory and Majesty, you will only attain from it what I have assigned to you, and you will deserve blame!"

For God said (2:195): "Spend in the path of God, and do not throw yourselves into ruin with your own hands"—which is their turning back to their possessions by worrying about them—"But do good/beauty, for surely God loves those who are doing what is good-and-beautiful" (*al-muḥsinūn*)!

Naṣīr ad-Dīn Ṭūsī on the Spiritual Quest

Translated by S. J. Badakhchani

Personal reflections on an individual's own quest for meaning and truth represent an important literary genre. Ghazālī's *Deliverer from Error* may well be the most celebrated of the type, but many other prominent figures have left us similar testimonies to their struggles to find a spiritually and intellectually satisfying orientation. Among the many arresting documents of the genre, Naṣīr ad-Dīn Ṭūsī's (1201–74) first-person Persian account, *The Journey and the Way* (*Sayr wa sulūk*), offers insight into a distinctively Ismāʿīlī perspective. Although he was reared in a Twelver Shīʿa family, Naṣīr ad-Dīn later served at the court of an Ismāʿīlī governor in eastern Persia and "converted" to the ruler's community.[32]

Text

When I first embarked upon [the study of] theology, I found a science that was entirely confined to practices of the exoteric side of the *sharīʿat*. Its practitioners seemed to force the intellect to promote a doctrine in which they blindly imitated their ancestors, cunningly deducing proofs and evidence for its validity, and devising excuses for the absurdities and contradictions that their doctrine necessarily entailed.

In short, I derived some benefit from enquiring into this science, to the extent that I came to know something of the divergence between the sects. I came to understand that [with regard to] the knowledge of truth and the attainment of perfection on which happiness in the hereafter depends, people of intellect agreed in one way or another, summarily but not in detail, on the affirmation of such a truth and a hereafter. However, there was a primary disagreement about whether one could reach the desired objective solely through intellect and reason, or whether, in addition to these, a truthful instructor (*muʿallim-i ṣādiq*) was required. All people are accordingly divided in this respect into two branches: those who believe in reason (*naẓar*), and those who [in addition to reason] believe in instruction (*taʿlīm*). Moreover, those who believe in reason [alone] are divided into different schools—which is in itself a lengthy subject—whereas those who believe in [the necessity of] instruction are a group known as the Ismāʿīlīs. This was my first acquaintance with the religion of the *jamāʿat*.[33]

As the science of theology proved fruitless, except for an acquaintance [it allowed] with the positions of the adherents to [various] doctrines, I became averse to it, and my enthusiasm to learn [more about] it lost its momentum. Then I started [to study] philosophy. I found this science to be noble and of great benefit. I saw that among the groups [into which] humankind [is divided], the practitioners of this discipline were distinguished by their allocation of a place for the intellect in the recognition of realities, and by their not requiring blind imitation (*taqlīd*) of a particular stand. Rather, in most cases they build the structure of religion in accordance with the intellect, "except what God wills" (7:188). However, when the discussion reached the desired objective—that is, the recognition of the True One (*ḥaqq*), the exalted, the most high, and knowledge of the origin and the return (*mabdaʾ wa maʿād*)—I found that they were on shaky foundations in these matters, for the intellect (*ʿaql*) is incapable of encompassing the giver of intellect (*wāhib-i ʿaql*) and the origins (*mabādī*). And because they rely on their own intellect and opinion, they blunder, they speak according to their own conjectures and whims in this field, using the intellect [to arrive] at knowledge of something that is not within its scope.

To sum up, my heart was not satisfied with what they said in these matters, while my desire to attain the truth was not diminished. In my exposition, I shall mention some more aspects of this matter. Many benefits, however, were obtained from this investigation into philosophy, one of them being that I came to know that if in any existing thing perfection is potential (*bi 'l-quwwa*), it cannot change from potentiality into actuality (*bi-fiʿl*) by itself without being affected by something outside itself, because if its essence were sufficient to bring that perfection from potentiality into actuality, the change would not be delayed. Indeed, the attaining of that perfection would have been simultaneous with the existence of the essence. We can take bodies as an example of this: motion is [always] potential in them. Without the effect of something else, that motion is never actualized; otherwise all bodies would be in [perpetual] motion. But when another thing exerts an effect on a body, that potential motion (*ḥarakat*) becomes actual. In this case the other is called the "mover" (*muḥarrik*) and the body is called the "moved" (*mutaḥarrik*).

Once this proposition had been established and my soul was satisfied of its truth, my attention was drawn to the point that was made in the science of theology, about the primary disagreement among mankind being whether knowledge of the truth is attainable solely through the intellect and reason, without instruction from any teacher, or whether, in addition to intellect and reason, an instructor is needed. Then I applied the [above] proposition to this situation and found that the truth lay with those who believe in instruction (*taʿlīmiyān*), for knowledge and understanding in human being is in itself [merely] potential, and its perfection can only be actualized in persons of sound natures, [in whom] intellect and reason are to be found, when something external has exerted an effect on them. Thus, this perfection too can inevitably only be actualized by means of the effect of some other thing. [Accordingly], when that other bestows a perfection, the perfection [here] being knowledge (*ʿilm*), the bestower, in accordance with the previous law, is called the "instructor" (*muʿallim*) and the one on whom it is bestowed the "instructed" (*mutaʿallim*), by analogy with the "mover" (*muḥarrik*) and the "moved" (*mutaḥarrik*).

It thus becomes clear that without the instruction (*taʿlīm*) of a teacher (*muʿallim*), and the bringing to perfection (*ikmāl*) by an agent of perfection (*mukammil*), the attainment of the truth is not possible; that mankind, with its great number and differences of opinion, is mistaken in its claim that the truth can be reached solely through the intellect and reason; and that the believers in instruction (*taʿlīmiyān*) are therefore correct.

Once this proposition had become clear, I began to investigate the religion (*madhhab*) of this group. But since I did not know anyone who could describe the nature of their doctrine objectively, and could only hear about their beliefs from people hostile to them, and since I knew that I could not rely on a person's prejudices about his enemy, I was unable to get to know [this group] as I should, and out of fear I was unable to disclose my secret.

In short, I spent [quite] a period of time thinking about this. Then, in the course of my search, I frequently heard from travelers to the [surrounding] countries about the scholarly virtues of the auspicious master, Shihāb ad-Dīn and his deep insight into different fields of knowledge. Then I sought a suitable opportunity and, through the intermediary of a friend who had an association with him, I sent him a letter containing two or three questions about those points in the discourse of the philosophers that I had found to be contradictory and about which I had some observations of my own. Then I was granted the honor of a reply from him in the handwriting of the master, the chief scribe, Ṣalāḥ ad-Dīn Ḥasan,[34] and in answer to the questions he said: "For a reason that can only be explained face to face, I am not [in a position] to convey any scholarly communication [in writing]."

Shortly after this, I took the opportunity, while on a journey from Iraq to Khurāsān, to pass through the glorious territory of [Gird] Kūh[35] and for two or three days [was able to] be in Shihāb ad-Dīn's company and hear something of the *daʿwat* doctrines from his own mouth. I copied down his words and derived much [benefit] from them. Since the requisites for staying with him and remaining in that place had not been prepared—for several reasons that I need not go into—I journeyed on from there to Khurāsān. A few days later, I happened to see a copy, in mediocre handwriting and antiquated paper, of the *Fuṣūl-i muqaddas* (Sacred Chapters) of [Imam Ḥasan] . . . in the possession of an unworthy person who did not know what it was.

Obtaining [the text] with a ruse, I occupied myself day and night with reading it, and to the extent of my humble understanding and ability, I gained endless benefits from those sacred words that are the light of hearts and the illuminator of inner thoughts. It opened a little my eye of exploration (*chishm-i taṣarruf*) and my inner sight (*dīda-yi bāṭin*) was unveiled.

Thereafter, my only desire was to introduce myself among the *jamāʿat* (assembly) when the opportunity presented itself. At that time, in accordance with my inward motivation, I made such strenuous efforts that finally I succeeded. Through the good offices of the exalted royal presence of Nāṣir al-Ḥaqq wa 'd-Dīn and his compassionate regard for my improvement, I was granted the good fortune of joining the *jamāʿat* and entry among the ranks of the novices (*mustajībān*) of the *daʿwat,* and thus my situation reached the point where it is now.

Nothing can be gained by the illuminated mind in listening to this story except weariness. However, due to the circumstances already mentioned concerning his [Nāṣir ad-Dīn's] cordial nature and sympathy for me, its narration seemed to me to be prudent. If God the exalted is willing, it will be covered with the veil of forgiveness and heard with consideration. This [exposition so far] has been a description of the exoteric situation.

From an esoteric perspective, however, when I had reached a position where I could understand—by the proof that has already been cited—that it was the followers of instruction who were correct, I concluded with no additional troublesome thinking that the true instructor can only be he who is the instructor of the followers of the truth.[36] This person, through whose teaching souls move from potentiality to actuality, must therefore be the instructor of the Taʿlīmiyān [i.e., the Ismāʿīlīs].

Then my mind became preoccupied with considering what particular characteristics would distinguish that instructor from other teachers, and what his instruction would be like. With due submissiveness, I beseeched God the exalted to clarify and unveil this question, so that my heart might be appeased. Then I referred [myself] to the intellectual principles that I had already verified and the premises that had been made clear in the *Fuṣūl-i muqaddas*. I combined them, asked questions from here and there, and held discussions and debates with [other] novices (*mubtadīyān*), until gradually, through the stages that I will explain, the scheme of beliefs as will be mentioned later on became clear in my mind.

First, it appeared to me that the instructor through whose mediation the potential perfection of the instructed soul is actualized must [himself] be in a state of actual perfection, because he who is not actually perfect cannot perfect others; and if that perfection had been potential in him and become actualized afterwards, he also would have been in need of another instructor. As necessity dictates,[37] this would either result in an infinite regression, or end up with a teacher who has always been in a state of actual perfection. The evidence for the existence of such a person among humankind can be deduced both from philosophy (*ḥikmat*) and revelation (*sharīʿat*).

As for philosophy, it has been stated by philosophers that the possessor of sacred powers has absolutely no need to acquire knowledge (*iktisāb*). Indeed, merely by focusing his soul, and without having to go through the process of acquisition and active seeking, realities and knowledge become clear [to him] in their totality. As for revelation, it is maintained by the followers of the exoteric (*ahl-i ẓāhir*) that the possessor of bestowed knowledge (*ʿilm-i ladunī*) receives it without the mediation of any instruction.[38]

Consequently, the mind does not reject the necessity of the existence among human beings of an instructor who is the first among instructors and is absolutely perfect. The instructor [is necessary] in order that some may gain perfection through him, and others through the latter, so that the effusion of the supreme bliss might encompass the next level gradually, according to the order and degree that are ordained by the wisdom of the first origin.

When I passed this stage and another veil had been removed from my mind, I realized that the perfection to which the seeker directs himself is knowledge of the True One, the exalted, the most high, who is the origin of [all] beings. Between Him and the first instructor, whose knowledge of the True One, the exalted, the most high, is always actual, there cannot exist any intermediary, because if an intermediary is posited, he would first have to come to know the intermediary, and then through him the True One. Knowledge of the True One would also, therefore, be a [mere] potentiality in him, [waiting to be actualized] through someone else. If this were so, this other person would have to be the first instructor, not him. But since we have already supposed him to be the first instructor, so the first instructor is the nearest person to God.

Kemas Fakhr ad-Dīn on the Quest for Self and God's Oneness

Translated by G. W. J. Drewes

Authors across Islamdom have fashioned numerous ways of describing the inner quest as a journey along the path of spiritual insight into God's unity and attributes. Originally from the Sumatran city of Palembang, Kemas Fakhr ad-Dīn (fl. ca. 1750) spent many years studying Islamic tradition in Arabia. After returning to Indonesia, he made his most notable contribution by translating traditional Islamic theological concepts into the Malay language. Among his extant works is a Malay translation of a "treatise on *tawḥīd*" by Shaykh Walī Raslān of Damascus (d. 1296), including input from Arabic commentaries by important sixteenth- and eighteenth-century

Muslim scholars. Here is an excerpt on the theological dimensions of wayfaring toward God, employing a classic division of the generality of "travelers" into three levels of spiritual attainment. Kemas intersperses direct Arabic quotations from Shaykh Walī Raslān (prefaced by "as the author says") with blended comments from other sources.[39]

Text

Know, O traveler on the mystic path, that the meaning of *tawḥīd* is the denial of being to anything else by the acknowledgement of the Truly One. This has three grades:

1. the grade of the common people who affirm with their tongues and believe in their hearts;
2. that of those who are 'brought near,' i.e., those who see the multiplicity of things but look upon them as springing from the Truly One, with an eye that makes them look away from causes and means; and
3. that of the truthful. i.e., those who in all being see only the Being of the Supreme Reality, and of whom the mystics say that they have passed away in *tawḥīd*. God knows best.[40]

A human being's self is veiled from him by [outward] things. When he gets rid of these, undoubtedly the veil will be lifted from his self, so that he will know himself. When he knows himself, undoubtedly he will get rid of self and know the Lord. This is why the author says: "Whenever you worship sincerely, it will be disclosed to you that He is and you are not; therefore, take refuge from your self."

Whenever you have truly got rid of self, undoubtedly it will be disclosed to you that He is the only and eternal Being, not you; that is to say that you have no being at all but are only pure non-being.

When you see nothing but God, you are a true monotheist, and when this vision is disclosed to you, you know that looking upon self is sinful and you ask God's forgiveness for it. When you are free from it, then realize the station of *tawḥīd* and hold to it both when active and inactive, that is to say, to God, praise be unto Him and He is exalted, because as a free agent He disposes of everything and is the primordial cause of all activity and inactivity.

"Whenever you find polytheism in yourself, renew your profession of His Uniqueness and your faith at every moment and time."

Whenever you consider the inferences from the revelation that He is and you are not, then the polytheism that is yours without your being aware of it will become apparent to you, and ever and anon you will renew your *tawḥīd,* i.e., you will realize anew that He is and that you are not, and renew your faith, that is to say that you truly profess that He is and you are not, so that absolute certainty will be yours.

What is meant by *tawḥīd* is that the attribute of uniqueness becomes manifest to the servant, so that the servant is wiped out completely without leaving a trace, while the heart fully professes that this is the actual situation.

When you know that God alone acts as a free agent in everything and when by means of the [understanding of the] essential meaning of *Lā ilāha illā 'llāh* ("There is no god but God") you have realized this and you further know that no one but God gives misery and bestows benefit, gives and withholds, humiliates and raises, then let the traveler on the mystic path never desist from uttering this sentence with his tongue, so that it sets its mark on his heart and so wipes out his polytheism. Whenever the traveler on the mystic path makes a habit of this, no doubt his faith will steadily increase and he will get rid of things created, and whenever he perseveres in this and practices it assiduously, no doubt his conviction will be more and more settled. He will get rid of self and attain to the Essential Being, as the author says:

"Whenever you get rid of these, your faith will increase, and whenever you get rid of self, your conviction will be confirmed."

Whenever you have turned away from all things created, no doubt your faith in God will increase at the stations of disclosure and vision, since getting rid of one of two opposites means adhering to the other. Whenever you have got rid of self, no doubt your certitude of God most high will be firm, so that you will know Him, since getting rid of all things created means desisting from confiding in them and the absence of depending on them. When the mystic's heart has got rid of all things created, no doubt he will turn inwardly to the Lord. This is the essential meaning of the profession of faith.

Sometimes the mystic (*sālik,* traveler) gets rid of all things created but there is left in him a remnant of looking on himself, of disposing himself, and of reverting to his own will and choice, and the station of absolute certainty is not reached, since perfection in this is that he gets rid of self in the same way as he got rid of other things. Self is created, and the servant will not attain to the Supreme Reality until he has got rid of all things created, as was said by some mystics, "Part [with yourself] and the end will be gained," while

ʿAbd al-Qādir [al-Jīlānī] (d. 1166) said with respect to this, "When you have died to things created, no doubt you will die to your desires; when you have died to your desires, no doubt you will die to your own will; when you have died to your own will, no doubt you will live an immortal life and be rich without being ever reduced to poverty, healthy without being ill ever afterwards." How could it be otherwise, as the servant has come to exist for the Lord, and how could this not be realized by him, seeing that in his heart nothing but God is left? Whosoever has reached this state undoubtedly will not care for other things nor pay attention to heaven and hell, nor will he confide in worship and mystic stations or be given to visions and contemplation, as the author says:

"Oh captive of passions and of worship! Oh captive of stations and of visions! You are deluded!"

Oh you who are the captives of passions and of worship! Oh you who are the captives of stations and of visions! You are deluded by these! That is to say, deluded by lawful passions such as the desire of eating, drinking, clothes, marriage, houses, ships, possessions, children, rank, respect, knowledge, etc., and these keep you captive only because you have an inclination to them and exert yourselves for their sake and strive after them, but not after the Lord. For when the heart is inclined to anything, it becomes its captive and its slave, as someone said, "I never love anything without becoming its slave." But the Lord is not satisfied with your being a slave of anything but Him, and He is no more satisfied with the heart of a polytheist than his works are agreeable to Him. Neither of these is acceptable to the Lord. Therefore, empty your heart of all other things and replenish it with knowledge and secrets. Among these other things are acts of worship, stations and visions, and whenever the mystic occupies himself with these and is inclined towards them, he certainly is captivated and deluded by them.

Because of this the author says: "You are occupied with self, not with Him. In what respect are you occupied with Him, not with self, while He, the mighty and great, is omnipresent and all-seeing, and is with you wherever you are in this world and the next?"

You who are occupied with all that pertains to your exterior person such as your inner desires and all forms of worship by which you fancy to grow near to Him and meet Him—God, that is—with respect to what do you think you are engaged with Him, not with self, while your being is captivated by other things—since anyone who loves a thing is captivated by it—although He, the mighty and great, is among us with His knowledge and looks upon us with His judgment? Nothing is hidden from Him, so how can you occupy yourself with self, though He is with you with His knowledge, power and help wherever you are in this world and the next? When you know that He is with you outwardly and inwardly, then see to it that you are with Him by means of concentration on *tawḥīd.* In short, for all those who walk in the way of the select spirits, it is suitable that they behave in anything whatsoever without setting store by it. Outwardly they move in daily life but their hearts are with the Lord, since they are His servants under all circumstances and He is their Lord. When you ask, ask from God most high, and when you ask for help, ask God. If you behave that way you have realized the discipline of being with Him, and thereby you will be screened from self, as the author says:

"If you are with Him, He screens you from self, and if you are with self, He brings you under bondage."

If you are with Him, He certainly will screen you from self; that is to say, He will prevent you from looking upon yourself, so that you will be protected from hidden polytheism. This situation is called "passing away in *tawḥīd,*" and "union." If, however, you are occupied with self on account of your not concentrating on Him, He certainly will demand worship of you; that is to say, you were created for worship and worship will be demanded of you. This situation is that of separation, in which the servant is back to the performance of religious service, etc. This is to say that when you are with Him and have adapted to the full the discipline of being with Him, you certainly will be screened from self.

EIGHT

Poetic, Pastoral, and Narrative Theology

ONCE UPON A TIME THERE was a walled city whose citizens longed to know what was beyond their shared enclosure. Every now and then, an intrepid soul would violate the rules and clamber up to have a look over the rampart. Horrified townsfolk observed that a smile would come over the climber's face just before he disappeared over the wall, never to be heard from again. One day they decided to experiment: A volunteer climbed and peered into the great unknown with the others holding his legs. When the first hint of a smile stole across his face, they pulled him down and demanded that he spill the whole story. Alas, he had been struck mute and could respond only with a rueful grin.[1]

Muslim religious writers have long struggled to account in conventional language for that most elusive of experiences, knowledge of the mystery that is God. The old saying "Those who know don't talk; those who talk the most, know the least" is appropriate here. Saʿdī (d. 1292) of Shiraz (Iran) was one of Islamdom's most celebrated "wisdom" authors, and he shared his gifts readily. One charming story recalls how Saʿdī penned a particularly insightful verse, a line so beautiful that God sent a bevy of angels down with gifts of gold. The line read: "In the sight of one who is fully aware, every leaf on the green trees is a book [teaching] the intimate knowledge (*maʿrifat*) of God the Creator."[2] Chapter 7 sampled the works of some of the many talented Muslim authors who have explored the depths of this "intimate knowledge" in its more theoretical aspect. There is another side to the story as well, one that addresses the theme in less technical terms, in the imagery of various poetic genres, in letters of spiritual guidance written to addressees by no means schooled in academic theology, and in stories—and occasionally combining two or more modes of literary communication.

Building on the theoretical approaches exemplified in chapter 7, here are samples from the vast treasury of literary and "pastoral" resources exemplifying a variety of genres and theological perspectives: theological poetry/poetic theology; reflections on the experiential dimensions of "living with" and "talking about" God's attributes and names; and the uses of narrative in understanding complex theological realities. An important theme throughout is that of the varied understandings implied as to the self and the effects of an individual's experience of, and intensely personal relationship to, God.

POETIC THEOLOGY AND THEOLOGICAL POETRY

Some of the most famous and influential Sufis are justly celebrated for their virtuosity as poets, storytellers, and sources of wisdom sayings. What is less well known is that many of those same figures were well versed in the broader range of religious sciences and incorporated substantial theological reflection and insight into their works. Two such poets who deserve greater credit for their theological acumen, even if they opted to express their thoughts in non-academic terms, are Persian masters Sanāʾī and ʿAṭṭār. Here are samples of how they made sense out of the scholastic articulation of several major theological questions much discussed in exegesis, creeds, and the treatises of *kalām.* Theologically insightful poetry has remained an important medium of expression into our own time, as a selection from the twentieth-century Indian poet Muḥammad Iqbal exemplifies.

Sanāʾī on God's Attributes, Unity, and Anthropomorphisms

Translated by John Renard

Sanāʾī (d. 1131) was one of many gifted medieval religious poets hailing from Ghazna, in what is now Afghanistan. He is perhaps best known for his didactic poem, *The Enclosed Garden of Ultimate Reality,* composed in a genre known as couplets (*masnavī*). Popular especially among poets writing in Persian, Turkish, and Urdu, the genre consists of verses/lines whose first and second halves (distichs) end in rhyme. Like shorter lyric forms, *masnavīs* can employ a number of metric schemes; unlike the lyric genres, the couplet form can be hundreds, even thousands of verses long. Sanāʾī's didactic text exemplifies deep reflection on the implications of God's attributes and acts for the life of the individual seeker, focusing on the kinds of questions his readers might ask about their personal experience of the spiritual life. Here is a selection from the beginning of the work, including an invocation in the form of a meditation on God's names and attributes, and two short sections on the intimate knowledge (*ma'rifat*) of God and God's transcendent unity. Note especially how the poet interprets the imagery of the Throne Verse.[3]

Text

O you who nourish the soul and ornament the visible world, and
you who grant wisdom and are indulgent with those who lack it;
Creator and sustainer of space and of time, custodian and provider
of dweller and dwelling;
All is of your making, dwelling and dweller, all is within your
compass, time and space.
Fire and air, water and earth, all are mysteriously within the scope
of your power.
All that is between your Throne and this earth are but a fraction of
your handiwork; inspirited intelligence acts as your swift herald.
Every living tongue that moves in every mouth has but one purpose:
to give you praise. Your sublime and exalted names evidence your
beneficence and grace and kindness.
Every one of them outstrips throne and globe and dominion; they
are a thousand plus one and a hundred less one.
But to those who are outside the spiritual sanctuary, the names are
veiled.
O Lord, in your largesse and mercy allow this heart and soul a
glimpse of your name!
Unbelief and religion tread together your road, proclaiming: He is
one and has no partner.
He is the Creator, the Beneficent, the Capable; unlike us He is the
One, the Omnipotent;
The Living and Eternally Ancient and Knowing and Powerful;
Sustainer of Creation and Victorious and Forgiving;
The One who Sets in Motion and brings to rest, this is the One who
is Unique and without equal.
Whatever you call origin or foundation, you are [in effect]
identifying as equal to Him—be mindful.
Our inability is proof of His completeness; His omnipotence is the
lieutenant of His names;

"No" and "He" alike [i.e., negation and affirmation] have returned from that sublime palace with empty pocket and satchel.
What could be superior to imagination and intellect and sense-awareness and analogical reasoning if not the thoughts of one who knows God?
Wherever the knower [of God] is, in whatever condition, the [very]
Throne of God is carpet beneath his sandals.
A discerning soul sees that adulation is frivolous except when directed to the Creator,
The One who knows how to fashion a body from earth, and how to make the wind [breath] the dictionary of speech—
Bestower of intellect and Inspirer of hearts, Inscriber on the soul and originator of causes.
Everything is of His crafting, whether waxing or waning; of all things created He is the origin and destination;
From Him all emerges, to Him all returns, whether good or ill, all moves toward Him.
He fashions the power of choice of good and evil persons [alike], sending forth the soul and authoring wisdom.
From nothing He made you into something; you who were of no account He made most precious.
No heart [or: mind] finds a way to His manner of being; intellect and soul are unaware of His perfection.
The reasoning mind is stymied by His Majesty; the eye of the soul is blinded by His all-sufficiency [i.e., completeness].
First Intellect is the offspring of His way of being: He granted it a path to intimate knowledge of Him.
Imagination's agility fails before the glory of His essence, and understanding is confined at the prospect of describing Him.
His fire, which in His grandeur He made His carpet, scorched the wing of intellect.
The [universal] soul is less than a [lowly] servant in His retinue, reason a [mere] apprentice in His school.
What is intellect in this lodging for wayfarers, but a crooked writer of the divine text?
Of what [use] is this intellect, this [source of] idle talk? Of what [use] this deceitful firmament and nature?
When he reveals to reason the way to Himself, then [alone] laud him appropriately.
Since intellect was the first among created beings, intellect ranks higher than other elite beings.

Universal intellect is [but] a single expression from His notebook;
the universal soul [but] a single foot soldier at His door.
To Love He gave perfection from Love [itself]; reason [by contrast]
is trammeled even by reason itself.
Like us, intellect on the road to His being is perplexed, like us
bewildered.
He is the Intellect of intellect and the soul of soul, and whatever is
beyond that, He is.
How can one know God through the meager hints of intellect and
soul and sensation?
If God did not show [the seeker] the road, how could one come to
know the deity?

ON THE INTIMATE/EXPERIENTIAL KNOWLEDGE [OF GOD, *MA'RIFAT*]

No one can understand Him unaided; His essence one can know
only through Him.
Reason [or: intellect] desired the truth of Him but did not fare well;
inability [to know God] set out on the road to Him and arrived
at knowledge.
His beneficence said, "Know Me"; were it not so, who could know
Him through mind and senses?
How could the evidence of the senses succeed? How can a walnut
keep its footing on a dome?
Reason is a guide, but [only] to His door; only His favor brings you
to Him.
You will not make the journey with the evidence of reason; do not
make this error like other fools.
Our guide on the path is His graciousness; His works are indicator
and witness to Him.
You who fall short of knowing *yourself*, how can you ever know God?
Since you are helpless to attain knowledge (*'ilm*) of yourself, how
can you be an intimate knower (*'ārif*) of the Infinite Creator?
If you are not aware of [even] beginning to know Him, how will
you have [even the] merest concept of Him?
When one describes Him evidentially, speech amounts to [no
more than] an analogy, while silence is [equivalent to] denial of
[God's] attributes.
The ultimate goal of reason is astonishment; humankind's reason
for being is desire for Him.

Mere imaginings fall short of describing Him; [even] deep understanding's (*fahm*) vaunted powers are futile.
[Even] prophets are perplexed at such statements; [even] Friends of God are astonished at such qualities.
He is the desire and lord of reason and soul; He is the final destination of the seeker and wayfarer.
Reason shows the way to His existence; [all] existent things are beneath the foot of His being.
His acts transcend inward and outward, His essence above the why and the how.
Understanding has not made its way to His essence; reason's heart and soul are [mere] dust on this road.
Without the *kohl* (eye cosmetic) of intimacy with Him, one has no clue as to His divinity.
Why engage in fancy in an attempt to discuss Him? How can an upstart converse with the eternally ancient?
Via the road of reason, imagination, and sense no living being can know God.
When the quality of [God's] magnificence shows its face to the intellect, it overcomes both intellect and soul.
Even if one accorded reason the status of the station of Gabriel the Trusted,
[The reality is that] out of dread before the full splendor [of God], [even] Gabriel is smaller than a sparrow.
Coming to that place, reason bows its head and the bird [of soul] there can no longer fly.
Only through meager senses and corrupting lower-self (*nafs*) can the recently arrived even begin to speak of the One who has always been;
Will your [meager] being travel the road of His magnificent and powerful qualities to intimate knowledge of Him?

ON [GOD'S] TRANSCENDENT UNITY (*TAWḤĪD*)

He is One, and beyond any numerical reckoning; He is most sublime (*ṣamad*) and in need of nothing.
That oneness neither thought nor [intellectual] comprehension can know, and that sublimity is none that sense or imagination can fathom.
His is neither scarcity nor abundance; One upon One is still One.

Duality contains nothing but evil and inaccuracy; in singularity there is never any miscalculation.
So long as you are inwardly enumerating and doubtful, whether you reckon one or two, [still] both [of these] are one.
How dare you [who are] the devil's feeding ground [or: pasture] claim to know with certainty the what, the how many, the why, and the how?!
His eminence is not a result of superfluity, His essence transcends quantity and quality.
The hapless seeker can scarcely inquire "whether" or "who" about Him.
No one has articulated [fully] the qualities of the Originator [known only as] He: how much, how, why, what, who or where.
"Hand" is His capacity, "face" His subsistence; "coming" is wisdom and "descent" His gift (cf. 48:10, 2:109, 89:23).
His "two feet" are the majesty of chastisement and danger, His "two fingers" the pervasiveness of His judgment and power.
[All] existing things are under His disposition (*qudrat*), all are in His presence and Him all things seek.
Light tends to move toward light; how could light be disconnected from the sun?
Pre-Eternity (*azal*) appeared but the day before yesterday in relation to His being, arriving at dawn but tardy even so.
How can pre-eternity put limits on His works? Pre-eternity is but a single house servant of His.
About post-eternity (*abad*) do not imagine or surmise [that it is greater], for post-eternity is of like character to pre-eternity.
How can He occupy a space greater or lesser, given that place itself has no location [in this context]?
How could the Creator of space itself have a place, how could there be a heaven for the one who made the heavens?
Neither space nor time is a match for Him, neither account nor eyewitness can explain Him.
No foundation undergirds His powers, nor does his essence reside in a place.
You who are enthralled by form and figure, a slave to "He mounted the Throne" (20:4, 7:52),
Form is of a piece with time-bound entities, and is unworthy of [or: incompatible with] the might of the Everlasting.
For the same reason that the painter is not the painting, "He mounted" exists, but neither Throne nor earth [exists].

Pronounce "He mounted" from the depth of your soul, but do not consider His essence bound by directionality,
Since "He mounted" is a Qurʾānic verse, and proclaiming [He occupies] "No place" is an article of faith.
The Throne is like a door knocker: it has no inkling as to the attributes of God.
The term "speech" is inscribed in the text [of the Qurʾān], but image and voice and likeness are far removed from Him [or the text?].
Tradition records that "God descends," but do not conclude that He comes and departs.
Written mention of the Throne is meant to ennoble it [not to locate God in space], and naming the Kaʿba is meant to praise it [i.e., not to seem to bring God to earth].
"No place" [for God] refers to a religious belief; express your surprise [or: shake your head wordlessly] for this is the place for approbation.
Out of enmity they sought Ḥusayn because ʿAlī uttered the expression [God has] "No place."
For humankind He created a world of these qualities, so that for you He has fashioned a nest.
Yesterday the heavens were not; today they exist, and again tomorrow they will not be, but He still is.
He will roll up before Him the veil of smoke: "On the day We fold up the heavens" (21:103)—[therefore] let out a sigh.
When those who know [God] experientially live by the Eternally Ancient, the *Hā* [of "behold"] and the *Hū* [i.e., He] they will slice asunder [i.e., intimate knowers of God dwell beyond the realm of ordinary living].

ʿAṭṭār on the Valley of Experiential Knowledge

Translated by John Renard

Another major didactic poet, Farīd ad-Dīn ʿAṭṭār (d. 1220), composed one of the most popular and charming "mystical epics" of quest and discovery. His *Conference of the Birds* (*Manṭiq aṭ-ṭayr*) describes the perilous journey of the Birds (all humanity) to encounter the Monarch who dwelled in the far mountains. Only by subjecting themselves to the rigors of traversing seven "valleys" under the leadership of their spokesbird, the Hoopoe, could they come to the ultimate object of their hopes and desires. ʿAṭṭār weaves his larger tale by interspersing marvelous mininarratives into the narrative of the seven valleys: search, love, experiential knowledge, unity, detachment, bewilderment, and death. In keeping with one of the central themes of part 4, here is the poet's explanation of the Third Valley, that of *maʿrifat,* intimate or experiential knowledge of God. The edition of the Persian text used for this translation defines *maʿrifat* in its glossary as "a quality of one who knows God through His Names and Attributes."[4]

Text

[THE HOOPOE RETURNS TO HIS DESCRIPTION OF THE SPIRITUAL ITINERARY]

After the [valley] I have described to you, another will come into view: the limitless Valley of Intimate Knowledge.
No one can fully take the measure of this place, and many and varied are its paths.
No path in [the valley] is like any other, and the journeyer in body differs from the journeyer in soul.
Soul and body, whether deficient or complete, remains ever in its ascent or decline.
No matter what road appears before [each] person, each proceeds according to his/her limitations.
On this awesome path, how can the overmatched spider keep pace with the elephant?
Every person's progress matches his/her relative perfection, each one's proximity [to God/the goal] is a measure of personal spiritual state [or: matches the individual].
Even if a gnat flew full throttle, how could it keep up with the Ṣarṣar [storm] wind?
Inevitably, our byways diverge; no bird divines the trajectory of another.
Experiential knowledge in this place takes diverse forms: this one discovers the *miḥrāb* [in the mosque], that one finds an idol.
When the sun of intimate knowledge shines down from the firmament, this path [appears as] the highest level,
[Where] each body sees in proportion to its capacity, and finds his/her center in the ultimate reality (*ḥaqīqat*).
When his/her innermost essence shines forth, the furnace (*gulkhān*) of this world will become a rose garden (*gulshān*)

[alluding to the story of Abraham resting comfortably in Nimrod's bonfire].
He/she will see the kernel within, not [merely] his/her skin, will see no particle but his Friend.
Whoever sees His Face sees the everlasting, sees the smallest detail of His eternal dwelling.
A hundred thousand mysteries from beneath the veil [will emerge] when that Face appears like the sun.
A hundred thousand individuals will be lost before just a single one removes the veil entirely from the mysteries.
On this path, one must be perfect in courage in order to plunge into this unfathomable ocean.
Should you taste the mysteries, all of your lifetime desire [for more] may continue to be made manifest.
Though thirst may be slaked here, [yet] a hundred thousand lives may be lost here.
Though you extend your hand to the majestic Throne [of God], even so hasten [to ask] "Is there not more?" (50:30—as Hell asks when it is filled to the brim).
Drown yourself in the ocean of intimate knowledge (*'irfān*), or else be buried in the earth fearful [of the punishment of the tomb and the interrogating angels].
Indeed, you who sleep self-satisfied, should you not rather be in mourning?
If you do not experience the joy of meeting the Friend, at least move on and grieve the separation of yearning.
If you do not see the beauty of your Friend, at least take note and seek your [own] mysteries.
And if you do not know, search ashamedly; how long will you be like an unbridled [directionless] donkey?

Muḥammad Iqbal on "Secrets of the Self"

Translated by R. A. Nicholson

Expression of spiritual values and theological themes is not merely for antiquarians. Examples of such artistry are abundant through later medieval and early modern times and well into the twentieth century. Muḥammad Iqbal (d. 1938), who wrote in both Urdu and Persian, was one of the leading South Asian exponents of this refined art. Among the prolific author's most important poetic works is his Persian *Secrets of the Self* (*Asrār-i khudī*). Here are two didactic tales, very much in the spirit of Sanā'ī, 'Aṭṭār, and Rūmī, but with a distinctly different perspective on the self and offering a narrative-theological interpretation of problems faced by Indian Muslims early in the twentieth century.[5]

Text

CHAPTER 12: THE STORY OF THE BIRD THAT WAS FAINT WITH THIRST

A bird was faint with thirst,
The breath in his body was heaving like waves of smoke.
He saw a diamond in the garden:
Thirst created a vision of water.
Deceived by the sun-bright stone,
The foolish bird fancied that it was water.
He got no moisture from the gem:
He pecked it with his beak, but it did not wet his palate.
"O thrall of vain desire," said the diamond,
"You have sharpened your greedy beak on me;
But I am not a dew drop, I give no drink,
I do not live for the sake of others.
Would you hurt me? You are mad!
A life that reveals the self is strange to you.
My water will shiver the beaks of birds
And break the jewel of human life."
The bird won not his heart's wish from the diamond
And turned away from the sparkling stone.
Disappointment swelled in his breast,
The song in his throat became a wail.
Upon a rose-twig a drop of dew
Gleamed like the tear in a nightingale's eye:
All its glitter was owing to the sun,
It was trembling in fear of the sun—A restless sky-born star
That had stopped for a moment, from desire to be seen;
Often deceived by bud and flower,
It had gained nothing from Life.
There it hung, ready to drop,
Like a tear on the eyelashes of a lover who has lost his heart.
The sorely distressed bird hopped under the rose-bush,
The dewdrop trickled into his mouth.

O you that would deliver your soul from enemies,
I ask you—"Are you a drop of water or a gem?"
When the bird melted in the fire of thirst,
It appropriated the life of another.
The drop was not solid and gem-like;
The diamond had a being, the drop had none.
Never for an instant neglect self-preservation:
Be a diamond, not a dewdrop!
Be massive in nature, like mountains,
And bear on your crest a hundred clouds laden with floods
of rain!
Save yourself by affirmation of self,
Compress your quick silver into silver ore!
Produce a melody from the string of self,
Make manifest the secrets of self!

CHAPTER 13: THE STORY OF THE DIAMOND AND THE COAL

Now I will open one more gate of Truth,
I will tell you another tale.
The coal in the mine said to the diamond,
O you entrusted with splendors everlasting,
We are comrades, and our being is one;
The source of our existence is the same,
Yet while I die here in the anguish of worthlessness,
You are set on the crowns of emperors.
My stuff is so vile that I am valued less than earth,
Whereas the mirror's heart is rent by your beauty.
My darkness illumines the chafing dish,
Then my substance is incinerated at last.
Every one puts the sole of his foot on my head
And covers my stock of existence with ashes.
My fate must be deplored;
Do you know what is the gist of my being?
It is a condensed wavelet of smoke,
Endowed with a single spark;
Both in feature and nature you are star-like,
Splendors rise from every side of you.
Now you become the light of a monarch's eye,
Now you adorn the haft of a dagger."
"O sagacious friend!" said the diamond,

"Dark earth, when hardened, becomes in dignity a bezel.
Having been at strife with its environment,
It is ripened by the struggle and grows hard like a stone.
It is this ripeness that has endowed my form with light
And filled my bosom with radiance.
Because your being is immature, you have become abased;
Because your body is soft, you are burnt.
Be void of fear, grief, and anxiety;
Be hard as a stone, be a diamond!
Whosoever strives hard and grips tight,
The two worlds are illumined by him.
A little earth is the origin of the Black Stone
Which puts forth its head in the Kaʿba:
Its rank is higher than Sinai,
It is kissed by the swarthy and the fair.
In solidity consists the glory of Life;
Weakness is worthlessness and immaturity."

[In these two brief didactic narratives, Iqbal tilts toward problems that beset the individual seeker on the spiritual path. Elsewhere in the *Secrets of the Self,* however, he turns to more expansive themes that bear on questions of social ethics. In the next sections, Iqbal reflects on the matter of *jihād* and on the role of Islam in the lives of modern Indian Muslims, foreshadowing themes to be explored further in part 5.]

CHAPTER 15: SHOWING THAT THE PURPOSE OF THE MUSLIM'S LIFE IS TO EXALT THE WORD OF ALLĀH, AND THAT THE JIHAD, IF PROMPTED BY LAND-HUNGER, IS UNLAWFUL IN THE RELIGION OF ISLAM.

Imbue your heart with the tincture of Allāh,
Give honor and glory to Love!
The Muslim's nature prevails by means of love:
The Muslim, if he is not loving, is an infidel.
Upon God depends his seeing and not-seeing,
His eating, drinking, and sleeping.
In his will that which God wills becomes lost—
"How shall a person believe this saying?"
He encamps in the field of "There is no god but Allāh";
In the world he is a witness to mankind.
His high estate is attested by the Prophet who

was sent to humankind and Jinn—
The most truthful of witnesses.
Leave words and seek that spiritual state,
Shed the light of God over the darkness of your deeds!
Albeit clad in kingly robe, live as a dervish,
Live wakeful and meditating on God!
Whatever you do, let it be your aim therein
To draw nigh to God,
That his glory may be made manifest by you.
Peace becomes an evil, if its object be aught else;
War is good if its object is God.
If God be not exalted by our swords,
War dishonors the people.
The holy Shaykh Miyān Mīr Walī,
By the light of whose soul every hidden thing was revealed—
His feet were firmly planted on the path of Muḥammad,
He was a flute for the impassioned music of love.
His tomb keeps our city safe from harm
And causes the beams of true religion to shine on us.
Heaven stooped its brow to his threshold,
The Emperor of India was one of his disciples.
Now, this monarch had sown the seed of ambition in his heart
And was resolved on conquest.
The flames of vain desire were alight in him,
He was teaching his sword to ask, "Is there any more?"
In the Deccan was a great noise of war,
His army stood on the battle field.
He went to the Shaykh of heaven-high dignity
That he might receive his blessing:
The Muslim turns from this world to God
And strengthens policy with prayer.
The Shaykh made no answer to the Emperor's speech,
The assembly of dervishes was all ears,
Until a disciple, in his hand a silver coin,
Opened his lips and broke the silence,
Saying, "Accept this poor offering from me,
O guide of them that have lost the way to God!
My limbs were bathed in sweat of labor
Before I put away a dirhem in my skirt."
The Shaykh said: "This money ought to be given to our Sultan,
Who is a beggar wearing the raiment of a king.

Though he holds sway over sun, moon and stars,
Our Emperor is the most penniless of humankind.
His eye is fixed on the table of strangers,
The fire of his hunger has consumed a whole world.
His sword is followed by famine and plague,
His building lays wide land waste.
The folk are crying out because of his indigence,
His empty handedness causes him to plunder the weak.
His power is an enemy to all:
Humankind are the caravan and he the brigand.
In his self-delusion and ignorance
He calls pillage by the name of empire.
Both the royal troops and those of the enemy
Are cloven in two by the sword of his hunger.
The beggar's hunger consumes his own soul,
But the Sultan's hunger destroys state and religion.
Whoso shall draw the sword for anything except Allāh,
His sword is sheathed in his own breast."

CHAPTER 16: PRECEPTS WRITTEN FOR THE MUSLIMS OF INDIA BY MĪR NAJĀT NAQSHBAND, WHO IS GENERALLY KNOWN AS BĀBĀ SAḤRAI

O you that have grown from earth, like a rose,
You too are born of the womb of self!
Do not abandon self! Persist therein!
Be a drop of water and drink up the ocean
Glowing with the light of self as you are,
Make self strong, and you will endure.
You get profit from the trade,
You gain riches by preserving this commodity.
You are being, and are you afraid of not-being?
Dear friend, your understanding is at fault.
Since I am acquainted with the harmony of Life,
I will tell you what is the secret of Life—
To sink into yourself like the pearl,
Then to emerge from your inward solitude;
To collect sparks beneath the ashes,
And become a flame and dazzle human eyes.
Go, burn the house of forty years' tribulation,
Move round yourself! Be a circling flame!

What is Life but to be freed from moving round others
And to regard yourself as the Holy Temple?
Beat your wings and escape from the attraction of Earth:
Like birds, be safe from falling.
Unless you are a bird, you will do wisely
Not to build your nest on the top of a cave.
O you that seek to acquire knowledge,
I say over to you the message of the Sage of Rum [Jalāl ad-Dīn Rūmī]:
"Knowledge, if it lies on your skin, is a snake;
Knowledge, if you take it to heart, is a friend."
Have you heard how the Master of Rum (Rūmī)
Gave lectures on philosophy at Aleppo?—
Fast in the bonds of intellectual proofs,
Drifting over the dark and stormy sea of understanding;
A Moses unillumined by Love's Sinai,
Ignorant of Love and of Love's passion.
He discoursed on Skepticism and Neoplatonism,
And strung many a brilliant pearl of metaphysics.
He unraveled the problems of the Peripatetics,
The light of his youth made clear whatever was obscure.
Heaps of books lay around and in front of him,
And on his lips was the key to all their mysteries.
Shams-i-Tabrīz, directed by Kamāl,
Sought his way to the college of Jalāl ad-Dīn Rūmī
And cried out, "What is all this noise and babble?
What are all these syllogisms and judgments and demonstrations?"
"Peace, O fool!" exclaimed the Maulvi [epithet of Rūmī],
"Do not laugh at the doctrines of the sages.
Get out of my college!
This is argument and discussion; what have you to do with it?
My discourse is beyond your understanding.
It brightens the glass of perception!"
These words increased the anger of Shams-i-Tabrīz
And caused a fire to burst forth from his soul.
The lightning of his look fell on the earth,
And the glow of his breath made the dust spring into flames.
The spiritual fire burned the intellectual stack
And clean consumed the library of the philosopher.
The Maulvi, being a stranger to Love's miracles
And unversed in Love's harmonies,
Cried, "How did you kindle this fire,

Which has burned the books of the philosophers?"
The Shaykh answered, "O unbelieving Muslim,
This is vision and ecstasy: what have you to do with it?
My state is beyond your thought,
My flame is the Alchemist's elixir."
You have drawn your substance from the snow of philosophy,
The cloud of your thought sheds nothing but hailstones.
Kindle a fire in your rubble,
Foster a flame in your earth!
The Muslim's knowledge is perfected by spiritual fervor,
The meaning of Islam is Renounce what shall pass away.
When Abraham escaped from the bondage of "that which sets,"
He sat unhurt in the midst of flames.
You have cast knowledge of God behind you
And squandered your religion for the sake of a loaf.
You are hot in pursuit of antimony,
You are unaware of the blackness of your own eye.
Seek the Fountain of Life from the sword's edge,
And the River of Paradise from the dragon's mouth,
Demand the Black Stone from the door of the house of idols,
And the musk-deer's bladder from a mad dog,
But do not seek the glow of Love from the knowledge of today,
Do not seek the nature of Truth from this infidel's cup!
Long have I been running to and fro,
Learning the secrets of the New Knowledge:
Its gardeners have put me to the trial
And have made me intimate with their roses.
Roses! Tulips, rather, that warn one not to smell them—
Like paper roses, a mirage of perfume.
Since this garden ceased to enthrall me
I have nested on the Paradisal tree.
Modern knowledge is the greatest blind[ness]—
Idol-worshipping, idol-selling, idol making!
Shackled in the prison of phenomena,
It has not overleaped the limits of the sensible.
It has fallen down in crossing the bridge of Life,
It has laid the knife to its own throat.
Its fire is cold as the flame of the tulip;
Its flames are frozen like hail.
Its nature remains untouched by the glow of Love,
It is ever engaged in joyless search.

Love is the Plato that heals the sicknesses of the mind.
The mind's melancholy is cured by its lancet.
The whole world bows in adoration to Love,
Love is the Maḥmūd that conquers the Somnath of intellect.
Modern science lacks this old wine in its cup,
Its nights are not loud with passionate prayer.
You have misprized your own cypress
And deemed tall the cypress of others.
Like the reed, you have emptied yourself of self
And given your heart to the music of others.
O you that beg morsels from another's table,
Will you seek your own kind in another's shop?
The Muslim's assembly-place is burned up by the lamps of strangers,
His mosque is consumed by the sparks of monasticism.
When the deer fled from the sacred territory of Mecca,
The hunter's arrow pierced her side.
The leaves of the rose are scattered like its scent:
O you that have fled from the self, come back to it!
O trustee of the wisdom of the Qur'ān,
Find the lost unity again!
We, who keep the gate of the citadel of Islam,
Have become unbelievers by neglecting the watchword of Islam.
The ancient Sāqī's bowl is shattered,
The wine-party of the Ḥijāz is broken up.
The Kaʿba is filled with our idols,
Infidelity mocks at our Islam.
Our Shaykh has gambled Islam away for love of idols.
And made a rosary of the *zunnār* (a mid-body wrap distinctive of Christian garb).
Our spiritual directors owe their rank to their white hairs
And are the laughing-stock of children in the street;
Their hearts bear no impress of the Faith
But house the idols of sensuality.
Every long-haired fellow wears the garb of a dervish—
Alas for these traffickers in religion!
Day and night they are traveling about with disciples,
Insensible to the great needs of Islam.
Their eyes are without light, like the narcissus,
Their breasts devoid of spiritual wealth.
Preachers and Sufis, all worship worldliness alike;
The prestige of the pure religion is ruined.

Our preacher fixed his eyes on the pagoda
And the mufti of the Faith sold his verdict.
After this, O friends, what are we to do?
Our guide turns his face towards the wine-house.

PASTORAL THEOLOGY: TALKING AND TEACHING ABOUT GOD

Another famous medieval literary mystic, Jalāl ad-Dīn Rūmī, is even better known (at least outside the Middle East) for his poetry than Sanāʾī and ʿAṭṭār. But he also reflected on important theological issues in his nonpoetic writing, as the excerpt on the complexities of the language of faith (from his discourses) exemplifies. Rūmī concludes with a saying attributed to Muḥammad, an axiom of pastorally effective theological discourse: "Speak to the people in accord with their understanding." Ibn ʿAbbād of Ronda, a fourteenth-century Iberian-born, Moroccan-raised Sufi of the Shādhilī order, in turn provides a fine example of putting that maxim into practice. A letter of spiritual direction shows how an experienced guide assists a seeker in finding real-life relevance in what might otherwise be desiccated theological jargon.

Rūmī on the Many Languages of God Talk

Translated by Wheeler M. Thackston

Jalāl ad-Dīn Rūmī (d. 1273) is best known for his sixty thousand verses of mystical poetry, both didactic and lyric. But his followers also captured some of his most profound theological insights in a volume of reflections he delivered orally and that were gathered and written down later. In his twenty-third discourse, Rūmī takes an otherwise mundane observation—about places he likes to visit because of their salubrious climate—and turns it into an occasion to wax almost allegorical about the meaning of the languages of faith. Here are his arresting "parables" about the phenomenon of "God-talk," even when the hearers do not necessarily understand the language in which it is spoken.[6]

Text

I have to go to Toqat because it's warm there. It's warm in Antalya too, but the people there are mostly Greeks. They don't understand our language, although there are a few who do. We were speaking one day to a group that included some infidels, and during our talk they were weeping and going into ecstatic states. "What do they understand? What do they know?" someone asked. "Not one out of a thousand *Muslims* can understand this kind of talk. What have these people understood that they weep so?" It is not necessary for them to understand the words. What they understand is the basis of the words. After all, everyone acknowledges the oneness of God and that He is the Creator and Sustainer, that He controls everything, that everything will return to Him, and that either eternal punishment or forgiveness emanate from Him. When they hear words that are descriptive of God they are struck with a commotion, yearning, and desire because their objects of desire and search are made manifest in these words. Although the way may differ, the goal is one. Don't you see that there are many roads to the Kaʿba?

Some come from Anatolia, some from Syria, some from Persia, some from China, some across the sea from India via the Yemen. If you consider the ways people take, you will see a great variety. If, however, you consider the goal, you will see that all are in accord and inner agreement on the Kaʿba. Inwardly there is a connection, a love and affection, with the Kaʿba, where there is no room for dispute. That attachment is neither infidelity nor faith—that is, it is not confounded by the different ways of which we have spoken. All the dispute and quarrelling that were done along the way (such as one saying to another, "You're an infidel; you're wrong") while the one appears so to the other—when they reach the Kaʿba, it becomes obvious that the dispute was over the way, while their goal was the same all along.

For example, if a cup were alive, it would love the cup maker devotedly. Now, once this cup has been made, some will say that it should be placed on the table just as it is; some will say the inside should be washed; some will say the outside should be washed; some will say the whole thing should be washed, while still others will say that it does not need washing at all. The difference of opinion is confined to such things; all are in agreement that the cup had a creator and a maker and that it did not make itself. Over that there is no disagreement.

Now let us consider humans: inwardly, in the depths of their hearts, they all love God, search for Him, and pray to Him. All their hopes are in Him, and they acknowledge no one as omnipotent or in absolute dominion except Him. Such an idea is neither infidelity nor faith. Inwardly it has no name, but when the "water" of that idea flows toward the "drain spout" of the tongue, it congeals and acquires form and expression. At this point it becomes "infidelity" or "faith," "good" or "evil." It is like plants growing in the ground. At first they have no specific form of their own. When they poke their heads out into the world, initially they are fragile, delicate, and colorless. The farther they proceed into this world, the thicker and coarser they become. They take on different colors. When believers and infidels sit together, as long as they say nothing expressly, they are in accord and their thoughts are not hampered. There is an inner world of freedom where thoughts are too subtle to be judges—as the saying goes, "We judge by externals, and God will take care of innermost thoughts." God creates those thoughts within you, and you cannot drive them away with any amount of effort.

As for the saying that God has need of no instrument, don't you see how He makes those thoughts and ideas within you without any instrument, without any pen or ink? Those ideas are like birds of the air and gazelles of the wild, which cannot be lawfully sold before they are caught and caged. It is not within your power to sell a bird on the wing because delivery is a condition of sale. How can you deliver what you do not control? Therefore, so long as thoughts remain within, they are nameless and formless and cannot be judged as indicating either infidelity or Islam. Would any judge say, "You have inwardly acknowledged thus and so," or "You have inwardly sold thus and such a thing," or "Come and swear that you have not inwardly had thus and such a thought?" He would not because no one can judge what goes on inside you. Thoughts are birds on the wing. However, when they are expressed, they can be judged as pertaining to infidelity or Islam, as good or evil.

There is a world of bodies, another of imaginings, another of fantasies, and another of suppositions, but God is beyond all worlds, neither within nor without them. Now, consider how God controls these imaginings by giving them form without qualification, without pen or instrument. If you split open your breast in search of a thought or idea and take it apart bit by bit, you won't find any thoughts there. You won't find any in your blood or in your veins. You won't find them above or below. You won't find them in any limb or organ, for they are without physical quality and are non-spatial. You won't find them on your outside either. Since His control of your thoughts is so subtle as to be without trace, then consider how subtle and traceless He must be who is the Creator of all this. Inasmuch as our bodies are gross objects in relation to ideas, so also subtle and unqualifiable ideas are gross bodies and forms in relation to the subtlety of the Creator. [As Rūmī wrote in his collection of lyric poetry *Dīvān:*]

If the holy spirit were to unveil itself,
    human intellect and soul would seem as substantial as flesh.

God cannot be contained in this world of phantasmagoria (lit., image-making)—nor yet in any world. If He could be contained in the world of phantasmagoria, then it would follow of necessity that He could be comprehended by a maker of notions and He would no longer be the creator of phantasmagoria. It is obvious therefore that He is beyond all worlds.

"Now has God in truth verified unto His apostle the vision wherein He said, You shall surely enter the holy temple of Mecca, if God pleases, in full security" (48:27). Everyone says, "Let us enter the Kaʿba," Some, however, say, "Let us enter the Kaʿba if God please." These latter, who are exceptional, are lovers inasmuch as a lover does not see himself as in control or as an agent with free will; a lover considers himself as subject to the beloved's control. Therefore, he says, "If the beloved wishes, let us enter." Now the holy temple, in the view of the externalists, is that Kaʿba to which people go; but for lovers and the elite it is union with God. Therefore, they say, "If God please let us reach Him and be honored by seeing Him." On the other hand, it is rare for the beloved to say, "If God please." It is like a stranger's tale, which requires a stranger to listen or to be able to listen. God has servants who are beloved and loved and who are sought by God, who performs all the duties of a lover with respect to them. Just as a lover would say, "If God please, we will arrive," God says, "If God please" on behalf of that stranger. If we were to occupy ourselves in explaining this, even the saints who have attained union would lose the train of thought. How then is one to tell such mysteries and states to ordinary people? [As the poet Khāqānī wrote:] "The pen reached this point and broke its nib." How is a person who cannot see a camel on a minaret going to see a hairline crack on the camel's tooth? Let us return to our original topic.

Those lovers who say, "If God please"—that is, "the Beloved is in control; if the Beloved wishes, we will enter the Kaʿba"—are absorbed in God. There no "other" can be contained and to mention any "other" is forbidden. How can there be room for an "other" when, until one effaces one's own self, there is no room for God? "No one other than the householder is in the house."

As for the saying, "Now has God in truth verified unto His apostle the vision" (48:27), this "vision" is the dream of lovers and those devoted to God. Its interpretation is revealed in the other world. As a matter of fact, all the conditions of this world are dreams, the interpretation of which is revealed in the other world. When you dream that you are riding a horse and attain your goal, what does the horse have to do with your goal? If you dream that you are given sound dirhems, the interpretation is that you will hear good and true words from a learned man. What resemblance is there between dirhems and words? If you dream that you are hanged on the gallows, it means that you will become chief of a people. And what does a gallows have to do with chieftainship? Likewise, as we have said, the affairs of this world are dreams. [As the Hadith says:] "This world is like a sleeper's dream." The interpretations of these dreams are different in the other world from the way they appear here. A divine interpreter interprets them because everything is revealed to him.

When a gardener comes into a garden and looks at the trees, he does not have to examine the fruit on each one to tell which is a date tree, which is fig, pomegranate, pear, or apple. Since the divine interpreter knows, there is no need to wait for Resurrection for him to see the interpretations of what has happened and what the result of a dream will be, for he has seen beforehand what the result would be—just as the gardener knows beforehand what fruit will be given by each branch as a matter of course.

Everything in this world—like wealth, women, and clothes—is sought because of something else, not in and for itself. Don't you see that if you had a hundred thousand dirhams and were hungry or unable to find food, you couldn't eat those dirhams? Sexuality is for producing children and satisfying passion. Clothing is to ward off the cold. Thus do all things form links in a chain to God. It is He who is sought for His own sake and who is desired for Himself, not for any other reason. Since He is beyond everything and is nobler and more subtle than anything, why would He be sought for the sake of what is less than Him? Therefore it can be said that He is the ultimate. When one reaches Him, one has reached the final goal; there is no surpassing there.

The human soul is a locus of doubt and ambiguity, and by no means can one ever extricate the doubt and ambiguity from it without becoming a lover. Only then does no doubt or ambiguity remain. [As the Hadith says:] "Your love for a thing makes you blind and deaf."

When Iblīs refused to bow down to Adam, in disobedience to God's command, he said, "You have created me of fire, and have created him of clay" (7:12)—that is, my essence is of fire and his of clay. How is it right for a superior to bow down to an inferior? When Iblīs was cursed and banished for his sin and opposition and contention with God, he said: "Alas, Lord, you made everything. This was your temptation of me. Now you curse me and banish me."

When Adam sinned, God expelled him from paradise and said: "O Adam, when I took you to task and tormented you for your sin, why did you not contend with me? You had a line of defense, after all. You could have said, 'Everything is from You. You made everything. Whatever You will comes to be in the world; whatever You will not can never come to be.' You had such a clear, right defense. Why did you not state it?"

"O Lord," said Adam: "I knew that, but I could not be impolite in Your presence. My love for You would not allow me to take You to task."

The Divine Law is a fountainhead, a watering place. It is like a king's court, where the king's commands and prohibitions are many, where his dispensation of justice for the elite and common alike is limitless and beyond reckoning. It is extremely good and beneficial. The stability of the world rests on his orders. On the other hand, the state of dervishes and mendicants is one of close conversation with the king and knowledge of the ruler's own knowledge. What is it to know the science of legislation in comparison with knowing the legislator's own knowledge and having converse with the king? There is a great difference. His companions and their states are like a school in which there are many scholars. The director pays each scholar according to his ability, giving to one ten, to another twenty, to another thirty. We also speak to each person according to his ability to comprehend. [As the Hadith says:] "Speak to the people in accord with their understanding."

Ibn ʿAbbād on Relating to God's Attributes and Names

Translated by John Renard

Another important literary genre employed to convey a more personal mode of reflection on the "real life" implications of central theological concepts is the epistolary. Scores of major Muslim authors, often better known for more formal prose works or for lofty poetry, have left significant collections of letters in which they address the spiritual concerns of friends and followers. Here is an excerpt of one such sample of "pastoral theology" in a letter of spiritual guidance by Ibn ʿAbbād of Ronda (Spain, d. 1390). It exemplifies how even in a more intimate form of communication the language of traditional theological notions about God and the divine attributes plays a prominent role: a master teacher helps a concerned seeker reflect very personally on some of the major theological themes laid out in earlier chapters here. Ibn ʿAbbād describes here two modes by which human beings relate to God: the *sālik,* or "wayfarer," follows an often lengthy path of disciplined attention to

God's signs in which the seeker's personal struggle is key; and the *majdhūb* is one who is "drawn" along a relatively effortless journey hallmarked by God's election.[7]

Text

The Exalted Creator has fashioned and constituted the human person with both perfection and imperfection, all of which is miniscule when compared to Him. Then He predisposed the human being for intimate knowledge[8] of Him and of His attributes and Names. By that means He raises the individual above the limitations of intellect, through which one comprehends the empirical sciences, and leads him to contemplate the signs in nature and in created beings. Marvels and wonders manifest themselves to anyone who looks upon these things. They compel him to acknowledge the Fashioner, the Originator, the Creator, the First Principle as possessing the qualities of life, knowledge, power, and will—even as one regards oneself after performing a masterly and exacting task. Then the individual looks also at himself and sees there the qualities of perfection in hearing and sight and speech, so that the experience of the divine power impels him to ascribe the same qualities to the Creator and Originator.

One then discerns the immense disparity between the recent and the eternally ancient, the creature and the Creator.[9] This prompts him to affirm transcendence and deny anthropomorphism. At this point one comprehends all that is accessible to human understanding about the transcendence of his exalted Creator. He ascends from there to the highest degree and utmost extent of his ability to affirm and see. This is the process by which one examines and reflects and is led to the Cause by means of His effects. And the process will suffice to lead every ordinary intelligent person to the rudiments of the intimate knowledge that is requisite for salvation and spiritual progress. One may, however, continue to experience doubts in one's faith, and not experience the expansion of the core of his being and the purification of the heart.[10]

Then God Most High singles out certain of His servants by manifesting Himself to them through His light, something that is most evident to them. They travel by that light along the way that their intimate knowledge of Him indicates most clearly. They contemplate His wondrous attributes and essential Names in a way that the first group of people does not. They comprehend the majesty of the divine presence and the holy lights in a way that eludes the grasp of those who seek evidence. To these the chosen servants say, "How is it that you seek information about what cannot essentially be demonstrated? When is He so hidden that one lacks evidence of Him? How can He be lost to us when there are traces that lead us to Him? Can anything other than Him be manifest in a way that is not within its natural power until He makes it manifest? How can He in whom every feature is recognized be recognized by His features? Or how can He whose Being precedes every other being be distinguished as a specific entity? And how can one gain access by some remote means to Him who is 'closer than the jugular vein' (cf. 50:16)? And 'Does not your Lord suffice, since He is Witness over all things?'" (41:53).

Through intimate knowledge of Him, they arrive only at the names; because of His transcendence they do not attain to the farthest limit of praise and magnification. Still they contemplate that Being in comparison with which all else is nothingness, that permanence in comparison with which all else is negation, the experience of which is false, the perception of which is illusion, the memory of which is forgetfulness, and whose increase is diminishment. They see thus with the eye of certitude and clear proof the truth of the one who said, "God existed before all things, and He exists now independent of all that depends on Him."

Once they arrive at this station, they have come into the grasp of the King, the Knower. He frees them from slavery to sensible knowledge and causes them to die [i.e., experience *fanāʾ*] to all other things. Their inmost thoughts are purified and God, may He be praised, is manifest to them through His most excellent Attributes and Names. He gives them a knowledge of what He will so that they assume the posture of servants before their Master. They come to rest in the place where the One who knows their every secret thought watches over them. They align themselves in rows of service along with those who "set the ranks and hymn His praise" (cf. 37:165–66). They attain the most excellent ranks of the servants and they sing with the tongue of their spiritual state (*lisān al-ḥāl*), saying, "How many were the desires of my heart. . . . "[11] And how delightful for them to be chosen for the dwellings of the beloved ones, with that "beautiful life's end" (3:14, 13:29) foretold for them in the Mother of the Book![12]

The difference between these two paths and their methods can be clearly explained this way. At the heart of the first path [of the *sālik*] is the intellect's search for evidence and its inability to understand except by a kind of analogical reasoning and comparison. That is as far as empirical study will lead one. The second path [of the *majdhūb*], however, rests on the light of certitude, by which only the Clear Truth is manifest. That is the most sublime thing that can descend from the heavens into the hearts of chosen believers, who comprehend thereby the Mystic Truth of the Attributes and Names. . . .

You need the kind of instruction whose import can be fully comprehended only through intelligence and experience, and from which one can be distracted only by negligence and dissimulation. These are dangers you will encounter in this learning process, especially among people who are characterized by one of these three qualities: pride, innovation, or unquestioning acceptance of authority. Pride is a curse that prevents one from perceiving the divine signs and admonitions. Innovation is an error through which pride causes one to fall into serious troubles. And unquestioning acceptance of authority is a trammel that prevents one from achieving victory and arriving at one's destination. The individual who possesses any one of these characteristics is subject to poor judgment and is in continual struggle and turmoil. How much more is that the case with the person in whom these qualities are combined!

Do not let yourself be influenced by people of this sort. And do not let your association with them be an obstacle to your understanding in this learning process, so that your piety is weakened and the doors of guidance and success close before you. When one of these people proposes nonsensical arguments or claims to be in some state or station, the result is sophistry, lies, deceit, and delusion. This is seductive both for the one who speaks and the one who listens, for it claims to enrich every gullible and ignorant person. All of that is vanity upon vanity. Herein lies one of the most convincing proofs of the superiority of the knowledge I have been talking about. It opens its door only to the pure and God-fearing servant and lifts its veil only to the heart that is repentant and undefiled by the contradictory notions proposed by other forms of knowledge.

Therefore do not consider any of the proponents of the law to be more competent than someone from this school of Knowledge. For exoteric learning is diametrically opposed to the Mystic Truth. It leads to inappropriate behavior and depravity in one's way of living, and culminates in a ruinous emptiness for those who engage in it. The mystics, on the other hand, contemplate that which is hidden from others and come to a full realization of truths that are beyond the grasp of others. They are like the people of whom the poet said,

> My night has become a sunny dawn because of your face,
> even though dusk has come to the sky.

Many are they who remain in the darkness of their night,
while we are in the dazzling brilliance of your face.

Shiblī said, "Do not consider yourself learned, for the learning of the religious scholars is suspect."[13] When a question is posed to you, do not approach it in a purely intellectual fashion. You ought rather to deal with it peacefully, setting aside rational objections, so that the simple truth of it, that can calm your heart and expand the core of your being, may be unveiled for you. You will need a pure intention and sincere desire to pursue this learning, for it is a noble learning by which the servant is led to an intimate knowledge of his exalted and glorious Lord and to the experience of His blessings. Through it the servant is brought to the ultimate happiness of meeting Him along with His elect and beloved ones. Junayd has said, "Had I realized that God possessed a knowledge under heaven more noble than this learning we expound with our companions and brothers, I would have run straight for it." All of this is founded on sincerely taking refuge, on the awareness of one's need, on perseverance in supplication, and on self-effacement, in the presence of the King, the Mighty One. Through these means the core of one's being is expanded and the bolts of locked secrets are thrown open. And there is no help and no strength except in God.

NARRATIVE APPROACHES TO MAJOR THEOLOGICAL THEMES

Rūmī was a master storyteller gifted with the ability to cast elusively complex concepts in accessible and engaging forms. The protean poet loved to morph mercurially from image to image in a kind of pedagogical spiral toward his ultimate point. Other talented literary artists have fashioned more extended narrative genres. Ibn Ṭufayl's parable/allegory of Ḥayy ibn Yaqẓān's natural, yet also "miraculous," arrival at an understanding of the divine attributes sets a key theological theme in an imaginative unitary narrative context. Next, Najm ad-Dīn Rāzī offers a lovely allegory on the finality of Muḥammad's prophethood and the Prophet's centrality to Muslim life and thought—a key theme addressed here for the first time in this anthology. Finally, an arresting example of Shīʿī prose "narrative theology" describes the lofty spiritual status of Fāṭima, Muḥammad's most important daughter and the "mother" of Shīʿī Islam.

Ibn Ṭufayl on Acquiring Knowledge of Divine Names and Attributes

Translated by Lenn Evan Goodman

Sometimes likened to the story of Robinson Crusoe, Andalusian Ibn Ṭufayl's (d. 1185) allegorical tale *Alive, Son of Awake* (Ḥayy ibn Yaqẓān) presents an intriguing prose narrative with a philosophical twist on that most theological of themes, the attributes and names of God. Ḥayy's story functions as an arresting vehicle for discussing (at least indirectly) relationships between reason and revelation, nature and nurture, self and self-awareness. The present excerpt drops the reader into the midst of the seeker's developmental quest and raises numerous questions as to the ultimate nature of Ḥayy's relationship to "the Real."[14]

Text

[Ḥayy] considered the attributes of the Necessarily Existent. Already at the purely intellectual stage, before taking up active practice, Ḥayy had learned that these attributes are of one of two kinds: either positive, like knowledge, power, and wisdom, or negative, like transcendence of the physical and all that even remotely pertains to it. This transcendence implies that the list of positive attributes can include no attribute proper to physical things—as is plurality. Thus His positive attributes do not render His identity plural, but all must reduce to one principle, which is His real self.

Ḥayy then took up the task of becoming like Him in both these ways. For the positive attributes, knowing they all reduced to His identity (since plurality, belonging to physical things, was totally out of place here) and thus realizing that His self-awareness was not distinct from Himself, but His identity was Self-consciousness and His Self-knowledge was Himself, Ḥayy understood that if he himself could learn to know Him, then his knowledge of Him too would not be distinct from His essence, but would be identical with Him. Thus Ḥayy learned that to become like Him in His positive attributes is simply to know Him, without sacrilegiously associating anything physical with Him. This he set out to do.

The negative qualities all reduced to transcendence of physicality. So Ḥayy set about eliminating the physical in himself. The exercises by which he approached some likeness to the heavenly bodies had already brought him quite a way in this direction. Still, many vestiges remained: For example, his circular motion, since "motion" was a predicate appropriate only to physical objects. His compassion and solicitude for animals and plants and his eagerness to remove anything that hampered them were themselves characteristic of the physical, since he would not have seen the objects of his concern in the first place without using a corporeal faculty; and to help them too required use of his bodily powers.

So Ḥayy undertook to expel all this from himself, for none of these things was conducive to the ecstasy he now sought. He would stay in his cave, sitting on the stone floor, head bent, eyes shut, oblivious to all objects of the senses and urges of the body, his thoughts and all his devotion focused on the Being Whose Existence is Necessity, alone and without rival. When any alien thought sprang to his imagination, Ḥayy would resist it with all his might and drive it out of his mind.

He disciplined himself and practiced endurance until sometimes days could pass without his moving or eating. And sometimes, in the midst of his struggles, all thoughts and memories would vanish—except self-consciousness. Even when immersed in the beatific experience of the Necessarily Existent Truth, his own subjecthood would not disappear. This tormented Ḥayy, for he knew it was a blot on the purity of the experience, division of his attention as if with some other God. Ḥayy made a concerted effort to purge his awareness-of-the-Truth, die to himself. At last it came. From memory and mind all disappeared, "heaven and earth and all that is between them" (15:85, 78:37), all forms of the spirit and powers of the body, even the disembodied powers that know the Truly Existent. And with the rest vanished the identity that was himself. Everything melted away, dissolved, "scattered into fine dust" (56:6). All that remained was the One, the True Being, Whose existence is eternal, Who uttered words identical with himself: "Whose is the Kingdom on this day? God's alone, One and Triumphant!" (40:16).

Ḥayy understood His words and "heard" the summons they made. Not knowing how to speak did not prevent him from understanding. Drowned in ecstasy, he witnessed "what no eye has seen or ear heard, nor has it entered into the human heart to conceive."[15] . . .

Near the island where, according to one of the two conflicting accounts of his origin, Ḥayy was born, there was, so they say, a second island, in which had settled the followers of a certain true religion, based on the teachings of a certain ancient prophet. Now the practice in this religion was to represent all reality in symbols, providing concrete images of things and impressing their outlines on the people's souls, just as orators do when addressing a multitude. The sect spread widely throughout the island, ultimately growing so powerful and prominent that the king himself converted to it and made the people embrace it as well.

There had grown up on this island two fine young men of ability and high principle, one named Absāl and the other Salāmān. Both had taken instruction in this religion and accepted it enthusiastically. Both held themselves duty-bound to abide by all its laws and precepts for living. They practiced their religion together; and together, from time to time, they would study some of that religion's traditional expressions describing God, the angels He sends, and the character of resurrection, reward and punishment. Absāl, for his part, was the more deeply concerned with getting down to the heart of things, the more eager to discover spiritual values, and the more ready to attempt a more or less allegorical interpretation. Salāmān, on the other hand, was more anxious to preserve the literal and less prone to seek subtle intensions. On the whole he avoided giving too free rein to his thoughts. Still each of them executed the express commands of the text fastidiously, kept watch over his soul, and fought his passions.

In the Law (*sharīʿa*) were certain statements proposing a life of solitude and isolation and suggesting that by these means salvation and spiritual triumph could be won. Other statements, however, favored life in a community and involvement in society. Absāl devoted himself to the quest for solitude, preferring the words of the Law in its favor because he was naturally a thoughtful man, fond of contemplation and of probing for the deeper meanings of things; and he did find the most propitious time for seeking what he hoped for when he was alone. But Salāmān preferred being among people and gave greater weight to the sayings of the Law in favor of society, since he was by nature chary of too much independent thinking or doing. In staying with the group he saw some means of fending off demonic promptings, dispelling distracting thoughts, and in general guarding against the goadings of the devil. Their differences on this point became the cause of their parting.

For Absāl had heard of the island where it is said Ḥayy came to be. He knew how temperate, fruitful and hospitable it was and how easy it would be, for anyone who so desired, to live there in solitude. So he decided to go there and remain in isolation for the rest of his life. He took what money he had, and with some hired a boat to take him to the island. The rest he divided among the poor; and, saying goodbye to his friend, he set sail. The sailors brought him to the island, set him down on the beach and left. Absāl remained there on the island, worshipping, magnifying, and sanctifying God contemplating His most beautiful names and sublime attributes.

His reveries were undisrupted; his thoughts, unsullied. When he needed food, he would take some of the island fruits or game, just enough to hold his appetite in check. He lived in this way for some time in most perfect happiness and intimacy with his Lord. Each day he could see for himself God's splendid gifts and acts of grace in the ease with which He allowed him to find not just his food but all his wants, confirming his trust and putting a sparkle in his eye.

[The two meet and become acquainted as, over time, Absāl teaches Ḥayy to speak.]

Absāl then plied him with questions about himself and how he had come to the island. Ḥayy informed him that he had no idea of his origins. He knew of no father or any mother besides the doe that had raised him. He told all about his life and the growth of his awareness, culminating in contact with the divine. Hearing Ḥayy's description of the beings that are divorced from the sense-world and conscious of the Truth, his description of the Truth Himself, by all His lovely attributes, and his description, as best he could, of the joys of those who reach Him and the agonies of those veiled from Him, Absāl had no doubt that all the traditions of his religion about God, His angels, bibles and prophets, Judgment Day, Heaven and Hell were symbolic representations of these things that Ḥayy Ibn Yaqẓān had seen for himself. The eyes of his heart were unclosed. His mind caught fire. Reason and tradition were at one within him. All the paths of exegesis lay open before him. All his old religious puzzlings were solved; all the obscurities clear. Now he had "a heart to understand" (cf. 7:179).

Absāl looked on Ḥayy Ibn Yaqẓān with newfound reverence. Here, surely, was a man of God, one of those who "know neither fear nor sorrow" (2:62). He wanted to serve as his disciple, follow his example and accept his direction in those things that in Absāl's own view corresponded to the religious practices he had learned in his society.

Ḥayy then asked him about himself and his life; and Absāl, accordingly, set out to tell him about his island and the people who lived there. He described how they had lived before the advent of their present religion and how they acted now. He related all the religious traditions describing the divine world, Heaven and Hell, rebirth and resurrection, the gathering and reckoning, the scales of justice and the straight way. Ḥayy understood all this and found none of it in contradiction with what he had seen for himself from his supernal vantage point. He recognized that whoever had offered this description had given a faithful picture and spoken truly. This man must have been a "messenger sent by his Lord." Ḥayy believed in this messenger and the truth of what he said. He bore witness to his mission as apostle of God. . . .

Still there were two things that surprised him and the wisdom of which he could not see. First, why did this prophet rely for the most part on symbols to portray the divine world, allowing mankind to fall into the grave error of conceiving the Truth corporeally and ascribing to Him things that He transcends and is totally free of (and similarly with reward and punishment) instead of simply revealing the truth? Second, why did he confine himself to these particular rituals and duties and allow the amassing of wealth and overindulgence in eating, leaving men idle to busy themselves with inane pastimes and neglect the Truth. Ḥayy's own idea was that no one should eat the least bit more than would keep him on the brink of survival. Property meant nothing to him, and when he saw all the provisions of the Law to do with money, such as the regulations regarding the collection and distribution of welfare or those regulating sales and interest, with all their statutory and discretionary penalties, he was dumbfounded. All this seemed superfluous. If people understood things as they really are, Ḥayy said, they would forget these inanities and seek the Truth. They would not need all these laws. No one would have any property of his own to be demanded as charity or for which human beings might struggle and risk amputation. What made him think so was his naive belief that all human beings had outstanding character, brilliant minds and resolute spirits. He had no idea how stupid, inadequate, thoughtless, and weak willed they are, "like sheep gone astray, only worse" (25:44).

[Ḥayy resolves to visit Absāl's island and share the Truth with others.]

By God's command it happened that a ship lost its course and was driven by the winds and the beating of the waves to their shore. When it came close to land the men on board saw two men on the beach, so they rode in closer and Absāl hailed them and asked if they would take them along. The men answered yes and brought them on board. No sooner had they done so than God sent a favorable wind that brought the ship with all possible speed to the island where the two had hoped to go. They debarked and went up to the city. Absāl's friends gathered, and he told them all about Ḥayy Ibn Yaqẓān. They all marveled at the story. They crowded around him, making much of him, and in fact deeply in awe of him. Absāl informed Ḥayy that of all human beings this group approached nearest to intelligence and understanding. If Ḥayy were unable to teach them, it would be all the more impossible for him to teach the masses. The ruler of the island and its most eminent man at this time was Salāmān, Absāl's friend who believed in living within society and held it unlawful to withdraw.

Ḥayy Ibn Yaqẓān began to teach this group and explain some of his profound wisdom to them. But the moment he rose the slightest bit above the literal or began to portray things against which they were prejudiced, they recoiled in horror from his ideas and closed their minds. Out of courtesy to the stranger and in deference to their friend Absāl, they made a show of being pleased with Ḥayy, but in their hearts they resented him. Ḥayy found them delightful and continued his exposition of the truth, exoteric and esoteric, night and day. But the more he taught, the more repugnance they felt, despite the fact that these were persons who loved the good and sincerely yearned for the Truth. Their inborn infirmity simply would not allow them to seek Him as Ḥayy did, to grasp the true essence of His being and see Him in His own terms. They wanted to know Him in some human way. In the end Ḥayy despaired of helping them and gave up his hopes that they would accept his teaching. . . .

Ḥayy now understood the human condition. He saw that most humans are no better than unreasoning animals, and realized that all wisdom and guidance, all that could possibly help them was contained already in the words of the prophets and the religious traditions. None of this could be different. There was nothing to be added. There is a man for every task and everyone belongs to the life for which he was created. "This was God's way with those who came before, and never will you find a change in the ways of God" (48:23).

So Ḥayy went to Salāmān and his friends and apologized, dissociating himself from what he had said. He told them that he had seen the light and realized that they were right. He urged them to hold fast to their observance of all the statutes regulating outward behavior and not delve into things that did not concern them, submissively to accept all the most problematical elements of the tradition and shun originality and innovation, follow in the footsteps of their righteous forebears and leave behind everything modern. He cautioned them most emphatically not to neglect religion or pursue the world as the vast majority of people do.

Ḥayy Ibn Yaqẓān and his friend Absāl now knew that even this aspiring group fell short and could be saved only in their own way. If ever they were to venture beyond their present level to the vantage point of insight, what they had would be shattered, and even so they would be unable to reach the level of the blessed. They would waver and slip and their end would be all the worse. But if they went along as they were until overtaken by death, they would win salvation and come to sit on the right (cf. 56:90–91). But "those who run in the forefront, those who run in the forefront, they will be brought near!" (56:10–11).

Najm ad-Dīn Dāya Rāzī on Muḥammad's Spiritual Finality

Translated by Hamid Algar

A core tenet of Islamic theology is the finality of Muḥammad's prophethood, and a correlated spiritual principle is his centrality in the hearts of Muslims everywhere. Many Muslim authors have written moving and creative accounts of the Prophet's place in Islamic life and thought since very early in the history of the faith, few more beautifully than Najm ad-Dīn Dāya Rāzī (d. 1256), in his Persian overview of the spiritual life, *The Path of God's Worshipful Servants.*[16] He situates the Prophet's summative role in the unbroken chain of revelation beginning with Adam, highlighting shared patterns in the experiences of the major prophets and fashioning a lovely allegory out of a cluster of evocative metaphors. Najm ad-Dīn intersperses verses of his own poetry.

Text

Adam was reviled because until his time the wheat of religion had been under cultivation and none had partaken of it. It was necessary for Adam to take charge of the wheat, and then for the prophets following him, for it finally to be passed to the masterly hands of Muḥammad when the time arrived for baking. All nurtured themselves on it, for as the proverb says, "Whoever busies himself with clay will eat thereof." Adam worked with wheat and ate wheat; those who worked with flour ate flour; and those who worked with dough ate dough. Finally it fell to Muḥammad and his followers to eat the baked bread when it was brought forth from the oven of Muḥammadan love.

Then the bread of religion that had been baked in the fire of love was placed at the shop door of Muḥammad's summons, and a crier proclaimed that whoever should desire to eat of that bread and be beloved of the Divine Presence should come to the door of Muḥammad's shop: "Say: 'If you love God, follow me that God too may love you'" (3:31). If the other prophets should wish their bread to be baked, they too must come to his shop on the morrow of resurrection, for [as the Hadith says] "all people will need my intercession on the Day of Resurrection, even Abraham."

The cultivation of religion was, then, possible only through generic mankind: Each of the prophets was a member of that humanity, and each kneaded the dough as was meet until it was the turn of Muḥammad, the heart of the human person, to take it into his hand. Then did religion attain its perfection, no longer needing the attentions of any craftsman. Never had it reached the perfection of "this day I have perfected for you your religion" (5:4) before the age of the Prophet. Any addition to perfection is to be accounted a decrease, and for this reason the Prophet said: "If someone introduces into our religion what is not a part of it, it is to be rejected." He also said, "Beware of all that is introduced into religion, for it is innovation, and innovation is misguidance."

Religion has many attributes, each of which required one of the prophets to nurture it to perfection. Thus Adam brought to perfection the attribute of pure devotion to God; Noah, that of summoning humankind to God; Abraham, that of intimate friendship with God; Moses, that of discourse with God; Job, that of patience; Jacob, that of sadness; Joseph, that of sincerity of purpose; David, that of recitation of God's word; Solomon, that of gratitude; John, that of fear; and Jesus, that of hope. Similarly, all the other prophets brought a certain attribute to perfection, and although they were simultaneously nurturing other attributes, the cultivation of one particular attribute was foremost in them.

Now the pearl in the diadem of all these attributes and the supreme gem in their necklace was the attribute of love, and it was this attribute of religion that Muḥammad nurtured to perfection, for he was the heart of the human person, and the cultivation of love is the special task of the heart.

Since the perfection of religion consists in the perfection of love, the dignity of "God will bring forth a people whom He loves and who will love Him" (5:57) was as a cloak of honor tailored to the stature of Muḥammad's people, and the nobility of "radiant faces gazing on that day upon the face of their Lord" (75:22) was as a candle lit for those who, moth-like, had immolated the substance of their being. Whereas the people of Moses had been given quail and manna, and that of Jesus a heavenly spread—"let them eat and take pleasure therein" (15:3)—it was enough for these ragged drinkers of dregs, these roofless profligates, to imbibe the wine of vision that the cupbearer of "their Lord gave them to drink" (76:21) poured from the goblet of His beauty down the throats of their being. It is true that from the effects of that wine there arises the tumult of "I am the Truth" [Ḥallāj] and "Glory be unto me!" [Bāyazīd Bisṭāmī]; but to destroy the house of being was a cloak that fitted only these distraught gamblers, and to lose life on the flame of vision was possible only for these broken-winged moths. The two worlds have been farmed out to other peoples, but the pavilion of God's majesty is erected in the courtyard of these indigent beggars [as in the Sacred Hadith] "I am with those whose hearts are shattered on My account."

God Almighty has inspired a verse in this beggar:

He said: "Not every heart may look on our love;
Not every soul is a shell for its pearl.
You are not alone in your longing for union,
But it is not a cloak that fits every figure."

Since the perfection of religion was dependent upon the perfection of the attribute of love, and that attribute reached perfection by means of the Prophet Muḥammad, the heart of the human person, therefore he was the Beloved of God and the Seal of the Prophets. Whoever desires religion in its perfection and the rank of beloved of God, let him place his head on the path of imitating the Prophet, for "Say: 'If you love God, then follow me that God may love you'" (3:31).

Since perfection was reached with this religion of Islam, all other religions became abrogated, in the same way that whenever water is to be had, ablution with soil is not permitted.[17] We have explained how, in the time of earlier prophets, it had been necessary to eat wheat, flour, and dough; now that the bread had been baked, the eating of these was abrogated. Indeed, all the prophets will come tomorrow to the door of this shop and obtain bread from our baker, for [according to the Hadith] "Adam and all who come after him shall stand under my banner on the Day of Resurrection; yet I take no pride therein." Yet the Prophet, in the breadth of his powers and the loftiness of his intent, is not contented with the mere baking of the bread of religion, not satisfied with saying, "I am the master of the sons of Adam," for again he adds, "yet I take no pride therein."

What truth is indicated here? An extremely profound truth and a subtle allusion, for the Prophet says in effect: "All this baking of bread, this mastery, leadership and standard bearing, is the benefit people derive from me, for 'We have not sent you save as a mercy to all the worlds'" (21:107). All this is then a cause of pride and boasting for them, that they have a commander, a leader, an intercessor, a paragon, a model, and a guide such as me. My share in all this is in sharelessness; my fulfillment in nonfulfillment; my wish, in wishlessness; my being, in nonbeing; and my wealth and my pride, in poverty [as in a Hadith favored by Sufis]: 'Poverty is my pride.'"

This feeble one says:

Neither Khurāsān nor Iraq is our wish,
And of the friend not union, not parting, we seek.
To no wish can I be joined, I am free of all wish;
Such and such alone, this is my wish.

O Muḥammad, we ask, what mystery is this that you do not boast of the command and leadership of the prophets, but take pride instead in poverty? "This is because our path is founded on love and affection, and it can be traveled only in a state of nonbeing, while command, leadership, and prophethood are all part of being—"

Only the lightly laden may travel this path;
Lighten your burden of self, then tread the path.
A hundred times daily you will be slain on the path;
But breathe not a hint of desire for requital.

When a party of infidels broke the lip and the tooth of the Prophet with the stone of affliction, he was about to part his lips in prayer for them.[18] He had not yet moved his lips when the heavy rock of "You have nothing to do with the affair" (3:128)[19] was cast at his feet. How strange! None had treated Noah in this manner, yet he said: "My Lord, leave not a single inhabitant upon earth from among the unbelievers!" (71:26). Immediately a storm arose throughout the world and destroyed all mankind. Truly Noah was the manifestation of the attribute of wrath, and the path he trod was in accordance therewith—"Say: 'Each acts according to his disposition'" (17:84). Muḥammad was the manifestation of the attributes of grace and of love, and the path he trod was that of concern for the well-being of others. Thus, after they had stoned him, he said: "O God, guide my people, for they know not."

Whence sprang this conduct? From the path of self-diminution and nonbeing that had been laid out before him, so that he might lose his being in nonbeing.

Unless you become less and then less again,
Never can you join the ranks of the lovers.

For as long as figurative being persists, it is impossible to partake in full of the presence of true being; only insofar as you sacrifice figurative being for the sake of true being can you have any share therein. Thus firewood comes to partake of its being as firewood by means of fire, but only insofar as it sacrifices its own firewood being to the being of the fire; and it partakes fully of its own being only when it sacrifices it completely to the being of the fire. Then it is transformed from firewood, with density, darkness, and lowliness, into fire, with subtlety, luminosity, and elevation. If there is anything left of its own firewood being, smoke will be seen to arise as a sign of longing for the fire. For the firewood, having once tasted the fire, is no longer content with its own firewood being and wishes to become totally transformed into the fire being.

O Lord, what place is there now for desire
For today He is both rival and cupbearer?[20]
Come, O cupbearer, pour out more wine,
For a trace remains yet of our being.

Thus whatever fire the wood encounters while in this state it encounters for its own sake, and it can give nothing of it to others.

The true worth of your burning is hidden from the raw;
Burn then for me, already burned a hundredfold!

But once the firewood has entirely sacrificed itself to the fire, it will desire its own being and any fire that it may encounter only for the sake of other firewood.

There is a great mystery contained within this allegory. The one hundred and twenty thousand and more instances of prophethood have sacrificed the firewood of their human nature to the fire of love and the manifestation of God's attributes, but some half-burned fragment has remained from each, so that on the morrow of resurrection smoke will arise from them, proclaiming their selfhood.

But as for Muḥammad, he has immolated, mothlike, the entirety of his being on the candle of the glory of the unity of the Essence, and sacrificed all of his Muḥammadan being to the fiery tongue of love that leaps forth from that candle. He cries out instinctively, "My people! My people!"[21] and the tongue of the candle has become his tongue. Severing all relation to the sons of Adam, he proclaims: "Muḥammad was not the father of a man from among you; rather the Messenger of God and the Seal of the Prophets" (33:40).

This feeble one has composed the following verse:

We are those who have voided their selves of all being;
Who have set light to all their being;

Who in the nights of union before your candlelike cheek,
Have like the moth lost all their being.

What you have heard concerning Muḥammad being shadowless, is because he had become entirely transmuted into light—"O people, a light has come unto you from your Lord" (cf. 5:17, 4:174)—and light has no shadow. When the Prophet had been delivered from the shadow of his self, the whole world took refuge in his light, for "Adam and all who come after him shall stand under my banner on the Day of Resurrection; yet I take no pride therein." The Muḥammadan Light had marked out the first boundary of being, for "The first that God created was my Light"; now it marked out the boundary of eternity, for [as the Hadith says] "There is no prophet after me."

After the sun of Muḥammad's ascendancy had risen, the stars of sanctity of the earlier prophets departed, the night illumined by their religions yielded to day, and the verse of their prophethood became abrogated by that of "Master of the Day of Religion" (1:4). For there is no use to be had of a lamp in the daytime: "Once the day has broken, no need for a lamp."[22] Wretched is that blind and unseeing one who is deprived of all light when it exists in such plenitude!

The sun has long since risen, O idol;
If it shines not on me, it is my misfortune.

The Prophet may be thought of as saying: "Even though the sun of my form shall set in the occident of 'every soul shall taste death' (29:57), the sun of ascendancy of my religion shall remain until the end of the world, through the medium of pious and truthful scholars—'There will constantly be a group of my people adhering steadfastly to the truth.' What need henceforth for prophets, for each of the scholars of my religion shall be equal to a prophet? 'The scholars of my people are like the prophets of the Children of Israel.'"

Religion has an outer and an inner aspect. The former is preserved by the knowledge cultivated by God-fearing scholars and the latter is cultivated and maintained by shaykhs who have themselves traveled on the Path and guide others on it, for [as a Hadith says] "The shaykh among his following is like the prophet among his people." God Almighty in His generosity has made incumbent upon Himself the preservation of religion by means of these two classes, for He says: "We it is Who have sent down the Remembrance, and We it is Who shall preserve it" (15:9).

A Shīʿī Narrative on the Spiritual Status of Fāṭima az-Zahrāʾ

Translated by Mahmoud M. Ayoub and Lynda G. Clarke

An important feature of Islamic spirituality too little acknowledged in broader treatments of the topic is the spiritual status of several women close to the Prophet. We have many accounts of the "excellent qualities" (*faḍāʾil*) of Muḥammad's male Companions; and Hadith collections often include similar sections on the Prophet's wives. Muḥammad's most important daughter, Fāṭima (d. 633), is prominent in traditional Sunnī sources, but she plays a distinctive spiritual role in Shīʿī thought. Numerous texts on key members of the "Family" of Muḥammad recount the excellent qualities of the (male) imams who in the Shīʿī theology of history functioned as the Prophet's spiritual and temporal heirs. Fāṭima, however, stands out among women both Sunnī and Shīʿī, and her spiritual status is a major theological lynchpin in Shīʿī thought. Here is a classic narrative of her "sinlessness" (*ʿiṣma*), a quality she shares with the imams, and its implications, written by Ṭabrisī (who supplied a brief *tafsīr* of Qur'an 24:35 in chapter 1).[23]

Text

HER BIRTH, NAMES, AND EPITHETS

The most predominant view in the traditions transmitted by our traditionists is that Fāṭima az-Zahrāʾ was born in Mecca, on the twentieth of [the lunar month of] Jumāda 'l-Ākhira, in the fifth year of the Prophet's apostolic career. It is also asserted that when the Prophet died, Fāṭima was eighteen years and seven months old.

It is reported on the authority of Jābir ibn Yazīd that [the fifth Imam] al-Bāqir was asked: "How long did Fāṭima live after the Messenger of Allāh?" He answered: "Four months; she died at the age of twenty-three." This view is close to that reported by the traditionists of the [Sunnī] majority. They have asserted that she was born in the forty-first year of the Messenger of Allāh's life. This means that she was born one year after the prophet was sent by Allāh as a messenger. The scholar Abū Saʿīd al-Ḥāfiẓ relates in his book *Sharaf an-Nabī* that all the children of the Messenger of Allāh were born before Islam except Fāṭima and Ibrāhīm, who were born in Islam.[24]

It is reported that the sixth Imam, Jaʿfar aṣ-Ṣādiq (d. 765) said: "Fāṭima has nine names with Allāh. They are: Fāṭima, aṣ-Ṣiddīqa (the Righteous), al-Mubāraka (the Blessed), aṭ-Ṭāhira (the Pure), az-Zakīya (the Unblemished), ar-Rāḍiya (the one content with Allāh's pleasure), al-Marḍīya (the one pleasing to Allāh), al-Muḥaddatha (the one spoken to by angels) and az-Zāhira (the Luminous). In the *Musnad* [collection of transmitted Hadiths] of the eighth Imam ar-Riḍā, it is reported that the Prophet declared: "I named my daughter Fāṭima (the Weaned One) because Allāh weaned her and those who love her from the Fire." The Prophet also called her al-Baṭūl (pure virgin), and said to ʿĀʾisha: "O Ḥamayraʾ (a reddish white, a well-known epithet of ʿĀʾisha), Fāṭima is not like the women of human kind, nor does she suffer the illness you [women] suffer!" This is explained in another prophetic tradition that asserts that she never menstruated. It is likewise reported by Sunnī traditionists on the authority of Anas ibn Malik, who heard Umm Sālim, the wife of Abū Ṭalḥa al-Anṣārī, say: "Fāṭima never experienced the blood of menstruation or parturition, for she was created from the waters of Paradise." This is because when the Messenger of Allāh was transported to heaven, he entered Paradise, where he ate of its fruits and drank its water.

PROOFS OF HER *ʿIṢMA* (SINLESSNESS), SOME OF THE SIGNS PROVING HER STATUS WITH ALLĀH, AND TRADITIONS INDICATING HER EXCELLENCE AND EXALTED STATUS

One of the most incontrovertible proofs of Fāṭima's sinlessness is Allāh's saying: "Surely Allāh wishes to remove all abomination from you, O People of the House, and purify you with a great purification" (33:33). The argument in favor of this, is that the Muslim community has unanimously agreed that the 'People of the House' (*ahl al-bayt*), intended in this verse are the People of the Household of the Messenger of Allāh. Traditions of both the Shīʿī and Sunnī communities have asserted that this verse particularly refers to ʿAlī, Fāṭima, Ḥasan and Ḥusayn. The Prophet, moreover, spread over them all one day a Khaybarite mantle and prayed: "O Allāh, these are the People of my Household, remove all abomination from them and purify them with great purification!" Umm Salāma said: "I too, O Apostle of Allāh, am of the People of your House!" He answered: "Your lot shall be good!"

The Divine Will expressed in this verse must by necessity be either an abstract will not implemented by an action, or a will accompanied by an action. The first option is untenable because it implies no particular applicability to the People of the Prophet's House; such a will is shared by all obligated human beings. Nor is abstract will by itself cause for praise. The entire community has concurred on the view that this verse proclaims the excellence of the People of the Prophet's House over all others, and that the verse refers to them alone. Thus the second option [that the Divine Will referred to in the verse is a will accompanied by action] is true, and in it is clear proof of the sinlessness of those who were intended in the verse. It implies further that it is impossible for them to commit any evil action. Moreover, any others whom we have not named here are no doubt not held by general consensus as possessing *ʿiṣma* (protection from error). Thus since the verse necessarily implies sinlessness it must apply to them [the People of the Prophet's House], because it pertains to no other individuals.

Another proof of Fāṭima's sinlessness is the Prophet's saying concerning her: "Fāṭima is part of me. Whatever causes her hurt, hurts me, and whoever hurts me, hurts Allāh, exalted be His Majesty!" The Prophet said further: "Allāh becomes wrathful for Fāṭima's anger, and is pleased at her pleasure." Had she been one who was guilty of committing sins, it would not be that anyone causing her hurt would by this cause the Prophet himself hurt in any way. On the contrary, if anyone were to disgrace and hurt her deservedly—even if he were to inflict upon her the severest punishment permitted by the limits set by Allāh—if her action necessitated such retaliation, it would be pleasing to him.

Among the signs indicating Fāṭima's exalted status with Allāh is an incident related by both Shīʿī and Sunnī traditionists on the authority of [a wife of the Prophet] Maymūna, who reported that Fāṭima was found asleep one day, the handmill beside her turning of its own accord. She informed the Apostle of Allāh of this, and he said: "Allāh knew the weak condition of His handmaid; He thus inspired the handmill to turn by itself, and so it did." Among the reports asserting her excellence and high distinction over all other women is the tradition reported on the authority of ʿĀʾisha who said: "I never saw a man more beloved of the Apostle of Allāh than ʿAlī, or a woman more dear to him than Fāṭima."

Sunnī traditionists also reported on the authority of the Commander of the Faithful who said: "I asked the Messenger of Allāh, 'Who is more beloved to you, Fāṭima or I?' He answered, 'Fāṭima is more beloved to me, and you are dearer to me than she is.'" These traditionists also reported from Anas ibn Malik that: "Fāṭima is the most excellent of all the women of the world." In another tradition it is reported that the Prophet said: "The most excellent among the women of the world are: Maryam daughter of ʿImrān [i.e., the Virgin Mary], Āsiya daughter of Muzāhim [wife of Pharaoh], Khadījah daughter of Khuwaylid and Fāṭima daughter of Muḥammad." It is also related on the authority of Ibn ʿAbbās who said: "The most excellent of the women of Paradise are: Khadīja daughter of Khuwaylid, Fāṭima daughter of Muḥammad, Maryam daughter of ʿImrān and Āsiya daughter of Muzāhim." Traditionists report that ʿAbd ar-Raḥmān ibn ʿAwf said: "I heard the Apostle of Allāh say, 'I am a tree, Fāṭima is its trunk and ʿAlī is its pollen. Ḥasan and Ḥusayn are its fruits, and our followers [the Shīʿa] are its leaves. The roots of the tree are in the Garden of Eden, and its trunk, fruits and leaves are in Paradise.'" . . .

The traditions that our Companions [i.e., Shīʿī Hadith transmitters] have reported in proof of Fāṭima's special place among the children of the Apostle—her honored status and distinction over all the women of humankind—are beyond number. We shall, therefore, limit ourselves to the reports that we have already mentioned.

Among the things that Allāh completed, the great honor of the Commander of the Faithful (ʿAlī) in this world and the world to come was His special favor towards him in having him unite in marriage with the noble daughter of the Messenger of Allāh, who was the most beloved of all creatures to him [Muḥammad], the consolation of his eyes and mistress of the women of the world. Among the many traditions concerning this event is the sound hadith reported on the authority of Anas ibn Malik, who said: "As the Apostle of Allāh was sitting one day, ʿAlī came to see him. He addressed him saying, 'O ʿAlī, what brings you here?' 'I came only to greet you with the salutation of peace,' ʿAlī replied. The Prophet declared: 'Here comes Gabriel to tell me that Allāh has willed to unite you in marriage with Fāṭima. He has, moreover, called as witnesses to her marriage a thousand thousand angels. Allāh has revealed to the tree of Ṭūbā [in Paradise], "Scatter your pearls and rubies!" Black-eyed houris rushed to pick the precious stones up, which they shall exchange as presents among them till the Day of Resurrection.'"

It is related on the authority of Ibn ʿAbbās, who said: "On the night when Fāṭima was married to ʿAlī, the Messenger of Allāh stood before her. Gabriel stood at her right hand and Michael at her left. Seventy thousand angels stood behind her, praising and sanctifying Allāh. The Commander of the Faithful prided himself on his marriage to her on numerous occasions." Abū Isḥāq ath-Thaqafī reported on the authority of Ḥākim ibn Jubayr, who reported from al-Ḥajarī who related from his uncle who said: "I heard ʿAlī say one day, 'I shall utter words that no other man would utter but that he would be a liar. I am ʿAbd Allāh, and brother of the Apostle of Allāh. I am the one whose guardian is the Prophet of mercy, for I have married the mistress of all the women of the community. I am the best of the viceregents.'" Numerous reports expressing similar ideas have been transmitted.

Ath-Thaqafī reported on the authority of Burayda, who said: "On the nuptial night of ʿAlī and Fāṭima, the Prophet said to ʿAlī, 'Do not do anything until you see me.' He then brought water—or the traditionist reported that he called for water—which he used to perform his ablutions for prayers, pouring the rest over ʿAlī. The Prophet then prayed, 'O Allāh, bless them! Shower your blessings over them, and bless for them their two young lions [i.e., their two sons Ḥasan and Ḥusayn].'" Ath-Thaqafī also related on the authority of Shuraḥīl ibn Abī Saʿd, who said: "On the morning after Fāṭima's wedding, the Prophet brought a skinful of milk, and said to Fāṭima, 'Drink! May your father be a ransom for you.' He likewise said to ʿAlī, 'Drink! May your cousin be a ransom for you.'"

PART FIVE

The Science of Character and Comportment

ETHICS AND GOVERNANCE

AS THE "SCIENCE OF HEARTS" (*ʿilm al-qulūb*) addresses the myriad questions and challenges thoughtful Muslims have sought to resolve in their spiritual lives, so the "science of character and comportment" (*ʿilm al-akhlāq*) has assisted them in understanding the ethical demands and theological dimensions of religiously motivated behavior. Among the overarching theological themes Muslim thinkers have explored across the centuries, few loom larger in discussions of how theology affects "real life" than questions of the interface between divine omnipotence and human freedom and accountability, on the one hand, and the notion of divine "justice," on the other. The following two chapters, dedicated to matters of theory and practice, respectively, sample the works of major Muslim thinkers both classical and modern on a wide variety of themes: moral agency, from divine sovereignty to human participation in shaping ultimate destinies; the extent and purpose of Satan's role in the divine plan; the nature of sin and forgiveness; divergent classic models for Muslim administrators; and human responsibility for involvement in the establishment of public morality. Muslim authors have communicated their views, on both theoretical dimensions of the moral life and the more "practical" demands of putting that theory into action, in a variety of genres, from short treatises to chapters in larger systematic theological compendia, from letters and "mirrors for princes" to aphoristic wisdom and advice.

NINE

Ethics in Theory

TWO LARGE TOPICS OCCUPY THE present chapter. First, questions arising from the foundational concepts of God's perfect omnipotence and omniscience have a host of complex implications for the degree to which human beings choose, effect, and bear responsibility for their actions. In the Islamic version of what Christians refer to as "moral theology" or "theological ethics," answers range from an outright predeterminism that virtually exonerates the human agent of culpability for evil deeds, to attempts to balance divine power and human choice, to solutions that almost resort to reducing God's choices to the very dictates of reason itself. As a corollary to this, the question of how to understand the balance of divine justice, on the one hand, and the belief in God's mercy and "fairness," on the other, has generated whole libraries on the subject of "theodicy." Here is a selection of texts illustrating how major proponents across the spectrum worked out these theoretical dilemmas.

DIVINE OMNIPOTENCE, HUMAN FREEDOM

Ḥasan al-Baṣrī on Moral Responsibility

Translated by Valerie J. Hoffman

According to traditional accounts, the Umayyad caliph ʿAbd al-Malik ibn Marwān wrote to al-Ḥasan al-Baṣrī (d. 728), requesting a clarification of comments attributed to Ḥasan, which the caliph found unacceptable. Here are the main elements of a reply long (but debatably) attributed to Ḥasan.[1] After laying the groundwork of his argument by appealing to the example of fidelity to tradition exhibited by the ancestors in faith (*salaf*), and adducing numerous Qur'ānic texts showing how God's omnipotence does not exonerate the individual person of responsibility and accountability for actions taken, the document continues as follows.

Text

Anyone to whom it is said, "You are unjust and the source of injustice" hates to hear that. So they attribute to God that with which they are not pleased for themselves, and they attribute to themselves what they like! The only ones who die in this condition are a people in whose hearts is crookedness; they follow what is ambiguous, seeking discord (cf. 3:7). They debate and say, "God the Exalted said, 'He leads astray whom He wills and gives guidance to whom He wills'" (13:27), and they don't look at what is before or after these words in the text. Had they reflected on the indications in the text before and after this passage, they would not have been led astray. God the Exalted said, "God establishes those who believe with a firm word, both in this world and in the next, and God leads astray the oppressors, and God does what He wills" (14:27). What He wills is to establish those who believe by their faith and righteousness, and to lead astray those who commit injustice by their repudiation [of the truth] and enmity [to God]. He said, "When they deviated, God caused their hearts to deviate" (61:5). He only caused their hearts to deviate when they themselves deviated.[2] The Exalted said, "By this He leads many astray and by this He guides many, but He only leads astray those who are sinful, who violate the covenant of God after its binding and sever what God ordered to be joined and cause corruption in the earth; they are the losers" (2:26–27).

[Here Ḥasan sums up a range of specific points on which Muslims have presented various contending arguments concerning scriptural references to divine punishment of wrongdoing, the meaning of God's "permission," what it means to say that individuals are capable of "choosing," and the reality that some persons are "happy" and others not. Then he delves further into the underlying theological problem. Note that pointed references to Moses's moral dilemma in the face of Khiḍr's enigmatic deeds in sūra 18 will play an important role in the arguments of both Bāqillānī and Bazdawī.]

Know, Commander of the Faithful, that among those who oppose the command of God and His Book and His justice are a people who exaggerate concerning their religion and by their ignorance attribute things to predestination. But they are not content with that in the things of this world—they take with firmness and by force, because of the weightiness of the truth against them and the flimsiness of their futile imaginings! If you ordered any of them to do something concerning his religion he would say, "The pens have gone dry and it is written on the forehead: 'happy' or 'miserable.'" But if you said to one of them, "Don't wear yourself out seeking the things of the world and setting out early in the morning, in heat and cold, risking your life on journeys, for your sustenance is finished," he would have disputed that point with you. And if you said to him, "Do not weary yourself with watering your crops and sorting them and returning repeatedly to tend them in the heat and cold, for what has been predestined for you from God will grow in your ground," he would have disputed that point with you. And if you said, "Do not seek a shepherd for your sheep, for whatever God has predestined for the wolf to eat and the thief to take will die and be lost and you cannot keep it safe, and whatever God has determined to be preserved will not be lost," he would have denied this. And if you said, "Do not tether your horse or strengthen its bonds, and do not pay any attention to your camels, fearing they will wander away, for only what has been foreordained for you will happen, regardless of whether you tie them or let them go without a tether," he would rebuke you for saying that. And if you said, "Do not lock your shop or the door of your house, taking precautions for your goods, your wealth and your saddlebags, for there is no benefit concerning God's provision for you in locking the door," he would deny that. For he is not content to deal with his worldly affairs except with strength, prudence and resoluteness. If someone forbade that, he would consider him ignorant and blameworthy. But at the same time he leaves the affairs of his religion to predestination! All this is because of the heaviness of the truth and the flimsiness of their futile imaginings.

They also debate about His saying, "Had God so willed, He would have gathered them to guidance; do not be among the ignorant" (6:35). This is God's reproach to His Prophet when he grieved over the idolaters when they did not submit to God. God said, "Perhaps you will destroy yourself with grief over them if they do not believe these words" (18:6). God informed His Prophet of His power: had He wished to compel them to obedience, He could have done that, and that would not be impossible for Him. But He wanted to test them, in order to requite each one according to his deeds. He said, "Had your Lord so willed, everyone on earth would have believed. Would you force people to become believers?" (10:99).

One of the things about which they dispute is this saying of the Exalted: "We have created many *jinn* and people for hell; they have hearts with which they do not understand, they have eyes with which they do not see, they have ears with which they do not hear. They are like sheep, indeed they are even more misguided. They are heedless" (7:179). They interpreted this to mean that when God began to create, He made some people for hell, who are unable to obey what was requested of them, and He made some for heaven, who are unable to disobey Him concerning what is forbidden them, just as He created the short who is unable to be long and the black who is unable to be white, and He punished them unless they were believers. They have described God the Exalted by the ugliest of attributes, although He told them that they become fit for hell by their vulgar deeds. He drew a comparison to them by saying, "They have hearts with which they do not understand, and eyes with which they do not see. . . . " In the same vein He said, "The family of Pharaoh picked him [the infant Moses] up so he might be an enemy and a sorrow to them" (28:8), whereas in fact they picked him up so he might be the apple of their eye.[3] And as the Exalted said, "We only make them enjoy life for a long time that they might increase in wickedness" (3:178). He revealed that in enjoying long life they increase in wickedness by abandoning obedience. God was really speaking to the Arabs of what they already knew in their own usage, for one of the wise men among the Arabs said:

> It is for death that the mothers feed their lambs,
> Just as it is for the destruction of time that houses are built.

The poet tells us that the [ultimate] fate of children is death and the [ultimate] fate of buildings is destruction, although lambs are nourished for survival, not death, and houses are built for habitation, not destruction. The Qurʾān is Arabic, Commander of the Faithful, revealed by God to an Arab people, speaking in their language, whose meaning they understand.

They also debate about the knowledge of God. They say that God knew that some people would not believe, so they are unable to have faith because the knowledge of God prevents them. They went so far as to say that God imposes obligations on His servants to do what they are unable to do, and not to do what they are unable not to do. But God the Exalted calls them liars by saying "God only imposes an obligation on a soul according to its capacity" (2:286). God knew that unbelief would arise among them by their choice and by following their passions. They have likened this type of foreknowledge to God's knowledge of how they will end up with respect to height, shortness, form and color, which God knew they would have no way of changing. But it is not like that, for height, shortness, form and colors are the works of God in them; they have no choice over them or power to change them. But God knew they would choose unbelief by their passions, and He knew they would hate to abandon it although they were able to do so by the capacity put in them. All this was so He might test whether they would choose faith and justice. This is just like the ship that was pierced by Khiḍr.[4] God knew that if it passed by the king, he would have taken it by force, and He knew that if he pierced it, he could not take it. Likewise the boy who was killed by Khiḍr: God knew that had he lived, he would have brought suffering to his parents by his rebellion and unbelief, whereas if he killed him, he would protect his parents from his rebellion and unbelief. Likewise the wall that Khiḍr built: God knew that if he did not raise it, the treasure beneath it would have been lost, and He knew that if he built it the treasure would remain beneath it until the two boys reached maturity and took out their treasure as a mercy from God. Then he said to Moses, "I have not done it by my own command" (18:82), because God taught me to do these things, and this is the meaning of His saying, "We taught him knowledge from Us" (18:65).

Likewise concerning the Hypocrites who stayed behind from following the Messenger of God into battle, God knew that they would remain behind to avoid hardship, and He knew that were the gain nearby or only a short journey away they would have followed him.[5] But hardship was something they would not endure. They swear by God, "'Had we been able, we would have gone out with you and died ourselves'—but God knows that they are liars" (9:42), because they were able to go out, had they wanted.

They also debate about His saying, "Whatever good has befallen you is from God, and whatever bad has befallen you is from yourself" (4:79) and "Say: everything is from God—so what is wrong with these people who hardly understand speech?" (4:78). They interpret this according to their own opinion concerning obedience and disobedience: they allege that unbelief, sin, rebellion, oppression, injustice, slander and all abominations are from God, but it is not like that. Rather, when God bestows upon the Hypocrites things that they love, such as abundant livelihood, bodily health and other such things, they say, "This is from God." And if God afflicts them with things that they hate, such as scarcity of livelihood, bodily hardship or aridness of earth or deficiency of arable land and offspring, they say, "This is from Muḥammad." God the Exalted says, "Say: Everything is from God" (4:78), i.e., God does everything.

They also debate about the story of Noah and his saying "My advice would not benefit you if I wanted to counsel you if God wishes to lead you astray. He is your Lord, and to Him you will return" (11:34). They interpret this according to their ignorance to mean that Noah remained with his people for 950 years, calling them to God the Exalted and counseling them, without knowing whether or not their response to him and their acceptance of his counsel would benefit them, and not knowing whether or not God had prepared the way for them to accept it. But it is not as they interpret it. Rather, Noah argued with his people until they concluded his argument by saying, "Noah, you have argued with us and have prolonged your dispute with us. So bring what [punishment] you promise us, if you are truthful" (11:32). Noah said to them, "God will indeed bring it to you if He wishes; you are not able to stop it" (11:33), meaning "you will not escape His punishment if He brings it to you, and you are not exempted from it." "And my advice would not benefit you" at that time "if I wanted to counsel you" (11:34) when the punishment descends among you. Noah knew that when the punishment descended upon them and they saw it with their own eyes, faith would not benefit them at that time. God the Exalted revealed concerning the nations that He caused to perish: "Their faith did not benefit them when they saw our might. [This is] the way God acts with His servants; there the unbelievers were lost" (40:85). This is the way of God, that repentance is not accepted at the time of punishment. As for his saying, "If God wished to lead you astray, He is your Lord and you will return to Him" (11:34), leading astray in this context only means punishment, for that is what the Exalted says: "A new generation arose after them who neglected prayer and followed their own passions; they will find misguidance" (19:59), i.e., a painful punishment. The Arabs say, "So-and-so found misguidance today," meaning that the ruler beat him severely or punished him painfully.

Another thing about which they debate are these words of God the Exalted: "Whomever God wishes to guide, He opens his breast to Islam. And whomever He wishes to lead astray, He makes his breast narrow and constricted as if it were evaporating into the sky. Thus does God put filth on those who do not believe" (6:125). They interpret this according to their ignorance to mean that God the Exalted designated some people for the opening of their breasts—i.e., their hearts—without unbelief or sin or misguidance on their part, and for these people there is no way for them to obey Him as He commanded them, and they are eternally in hellfire. But it is not as the ignorant, mistaken ones have said, Commander of the Faithful. Our Lord is too merciful, just and gracious to do that to His servants. How can that be, when He has said, "God only imposes an obligation on a soul according to its capacity; it gets what it has earned" (2:286)? He only created *jinn* and humans to worship Him, and made ears, eyes and hearts for them with which they can bear many times more than the obligations God has imposed on His servants. Whoever obeys God concerning what He commands him, God opens his breast to Islam as a reward from Him for his obedience in this world, and by this He lightens the weight of good deeds for him and makes heavy unbelief, sin and rebellion. In such a condition he is able to bear all that God commanded him and forbade him. Likewise, God has passed judgment on everyone who reaches his level of obedience, whether exalted or humble, and on everyone who abandons the obedience with which God has commanded him and persists in his unbelief and misguidance in this world, although he is capable of the Trust and repentance.[6] God makes his breast narrow and constricted as if he were evaporating into the sky as a punishment from Him for him because of his unbelief and going astray in this fleeting life. Repentance is commanded and called for. Likewise God the Powerful and Splendid judges whoever reaches his level of unbelief and sin. God only mentioned the opening and narrowing [of breasts] in His Book, Commander of the Faithful, as a mercy from Him to His servants, and as an invitation from Him to them in the deeds by which they deserve, in His wisdom, that He open their breasts, and as an inducement from Him to them in the deeds by which they deserve, in His wisdom, the constriction of their breasts. God did not tell them this in order to cut off their hope or make them despair of His mercy and grace or to cut them off from His pardon, forgiveness and graciousness if they mend their ways. God the Powerful and Splendid made this clear in His Book when the Exalted One said, "God guides in the paths of peace those who seek to please Him, and brings them out of darkness to the light by His permission, and He guides them to a straight path" (5:16).

So reflect on this and understand, Commander of the Faithful, for God says, "Give good news to My servants who listen to My word and follow the best part of it, those whom God has guided; they are those who have understanding" (39:18). And hear the word of God the Exalted when He says, "If the People of the Book had believed and become pious, We would have forgiven them their evil deeds and would have caused them to enter into gardens of blessing. Had they upheld the Torah and the Gospel and what was revealed to them from their Lord, they would have eaten from above them and from underneath their feet" (5:65–66). The Exalted One also said, "Had the people of the villages believed and feared God, We would have opened blessings from heaven and earth to them. But they disbelieved, so We took them in what they earned" (7:96). Know, Commander of the Faithful, that God did not place things inevitably upon His servants, but He said, "If you do such-and-such, I will do such-and-such to you; and if you do such-and-such, I will do such-and-such to you." He only requites them for their deeds, and He has ordered them to worship Him, to call upon Him, and to seek His help. Had they desired His blessings, He would have added help to the help He had given them, and success to the success He had granted to them, and He would have made it easy for them to take the good things and leave the evil things. In the same way God has judged those who obey Him and seek His blessings.

So make up your mind, Commander of the Faithful, not to say that God has predestined for His servants what He has forbidden them, or has come between them and what He commands them to do, or that He sent messengers to call them to the opposite of what He had ordained for them, and then punishes them for all eternity if they do not respond to that for which He had not prepared a way for them. God is exalted far beyond what they say. Do these ignorant people know with whom they are disputing? They are disputing with God the Exalted, for God the Exalted says, "Believe, for that is better for you" (4:170), and the ignorant ones say, "There is no way for them to believe." God says, "Respond to the one who calls people to God" (46:41), and the ignorant ones say, "He has prevented them from responding." The Exalted says, "Hasten to the forgiveness of your Lord" (57:21), whereas the ignorant ones say, "How can they hasten, when He has definitely compelled them [to do what they are doing]?" He says, "What is wrong with them, that they do not believe?" (84:20), and they say, "Because God prevented them from believing and placed them in unbelief." He says, "People of the Book, why do you deny the revelations of God, when you are witnesses?" (3:70), but the ignorant ones say, "Because God predestined unbelief for them and made it inevitable." This is a dispute against God and a low opinion of Him. God the Exalted says, "Cease, that is better for you" (4:171). The ignorant ones think that He is saying, "Cease doing what I ordained for you, for that is better for you." Likewise the Exalted says, "Do not invent a lie against God" (20:61), "Do not go near the wealth of the orphan unless you bring something better" (6:152, 17:34), "Do not go near adultery" (17:32), "Do not kill the soul which is forbidden except with justification" (17:33), and "Do not buy my revelations for a small price" (2:41).

Everything that is in the Qur'ān of this sort the ignorant ones think forbids them to do what He has decreed and determined. Likewise they say that

God ordained for His Prophet the prohibition of what was permitted to him, and then blamed him for acting according to His decree. He says, "Prophet, why do you prohibit what God has permitted for you?" (66:1).[7] They say, "God ordained something for His Prophet now, then permitted it, and then blamed him for that." He says, "May God forgive you! Why did you permit them?" (9:43). None of the prophets committed an error without attributing that error to himself; he did not attribute it to his Lord. The hoopoe bird, to which God granted speech, said, "I found her and her people prostrating themselves before the sun rather than God. Satan has made their deeds favorable in their eyes, and has diverted them from the right path" (27:24).[8] This is frequent in the Qur'ān, and this is the answer to the question you asked me. I have clarified and explained it, so reflect and think well on it. It is healing for whatever is in the breast.

Shaykh al-Mufīd on Divine Predetermination and the Battle of Ṣiffīn

Translated by I. K. A. Howard

Early Shīʿī sources attribute a strikingly similar position on this theme to an earlier Commander of the Faithful, ʿAlī.[9] The text situates the question of divine determination in the context of ʿAlī's conflict with Umayyad authorities headquartered in Damascus, at the Battle of Ṣiffīn (657). It was at the conclusion of this engagement that the sect known as the Kharijites "seceded" from the supporters (or Shīʿa) of ʿAlī.

Text

A man came to the Commander of the faithful, after his departure from the Battle of Ṣiffīn. He asked him: "Commander of the faithful, tell me: Was the battle that took place between you and these people a result of the decree and determination of God?"

"You have never gone up a hill nor gone down into a valley without God's decree and determination being present in the action," he answered. "Then, Commander of the faithful, I regard [all] my concerns as God's responsibility," the man said. "Why?" [asked ʿAlī] "If the decree and determination of God drive us to act," the man replied, "then what is the point of rewarding us for obedience and punishing us for disobedience?"

"Fellow," said the Commander of the faithful, "have you thought that it was a sealed decree and determination? Don't think that. That sort of statement is the doctrine of idolators, supporters of Satan and opponents of God, the Merciful. [It is such people] and the Majīs with them who have adopted it. God, exalted be His Majesty, gives commands as a matter of free choice (*takhyīr*), and gives prohibitions as a warning [against an action]. He puts the burden on us. He is not obeyed unwillingly nor is He disobeyed as one who can be overcome. He has not created the heavens and the earth and what is between them in vain. 'That is the opinion of those who disbelieve. There will be woe from Hell-fire for those who disbelieve'" (38:27).

"What, then, is the decree and determination that you mentioned, Commander of the faithful?" asked the man. He ['Alī] answered: "It is the command to obey, the prohibition of disobedience, the provision [to humankind] to draw near Him and to abandon those who disobey Him, the promise [of reward] and the threat [of punishment], the inspiration [He gives people] to do good and the fear of doing evil [that He arouses in human beings]. All that is the decree of God with regard to our actions and His determination of our deeds. As for anything else [that has been claimed], do not give it any consideration. For the consideration of it will invalidate your action."

"You have dispelled my worries, Commander of the faithful," said the man. "May God dispel yours." And he began to recite:

> You are the Imam, through obedience to whom we hope for forgiveness from God, the Merciful, on the Day of the Return [to Him]. You have explained what was unclear in our religion. May your Lord bounteously reward you with kindness.

This account clarifies, through the words of the Commander of the faithful, the meaning of [divine] justice and the prohibition of [belief in] the doctrine of determinism (*jabr*), [in addition to] establishing the wisdom in the actions of God, the Exalted, and denying that there is any futility in them.

THEORIES OF MORAL CAPACITY AND RESPONSIBILITY

Bāqillānī's Ash'arī Perspective on Human Acquisition of Divinely Created Acts

Translated by Richard J. McCarthy, SJ

Bāqillānī (d. 1013) sets the stage for presenting the classic Ash'arite position on how one can simultaneously affirm God's pure omnipotence and sufficient human freedom to be held accountable for all actions. At the heart of this view is the concept of "acquisition" (*iktisāb*), which holds that human beings exercise only secondary agency in "choosing" or "acquiring" acts already created by God from all eternity.[10]

Text

ALL PRODUCED THINGS ARE *CREATED* BY GOD

You must also know that all produced things (*ḥawādith*) are created by God: harmful and hurtful, faith and unbelief, obedience and disobedience. This is proved by His words: "When Allāh has created you and what you make" (37:96). God Himself refuted the unbelievers when they claimed that He had partners in creating, and said: "Or do they assign partners to Allāh who created the like of His creation so that the creation [that they made and His creation] seemed alike to them? Say: Allāh is the Creator of all things, and He is the one, the Almighty" (13:16). God also said: "He it is Who makes you go on the land and the sea" (10:23), thus telling us that He is the Creator of our going, i.e. motions and rests. He also said: "Is there any creator other than Allāh?" (35:3). And Muḥammad said: "God is the Creator of every maker and his making." And the Community is agreed on the doctrine that there is no creator save God in both worlds, just as they arc agreed that there is no god at all save Him.

ALL PRODUCED THINGS ARE *WILLED* BY GOD

You must also know that all produced things take place as willed by God, and that it is inconceivable that there should exist, in this life or the next, anything not willed by God—benefit, harm, sustenance, term, obedience, disobedience, or any other existing thing. The proof of that is what we have explained previously, namely, the fact that He is their Creator. If that be true, it follows from it that He wills and intends to produce what He creates. This is also proved by His words: "Had Allāh so willed, He could have brought them all together to the guidance" (6:35); and: "And whomsoever it is Allāh's will to guide, He expands the core of that person's being unto the Surrender, and whomsoever it is His will to send astray, He constricts the core of that person's being and narrows it as if he or she were engaged in sheer ascent to the skies. Thus Allāh lays ignominy upon those who do not believe" (6:125); and: "And though We should send down the angels unto them, and the dead should speak unto them, and We should gather against them all things in array, they would not believe unless Allāh so willed" (6:111); and: "And if your Lord willed, all who are on earth would have believed together. Would you [Muḥammad] compel human beings until they are believers?" (10:99); and: "And if We had so willed, We could have given every soul its guidance, but the word from Me concerning evil-doers took effect: that I will fill hell with the jinn and mankind together" (32:13). The Qur'ānic verses to this effect are innumerable.

Moreover, the Community is agreed on professing the usage of this expression: What God wills is, and what He wills not is not. Furthermore, if God willed a thing, and another willed a thing, and that other's will, and not God's, existed, that would be a proof of impotence and superiority—but God is exalted above that! And a learned man has said: "By God, the Qadarīya have not spoken as God has, nor as the Prophets have, nor as the People of the Garden have, nor as the People of the Fire have, nor as their brother Iblīs has. For God has said: "He sends whom He will astray and guides whom He will" (16:93); and: "And you will nothing, unless Allāh wills, the Lord of Creation" (81:29). And Moses said: "It is but Your trial [of us]. You send whom You will astray and guide whom You will" (7:155). And our Prophet said: "Say: for myself I have no power to benefit, nor power to hurt, except what Allāh wills" (7:188). And the People of the Garden say: "Praise to Allāh, Who has guided us to this. We could not truly have been led aright if Allāh had not guided us" (7:43). And the People of the Fire say: "Our Lord! Our evil fortune conquered us" (23:106); and: "Yes, truly. But the word of doom for disbelievers is fulfilled" (39:71). And Iblīs said: "My Lord! Because You have sent me astray" (15:39). And God has said: "and if Allāh wills misfortune for a people, no one can repel it" (13:11).

ONE MUST CONSIDER THE *END* OF A HUMAN BEING

Know, moreover, that there is no difference between [God's] wish and will and choice and complacence and love, according to what we have said previously. Know also that in all that attention is to be paid to [a human being's] end and not to [his] present state. Thus in the case of one with whom God is pleased, He has always been pleased with him and will never be displeased with him, even though the individual may be disobedient at the moment. And in the case of one with whom He is displeased, He will always be displeased with him and will never be pleased with him, even though he be obedient at the moment.

An example of that is that God was always pleased with Pharaoh's magicians, although they were unbelieving and in error when they were obedient to Pharaoh. But since, in the end, they believed, it was clear that God had always been pleased with them. So, also, God was always pleased with Abū Bakr (aṣ-Ṣ iddīq) and ʿUmar (al-Fārūq) [the first two caliphs], even when they worshipped idols, because He knew how they would end and the point they would reach in professing His unicity and championing the Apostle and fighting in God's way. So, also, God was always displeased with Iblīs and Balʿam and Barṣīṣ, even when they served Him, because He knew what their end would be and the condition to which they would arrive. Junayd (d. 910) was once asked about God's words: "Behold, those unto whom kindness has gone forth before from Us" (21:101), and he answered: "They are people for whom God's care preceded in the beginning and for whom God's friendship appeared in the end."

THE CONCEPT OF "ACQUISITION"

You must also know that the creature has an acquisition (*kasb*), and that he or she is not forced to acts of obedience and disobedience, but acquires (*muktasib*) them. For God has said: "For it [is only] that which it has earned"—i.e. of reward for obedience—"and against it (only) that which it has deserved"—i.e. of punishment for disobedience (2:286); and: "because of (the evil) that people's hands have done" (30:41); and: "Whatever of misfortune strikes you, it is what your right hands have earned" (42:30); and: "If Allāh took humankind to task by that which they deserve, He would not leave a living creature on the surface of the earth" (35:45).

The truth of this is also proved by the fact that every intelligent person distinguishes between the involuntary moving of his hand and the rest of his body in an attack of fever and trembling and his own moving of one of his limbs when he intends that by his own choice (*bi 'khtiyārihi*). So the acts of creatures are their acquisition and God's creation. Creatures are not to be qualified by that by which the True (*al-Ḥaqq*, i.e. God) is qualified, nor is the True to be qualified by that by which creatures are qualified. And just as one should not say of God that He acquires (*muktasib*), so one should not say of the creature that he creates (*khāliq*).

THE NOTION OF [MORAL] *CAPACITY*

You must also know that the creature's capacity (*istiṭāʿa*) is with the act and cannot be made prior or posterior to it, just as, in the case of creatures' knowledge and perception, the knowledge cannot be made prior to the thing known nor the perception to the thing perceived. This is proved by God's words: "and who could not bear to hear" (18:101), i.e. to accept at the time of the summons, which means that they had no capacity in conjunction with the summons so that acceptance would have taken place along with it. God also said [i.e., Khiḍr said to Moses]: "Behold, you cannot bear with me" (18:67, 72, 75). And Abraham said: "My Lord! Make me to establish proper worship" (14:40); but if the capacity were prior to the act, he would have said: "You have already caused me to establish," and his request would have been meaningless, since he would have been asking for a thing that he had been given already and over which he had power. God also said: "You [alone] do we worship; You [alone] do we ask for help" (1:4). But if the capacity preceded the act, asking for it would be meaningless. Moreover, if created power preceded the act, the act would exist without a power. For the power is an accident, and the accident does not perdure. Nor can the capacity exist after the act, for in that case, too, one would be active without a power [Or perhaps: it would be active without an act]. So nothing remains save that the capacity is with the act. . . .

GOD'S GENEROSITY AND *TRANSCENDENT WILL*

You must also know that obedience is not a cause (*ʿilla*) of reward nor disobedience a cause of punishment, and that no one has any claim upon God. Not so: the reward and favor shown to the creature are generosity on God's part, and the punishment is justice on His part. The creature is bound by what God imposes on him, but there is no one to impose any obligation on God nor is anything obligatory on Him. The good is the act that corresponds to [God's] command, and the bad is the act that corresponds to [His] prohibition. But neither good nor bad are such in virtue of form.

The proof of the first point [God's generosity] is that God has no obligation towards any creature. For the true meaning of obligation is that he who is bound by it deserves blame for omitting it, but the Lord is far exalted above blame. That is also proved by God's words: "That He may reward out of His bounty those who believe and do good works" (30:45). Thus He made it known that [the reward] is because of His bounty, not because of the works. God also said: "If it had not been for the grace of Allāh and his mercy" (4:83). And the Prophet was once asked: "Will any one of us enter the Garden because of his works?" He replied: "No." Then he was asked: "Not even you?"

and he answered: "Not even I, unless God fill me with His mercy." Then one of the Companions asked: "Then what good is the performance of works?" Muḥammad replied: "Perform works, for everyone is facilitated unto that for which he was created."

God has promised reward and threatened punishment, and His word is truth and His promise veracity. He has appointed acts of obedience as a sign of obtaining degrees [of reward], and acts of disobedience as a sign of falling into perdition. But all that is a sign for creatures, one to another, and not for Him. For God knows all things before they come into being. As one man has said: The True alone has knowledge of invisible things. He knows what was, and what will be, and how what will not be would have been if it had been.

The proof of the second point, namely that the good is what corresponds to [God's] command and the bad is what is contrary to [God's] command, is that the pleasure of sexual intercourse, in the case of wife or bondwoman, has the same form as that in forbidden intercourse. But it is good, in the case of lawful possession, because of conformity to divine positive law, and bad, in the other cases, because it contravenes divine positive law. So, also killing and its form are the same in the case of punishment and in other cases. But the one is good because it is conformed to the law, and the other bad because it contravenes the law. So also, eating on the last day of Ramaḍān has the same form as eating on the day of the breaking of the fast; but the one is good because of conformity to the law, and the other bad because of opposition to the law. So, also, abstention on a day of Ramaḍān has the same form as abstention on the day of the breaking of the fast; but in the one there is good because of conformity to the law, and in the other there is bad because of opposition to the law. And all the precepts of the law prove that the good is that which is made good and allowed and permitted by the law, and that the bad is that which is made bad and prohibited and forbidden by the law, and that form plays no part therein.

If, then, you understand that, it will free you from the difficulties advanced by the ignorant Qadarīya, which lead astray the minds of the vulgar. And if this be certain and established, it follows from it that there is no commander above the Creator who commands Him, and no forbidder who forbids Him, so that his acts should not be described as good because of conformity to the command, and again as bad because of opposition to the command. In fact, He is in reality sovereign Lord Who disposes of His possessions as He wills—"He will not be questioned as to that which He does, but they will be questioned" (21:23).

You must also know that the sustenance of creatures and of all animals is from God, and that there is no sustainer (*rāziq*) save God, whether the sustenance be lawful or forbidden. This is proved by God's words: "Allāh enlarges livelihood for whom he will, and straightens [it for whom He will]" (13:26); and: "And there is not a living thing on earth whose sustenance does not depend on Allāh" (11:6); and: "Allāh is He Who created you and then sustained you, then causes you to die, then gives life to you again. Is there any of your [so-called] partners [of Allāh] that does any of that? Praised and exalted be He above what they associate [with Him]!" (30:40). And the Muslims are agreed on the use of the expression: There is no sustainer at all save God, just as they are agreed that there is no creator at all save God.

Another proof of that is that if one were to suppose a child who grows from infancy to maturity among thieves and highway robbers, receiving their stolen and plundered food, and then, after reaching maturity, following their way of life in stealing, plundering and raiding until he becomes old and decrepit, without ever receiving a morsel of lawful food—and then one were to say that God never gave this individual any sustenance and that he never ate any sustenance: such a one would be obstinately opposed to the explicit text that has come down and a violator of the consensus of Muslims. So all this proves that there is no creator at all save God, and no sustainer at all save God.

Bazdawī's Māturīdī Perspective on Moral Capacity

Translated by David Thomas

Abū 'l-Yusr Muḥammad al-Bazdawī was a leading Ḥanafī jurisprudent in Central Asia in the eleventh century. Not much is known about his life, though his surviving works show that he was thoroughly acquainted with the main currents of thought of his day. Al-Bazdawī may have been born in 1030, into a family of well-known legal scholars. His grandfather had been a student of the great *mutakallim* and Ḥanafī jurisprudent Abū Manṣūr al-Māturīdī (d. 943), and his father had followed in the same line of scholarship. His father was probably al-Bazdawī's first teacher, before he moved to study under other leading legal scholars in Transoxiana. He was appointed *qāḍī* in Samarkand in 1088, though he appears to have spent most of his life in Bukhara, where he died in 1099.

Al-Bazdawī's *Book of the Principles of Religion* (*Kitāb uṣūl ad-dīn*), the source of this excerpt, is a digest of Ḥanafī-Māturīdī thinking. It reveals that its author knew well the teachings of earlier theological and legal masters, including the great Muʿtazilī scholars of the ninth and tenth centuries and also their opponent Abū 'l-Ḥasan al-Ashʿarī (d. 935), whose reputation as an advocate for a middle way between the extremes of conservatism and rationalism rivaled that of al-Māturīdī himself.[11]

Text

POWER (*QUDRA*) FOR THE ACTION DOES NOT PRECEDE THE ACTION

The People of Custom and Community [i.e., Sunnīs] teach that power for the action does not precede the action but is with the action, and that power has no continuity; and also Abū Ḥanīfa, the head of the People of Custom and Community in this and every other matter, for the entire school of the People of Custom and Community pass down from Abū Ḥanīfa. Abū 'l-Ḥasan al-Ashʿarī and Abū ʿAbd Allāh ibn Saʿīd al-Qaṭṭān, who were with the People of Custom and Community on most issues also taught it. And Bishr al-Marīsī of the Compulsionists and al-Ḥusayn an-Najjār al-Baṣrī and Hishām ibn al-Ḥakam of the Muʿtazila also taught it. However, Abū Ḥanīfa used to teach: The ability for obedience is suitable for disobedience, and the ability for disobedience is likewise suitable for obedience. Ibn Kullāb also taught this, and all the Ashʿarīya, among them Abū Sahl al-Qalānisī and his son Abū Saʿīd. Abū 'l-Ḥasan al-Ashʿarī, al-Ḥusayn an-Najjār and al-Marīsī taught: The ability for obedience is not suitable for disobedience nor the ability for disobedience for obedience. Rather, one is favor and the other failure.

All the Ashʿarīya, the Muʿtazila and the Khawārij, and some of the Rāfiḍa and the Mushabbiha from the Qadarīya, among them Hishām and Ibn Haysam, taught: Capability is before the action. Some of the Muʿtazila said: Ability continues for some moments, and also all accidents, while others said: It does not continue.

Many of our fellow experts in Khurāsān and Iraq teach that capability (*al-istiṭāʿa*) is before the action. This is a mistake among the true Muʿtazila, and whoever says that capability is before it is without doubt effectively saying that the human being is the one who brings actions into existence. But he is in fact saying that capability is before the action, meaning that a person is ordered to an action that he is unable to perform. So say to him: This is wrong on your part because the one who brings actions into being is God almighty, and it cannot be said that anyone in whom He has not brought the action into being is not able to act so that he is more or less being ordered what he is unable to do. And this is the same, so he is compelled to say that the one who brings the action into existence is the human. Thus, the teaching about it is equivalent to the teaching about this. For this reason whoever teaches that teaches this.

The reason for their teaching about this is the words of God almighty: "And pilgrimage to the House is a duty upon people towards God, for whoever is capable of finding a way there" (3:97), making pilgrimage a duty upon anyone who is capable of performing it, and confirming that capability is before the performing. Similarly, God almighty says: "So fear God as much as you are capable of it" (64:16), commanding fear of God after we are capable. This first verse proves to us that capability is before the action, and so it confirms that capability is before the action. Thus, the experts agree that no action is commanded from someone who is incapable, and in the same way God almighty does not command this action from anyone who is too weak for it: anyone who is too weak to stand when he is sick, incapacitated or chronically ill He does not command to perform the prayers standing up, and the same with those who have lost their memory; nor does he order the blind to see. Since God almighty commands his servants to perform actions, it necessarily follows that they will have power for the action before the action so that the command is shown to be correct by the action. Indeed, both specialists and ordinary people, and even dumb animals, believe that capability is before the action, so that even someone with a confused mind will say: "I can walk ten parasangs," or "I can lift this sack," or "I can jump across this river," and even a donkey knows that he can jump across a narrow river unless he is stopped.

The reason for the teaching of the People of Custom and Community is the words of God almighty, "Indeed, you [Moses] will not be capable of being patient with me [Khiḍr]" (18:67), which declare that he was not capable, and he was not capable only because he did not have capability. In another place He says, "They have gone astray, and they are not capable of finding a way" (17:48), which declares that they were not capable of following the path of guidance, because he had denied capability.

It may be said: What is meant by it is that He imposed this action upon them, for one says, "So and so is not capable of carrying this because of its weight even though he has the ability for the action," and "So and so is not able to follow this path even though he has the ability to walk." However this is imposed upon him, this is what is meant by it. It is what is accepted among people and it is in the proofs we have mentioned. In reply we say: When these words are uttered, what is meant is that the person is completely unable to do it because the apparatus for the action is not sound. What is said and meant is that he is not capable because he has no ability for it beforehand. However, it is the custom among people that when they say this they mean the suitability of the apparatus for the action, because ordinary people do not understand "ability." Thus, the intention of his words, "And pilgrimage to the House is a duty upon people towards God, for whoever is capable of finding a way there" (3:97) is that anyone who has the apparatus must make the journey to Mecca, because the pilgrimage is a duty upon him. In a similar way, it is related from the Prophet that he said: "Capability is the provisions and the journeying," and the community likewise agree that the meaning of this capability is the provisions and the journeying, the safety of the way and health of the body, with such elements preceding the action and being given the name "capability."

The response to His words, "As much as you are capable of it" (64:16) is similar, and also to their argument about His words, "They will indeed swear by God, 'If only we had been capable we would certainly have gone out with you'; they destroy their souls" (9:42) and the rest of the verse ["for God knows that they are indeed lying"]. Its intention is the soundness of the apparatus for the action because it is through this that the action is made possible. For God almighty has made it the norm that the soundness of the apparatus of the action makes the action possible through God almighty endowing the person with power for the action at the time of the action, and because he is not deprived of power for the action or of the action, as we have explained. Concerning our interpretation of the verse, the intention of it is no more than that ability is burdensomeness. The intention is not that Moses did not have patience in the sense that he was not able to attain it but rather the intention was burdensomeness. Similarly, moving along the path of guidance was not made burdensome for the unbelievers because they are able to perform the actions for it by the apparatus they possessed. Similar to this instance, it is correct that it is not the same as burdensomeness, and is only the same as burdensomeness if their apparatus for the action is not suited to carrying it out. So it is proved that its intention is what we have referred to.

The rational proof of the matter is: his teaching that capability is before the action is wrong because a living being cannot be imagined as otherwise than acting and as acting in every circumstance, and he is only acting by capability and ability, so ability is always with the action. We only say this because if someone is standing he performs the action of standing, and if he stops standing he stops it in order to sit, and he is acting; and if he lies down on his back and stops sitting in order to lie down, lying down is also an action, and it is the same with eating and stopping eating in order to fast. A person always stops an action for an action; he stops moving to be still and stops being still to move, and being still is an action like moving, and being seated is being still and so is standing: they are both actions, except that moving is the action of changing one's position and stillness is the action of being static. Hence, it is not to be thought that power precedes the action.

They may say: It is not like this, because in our view someone who is tied up is able to walk, though he does not walk, and similarly someone sleeping and someone unconscious are able to perform actions but they do not perform any voluntary actions, so there is power but no action. To this we say: A person who is tied up is either standing or sitting and his power is with the action for this action, he originates the action from himself, so power is not before the action. If they say: But in our view he is able to walk; we say: This is incorrect, for if the act of standing or sitting are brought into existence from the power, it cannot be thought that the act of walking is brought into existence from it, for if the act of walking replaced the act of standing or sitting, this ability would be suited to it: either he would be able to walk and standing would be brought into existence for this, or not. Standing and walking do not occur together, because walking is changing one's position and standing is being static; the one is movement and the other stillness. To their words: The unconscious or sleeping are able to act, although they do not act; we say: Someone sleeping and someone unconscious do not have power that is ability to act, but rather they are as it were lifeless owing to weakness that appears in the apparatus for their actions. Their limbs are those of a lifeless being: thus, the eye of a blind man is like the eye of a lifeless being, for the blind do not have power to see, like the eye of a lifeless being, and similarly the limbs of someone unconscious or sleeping are like the limbs of a lifeless being, in that neither of them has power for action because of debility in the limbs of both. This applies if movements cannot be imagined from either of them even if movements from either of them can be imagined in the next moment and they are both undeniably performing actions.

If they say: Why do you say that power never precedes any action, even though a living man who has apparatus that is sound for an action is acting in every moment? we say: Because it cannot possibly go before or precede the action if it is never separate from the action. Then, if it is said: How can an action originate from someone who is powerless, when a voluntary action can only be imagined from a being who is powerful? we say: It cannot be imagined apart from power, because power is with the action. If they say: By power that exists or by power that does not exist? we say: By power that exists. If they say: Then you are referring to power that precedes the action, because at the point of its existing the thing does not exist; we say: The point when the action exists is the point when power exists, because power is with the action.

To their words: But the thing does not exist at the point of its existing; we say: Just as it does not exist, so it does not *not* exist, since the state of existing is mid-way between existing and not existing. But the action does not exist either, and the action and power exist together, and existence is related to power, and this degree of power is enough for the existence of the action from the human, because the coming into existence is not from him but from God almighty, so the need is not related to power that exists before the action.

Then we say to the person who teaches that power does not continue: In your view power exists but not the action and the action exists but not power, and this is the most absurd and repugnant of statements. And whoever talks of power continuing, well, this kind of talk is absurd because power is an accident and the continuity of accidents is impossible, as we have explained, although the action is not related to power that is before the action. So there is no action, and there is no point in its existing before the action, and thus it is not a precondition for the action.

To their words that if power were with the action then this would be a command to act to one who was too weak to act, and God almighty has not ordained this, and the discerning are likewise against it; we say: It is not like this, but according to all the People of Custom and Community the ability to obey is suited to disobeying, and similarly the ability to disobey is suited to obeying, and the living human who is commanded a thing is not deprived of power, so the command is directed at a being who has power to act. Against the words of the person who says that the ability for one of two actions is not suited to an action that is the opposite of it, we say in the same way that this is not a command to a person who is weak, because God almighty endows him with power during the action as long as his limbs are sound—for this is how God almighty causes events to occur habitually—so sound limbs functioning in the place of capability because capability exists in them at the time of the action are customary through the endowment of God almighty.

If they say: Discerning people agree that power is before the action, and consequently they say: We are capable of this and we are not capable of this; we say: Moses' companion said to Moses, "Indeed, you will not be capable of being patient with me" (18:67), and Moses rebuffed him. So how can there be a consensus among the discerning? And this is the response to his words that the riding beast knew that capability was before the action: we say: Did neither Moses nor his companion know when the donkey *did?* This is the most corrupt and objectionable argument. The response is: Ordinary people do not know about capability that is ability for the action because it is not perceptible. One of the experts has said: According to ordinary people capability in sound limbs is capability that is sound limbs; what they say makes this clear, and it is before the action. Since capability and ability for the action cannot be perceived, some of the discerning deny them both, and since they cannot be perceived their existence can only be known through its effect, and its effect is the person acting, and hence capability can only be known by the action.

They may say: It is known by this but it is before it, as fire is known by smoke but is before it, and we know this by the sound apparatus that is suited to power. Have you not substituted suitability of apparatus for power because they are indications of ability? We say: The existence of the action is not an indication of the existence of ability before it, but an indication of its existence with it, as we have explained. This is different from the smoke, because it is definitely an indication of fire with it, and it may indicate fire before it because it is a physical body that has continuity.

As for their words: We know this by apparatus suited to the action; we say: The suitability of the apparatus is not perceptible, so this suitability as well is only known by the action.

To their words: You are putting soundness of the apparatus in place of ability; we say: We do this because we find actions indicating the soundness of the apparatus, because in our view a living being is never without action. If they say: Sound limbs can be seen and examined; we say: The soundness cannot be seen or examined, and some discerning minds have denied this, saying: There is nothing other than the limbs.

The ability for any action is suitable for another action, and a refutation of those who disagree.

We have said: in the view of the People of Custom and Continuity the ability for any action is suitable for another action according to the principle of substitution, not according to the principle of continuity. This is the teaching of some of the Ashʿarīya, of the master Abū Manṣūr al-Māturīdī as-Samarqandī and of Ibn Kullāb (d. 855), in the sense that if there were an action in place of this action it would be another action.

In the view of Abū 'l-Ḥasan al-Ashʿarī, al-Ḥusayn an-Najjār and al-Marīsī it is not suitable. Their reason for saying this is that the ability to obey is favor and direction from God, and the ability to sin is failure and heedlessness, and it is incorrect that the ability to sin should be favor and direction from God almighty or that the ability to obey should be failure and heedlessness. So it is not right that the ability for one should be suitable for the other. According to their principle this is correct, because in the opinion of most of them the action and the thing done are one, and it is the same according to the teaching of those who say: The action is different from the thing done, so this is correct because the endowment of the ability for one of two actions is favor and direction from God almighty, and the endowment of the ability for the other is failure and heedlessness, and the one should not be spoken of as the other nor the other as the one.

The reason for what the majority of the People of Custom and Community say is that obedience is only movement and so is sin, except that one is forbidden and prohibited and the other appointed, ordered and allowed, and ability is the means for it to exist in that it is a movement and must be considered as such, and all movements are of one kind, and the ability for a movement is suitable for another movement of its kind, necessarily according to substitution.

Their teaching is that the endowment of the ability for one of two movements is favor, and the endowment of the ability for the other is heedlessness; and we say: With regard to motion there is no distinction between the two, except that it is forbidden or is appointed.

Brethren of Purity on Divine Initiative, Human Responsibility, and Law

Translated by Lorne Kenny

At roughly the same time that the Ashʿarī and Māturīdī theologians were fashioning and debating the key concepts of their theological ethics, a curious group of four thinkers from Basra (in Iraq) produced a unique and intriguing body of encyclopedic work. Their collected opus is known as the *Epistles of the Sincere [or Pure] Brethren* (*Rasā'il Ikhwān aṣ-Ṣafā'*). This mid-tenth-century work covers an astounding breadth of subjects, including a variety of theological themes as seen from a perspective influenced by Hellenistic and Ismā'īlī thought. Here are two selections on the paradoxical relationship between God's foreordainment of affairs and human moral accountability, on the one hand, and obedience to the divine law, on the other.[12]

Text

Among the requisites of faith and the characteristics of believers is the willing acceptance of the Decree and the Determination, which is the contentment of the soul with whatever determinations (*maqādir*) befall it. [These] are necessary results of the laws of the celestial bodies, while the Decree is the prior knowledge of God of what the laws of the celestial bodies make inevitable. It is said that contentment with the Decree is the minimal act of a human being that ascends to heaven, and it is the most noble of the requisites of faith and the most excellent of the characteristics of the believers.

Then know, my brother, that there is no one satisfied with the acrid, bitter determinations that befall him, except those who know the sacred character of the Law of God. One should be submissive to the judgment of the Law of God, satisfied of soul, like the submission of Socrates, the philosopher of the Greeks. It was said to him, "You are being killed unjustly. Do you want us to [ransom] you, or spirit you away?" Socrates answered, "I fear lest the Law of God should say to me tomorrow, 'Why did you flee from my judgment?'"

Before Socrates, one of the sons of Adam had submitted to the determinations, when his brother Cain said to him, "I will surely slay you." Abel was satisfied with the Decree of God, and so he submitted to the determinations, which are the necessary results of the laws of the celestial bodies, content of soul.

Similarly Christ was satisfied with the decree of God and submitted to the determinations and surrendered his humanity to the Jews, content of soul, satisfied with the judgment of God.

Similarly the Prophet of God, blessings and peace be upon him, willingly acquiesced when, upon the Day of [the Battle of] Uḥud, his excellent Helpers and noble Emigrants were slain, his banner broken, and there befell him of the determinations of the celestial bodies what befell him.[13]

In like manner there is the acquiescence of [martyred fourth Rightly Guided caliph] ʿUthmān ibn ʿAffān, when they entered upon him to slay him and of [Shīʿī protomartyr] al-Ḥusayn on the day of Karbalāʾ. He knew that he was about to be killed, so he fought until he was slain, acquiescing in the Decree of God.

Know, my brother, that the prime support of faith and its most powerful pillar is subservience to the bearers of the divine Laws (*nawāmīs*) in that which they command of obedience and that which they forbid of rebellion; it consists of hearkening to them and obedience to them. This is so because the noblest works of mankind, the most delightful deeds of humanity and the highest rank to which the wise may attain next to the rank of angels is the establishment of the divine Laws. Know, my brother, that the lawgivers and their followers possess many good qualities and characteristics, a part of which we have mentioned in the Treatise on the Laws, part in the Treatise on the Doctrine of the Brethren of Purity, and part in the Treatise on the Mutual Fellowship of the Brethren.

Know then that the relation between the lawgivers and their followers, and that which the latter hear from them with regard to knowledge, and that to which they are commanded in the prescriptions of the Laws, resemble the heavens with its rain and the earth with its vegetation. That is because the speech and utterances of the lawgivers are like the rain, and the hearkening of their followers is like the earth; and what is produced through both of them of the benefits of the sciences, by way of both ideas and deeds, is like the plants, animals, and minerals. To these He points in His Word:

> He sends down out of heaven water and the *wādīs* flow each in its measure, and the torrent carries a swelling scum; and out of that over which they kindle fire, being desirous of ornament or ware, out of that rises a scum like it. So God strikes both the true and the false. As for the scum, it vanishes as jetsam, and what profits humankind abides in the earth. Even so God strikes His similitudes. For those who answer their Lord, the reward most fair: and those who answer Him not—if they possessed all that is in the earth, and the like of it with it, they would offer it for their ransom. (13:17)

Know, my brother, that the Law is fulfilled only by means of commands and prohibitions. Command and prohibition are carried out only by means of promise and threat. Promise and threat are made effective only through providing incentive and deterrent. Incentive and deterrent are efficacious only for those who fear and hope. Fear and hope become apparent or known only through subservience to command and prohibition, for whoever does not fear anything nor hope for anything has no desire or apprehension. Whoever has no desire or apprehension, for him promise and threatening are not efficacious, nor are command and prohibition [and hence] he has no share at all in the Divine Law.

The attainments to be hoped for are of two kinds: the one pertaining to this life and the other to the next. The earthly is such things as rule, honor, power, wealth, and earthly possessions while the soul is joined to the body, and that which remains of it after death, such as offspring and descendants. That pertaining to the next life is the escape of the soul from the sea of material existence and captivity to nature, the departure from the abyss of bodily existence, [namely] the world of being and corruption that exists in the sublunary world, and the realization of one's ascension to the Kingdom of Heaven, entry amongst the company of the angels, floating through celestial space and the vast expanse of the heavens, and the enjoyment of that rest and bliss mentioned in the Qur'ān, which fails of description except in summary fashion, as God, exalted be He, has said, "No soul knows what comfort is laid up for him/her secretly" (32:17).

ʿAbd al-Jabbār's Muʿtazilī View of Ethical Principles and Theodicy

Translated by Richard Martin

From a text introduced in chapter 5, ʿAbd al-Jabbār's (d. 1025) *Book of the Five Principles,* here is a classic Muʿtazilī interpretation of theological ethics in the context of the question of divine prerogatives and human ethical responsibility.[14] Note the overriding concern for explicitly "rational" bases of the ethical quality of choices and actions, very different from the Ashʿarī and Māturīdī views detailed above, with their conviction of God's sky-blue freedom.

Text

[Then] if someone asks: What is the proof that God does not do that which is ethically wrong (*la yafʿalu al-qabīḥ*)? *Respond:* Because He knows the immorality of all unethical acts (pl. *qabāʾiḥ*) and that He is self-sufficient without them, and it is impossible for Him to do them. For one of us who knows the immorality of injustice and lying, if he knows that he is self-sufficient without them and has no need of them, it would be impossible for him to choose them, in so far as he knows of their immorality and his sufficiency without them. Therefore, if God is sufficient without need of any unethical thing it necessarily follows that He would not choose [the unethical], based on His knowledge of its immorality. Thus every immoral thing that happens in the world must be a human act, for God transcends doing [immoral acts]. Indeed, God has distanced Himself from that with His saying: "But Allāh wills no injustice to His servants" (40:31), and His saying: "Verily Allāh will not deal unjustly with humankind in anything" (10:44). And even if we allowed that He did what was unethical, we would not believe that He punished the prophets and the righteous ones (*aṣ-ṣāliḥīn*) and sent them to the Hellfire, and we would not believe that His word was a lie and an order that could be nullified, for that, then, would necessitate that we [could] not trust in His promise and threat. And we do not believe that He sends prophets to the Hellfire and enemies and unbelievers to Paradise. Anyone who did such things would not command our obedience to Him because we could not be safe from His evil, and by obeying Him we would create the utmost havoc. And it would necessitate the possibility that God could send to humankind one who called them to unbelief and deception, and manifest through him miracles and proofs. For if it were possible for Him to do what is unethical, what would prohibit Him from doing all of [what we have just mentioned]? And saying this would lead us not to trust in the Book and the Sunna, and not to know the Sharia. And it would lead us to be unsure [whether] what we do is straying (*ḍalāl*) [from the right path] and what unbelievers do is truth. Whoever reaches this point, his error (*khaṭā'uhu*) is detestable and his infamy is great.

Then if someone asks: What is the proof that human acts are not created (*laysat bi-makhlūqāt*) by God but that they are done with His knowledge? *Respond:* If they were done by God then what good would there be in His commanding those that are ethically good and prohibiting those that are ethically bad, and praising and rewarding obedience but blaming and punishing disobedience? In the same way, it would not be good for Him to command His acts in us, such as color, shape, health, and sickness, or to prohibit such, or lay blame for such. Moreover, if God were the agent of our acts then they would not have happened according to our purposes and motivations. And moreover, [even] a wise man cannot create his own abuse, or condemn and vilify [himself]; for how could it be said that every abuse and vilification [addressed] to him is of his own doing? And moreover, whoever commits injustice and transgression must be unjust and a transgressor. Thus, if God committed injustice He would be unjust, just as if He acted justly He would be just, and whoever says [otherwise] is an unbeliever. He has said: "You will see no disharmony in the creation of [God] the Beneficent" (67:3), and: "He who has made everything that He has created good" (32:7), and: "[Such is] the artistry of Allāh, who disposes of all things in perfect order" (27:88). [These verses] indicate that these ethically bad acts are not created by God but that they are human acts, and on that basis they deserve blame and punishment. How can it be possible for God to create erroneous behavior in them and then punish them, thus saying: "Why do you disbelieve?" Isn't that the same as someone commanding his slave to do something, then punishing him for it? And that would clearly be corrupt.

Then if someone asks: What is the proof that the power [to act autonomously] (*qudra*) precedes the act [itself]? *Respond:* Because if it were simultaneous with the act then necessarily the unbeliever would not have had the capacity [power] (*qudra*) to have faith. And if he did not have the power for it, it would not be good for God to command it because God does not impose on human beings what they do not have the power to do, according to His saying: "On no one does Allāh place a burden greater than he can bear" (2:286); and "Allāh puts no burden on anyone unless He has enabled him and given to him [what he needs in order to bear it]" (65:7). If it were possible for Him to impose on [His] servants what they were unable to do then it would be possible for Him to enjoin (*yukallif*) the impotent to act, the disabled to run, and the blind to place the diacritical points correctly in the text of the Qurʾān; and to enjoin us to climb to the roof without using stairs; all of that is clearly spurious.

This establishes the fact [a] that He only enjoins on His servants what they have the power to do, and [b] that the unbeliever has the power [both] to believe and to disbelieve, so if it comes from him to disbelieve, it is by his choice. [This is] the same as if we gave a man a knife to use to his own advantage but he killed himself with it. The one who gave him the knife did him a good deed, but he harmed himself using the knife for what caused the danger, and not for what benefited himself. Likewise, God gives the unbeliever power (*qūwa*), but [the latter] uses it to destroy himself and does not use it [to adopt] faith; thus it is he who destroys and does evil to himself. That which indicates that [God] does not impose upon humankind what they do not have the power to do is that it is impossible to command someone with no wealth to pay religious charity (*zakāt*), because the *zakāt* is invalid without property. Similarly, He does not command His servant to believe if he does not have the power for it, because faith is invalid without the power for it. And that which indicates that the power precedes the act is that the instrument, such as the hand or foot, by which the act occurs must exist prior to it. So, too, the power [must exist prior to the act].

If someone asks: What is the proof that God does not will disobedience, and why do you deny that everything that happens in the world is by the will and wish of God? *Respond:* Because we say that every religious duty (*ʿibādāt*) is an act that He wills and wants and consents to, and every form of disobedience He prohibits is an act that He loathes and censures and for which He threatens punishment. The proof of that is that it would be impossible for a wise man to command something he loathed and to prohibit something he wanted. God has commanded [us to have] faith, so He must will it; and He prohibits unbelief, so He must loathe it. [God] has said: "And God wills no injustice for his servants" (40:31); and "I created the jinn and humankind only to worship [Me]" (51:56). And He said after He mentioned a number of disobedient acts: "All of that is evil, loathsome in [the sight of] your Lord" (17:38). That which indicates this is that a wise man would not will to do something ethically wrong, because willing something ethically wrong is ethically wrong, and wanting to do something insolent is insolence, just as willing wisdom is wisdom. Thus, if God is all-wise we know that He does not will insolence. How would it be possible [for Him] to will to curse and condemn Himself, and how could it be said that every corruption or injustice that occurred to humankind was willed by Him?

Then if someone says: If something that [God] did not will happened in the world, that would necessitate His impotence. *Respond:* Are there not [cases] in the world where He does not command something but rather prohibits it? These do not indicate His impotence. And, in the world things happen that He does not will but rather loathes, and these do not necessitate His impotence. If it were possible for Him to will disbelief, it necessarily follows that the unbeliever as well as the believer will have done what God has willed. And if that is the case [His willing unbelief] would be beneficial, the same as it is beneficial when a slave does what the master wishes. And it would necessarily follow that He should not punish the unbeliever but send him to Paradise along with the believer, because [the unbeliever] had also done what God willed the same as the believer had done. Thus if He prohibits disobedience it is not possible for the Wise One to prohibit what He willed, just as He would not command what He loathed. Moreover, if it could be said that He willed disobedience, then one could also say that He loves it and is pleased with it. But He says: "He likes not ingratitude from His servants; if you are grateful, He is pleased with you" (39:7).

Then if someone says: People say: "Whatever Allāh wants is so, and whatever He does not want isn't." So, it must be that everything that perishes or exists is by virtue of what He wants. *Respond:* What those people say is not an argument. If one could argue on the basis of that statement then one could argue on the basis of their statement: "God's command is inexorable" (*la maradda li-amri 'llāh*), meaning it is impossible to repulse what He commands. But it has been established that unbelievers do repulse God's command. Therefore, its interpretation should be that "there is no resistance to what He does." Similarly, the interpretation of their statement: "Whatever Allāh wants is so" should be: "Whatever God wants to do must be."

Then if someone asks: What do you say about the affliction of the children of polytheists, do you allow that God would do it? *Respond:* May God protect [me] from permitting that of him, for it would be an injustice and an [act of] insolence, and He is far removed from such things. What God has said indicates this: "No bearer of burdens can bear the burden of another" (6:164, 17:15), and "for every soul to receive its reward by the measure of its endeavor" (20:15), and "Every soul earns only its own account" (6:164), and "nor would [We] send our wrath until we had sent a messenger [to give warning]" (17:15); and [anyway], messengers are not sent to children. The Prophet said: "The pen is raised in three instances: a man sleeping until he awakens, a child until he reaches puberty; and an insane person until he recuperates. One for whom the pen has been raised has no sin (*dhanb*) for which to be punished. Moreover, [divine] punishment is morally good only for one who has committed a sin, just as those who misbehave are disciplined in the visible world. Now, a child is without sin, so, how can it be said that God would punish him?

Then if someone asks: He punishes him for his father's sin? *Respond:* It is impossible to punish someone for someone else's sin, just as it would not be morally good to punish and beat one man for the misbehavior and injustice of another.

Then if someone asks: Has God not said: "And they will breed none but wicked ungrateful ones" (71:27)? *Respond:* He intends [in this verse] that only those who become wicked and ungrateful, when they mature, should not breed; He does not mean that they have this attribute (*ṣifa*) when they are born.

Then if someone asks: Is it not the case that in this world (*ad-dunyā*) children are virtually the same as their fathers in regard to disbelief? Hence, are they not under virtually the same rule as their fathers in the hereafter (*al-ākhira*) regarding [divine] punishment? *Respond:* If what you said were possible, one could also say that if [the father] committed adultery [the child] should be flogged and if [the father] committed murder, [the child] should be killed, because he is under the same rule as his father. If that is not valid then what you asserted is faulted; he only has the same judgment as his father, however, in that which does not relate to divine punishment. As for divine punishments, God preserve us!

Then if someone asks: Does God recompense them for these diseases and sicknesses he causes, or not? *Respond:* Indeed, if He caused sickness, He would turn it into greater advantage in the hereafter. If that were not so then it would not be ethically good for Him to cause animals and children to be sick, just as it would not be ethically good for us to hire somebody and work him to exhaustion without paying him his wage.

Then if someone asks: Thus, is there a lesson and benefit from these sicknesses for humans (*al-mukallafīn*) or not? *Respond:* Yes, because when a man is sick he is much more likely to be mindful of disobedience, fearing the Hellfire, and to act obediently desiring Paradise. God stated this warning: "See they not that they are tested every year [once or twice? Yet they turn not in repentance and they take no heed]" (9:126).

Then if someone asks: Are you saying that Allāh has indicated the truth (*al-ḥaqq*) to everyone He has created, and has He guided them to religion? *Respond:* Yes, and the evidence for that is that if He is forbearing and merciful, it would not be possible for Him to impose on us [what He requires of us] unless He has indicated to us what He will impose; and it would not be possible for Him to prohibit us from disobedience unless He has warned us about it so that we could avoid doing it, because He has willed our well-being. Therefore, He must explain and indicate to us the proper way (*ṭarīqat ar-rushd*) so that we can take it, and the improper way (*ṭarīqat al-ghayy*) so that we can beware of taking it. If He does that, and then He issues a command to a man, and the man disobeys it, the man harms himself and will perish despite clear evidence [warning him]; and if [the man] obeys, he will have done himself good and would be saved. God is good to all of humankind (*al-mukallifīn*), both to those who believe and those who disbelieve, just as someone who offers food to two starving men and [only] one eats it, he has been morally good to them both equally.

Then if someone asks: Are you saying that every blessing [good] (*ni'ma*) we have is from God? *Respond:* Yes, He gave us life, and empowered us, and gave us the instrumental means [with which to accomplish things], and made it possible for us to enjoy things, granted us health and vitality and sense perceptions, and provided us with various kinds of sustenance. Then He imposed [duties] upon us, and prohibited us from [certain things] so that we would worship Him and enter the delights of Paradise; by these [we acquire] the perfection of grace in this world as well as in religion. As for the gifts, tributes, and legacies we receive from others than Him, all of them are [ultimately] from God. Truly, God is [the one] who created [all of] that, and He made us to have possessions and advantages so that we would be gracious and giving. Thus, every good thing we have is from God.

Then if someone asks: Are you saying that God bestowed favors upon us (*anʿama ʿalaynā*) by imposing obligations upon us and by issuing us commands and prohibitions, and that speech (*al-kalām*) is [one of] His [creative] acts? *Respond:* Yes, because God created [His] servants, then He gave them commands and prohibitions and imposed duties upon them, just as He created them and He was good. Just as doing the good is contingent (*muḥdath*), so His speech is contingent. He has said: "Naught comes to them of a reminder (*dhikr*) from their Lord but that it is contingent [or new]" (21:2). He describes the reminder as "contingent." The reminder is the Qurʾān, according to His saying: "And this [Qurʾān] is a blessed message that we have sent down" (21:50), and His saying: "This is no less than a reminder and a Qurʾān that makes clear" (36:69). And He said: "And Allāh's command must be fulfilled" (33:37), and His command is the Qurʾān. And He said: "He has sent down [from time to time] the most beautiful saying" (39:23), and a saying must be contingent. And He said: "*Alif Lām Rā,* [This is] a Book whose verses are univocal [or plain] and then were detailed" (11:1), and this is the mark of the contingent. And He said: "And before this was the Book of Moses as a guide and a mercy" (46:12), and if something else existed before [the Qurʾān] then [the Qurʾān] is contingent. And moreover, the Qurʾān has many sūras, and is in Arabic, and is divided into two and many parts, and is heard. There is no disagreement within the community of the faithful (*umma*) that everything other than God is contingent, hence it follows necessarily that the Qurʾān and the rest of God's speech is other than He, and that indeed, no one besides Him has the power to do the likes of [this], as He has said: "Say: If the whole of mankind and jinns were to gather together to produce the like of this Qurʾān, they could not produce the like thereof, even if they backed up each other" (17:88).

Then if someone asks: Are you saying that Muḥammad is a true prophet? *Respond:* Yes, and the evidence for that is that he challenged the Arabs, who had the ultimate in pure speech (*al-faṣāḥa*), to produce something similar to this Qurʾān. We know that they were intent on invalidating his affair, for if they had been capable of the likes of this Qurʾān, they would have been able to invalidate his affair. They avoided him despite their desire to make war upon him and fight against him. So, when we know that they turned to fighting and that they deserted their homeland and homes, that is evidence that it was not within their power to make something similar to the Qurʾān. And we would know that God made it a miracle for His messenger so that we would know by this means that he is a true messenger, just as we know that raising the dead and healing the blind and lepers are the miracles of Jesus (ʿĪsā), and just as [we know] that He made parting the sea and transmuting rods [into serpents] the miracles of Moses (Musā ibn ʿImrān). And [additional] evidence that [Muḥammad was a true prophet] is that he fed a crowd of people with only a modicum of food; and he beckoned to a tree and it stretched out [toward him] without his having pushed or pulled it; and he put his hand in a basin with [little] water in it, and then it gushed from between his fingers until the people drank and performed ablution from it; and small stones swam in his palm. Human beings are not capable of any of this. Thus it establishes that he is a true prophet and that we have to accept what he commanded us to do and prohibited us from doing, and that the Qurʾān is the word of God, requiring us to do according to what is in it.

Then if someone asks: The Qurʾān consists of verses that disagree with each other (*āyāt mukhtalifāt*), so how can you implement what is in it? For example, His saying: "There is nothing whatever like unto Him" (42:11); and He says in another passage: "I have only created (*khalaqtu*) the jinn and humankind that they may serve me. No sustenance do I require of them, nor do I require that they should feed me" (51:56–57); and He says: "Many are the jinn and humans we have created for Hell" (7:179). *Respond:* The Qurʾān has [verses whose meanings are] univocal and [verses whose meanings are] equivocal, just as He said: "He it is who has sent down to you the Book; in it are univocal verses; they are the Mother of the Book; others are equivocal" (3:7). It is obligatory for you to carry out what accords with reason, . . . [ellipsis in original translation] upon that which is sound within it. Thus, judge that which accords with rational proof to be true, and bring that which contradicts [reason] into accord with it. Therefore, we say that His saying "There is nothing whatever like unto Him" (42: 11) is univocal, and His saying: "And your Lord comes" (89:22) means "And your Lord's command has come." And we say that His saying: "I have only created the jinn and humankind that they may serve me" is univocal, and that He created all of them to worship Him. And His saying: "Many are the jinn and human beings we have created for Hell" is figurative (*majāz*), whose meaning is that the fate of their affair is the Hellfire. Then, . . . [ellipsis in original translation] the [meaning of] equivocal verses in the Book of God is indicated by univocal verses, but if not, then human intellect (*al-ʿaql*) is sufficient to indicate [the meaning]. God made some of the Qurʾān[ic verses] univocal and some equivocal to bring humans closer to speculating (*al-naẓar*) on its [meaning], and to [bring them to] rely on the proofs of the intellect and the arguments of the ulama and not on blind trust [in their pronouncements] (*taqlīd*). It is obligatory for a rational person (*al-ʿaqīl*) to base his convictions only on the univocal [verses] and on that which is indicated by reason, and to bring the equivocal [verses] into agreement with that.

CLASSICAL AND MODERN VIEWS OF THE DEVIL, DESTINY, AND FATE

Ibn Qayyim al-Jawzīya on God's Wisdom in Creating Iblīs

Translated by Jon Hoover

Among the more enticing questions about God's choices in creating all things is why the Creator would have opted to create Satan himself and allow him such latitude in testing humanity. Many Muslim theologians have written about the role of Iblīs in the larger theme of theodicy, few more famously than Traditionalist theologian, "neo-Ḥanbalī" student of Ibn Taymīya, and jurist Ibn Qayyim al-Jawzīya (d. 1350).[15]

Text

Aspect 24: They say, "What wise purpose (*ḥikma*) is there in the creation of Iblīs and his soldiers?" There are wise purposes in that [creation]; its detail only God fully comprehends.

Among [these wise purposes] is that [God] perfects the ranks of servitude (*ʿubūdīya*) for His prophets and His friends through [their] striving against the enemy of God and his party, clashing with him and forsaking him in God, infuriating him and infuriating his friends, seeking refuge in Him from him and taking refuge in Him so that He may protect them from his evil and his deceit. From that they derive benefits in this world and the next which would not occur without it. We have already noted that what is dependent upon something does not occur without [that thing].

Among [these wise purposes] is that the fear of the angels and of the believers from their sin is stronger and more complete after having witnessed Iblīs's circumstance and his fall from the angelic rank to the Iblīsī level. There is no doubt that when the angels witnessed that, an extraordinary [manner of] servitude to the Lord, an extraordinary subjection, and an extraordinary fear overcame them. Similar is what is witnessed in the case of a king's servants. When while watching him they see that he has demeaned one of them very severely, there is no doubt that their fear and caution will be greater.

Among [these wise purposes] is that He made an example out of [Iblīs] to anyone who counters His command, grows too proud to obey Him and persists in disobedience. Similarly, He made the father of humanity [Adam] in his sin to be an example for whoever violates His prohibition or disobeys His command: he repented, showed regret and returned to his Lord. [God] tried both fathers of the jinn and humanity with sin. He made an example out of one father to whoever persists and remains in his sin, and [He made] the other father to be an example for whoever repents and returns to his Lord. By God, how many dazzling wise purposes (*al-ḥikam al-bāhira*) and manifest signs are there in this!

Among [these wise purposes] is that [Iblīs] is a touchstone by which God tests His creatures so that the foul among them may thereby be distinguished from the fair. He created the human species from earth. In [the earth] are the smooth and the rough, the fair and the foul. He must manifest in [creatures] what was in their primal matter, as in the hadith that at-Tirmidhī related *marfūʿan* [i.e., going back to the Prophet], "God created Adam from a handful that He took from the whole earth. The children of Adam came forth in the same manner, some of them fair and some foul, some smooth and some rough," and so on. That which was in the primal matter was hidden in the creature created from it [i.e., the primal matter]. The divine wise purpose required bringing [that which was hidden] out and manifesting it. Therefore, there had to be a secondary cause to manifest that. Hence Iblīs was a touchstone by which the fair was distinguished from the foul. Similarly, He made the prophets and the messengers a touchstone by which to distinguish [the fair from the foul]. He said, "God will not leave the believers in the state in which you are now until He distinguishes the foul from the fair" (3:179). Hence He sent His messengers to those legally and morally obligated, among them the fair and the foul. The fair were added to the fair, and the foul to the foul. His profound wise purpose required mixing [those who were fair and those who were foul] in the abode of testing. When they arrive in the abode of rest, He will distinguish between [the fair and the foul]. In profound wise purpose and vanquishing power, He will make a separate abode for [the fair] and a separate abode for [the foul].

Among [these wise purposes] is that He manifests the perfection of His power in the creation of the likes of Gabriel, the angels, Iblīs and the satans. This is one of the most tremendous signs of His power, His will and His authority. Indeed, He is the creator of opposites like the sky and the earth, the light and the darkness, the Garden and the Fire, water and fire, iron and air, good and evil, heat and cold, and the fair and the foul.

Among [these wise purposes] is that creation of one of two opposites [derives] from the perfection of the goodness of its opposite. Indeed, the goodness of an opposite becomes manifest only by its opposite. If it were not for the ugly, the virtue of the beautiful would not be known. If it were not for poverty, the value of wealth would not be known. This was clarified not far back.

Among [these wise purposes] is that He loves to be thanked with true thanksgiving and its diverse kinds. By virtue of the existence of the enemy of God, Iblīs, his soldiers and the testing [of God's friends] by him, there is no doubt that His friends thank Him in diverse ways that would not occur without [Iblīs]. How great is the difference between Adam's thanksgiving while in the [primordial] Garden before being removed from it and his thanksgiving after having been tried by his enemy. Then his Lord chose him, turned to him and accepted him (cf. 20:122).

Among [these wise purposes] is that love, turning [to God], complete trust, patience, good pleasure and such like are the most beloved of servitude to God and this servitude to God is realized only through striving (*jihād*), self-sacrifice to God and giving priority to love of Him over everyone else. Striving is the apex of servitude and the most beloved [kind of servitude] to the Lord. The creation of Iblīs and his party is the driving force behind this servitude and its effects. No one can count the wise purposes, advantages, and benefits in these but God.

Among [these wise purposes] is that in creating those who clash with His messengers, call them liars and show enmity toward them is completeness in manifesting His signs, the marvels of His power and the subtleties of His craftsmanship. The existence [of such enemies] is more beloved to Him and more profitable to His friends than their nonexistence, as was mentioned previously in the manifestation of the sign of the flood [of Noah], the staff and the hand [of Moses], the dividing of the sea [by Moses], and the throwing of the Friend [Abraham] into the fire, and [the manifestation of] many, many more of His signs and demonstrations of His power, knowledge and wise purpose. The secondary causes from which these [signs] follow must exist, as was mentioned previously.

Among [these wise purposes] is that in fiery matter are [destructive] burning, high rising [flame] and corruption [on the one hand] and illumination, radiation and light [on the other]. He brought forth from it both this and that. Similarly, in earthy, dust-like matter are the fair and the foul, the smooth and the rough, and the red, black and white. Bringing all of that forth from [earthy, dustlike matter] is [a display of] a dazzling wise purpose, a vanquishing power, and a sign indicating that "Nothing is like unto Him; He is All-hearing, All-seeing" (42: 11).

Among [these wise purposes] is that among His names are the Abaser and the Exalter, the Honorer and the Humiliator, the Arbiter, the Just, the Avenger. These names require consequents (*mutaʿalliqāt*) in which their excellence (*iḥkām*) becomes manifest, as with the names of beneficence, provision, mercy, and the like. The consequents of [both the positive names and the negative names] must become manifest.

Among [these wise purposes] is that He is the Sovereign who is complete in sovereignty. Belonging to the completeness of His sovereignty is the universality of His free disposal and its diversification into rewarding and punishing, esteeming and demeaning, justice and grace, and honoring and humiliating. Someone to whom pertains one of the two kinds [of divine free disposal in each set of paired opposites] must exist just as He brings someone to whom pertains the other kind into existence.

Among [these wise purposes] is that among His names is the Wise. Wise purpose is among His attributes. His wise purpose necessarily entails putting everything in its place, which [place] is not befitting for anything else. [His wise purpose] required creating the opposites and singling out rulings, attributes and particularities for each one of them that were not befitting for any other. Can wise purpose be completed in any other way?! The existence of this kind belongs to the completion of wise purpose just as it belongs to the perfection of power.

Among [these wise purposes] is that His praise is complete and perfect in every respect. He is praiseworthy for His justice, His impeding, His abasing, His avenging and His demeaning just as He is praiseworthy for His grace,

His giving, His exalting, and His esteeming. To Him is complete, perfect praise for this [set of acts: justice, impeding, etc.] and that [set of acts: grace, giving, etc.]. He praises Himself for all of [these acts]. His angels, His messengers and His friends praise Him for them. All the People of the Standing (*ahl al-mawqif*) [assembled on the Day of Resurrection] will praise Him for them. He has complete wise purpose in His creation and His origination of whatever belongs to the necessary concomitants of the perfection and completeness of His praise. Likewise, to Him belongs complete praise for [creating and originating whatever belongs to those concomitants]. It is not permissible to strip away (*taʿṭīl*) His praise just as it is not permissible to strip away His wise purpose.

Among [these wise purposes] is that He loves to manifest His gentleness, His patience, His equanimity, the wideness of His mercy and His liberality to His servants. This required creating someone who associates [other gods] with Him [in worship], opposes Him in His rule, strives to clash with Him, tries to arouse His wrath and, even more, assimilates Him [to creatures]. Despite this, He sends various kinds of fair things his way, provides for him, restores him to health, makes possible for him the secondary causes by which he can enjoy the various kinds of blessings, answers his invocation, draws evil away from him, and deals with him out of His righteousness and His beneficence. [This is] the opposite of how he deals with Him in his unbelief, his associationism, and his perniciousness. By God, how great is the wise purpose and praise in this! He shows love to His friends, and He makes Himself known to them through the different kinds of His perfections. Similarly, in the authentic [Hadith] from [the Prophet] he said, "No one is more patient in the face of an injurious [word] that he overhears than God. They ascribe a son to Him, but He provides for them and restores them to health."

In the authentic [Hadith] from [the Prophet] in what he relates from his Lord, "A son of Adam abused Me, and there was no need for him to do that. A son of Adam called Me a liar, and there was no need for him to do that. He abused Me when he said, 'He took a son.' I am the One, the Self-Subsistent who does not beget and is not begotten. No one is my equal (cf. 112:1–4). He called me a liar when he said, 'He will not return me [to life] as He gave me beginning.' Beginning to create is not easier for Me than [creating] again (cf. 30:27)." Despite this abuse of Him and calling [Him] a liar, He provides for the lying abuser, restores him to health, protects him, calls him to His Garden, accepts his repentance when he turns to Him, gives him good deeds in exchange for his evil deeds, shows grace to him in all his circumstances, prepares him for the sending of His messengers to him, and commands them to speak softly to him and be courteous with him.

Al-Fuḍayl ibn ʿAyyād (d. 803) said, "Not a night grows dark but in which the Great calls out, 'Who is greater than Me in liberality (*jūd*)? Creatures are disobedient to Me. Yet, I watch over them in their beds as if they had not disobeyed Me, and I guard them as if they had not sinned. I am liberal in grace to the disobedient, and I am gracious with the pernicious. Who calls on Me, and I do not respond?! Who asks of Me, and I do not give to him?! I am the Liberal, and from Me is liberality. I am the Generous, and from Me is generosity. From My generosity, I give the servant what he has asked of Me, and I give him what he has not asked of Me. From my generosity, I give to the repentant as if he has not disobeyed Me. Can creatures flee? To where can the disobedient turn [to avoid] my door?'" In a divine tradition (*athar ilāhī*): "Indeed, humankind, the jinn and I are involved in a great matter. I create, and someone else is worshipped! I provide and someone else is thanked!" In another good (*ḥasan*) tradition: "O son of Adam! You have not been equitable with Me. My goodness comes down on you, and your evil rises up to Me. How much love have I shown to you even though I am sufficient apart from you?! How much you have loathed Me through acts of disobedience even though you were in want of Me?! The noble angel never stops ascending to Me with a bad deed from you." In the authentic hadith: "If you had not sinned, God would have done away with you and brought people who sin. Then, they would have asked for forgiveness, and He would have forgiven them."

Out of the perfection of the love of [God] for His names and His attributes, His praise and His wise purpose required that He create creatures in whom to manifest their rulings and their effects. Out of His love for pardoning, He created someone whom He can pardon. Out of His love for forgiving, He created someone whom He can forgive, someone with whom He can be gentle, patient and unhurried, and, moreover, someone whom He can love to protect and grant respite. Out of His love for His justice and His wise purpose, He created those in whom He can manifest His justice and His wise purpose. Out of His love for liberality, beneficence and righteousness, He created someone to treat Him with perniciousness and disobedience, while He treats him with forgiveness and beneficence.

Were it not for the creation of those through whom He brings about various kinds of disobedient acts and wrong conduct, these wise purposes and benefits and many, many times their number would vanish. Blessed is God, Lord of the worlds, the wisest of rulers, possessor of profound wise purpose and abundant blessings, whose wise purpose extends as far as His power extends. In everything He has a dazzling wise purpose just as in [everything] He has vanquishing power. About this subject, we have mentioned only a drop in a sea. Beyond this, human intellects are too impotent, weak and inadequate to comprehend the perfection of His wise purpose in any part of His creation. How much more that is beloved to Him has occurred on account of this creature [Iblīs], whom the Lord loathes and who bears His wrath?! The hateful that occurred was merged into His love. The Wise whose wise purpose is dazzling makes one thing that He loves more than another come to pass by bearing with the hateful thing that He loathes and is wrathful against when it is a way to attain what is loved. The existence of that from which a concomitant follows necessarily without its concomitant is absurd. Even though evils and disobedient acts have occurred through the enemy of God Iblīs, how much more obedience has occurred through his existence and the existence of his soldiers, which [obedience] is more beloved to God and more well pleasing to Him?! [And how much more] striving in His path, countering the soul's caprice and its appetites, bearing hardships and hateful things in His love and His good pleasure?! The most beloved thing to the beloved is to see the one who loves him endure injury for his sake. Speaking truly of his love is the following:

For your sake, I made my cheek a bit of dirt
for the gloating and envious until you were well pleased.

In a divine tradition: "I desire what the enduring endure for My sake." What is most beloved to God is that those who love Him bear the injury of His enemies against them for Him and for His good pleasure. How great is the profit of that injury for them, and how praiseworthy are they on account of what follows from it?! What esteem do they obtain from their Beloved through it?! Nearness to Him is the delight of their eyes. But it is forbidden to those who deny the love of the Lord to smell therefore a fragrance, enter this door, or taste this drink.

So, say to eyes that are blind: There are eyes
apart from you that [are able to] see the sun setting and rising.
Be tolerant with souls that are unworthy of the love they receive.
It is not good to be too exacting in every situation.

Even though this creature [Iblīs] angers his Lord, well pleasing to Him is what His prophets, His messengers and His friends do to him. This good pleasure is greater than that anger. Even though the disobedient acts and wrong conduct that he commits provoke His wrath, He is more joyous at the repentance of His disobedient servant than someone who finds his lost she-camel carrying his food and his drink in perilous waterless deserts. Even though what this enemy does to His prophets and His messengers angers Him, gladdening Him and well pleasing to Him are their shaming him, disobeying him, shunning him, crushing him and infuriating him. This good pleasure is greater to Him and sounder to Him than forgoing that hated thing, which would necessarily entail forgoing what is well pleasing and beloved. Even though Adam's eating from the tree provoked His wrath, well pleasing to Him were his repentance, his turning [to God], his subjection, his self-humiliation before Him and his contrition to Him. Even though His enemies' eviction of His messenger from his sanctuary and his town angered Him, greatly well pleasing to Him was his entry [back] into it. Even though their killing His friends and His beloved ones and their tearing their flesh and spilling their blood provoke His wrath, well pleasing to Him is their obtaining life. No other [life] is fairer, more blessed and more pleasurable in nearness to Him and proximity to Him. Even though His servants' acts of disobedience and their sins provoke His wrath, well pleasing to Him are the witnessing of His angels, His prophets, His messengers and His friends to the wideness of His forgiveness, His pardon, His righteousness, His generosity and His liberality, [their] lauding Him for that, praising Him and glorifying Him with these ascriptions. Praise of Him with [these ascriptions] and laudation of Him are more beloved to Him and better pleasing to Him than forgoing those acts of disobedience and forgoing these beloved things [such as Adam's repentance and His servants' coming near to Him].

Know that praise is the principle bringing all of [the above] together. [Praise] is the tie holding together the order of creation and command. All praise is to the Lord in all its respects, implications and varieties. To Him is praise in everything that He created and ruled. His praise extends as far as His creation and His command extend, true praise that includes loving Him, being well pleased in Him and with Him, lauding Him and acknowledging His profound wise purpose in everything that He creates and commands. Stripping away His wise purpose is identical to stripping away His praise, as was previously clarified. Just as He is wholly praiseworthy, He is wholly wise. His praise and His wise purpose, like His knowledge, His power and His life, are necessary concomitants of His essence. It is not permissible to strip away any of the exigencies and effects of His attributes and His names. This would make imperfection follow necessarily, which would contradict His perfection, His grandeur and His majesty.

ʿAbduh and Afghānī on Destiny and Fate

Translated by Vincent J. Cornell

Muslim theologians have continued to wrestle with these matters of God's absolute disposition of all affairs through the centuries. Muḥammad ʿAbduh (d. 1905) and Jamāl ad-Dīn Afghānī (d. 1897) are among the more influential figures who advocated "modernist" reforms that would demonstrate Islam's compatibility with "modernity." During a period when both men were in Paris, they collaborated in founding and publishing a journal from which this text derives. The journal typically did not name authors of its submissions; but as a rule, ʿAbduh penned theological pieces and Afghānī the more "political." Both, however, may have been responsible for this text. Their views on the question of whether divine omnipotence implies a kind of "predestination" that, for example, mitigates human responsibility is part of a long history of Islamic theorizing on this central theological point, as references to many historic contributors to the debate make clear.[16]

Text

God's pattern of conduct (*sunnat Allāh*) among His creatures is that what governs the heart (*al-ʿaqāʾid al-qalbīya*) governs the actions of the body. Thus, every righteous or unrighteous act goes back to a righteous or unrighteous belief, as we have explained in a previous issue. Sometimes, one belief is accepted out of a variety of ideas such that other beliefs and concepts follow it, and it is manifested in the body through acts that are in accordance with the state of the soul. However, at other times, when one of the basic principles of the good or rules of perfection come to the mind through education or the preaching of religious law, a mistaken semblance of it occurs to the hearer such that it matches up with base characteristics or false beliefs that are neither appropriate to nor correspond to the original. One adheres to these [errors] because one believes in the resemblance. Whenever this occurs, the [original] aspect [of the principle] is altered and its effects are different. Sometimes one's adherence to false beliefs is based on a mistake in understanding or an evil disposition, such that immoral acts result from it. Because one does not have true knowledge of the principle, one does not understand what is truly believed and does not know the consequences of such a belief.

One who is deluded by appearances would think that these acts were based on [the falsely understood] principle or rule. Because of this deficiency in understanding, an alteration or change occurs in the basic principles of religion. Indeed, this is the root cause of heresy (*al-bidʿa*, lit. "innovation") in all religions. Many such deviations and the heresies that follow from them develop from corrupt natures and evil practices, such that they result in God chastising people with destruction and an evil end. This is what motivates those who have no expertise and who rely on the works of simpletons to defame a particular religion or a true creed.

Such is the case with the doctrine of destiny and fate (*al-qaḍāʾ wa al-qadar*), which is counted among the basic principles of the true and correct religion of Islam (*ad-diyāna al-islāmīya al-ḥaqqa*). The clamor of the heedless among the Europeans has multiplied on this subject and many theories have been propounded. They imagine that fatalism dominated people's minds so that it stripped them of their sense of power and aspiration and caused them to become weak and deficient. They also accuse the Muslims of [irrationally] adhering to the doctrine of divine attributes and relating it to the concept of change and restricting the notion of causality by the doctrine of fate. They say: "Verily the Muslims are in poverty and indigence and are the most backward in military and political strength among all the nations." Corrupt morals have spread among them while lying, hypocrisy, treachery, hatred, and enmity have multiplied among them. They are in disagreement with each other and are ignorant of their present and future condition and are heedless of what harms them and benefits them. They take pleasure in the present life; they eat, drink, and sleep but do not compete with each other in excellence. Instead, when it becomes possible for one of them to undermine his brother, he does not hesitate to harm him. Thus, they do evil to one another while the nations that used to be [developmentally] behind them devour them bite-by-bite. Although they take pleasure in every huckster and are ready to accept every new thing, they retreat passively into their ruined abodes, they graze in their own pastures, and they return to their [traditional] places of refuge. Their princes squander their spirit in sports and pastimes and in the gratification of desires; although they have duties and obligations that should involve their entire lives, they carry out none of them. They spend their money wastefully and extravagantly in whatever shortens the span of their days. Their expenditures are vast but they do not include in their accounting anything of value to their societies. They deceive each other, are in enmity with each other, and neglect the general welfare for the sake of their personal interests.

At times the competition between two princes even leads to the destruction of an entire nation. Each of them deceives his friend and backstabs his neighbor. Thus, the foreigner finds in both parties a lack of strength and a fatal weakness and gains from their lands profits without limit. Fear is prevalent among them and cowardice is common, such that they are frightened by a whisper and are injured by the slightest touch. They refrain from taking action to obtain the strength and resolve that other nations have achieved, including falling behind in matters of religion due to their [low] opinions of their neighbors. Indeed, those [religious minorities] that are under their rule are more advanced than they are and boast about what they have achieved. If misfortune occurs to one of their neighboring peoples or if an enemy attacks them, they neither strive to ameliorate their suffering, nor do they send aid to them. Neither does one find large popular associations that are dedicated either openly or in secret to reviving self-respect, advocating defense, aiding the weak, or preserving the truth from the lusts of the powerful or the oppression of foreigners.

Thusly do [the foreigners] ascribe these characteristics and changes to the Muslims. They claim that there is no basis for [these characteristics] other than their belief in destiny and fate and that they commit all of their affairs to the divine will (*al-qudrat al-ilāhīya*). They conclude that as long as the Muslims maintain this belief they will never assert themselves, nor will they attain glory or greatness. They will not observe justice, they will not defend themselves against an enemy, and they will advocate neither the empowerment of authority nor the establishment of a kingdom. Instead, they will remain weak, acting against their own interests and stunting their natures until annihilation and destruction come to them (God forbid!). Some will eliminate others through internal conflicts and then the foreigners will exploit whatever is left untouched.

The Europeans believe that there is no difference between the doctrine of destiny and fate and the doctrine of the theological school of the Predestinarians (*al-Jabrīya*), who say that the human being is compelled absolutely in all of his acts. They imagine that with the doctrine of destiny (*al-qaḍā'*) Muslims see themselves as a feather floating in the air and buffeted by the wind wherever it goes. Indeed, if it were to occur to the minds of people that they have no choice in word or deed or in motion or rest, and that all of this is subject to a compelling force or a coercive power, there is no doubt that it would retard their strength and they would lose the fruits of the powers of capability and understanding that God granted them. It would also erase from their imaginations the urge to strive and earn. Under such circumstances, it would behoove these people to betake themselves from the world of existence to the world of nonexistence!

This is the view of a faction among the Europeans and this approach is also followed by many of the weak-minded in the East. However, I am not afraid to state: This view is false, their opinion is wrong, their conjecture is baseless, and they have imposed a lie on God and the Muslims alike. There is not a single Muslim in this present time—neither Sunnī nor Shīʿī, nor Zaydī nor Ismāʿīlī, nor Wahhābī nor Khārijī—that follows the theological school of absolute predestination or believes in the ultimate denial of choice to the human will. On the contrary, every one of these Muslim sects believes that there is an element of choice in their actions (i.e., *kasb*), and that this [element of choice] is ultimately responsible for their reward or punishment. They further believe that this element of choice makes them accountable for what God has bestowed upon them, that in a like manner they are asked to follow the divine commands and prohibitions that call to every good and guide to every success, and that this element of choice is the basis of juridical responsibility, through which [God's] wisdom and justice is made complete.

Indeed there used to be among the Muslims a sect known as *al-Jabrīya,* which taught that the human being was compelled in all of his acts by a compulsion that was not tainted by choice. They believed that there was no difference between an individual moving his jaw to eat or chew and when he shivers from extreme cold. However, the methodology of this sect is considered by [today's] Muslims to be of no more value than the corrupt disputations of the Sophists. The leaders of this school died out in the fourth century of the Hijra and no trace of them has remained. Therefore, the doctrine of compulsion (*jabr*) cannot be considered the source of the doctrine of destiny and fate and there is no basis for this belief on the part of the conjecturers.

The doctrine of destiny is supported by a conclusive proof and in fact the concept of the instinct (*al-fiṭra*) alludes to this. It is easy for anyone who thinks to believe that every event has a cause that is near to it in time. However, one sees in the chain of causes only [the cause] that is present to him: no one knows the full past except the one who originated the pattern [in the first place]. Thus, in the unfolding of every chain of events there is a clear opening for the determination (*taqdīr*) of [God], the Glorious, the All-Knowing. As for what the human being wills, this is created, just like the created moments in the chain of causation. The act of will is nothing but an effect produced by the human understanding, whereas the understanding is a product of the mind (*an-nafs*), according to what occurs to the senses and feelings and as a response of one's instinctive nature to the needs. Even a fool (not to mention an intelligent person) understands that the powers of thought and will are part of the apparent universe (*li-ẓawāhir al-kawn*); however, the [the basis of the doctrine of destiny and fate] is that the causes that one sees outwardly are effects that occur by the hand of the greatest Governor of the Universe, who originates all things according to His wisdom but makes every apparent event correspond to it as if it were independent of it, especially in the world of human [perception].

Even if we required that an ignorant person be misguided and not acknowledge the existence of a fashioner of the universe, it would still not be possible for him to avoid acknowledging the effects of acts of nature and temporal events on the actions of the human will. Thus, how can it be possible for the human being to escape from the plan (*sunna*) that God has established for His creatures? This is a matter that all students of the true realities have recognized, not to mention those who have become experts. Indeed, even some European philosophers and political scientists have acknowledged the power of destiny and have argued extensively about its application, but we have no need to use their views as proofs.

Verily, history is a science that is superior to storytelling, by which I mean that scholars from every nation conduct research into it. It is the science that investigates the life-stories of nations—their rise, their fall, the nature of great and crucial events and the changes and transformations of customs, morals, and ideas that have resulted from them. Indeed [history investigates] even such special characteristics as the inner feelings and experiences and their effects on the growth of nations, the development of states, or of the annihilation of some of them and the obliteration of their remains.

The value of this art, which is considered one of the literary arts and the most superior of them, is that it is fundamental to belief in destiny and fate and to the acceptance of the fact that the powers of the human being are in the grasp of the Master of all that exists and the Manager of all events. Furthermore, were the powers of the human being independent of the effects [of destiny and fate], those who are exalted would not be brought low, the strong would not be made weak, the great would not be brought down and political authority would not collapse.

If belief in destiny and fate were separated from the inappropriate notion of compulsion the attributes of audacity and daring and the birth of courage and fortitude would follow from it, and it would lead to an upwelling of the ferocity that throbs in the hearts of lions and causes leopards to cringe in terror. [Correct belief in the doctrine of destiny and fate] imbues the mind with a constancy that causes one to bear odious burdens, to struggle against one's fears, and to adorn the soul with generosity and liberality. It calls upon the soul to leave aside all that is dear to it; indeed, it even charges it with the expenditure of life and to forsake the pleasures of existence! All of this is for the sake of the Truth, which calls on the mind to believe in this doctrine.

As for one who believes that his fate is subject to strict limits, that his portion in life is fixed, and that all is in the hands of God, who disposes of everything as He wishes—how can such a one fear death in defense of his rights, in raising up the voice of his nation (*umma*) or his community (*milla*), or in standing up for what God requires in this respect? How can he fear poverty in what he expends of his wealth in the glorification of the Truth or in building up God's majesty, whether [his actions are] based on divine commands or on the principles of human society?

God has brought exaltation to the Muslims with belief [in the doctrine of destiny and fate] and confirms its excellence with the following statement of truth: "About those to whom men said: 'A great army is gathering against you, so fear them.' But this only increased their faith. They said: 'Allāh suffices for us and He is the best protector.' And they returned with grace and bounty from Allāh. No harm ever touched them because they followed the good pleasure of Allāh. Verily Allāh is the Lord of Great Bounty" (3:173–74). The Muslims burst forth in the years of their early development to conquer and subjugate kingdoms and territories, such that minds were confounded and experts were amazed at how they conquered so many states and overpowered so many nations. Their rule spread from the Pyrenees that separate Spain and France to the Great Wall of China, despite their small numbers and lack of familiarity with different climes or variations in geography. They brought kings under their sway and brought low the Caesars and the Khusraws [of Persia] in a period of less than 80 years. Surely this must be counted among the greatest of all paranormal events and miracles!

They destroyed lands, they demolished towering mountains, and they raised above the earth a second earth of greater value and another dimension of benefit. They pulverized the peaks of mountains beneath the hooves of their steeds and in their place they built mountains and hills out of the heads of those who repudiated their rule. They made every heart tremble and every muscle quiver, and their only motivation in all of this was belief in the doctrine of destiny and fate.

This is the belief that caused the feet of a small number among a small population to stand firm before armies that filled vast spaces to choking and made them constricted by clouds of dust. Then [the Muslims] forced them out of their positions and turned them back on their heels.

With this faith their swords first glistened in the East and their luster ended up in the dust of battle among the most noble of the West. This is what led them to expend their wealth and all the riches that they owned in the cause of disseminating the Word: they were not ashamed of poverty nor did they fear need. This belief is what made it easy for them to take their children and wives and whatever was on their backs to fields of battle in the farthest countries of the world, just as if they were going into gardens and orchards. It was as if they had given themselves over completely to trust in God against every form of treachery and through reliance on Him surrounded themselves with a fortress that protected them from every misfortune. Their wives and children provided water for their armies and served them with whatever they needed. The wives and children did not separate from the men and the aged except to bear arms; the women were not overcome by fear and the children did not succumb to dread. This belief is what raised them to such a state that the mere mention of their names melted hearts and stirred up the blood so that they conquered merely by striking dread in the hearts of their enemies and overcame them with the power of awe in expectation of the lightning of their swords and the flashing of their spears—indeed, even before a portion of their main force reached their front lines!

My weeping is on behalf of the [Righteous] Predecessors (*as-salafīyīn*) and my lament is for the Foremost (*as-sābiqīn*). Where are you now, oh band of mercy (*ʿiṣābat ar-raḥma*) and guardians of compassion (*awliyāʾ ash-shafāqa*)? Where are you now, who know the manly virtues, and are proud in your strength? Where are you now, oh people of courage and succor to the oppressed on the day of trial? Where are you now, oh "best of nations brought forth from humanity, commanding the good and forbidding evil?" (3:110) Where are you now, oh glorious and valiant ones who maintain uprightness, adhere to justice, speak wisely, and work to build up the community? Can you not see from your graves what has happened to the successors who came after you, what has befallen your children, and what [beliefs] are ascribed to you? [Your successors] have turned away from your example (*sunna*) and have deviated from your path. They have departed from your way and have separated into sects and factions such that they have become so weak that it softens the heart out of pity and inflames the liver with sadness. They have become the prey of foreign nations, unable to protect their resources and unable to defend their territory. Can you not cry out from your promontories with a cry that brings awareness to the heedless, awakens those who are asleep, and guides the misguided toward the Straight Way? "Verily we belong to God and to Him is the return" (2:156).

I say (and perhaps I should not be afraid to imagine that I will be attacked for what I say): From the beginning of the history of human societies until today there has not been a great conqueror or famous warrior who was born in the middle classes of society but whose aspirations have raised him to the highest status, made difficulties bow before him, made hardships subservient to him, and who attained a capacity for leadership that called forth amazement and stimulated the mind to seek its cause. Was not all of this caused by a belief in destiny and fate? Glory to God! The human being is protective of his life and is eager to preserve what is suitable to his nature and disposition. Thus, what is it that causes him to disregard this and rush headlong into danger, threat to life and limb, and adversity other than belief in destiny and fate and the expectation that his portion of fate is reserved for him and that he should not be affected by the terror of appearances?

History has confirmed for us that Koresh the Persian [i.e., Kay Khusraw], who was the first conqueror known to the history of the ancients, could not have attained dominance through his wide conquests except for his belief in the doctrine of destiny and fate. Because of this belief he feared no terror nor did he shirk from the severest trials. Likewise, the Greek Alexander the Great was one whose spirit was strengthened by this glorious doctrine. Also the Tatar Genghis Khan, who was famed for his conquests, was one of the foremost adherents of this doctrine. Even the Frenchman Napoleon I Bonaparte was one of the strongest in adherence to belief in destiny; this is what allowed him to fight against vast forces with a small army and overcome them and attain the limit of his victories.

[Belief in the doctrine of destiny and fate] is the best belief for purifying the human spirit from the lowliness of cowardice; however, it is also the prime obstacle for one dishonored [by fear] from attaining perfection on whatever level. Indeed, we would not be adverse to admit that this doctrine has been confused in the minds of some of the Muslim public with the defective doctrine of predestination, and that perhaps this is the reason for some of the losses they have incurred through the calamitous events that have beset them in recent times. Therefore, it is our hope that the foremost scholars of the age will expend their efforts in purifying this noble doctrine from the traces of alteration (*al-bid'a*) that have befallen it. [We hope] that they will remind the public of the precedents (*sunan*) and actions of the Righteous Predecessors (*as-salaf aṣ-ṣāliḥ*) and that they will disseminate among them confirmatory [teachings] by our Imams, such as Shaykh [Abū Ḥāmid] al-Ghazālī and his like, to the following effect: The Divine Law asks us to practice trust in God and reliance on destiny through our actions, not through idleness or laziness. Furthermore, God did not command us to neglect our responsibilities or deny what is required of us in order to prove our trust in Him. This is the "proof" of those who are superficial in religion and who have deviated from the Straight Way. No one among the true adherents of the Islamic religion doubts that defending his community in these times has become a personal obligation for every responsible believer, nor that anything but a summons to the good by the religious scholars and the true doctrines of the Muslims on which everyone agrees will return them to their convictions and will incite them to be zealous in restoring their original condition. All of this has been entrusted [by God] to their protection.

As for what [the Europeans] assert about the decline and backwardness of the Muslims, it has not been due to the dissemination of this or any other Islamic doctrine. Ascribing this to [to the doctrine of destiny and fate] is like ascribing contradictoriness to a polemic—or contrarily, it is like ascribing heat to snow or cold to fire. Indeed, after their period of expansion the Muslims became drunk with power and intoxicated with glory and conquest, and while they were in this state they were confronted by two powerful shocks: a shock from the east, which was the Tatar invasion under Genghis Khan and his descendants, and a shock from the west, which was the takeover of all of their lands by the nations of Europe. Now the shock that comes from intoxication deprives one of judgment and causes one to become fearful and rely on the laws of nature. Thus, [the Muslims found themselves] ruled by different forms of government in which power lay with those who were not suited for it, authority was given over to those who practiced bad politics, and their rulers and princes were criminals of corrupt morals and disposition whose only inclination was to cause oppression and distress. Because of this, their minds became weak and the outlook of many of them became petty and did not surpass the domain of personal interest. Each of them began to take advantage of the other, seeking harm for him and causing him evil from every side for no valid reason or meaningful purpose yet making this the fulfillment of their lives. Thus, their rule devolved into weakness and lassitude and led them to their present state.

However, I say—and what I say is true—that this confessional community (*milla*) will never die out as long as they take this noble doctrine to heart, inscribe its image on their minds, and [ensure] that its true teachings are upheld by the foremost scholars among them. As for the psychological illness and intellectual infirmity that have been ascribed to [the Muslims], these [ideas] must be resisted with the power of correct doctrines and affairs must be returned to their original state so that they are freed from their limitations. [Muslims] must apply philosophical methods and study how to free their lands from the terrorism of the nations that are envious of them and stop them in their tracks. This [goal] is not far-fetched and the events of history support it. Look, for example, at the Ottomans and how they rose again after suffering severe setbacks (the wars against the Tatars and the wars of the Crusades), how they drove their armies across the expanse of the Earth, how great fields of battle spread out before them, how they conquered countries and put an end to the tyranny of kings, and how their rule included European states, such that the Ottoman sultan was known among the nations as the "Greatest Ruler."

Then discernment came [to the Muslim community] once again, caused by the recent events of bad fortune and evil reversals that threatened them, exciting their spirits and motivating their natures. This movement inspired the thoughts of the insightful among them in the majority of the regions in the East and the West, and the best of them became inclined toward forming associations devoted to the truth and determined to bring about the victory of justice and the Sharia. They strove to their utmost to propagate these ideas, bringing together diverse views, organizing the dispersed and the scattered, and making out of the least of their works the publication of a newspaper in the Arabic language, so that through its contents they could communicate and transmit to the most far removed of [their brethren] some [indication] of what the foreigners harbored against them. Verily, we see the numbers of this righteous association increase day after day. We ask God Most High to bestow success on our endeavor and support the truth as our objective, and we hope from His grace that He will favor our best efforts with lasting usefulness for the Easterners in general and for the Muslims in particular.

TEN

Ethics in Practice

FOUR LARGE CONCERNS OCCUPY THE present chapter. First, an articulation of an overarching principle of Muslim ethics emphasizes active, socially engaged moral responsibility for all. Second, divergent understandings of the theological foundations of legitimate succession to the mantle of the Prophet arose very early in Islamic history. In addition to Muḥammad's spiritual centrality as described in the final text of chapter 8, the Prophet also functions as the paragon of ethical conduct and virtue—an example enshrined in the Sunna. Here several texts explore other dimensions of how that ethical modeling has lived on in the post-Prophetic community as it develops ways of identifying leaders who will keep Muḥammad's moral leadership alive. Known by the technical title "the imamate," the subject occupies what early on became de rigeur chapters in handbooks of *kalām,* as well as more than a few monographs on the subject of "theological legitimacy." Though in other contexts, readers might identify this discussion as "political philosophy," in Islamic thought it has also had profoundly theological implications.

Third, concerns over the appropriate religious motivation and demeanor required of anyone elevated to leadership of Muslim communities throughout history have led to an important genre known as the "mirror for princes." Finally, philosophers and theologians alike have written numerous volumes known generically as the "science of character and comportment" (*'ilm al-akhlāq*). Intended for the "average" person, not just for rulers, their topics include general canons of virtuous behavior as well as detailed analyses of how one identifies "sin." A reflection by a major early modern thinker on the theologically critical topic of forgiveness concludes the chapter.

THE FOUNDATION OF ETHICS IN PRACTICE

Juwaynī on Commanding the Good and Forbidding the Reprehensible

Translated by Paul Walker

At the heart of ethical action is the ancient notion of "commanding the good and forbidding the reprehensible" (*al-amr bi'l-ma'rūf wa'n-nahy 'an-il-munkar*). Based on a Qur'ānic text (3:110), the moral mandate is presented there as a criterion by which Muslims are to be known as the "best of human communities." It functions as one of the principal planks in the "Five Principles" of the Mu'tazilī theologians, but it is also central to a much broader range of ethical thinking. Juwaynī (d. 1085) was one of the major exponents of the Ash'arite school and a celebrated mentor of Ghazālī. Here is Juwaynī's brief but clear interpretation of "commanding and forbidding" and Muslim moral activism.[1]

Text

Customarily, the theologians would take up this topic in legal theory and indeed it falls more properly in the domain of the experts in jurisprudence. Commanding the good and forbidding the reprehensible is obligatory in general by unanimous agreement. One need not pay attention to the doctrine of the Shī'a that commanding the good and forbidding the reprehensible must await the appearance of the [Twelfth] Imam. The Muslims were in agreement, prior to the spread of these people, on the admonition to command the good and forbid the reprehensible and to censure those who neglect to undertake to do it. We can perhaps impart here enough elucidation to rebut the declarations of the Imāmīya [or *Ithnā' 'asharīya,* Twelver Shī'a], if God so wills.

If what we have said is admitted as a principle, commanding the good is not specifically a duty of those appointed to govern but is rather incumbent on every Muslim individually. This rule was also established by the unanimous agreement of the community. In the earliest days and in the era that followed, persons other than those appointed to govern used to command those who governed to do good and to enjoin them from doing what is reprehensible and, moreover, the Muslims supported them and refrained from blaming them for being occupied with commanding the good without an explicit commission to do so.

We would add here that the rule in the law divides into what the elite and the masses have equal ability to grasp without needing special legal investigation and what requires the counsel of experts. As for what does not require special competence, those knowledgeable and those not knowledgeable can command, in that area, the good and forbid the reprehensible. For what can only be apprehended by the specialists in law, the common folk are not allowed to command and forbid in that area, but rather command in it has been entrusted exclusively to persons with special legal competence.

No legal authority may interpose an obstacle or a suppression against the judgment of another legal authority on issues in which there is dispute, since every authority, in our view, is correct in regard to the positive applications of the law. Those who maintain that only one is correct cannot specify which one he is. Thus, in either doctrine, one legal authority is prevented from trying to suppress another.

Furthermore, if the person who takes upon himself the commanding of the good is not himself virtuous, his commanding of the good does not cease. What is specifically imposed on him personally is a duty that is distinct from what he is required to command in others. One of the two duties does not necessarily apply to the other. Moreover, commanding the good is a duty of sufficiency. If in each district there is someone who can undertake it adequately by himself, the obligation on the rest is removed.

A part of commanding the good and forbidding the reprehensible is stopping the perpetrator of mortal sins from committing them, if such a person cannot be kept from doing them by verbal admonitions. All of the people are permitted to undertake to do this, if the matter does not end by provoking fighting and the use of weapons. If it were to go that far, it would be a matter for the ruler to handle and only he. If the person in charge at the time happens to be a tyrant and manifests his injustice and inequity and he will not listen to the advice to refrain from the evil he commits, those who have the power to invest and depose should act in concert to get rid of him, even if it requires armed struggle and the onset of open war.

Commanding the good does not require investigation, inspection or the use of spies and breaking into houses on the basis of suspicions. Instead, if you encounter someone doing a reprehensible thing, make an effort to change what that person is doing.

These are the rules concerning commanding the good and forbidding the reprehensible. There is no exception for any of them; from beginning to end, the law provides explicit details.

THEOLOGIES OF HISTORY: CONTENDING NARRATIVES OF EARLY MUSLIM GOVERNANCE

Notwithstanding the general requirement that no Muslim can be an idle bystander when injustice is committed or justice left unserved, Islamic tradition's concern for structured governance dates from the very beginning of the faith community. A standard topic in virtually all major treatises on *kalām,* regardless of "school," is generally referred to as the Imamate. Discussions include a range of questions concerning varying narratives of the process by which legitimate successors to Muḥammad were chosen; the principal criteria for, and essential qualities of, successors; the relationship between those chosen and the early community of believers; and the nature of the authority vested in these figures. For Shīʿī Muslims, the discussion focuses on succession by both explicit "designation" and membership in the "Family of the Prophet," of a line of leaders known as Imams. From the Sunnī perspective, succession turns on selection from among a council of elders not necessarily descendants of Muḥammad, of leaders more commonly known as caliphs. Here are samples of classic texts by major Shīʿī and Sunnī theologians on this complex topic, beginning with that of an influential author of the Nawbakhtī family and proceeding to that of third-generation Ashʿarite theologian Bāqillānī.

Nawbakhtī on Divergent Views of the Imamate

Translated by Abbas K. Kadhim

Abū Muḥammad al-Ḥasan ibn Mūsā an-Nawbakhtī (d. 923) was among the most important early medieval Shīʿī theologians. In this excerpt, he offers an overview of the range of positions on the topic of theologically legitimate succession propounded by a number of the major schools and factions mentioned in other contexts in earlier chapters of this anthology.[2]

Text

Their elders said the following about the imamate: "The messenger of Allāh left this world without appointing any particular person to take his place to unite the people and to discharge the duties of government—such as caring for the people, making treaties, appointing governors, deploying armies, defending the core of Islam, suppressing the opponents, teaching the ignorant,

371=7384

and providing justice for the wronged." They also assigned this role to anyone who took charge after the Messenger and his family.

Then these people disagreed. Some said that people must use their judgment to appoint the imam and that all new problems of life and religion must be dealt with by using opinion (*ijtihād ar-ra'y*). Others believed that judgment is erroneous, and that Allāh ordered people to use their reason when choosing the imam. A sect of the Muʿtazila deviated from the belief of their elders when they said that the Prophet specified the character of the imam without specifying his name and lineage. They concocted this doctrine very recently. A sect of the people of Hadīth, after being crushed by the Imāmīya[3] argument, resorted to the claim that the Prophet and his family indeed appointed Abū Bakr, by ordering him to lead the prayer. By saying this, they abandoned the doctrine of their elders, who said that Muslims, after the death of the Prophet said, "We accepted for our life an imam, who was accepted for our religion by the Messenger of Allāh and his family."

The proponents of the *iḥmāl* [i.e., who claimed that the Prophet neglected (*aḥmala*) to appoint a successor] disagreed about the imamate of the superior (*fāḍil*) and the inferior (*mafḍūl*). Most of them said that it is permissible for both, if the superior has a problem that hinders his appointment. The rest agreed with the people of *naṣṣ* (explicit designation) about the imamate being not permissible except for the superior.

They also held different positions regarding the Prophet's will (*waṣīya*). The proponents of *iḥmāl* (neglect) said: the Messenger of Allāh and his family died without leaving a will or a testament for anyone. Others said that his will was ordering people to fear Allāh, the Exalted.

Then they disagreed about the imamate and its people. The Buṭrīya, the followers of al-Ḥasan ibn Ṣāliḥ ibn Ḥayy (d. 814) and his peers, said that ʿAlī was the best person after the Messenger of Allāh and his family, and the most qualified man for the imamate. But they said that the appointment of Abū Bakr was not erroneous. However, they abstained from judging ʿUthmān and supported the party of ʿAlī and agreed that his opponents deserve Hell fire. They argued that ʿAlī yielded to them [i.e., the first two successors] and by doing so, he resembled a man with a legitimate claim against another and decided to drop his claim.

Yet Sulaymān ibn Jarīr ar-Riqqī and his followers said that ʿAlī was the imam and that appointing Abū Bakr and ʿUmar was erroneous, but they cannot be accused of debauchery (*fisq*), because they used their judgment and made a mistake. This sect dissociated itself from ʿUthmān and considered him blasphemous, along with anyone who fought against ʿAlī.

Ibn at-Tammār and his followers said that ʿAlī was the most eligible man for the imamate and that he was the best person after the Messenger of Allāh and his family. But they said that Muslims were not wrong when they appointed Abū Bakr and ʿUmar; they were wrong by forsaking the superior. This group also dissociated themselves from ʿUthmān and considered him and anyone who fought against ʿAlī as apostates.

Al-Faḍl ar-Raqāshī, Abū Shimr, Ghaylān ibn Marwān, Jahm ibn Ṣafwān, and their followers among the Murjiʾa said that anyone who has knowledge about the Book and the *Sunna* deserves the imamate. According to them, the imamate cannot be acquired without unanimous agreement of the Muslim community.

Abū Ḥanīfa and the rest of the Murjiʾa said that the imamate cannot be outside of the tribe of Quraysh. Anyone from its men, who calls for the Book and the *Sunna* and justice, is the rightful imam. His imamate, as well as fighting on his side, becomes mandatory. They cite the Hadith that was attributed to the Prophet and his family, "The imams are from Quraysh."

All the Khawārij, except for the Najdīya, said that the imamate could be assigned to anyone who is knowledgeable about the Book and the *Sunna* and who applies them. They said that the agreement of two men is enough to appoint an imam.

The Najdīya, however, said that the Muslim community does not need an imam or anyone else; it is simply incumbent, upon us and upon other people, to apply the Book of Allāh, the Exalted.

The Muʿtazila said that the imamate is deserved by anyone who applies the Book and the *Sunna*. If a man from Quraysh and another man were qualified, we would prefer the former. They also said that the imamate must be decided based on consensus, free choice, and reason.

Ḍirār ibn ʿAmr said that if a man from Quraysh and a non-Arab man were qualified, we must prefer the latter, because he has a smaller tribe. If he disobeys Allāh, it would be easy to remove him from office. This is better for Islam.

Ibrāhīm an-Naẓẓām and his followers said that the imamate is deserved by any man, who applies the Book and the *Sunna,* for the saying of Allāh, the Exalted, "The most esteemed among you, before Allāh, is the most pious" (49:13). They claimed that people are not obligated to appoint an imam if they obey Allāh and purify their conduct and intention. That is not possible without knowing the imam, who must be obeyed; since Allāh, the Exalted, would not mandate that they recognize an imam without providing them with the knowledge of recognizing him. Otherwise, He would be mandating that which is impossible.

They said that Muslims were correct in appointing Abū Bakr, because he was the most suitable among them, according to analogy and history. As to analogy, we know that a man does not submit to another and follow his orders unless three conditions obtain. Either the latter has a large clan to help him control others, or he has money that makes people submit to him, or he has a religious status that distinguishes him among others. We know that Abū Bakr was a man with the smallest clan and the least assets; therefore it is certain that he was preferred because of his religious status. And the historical evidence is that he acquired the consensus of people and their acceptance of his imamate. The Prophet and his family, said, "Allāh, the Exalted, would not allow my people to agree on error." If the consensus of the people about him was an error, then the prayer and all other religious duties would be invalid and the Qur'ān—which is the only source of our religion after the death of the Prophet—would be obsolete. This is the Mu'tazila argument, which is also the argument of all of the Murji'a sects.

'Amr ibn 'Ubayd, Ḍirār ibn 'Amr, and Wāṣil ibn 'Aṭā' were the rootstock of the Mu'tazila. 'Amr ibn 'Ubayd and his followers said that 'Alī was more deserving [of the imamate] than the others. But Ḍirār said, "I do not know which one was more guided, 'Alī or Ṭalḥā and az-Zubayr." Wāṣil ibn 'Aṭā' said that 'Alī and his opponents were like two disputants, whose veracity is not ascertained so that we do not know who is lying and who is telling the truth. These three scholars agreed on loyalty to all of the disputants—as a group—but believed that one of them must be misguided and will undoubtedly go to Hell. They also said that, if 'Alī, Ṭalḥā, and Zubayr gave testimony, after their fight, about a matter of a dirham's worth, their testimony would not be considered. Yet, if 'Alī were a witness and he were supported by another man from the community, his testimony would be accepted; and the same goes for Ṭalḥā and Zubayr. They considered them [i.e., 'Alī, Ṭalḥā, and Zubayr] faithful, *as a group,* and on the basis of their faithful past, but they did not consider any one of them faithful or a qualified witness (as an individual).

The Buṭrīya, or the People of Hadith, al-Ḥasan ibn Ṣāliḥ ibn Ḥayy, Kathīr an-Nawwā', Sālim ibn Abī Ḥafṣa, alḤakam ibn 'Utayba, Salāma ibn Kuhayl, Abū 'l-Miqdām Thābit al-Ḥaddād, and their followers, called for loyalty to

ʿAlī, then they mixed it with the loyalty to Abū Bakr and ʿUmar. They agreed that ʿAlī was the best and the superior among his community. Nevertheless, they accept the judgment of Abū Bakr and ʿUmar and allow the wiping of shoes [in the ablution] and permit drinking intoxicating wine and eating catfish.

Bāqillānī on Rightly Guided Caliphs and the Imamate

Translated by Richard McCarthy, SJ

Like other Sunnī theologians, Ashʿarite theologian Bāqillānī (d. 1013) provides several discussions on the Imamate in various major works of his. Here is a selection from his *The Book of Equity Concerning Disputed Questions,* in which he articulates what would become, in at least a general way, the majority view among the global Muslim community.[4]

Text

THE FIRST FOUR IMAMS

You must also know that the Imam of the Muslims and the Commander of the Faithful and the foremost of all creatures, Helpers and Refugees, after the Prophets and the Apostles, is Abū Bakr the Trusting (*aṣ-Ṣiddīq*). For God has said: "the second of two; when they two were in the cave" (9:40)—and there is none more excellent than two, when God is their third.[5] God has also said: "O you who believe! Whichever of you becomes a renegade from his religion, [know that in his stead] Allāh will bring a people whom He loves and who love Him" (5:54)—i.e. [Abū Bakr] the Trusting and his companions, when he fought the renegades [who had reverted to paganism after Muḥammad's death]. God also said: "And whoever brings the truth and believes in it" (39:33)—and in the soundest explanations it is said that he who brought the truth is Muḥammad, and Abū Bakr the Trusting believed in it. The truth of this explanation is confirmed by Muḥammad's words: "Men said to me: You lie. But Abū Bakr said: You speak the truth." It is also proved by God's words: "Those who spent and fought before the victory are not upon a level [with the rest of you]. Such are greater in rank than those who spent and fought afterwards" (57:10). This is the Trusting, who was the first to spend on behalf of the Apostle of God. This is confirmed by Muḥammad's words: "The most generous of men to me, in person and in wealth, was Abū Bakr. No one's wealth has benefited me as has the wealth of Abū Bakr." And it is proved by Muḥammad's words to Abu 'd-Dardā': "Do you walk before him who is better than you? By God, the sun has not risen or set on any man, after the Prophets and the Apostles, better than Abū Bakr."

Moreover, obedience to Abū Bakr was obligatory because of the consensus of the Muslims on obedience to him and on the [validity of] his Imamate and on [their duty of] submission to him. So much so that the Commander of the Faithful, ʿAlī, said in reply to Abū Bakr's words: "Release me from this obligation, for I am not the best of you"—"We shall not release you, nor shall we ask you to rescind the bargain. The Apostle of God set you over religion, and shall we not be content with you for this life of ours?" By that he meant the occasion when Muḥammad appointed Abū Bakr to lead the prayer in his own presence, and his deputing him to lead the pilgrimage—[for ʿAlī added] "and he appointed you leader over us." Abū Bakr was the best man of the Community, the weightiest in faith, the most perfect in understanding, the richest in knowledge, the most abounding in forbearance (*ḥilm*). Muḥammad spoke of this in his words: "If Abū Bakr's faith were to be weighed against that of all the people of the earth, Abū Bakr's faith would out-weigh theirs."

The next after Abū Bakr in this [office] is the Commander of the Faithful, ʿUmar, because Abū Bakr appointed him as his vicegerent. There are innumerable traditions recounting the virtues of ʿUmar. For example, Muḥammad said: "If there were to be a Prophet after me, it would be ʿUmar. Truly God has bound the truth to ʿUmar's tongue and breast." And again: "The breaths (*anfās*) of ʿUmar almost preceded the revelation of God." For ʿUmar spoke to Muḥammad about the captives of Badr, saying: "You should execute them." And God's words came down: "It is not for any Prophet to have captives until he has made slaughter in the land" (8:67). And Muḥammad also said: "If a doom were to come down from heaven, no one would escape it save ʿUmar," when God's words came down: "Had it not been for an ordinance of Allāh which had gone before, an awful doom had come upon you on account of what you took" (8:68). And ʿUmar said: "Better were your wives veiled [screened off], for both good and bad come in to [see] you," and the Verse of the Veil was revealed (cf. 33:53 and 59). And ʿUmar said: "It may happen that his Lord, if he divorce you . . . ," and the verse on that was revealed (66:5). But ʿUmar's excellence is beyond reckoning.

The Commander of the Faithful after ʿUmar is ʿUthmān. For the Muslims are agreed that he was one of the group of six designated by ʿUmar. And Muḥammad said: "ʿUthmān is my brother and my companion in the Garden"; and: "Had we a third daughter, we should have given her to you in marriage"; and: "I besought God to release 'Uthmān from the Reckoning, and He has done so"; and: "Who will be generous in the matter of the Mosque, and I will guarantee the Garden for him?"—and 'Uthmān bought the ground and appointed it for the Muslims; and: "Who will equip the army of al-'Usra, and the Garden will be his?"—and 'Uthmān equipped it with nine hundred and fifty camels, and completed the thousand with fifty horses.

The Commander of the Faithful after him is 'Alī. Many traditions on his merits have been related from the Prophet, e.g. "O God, make truth to turn with 'Alī wherever he turns"; and: "Are you not content to be to me as Aaron was to Moses, save that there is no Prophet after me?"; and: "Tomorrow I will surely give the standard to a man who loves God and His Apostle and who is loved by God and His Apostle"—and he gave it to 'Alī.

PROOF OF THAT ORDER OF IMAMS

The proof of the affirmation of the Imamate of those four Caliphs in the order we have explained is that the Companions were the chiefs of religion and the lamps of the possessors of true knowledge, who had witnessed the revelation and who knew the interpretation, and of whom the Prophet had testified that they were the best of creatures in his words: "The best of ages is mine." Hence, since they preferred these four to others, and put them in the order we have mentioned, we know that they did not prefer anyone from desire for personal gain, but that they chose whom they chose because of their belief that he was the best and most fitted for the Imamate at the time of his appointment to office.

The noble and most excellent Imam, the Glory of Islām,[6] said: There occurred to me a proof from the text of the Book of this ordering of the first four and its not being able to be otherwise, viz. God's words: "Allāh has promised such of you as believe and do good works that He will surely make them succeed [the present rulers] in the earth even as He caused those who were before them to succeed [others]; and that He will surely establish for them their religion" (24:55). God's promise is true and his announcement veracious, and the contrary of what He has announced cannot take place. Hence what He promised them and announced would be in their regard had to be fulfilled. But this could not have been save in the order mentioned. For if 'Alī were put first the Caliphate would not have come to any of the other three, since 'Alī died after they did. So, also, if 'Uthmān were put first, the Caliphate would not have come to Abū Bakr and 'Umar, because 'Uthmān died after they did. And if ʿUmar were put first, the Caliphate would not have come to Abū Bakr, because ʿUmar died after he did. But God announced that the Caliphate would come to them all. Hence it could not have happened save in the way it did. To God praise for guidance and help!

DISPUTES AMONG THE COMPANIONS

You must also know that, regarding the disputes that took place among the Companions of the Prophet, you must refrain from [discussing] them, and must call down God's mercy on them all, and praise all, and ask God to grant them His good pleasure and security and victory and the Gardens. You must also believe that ʿAlī was right in what he did, and that he has "two rewards"; and that the Companions did what they did only because of the exercise of personal judgment (*ijtihād*), and so have one reward. But they are not to be called sinners or innovators. This is proved by God's words: "Allāh taking pleasure in them and they in Him" (5:119); and: "Allāh was well pleased with the believers when they swore allegiance unto you beneath the tree" (48:18). And Muḥammad said: "If the judge (*al-ḥākim*) should exercise his personal judgment and be right, he will have two rewards; but if he should exercise his personal judgment and be wrong, he will have one reward." So if the judge in our time receives two rewards for his exercise of personal judgment, what should you think of the exercise of personal judgment by those [of whom God said] "Allāh taking pleasure in them and they in Him"?

The truth of this is also proved by what Muḥammad said of [ʿAlī's son] al-Ḥasan (d. 669): "Truly he is a chief, and by him will God make peace between two great parties of the Muslims"—thus affirming greatness of each of the two groups and ascribing to them sound Islām. Moreover, Muḥammad said: "There will be a disaster among my Companions and disputes that God will forgive to them; and he shall be unhappy in them who will be unhappy." And God promised these people that He would remove rancor from their breasts in His words: "And We remove whatever rancor may be in their breasts. As brethren, face to face, [they rest] on couches raised" (15:47).

HIERARCHY OF THE COMMUNITY

You must also know that the best of the Community are the Companions of the Apostle of God, and that the best of the ten Companions are the four Rightly-Guided Caliphs. And you must confess the excellence of the household of the Apostle of God, and acknowledge the excellence of his wives, and that they are the Mothers of the Faithful, as God and his Apostle described them. And you must speak well of them all, and brand with innovation and error and sin him who calumniates them, or any one of them, because of the explicit declarations of Book and Sunna concerning their excellence and in praise and laudation of them. Hence whoever says the contrary is a sinner and opposes the Book and the Sunna—we take refuge in God from that!

ATTITUDE TOWARDS DISPUTES OF COMPANIONS

One must refrain from mentioning what was disputed among the Companions and be silent about it. For Muḥammad said: "Beware of discussing what was disputed among my Companions!" And it is related by Ibn ʿAbbās (d. 686) that he was asked: "What do you say about what was disputed among the first Muslims?" He replied: "I say what God said: 'Our Lord! Forgive us and our brethren who were before us in the faith, and place not in our hearts any rancor toward those who believe'" (59:10). And [the seventh Shīʿī Imam] Jaʿfar ibn Muḥammad aṣ-Ṣādiq (d. 765) was asked about that, and he answered: "I say what God said: 'The knowledge thereof is with my Lord in a Record. My Lord neither errs nor forgets'" (20:52). And another of them was asked about that, and he replied: "Those are a people who have passed away. Theirs is that which they earned, and yours is that which you earn. And you will not be asked of what they used to do" (2:134). And [Umayyad caliph] ʿUmar ibn al-ʿAzīz (d. 720) was asked about that, and he replied: "That is blood from which God kept my hand clean: shall I not then keep my tongue clean from it?" The likeness of the Companions of the Apostle of God is as that of the eyes—and the remedy for the eyes is not to rub them!

CONDITIONS OF THE IMAMATE

You must also know that the Imamate is unsuitable save for him in whom its conditions are united. First: he must be a Qurashite, because of Muḥammad's words: "The Imams are from Quraysh." Secondly: he must be possessed of the legal ability (*min ahli 'l-fatwā*) of those who can exercise personal judgment, because the Judge, who will be appointed by him, has need of that, and therefore, *a fortiori,* the Imam himself has need of it. Thirdly: he must be a man of courage and sufficiency and ability to manage affairs, pure and godly in his religion. These conditions were verified in the Caliphs of the Apostle of God. Moreover, Muḥammad said: "The Caliphate after me will last for thirty years; then it will become a kingdom." And the days of the first four Caliphs were just that number. May God help us to the right and preserve us from error and slips by His bounty and mercy!

THEOLOGIES OF GOVERNANCE: HOLDING UP A MIRROR TO KINGS AND SULTANS

Many centuries after early theologians of various perspectives had hammered out their distinctive views on governance and religiously legitimate authority, Muslim authors continued to produce works in the genre "mirrors for princes" or "advice for kings." Typically in elevated and embellished literary style, the genre has a very long history in a host of languages, including most importantly Arabic, Persian, and Turkish. Sunnī and Shīʿī authors alike have been moved to compose works in the genre. A number of major theologians have assumed the bold and courageous role of reminding Muslim rulers of their awesome responsibilities before God. An extensive literature of "mirrors for princes" spans many centuries and includes works attributed to theologians both illustrious and less well known. We begin with a classic Sunnī view on the role of Muslim "political" leaders in a brief excerpt from Ghazālī's *Book of Counsel for Kings* and follow up with a much later work from South Asia, penned by a Shīʿī author for his Mughal Sunnī patron.

Ghazālī on the Larger Context of Islamic Governance

Translated by F. R. C. Bagley

Chapter 1 of the second part of Abū Ḥāmid al-Ghazālī's (d. 1111) Persian *Book of Counsel for Kings* (*Naṣīḥat al-mulūk*) describes briefly the "qualities required in the exercise of discipline (*siyāsat*) and justice by Kings and [that ought to figure] in every royal biography and chronicle."[7] Note how he situates his views against the broader horizon of kingly rule stretching back to pre-Islamic times, with examples drawn almost exclusively from ancient Persian traditions.[8]

Text

You should understand that God on High selected two classes of the Sons of Adam and endowed these two classes with superiority over the rest: the one being prophets, blessings and peace be upon them, and the other kings. To guide His slaves to Him, He sent prophets; and to preserve them from one another, He sent kings, to whom He bound the welfare (*maṣlaḥat*) of people's lives in His wisdom and on whom He conferred high rank. As you will hear in the Traditions, "the Sulṭān is God's shadow on earth," which means that he is high-ranking and the Lord's delegate over His creatures. It must therefore be recognized that this kingship and the divine effulgence have been granted to them by God, and that they must accordingly be obeyed, loved and followed. To dispute with kings is improper, and to hate them is wrong; for God on High has commanded, "Obey God and obey the Prophet and those among you who hold authority" (4:59), which means [in Persian] obey God and the prophets and your princes. Everybody to whom God has given religion must therefore love and obey kings and recognize that their kingship is granted by God, and given by Him to whom He wills. God Almighty stated this, in the verse: "Say, O God, owner of the sovereignty! [You give the sovereignty to whom You will, and You take it away from whom You will. You strengthen whom You will, and You humble whom You will. In Your hand is the choice of what is best. Truly You are powerful over everything]" (3:26). This means [in Persian] that God on High, who is the King of Kings, gives the kingship to whom He wills, and that He strengthens one man through His favor and humbles another through His justice.

The Sulṭān in reality is he who awards justice, and does not perpetrate injustice and wickedness, among God's slaves; for the unjust Sulṭān is ill-starred and will have no endurance, because the Prophet stated that "sovereignty endures even when there is unbelief, but will not endure when there is injustice." It is [recorded] in the chronicles that for well-nigh four thousand years this universe was held by the Magians and the kingdom remained in their family. This endured because they maintained justice among the subjects. In their religious system they did not permit injustice or oppression; and through their justice and equity they developed the universe [and made it prosperous]. In the Traditions it is related that God on High sent the following revelation to the Prophet David: "O David, tell your nation not to speak ill of the people of Persia; for it is they who developed the universe, so that My slaves might live in it." You must understand that the development or desolation of this universe depends upon kings; for if the king is just, the universe is prosperous and the subjects are secure, as was the case in the times of Ardashīr, Farīdūn, Bahrām Gūr, Kisrā, and other kings like them; whereas when the king is tyrannical, the universe becomes desolate, as it was in the times of Ḍaḥḥāk, Afrāsiyāb, and others like them. [The text goes on to summarize the reigns of these and other pre-Islamic Persian Magian sovereigns.]

Muḥammad Bāqir Najm-i Thānī on Justice and Discipline

Translated by Sajida Sultana Alvi

Here is an excerpt from an early modern South Asian Shīʿī author who served a Sunnī sovereign. Muḥammad Bāqir Najm-i Thānī (d. 1637) wrote his Persian *Admonition of Jihāngīr, or Advice on the Art of Governance* (*Mawʿiẓa-yi Jahāngīrī*) in 1612–13 for the son and successor of Mughal emperor Akbar. Note Thānī's emphasis on God as the source of all authority and justice.[9]

Text

SECTION I: ON JUSTICE (*ʿADĀLAT*) AND DISCIPLINE (*SIYĀSAT*)

Know that the empire and kingship constitute exalted rank and high station. With endeavor alone one cannot reach that level of aspiration. One may attain the position [of sovereignty] only with divine assistance, perpetual felicity, strength of power, and intercession of good luck. When in unexpected good fortune such a situation becomes possible and Almighty God, Praise be unto Him, bestows favor upon one of His servants by putting a crown of authority on his head, he in turn must hold the empire dear and venerable. In systematizing rules and in maintaining their procedures, he must exert the utmost care to achieve justice and impartiality. If the judge [ruler] does not regulate the affairs of the people, a clandestine rebel, abetted by tyranny, will destroy the lives of the nobility and plebeian alike. If the light from the candle of justice does not illuminate the somber cell of the afflicted, the darkness of cruelty will blacken the entire country just as it does the hearts of tyrants.

Because rulers are but the reflections of the Creator, without the sun of their justice the expanse of the world is not illuminated. For people, repose in cradles of peace and security can develop only in the shade of their [rulers'] compassion and benevolence. A just ruler is a refuge to the oppressed and a protector of fallen. In the Tradition [it says] that "on a pair of scales, one hour of justice outweighs sixty years of worship." Indeed the benefit of praying is limited to the worshipper, [whereas] the benefit of justice reaches to the public in general, from high to low. The sages have said that justice is not of virtue but *is* virtue; and tyranny, which is its opposite, is not a part of vileness but *is* all vileness. Among the virtues of justice is that the earth does not decompose a sultan's body [in the grave]; and if this just sultan is a Muslim as well, the fire of hell will also not affect him.

Indeed, rulers conquer the dominion of the hereafter only by helping the oppressed and redressing [the wrongs of] the afflicted. For every prudent ruler who establishes his administration on the law of justice and does not deviate from the path of impartiality, the religious and ruling institutions (*qawāʾid-i dīn wa dawlat*) [as well as] the foundations of the dominion and the community remain firm and structured. If, however, he transgresses from the way of justice, the base of his empire will be destroyed and the foundations of his power will soon be shaken.

Wise men have enunciated that five types of persons should quit aspiring for five things, abandoning hope of their attainment: first, a tyrant ruler for the stability of the country and preservation of the empire; second, an arrogant and haughty person for people's praise; third, an ill-tempered person for many friends; fourth, a shameless and rude person for glory and a rank of dignity; fifth, a miser for a good name.

Certainly, the cable of security for the world's inhabitants is tied to the person of all-powerful emperors and rulers. Their commands have sway over people's lives and possessions; their mandates are like the descending decree, enacted and carried out to solve and resolve problems. Therefore, rulers must consider that they occupy the throne in order to dispense justice, not to lead a life filled with pleasure. They must consider justice and equity as the means to survival of their rule, permanence of their fame, and reward in the hereafter. To them, nothing should be more binding than pursuit of the people's [i.e., God's servants'] welfare. They must not consider it ignominious to speak with peasantry, the elderly, the weak, and the poor. Having listened to the petitioners for justice, the rulers themselves should probe the affairs of the oppressed and affectionately turn their attention toward resolving their problems. They should not be irritated by their [the petitioners'] loquacity. Indeed, the emperor is like a physician and the petitioner like a patient. If the patient does not fully explain his condition, the physician cannot apprehend his disease. How can he diagnose an unknown illness?

One must, however, know that the roots of the tree of justice are invigorated and watered by showers from the clouds of discipline, because [governmental] control is based on the laws of justice. It is said that an empire is like a young plant and that control is akin to water. Therefore, to reap the fruit of peace and security, the roots of the empire must be kept refreshed by the water of discipline. If [governmental] regulation and discipline are not effective, enterprises will be in disarray. If punishment and chastisement are nonexistent, [state] affairs will be in ruin. [Imperial] control is the adornment of the country and community and an expedient for the welfare of religion and empire. Without the rulers' regulation of control, the decrees of the *Sharīʿa* will not be promulgated, nor is the basis of the power strengthened. If the sword of retribution is not drawn from the scabbard of vengeance, the roots of rebellion are not eradicated and the basis of oppression is not undermined. If the debris of tyranny is not burnt in the fire of [imperial] wrath, the seedling of repose will not flourish in the garden of hope. Popular insurgents, having witnessed the fire of punishment blaze, slip away. [However], if there is even a little intimidation discernible in the [state] control, there will be uprisings everywhere and diverse disturbances will develop. Therefore, rulers should display the mercy of God toward the virtuous and the reformers (*muṣliḥān*), and the wrath of God toward the evildoers and the seditious. Rulers should dip the lancet of their rage in the honey of kindness and mix the poison of their majesty with the sugar of compassion. They should combine [their] control with justice in order to keep the meadow of righteous people's aspirations lush with the sprinkles of benevolence, and to uproot the foundation of the lives of the wicked with discipline's stormy winds.

SOCIAL AND PERSONAL ETHICAL GUIDANCE

Finally, the library of works dedicated to "moral theology/philosophy" in general encompasses scores of treatises that begin with chapters laying out the religious foundations of all human behavior and that pointedly discuss a wide range of personal challenges encountered by individuals aspiring to high moral values. Brief samples from four highly influential figures bring this anthology to a close. First, a selection from a prolific eleventh-century "Traditionalist" thinker from Andalusia reveals some less appreciated sides of the many-faceted Ibn Ḥazm, an adherent of the long-dormant Ẓāhirī school of law. Ghazālī's pastoral reflections on contentment with divine dispensation of affairs focus on the experiential dimension of the theological concept of God's absolute power. Shāh Walī Allāh's analysis of the "ranks of sin" offers a clear theological taxonomy, and Mullā Ṣadrā's reflections on forgiveness conclude the chapter.

Ibn Ḥazm on Anxiety, Self-Knowledge, and Virtue

Translated by Muḥammad Abū Laylah

Author of a vast range of literary genres, from theological treatises to mystical poetry and reflections on love, Ibn Ḥazm (d. 1085) of Cordova here reveals himself to be a remarkably shrewd observer of human nature. In his reflection on the problem and purpose, in the divine scheme, of the universal experience of anxiety, and his suggestions as to how people need to examine their motives and intentions, Ibn Ḥazm exhibits not only deep insight but a sense that he had learned not to exempt himself from his own trenchant criticism of human behavior. A second excerpt offers his reflections on one of many areas of personal ethical behavior, the need to avoid hypocrisy in one's criticism of others and of oneself.[10]

Text

I have tried to find one goal that everyone would agree to be excellent and worthy of being striven after. I have found one only: to be free from anxiety. When I reflected upon it, I realized that not only do all agree in valuing it and desiring it, but I also perceived that, despite their many different passions and aspirations and preoccupations and desires, they never make the slightest gesture unless it is to dispel anxiety, they never utter a single word unless it is designed to drive anxiety far away. One loses his way, another comes close to going wrong, finally another is successful—but he is a rare person, and success is rare, [O, all-knowing God].

Dispelling anxiety is a goal upon which all nations agree—from the time when the Almighty created the world until the day when this world will pass away and be followed by the Day of Judgment—and their actions are directed to this goal alone. In the case of every other objective there will always be some people who do not desire it.

For example, some people are not religious and do not take eternity into account.

There are some who by nature and inclination prefer obscurity to fame [the obscurity of satisfied passion].

There are some people of evil nature who are not striving for good, for peace [loyalty] or for justice.

There are some who have no interest in amassing a fortune, preferring abstinence to ownership; this was the case with many of the prophets and those who followed their example, ascetics and philosophers. There are some who by nature dislike sensual pleasures and scorn those who seek after them, such as those men we have just mentioned, and who prefer to lose a fortune rather than gain one. Some prefer ignorance to knowledge; in fact most of the people that you see in the street are like this. These are the objectives of people who have no other aim in life. Nobody in the whole world, from the time of its creation until its end, would deliberately choose anxiety, and would not desire to drive it far away.

When I had arrived at this great piece of wisdom, when I had discovered this amazing secret, when Allāh the Almighty had opened the eyes of my mind [spirit] to see this great treasure, I began to search for the way that would truly enable me to dispel anxiety, that precious goal desired by every kind of person, whether ignorant or scholarly, good or evil. I found it in one place alone, in the action of turning towards God the Almighty and powerful, in pious works performed with an eye to eternity.

Thus the only reason that someone chases after riches is to dispel the anguish of poverty. The only reason that someone seeks fame is to dispel the anxiety of seeing someone else outdo him. The only reason that someone chases after pleasures is to dispel the anxiety of missing them. The only reason that someone chases after knowledge is to dispel the anxiety of being ignorant about something.

People enjoy listening to other people's conversation and gossip only because it dispels the anxiety of being alone and isolated. People eat, drink, make love, wear clothes, play games, build a shelter, mount a horse, go for a walk, only in order to avoid the reverse of all these actions and every other kind of anxiety.

In all the actions listed here, anyone who pauses to reflect will see that anxieties will inevitably occur, such as problems that arise in the course of the action, the impossibility of performing the impossible, the fleeting nature of any achievements, and the inability to enjoy something because of some difficulty. There are also bad consequences that arise from every success: fear of one's rival, attacks by the jealous, theft by the covetous, loss to an enemy, not to mention criticism, sin and such things. On the other hand, I have found that actions performed with an eye on eternity are free from every kind of fault, free from every stain, and a true means of dispelling anxiety. I have found that the individual who is striving for eternity may be sorely tested by bad fortune on his way but does not worry; on the contrary, he is glad, because the trial to which he is subjected gives rise to hope, which aids him in his endeavor and sets him the more firmly on the path towards his true desire. I have found that, when he finds his way blocked by an obstacle, he does not worry, because it is not his fault, and he did not choose the actions that he will have to answer for. I have seen such a person be glad, when others have wished evil upon him, and be glad when he has undergone some trial, and be glad when he has suffered on his chosen path, and be glad, always [living] in a permanent state of joy while others are permanently the opposite. You should therefore understand that there is only one objective to strive for, it is to dispel anxiety; and only one path leads to this, and that is the service of God. Everything else is misguided and absurd. . . .

Know well that nobody upon earth is free of all faults except the prophets.

A person who does not see his own faults is a fallen being; he comes to be so from baseness, turpitude, stupidity and feebleness of intelligence, lack of discernment and understanding, to such a point that he is no different from vile people and it is not possible to drop lower into degradation than he has. Let him save his soul by seeking out his own faults and turning attention upon them instead of his pride and the faults of others, the doing of which harms him neither in this world or the next.

I do not know of any benefit to be drawn from hearing about the faults of other people except that he who hears about them may learn the lesson, avoid them and seek to cure himself of them with God's assistance and might.

To speak of the faults of others is a serious shame that is absolutely not acceptable. One should avoid doing it except when one wishes to advise someone whom one fears to see fall into the clutches of the person one is criticizing or when one only wishes to reprimand a boastful person, which should be done to his face and not behind his back.

If you are proud of your intelligence, remember all the bad thoughts that come into your mind, the deceitful hopes that assail you, then you will realize how feeble your intelligence is.

If you are proud of your personal ideas remember your mistakes, keep them in your memory, do not forget them: think of all the times you have believed yourself right and you have been proved wrong, all the times that someone else has been right and you have been wrong. If you do this, you will see that in most cases you have been wrong about as often as right. The score will come out about equal. But it is more likely that your mistakes will be more numerous because this is the case with every human being except the prophets.

If you are proud of your good works, remember your times of rebellion, your faults, your life in all its aspects. Ah, by God, then you will find that they outnumber your good works and it will make your good deeds forgotten. So you should worry about this for a long time and replace your pride with self-disdain.

If you are proud of your knowledge, you should know that it is no credit to you, it is a pure gift that God has granted you. Do not receive it in a way that would anger the Almighty because He might wipe it from your memory by subjecting you to an illness that would make you forget all that you have learned and stored in your memory. I have been told that this happened to ʿAbd al-Mālik ibn Ṭārif (d. 1009), who was a scholar, intelligent, moderate, exact in his researches, who had been allotted by fate such a prodigious memory that virtually nothing reached his ears that had to be said to him twice. Now he undertook a journey by ship and experienced such a terrible storm at sea that he lost the memory of most of what he had learnt and suffered considerable upset to his mind. He never recovered his full intelligence. I myself have been struck by illness. When I got up from it I had forgotten all my knowledge except for a few ideas of little value. I did not recover it until several years later.

You should also know that there are many people greedy for knowledge, who devote themselves to reading, to study and to research but do not reap any benefit from it. A scholar should realize that it is enough to pursue knowledge; many others will rank higher than him. Knowledge is truly a gift from God. So what place is there for pride? One can only feel humble, give thanks to God Almighty and beg Him to increase His gifts and beseech Him not to withhold them.

You should also remember that everything that remains hidden from you, everything that you do not know of the different branches of knowledge, the aspects that you have specialized in, and that you are proud to have penetrated [nevertheless what you do not know] is greater than what you do know. You should therefore replace your pride with scorn and self-disdain; that would be better. Think of those who are more knowledgeable than you—you will find that there are many of them—and may your spirit be humble in your own sight.

You should also remember that you may be deceived by knowledge, for if you do not put into practice what you know your knowledge will be a testimony against you and it would have been better for you if you had never been a scholar. For you should remember that an ignorant person is wiser than you, he is in a better position, he is more excusable. May your pride then completely disappear.

Moreover, the knowledge that you are so proud of having penetrated is perhaps one of the less important branches of knowledge, of no great value, such as poetry. You should then remember the person whose branch of study is more noble than yours on the scale of this world and the next, and your soul should become humble in your own sight.

If you are proud of your courage, remember those who are more valiant than you. Then examine what you do with your courage that God has granted you. If you waste it in rebellion against God, you are a fool for you are losing your soul by committing acts of no value to it. If you use your courage in obedience to God, you are spoiling it by your pride. You should also remember that your courage will fall away as you grow old and if you live so long you will become dependent, as weak as a baby.

Ghazālī on Contentment with Divine Destiny

Translated by Muhtar Holland

In addition to his many works of systematic, pastoral, and mystical theology, Abū Ḥāmid al-Ghazālī (d. 1111) was also one of the most perceptive of pastoral theologians. He had a remarkable gift for helping intelligent nontheologians, fellow Muslim travelers of the spiritual path, understand the experiential implications of otherwise often perplexing theological concepts. Here, from a truly beautiful book—*The Path of the Worshipful Servants to the Garden of the Lord of All the Worlds*—Ghazālī offers a sample of that practical wisdom for which so many have prized his work.[11]

Text

Someone may ask: "What is the meaning of contentment with destiny's decree? How can it be realized, and what is its legal status?"

You should therefore know that the scholars have said: "Contentment is the abandonment of displeasure. Displeasure is expressed by asserting that something other than what God has decreed would be better and more beneficial for you, though you do not know for certain whether it is good or bad." This [abandonment of displeasure] is a precondition of contentment, so understand that well.

You may say: "Surely all evils and sins are due to the decree and foreordainment of God, so how can the servant be content with evil, and how can that be incumbent upon him?"

You should therefore know that contentment with the decree is all that is incumbent. The decreeing of evil is not itself an evil. The evil is what has been decreed, so contentment is not with the evil [but only with the fact that God has decreed it]. According to our shaykhs:

> Four things have been divinely decreed: (1) a benefit (*niʿma*), (2) an adversity (*shidda*), (3) something good (*khayr*), and (4) something evil (*sharr*).
>
> In the case of a benefit, there must be contentment with the One who decrees (al-Qāḍī), the decree (*al-qaḍā'*), and what is decreed (*al-maqḍī*). There must also be gratitude for it, inasmuch as it is a blessing, and the servant must acknowledge its blessedness by demonstrating the effect of the benefit.
>
> In the case of an adversity, there must also be contentment with the One who decrees, the decree, and what is decreed. There must also be patience, since an adversity is hard to endure.
>
> In the case of something good, there must also be contentment with the One who decrees, the decree, and what is decreed. The servant must also acknowledge the favor, since it is a boon that he has been fortunate to obtain. In the case of something evil, there must also be contentment with the One who decrees, the decree, and what is decreed, inasmuch as it has been decreed, not inasmuch as it is evil. The fact that it has been decreed is attributable, in reality, to the decree and the One who decrees.

This last case is similar to the situation where you are content with the doctrine (*madhhab*) of the proponent of a different school, in the sense that you are content to have knowledge of it, not to adopt it as your own doctrine. The fact that it is known (*maʿlūm*) is attributable to knowledge (*ʿilm*), so you are actually content and pleased with the knowledge of that doctrine, not with the doctrine itself.

Someone may ask: "If someone is content, is he entitled to ask for more?" The answer will be: Yes, if he does so with the stipulation that it must be good and proper, not unconditionally. That will not dislodge him from contentment. It is actually a sign of contentment, so it is better [than not asking for more], because, if something delights a person and he is content with it, he will naturally ask for more of the same. The Prophet used to say, when milk was available: "O God, grant us Your blessing in it, and provide us with more of it!" He would also say, when referring to [food or drink] other than milk: "[O God, grant us Your blessing in it], and provide us with more of something better than it!"

In neither case did he indicate that he was not content with what God had foreordained for him in that particular instance.

You may ask: "Has it not been reported that the Prophet made his request contingent on God's will, and conditional on its being good and proper?" You must therefore know that these matters are peculiar to the heart, and there is no need to express them with the tongue. Failure to express them verbally is therefore unimportant, provided they are stipulated by the heart, so understand that unequivocally. . . .

As for contentment with destiny (*ar-riḍā bi 'l-qaḍā'*), you must consider two essential points, to which nothing further need be added:

(1) The benefit of contentment in the present and the future. As for its benefit in the present, it is freedom of the heart and relief from useless anxiety. That is why one of the ascetics once said: "Since destiny is a true fact, anxiety is redundant." According to the traditional report, the Prophet said to Ibn Masʿūd (d. 652): "Let your anxiety be very slight, for whatever has been predestined will come about, and whatever has not been predestined will not come to you." This Prophetic saying is comprehensive, conveying much valuable meaning in very few words.

As for the benefit of contentment in the future, it is the reward of God and His good pleasure. God has said that "He is well pleased with them, and they are well pleased with Him" (5:119). By contrast, discontent is fraught with anxiety, sorrow, and distress in the present, and with the burden of sin and punishment in the future. It has no benefit, since destiny's decree is effective, so it will not be cancelled by your anxiety and your discontent. As the poet said:

> Whatever is decreed, O self, endure it with patience,
> and may you be safe from that which is not foreordained.
> You must realize that what is predestined will come about
> for certain, regardless of whether or not you practice patience.

The intelligent person will not choose useless anxiety, combined with the burden of sin and punishment, instead of the heart's comfort and the reward of the Garden of Paradise!

(2) Discontent is fraught with the dire threat of danger and injury, unbelief (*kufr*), and hypocrisy (*nifāq*), unless God overtakes you [with His mercy]. Reflect on His saying: "But, by your Lord, they will not believe until they make you judge of what is in dispute between them and find within themselves no dislike of what you decide, and submit with full submission" (4:65).

He has thus denied their claim to belief, by solemnly swearing that belief is absent from those who are discontented, and who find within themselves a dislike of the decision of God's Messenger. What then is the condition of someone who is displeased with God's decree? According to a traditional report [*Ḥadīth Qudsī*], God says: "If someone is not content with My decree, if he is not patient with My tribulation, and if he is not grateful for My blessing, let him choose a deity (*ilāh*) apart from Me."

Someone said: "It is as if He is saying: 'This person will not be content with Me as a Lord, as long as he is displeased, so let him choose another lord, with whom he is content.'"

For the intelligent person, this [saying attributed to God] is the ultimate threat and warning. One of the righteous predecessors spoke the truth, when he was asked: "What is servanthood (*ʿubūdīya*) and what is Lordship (*rubūbīya*)?" and he replied: "It is for the Lord to decree, and for the servant to be content." This means that if the Lord decrees, but the servant is not content, it is pointless to speak of servanthood and Lordship. You must consider this principle, and scrutinize yourself, for then you may be safe, with God's help and His enabling grace.

Shāh Walī Allāh on the Ranks of Sin

Translated by Marcia Hermansen

The prolific South Asian theologian Shāh Walī Allāh (d. 1762) of Delhi contributed to chapter 2's discussions on selected hermeneutical themes, with a selection on the causes of abrogation. That topic, and the diverse positions Muslim thinkers have taken on it over the centuries, has important implications for ethical decision making, dealing as it does with the contentious matter of which scriptural injunctions remain in force and which have been superseded. Here the teacher speaks more directly as a theological ethicist with his categorization of sinful human actions.[12]

Text

You should know that just as there are actions that are embodiments, symbols, and practices that are conducive to the animalistic side's yielding to the angelic, likewise there are actions, symbols, and ways of acquiring the state which are absolutely contradictory to this yielding, namely, sins.

They are at various degrees:

(1) The first degree of sins totally block a person's means to the desired perfection and the majority of these are of two types.

(a) One of them are those going back to the Source in that he does not know that he has a Lord, or he conceives of God as described by the attributes of created things, or he believes that a created thing may have some of the attributes of God. The second [of these first type of sins] are anthropomorphism, and the third of them is associationism (*ishrāk*). The soul will never be sanctified until it sets its sights on the heavenly transcendence and the comprehensive divine management encompassing the world. If this is lacking the soul will remain self-absorbed or preoccupied with what is similar to itself in being so limited in every one of its concerns that the veil of rejection cannot be punctured by so much as a needle prick, and this is the greatest of calamities.

(b) Type two of [sins at the first level] are that a person believes that there will be no creation of the soul beyond this bodily one and that there is no other perfection beyond this that a person must seek. If the soul harbors this idea it will not raise its sights to perfection at all.

Affirming a perfection other than that of the physical body is only realizable by the majority of people through conceiving of a condition that is the opposite of the present one from every aspect. If this is not done then the rational and the tangible fulfillments would seem to be opposed to each other so that a person would incline to the tangible and the rational would be neglected. Therefore a touchstone for this is assigned which is faith that he will meet God, and faith in the Last Day, and this is God's saying, "Those who don't believe in the Hereafter, their hearts refuse to know, and they are proud" (16:22). In summary, when someone dies at this level of sin, his animalistic side is effaced, and hatred will completely envelop him from above such that he finds no way ever to be free of it.

(2) The second degree of sins is that he is arrogant with his animalistic arrogance toward what God established in order to make people attain their perfection, and what the Highest Council intend with the furthest extent of their resolve to propagate and elevate through the messengers and the divine laws. Thus he denies these and is hostile to them. Then when he dies all of their resolve is disposed to hate him and to pain him, and "his sin surrounds him" (2:81) so that he finds no means to escape, but this state of his failing to attain his perfection or of his only attaining something insignificant does not detach from him. In all of the divine laws this level expels the person from the religion of his prophet.

(3) The third level is abandoning that which will earn him salvation and doing that which would convene, at the Plane of *Dhikr* [the realm of images and angels], curses on the one who does it due to its being an anticipated source, in most cases, of a great corruption on the earth and an attitude opposed to the refinement of the lower soul. [Under this level come]:

(a) A person's not carrying out anything significant of the divine laws that results in obedience [to God] or that will prepare him for obedience. This varies with the differences in souls, except that the ones immersed in weakly bestial attitudes are the people most in need of having the laws augmented, and the communities whose animalistic sides are strongest and most contaminated are the ones most in need of the augmentation of the strictest laws.

(b) Predatory acts that provoke a severe curse such as murder,

(c) lustful actions,

(d) and harmful sources of income such as gambling and usury.

In each one of these things that have been mentioned is a great breach in the soul from the aspect of undertaking what opposes the necessary practice as we mentioned, and a cursing from the Highest Council that surrounds him, so that the combination of the two things results in punishment. This [third] level comprises the greatest of the major sins. Their prohibition is convened in the Holy Enclave, together with the cursing of those who commit them. The prophets constantly told of what was convened there, and most of this is agreed upon in the divine laws.

(4) The fourth degree is disobedience to the divine laws and the codes that vary due to the variation of the communities and eras. This occurs because when God sent a prophet to a people, "to bring them out of the darkness into the light," to correct their deviation, and to govern them with the best polity, this mission included making compulsory those things indispensable for reforming and governing them. Thus for every goal there is a common or enduring symbol (*mazinna*) according to which they must be held accountable, and about which they must be addressed, and setting times [for each act] has rules that require it. Many things motivate to a harm or benefit and thus people should be commanded according to what they will be motivated to do.

Some things are definitely commanded or forbidden, and some things are commanded or forbidden indeterminately. A minority of these [variable rules] are what the external revelation [the Qur'ān] revealed, and a majority were only confirmed through the independent reasoning (*ijtihād*) of the Prophet.

(5) The fifth rank [of sins] are what the law-giver did not specifically rule on, nor was their ruling convened among the Highest Council. Rather, a worshipper turned to God with the complete intent of his concentrated resolve and thus it struck him that a thing was supposed to be forbidden or commanded due to analogical reasoning, or derivation, or something like that [i.e., legal inference rather than explicit direct scriptural injunction]. This is like the effect that certain medicines seem to have according to common people due to their incomplete experience, or due to reliance on the ruling about the cause made by the proficient doctor; while they don't know the reason for the effectiveness, nor has the doctor stipulated it. Someone like this is not relieved of responsibility unless he acts with caution. If he does not do so a veil will arise between him and his Lord in what he supposes, and thus he will be held accountable for his opinion.

The element that is pleasing to God concerning this [fifth] level is that it should be omitted and not heeded despite the fact that there exist people who want to impose it on themselves, so that the Generous One increases for them what they have imposed on themselves. Concerning this is His saying [Sacred Hadith], "I am as My servant thinks Me to be" and His saying in the Great Qur'ān, "But monasticism they invented—We ordained it not for them—only seeking Allāh's pleasure" (57:27), and the Prophet's saying, "Don't be too severe with yourselves or God will be severe with you," and his saying, "Sin is something that has a strong impact on your heart."

The same goes for someone's disobeying the ruling of a legal scholar (*mujtahid*) if that person himself is a *muqallid* who is performing *taqlīd* [unquestioning acceptance of authority] toward a scholar who held this [opinion], and God knows better.

Mullā Ṣadrā on Forgiveness

Translated by William Chittick

Ṣadr ad-Dīn ash-Shīrāzī, better known as Mullā Ṣadrā (d. 1640), is perhaps best known as a philosopher and philosophical theologian. But he has also contributed significantly in the related area of "spiritual" theology, with its explicit concern with the divine-human relationship. His considerable body of work through the mid-seventeenth century is a testimony, not only to the continuing vitality of both philosophical and theological themes, but to the sustained vibrancy of the literature of spiritual experience. Chapter 6 included Mullā Ṣadrā's views on the divine voice. Here, chapter 8 of his Arabic *Elixir of the Gnostics* (i.e., of those who know God intimately) presents his exuberantly metaphorical take "on the meaning of forgiveness and its realization from God's bounty as He has promised and announced to His servants."[13]

Text

This is known from the precedents of His mercy and beneficence toward humankind, His forgiveness of humanity's precedent, creaturely sins, and His purifying the human being of the defilement of his natural filths and hylic [i.e., material] impurities. Do you not see how He has brought forth the embryo from the tightness of its mother's belly into the space of this world and how He has forgiven the sins that it committed and the ugly deeds that it performed when it was a sperm drop, a blood clot, a flesh lump, and an embryo? For it was stained with impurities and nourished with the forbidden blood of menstruation, and it lingered in the earth of the womb in the company of the darknesses. He purified it from the defilement of the impurities and foulnesses, and, in place of the "blood" of menstruation, He gave it "pure milk, sweet" to drink (16:66), so that it may nourish itself and its body become strong. Then it may roam in the expanse of the world however it desires and wills. Thus it comes forth from its precedent sins on the day its mother gives birth to it.

In the same way, when a human being reaches the degree of knowledge and faith and comes forth from the sleep of ignorance and the slumber of nature, "God forgives him the sins that have gone before" (48:2)—the ignorance and darkness and the ugly deeds of blindness and deprivation. He purifies him from the defilement of the offenses of bodies,[14] and the appetites of soul, and caprice. In place of bodily nourishments and various foods, He gives soulish nourishments, which are the diverse sorts of knowledge and the varieties of the sciences.

An Unveiling and Verification: That which grasps the earth's spirit is the vegetal soul, which is a fully active word[15] and a potency from among the potencies of the angels entrusted to the surface of the earth, a potency whose task is to transform the earth. It strips from it the earthly form so that it may replace it with a more beautiful form and a purer dress. Thus "He forgives" it its "sin that has gone before" (48:2) and He brings it out of its lowliness and its distance from the world of mercy.

So also, that which grasps the plant's spirit, makes it die, and lifts it to the heaven of animality is the soul specific to animals. She is among the helpers of the angels entrusted, by God's leave, with this act by taking into service the sensory and motor potencies.

In the same way, that which grasps the spirit of the animal, makes it die, and lifts it up to the heaven of the degree of humanness is the soul specific to human beings. She is God's word named "the holy spirit." Her task is to bring forth the souls from the hylic potency[16] to the acquired intellect, by God's command, and to convey the spirits to God's neighborhood and the world of the afterworldly Sovereignty.

In these transformations, each subsequent level is more eminent than its preceding level. What undergoes transition from the precedent state to the subsequent state has no regret or remorse over the disappearance of the first configuration. Or rather, if there is any, it concerns something else.[17]

In this way should one gauge the afterworldly configuration, which belongs to souls that climb up to it through science and knowledge.

A Qurʾānic Confirmation: Know that the Wise Qurʾān sometimes ascribes making souls die to God, like His words, "God makes the souls die at the time of their death" (39:42). This signifies that the one that makes to die is God. So also are His words, "Who created death and life" (67:2) and "My Lord is He who gives life and brings death" (2:258). So also are His words, "How do you disbelieve in God, for you were dead things, so He gave you life, then He brings you death, then He gives you life?" (2:28).

Sometimes making to die is ascribed to the angel of death, like His words, "Say: The angel of death, who has been entrusted with you, will make you die" (32:11). And sometimes it is ascribed to God's messengers, as in His words, "Until, when death comes to one of you, Our messengers make him die" (6:61).

Concerning the manner in which these verses agree, one of the commentators has mentioned that in reality the one who makes to die is God, but, in the world of the Witnessed, He delegates every sort of deed to one of the angels. So, He delegates grasping the spirits to the angel of death, who is a chieftain under whom are subordinates and servitors. Thus making to die is attributed in a verse to God, and this is the true attribution; in a verse to the angel of death, because he is a chieftain in this deed; and to the other angels, because they are the subordinates of the angel of death. And God knows best what is correct. Thus ends his discussion.[18]

A Holy Interpretation: Know that humankind is an all-gathering configuration. The existence of this all-gathering ["congregational"] mosque has been built from four roots, each of which has troops, servitors, and branches whose detailed differentiation none knows but God. The true goal in building this all-gathering, human mosque, within which the individuals of the species are gathered, is [1] the commencing of the *ṣalāt* (ritual prayer) by the address of the preacher-intellect on the pulpit that is the human brain by bearing witness that there is no god but God; [2] [the intellect's] signifying the unity of the Real through its gathered, unifying existence on the level of its simple, undifferentiated spirit; [3] the acquiescing of the "creatures," which are its perceptual and motor potencies, to its command; [4] their listening to its call when its voice penetrates their means of hearing; [5] their accompanying the spirit and following it in the *ṣalāt,* which is "the *miʿrāj* (ascension) of the believer,"[19] to the encounter with God; and [6] their abandoning the use of the body in their bodily interactions and purposes, thereby acquiescing to God's command and responding to the Real's summons in His words, "O believers, when the *ṣalāt* is called on the Day of Gathering, hasten to God's remembrance," and so on (62:9).

Allusion has already been made that death is a natural affair and an innate hastening. To this God alluded in His words, "O humankind! You are laboring unto your Lord laboriously, and you shall encounter Him" (84:6). We have clarified this in the proper place such that nothing can be added.

Now, diverse accounts have come concerning the superintendent of the inhabitation of this sacred mosque and the one who takes up the clay of this Inhabited House [i.e., the human body]. In some of them, what gathers the parts of Adam's body is the angels. In some, the one who takes up the dust of his frame is God's messengers, so that they may have messengerhood to His servants. In some, the angel of death takes up a handful of dust. In still others, God grasps with His hand a handful from the surface of the earth.

What has become implanted in the perceptual means of intellects is that the grasper of the spirit of humanity and the one who makes him die is the grasper of his body's parts. So, all these accounts are truthful in purport and agree in meaning for those who have come to understand the reality of humanity's essence.

For his essence was leavened from four clays and roots, so within it are the natural, vegetal, animal, and soulish clays. At root its vegetal clay is what was grasped by the angels who are entrusted with bringing about the inhabitation of this elemental world. So God gave it life through water: "And from water We made every living thing" (21:30).

The matter of the clay of animality is what God's messengers brought, according to His words, "Say: The spirit is from the command of my Lord" (17:85). In other words, it began to come from the world of the Command at the hands of angels intermediary between His Command and His Creation.

The matter of his rational soul and his hylic intellect is that whose intellective life comes to be by His blowing His spirit into it, according to His words, "So when I have proportioned him and blown into him of My spirit" (15:29).

As for the clay portion of him who is a servant, a knower of God, subsistent through His subsistence, and annihilated from his own essence, it is that to which He gives life through the spirit of holiness, as He says concerning Jesus: "We confirmed him with the spirit of holiness" (2:87).

Now, given that what grasps a human being's clay and gives him life is the same as what grasps his spirit and makes his precedent matter die, it is the vegetal clay whose dust is grasped by the earthly angels [and which God brought to life with water]. So, these same angels make the clay die and grasp its spirit to God, according to His words, "The angels make them die while they are wronging their souls" (16:28).

As for the animal creation, it was grasped by the "messengers," and to it God gave life by His command. So, they grasp its spirit and make it die, according to His words, "Our messengers make him die and they neglect him not" (6:61).

His rational soul, which was grasped by the angel of death and to which God gave life with a Seraphielian inblowing from Him, is made to die by the angel of death, according to His words, "Say: The angel of death [Seraphiel], who has been entrusted with you, will make you die" (32:11).[20]

As for the intellective matter and holy, divine leaven that was grasped by God, to which He gave life through the spirit of holiness, and which was attracted by the attraction of the "return" in His words, "O soul at peace, return to your Lord, well-pleased, well-pleasing" (89:27–28), it is that which God makes to die and lifts up to Him, according to His words, "God makes the souls die at the time of their death" (39:42); His words, "God will lift up in degrees those of you who have faith and those who have been given knowledge" (58:11); His words, "He has lifted up some of you above others in degrees" (6:165); and His words concerning Jesus, "Surely I will make you die and lift you up to Me and I will purify you of those who disbelieve" (3:55).

NOTES

CHAPTER ONE

1. See John Burton, *An Introduction to the Hadith* (Edinburgh: University of Edinburgh, 1994), esp. "The Theological Dimension of the Hadith," 92–105.

2. *Ṣaḥīḥ Muslim* (Beirut: Dār Ibn Ḥazm, 1995), *Kitāb al-īmān,* 1:48–49 (#7). For a full discussion of another version of the Hadith, see Sachiko Murata and William Chittick, *The Vision of Islam* (New York: Paragon House, 1994), xxv–xxxix. Unlike that version, the present text alludes obliquely to the *shahāda* (not associating anything with God) and does not mention pilgrimage. Except where otherwise noted, translations in this chapter are the editor's.

3. *Ṣaḥīḥ Muslim, Kitāb al-qadr,* 4:1616 (#1).

4. *Ṣaḥīḥ Bukhārī* (Beirut: Dār aṣ-Ṣādir, 2004), *Kitāb al-qadr,* 4:1168 (#6596).

5. Ibid., 4:1169 (#6599).

6. Ibid., 4:1172 (#6619). For similar traditions in another collection, see *Ṣaḥīḥ Muslim,* 4:1616–29.

7. *Ṣaḥīḥ Muslim, Kitāb al-qadr,* 4:1623 (#17).

8. Ibid., 4:1621–22 (#15). For a translation of Bukhari's version of the same story, see Murata and Chittick, *Vision of Islam,* 143.

9. *Ṣaḥīḥ Muslim, Kitāb al-īmān,* 1:143–44 (#299). For a similar account with different details of the individual's audacious persistence, see ibid., 1:149–50 (#310).

10. Ibid., *Kitāb al-masāqa,* 3:979 (#31).

11. From online Arabic text of *Mishkāt al-maṣābīḥ,* 2:277 [13] 2376, www.maktabah.org/hadith/collections/293-mishkat-al-masabih.html.

12. *Ṣaḥīḥ Muslim, Kitāb al-īmān,* 1:155–56 (#326). See also ibid., 1:154–55 (#322) and other variants in the same section.

13. Ibid., 1:108 (#200).

14. Ibid., *Kitāb at-tawba,* 4:1673 (#11).

15. Ibid., 4:1676 (#24).

16. Various versions of the Hadith contain this quote. On the Ḥadīth Qudsī, see William Graham, *Divine Word and Prophetic Word in Early Islam* (The Hague: Mouton, 1977), 184.

17. *Ṣaḥīḥ Muslim, Kitāb at-tawba,* 4:1674 (#14).

18. Graham, *Divine Word and Prophetic Word,* 177, Arabic text; cf. variant on 178.

19. *Ṣaḥīḥ Muslim, Kitāb at-tawba,* 4:1675 (#21).

20. Ibid., *Kitāb al-īmān,* 1:109 (#204).

21. Ibid., 1:89 (#147).

22. Ibid., *Kitāb adh-dhikr,* 4:1637 (#2). See also ibid., *Kitāb at-tawba,* 4:1670 (#1).

23. Ibid., 4:1642 (#22), and see variations there and in Graham, *Divine Word and Prophetic Word,* 127–29.

24. From online Arabic text (see note 11) of *Mishkāt al-maṣābīḥ,* 2:263 [4] 2326; see also 2:270 [28] 2350. See also *Ṣaḥīḥ Muslim, Kitāb al-birr wa'ṣ-ṣilati wa'l-ādāb,* 4:1573–74 (#2077), for a text on "oppression" with a similar central section addressed to "O my servants."

25. *Ṣaḥīḥ Muslim, Kitāb aṣ-ṣalāt,* 1:248 (#38).

26. See R. Marston Speight, "The Function of *Hadith* as Commentary on the Qur'an, as Seen in the Six Authoritative Collections," in *Approaches to the History of the Interpretation of the Qur'an,* ed. Andrew Rippin (Oxford: Clarendon, 1988), 63–80.

27. *Ṣaḥīḥ Bukhārī, Faḍā'il al-qur'ān,* 3:924 (#5015).

28. Ibid., 3:923–24 (#5010).

29. Ibid., 3:925 (#5018).

30. Ibid., 3:928–29 (#5044).

31. Ibid., 3:928 (#5041). This mention of "vocalizations" is testimony to the ancient roots of the complex and much discussed matter of variant "readings" or "ways of recitation," traditionally numbered at seven. The variations are typically very minor, including, for example, different spellings of the same word, use of a singular rather than a plural (or vice versa), or slightly different prepositions with essentially the same import.

CHAPTER TWO

1. Reprinted from Mahmoud Ayoub, *The Qur'an and Its Interpreters, Volume 1* (Albany: State University of New York Press, 1984), 247–52. In the interest of smoother reading, I have deleted Ayoub's in-text references to the primary sources of the individual exegetes; I have also inserted death dates of major exegetes.

2. From Avicenna, "On the Proof of Prophecies and the Interpretation of the Prophets' Symbols and Metaphors," trans. Michael E. Marmura, in *Medieval Political Philosophy: A Sourcebook,* ed. Ralph Lerner and Muhsin Mahdi (Toronto: Collier-Macmillan, 1963), 116–17.

3. Not a quotation from Plato's *Laws.*

4. Avicenna is quoting from the "correspondence" between Plato and Aristotle translated into Arabic from Hellenistic sources.

5. Reprinted from David Buchman, trans., *Al-Ghazālī: The Niche of Lights* (Provo, UT: Brigham Young University Press, 1998), 39–41.

6. Excerpted from Feras Hamza and Sajjad Rizvi, eds., with Farhana Mayer, *An Anthology of Qur'anic Commentaries* (Oxford: Oxford University Press, in association with the Institute of Ismaili Studies, 2008), 380–84.

7. That is, Bilād ash-Shām.

8. Excerpted from Hamza and Rizvi, eds., with Mayer, *Anthology of Qur'anic Commentaries,* 444–49.

9. *Balkafa,* that is, the Ash'arī theological principle of "not asking how" (*bī lā kayf*).

10. This formulation of the inability to "perceive" God relates to the Sufi tradition that the light of God is so intense that it dazzles and blinds human perception.

11. For a short treatise on *ta'wīl,* see "Al-Ghazālī: The Canons of *Ta'wīl,*"trans. Nicholas Heer, in *Windows on the House of Islam,* ed. John Renard (Berkeley: University of California Press, 1998), 48–54.

12. Reprinted from Jane Dammen McAuliffe, "Ibn al-Jawzī's Exegetical Propaedeutic: Introduction and Translation," originally published in *Alif: Journal of Comparative Poetics* 8 (1988): 101–13, excerpting 106–13.

13. Translated by David R. Vishanoff from Jalāl ad-Dīn 'Abd ar-Raḥmān as-Suyūṭī, *Al-Itqān fī 'ulūm al-Qur'ān,* ed. Aḥmad Sa'd 'Alī ([Cairo, 1951]; repr., Beirut: Dār an-Nadwa al-Jadīda, n.d.), 28–31.

14. The text may be corrupt here. Al-Bāqillānī does not in fact recognize any departures from the consensus when he discusses a simpler version of this point in Abū Bakr Muhammad ibn aṭ-Ṭayyib al-Bāqillānī, *Al-Taqrīb wa-l-irshād (aṣ-ṣaghīr),* ed. 'Abd al-Ḥamīd ibn 'Alī Abū Zunayd (Beirut: Mu'assasat al-Risāla, 1998), 3:295.

15. *Ẓihār:* A form of marital separation in which a man says to his wife, "You are to me as my mother's back (*ẓahr*)," that is, forbidden. See Qur'ān 33:4 and 58:1–4.

16. *Li'ān:* A form of marital separation in which a husband swears his wife committed adultery and she swears she did not. See Qur'ān 24:6–9.

17. Qur'ān 4:176, which is most commonly understood to be about people who die leaving neither parents nor children to inherit from them; cf. Qur'ān 4:12.

18. This was important to Sunnīs because they held that Abū Bakr was rightfully designated the first caliph after the Prophet's death, whereas the Shī'a said that position rightfully belonged to 'Alī.

19. As in "the authors *whom* we mentioned above."

20. As in "*the* authors," which denotes all authors generally.

21. In Arabic "*the* author" means "authors in general" (as in "the author determines the meaning of his words"), unless a specific author has already been identified, in which case "*the* author" refers back to that author only.

22. Translated by David Vishanoff from 'Abd al-Jabbār ibn Aḥmad al-Hamadhānī, *Mutashābih al-Qur'ān* (*Ambiguous Verses of the Qur'ān*), ed. 'Adnān Muḥammad Zarzūr, 1:1–8.

23. Ash'arites: Literally the Compulsionists (al-Mujbira), those who hold that God creates, and thus compels, every human action. This includes many Muslim thinkers, but Mu'tazilites use the term *Mujbira* to refer to their theological opponents the Ash'arites.

24. For the Ash'arite views of Juwaynī on abrogation and the additional key topic of inimitability (*i'jāz*), see Paul Walker, trans., *A Guide to Conclusive Proofs for the Principles of Belief* (Reading, UK: Garnet, 2000), 184–87, 189–91.

25. Reprinted from Marcia K. Hermansen, trans., *The Conclusive Argument from God: Shāh Walī Allāh of Delhi's Ḥujjat Allāh al-Bāligha* (Leiden: Brill, 1996), 357–60.

26. *Nabīdh* is a drink, fermented from dates and barley.

27. The Prophet created a special relationship of brotherhood (*ikhā'*) between the immigrants from Mecca (*muhājirūn*) and the Medinans (*anṣār*), whereby each Anṣārī gave half of his property to a Meccan (*muhājir*).

28. Abū Jahl was the Prophet's uncle and one of his leading opponents. This incident of the sacrifice of a camel occurred after the Battle of al-Ḥudaybīya (in 628).

29. This refers to the cutting down and burning of palm trees of the Jewish tribe, the Banī Naḍīr, who were accused of treachery and later deported from Medina, mentioned in Qur'ān 59:5.

30. Reprinted from Al-Sayyid Abū al-Qāsim al-Mūsawī al-Khū'ī, *The Prolegomena to the Qur'an,* translated with an introduction by Abdulaziz A. Sachedina (Oxford: Oxford University Press, 1998), 44–47.

31. For this narrative, see Qur'ān 2:23, 10:31, 11:13, 17:88, 52:34.

32. This is the original note in Khū'ī's text:

> There is no doubt that the Qur'an was revealed as a guide to all humanity, although God, in His perfect wisdom, revealed it in the language of a particular community, namely, Arabic. Hence, anyone who regards the Qur'an as the guide should understand its message in his own language. However, in rendering the message of the Qur'an in another language, it is necessary that its meanings be accurately conveyed in translation. Three important matters should be kept in mind in order to translate the Qur'an into another language:
>
> - The ostensible sense of the language as it is understood by the learned tradition of the Arabic usage;
> - The judgment of naturally guided reason;
> - The interpretation of those who were endowed with inerrancy, such as the Prophet and the Imams.
>
> Moreover, the translator should avoid personal opinions attributed to some commentators, because such exegesis will necessarily render the translation as based on personal opinion. If the above prerequisites are adhered to in the translation, then the translations should be made available in the language of the peoples who will benefit from its guidance.

33. This is the original note in Khū'ī's text: "The reference here is to a genre of poetry, or argumentation, known as *fakhr* (boasting), in which a person boasts of his ancestry, his tribe, and his own achievements and belittles those of his opponents. This genre survived, especially in poetry, long after the establishment of Islam."

CHAPTER THREE

1. Quoted in Roy Mottahedeh, *Loyalty and Leadership in an Early Islamic Society* (London: I. B. Tauris, 2001), 30–31.

2. From ʿAlī ibn Rabbān aṭ-Ṭabarī, *The Book of Religion and Empire,* trans. David Thomas, from *Kitāb ad-Dīn wa 'd-Dawla,* ed. Alphonse Mingana (Manchester, 1923), checked against the unique manuscript in the John Rylands Library, Manchester, U.K.

3. ʿAlī means that he will interpret the biblical texts according to their correct meaning and not in the way Jews and Christians have done.

4. The assumption implicit here is that the king originally followed the pure monotheism that is natural to all humans.

5. Two principles: The principles of light and darkness that were the fundamental elements of Zoroastrian belief.

6. Musaylima "the liar" claimed to be a prophet like Muḥammad among the Banū Ḥanīfa. He met Muḥammad more than once and recognized his Prophetic status, requesting reciprocal recognition from Muḥammad. After Muḥammad died he boosted his claims and was killed in 632 by an army sent by Abū Bakr.

7. Hurmiz: A late form of the name Ahura Mazda, the supreme Zoroastrian deity.

8. Qūmis: A province in Islamic Persia.

9. Al-Fākhir may be either a name or ʿAlī's abusive soubriquet for the author, "the boaster"; nothing is known directly of "his book." Qaḥṭān (the biblical Joktan) is considered the forefather of South Arabians; north and central Arabian Bedouins trace their ancestry to ʿAdnān, a descendant of Abraham's son Ishmael (Ismāʿīl).

10. ʿAdī ibn Ḥātim ibn ʿAbd Allāh ibn Saʿd aṭ-Ṭāʾī became a Muslim toward the end of the Prophet's life and transmitted a number of Hadiths from him. He was a prominent supporter of ʿAlī and fought with him at the Battles of the Camel and Ṣiffīn. He died in Kūfa at a very great age in about 687.

11. Hannah: The mother of Samuel (1 Samuel 1:1–2:10).

12. Acts 13:1, giving the name of the fourth as Manaen.

13. Acts 21:9, where Philip is called evangelist (Arabic, *mubashshir*), rather than interpreter (*mufassir*), suggesting a possible scribal error or an intentional change on ʿAlī's part.

14. Acts 15:32, making no mention of the group going to the house of Judas and Silas. This may be the result of an overliteral translation of the Syriac *dibaith,* which means here "companions," as "house."

15. Reprinted from W. Montgomery Watt, trans., "Ash-Shahrastani's Account of Christian Doctrine," *Islamochristiana* 9 (1983): 249–59.

16. Much of this paragraph follows the Qurʾān rather than Christian tradition. Christians, the Christ, and Jesus are (respectively) Naṣārā, al-Masīḥ, and ʿĪsā. The miracles referred to are those mentioned in the Qurʾān (3:49, 5:10), but Shahrastānī omits the miracle of the clay birds, contested by Christians because it is found only

in apocryphal works. The phrase "without previous seed" means the virginal conception of Jesus that is taught in the Qur'ān (3:45–7, 19:16–21); "speaking without prior teaching" presumably refers to his speaking in the cradle (19:29–33). The words "perfect sign of his truthfulness" probably mean that these matters are the proof that his prophethood is genuine.

17. The Qur'ān speaks of God "raising" Jesus to himself (3:55, 5:158) using the word *rafa'a;* "ascension" has been restricted to another word, *ṣu'ūd*. Jesus is also said to be God's "word (*kalima*) which he put into Mary and a spirit from him" (4:171, cf. 3:45), so Shahrastānī has no hesitation in using *kalima*. *Tawaḥḥud* may have been used to achieve the parallel of *tajassud* (embodiment) and may not differ from the cognate *ittiḥād,* though they are distinguished here as "unity" and "union."

18. *Imāma* here probably represents "priesthood" in a Christian source. Among the many meanings of *imām* is "leader in worship."

19. The word *waṣī* is often used, especially in Shī'ī Islam, for the successor or executor of a prophet or *imām*. In Arabic, Simon Peter is Shim'ūn aṣ-Ṣafā (i.e., Cephas).

20. The quotations are not exact. The first is implied by Mark 1:11 and several similar verses, taken along with John 1:14, where the Greek *monogenes* could be rendered by the Arabic *waḥīd,* "unique." In Matthew 16:16, Peter says, "you are the Christ, the son of the living God."

21. Melkites are typically called Malakīya and Milkīya (from which the English "Melkite" comes), meaning "the king's (or emperor's) people" and referring to the Catholic and Orthodox Church of this period.

22. The quotations are from Matthew 5:44–8 and 6:1 and John 20:17.

23. This is roughly correct. What follows is a translation of the Nicene Creed (eastern form), with one or two slight discrepancies: Jesus is not called "Lord" or "begotten," and the speaking of the Holy Spirit through the prophets is omitted. The words "begotten of the Father before all ages" are represented by *bikr al-khalā'iq kullihā,* lit., "first-born of all the creatures." But if this means that Jesus is one of the creatures, it is contradicted by the following words: "not made" (*laysa bi-maṣnū'*).

24. Mār Isḥāq: Probably Isaac the Syrian (seventh century).

25. This is mistaken, since Nestorius lived about four hundred years before al-Ma'mūn (caliph, 813–33) and was not especially noted as a philosopher.

26. Sharia generally refers to "revealed law" but here probably means "revealed scriptures."

27. Reprinted from "*The Devil's Delusion* of Ibn al-Jauzi," trans. D.S. Margoliouth, *Islamic Culture* 9:3 (July 1935): 377–84.

28. This is a Hadith given in Bukhārī's *Kitāb at-tafsīr,* concerning the interpretation of Qur'ān 26:214, "And warn your nearest of kin." After addressing several constituencies (of the Quraysh tribe), he (the Prophet) ended with the same message to Fāṭima by saying, "Ask me for some of my wealth, but . . . "

29. Translated by Thomas Michel, SJ, in *A Muslim Theologian's Response to Christianity: Ibn Taymiyya's "Al-Jawāb al-Ṣaḥīḥ"* (Delmar, NY: Caravan, 1984), excerpting 231–37.

CHAPTER FOUR

1. A related genre in this context consists of catechism-like question-answer texts, popular at varying times in Muslim communities across the world, which function as pedagogical devices for disseminating basic elements of the various creeds more "popularly." See, for example, Marston Speight and Kenneth Cragg, *Islam from Within: Anthology of a Religion* (Belmont, CA: Wadsworth, 1980), 135–44.

2. Excerpted from William Montgomery Watt, *Islamic Creeds: A Selection* (Edinburgh: Edinburgh University Press, 1995), 33–38.

3. Excerpted from ibid., 73–77.

4. Excerpted from ibid., 80–83.

5. Excerpted from ibid., 98–102.

6. Reprinted from Christian W. Troll, SJ, *Sayyid Ahmad Khan: A Reinterpretation of Muslim Theology* (New Delhi: Vikas, 1978), 257–64.

7. The following is a translation from Sayyid Aḥmad Khān's paraphrase of the Qur'ānic verses.

8. Excerpted from Shaykh al-Mufīd, *Kitāb al-Irshād: The Book of Guidance into the Lives of the Twelve Imams,* trans. I. K. A. Howard (Elmhurst, NY: Tahrike Tarsile Qur'an, 1981), 171–73.

9. Reprinted from Valerie J. Hoffman, *The Essentials of Ibāḍī Islam* (Syracuse, NY: Syracuse University Press, 2012), 205–11.

10. That is, it is entirely against the faith to apply the same judgment indiscriminately to all people; one must selectively affiliate with, dissociate from, or suspend judgment from different people based on what they believe and do.

11. Abū Saʿīd Aflaḥ ibn ʿAbd al-Wahhāb was the third imam of the Rustamid Imamate in Algeria (r. 824–72).

CHAPTER FIVE

1. For example: "innovation" (*bidʿa*) beyond adherence to the Sunna raised some concern; "deviation" (*ḍalāla*) suggested more willful noncompliance that might merit the designation "sect" (*farq,* pl. *firaq*); "free-thinking" (*zandaqa*) could characterize still looser adherence to community standards. At the outer fringes, so to speak, were those who "corrupted" the faith (*fāsiqūn*) or were downright "irreligious" (*mulḥidūn*) or "hypocritcal" (*munāfiqūn*). And separating themselves most clearly were "idolaters" (*mushrikūn,* i.e., guilty of *shirk*), "unbelievers" (*kāfirūn,* i.e., guilty of *kufr*), and those charged with "apostasy" (*irtidād*).

2. Excerpted from *Early Islamic Mysticism,* translated and introduced by Michael A. Sells (Mahwah, NJ: Paulist Press, 1996), 308–20.

3. In the discourse of scholastic theology, the translation "essence" is most appropriate for *dhāt.* However, in many Sufi texts that are consciously "nonessentialist," the term *dhāt* takes on a different meaning, one that is quite difficult to translate—identity, self, the transcendent aspect of the real that is beyond all distinction, all quiddity, and all description.

4. That is, if one affirms a deity, and then eternal attributes, those eternal attributes exist eternally, uncreated by the deity, and thus there is more than one deity; in a theological context where all things must be either creatures or deities, anything uncreated must be, by nature, divine. If Allah had eternal attributes of knowledge, will, power, and life, each of these attributes would be deities, and such a position would fall into the error of association (*shirk*).

5. The philosophers (*al-falāsifa*): As the Greek origin of the term suggests, the *falāsifa* were those Muslim thinkers who were influenced by the newly translated texts of Plato, Aristotle, Plotinus, and other Greek thinkers and who wrote under the particularly strong influence of Aristotle, although with their own original perspectives and contributions.

6. The Traditionalists (*as-salaf*): that is, the school of the "predecessors" or early ones—in other words, those who claimed to represent the earliest understanding of Islam.

7. See chapter 9 for an excerpt of Ḥasan's text in the context of ethical theory.

8. Shahrastānī's point here is that the Wāṣilīya were willing to acknowledge the Qur'ānic and Hadith affirmation of absolute divine predetermination in a variety of areas, from a person's situation in life to the appointed moment of death. But they refused to acknowledge the deity as the source of good and evil actions on the part of humans, separating this category out from divine predetermination on the grounds that if such were the case, God would require people to do what he ordains that they cannot or will not do, and such a deity would be unjust.

9. The text continues, with the fourth category concerning the conflicts between the followers of ʿAlī (later to be called Shīʿa) and those who did not recognize ʿAlī's claim to succeed Muḥammad, a conflict that came to a climax when the caliph ʿUthmān was assassinated by members of an ʿAlid faction. The fourth doctrine concerns the two opposing parties at the battles of the Camel and Ṣiffīn:

> He said that one side was in the wrong, but not essentially (*bi ʿaynihi*). Similarly, concerning those who assassinated him and those who deserted him, he maintains that one of the parties had to be sinful, just as one of the two groups cursing one another is sinful, but the sinfulness is not essential. One cannot accept the testimony of ʿAlī, Ṭalḥa, and Zubayr (the parties to the conflict) even concerning a bundle of onions. ʿAlī and ʿUthmān might both be wrong.
>
> This is the position of the head of the Muʿtazila and the founder of this particular school on the most famous companions of the Prophet and members of his family. ʿAmr ibn ʿAbīd agreed with him in his position and affirmed even more strongly than he [Wāṣil] that the determination of which of the two parties was sinful is not an essential determination. According to ʿAmr, even if one saw two men from one of the parties, such as ʿAlī and one of his soldiers, or Ṭalḥa and Zubayr, their testimony and declaration of which party was in the wrong and destined for the fire could not be accepted. ʿAmr was a master of hadith and known for his renunciation. Wāṣil was famous for his virtue and behavior.

10. There follows a technical discussion of how different groups should be classified:

> The Muʿtazilites consider a Jabrite anyone who denies that the originated power has influence in the initiation or production [of acts]. They are therefore obliged to consider as Jabrites those of their own circle who claim that engendered acts (*mutawallidāt*) are acts without any actor, since this claim denies any effect to the originated power. Those who compose treatises of classification have numbered the Najjārīya and the Ḍirārīya among the Compulsionists, while placing the Kullābīya among the Attributionists. Sometimes they call the Ashʿarites Ḥashwīya, sometimes they call them Jabrites. We have heard them (the Jabrites) affirm as their colleagues the Najjārīya and the Ḍirarīya and have numbered them among the Jabrites. We did not hear them acknowledge as their own any other groups, so we have numbered the others among them and we have numbered them among the Attributionists (*ṣifātīya*).

11. Jahm implies that once the principle of compulsion is affirmed, the human response to its obligations will be compelled.

12. Excerpted from Sālim Ibn Dhakwān, *The Epistle of Sālim Ibn Dhakwān,* trans. Patricia Crone and Fritz Zimmermann (Oxford: Oxford University Press, 2001), 115–27.

13. On this topic, see the Ibāḍī text in chapter 4 on "associating with unbelievers."

14. Excerpted from Richard J. McCarthy, *The Theology of al-Ashʿari* (Beirut: Imprimerie Catholique, 1953), 119–34.

15. The Arabic text has a note here, citing Bayḍāwī, to the effect that Muḥammad was not silent but answered straightaway.

16. *Ḥabluki ʿalā ghāribiki:* Literally, "your rope is upon your withers," originally referring to a she-camel allowed to graze freely, hence meaning here, "you are free to do as you like."

17. These were four renowned jurisprudents and founders of legal schools, and Sufyān's has long been dormant.

18. Reprinted from Richard C. Martin and Mark R. Woodward, with Dwi S. Atmaja, *Defenders of Reason in Islam: Muʿtazilism from Medieval School to Modern Symbol* (Oxford: Oneworld, 1997), 90–94.

19. Reprinted from Avicenna, "On the Proof of Prophecies and the Interpretation of the Prophets' Symbols and Metaphors," trans. Michael E. Marmura, in *Medieval Political Philosophy: A Sourcebook,* ed. Ralph Lerner and Muhsin Mahdi (Toronto: Collier-Macmillan, 1963), 113–15.

20. Self-evident truths: Literally, "the beginning [that is the primary knowledge or the first intelligibles] of the intellects."

21. Excerpted from Richard J. McCarthy, SJ, "Al-Bāqillānī: Muslim Polemist and Theologian," 2 vols. (PhD dissertation, Oxford University, 1951), 2:292–305.

22. Excerpted from Naṣīr al-Dīn Ṭūsī, *The Paradise of Submission: A Medieval Treatise on Ismaili Thought,* trans. S.J. Badakhchani (London: I.B. Tauris, 2005), 136–42.

23. Malik as-Salām is the biblical Melchizedek (Genesis 14:18–20).

24. Dhū al-Qarnayn: "The Two-Horned One," identified by many exegetes as Alexander the Great (Iskandar) and associated in Sufi and Shīʿī traditions with Khiḍr, Moses's companion in Qur'ān 18:60–82.

25. Maʿadd: Ancestor of an ancient Arabian tribe that bears his name.

26. The seven pillars are purification, confessing the imamate (embracing also the *shahāda*), ritual prayer, fasting, almsgiving, *ḥajj*, and struggle (*jihād*).

CHAPTER SIX

1. Excerpted from Muhyiddin Ibn ʿArabi, *What the Seeker Needs; Essays on Spiritual Practice, Oneness, Majesty and Beauty,* trans. T. Bayrak and R. T. Harris (Putney, VT: Threshold Books, 1992), 49–54. I am paraphrasing a translator's footnote in the paragraph just following.

2. Ibn al-ʿArabī's word here is *maʿnā,* which means a nonmaterial thing: a significance, an abstraction, an idea. In the plural it often refers to personal qualities. The closest English parallel is probably "an intangible."

3. The two hands are often held to be mercy and wrath, or majesty and beauty. Ibn Ḥanbal records a Hadith in which God took a handful in His right hand and another in His left, saying, "This [right handful] is for this [i.e., Paradise], and that [left handful] is for that [i.e., Hell]."

4. Reprinted from Jon Hoover, "Perpetual Creativity in the Perfection of God: Ibn Taymiyya's Hadith Commentary on God's Creation of This World," *Journal of Islamic Studies* 15:3 (2004): 287–329, excerpting 300–302 and 314–18.

5. Reprinted from G. W. J. Drewes, ed. and trans., *The Admonitions of Seh Bari* (The Hague: Martinus Nijhoff, 1969), 75–81 (English only), paras. 48–55.

6. Excerpted from George Makdisi, *Ibn Qudāma's Censure of Speculative Theology* (London: Luzac, 1962), 31–36.

7. Reprinted from *The Precious Pearl: Al-Jāmī's "Al-Durrah Al-Fākhirah,"* trans. Nicholas Heer (Albany: State University of New York Press, 1979), 60–64.

8. That is, by so many original witnesses and at each stage of transmission by so many transmitters that neither witnesses nor transmitters could conceivably have agreed together on a falsehood.

9. That is, insofar as they exist in themselves rather than in God's knowledge.

10. That is, accidents whose parts do not all exist together at one time, such as motion and sound.

11. This extended quote within al-Jāmī's text is from Ghazālī's *Intellectual Insights* (*Al-maʿārif al-ʿaqlīya*).

12. Dāwūd al-Qayṣarī (d. 1350), a student of ʿAbd ar-Razzāq Kāshānī (d. 1330), an intellectual/spiritual "great-grandson" of Ibn al-ʿArabī.

13. Excerpted from Ṣadr ad-Dīn Shīrāzī, *The Wisdom of the Throne,* trans. James W. Morris (Princeton, NJ: Princeton University Press, 1981), 109–13.

14. Excerpted from McCarthy, "Al-Bāqillānī: Muslim Polemist and Theologian," 2:218–20.

15. Excerpted from Shaykh al-Mufīd, *Kitāb al-Irshād: The Book of Guidance into the Lives of the Twelve Imams,* trans. I. K. A. Howard (Elmhurst, NY: Tahrike Tarsile Qur'an, 1981), 166.

16. Excerpted from Martin and Woodward, with Atmaja, *Defenders of Reason in Islam,* 103–5.

17. From *The Real Commentary on the True Teaching* (*Zhengjiao zhenquan* 正教眞詮), trans. Sachiko Murata, 2013.

18. "Mandate" (*ming* 命) is the standard translation of *amr* (command) in the two senses of the creative command, "Be!," which brings all things into existence, and the religious command, "Do this! Don't do that!"

19. "Nature" (*xing* 性) is one of the key terms in neo-Confucian philosophy, a school of thought that is sometimes called the Learning of Nature and Principle (*xingli xue* 性理學). Wang Daiyu and other Muslim scholars used the word to render Arabic *rūḥ,* "spirit." Liu Zhi, the most systematic of the Muslim scholars writing in Chinese, depicts six ascending levels of nature, a scheme derived mainly from *Maqṣad-i aqṣā* by ʿAzīz Nasafī (d. ca. 1300). Comparing Liu Zhi's scheme with Nasafī, it is clear that the nature of awareness (*xingjue* 性覺) corresponds to the animal spirit and the nature of the spiritual (*xingling* 性靈) to the human spirit. See Sachiko Murata, William Chittick, and Tu Wei Ming, *The Sage Learning of Liu Zhi* (Cambridge, MA: Harvard University Press, 2009), 167, 430.

20. "Former Heaven" (*xiantian* 先天) and "Latter Heaven" (*houtian* 後天) are terms that were discussed from ancient times. They were used by Wang and other Muslim scholars to designate the Origin and Return (*mabdaʾ wa maʿād*), also called the Arc of Descent (*qaws an-nuzūl*) and the Arc of Ascent (*qaws aṣ- ṣuʿūd*). See Murata et al., *Sage Learning,* 64–68.

21. Translation of the famous saying of ʿAlī, "He who recognizes himself recognizes his Lord."

22. Here Wang turns to a discussion of the relationship between the divine essence and the names or attributes in terms of two pairings standard in Chinese thought: substance (*ti* 體) and function (*yong* 用), and movement (*dong* 動) and stillness (*jing* 靜). He seems to be using the compound "movement-stillness" to express the manner in which the names designate the same Essence while differentiating among its manifestations.

23. Wang may have in mind the distinction commonly drawn between "names of attributes" and "names of acts."

24. Here scholars of Chinese thought would probably translate "heart" (*xin* 心) as "mind," but it seems important to maintain consistency with this extremely important technical term, not least because Islamic texts use the word *qalb* in precisely the same meanings, with the sole exception of attributing a heart to God.

25. These four activities are drawn from the beginning of the short Confucian classic *The Great Learning.* Wang expands on them in his *Great Learning of the Pure and Real.* See Sachiko Murata, *Chinese Gleams of Sufi Light* (Albany: State University of New York Press, 2000), 69–70.

26. The "Non-Ultimate" (*wuji* 無極) and the "Great Ultimate" (*taiji* 太極), originally Daoist terms, are much discussed in neo-Confucianism. By "the Human who planted the taproot," the poet means the Human Ultimate (*renji* 人極), typically discussed along with the first two. As Wang writes in the next section of his book, "The original chief of the ten thousand sages, Muḥammad, . . . is the root origin of the Non-Ultimate and the beginning of all the subtle clarities."

27. By the first group Wang means Confucians and by the second, Daoists and Buddhists.

28. The reference is to Qur'an 95:4–5: "We indeed created the human being in the most beautiful stature, then We sent him down to the lowest of the low."

29. This paragraph is drawn from Nasafī's *Maqṣad-i aqṣā,* and the next four are inspired by *Mirṣād al-ʿibād* by Najm ad-Dīn Rāzī (d. 1256); see chapter 9 for an excerpt of the latter. Liu Zhi makes use of the same passages; see Murata et al., *Sage Learning,* 220–27, 270–71.

30. This refers to the Shīʿī messianic deliverer known as the Mahdī (Rightly Guided One) and the Qāʾim (Resurrector, related to the word for resurrection, *al-qiyāma,* and to "he who rises up" / "he who stands up [to establish the truth]," related to the word for uprising, *al-qiyām*), who, according to the Imāmī (i.e., Twelver) Shīʿa, has been in a state of occultation since the late ninth century.

31. Nuʿmānī mentions that the imam has been in hiding "some eighty years" at the time he is writing.

32. The heresiographical works that have survived from the Lesser Occultation indicate that after the passing of al-ʿAskarī, his followers split into numerous sects. Nawbakhtī (d. between 912–13 and 922–23), counted fourteen factions; al-Ashʿarī al-Qummī (d. 911–12 or 913–14), fifteen; and historian and geographer al-Masʿūdī (d. 956), writing circa 943–44, twenty-one. We do not know how many of these sects continued to exist at the time of Nuʿmānī, twelve years after the start of the second *ghayba,* but it is clear from his description here that many factions continued to vie with one another. A contemporary of Nuʿmānī, the Ismāʿīlī *dāʿī* and Fatimid chief judge, Abū Ḥanīfa an-Nuʿmān ibn Muḥammad at-Tamīmī al-Maghribī, known as al-Qāḍī an-Nuʿmān (d. 974), states that eleven sects appeared after the death of al-ʿAskarī, with number 6 being the Twelver Shīʿa. Shaykh al-Mufīd (whose work appears in several excerpts in this anthology) claims that by 983–84, the Twelvers were the only remaining sect.

33. Nuʿmānī mentions the *wasāʾiṭ* only twice. It is not clear if this is another term for the *sufarāʾ* or if it refers to a different class of individuals who served as the imam's agents and deputies, similar to the term *wukalāʾ* used by scholars before and after Nuʿmānī (the related term *nuwwāb* is a Safavid invention from when the four *sufarāʾ* came to be known as *an-nuwwāb al-khāṣṣa* and the *ʿulamā* as *an-nuwwāb al-ʿāmma* of the Hidden Imam).

34. Although Nuʿmānī is the first scholar to outline the distinguishing features of the two *ghaybas,* he nonetheless includes Hadiths that mention only one *ghayba* for the Qāʾim as well, for example, the following intriguing Hadith ascribed to Sixth Imam Jaʿfar aṣ-Ṣādiq: "The master of this *amr* will have a *ghayba*. He will say

during it, 'I fled from you when I feared you. But [now] my Lord has granted me the Law and made me one of the messengers'" (Qur'ān 26:21). According to this tradition, when the Qā'im appears, he will reveal new laws and declare that he is a messenger of God.

35. From Muḥammad ibn Ibrāhīm ibn Ja'far an-Nu'mānī (Ma'rūf bi-Ibn Abī Zaynab al-Nu'mānī), *Al-Ghayba* (Qum: Anwār al-Hudā, 1422/2001–2), trans. Omid Ghaemmaghami, 2013.

36. The term "proof [of God]" (*ḥujja*) is a designation of all of the imams as well as a specific epithet of the twelfth imam in early Shī'ī sources.

37. It is often difficult to translate the term *amr* (lit., command, order, cause, affair) owing to its multifarious uses. *Amr* in Hadiths about the Qā'im has clear eschatological and apocalyptic connotations. In certain Shī'ī Hadiths, the Qur'ānic *amr* is identified as the Qā'im and/or the Qā'im's rise.

38. "As-Sufyānī" (i.e., descendant of Sufyān, prominent in the Umayyad clan) was one Abū al-'Amayṭir (politically active 811–14) who announced himself as the Sunnī "messiah" whom the Umayyads claimed would (according to ancient prophecies) restore their caliphal rule and overthrow the Abbasid caliphate (which had supplanted the Umayyads in 750). In early Shī'ī sources, likely originating in a Kūfan anti-Umayyad collection of apocalyptic literature, as-Sufyānī is presented as the chief opponent and eschatological doppelgänger of the Mahdī.

39. Day of the Camel refers to an important battle in 656, in which Caliph 'Alī defeated a rebel force mounted by Ṭalḥa and Zubayr, who had the support of Muḥammad's wife 'Ā'isha—who was carried into the fray on a camel, hence the name.

40. Ismā'īl, the eldest son of the sixth imam, Ja'far aṣ-Ṣādiq (d. 765), whom the Ismā'īlī Shī'a regard as Ja'far's successor as imam.

41. For further context on divergent views on the imamate, the various claimants to leadership, and differences between Sunnī and Shī'ī "theologies of history," see texts by Nawbakhtī and Bāqillānī in chapter 10.

CHAPTER SEVEN

1. Excerpted from Shaykh al-Mufīd, *Kitāb al-Irshād,* trans. Howard, 168–71.

2. Excerpted from John Renard, ed. and trans., *Knowledge of God in Classical Sufism: Foundations of Islamic Mystical Theology* (Mahwah, NJ: Paulist Press, 2004), 273–85. For a thematically similar short treatise of Abū Ḥāmid al-Ghazālī, see "Al-Ghazālī: Treatise on the Intimate Knowledge of God," trans. William Shepard, in *Windows on the House of Islam,* ed. John Renard (Berkeley: University of California Press, 1998), 355–59.

3. Abū Jahl was actually 'Amr ibn Hishām (d. 624), an enemy of Muḥammad whose opposition won him the nickname Father of Ignorance.

4. *Dil-gushā* is an indirect reference to the Qur'ānic notion that God expanded the center of Muḥammad's being (*ṣadr*; 94:1), an experience that Sufi theorists adapted as an essential aspect of spiritual experience along the Path.

5. Hujwīrī is punning here, suggesting that cause and means by themselves are *rāhbur* (highway robber, road interrupter) rather than *rāhbar* (one who shows the road, guide), as they might be with the help of God's grace or favor.

6. Abū Ṭālib (d. 619) was Muḥammad's uncle who took care of the orphaned boy after the child's grandfather died but who never converted to Islam.

7. Abū ʿAlī ad-Daqqāq (d. 1015) was the father-in-law and an important teacher of Qushayrī.

8. Balʿam, Son of Bāʿūr, is the biblical Baalam in Numbers 22–24.

9. Barṣīṣa was a quasi-legendary Christian ascetic/recluse who, unlike Saint Anthony the desert father, fell victim to the diabolical temptation to deny God.

10. *Iblīs* is one of the Arabic terms for the Devil, derived perhaps from the Greek *diabolos.*

11. Hujwīrī alludes to Abraham, who repudiated the idols his father carved for a livelihood and learned from the setting of the heavenly lights that they were other than God. See Qurʾān 6:76ff.

12. From James W. Morris, trans., "The Book of the Quintessence Concerning What Is Indispensable for the Spiritual Seeker" (not previously published).

13. *Rabb:* The "personal (individual) God" and the Sustainer and spiritual Teacher of each soul.

14. Alluding to many Qurʾānic verses, such as "He is with you-all wherever you-all are," or "We are closer to him than his jugular vein," and also possibly to more direct and individualized forms of God's "causing us to know."

15. Ibn al-ʿArabī ordinarily uses the expression *muʾminūn* in its specifically Qurʾānic sense, to refer to the elite group of the prophets, saints, and spiritually accomplished souls of the Friends of God, *awliyāʾ*. Thus the *duʿā* prayers mentioned here are probably referring to asking for their help and intercession, not merely blessings.

16. Alluding to the famous Hadith: "The person of faith is the mirror of the person of faith [or God, *al-muʾmin*]."

17. That is, the "perfect (spiritual) Cure" or the "Philosopher's Stone" that turns the lead of experience into the gold of spiritual wisdom.

18. *Luqma:* Literally, sustaining "morsel" of food, analogous to "our daily bread" in the Lord's Prayer. "Licit" refers to the notion of what is spiritually permissible (*ḥalāl*).

19. *Taʿmīr:* To "fill with life" (give long life), build or construct, repair and restore, and to fill up something (so that it will work properly).

20. These supplementary prayers are established practices said to be part of the Sunna; they can be extended indefinitely in length, depending on the passages of the Qur'an recited and the actual internal content of the prayer.

21. Its *iʿtibār:* That is, the essential personal "lesson" (for you at that particular occasion) and the connection between that verse and your own situation at that instant.

22. The word *ṣifāt* (qualities) can refer specifically to the divine attributes (here, the positive attributes of the Most Beautiful Names) or to the broader range of

characters, situations, and exhortations mentioned in the Qur'ān that are their dramatic exemplifications.

23. That is, as opposed to all the other (often conflicting and confusing) social, familial, and other sources of such feelings.

24. *Mubāḥ* refers to all actions that are simply religiously permissible.

25. Legal terms used here refer to the "lesser" impurities and the corresponding partial ablutions (*wuḍū'*).

26. *Makārim al-akhlāq* refers to the Hadith that Ibn al-ʿArabī goes on to cite here, in which the Prophet explained, "I have been sent to help perfect the *makārim al-akhlāq*."

27. Referring to Qur'ān 17:38: "All of that is evil and detestable with your Lord." Even closer to the discussion of the specific topic of just requital (*qiṣāṣ*) here is the explicit saying at 42:40: "The recompense of an evil [deed] is an evil like it. But whoever pardons and improves/corrects, their reward is incumbent on God. Verily He does not love the wrongdoers!"

28. Alluding to a Hadith and echoing the Qur'ānic insistence (e.g., at 2:286) that God does not do this to human beings.

29. A reference to the Qur'ānic teaching about the role of humankind as God's "stewards" or "stand-ins" (*khalīfa*) on earth.

30. An allusion to a Hadith: "Anger is the touch of Satan (on the heart)."

31. Alluding to the famous Arabic proverb (or Hadith): "Hastiness (*al-ʿajala*) comes from the devil."

32. Reprinted from Naṣīr al-Dīn Ṭūsī, *Contemplation and Action: The Spiritual Autobiography of a Muslim Scholar,* trans. S.J. Badakhchani (London: I.B. Tauris and the Institute of Ismaili Studies, 1999), 27–34.

33. *Jamāʿat:* Literally, "assembly," "congregation," or "community." In Ismāʿīlī literature, from the early Alamūt period, this word is always used for the Ismāʿīlī community in particular.

34. Ṣalāḥ ad-Dīn Ḥasan, also known as Ḥasan-i Ṣalāḥ-i Munshī, or as he calls himself in the preface to the *Dīwān-i Qā'imiyyāt,* Ḥasan-i Maḥmūd-i Kātib, was the personal scribe to Shihāb ad-Dīn.

35. The word *kūh* (mountain) is a suffix that appears in the names of a number of Ismāʿīlī fortresses in Iran. It is difficult to say which of the text editors, Qazwīnī or Taqawī, added the word "Gird" to specify the place where Ṭūsī met Shihāb ad-Dīn. This, however, was a reasonable assumption on their part because Gird Kūh, or Gunbadān Dizh, about eighteen kilometers from Dāmghān on the main route between Khurāsān and western Iran, was the site of one of the main Ismāʿīlī fortresses.

36. Ṭūsī's deduction is akin to Ḥasan-i Ṣabbāḥ's fourth proposition: "As the truth is with the first group, therefore, their leader necessarily is the leader of the truthful people."

37. The "necessity" alludes to the Qur'ānic assurance of guidance: "He said, our Lord is He who bestows creation on everything, and further gives [it] guidance" (20:50).

38. In contrast to acquired knowledge (*ʿilm-i iktisābī*), bestowed knowledge (*ʿilm-i ladunī*) does not entail the hardship of learning. In the *Rawḍa-yi taslīm,* while discussing the types of knowledge, Ṭūsī speaks of bestowed knowledge as divinely assisted knowledge (*ʿilm-i taʾyīdī*). He also states that when someone approaches the universal teacher (i.e., the imam) with questions concerning recognition (*maʿrifat*), unity (*waḥdat*), and so on, and if the teaching is conveyed in exoteric form in an orderly, graduated, and relative manner, it is called instructive (*taʿlīmī*); but if it consists of esoteric knowledge and is learned instantly, it is called bestowed (*ladunī*).

39. Reprinted from G. W. J. Drewes, *Directions for Travellers on the Mystic Path: Zakariyyāʾ al-Anṣārī's Kitāb Fatḥ al-Raḥmān and Its Indonesian Adaptations, with an Appendix on Palembang Manuscripts and Authors* (The Hague: Martinus Nijhoff, 1977), 109–17 (odd nos.).

40. For classic Persian and Turkish texts employing similar distinctions among "classes" of spiritual journeyers, see "Majd ad-Dīn Baghdādī: Treatise on Journeying," trans. Fatemeh Keshavarz, and "Vāhidī: The Seven Invocations and the Seven Journeys," trans. Ahmet T. Karamustafa, in *Windows on the House of Islam,* ed. John Renard (Berkeley: University of California Press, 1998), 301–11, 311–17.

CHAPTER EIGHT

1. I read this story years ago in the work of a medieval Persian poet but lost my original notes, and even after consulting extensively with colleagues about its source am unable to relocate it.

2. From Jāmī's *Subḥat al-abrār [Rosary of the Devout Ones]: Barg-i darakhtān-i sabz dar naẓr-i hoshyār har varaghī daftar īst maʿrifat-i kirdigār.* For a magnificent miniature painting illustrating the scene, and more on the relevant text of Jāmī, see Marianna Shreve Simpson, *Sultan Ibrahim Mirza's* Haft Awrang (London: Yale University Press/Smithsonian Institution, 1997), 148–51.

3. From the Persian text in *The Enclosed Garden of the Truth: The First Book of the Ḥadīqat al-ḥaqīqat,* ed. and trans. Major J. Stephenson (New York: Samuel Weiser, 1972), Persian pp. 1–6, translation by John Renard,

4. From Farīd ad-Dīn ʿAṭṭār, *Manṭiq aṭ-ṭayr,* ed. Muḥammad Riḍā Shāfiʿī Kadkanī (Tehran: Intishārāt-i Sukhun, 1383/2004), 392–93, ll. 3512–27, translation by John Renard.

5. From Muḥammad Iqbal, *Secrets of the Self (Asrār-i Khudī),* trans. R. A. Nicholson, in the public domain and accessed at a Web site of Muḥammad Iqbal's work sponsored by Iqbal Academy Pakistan, www.allamaiqbal.com.

6. Excerpted from W. M. Thackston Jr., trans., *Signs of the Unseen: The Discourses of Jalaluddin Rumi* (repr.; Boston: Shambhala, 1999), 101–7.

7. Excerpted from John Renard, ed. and trans., *Ibn ʿAbbād of Ronda: Letters on the Sufi Path* (Mahwah, NJ: Paulist Press, 1986), 60–62, 67–68.

8. *Maʿrifa:* God-given, experiential, intuitional, nondiscursive insight into the creature's relationship with the Creator. Junayd (d. 910), a major early Sufi mystic of

Baghdad, defines it as "the hovering of the heart between declaring God too great to be comprehended, and declaring Him too mighty to be perceived. It consists in knowing that, whatever may be imagined in the heart, God is the opposite of it."

9. This is a paraphrase of Junayd's definition of *tawḥīd,* the acknowledgment or mystical experience of God's unity: "The separation of the Eternal from that which has been originated in time by the Covenant."

10. "Expansion of the core of his being" translates *inshirāḥ aṣ-ṣadr. Ṣadr* is often rendered, in translations of the Qur'an and other works, as "mind, heart, breast," alluding to 94:1, "Have we not expanded your *ṣadr* for you." "Purification of the heart" translates "snow of the heart," one of Ibn ʿAbbād's favorite formulae. It may be an allusion to Ibn Hishām's account of how angels opened the chest of the very young Muḥammad, removed a dark substance, and cleansed his heart with snow from a golden basin.

11. Quoting al-Ḥallāj (d. 922), a famous martyr-mystic of Baghdad who was executed for claiming union with God in a way that Muslim authorities deemed blasphemous. The verse continues, "but they all came together once my eye had seen You."

12. "Mother of the Book" is the name given to the Qurʾān before it was revealed, that is, when the revelation still existed only in the mind of God.

13. Shiblī (859–945) was a mystic of Baghdad, a friend of al-Ḥallāj, famous for his rather bizarre behavior and enigmatic utterances.

14. Excerpted from *Ibn Ṭufayl's Ḥayy Ibn Yaqẓān: A Philosophical Tale,* trans. Lenn Evan Goodman (Chicago: University of Chigaco Press, 2009), 147–49, 156–57, 160–65.

15. From a sacred Hadith analogous to biblical texts in 1 Corinthians 2:9 and Isaiah 64:4.

16. Excerpted from Najm ad-Dīn Rāzī, *The Path of God's Bondsmen from Origin to Return,* trans. Hamid Algar (Delmar, NY: Caravan, 1982), 171–78.

17. Ablution with soil (*tayammum*): When water is not to be had, a token minor ablution may be made before offering prayer by dusting the palms of the hands with soil.

18. A reference to the Battle of Uḥud, the second major engagement between the Muslims and the Meccan polytheists, in the course of which the Prophet was struck by a stone cast by ʿUtba ibn Abī Waqqāṣ.

19. One of the verses revealed on the occasion of the defeat at Uḥud (Qurʾān 3:121–129).

20. In Sufi poetry the cupbearer (*sāqī*) represents "the superabundant source of grace that intoxicates all the particles of existence with the wine of conjunctive being (*hastī-yi eẓāfī*) [i.e., a being that derives from God without intermediary]." The rival (*ḥarīf*) is he who competes for the attention of the cupbearer, the wayfarer on the spiritual path.

21. Allusion to a Hadith (in the collections of Bukhārī and Muslim), in which the Prophet foretold his intercession on the Day of Judgment and his plea to God: "My

people, O Lord, my people!" See the text on intercession in chapter 1, in the "Theological Themes in the Hadith" section (*Ṣaḥīḥ Muslim, Kitāb al-īmān,* 1:155–56 [#326]).

22. An expression originating with the early Sufi Abū 'l-Ḥasan Nūrī (d. 907).

23. Excerpted from Mahmoud Ayoub and Lynda Clarke, *Beacons of Light: Muḥammad the Prophet and Fāṭimah the Radiant, a Partial Translation of "I'lamu 'l-Wara bi A'lāmi 'l-Hudā" of Abū 'Alī al-Faḍl ibn al-Ḥasan ibn al-Faḍl aṭ-Ṭabrisī (c. 1076–54)* (Tehran: World Organization for Islamic Services, 1986), excerpting 233–39.

24. That is, Abū Sa'd or Sa'īd al-Kharkushī. Ṭabrisī (or his editor) here calls him al-Ḥāfiẓ (the Qur'ān memorizer), but he seems rather to be known as al-Wā'iẓ (the preacher). Despite al-Kharkushī's statement as here reported by Ṭabrisī, traditionists have generally agreed that Fāṭima was born early in the Prophet's career.

CHAPTER NINE

1. From the Arabic text in Hellmut Ritter, "Studien zur Geschichte der islamischen Frömmigkeit, Ḥasan al-Baṣrī," *Der Islam* 21 (1933): 1–83 (Arabic on pp. 67–82), trans. Valerie J. Hoffman.

2. The language of the Qur'ānic verse is ambiguous. Did they deviate *because* God caused their heart to deviate, or when they deviated did God cause them to deviate yet more? Ḥasan obviously prefers the latter interpretation, but the former is also possible from this text, though the next verse quoted lends itself more clearly to Ḥasan's interpretation.

3. This refers to the story of Moses, who was cast upon the river (in a basket, according to the biblical account in Exodus 2) by his mother when he was an infant, to save him from the slaughter of Hebrew boys imposed by Pharaoh. He was picked up by Pharaoh's daughter, returned to his mother for nursing, and then taken into Pharaoh's household. Ḥasan's point is that when the Qur'ān says "the family of Pharaoh picked him up so he might be an enemy and a sorrow to them," it means that Moses eventually became an enemy and a sorrow to them, although he was taken into Pharaoh's household because they were delighted with him and hoped that he "might be the apple of their eye."

4. The Qur'ān tells a story in sūra 18:64–82 of a young man described as a servant of God who had been taught knowledge from Him, who encountered Moses and allowed him to accompany him provided that Moses ask no questions about any of his actions. Moses promises to be patient, but he cannot endure the seeming injustices his companion commits: he bores a hole in the bottom of their ship, he kills a youth, and he restores a wall in a city that refused to offer them hospitality. When Moses cannot keep silent, his companion says they must part, but first he explains his actions. The ship belonged to some poor fishermen, and a king was taking all ships by force; boring a hole in the boat prevented the vessel from traveling downstream, where it would be seized by the king. The youth killed by Khiḍr in the story was the son of believers, but he would have grown to be wicked and cause his parents grief. The wall belonged to two orphan boys, and beneath it their treasure

was buried. Khiḍr restored the wall so the treasure would remain intact until they grew up. All of these seemingly unjust or irrational deeds were done at God's command, on the basis of a wisdom hidden from ordinary people. Tradition has identified Moses's companion as al-Khiḍr, the Green One, who is said to have drunk from the fountain of eternal youth and attained immortality. He figures in Sufi traditions as a mystical guide who appears throughout history to guide seekers. Sufis see the Qur'ānic story of al-Khiḍr's interaction with Moses as evidence that even prophets are in need of instruction by a knower of mystical truth.

5. The Qur'ān labels as "Hypocrites" those who profess Islam but refuse to fight with the Muslims in their battles. The specific event that the verse speaks of here is the expedition in 630 C.E. to Tabuk, near the Gulf of ʿAqaba in southern Jordan, a lengthy journey across the desert.

6. The Qur'ān says, "We offered the Trust to the heavens, the earth, and the mountains, but they refused to carry it and were afraid of it. Humanity took it—he is indeed unjust ["to himself," according to Fazlur Rahman's interpretation, *Major Themes of the Qur'ān* (Minneapolis and Chicago: Bibliotheca Islamica, 1980), 18] and foolish!" (33:72). Some commentators have interpreted the Trust to be the viceroyship for which God created humanity (7:10), while others, evidently including Ḥasan al-Baṣrī, interpret it to be the Trust of moral choice.

7. The incident referred to here is a promise that Muḥammad gave to his wife Ḥafṣa, to separate from his concubine, Maryam, with whom she had found him. The Qur'ān rebukes Muḥammad for prohibiting to himself what God had made lawful to him.

8. In the Qur'ān, King Solomon knew the speech of birds and had a retinue of birds that went with him on his travels. The hoopoe tells Solomon that he has been to Sheba, where he saw the queen and her people worshipping the sun. Solomon summons her to his court and converts her.

9. Excerpted from Shaykh al-Mufīd, *Kitāb al-Irshād,* trans. Howard, 167–68.

10. Reprinted from McCarthy, "Al-Bāqillānī: Muslim Polemist and Theologian," 2:213–24, leaving out the oddly placed section on "ocular vision of God in the next life."

11. From the Arabic text of Muḥammad Abū 'l-Yusri al-Bazdawī, *Uṣūl ad-Dīn,* ed. Hans Peter Linss (Cairo: Al-Azhar University, 2003), 120–27, trans. David Thomas.

12. Translated by (the late) Lorne Kenny and reprinted from John Alden Williams, ed. *Themes of Islamic Civilization* (Berkeley: University of California Press, 1982), 152–54, 172.

13. Two core elements in the Muslim community of Medina, the Emigrants (*muhājirūn*) made the Hijra with the Prophet, and the Helpers (*anṣār*) were Medinans dedicated to Muḥammad's mission from early days there.

14. Excerpted from Martin and Woodward, with Atmaja, *Defenders of Reason in Islam,* 96–103.

15. Reprinted from Jon Hoover, "God's Wise Purposes in Creating Iblīs: Ibn Qayyim al-Gawziyyah's Theodicy of God's Names and Attributes," in *A Scholar in*

the Shadow: Essays in the Legal and Theological Thought of Ibn Qayyim al-Gawziyyah, ed. Caterina Bori and Livnat Holtzman, *Oriente Moderno* monograph series 90:1 (2010): 113–34, excerpting 127–34.

16. From the original Arabic text in "Al-Qaḍā' wa al-Qadar," *Al-ʿUrwa al-Wuthqā,* no. 7 (1884) (Beirut: Dār al-Kitāb al-ʿArabī, 1980), 89–98, trans. Vincent Cornell, some portions originally published in David Marshall, ed., *Tradition and Modernity: Christian and Muslim Perspectives* (Washington, DC: Georgetown University Press, 2013), 97–99.

CHAPTER TEN

1. Reprinted from Imām al-Ḥaramayn al-Juwaynī, *A Guide to Conclusive Proofs for the Principles of Belief,* trans. Paul E. Walker (Reading, U.K.: Garnet, 2000), 202–3.

2. Excerpted from Abū Muḥammad al-Ḥasan ibn Mūsā Al-Nawbakhtī, *Shīʿa Sects* (*Kitāb Firaq al-Shīʿa*), trans. Abbas K. Kadhim (London: ICAS Press, 2007), 46–53.

3. The Imāmīya, also called Twelver Shīʿa, who share belief in the Prophet's explicit designation of Imam ʿAlī for the caliphate and the necessity of the imamate as a political and religious leadership. Their division into many groups, as the author enumerates, is based on their divergence regarding who the imam is, in any given era.

4. Reprinted from McCarthy, "Al-Bāqillānī: Muslim Polemist and Theologian," 2:245–53.

5. "The two in the cave" is a traditional reference to Abū Bakr's companionship with Muḥammad as they hid from the pursuing Quraysh during their *hijra* from Mecca to Medina in 622.

6. Probably al-Ashʿarī himself. Here the use of the term *Imam*—as an honorific bestowed on the leader/founder of Bāqillānī's theological school—is yet another testimony to the term's polyvalence.

7. *Andar siyāsat wa ʿadl-i pādshāhān: Siyāsat* (Ar.) ("discipline" or "infliction of punishment") came to mean "exercise of political authority." *ʿAdl* (Ar.) and *dād* (Per.) mean "awarding of just decisions" and sometimes merely "just conduct" or "just character"; *inṣāf* (Ar.) (equity) is used almost synonymously. The antonyms are *ẓulm* (Ar.), *sitam* (Per.), and *jawr* (Ar.), which respectively mean "injustice," "oppression," "tyranny."

8. Reprinted from F. R. C. Bagley, trans., *Ghazālī's Book of Counsel for Kings (Nasīḥat al-Mulūk)* (London: Oxford University Press, 1964), 45–47.

9. Reprinted from Sajida Sultana Alvi, trans., *Advice on the Art of Governance: Mauʿiẓah-i Jahāngīrī of Muḥammad Bāqir Najm-i Sānī, an Indo-Islamic Mirror for Princes* (Albany: State University of New York Press, 1989), 45–47.

10. Excerpted from Muhammad Abu Laylah, *In Pursuit of Virtue: The Moral Theology and Psychology of Ibn Ḥazm al-Andalusī [384–456 AH 994–1064 AD], with a Translation of His Book "Al-Akhlāq wa'l-Siyar"* (London: TaHa, 1990), 121–24 (paras. 5–8), 172–75 (paras. 226–29, 231–39).

11. Reprinted from Muhtar Holland, trans., *Al-Ghazālī: The Path of the Worshipful Servants to the Garden of the Lord of All the Worlds* (Bristol, U.K.: Amal, 2009), 26–27, 42–43.

12. Reprinted from Hermansen, *The Conclusive Argument from God,* 232–35.

13. Reprinted from William C. Chittick, trans., *Mullā Ṣadrā: The Elixir of the Gnostics* (Provo, UT: Brigham Young University Press, 2003), 81–85.

14. Ṣadrā supports his argument, using the plurals of the words *jarīma* (offense) and *jirm* (body), from the same root, thus implying that merely being embodied is an offense against spirit; only by transmuting body into spirit can one overcome this ontological sin.

15. "Fully active word" (a term from the Arabic text of Plotinus) refers to the spiritual reality that senses and imagination construe as embodied in matter.

16. "Hylic potency" (from the Greek *hyle,* "matter") refers to the soul's innate disposition to perceive every intelligible meaning: analogous to bodily matter, the soul lacks sensory forms and yet is capable of receiving them.

17. An apparent reference to Qurʾānic texts in which the inhabitants of Hell regret that they failed to perform good works in life.

18. Ṣadrā seems to be paraphrasing Fakhr ad-Dīn Rāzī's commentary on Qurʾān 6:61.

19. "*Ṣalāt* (daily ritual prayer) is the *miʿrāj* (ascension) of the believer" is often cited as a Hadith.

20. In Islamic tradition, Isrāfīl (alternately, Seraphiel) is the archangel who will announce the end of time and the Resurrection with two trumpet blasts.

APPENDIX

Synoptic/Comparative Table of Texts

Author	Text	Author and Text Dates (w. = written)	Language and Place	Genre	Theme(s)	Sect/School *Madhhab* Affiliations
Chapter 1: Qur'ān and Hadith						
Divinely revealed	Qur'ān	610–32 Mostly oral, text formalized mid-7th c.	Arabic Mecca, Medina (Arabia)	Varied: homiletic, narrative, direct address, quasi-legal	Divine transcendence, immanence; revelation; divine power and human responsibility	N/A
Muḥammad's words, divinely originated content	Hadith: multiple editions, diverse transmitter "chains"	610–32 Oral tradition, earliest written texts 8th–9th c.	Arabic Arabia, texts gathered from Morocco to Central Asia	Recollected sayings of/anecdotes about Prophet; multiple subgenres, e.g., narrative, exegesis, dialogue	As above, plus various exegetically relevant topics and hints at underlying hermeneutical concerns	N/A
Chapter 2: Interpreting the Sacred Sources						
Various exegetes	Exegetical texts; comparison and contrasting views of words/phrases of Qur'ānic verses	8th–16th c.	Arabic Middle East, various	*Tafsīr,* summary of opinions, exemplifying broad range of methodologies and theory	Throne Verse (2:255)	Mix of Sunnī, Ismā'īlī, Shī'ī, Mu'tazilī, Sufi
Avicenna (Ibn Sīnā)	*On the Proof of Prophethood*	d. 1037	Arabic Central Asia	Brief treatise, philosophical view of prophetic mission	Verse of Light (24:35)	Sunnī, Ḥanafī, Māturīdī, philosopher

Abū Ḥāmid al-Ghazālī	*Niche of Lights*	d. 1111 w. after 1097	Arabic Baghdad	Theological treatise, Sufi and philosophical perspective	Verse of Light (24:35)	Sunnī, Ashʿarī, Shāfiʿī, Sufi
Ṭabrisī (Ṭabarsī)	*Comprehensive Elucidation of Qurʾānic Commentary*	d. 1154	Arabic Baghdad	*Tafsīr* seeking broad coverage, Sunnī as well as Shīʿī sources	Verse of Light (24:35)	Twelver Shīʿī, Muʿtazilī
Abū ʾl-ʿAlā al-Mawdūdī	*Understanding the Qurʾān*	d. 1979 w. 1942	Urdu India (Delhi, Awrangabad)	*Tafsīr*, most widely read Urdu exegetical work	Verse of Light (24:35)	Sunnī, Ḥanafī, Sufi background, Deobandī education
Ibn al-Jawzī	Prologue to *Provisions for the Journey on the Science of Exegesis*	d. 1200	Arabic Baghdad	*Tafsīr* of a renowned preacher and *madrasa* professor	Hermeneutical method/principles	Sunnī, Ḥanbalī, Traditionalist
Jalāl ad-Dīn as-Suyūṭī	*Mastery of the Qurʾānic Sciences*	d. 1505	Arabic Egypt	Chapter in a major work by a polymath legendary for prolific output	Occasions (circumstances) of scriptural revelations	Sunnī, Shāfiʿī, Shādhilī Sufi, "Salafī" views similar to Ibn Taymīya
ʿAbd al-Jabbār ibn Aḥmad al-Hamadhānī	*Ambiguous Verses of the Qurʾān*	d. 1025	Arabic Baghdad, Rayy (Persia)	Short exegetical-hermeneutical treatise	Rational interpretations of ambiguous verses	Muʿtazilī, Sunnī, Shāfiʿī
Shāh Walī Allah	*The Conclusive Argument from God*	d. 1762	Arabic Delhi (India)	Theological *summa* by famed *madrasa* professor	Causes of abrogation (*naskh*)	Sunnī, Ḥanafī, protomodernist reformer, sought to reformulate *kalām*

(continued)

Author	Text	Author and Text Dates (w. = written)	Language and Place	Genre	Theme(s)	Sect/School *Madhhab* Affiliations
Ayatollah Khuʾī	*Prolegomena to the Qurʾān*	d. 1992	Persian Iran	Hermeneutical monograph	Inimitability and miracle of Qurʾān (*iʿjāz*)	Twelver Shīʿī, Mujtahidī
Chapter 3: Muslim Awareness of Other Religious Communities						
ʿAlī ibn Rabbān aṭ-Ṭabarī	*The Book of Religion and Empire*	d. 870	Arabic Central Middle East	Excerpt of treatise	Interpreting other religious traditions' stories	Sunnī, convert from Christianity
Muḥammad ibn ʿAbd al-Karīm Shahrastānī	*The Book of Religious and Philosophical Sects*	d. 1153	Arabic Persia (NE Iran)	Monograph, history of diverse religious communities	Heresiography, non-Muslim schools	Sunnī, Ashʿarī (Juwaynī pupil), sympathetic to Ismāʿīlī thought
Ibn al-Jawzī	*The Devil's Delusion*	d. 1200	Arabic Baghdad	Treatise on methods by which Iblīs dupes various groups, both Muslim and others	Blend of polemic, heresiography, highlighting evil in false beliefs	Sunnī, Ḥanbalī, Traditionalist, major critic of *kalām*, preacher
Ibn Taymīya	*Response to Christianity*	d. 1328	Arabic Damascus	Theological/polemical treatise in response to Christian claims	Christian/Jewish alteration of their sacred texts (*taḥrīf*)	Sunnī, Ḥanbalī, Traditionalist
Chapter 4: Creed and Polemic						
Anon.	"Longer Ḥanbalī Creed"	9th–10th c.	Arabic Iraq	Extended *ʿaqīda* creedal formulation	God's attributes, variability of faith, rejection of Ḥanafī use of analogical reasoning	Sunnī, Ḥanbalī, Traditionalist

Abū Ḥāmid al-Ghazālī	From book 2 of *The Revitalization of the Religious Disciplines*	d. 1111	Arabic Baghdad	Creed incorporated into one of the forty "books" of his *summa*, *Foundations of the Articles of Faith*	Key features emphasize Ashʿarī themes	Sunnī, Ashʿarī, Shāfiʿī, Sufi
Najm ad-Dīn Abū Ḥafṣ Nasafī	*ʿAqāʾid* (creedal formulae)	d. 1142	Arabic Central Asia, Samarkand (Uzbekistan)	Creed, short catechism form	Distinctively Māturīdī themes	Sunnī, Māturīdī, Ḥanafī
ʿAllāma al-Ḥillī	*The Eleventh Chapter* (in author's summary of Jaʿfar aṭ-Ṭūsī's ten-chapter work on worship/prayer)	d. 1325	Arabic Iraq, Persia	Creed	Muʿtazilī emphasis on God's justice; added to Ṭūsī's book because Ḥillī thought knowledge of God was presupposed	Twelver Shīʿī, Muʿtazilī
Sayyid Aḥmad Khān	*ʿAqīda I*	d. 1898 w. 1872	Urdu India	Creed, one of several by author	"Metaphysical" themes in forefront: nature of existent beings, God as Creator	Sunnī, Ḥanafī, Māturīdī
Shaykh al-Mufīd	*The Book of Guidance into the Lives of the Twelve Imams*	d. 1022	Arabic Baghdad	History/chronicle of Shīʿā leaders and their teaching/sayings	ʿAlī's thoughts on heresy	Twelver Shīʿī, Baghdad Muʿtazilī (anti–"reason alone")
Nāṣir ibn Sālim ibn ʿUdayyam ar-Rawāḥī	*The Creed of Wahb*	d. 1920	Arabic Persian Gulf region	Lesson 4 of chapter 5 of the "Creed of Wahb" (of the first Ibāḍī imam)	Dialogue (Q&A) format; relations with persons of different faith	Ibāḍī, distant descendants of the 7th c. Khārijī sect

(continued)

Author	Text	Author and Text Dates (w. = written)	Language and Place	Genre	Theme(s)	Sect/School *Madhhab* Affiliations
Chapter 5: Theological Schools and Principles						
Muḥammad ibn ʿAbd al-Karīm Shahrastānī	*The Book of Religious and Philosophical Sects*	d. 1153	Arabic Persia (NE Iran)	Monograph, history of diverse religious communities	Doxography of various Muslim schools	Sunnī, Ashʿarī (Juwaynī pupil), sympathetic to Ismāʿīlī thought
Sālim ibn Dhakwān (attributed to)	*The Epistle of Sālim ibn Dhakwān*	8th c.	Arabic Iraq or Persian Gulf area	"Pulpit manifesto" critical of various "extremist" groups, incl. various Khārijī sects	Polemic against the Murjiʾa school from Ibāḍī perspective	Ibāḍī, Khārijī
Abū ʾl-Ḥasan al-Ashʿarī	*Vindication of Kalām*	d. 935	Arabic Basra, Baghdad	Short treatise on principles of Ashʿarī method	Defense of systematic theology	Sunnī, Shāfiʿī, "convert" from Muʿtazila
ʿAbd al-Jabbār	*The Book of the Five Principles*	d. 1025	Arabic Baghdad, Rayy (Persia)	Short treatise on Muʿtazilī doctrine	Summation of Muʿtazilī method	Sunnī, Muʿtazilī
Avicenna (Ibn Sīnā)	*On the Affirmation of Prophethood*	d. 1037	Arabic Central Asia	Short treatise on the foundations of prophetic revelation	Philosopher's critique of revelation using epistemological categories	Sunnī, Ḥanafī, Māturīdī, philosopher
Bāqillānī	*Explaining the Distinction between (Prophetic) Miracles and (Saintly) Marvels, Trickery, Soothsaying, and Magic*	d. 1013	Arabic Baghdad	Monograph devoted to subject of *muʿjiza*	Nature, function of prophetic miracle	Sunnī, Ashʿarī, Mālikī

Naṣīr ad-Dīn Ṭūsī	*The Paradise of Submission*	d. 1274	Arabic NE Iran, Baghdad	Treatise, theology of history	Structure of post-Prophetic?? authority	Ismāʿīlī, philosopher, Sufi, Twelver Shīʿī links
Chapter 6: Major Themes in Systematic Theology						
Ibn al-ʿArabī	*Majesty and Beauty*	d. 1240	Arabic Mecca (?), Damascus (?)	Short treatise on dimensions of *tawhīd*	On key divine attributes: "Two Hands of God"	Sunnī, Sufi, Mālikī, but held all schools valid
Ibn Taymīya	*Commentary on the Hadith of ʿImrān ibn Ḥusayn*	d. 1328	Arabic Damascus	Excerpt from longer *Collected Fatwas of Ibn Taymīya*	Divine action ongoing in world	Sunnī, Ḥanbalī, Traditionalist
Seh (Shaykh) Barī	*Admonitions of Seh Bari*	16th c.	Javanese Java	Literary conceit, ahistorical dialogue featuring Ghazālī	God's continued creativity versus heretical views thereof	Portrayed as Sunnī, Ashʿarī, Sufi
Muwaffaq ad-Dīn Ibn Qudāma	*Censure of Speculative Theology*	d. 1223	Arabic Baghdad, Damascus	Treatise critiquing Ibn ʿAqīl's (and others') Muʿtazila methods	Nature of divine voice, not allegorical	Sunnī, Ḥanbalī, pupil of Ibn al-Jawzī, Traditionalist
ʿAbd ar-Rahmān Jāmī	*The Precious Pearl*	d. 1492	Arabic Afghanistan	Excerpt from treatise	Sufi view on God's speech	Sunnī, Ashʿarī, Ḥanafī-taught, Sufi
Mullā Ṣadrā	*The Wisdom of the Throne*	d. 1640	Arabic Shīrāz, Iran	Excerpt from treatise	Philosophical theological on God's speech	Twelver Shīʿī, philosopher
Bāqillānī	*The Book of Equity Concerning Disputed Questions*	d. 1034	Arabic Iraq	Excerpt from treatise dealing with a range of theological issues	Vision of God in the hereafter	Sunnī, Ashʿarī, Mālikī

(continued)

Author	Text	Author and Text Dates (w. = written)	Language and Place	Genre	Theme(s)	Sect/School *Madhhab* Affiliations
Shaykh al-Mufīd	*The Book of Guidance into the Lives of the Twelve Imams*	d. 1020	Arabic Baghdad	History/chronicle of Shīʿa leaders and their teaching/sayings	ʿAlī's thoughts on seeing God	Twelver Shīʿī, Baghdad Muʿtazilī (anti–"reason alone")
ʿAbd al-Jabbār	*The Five Principles*	d. 1025	Arabic Baghdad, Rayy (Persia)	Excerpt from treatise	Eschatological: God and believer in hereafter	Sunnī, Muʿtazilī, Ḥanafī
Wang Daiyu	*The Real Commentary on the True Teaching*	d. 1657/58 w. 1642	Chinese Nanjing	First Islamic work in Chinese: Islam in traditional Chinese terms (Daoist, Confucian)	Cosmological imagery, relation of "the Real" to the "ten thousand things"	Sunnī, Sufi with possible links to Naqshbandīya
Ibn Abī Zaynab an-Nuʿmānī	*The Book of Occultation*	d. 956/71	Arabic Iran, Iraq, Syria	Conclusion of Nuʿmānī's introduction	Summary of materials supporting author's views	Twelver Shīʿī
Chapter 7: Knowledge and the Spiritual Quest						
Shaykh al-Mufīd	*The Book of Guidance into the Lives of the Twelve Imams*	d. 1020	Arabic Baghdad	History/chronicle of Shīʿa leaders and their teaching/sayings	ʿAlī's thoughts on knowledge	Twelver Shīʿī, Baghdad Muʿtazilī (anti–"reason alone")
Hujwīrī	*Revelation of Realities Veiled*	d. 1072	Persian India	Compendium of Sufi/mystical theology	On raising the "veil" over *maʿrifa*	Sunnī, Sufi, Ḥanafī

Ibn al-ʿArabī	*What Is Indispensable for the Seeker*	d. 1240 w. 1204	Arabic Mosul (Iraq)	Short treatise on foundational issues for seekers	Essentials of the spiritual journey	Sunnī, Sufi, Mālikī, but held all schools valid
Naṣīr ad-Dīn Ṭūsī	*Contemplation in Action*	d. 1274 w. post-1246	Persian NE Iran, Baghdad	Excerpt from "diary," autobiographical	Chronicle of experience of the theological/ spiritual quest	Ismāʿīlī, philosopher, Sufi, Twelver Shīʿī connections
Kemas Fakhr ad-Dīn	Translation of Shaykh Walī Raslān (Damascus, d. 1296) commentary on 13th c. Arabic treatise on *tawḥīd*	fl. ca. 1750	Malay Sumatra (Palembang)	Commentary on 13th c. Arabic treatise on *tawḥīd*	Classes of spiritual wayfarers	Sunnī, possibly Sufi, otherwise little known
Chapter 8: Poetic, Pastoral, and Narrative Theology						
Ḥakīm Sanāʾī	*The Enclosed Garden of Ultimate Reality*	d. 1131	Persian Afghanistan	Excerpt from opening of didactic poem (*masnavī*)	Mystical reflection on divine attributes	Sunnī, Ḥanafī, Sufi, Māturīdī (?)
Farīd ad-Dīn ʿAṭṭār	*Conference of the Birds*	d. 1220	Persian Nīshāpūr (NE Iran)	Excerpt of didactic "epic"	Journey: "valley of *maʿrifat*"	Sunnī, Ḥanafī, Sufi, Māturīdī (?)
Muḥammad Iqbāl	*Secrets of the Self*	d. 1938 w. 1915	Persian India (Pakistan)	Extended didactic poem	Sufi themes re. the "self," "modern" South Asia overtones	Sunnī, Ḥanafī, Sufi sensibilities
Jalāl ad-Dīn Rūmī	*The Discourses*	d. 1273	Persian Turkey	Excerpt from prose discourse (#23)	Diversity in languages of faith	Sunnī, Ashʿarī, Ḥanafī, Sufi

(continued)

Author	Text	Author and Text Dates (w. = written)	Language and Place	Genre	Theme(s)	Sect/School *Madhhab* Affiliations
Ibn ʿAbbād of Ronda	*"Smaller" Collection of Letters*	d. 1390	Arabic Morocco	Correspondence with disciples	Experiential understanding of divine attributes	Sunnī, Mālikī, Ashʿarī, Sufi (Shādhilī)
Ibn Ṭufayl	*Alive, Son of Awake*	d. 1185	Arabic Cordova (Spain)	Allegorical/philosophical tale of spiritual awakening	Knowledge of God's names and attributes	Sunnī, Mālikī, philosopher, mentor of Ibn Rushd
Najm ad-Dīn Dāya Rāzī	*The Path of God's Worshipful Servants*	d. 1256	Persian Iran, Syria, Iraq, Egypt, Anatolia	Compendium of mystical spirituality	Muḥammad's finality, spiritual centrality	Sunnī, Ashʿarī, Sufi (Kubrawī)
Ṭabrisī (Ṭabarsī)	*Beacons of Light: Muḥammad the Prophet and Fāṭima the Radiant*	d. 1154	Arabic Iran	Narratives of Shīʿī central figure	Spiritual status and *ʿiṣma* (impeccability) of Fāṭima	Twelver Shīʿī, Muʿtazilī
Chapter 9: Ethics in Theory						
Ḥasan al-Baṣrī	*Letter to Caliph ʿAbd al-Malik*	d. 728	Arabic Iraq	Excerpts from "epistle" attributed to author	Divine initiative and human freedom	Sunnī, Qadarī
Shaykh al-Mufīd	*The Book of Guidance into the Lives of the Twelve Imams*	d. 1020	Arabic Baghdad	History/chronicle of Shīʿa leaders and their teaching/sayings	Predetermination and Battle of Ṣiffīn	Twelver Shīʿī, Baghdad Muʿtazilī (anti–"reason alone")
Bāqillānī	*The Book of Equity Concerning Disputed Questions*	d. 1034	Arabic Iraq	Excerpt from treatise dealing with a range of theological issues	God's creation, and human acquisition, of acts	Sunnī, Ashʿarī, Mālikī

Abū 'l-Yusr Muḥammad al-Bazdawī	*Book of the Principles of Religion*	d. 1099	Arabic Central Asia (Bukhara)	Excerpt from treatise	Human moral capacity, capability	Sunnī, Ḥanafī, Māturīdī
Ikhwān aṣ-Ṣafā'	*Epistles of the Sincere Brethren*	w. ca. 950–1025	Arabic Basra (Iraq), possibly Persian authors	Excerpt from collection of *rasā'il*	Divine decree and destiny	Ismā'īlī, Sufi, Mu'tazilī, philosopher
'Abd al-Jabbār	*The Book of the Five Principles*	d. 1025	Arabic Baghdad, Rayy (Persia)	Short treatise on Mu'tazilī method	Divine power and theodicy	Sunnī, Mu'tazilī
Ibn Qayyim al-Jawzīya	*Cure for the Sick in Matters of Destiny, Fate, Wisdom, and Justification*	d. 1350	Arabic Damascus	Treatise by Ibn Taymīya's most famous student	Satan's role in creation/theodicy	Sunnī, neo-Hanbalī, Traditionalist, Sufi influence
Muḥammad 'Abduh and Jamāl ad-Dīn Afghānī	"Destiny and Fate"	'Abduh, d. 1905 Afghānī, d. 1897	Arabic Egypt, Paris	"Modernist" journal published in Paris during 'Abduh's exile from Egypt	Wide-ranging reflections on theological/ethical implications of adapting traditional understandings to "modern" circumstances	'Abduh: Sunnī, Ash'arī with some Māturīdī views; Afghānī: some Shī'ī views apparent here
Chapter 10: Ethics in Practice						
Juwaynī	*Guide to Conclusive Proofs for the Principles of Belief*	d. 1085	Arabic Nīshāpūr	Excerpt from treatise by a teacher of Ghazālī	Commanding the good, forbidding the reprehensible	Sunnī, Shāfi'i, Ash'arī

(continued)

Author	Text	Author and Text Dates (w. = written)	Language and Place	Genre	Theme(s)	Sect/School *Madhhab* Affiliations
Ḥasan ibn Mūsā Nawbakhtī	*The Book of Shīʿa Sects*	d. 923	Arabic Iraq	Excerpt from treatise by early Shīʿī exponent of Muʿtazilī method	Polemic: varied Shīʿī views on legitimate rule	Twelver Shīʿī, Muʿtazilī
Bāqillānī	*The Book of Equity Concerning Disputed Questions*	d. 1034	Arabic Iraq	Excerpt from treatise dealing with a range of theological issues	Sunnī views on legitimate rule	Sunnī, Ashʿarī, Mālikī
Abū Ḥāmid al-Ghazālī	*The Book of Counsel for Kings*	d. 1111	Persian Nīshāpūr, Iran	Short treatise	Wider context of just rule	Sunnī, Shāfiʿī, Ashʿarī, Sufi
Muhammad Bāqir Najm-i Thānī	*Admonition of Jihāngīr, or Advice on the Art of Governance*	d. 1637 w. 1612–13	Persian India	"Mirror for princes" in long tradition of Arabic, Persian, and Turkish works	Shīʿī author's views of justice and political rule for Sunnī ruler	Shīʿī in Sunnī regime, (Ḥanafī context)
Ibn Ḥazm	*Ethics and Comportment*	d. 1064	Arabic Cordova (Spain)	Excerpt from treatise on ethics	Correcting human failings, causes of anxiety	Sunnī, Ẓāhirī, Traditionalist
Abū Ḥāmid al-Ghazālī	*The Path of the Worshipful Servants*	d. 1111	Arabic Ṭus (NE Iran)	Treatise on the spiritual life	Contentment with divine destiny	Sunnī, Shāfiʿī, Ashʿarī, Sufi
Shāh Walī Allah	*The Conclusive Argument from God*	d. 1762	Arabic Delhi, India	Theological *summa* by famed *madrasa* professor	The ranks of sin	Sunnī, Ḥanafī, protomodernist reformer, sought to reformulate *kalām*
Mullā Ṣadrā	*The Elixir of the Gnostics*	d. 1640	Arabic Iran	Excerpt from treatise	Meaning of forgiveness	Twelver Shīʿī, philosopher, influence of Illuminationist school of Suhrawardī

NOTE: Affiliations in the final column are occasionally based on inference and do not account for the fact that many important figures maintained "hybrid" allegiances, especially in law (i.e., the various *madhhabs*).

ACKNOWLEDGMENTS OF PERMISSIONS AND CREDITS

PERMISSIONS

Permission to reproduce the following material has been graciously granted by the copyright holders.

Alif: Journal of Comparative Poetics

"Ibn al-Jawzī on Exegetical Method" in chapter 2: From Jane Dammen McAuliffe, "Ibn al-Jawzī's Exegetical Propaedeutic: Introduction and Translation," originally published in *Alif: Journal of Comparative Poetics* 8 (1988): 101–13, excerpting 106–13. Reprinted with permission.

Brigham Young University Press

"Ghazālī on the Similitudes in the Verse of Light" in chapter 2: From David Buchman, trans., *Al-Ghazālī: The Niche of Lights,* © 1999 Brigham Young University Press. Reprinted by permission of Brigham Young University Press.

"Mullā Ṣadrā on Forgiveness" in chapter 10: From William Chittick, trans., *Mullā Ṣadrā: The Elixir of the Gnostics,* © 2003 Brigham Young University Press. Reprinted by permission of Brigham Young University Press.

Center for Iranian Studies at Columbia University

"Najm ad-Dīn Dāya Rāzī on Muḥammad's Spiritual Finality" in chapter 8: From Najm ad-Dīn Rāzī, *The Path of God's Bondsmen from Origin to Return,* trans. Hamid Algar (Delmar, NY: Caravan, 1982), 171–78. Excerpted with permission.

Center for Muslim Contribution to Civilization

"Juwaynī on Commanding the Good and Forbidding the Reprehensible" in chapter 10: From Imām al-Ḥaramayn al-Juwaynī, *A Guide to Conclusive Proofs for the Principles of Belief*, trans. Paul E. Walker (Reading, U.K.: Garnet, 2000), 202–3. Reprinted with permission.

Edinburgh University Press

"Ḥanbalī Traditionalist Creed" in chapter 4: From William Montgomery Watt, *Islamic Creeds: A Selection* (Edinburgh: Edinburgh University Press, 1995), 33–38, www.eupublishing.com. Excerpted with permission.

"Ghazālī's Ashʿarī Creed" in chapter 4: From William Montgomery Watt, *Islamic Creeds: A Selection* (Edinburgh: Edinburgh University Press, 1995), 73–77, www.eupublishing.com. Excerpted with permission.

"Nasafī's Māturīdī Creed" in chapter 4: From William Montgomery Watt, *Islamic Creeds: A Selection* (Edinburgh: Edinburgh University Press, 1994), 80–83, www.eupublishing.com. Excerpted with permission.

"Ḥillī's Twelver Shīʿī/Muʿtazilī Creed" in chapter 4: From William Montgomery Watt, *Islamic Creeds: A Selection* (Edinburgh: Edinburgh University Press, 1994), 98–102, www.eupublishing.com. Excerpted with permission.

E. J. Brill

"Shāh Walī Allāh on the Causes of Abrogation" in chapter 2: From Marcia K. Hermansen, trans., *The Conclusive Argument from God: Shāh Walī Allāh of Delhi's Ḥujjat Allāh al-Bāligha* (Leiden: Brill, 1996), 357–60. Reprinted with permission.

"Shāh Walī Allāh on the Ranks of Sin" in chapter 10: From Marcia K. Hermansen, trans., *The Conclusive Argument from God: Shāh Walī Allāh of Delhi's Ḥujjat Allāh al-Bāligha* (Leiden: Brill, 1996), 232–35. Reprinted with permission.

Georgetown University Press

"ʿAbduh and Afghānī on Destiny and Fate" in chapter 9: Translated by Vincent Cornell from the original Arabic text in "Al-Qaḍāʾ wa al-Qadar," *Al-ʿUrwa al-Wuthqā*, no. 7 (1884) (Beirut: Dār al-Kitāb al-ʿArabī, 1980), 89–98. Portions originally published in David Marshall, ed., *Tradition and Modernity: Christian and Muslim Perspectives* (Washington, DC: Georgetown University Press, 2013), 97–99, are reprinted by permission of Georgetown University Press © 2013, www.press.georgetown.edu.

Omid Ghaemmaghami

"Nuʿmānī on the Greater Occultation of the Twelfth Imam" in chapter 6: From Muḥammad ibn Ibrāhīm ibn Jaʿfar an-Nuʿmānī (Maʿrūf bi-Ibn Abī Zaynab al-Nuʿmānī), *Al-Ghayba* (Qum: Anwār al-Hudā, 1422/2001–2), translation © Omid Ghaemmaghami, 2013.

Lenn Evan Goodman

"Ibn Ṭufayl on Acquiring Knowledge of Divine Names and Attributes" in chapter 8: From Lenn Evan Goodman, trans., *Ibn Ṭufayl's Ḥayy Ibn Yaqẓān* (Chicago: University of Chicago Press, 2009), 147–19, 156–57, 160–65, © Lenn Evan Goodman.

Valerie J. Hoffman

"Ḥasan al-Baṣrī on Moral Responsibility" in chapter 9: Translated by Valerie J. Hoffman, from the Arabic text in Hellmut Ritter, "Studien zur Geschichte der islamischen Frömmigkeit, Ḥasan al-Baṣrī," *Der Islam* 21 (1933):1–83 [67–82].

Institute of Ismaili Studies

For reproduction of the four following excerpts, I acknowledge the kind permission of the Institute of Ismaili Studies, London, as well as (for the latter two) I. B. Tauris and Co. Ltd.:

"Ṭabrisī and Mawdūdī on the Verse of Light" in chapter 2: From Feras Hamza and Sajjad Rizvi, eds., with Farhana Mayer, *An Anthology of Qurʾanic Commentaries* (Oxford: Oxford University Press, in association with the Institute of Ismaili Studies, © Islamic Publications Ltd., 2008), 380–84 and 444–49.

"Ṭūsī's Ismāʿīlī Views on Post-prophetic Authority" in chapter 5: From Naṣīr ad-Dīn Ṭūsī, *The Paradise of Submissions A Medieval Treatise on Ismaili Thought,* trans. S.J. Badakhchani (London: I.B. Tauris, in association with the Institute of Ismaili Studies, © Islamic Publications Ltd., 2005), 136–42, paras. 402–27.

"Naṣīr ad-Dīn Ṭūsī on the Spiritual Quest" in chapter 7: From Naṣīr ad-Dīn Ṭūsī, *Contemplation and Action: The Spiritual Autobiography of a Muslim Scholar,* trans. S.J. Badakhchani (London: I.B. Tauris, in association with the Institute of Ismaili Studies, © Islamic Publications Ltd, 1999), 27–34, paras. 9–21.

Istituto per l'Oriente

"Ibn Qayyim al-Jawzīya on God's Wisdom in Creating Iblīs" in chapter 9: From Jon Hoover, "God's Wise Purposes in Creating Iblīs: Ibn Qayyim al-Gawziyyah's Theodicy of God's Names and Attributes," in *A Scholar in the Shadow: Essays in the Legal and Theological Thought of Ibn Qayyim al-Gawziyyah,* ed. Caterina Bori and

Livnat Holtzman, *Oriente Moderno* monograph series 90:1 (2010): 113–34, excerpting 127–34. Reprinted with permission.

Islamic College and Journal of Shīʿa Islamic Studies

"Nawbakhtī on Divergent Views of the Imāmate" in chapter 10: From Abū Muḥammad al-Ḥasan ibn Mūsā Al-Nawbakhtī, *Shīʿa Sects (Kitāb Firaq al-Shīʿa)*, trans. Abbas K. Kadhim (London: ICAS Press, 2007), 46–53. Excerpted with permission.

Jerrahi America

"Ibn al-ʿArabī on Divine Majesty and Beauty" in chapter 6: From Muhyiddin Ibn ʿArabi, *What the Seeker Needs; Essays on Spiritual Practice, Oneness, Majesty and Beauty,* trans. T. Bayrak and R. T. Harris (Putney, VT: Threshold Books, 1992), 49–54. Courtesy of Jerrahi America, with special thanks to Yurdaer Doganata.

Ralph Lerner

"Avicenna on the Metaphorical Meanings of the Verse of Light" in chapter 2: From Avicenna, "On the Proof of Prophecies and the Interpretation of the Prophets' Symbols and Metaphors," trans. Michael E. Marmura, in *Medieval Political Philosophy: A Sourcebook,* ed. Ralph Lerner and Muhsin Mahdi (Toronto: Collier-Macmillan, 1963, © the Free Press of Glencoe), 116–17. Reprinted with permission.

"Avicenna on Assessing Claims to Prophetic Revelation" in chapter 5: From Avicenna, "On the Proof of Prophecies and the Interpretation of the Prophets' Symbols and Metaphors," trans. Michael E. Marmura, in *Medieval Political Philosophy: A Sourcebook,* ed. Ralph Lerner and Muhsin Mahdi (Toronto: Collier-Macmillan, 1963, © the Free Press of Glencoe), 113–15.Reprinted with permission.

Thomas Michel, SJ

"Ibn Taymīya on Christian Alteration of Scripture" in chapter 3: From *A Muslim Theologian's Response to Christianity: Ibn Taymiyya's "Al-Jawāb al-Ṣaḥīḥ,"* trans. Thomas Michel, SJ (Delmar, NY: Caravan, 1984), excerpting 231–37. Excerpted with permission.

James W. Morris

"Mullā Ṣadrā on Divine Speech and Attributes" in chapter 6: From Ṣadr ad-Dīn Shīrāzī, *The Wisdom of the Throne,* trans. James W. Morris (Princeton, NJ: Princeton University Press, 1981), 109–13. Excerpted with permission.

"Ibn al-ʿArabī on What Is Indispensable for the Spiritual Seeker" in chapter 7: From "The Book of the Quintessence Concerning What Is Indispensable for the Spiritual Seeker" (not previously published), translation © James W. Morris.

Sachiko Murata

"Wang Daiyu on Translating *Tawḥīd* into Chinese Traditional Terms" in chapter 6: From *The Real Commentary on the True Teaching* (*Zhengjiao zhenquan* 正教眞詮), translation © Sachiko Murata, 2013.

Oneworld

"ʿAbd al-Jabbār's Muʿtazilī *Five Principles*" in chapter 5: From Richard C. Martin and Mark R. Woodward, with Dwi S. Atmaja, *Defenders of Reason in Islam: Muʿtazilism from Medieval School to Modern Symbol* (Oxford: Oneworld, 1997), 90–94. Reprinted with permission.

"ʿAbd al-Jabbār on God and Humanity in the Hereafter" in chapter 6: From Richard C. Martin and Mark R. Woodward, with Dwi S. Atmaja, *Defenders of Reason in Islam: Muʿtazilism from Medieval School to Modern Symbol* (Oxford: Oneworld, 1997), 103–5. Excerpted with permission.

"ʿAbd al-Jabbār's Muʿtazilī View of Ethical Principles and Theodicy" in chapter 9: From Richard C. Martin and Mark R. Woodward, with Dwi S. Atmaja, *Defenders of Reason in Islam: Muʿtazilism from Medieval School to Modern Symbol* (Oxford: Oneworld, 1997), 96–103. Excerpted with permission.

Oxford University Press

"Ayatollah Khuʾī on the Divine Miracle of the Qurʾān" in chapter 2: From Al-Sayyid Abū al-Qāsim al-Mūsāwī al-Khuʾī, *Prolegomena to the Qurʾan,* trans. Abdulaziz A. Sachedina (1998), ca. 2,100 words from pp. 44–47. By permission of Oxford University Press, U.S.A.

"Sālim ibn Dhakwān on the Murjiʾa" in chapter 5: From Sālim Ibn Dhakwān, *The Epistle of Sālim Ibn Dhakwān,* trans. Patricia Crone and Friedrich Zimmermann (2001), ca. 2,076 words from pp. 115–27. By permission of Oxford University Press, U.S.A.

"Ibn Taymīya on God's Perpetual Creativity" in chapter 6: From Jon Hoover, "Perpetual Creativity in the Perfection of God: Ibn Taymiyya's Hadith Commentary on God's Creation of This World," *Journal of Islamic Studies* 15:3 (2004): 287–329, excerpting 300–302 and 314–18. By permission of Oxford University Press, U.S.A.

Paulist Press Inc.

"Shahrastānī's Doxography of Muslim Schools" in chapter 5: From *Early Islamic Mysticism,* translated and introduced by Michael A. Sells (Mahwah, NJ: Paulist Press, 1996), 308–20, © Michael A. Sells, www.paulistpress.com. Reprinted with permission.

"Hujwīrī on Experiential Knowledge" in chapter 7: From John Renard, ed. and trans., *Knowledge of God in Classical Sufism: Foundations of Islamic Mystical Theology* (Mahwah, NJ: Paulist Press, 2004), 273–85, © John Renard, www.paulistpress.com. Reprinted with permission.

"Ibn ʿAbbād on Relating to God's Attributes and Names" in chapter 8: From John Renard, ed. and trans., *Ibn ʿAbbād of Ronda: Letters on the Sufi Path* (Mahwah, NJ: Paulist Press, 1986), 60–62, 67–68, © John Renard, www.paulistpress.com. Reprinted with permission.

Pontifical Institute for the Study of Arabic and Islam

"Shahrastānī's Heresiography on Non-Muslim Communities" in chapter 3: From W. Montgomery Watt, trans., "Ash-Shahrastani's Account of Christian Doctrine," *Islamochristiana* 9 (1983): 249–59. Reprinted with permission.

John Renard

"Sanāʾī on God's Attributes, Unity, and Anthropomorphisms" in chapter 8: translation from the Persian text in *The Enclosed Garden of the Truth, The First Book of the Ḥadīqat al-ḥaqīqat*, ed. Major J. Stephenson (New York: Samuel Weiser, 1972), Persian 1-6, translation © 2013 John Renard.

"ʿAṭṭār on the Valley of Experiential Knowledge" in chapter 8: From Farīd ad-Dīn ʿAṭṭār, *Manṭiq aṭ-Ṭayr*, ed. Muḥammad Riḍā Shāfiʿī Kadkanī (Tehran: Intishārāt-i Sukhun, 1383/2004), 392–93, lines 3512–27, translation © 2013 John Renard.

Society of Jesus of New England

"Bāqillānī on Prophetic Miracle and Veracity" in chapter 5: From Richard J. McCarthy, SJ, "Al-Bāqillānī: Muslim Polemist and Theologian," 2 vols. (PhD dissertation, Oxford University, 1951), 2:292–305. Excerpted with permission.

"Bāqillānī on the Vision of God in the Next Life" in chapter 6: From Richard J. McCarthy, SJ, "Al-Bāqillānī: Muslim Polemist and Theologian," 2 vols. (PhD dissertation, Oxford University, 1951), 2:218–20. Excerpted with permission.

"Bāqillānī's Ashʿarī Perspective on Human Acquisition of Divinely Created Acts" in chapter 9: From Richard J. McCarthy, SJ, "Al-Bāqillānī: Muslim Polemist and Theologian," 2 vols. (PhD dissertation, Oxford University, 1951), 2:213–24. Reprinted with permission.

"Bāqillānī on Rightly Guided Caliphs and the Imāmate" in chapter 10: From Richard J. McCarthy, SJ, "Al-Bāqillānī: Muslim Polemist and Theologian," 2 vols. (PhD dissertation, Oxford University, 1951), 2:245–53. Reprinted with permission.

Springer Science+Business Media B.V. of Dordrecht

"Javanese *Admonitions of Seh Bari* on God's Perpetual Creativity" in chapter 6: From G. W. J. Drewes, ed. and trans., *The Admonitions of Seh Bari* (The Hague: Martinus Nijhoff, 1969), 75–81 (English only), paras. 48–55. Reprinted with kind permission.

"Kemas Fakhr ad-Dīn on the Quest for Self and God's Oneness" in chapter 7: From G. W. J. Drewes, *Directions for Travellers on the Mystic Path: Zakariyyā' al-Anṣ ārī's Kitāb Fatḥ al-Raḥmān and Its Indonesian Adaptations, with an Appendix on Palembang Manuscripts and Authors* (The Hague: Martinus Nijhoff, 1977), 109–17 (odd nos.). Reprinted with kind permission.

State University of New York Press

"Varieties of Exegesis (*Tafsīr*) on the Throne Verse" in chapter 2: From Mahmoud M. Ayoub, ed., *The Qur'ān and its Interpreters, Volume 1*. The State University of New York Press, © 1984, SUNY. All rights reserved, reprinted by permission.

"Jāmī on God's Voice" in chapter 6: From Nicholas Heer, trans., *The Precious Pearl by 'Abd al-Raḥmān al-Jāmī*. The State University of New York Press, © 1979, SUNY. All rights reserved, reprinted by permission.

"Muḥammad Bāqir Najm-i Thānī on Justice and Discipline" in chapter 10: From Sajida Sultana Alvi, trans., *Advice on the Art of Governance: Mau'iẓah-i Jahāngīrī of Muhammad Bāqir Najm-i Sānī; An Indo-Islamic Mirror for Princes*. The State University of New York Press, © 1989, SUNY. All rights reserved, reprinted by permission.

Syracuse University Press

"Ibāḍī Views on Associating with Muslims of Deficient Faith" in chapter 4: From Valerie J. Hoffman, *The Essentials of Ibāḍī Islam* (Syracuse, NY: Syracuse University Press, 2012), 205–11. Reprinted with permission.

Taha Publishers Ltd.

"Ibn Ḥazm on Anxiety, Self-Knowledge, and Virtue" in chapter 10: From Muhammad Abu Laylah, In Pursuit of Virtue: The Moral Theology and Psychology of Ibn Ḥazm al-Andalusī [384–456 AH 994–1064 AD], with a Translation of His Book "Al-Akhlāq wa'l-Siyar" (London: TaHa, 1990), 121–24 (paras. 5–8), 172–75 (paras. 226–29, 231–39). Excerpted with permission.

Wheeler M. Thackston

"Rūmī on the Many Languages of God Talk" in chapter 8: From W. M. Thackston Jr., trans., *Signs of the Unseen: The Discourses of Jalaluddin Rumi* (repr.; Boston: Shambhala, 1999), 101–7. Excerpted with permission.

David Thomas

"'Alī ibn Rabbān aṭ-Ṭabarī on Interpreting the Stories of Other Faiths" in chapter 3: From 'Alī ibn Rabbān aṭ-Ṭabarī, *The Book of Religion and Empire*, ed. Alphonse Mingana, *Kitāb ad-Dīn wa 'd-Dawla* (Manchester, 1923), checked against the unique manuscript in the John Rylands Library, Manchester, UK. Translation © 2013 David Thomas.

"Bazdawī's Māturīdī Perspective on Moral Capacity" in chapter 9: From the Arabic text of Muḥammad Abū 'l-Yusri al-Bazdawī, *Uṣūl ad-Dīn,* ed. Hans Peter Linss (Cairo: Al-Azhar University, 2003), 120–27, translation © David Thomas, 2013.

Christian W. Troll, SJ

"Sayyid Aḥmad Khān's Modern Sunnī Creed" in chapter 4: From Christian W. Troll, SJ, *Sayyid Ahmad Khan: A Reinterpretation of Muslim Theology* (New Delhi: Vikas, 1978), 257–64. Reprinted with permission of author.

Trustees of the E. J. W. Gibb Memorial Trust

"Ibn Qudāma on the Divine Voice" in chapter 6: From George Makdisi, *Ibn Qudāma's Censure of Speculative Theology* (London: Luzac, 1962), 31–36. The University of California Press acknowledges the material derived from this work published by the Trustees of the E. J. W. Gibb Memorial Trust, who have granted their consent.

University of Durham Press

"Al-Ghazālī on the Larger Context of Islamic Governance" in chapter 10: From F. R. C. Bagley, trans., *Ghazālī's Book of Counsel for Kings (Nasīḥat al-Mulūk)* (London: Oxford University Press, 1964), 45–47. Reprinted with permission.

David R. Vishanoff

"Suyūṭī on the Occasions of Revelation" in chapter 2: Translated by David R. Vishanoff from Jalāl ad Dīn 'Abd ar Raḥmān as Suyūṭī, *al Itqān fī 'ulūm al Qur'an*, ed. Aḥmad Sa'd 'Alī ([Cairo, 1951]; reprinted Beirut: Dār an-Nadwa al-Jadīda, [n.d.]), 28–31. © 2013 David R. Vishanoff.

"ʿAbd al-Jabbār on Rational Interpretation of Scripture" in chapter 2: Translated by David R. Vishanoff from ʿAbd al-Jabbār ibn Aḥmad al-Hamadhānī, *Mutashābih al-Qurʾān* (*Ambiguous Verses of the Qurʾān*), ed. ʿAdnān Muḥammad Zarzūr (Cairo: Dār at-Turāth, 1969), 1:1–8. © 2013 David R. Vishanoff.

John Alden Williams

"Brethren of Purity on Divine Initiative, Human Responsibility, and Law" in chapter 9: Translated by Lorne Kenny from John Alden Williams, ed. *Themes of Islamic Civilization* (Berkeley: University of California Press, 1982), 152–54, 172. Reprinted with permission.

CREDITS

Grateful acknowledgment is made to the previous publishers of the following materials:

Amal Press

"Ghazālī on Contentment with Divine Destiny" in chapter 10: From Muhtar Holland, trans. *Al-Ghazālī: The Path of the Worshipful Servants to the Garden of the Lord of All the Worlds,* © 2009 Amal Press, excerpting 26–27, 42–43.

Islamic Culture

"Ibn al-Jawzī on the Devil's Deception of Jews and Christians" in chapter 3: From D. S. Margoliouth, "The Devil's Delusion of Ibn al-Jauzi," originally published in *Islamic Culture* 9:3 (July, 1935): 377–84.

Tahrike Tarsile Qur'an

"ʿAlī ibn Abī Ṭālib on Heresy" in chapter 4: From I. K. A. Howard, trans., *Shaykh al-Mufīd, Kitāb al-Irshād: The Book of Guidance into the Lives of the Twelve Imams.* © 1981 Tahrike Tarsile Qur'an/ Muḥammadī Trust, excerpting171–73.

"ʿAlī on the Vision of God" in chapter 6: From I. K. A. Howard, trans., *Shaykh al-Mufīd, Kitāb al-Irshād: The Book of Guidance into the Lives of the Twelve Imams.* © 1981 Tahrike Tarsile Qur'an/ Muḥammadī Trust, excerpting 166.

"ʿAlī on Knowledge and the Spiritual Life" in chapter 7. From I. K. A. Howard, trans., *Shaykh al-Mufīd, Kitāb al-Irshād: The Book of Guidance into the Lives of the Twelve Imams.* © 1981 Tahrike Tarsile Qur'an/ Muḥammadī Trust, excerpting 168–71.

"Shaykh al-Mufīd on Divine Predetermination and the Battle of Ṣiffīn" in chapter 9. From I. K. A. Howard, trans., *Shaykh al-Mufīd, Kitāb al-Irshād: The Book of Guidance into the Lives of the Twelve Imams.* © 1981 Tahrike Tarsile Qur'an/ Muḥammadī Trust, excerpting 167–68.

World Organization for Islamic Services

"A Shīʿī Narrative on the Spiritual Status of Fāṭima Az-Zahrāʾ" in chapter 8: From *Beacons of Light: Muḥammad the Prophet and Fātimah the Radiant,* a Partial Translation of *Iʿlamu 'l-Wara bi Aʿlāmi 'l-Hudā* of Abū ʿAlī al-Faḍl ibn al-Ḥasan ibn al-Faḍl aṭ-Ṭabrisī (c. 1076–1154), by Mahmoud Ayoub and Lynda Clarke. © 1986 World Organization for Islamic Services, excerpting 233–39.

INDEX OF NAMES OF PERSONS

Aaron (Hārūn), 94, 176, 377
ʿAbbās al-ʿAnbarī, 159
ʿAbd al-Jabbār ibn Aḥmad al-Hamadhānī, 47, 58–59, 63, 160, 211–12, 342
ʿAbd Allāh ibn Anīs al-Juhanī. *See* Juhanī
ʿAbd Allāh ibn az-Zibaʿrā, 156
ʿAbd Allāh ibn Saʿīd al-Kilānī, 146
ʿAbd Allāh ibn Saʿīd al-Qaṭṭān, 333
ʿAbd Allāh ibn Sūriya, 94
ʿAbd Allāh Mubārak, 247
ʿAbd al-Malik ibn Marwān, 141, 317
ʿAbd al-Mālik ibn Ṭarif, 388
ʿAbd al-Muṭṭalib, 40
ʿAbd al-Qādir al-Jīlānī, 267
ʿAbd al-Wahhāb, Aflaḥ ibn, 131, 407n11
ʿAbd ar-Raḥmān ibn Abī Bakr, 54
ʿAbd ar-Raḥmān ibn Mahdī, 159
ʿAbd ar-Raḥmān ibn Muḥammad al-Muḥāribī, 197
ʿAbd ar-Razzāq al-Kāshānī, 410n12
Abduh, Muḥammad, 358
Abraham (Ibrāhīm), 9, 16, 19, 39, 87, 94, 100, 150–53, 176–79, 246, 278, 285, 303–4, 330, 353, 405n9, 414n11
Absāl, 299–302
Abū ʿAbd Allāh ibn Ḥāmid, 93
Abū ʿAlī ad-Daqqāq, 244
Abū Bakr aṣ-Ṣiddīq, 56–57, 148–49, 210–11, 329, 372–378, 403n18, 405n6, 420n5
Abū Dāwūd, 101, 188, 200
Abū ʾd-Dardāʾ, 18, 376
Abū ʾḍ-Ḍuḥā, 197
Abū Dharr, 23, 29, 131–32
Abū Ḥanīfa, 160, 333, 373, 412n32
Abū Hāshim, 90, 140
Abū Ḥayyān at-Tawḥīdī, 77
Abū Hurayra, 14–17, 23–24, 94
Abū Isḥaq, 50, 312
Abū Jaʿfar al-Bāqir, 40, 309
Abū Jaʿfar al-Manṣūr, 140
Abū Jahl, 68, 239, 404n28, 413n3
Abū Lahab, 176
Abū ʾl-ʿĀliya, 38
Abū ʾl-ʿAmayṭir, 413n38
Abū ʾl-Ḥusayn of Basra, 140
Abū Maʿshar Najīʿ, 55
Abū Muslim, 38, 50, 53, 97, 188, 417n21
Abū Saʿd, 418n24
Abū Sahl Suʿlūkī, Shaykh, 244
Abū Saʿīd Aflaḥ ibn ʿAbd al-Wahhāb, 131, 407n11
Abū Ṣāliḥ, 151
Abū Shimr, 373
Abū Sulaymān, 77
Abū Ṭālib, 242, 414n6
Abū Thumayla ibn ʿAbd al-Muʾmin, 55
Adam, 7, 15–19, 40, 87, 94, 108, 127, 175–79, 208–9, 259, 291–92, 303–8, 340, 351–57, 380, 398
ʿAdī ibn Ḥātim ibn ʿAbd Allāh ibn Saʿd aṭ-Ṭāʾī, 82, 405n10
ʿAdnān, 82
Afghānī, Jamāl ad-Dīn al-, 358
Agabus, 85
Aḥmad ibn Ḥanbal, 53, 58, 104, 146, 159, 190, 197, 410n3

ʿĀʾisha, 15, 49, 54, 310–11, 413n39
Akbar, 382
Alexander the Great, 365, 410n24. *See also* Dhū ʾl-Qarnayn
Alexander of Aphrodisias, 34
ʿAlī, 29, 40, 126, 128, 146–47, 176, 179–80, 211, 228, 235–37, 241, 276, 310–13, 325–26, 372–78, 403n18, 405n10, 408n9, 411n21, 413n39, 420n3
ʿAlī ar-Riḍā, 37, 40, 310
ʿAlī ibn al-Ḥusayn, 55
ʿAlī ibn Rabbān aṭ-Ṭabarī, 78–79, 86
ʿAmr ibn ʿAbīd, 142, 408n9
ʿAmr ibn al-ʿĀs, ʿAbd Allāh ibn, 188
ʿAmr ibn Dīnār, 159
ʿAmr ibn Maʿdī Karab, 53
ʿAmr ibn ʿUbayd, 374
Anas ibn Mālik, 19, 310–12
Aristotle, 33–34, 189, 192, 206, 402n4, 408n5
Arius, 89
Ashʿarī, Abū ʾl-Ḥasan al-, 109, 144, 146, 151, 333, 339, 420n6,
Ashʿarī, Abū Mūsā al-, 29
Ashʿarī al-Qummī, al-, 412n32
ʿAsqalānī, Shaykh al-Islām Abū ʾl-Faḍl Ibn Ḥajar al-, 52
ʿAṭṭār, Farīd ad-Dīn, 270, 276, 279, 287
Avicenna (Ibn Sīnā), 32, 35, 164, 189, 205–6

Balʿam, 245, 329, 414n8
Bāqillānī, Abū Bakr al-, 52, 167–68, 209–10, 318, 326, 371, 375, 403n14, 420n6
Bāqir Najm-i Thānī, Muḥammad, 382
Barāʾ, al-, 50
Barnabas, 85
Barṣīṣa, 245, 414n9
Bazdawī, Abū ʾl-Yusr Muḥammad al-, 318, 332–33
Bishr al-Marīsī, 333, 339
Bishtāṣaf, 80
Bisṭāmī, Abū Yazīd al-, 30, 248, 304
Bukhārī, Muḥammad al-, 24, 50–51, 53, 186, 188, 190
Burayda, 313

Caesar, 95, 363
Christ. *See* Jesus
Companions of Muḥammad, 12–13, 24, 28–29, 55, 72, 100, 151–52, 157–59, 197, 210, 251, 309, 331, 377–379

Ḍaḥḥāk, aḍ-, 29, 38, 40, 50, 381
Daniel, 84
Dārimī, 190
David, 83–84, 94, 304, 381
Dāwūd al-Iṣfahānī, 146
Dāwūd al-Qayṣarī, 410n12
Dhū ʾl-Qarnayn, 176, 410n24. *See also* Alexander the Great
Dhū ʾn-Nūn, 246–47
Ḍirār ibn ʿAmr, 373–74

Elisha, 84
Ezekiel, 84

Faḍl ar-Raqāshī, al-, 373
Fuḍayl ibn ʿAyyād, al-, 355
Fākhir, al-, 82, 405n9
Fārābī, al-, 206
Fāṭima, 96, 229, 296, 309–13, 406n28, 418n24

Gabriel, 7–8, 13–14, 25–26, 40, 91, 104, 257, 274, 312, 352
Genghis Khan, 365–66
Ghaylān of Damascus, 140, 373
Ghazālī, Abū Ḥāmid al-, 32, 34–35, 109, 192–95, 201, 259, 366, 369, 380, 384, 389

Ḥaddād, Abū Ḥafṣ, 249
Ḥaddād, Abū ʾl-Miqdām Thābit al-, 374
Ḥāfiẓ, Abū Saʿīd al-, 309
Haggai, 84
Ḥajarī, al-, 312
Ḥajjāj, al-, 171
Ḥallāj, Abū Manṣūr al-, 304, 417n11
Hannah, 84, 405n11
Ḥarith al-Aʿwar, al-, 238
Hārūn ar-Rashīd, 253
Ḥasan (son of ʿAlī), 310–13, 378
Ḥasan al-Basrī, al-, 29–30, 38–39, 41, 49–50, 140–42, 317 419n6
Ḥasan ibn ʿAlī al-ʿAskarī, 226, 412n32
Ḥasan ibn Ṣāliḥ ibn Ḥayy, 372, 374
Ḥasan-i Ṣabbāḥ, 415n36

Ḥayy ibn Yaqẓān, 296–302
Hilāl ibn Umayya, 54
Ḥillī, ʿAllāma-i-, 116
Hishām ibn ʿAbd al-Mālik, 140
Hishām ibn al-Ḥakam, 143, 333
Hishām ibn Ḥakīm ibn Ḥizām, 26
Hosea, 84
Hūd, 151
Ḥudhayfa, 93
Hujwīrī, 238–239
Ḥusayn (son of ʿAlī), 276, 310–313, 341

Ibn ʿAbbād of Ronda, 287, 292
Ibn ʿAbbās, 20, 25, 29, 37–39, 49 –55, 210, 311–12, 379
ibn Abī Waqqāṣ, ʿUtba, 417n18
ibn al-ʿArabī, Muḥammād ibn ʿAbd Allāh Abū Bakr, 58
ibn al-ʿArabī, Muḥyī ʼd-Dīn, 30, 181, 201–5, 250, 410n12
ibn al-Ḥanafīya, Muḥammād, 28
Ibn al-Jawzī, 47, 92, 96
ibn al-Madīnī, ʿAlī, 51
Ibn al-Mubārak, 190
Ibn ʿAqīl, 196–97
Ibn at-Tammār, 373
ibn Bābawayh, Abū Jaʿfar, 40
Ibn Daqīq al-ʿĪd, 52
ibn Ḥanbal, Aḥmad. *See* Aḥmad ibn Ḥanbal
Ibn Ḥazm, 384–85
ibn Kaʿb al-Quraẓī, Muḥammad, 55
Ibn Kullāb, 333, 339
Ibn Māja, 101
Ibn Masʿūd, 49, 391
Ibn Qayyim al-Jawzīya, 350
ibn Qudāma, Muwaffaq ad-Dīn, 195–96
Ibn Sīnā. *See* Avicenna
Ibn Taymīya, 52, 55, 96–97, 186, 350
IbnṬufayl, 296–297
ibn ʿUtayba, al-Ḥakam, 374
ibn Yazīd, Jābir, 309
Ibn Zayd, 29, 39–41
Ibrāhīm (Son of Muhammad), 309
Ibrahīm an-Naẓẓam. *See* Naẓẓam, Ibrahīm an-
Idrīs ibn ʿAbd Allāh al-Ḥasanī, 140
ʿIkrima, 39, 49–50
ʿImrān, 311
ʿImrān ibn Ḥusayn, 186–88
Imruʾ ʾl-Qays, 171
Iqbal, Muḥammad, 270, 278–281
ʿĪsā. *See* Jesus
ʿĪsā ibn Rāshid, 40
Isaac (Isḥāq), 9, 150, 176
Isaiah, 83–84
Ismāʿīl (Ishmael), 9, 39, 83, 100, 150, 176, 405n9
Ismāʿīl ibn ʿAlī ʿAbd Allāh, 231
Isrāfīl, 107, 421n20
Īyās ibn Muʿāwiya, 49

Jaʿbarī, Burhān ad-Dīn Ibrāhīm ibn ʿUmar al-, 52
Jābir ibn ʿAbd Allāh, 49–50, 56
Jacob (Baradaeus), 91, 95
Jacob (son of Isaac), 9, 150, 304
Jaddī, Shaykh al-, 193–95
Jaʿfar aṣ-Ṣādiq, 309, 412n34, 413n40
Jaʿfar ibn Muḥammad, 159, 379
Jahm ibn Ṣafwān, 142–44, 373, 409n11
Jalāl ad-Dīn Rūmī. *See* Rūmī, Jalāl ad-Dīn
Jāmī, ʿAbd ar-Raḥmān, 201
Jeremiah, 83
Jesus (Christ), 9, 19, 72, 86–90, 95, 101, 156–57, 176–79, 208–9, 245, 304, 349, 399, 405n16, 406n17
Job, 304
John (Evangelist), 101
Joseph, 3, 304
Joshua (Yūshaʿ bin Nūn), 176
Jubbāʾī, al-, 140
Judas (betrayer of Christ), 176
Juhanī, Maʿbad al-, 197
Juwaynī, Imam al-Ḥaramayn al-, 369

Kaʿb ibn al-Ashraf, 57
Kalbī, al-, 39
Kathīr an-Nawwāʾ, 374
Kemas Fakhr ad-Dīn of Palembang, 264–5
Khān, Sayyid Aḥmad, 104, 120
Khāqānī, 290
Kharkushī, Saʿīd al-, 418n24
Khiḍr, 321, 330, 334, 410n24, 418n4
Khosroes, 95
Khūʾī, Ayatollah Sayyid Abū ʾl-Qāsim al-Mūsawī al-, 47, 68

Koresh the Persian, 365
Kulaynī, Muḥammad ibn Yaʿqūb al-, 226
Kumayl ibn Ziyād, 235–36

Laozi, 216
Liu Zhi, 411n19, 412n29
Lot, 151
Lucius, 85
Luke (Evangelist), 85, 100

Maʿadd (Simon Peter?), 176, 410n25
Malachi, 84
Mālik ibn Anas, 54, 146, 160
Maʾmūn, al-, 89
Manael, 85
Mānī, 80–81
Mār Isḥāq (Isaac the Syrian), 89
Mark (Evangelist), 100
Mary (mother of Jesus), 88–92, 95, 157, 209, 311
Masrūq, 197
Masʿūdī, 412n32
Matthew (Evangelist), 101
Māturīdī as-Samarqandī, Abū Manṣūr al-, 113, 332–33, 339
Mawdūdī, Abū ʾl-ʿAlā al-, 32, 41–42
Melchizedek (Malik as-Salām), 87, 176, 410n23
Michael (archangel), 40, 104, 312
Miqdād, al-, 72
Miriam, 84
Mir Najāt Naqshband (Baba Sahrai), 283
Miyān Mīr Walī, Shaykh, 282
Moses (Mūsā), 6, 9, 15–16, 19, 72, 83–86, 93–94, 112, 118, 150–51, 156, 172, 176–79, 196–97, 210, 284, 304, 318–21, 328, 335, 338, 349, 353, 377
Muʿāwiya, 49, 81, 147–48
Muḥammad (the Prophet), ; as final prophet, 71, 97–101, 127, 167, 177–79; as law-giver, 79, 175–77, ; as object of faith, 103, 107, 282, 303–8; in the Qurʾān, 7–12, 38–40, 46, 50, 57, 208, 250, 328, 376; in Hadith, 13–26, 156–57, 210–11; truthfulness of, 348–49, 375
Muḥammad ʿAbd al-Bāqī al-Bazzāz, 94
Muḥammad ibn Abī Ḥammād, 55
Muḥammad ibn Abī Maʿshar, 55
Muḥammad ibn Kaʿb, 39
Muḥammad ibn Wāsī, 248
Muḥāsibī, Ḥārith ibn Asad al-, 146
Mujāhid, 38, 41
Mullā Ṣadrā, 205, 395
Musaylima the Liar, 80
Muslim, 50, 53, 97, 188

Nahum, 84
Najda al-Ḥanafī, 55
Najjār, Ḥusayn ibn Muḥammad an-, 144
Najm ad-Dīn Dāya Rāzī, 296, 303
Napoleon Bonaparte, 365
Nasafī, Najm ad-Dīn Abū Ḥafṣ an-, 113
Nasāʾī, an-, 53
Naṣīr ad-DīnṬūsī. *See*Ṭūsī, Naṣīr ad-Dīn
Nāṣir al-Ḥaqq wa ʾd-Dīn, 263
Nawbakhtī, Abū Muḥammad al-Ḥasan ibn Mūsā an-, 95, 371, 412n32
Naẓẓam, Ibrahīm an-, 373
Nestorius, 89–90, 95
Nimrūd, 176
Noah (Nūḥ), 151, 175, 177, 179, 304, 306, 322
Nuʿmān, al-Qāḍī an-, 412n32
Nūrī, Abū ʾl-Ḥasan, 242, 418n22
Nūrī, Shaykh, 194–195

Paul (apostle), 85, 87
Paul of Samosata, 90
Peter, Simon (apostle), 87–88, 176
Pharaoh (of Exodus), 173, 176, 320, 329
Philip, daughters of, 85
Pilate, Pontius, 89
Plato, 32, 206, 286, 402n4
Plotinus, 421n15
Porphyry, 206
Prophet, the. *See* Muḥammad
Pythagoras, 33

Qaffāl, al-, 31
Qalānisī, Abū ʿAbbās al-, 146
Qalānisī, Abū Sahl al-, 333
Qatāda, 39, 49
Qūnawī, Shaykh Ṣadr al-Dīn al-, 201, 204
Qurṭubī, 28
Qushayrī, 414n7
Quṭb, Sayyid, 31

Rabī', ar-, 29
Rāzī, Fakhr ad-Dīn ar-, 31, 56, 186–89, 421n18
Rūmī, Jalāl ad-Dīn, 279, 284, 287–289, 296

Sa'dī of Shiraz, 269,
Ṣadr ad-Dīn ash-Shīrāzī. *See* Mullā Ṣadrā
Sa'īd al-Maqbarī, 55
Sa'īd ibn Jubayr, 29, 38, 50
Ṣalāḥ ad-Dīn Ḥasan, 262
Salāma ibn Kuhayl, 374
Salāma ibn Ṣakhr, 54
Salāmān, 299 - 302
Ṣāliḥ (pre-Islamic prophet), 151
Sālim ibn Abī Ḥafṣa, 374
Sālim ibn Aḥwāz al-Mazīnī, 142
Sālim ibn Dhakwān, 146
Sanā'ī, 270, 279, 287
Saul (New Testament prophet), 85
Seh Bari, 192–193
Seraphiel, 399
Seth (Shīth), 175
Sha'bī, 49
Shāfi'ī, Muḥammad ibn Idrīs ash-, 53–54, 160
Shahrastānī, Muḥammad ibn 'Abd al-Karīm, 85–86, 137–141
Shāh Walī Allāh, 47, 65, 384, 392
Shams-i Tabrīz, 284
Shaykh al-Mufīd, 126, 211, 325
Shem (Sām, son of Noah), 175
Shiblī, 247–48, 296Shihāb ad-Dīn, 262
Sijzī, 197
Silas (New Testament figure), 85
Simon, 85
Socrates, 33, 340
Solomon, 304
Subkī, Tāj ad-Dīn as-, 57
Suddī, as-, 29, 39
Sufyān ath-Thawrī, 160
Sufyānī, as-, 230
Sufyān ibn 'Uyayna, 159
Suhrawardī, 206
Sulamī, Abū 'Abd ar-Raḥmān as-, 49
Sulaymān ibn Jarīr ar-Riqqī, 372
Sulaymān ibn Mihrān al-A'mash, 197
Sunan Bonan, 193
Suyūṭī, Jalāl ad-Dīn as-, 47, 51

Ṭabarī, 'Alī ibn Rabbān aṭ-. *See* 'Alī ibn Rabbān aṭ-Ṭabarī
Ṭabarī, Ibn Jarīr aṭ-, 28–29, 55, 72
Ṭabrisī (Ṭabarsī), 29–32, 37, 309
Ṭalḥa, 147, 374, 408n9, 413n39
Thābit ibn Qays, 56
Thaqafī, Abū Isḥāq ath-, 312–13
Thawrī, Sufyān ath-. *See* Sufyān ath-Thawrī
Tirmidhī, at-, 101, 188, 351
Ṭūsī, Muḥammad aṭ-,228
Ṭūsī, Naṣīr ad-Dīn, 175, 206, 259

'Ubāda ibn aṣ-Ṣāmit, 188
Ubayy ibn Ka'b, 38–40, 50
'Umar ibn al-'Azīz, 379
'Umar ibn al-Khaṭṭāb, 26–28, 148–49, 329, 372–78
Uriah the Hittite, 94
'Urwa, 49
Usayd ibn Khuḍayr, 25
'Uthman ibn 'Affān, 147, 341, 372–77
'Uthmān ibn Maẓ'ūn, 53
'Uzayr (Ezra), 93, 95, 156

Wāḥidī, Abū al-Ḥasan 'Alī ibn Aḥmad al-, 51–52
Wakī', 159
Walī Raslān, Shaykh, 264–65
Wang Daiyu, 214–15
Wāṣil ibn 'Aṭā' al-Ghazzāl, 140–42, 374

Yaḥyā ibn Bishr ibn 'Umayr an-Nihāwandī, 25

Zamakhsharī, az-, 30–31, 54
Zarādusht (Zarathustra, Zoroaster), 80–81
Zayd ibn Aslam, 38
Zayd ibn Thābit, 28
Ziyād, 171
Zubayr, 147, 374, 408n9, 413n39

GENERAL INDEX

Abbasid (dynasty), 253, 413n38
abrogation (*naskh*), 1, 47, 50, 65–68, 75, 94, 99, 178, 305, 308, 392, 404n24
Abyssynia (Abyssinia), 72
accidents, 34, 110, 112, 114, 118, 121–22, 139, 151–52, 158, 162, 165–67, 203, 207, 330, 333, 337, 410n10
acquisition (*iktisāb, kasb*), 141–42, 144, 242, 264, 326–30, 361
Algeria, 407n11
Allāh. *See* God
allegory, 39–40, 44, 296–97, 299, 303, 307
alms, 12–13, 24, 88, 106, 180, 410n26
alteration (of scriptures, *taḥrīf*), 94, 96–102
angel(s), 6, 8, 13, 15–16, 25, 29–30, 37–38, 50, 86, 91, 104, 111–12, 156, 166–67, 186, 196, 205, 215, 238, 240, 244, 252, 269, 278, 299–300, 312, 327, 341–42, 351–57, 394, 396–99, 417n10. *See also* Gabriel; Israfil; Munkar; Nakīr
anthropomorphism, 31, 42, 91, 145–46, 196, 199–200, 242, 244, 270, 293, 393
Antioch, 85,
Apollinarians (Christian sect), 88
ʿaqāʾid (sing. *ʿaqīda,* creed), 103, 120, 358
Arab(s), 68–71, 95, 153, 169–70, 249, 251, 320, 322, 348, 373, 405n9, 410n25
Arabic, 7–8, 64–65, 100, 169, 201, 202, 205, 215, 239, 246, 264–65, 320, 348, 367, 380, 396, 402n4, 403n21, 404n32, 406n19, 411n19
Arianism, 102
Ark (Noah's), 127, 229
Armenia, 92
asceticism (*zuhd*), 13, 55, 82, 87, 386, 391
Ashʿarites, 60, 63, 118, 164, 206–207, 210, 326, 369, 371, 375, 403n23, 409n10
Attributionists, 138, 144–46, 409n10. *See also* Traditionalists; God, attributes of

Badr, Battle of, 57, 72, 376
Baghdad, 77, 192, 196, 226, 417n8,11,13
Balance, the, 107, 116
balkafa, 42, 403n9
Banī Naḍīr (Jewish tribe), 56, 404n29
Banū Qurayẓa (Jewish tribe), 56
Barghuthīya, 144
Basin of Muḥammad, 107, 116
basmallah, 28
Basra, 340
Bedouins, 12, 155, 405n9
bidʿa, 152, 359, 366
Birk al-Ghimad, 72
Black Stone, 31, 281, 285
Brahmins, 169, 243
Brethren of Purity, 339–41
Bridge, the, 107, 116
Buddhism, 77, 215, 412n27
Buṭrīya, 372, 374
Būyid (dynasty), 77
Byzantines (Rūm), 88

Caesar, 95, 363
caliph(s), 28, 81, 140, 151, 253, 317, 329, 341, 371, 375, 377–79, 403n18, 408n19

caliphate, 67–68, 106, 377–79, 413n38, 420n3
capacity, moral (*istiṭāʿa*), 11, 20, 44, 115, 144, 255, 320–21, 323, 326–50
Chinese, 181, 214–15, 411n19,22,24
Christianity, 15, 39–40, 56, 70, 78–102, 128, 150, 173, 286, 317, 405n3,16, 406n18, 414n9. *See also* People of the Book
Christian sects. *See* Appolinarians; Donatists; Jacobites; Julianists; Macedonians; Melkites; Nestorians; Paulicians; Photinians; Sabellians
circumcision, 99
Commander of the Faithful, 211, 228–30, 235–38, 241, 311–12, 318–26, 375–77
compulsion (*jabr*), 138, 141–43, 326, 360–62, 409n11. *See also* determinism
Compulsionists, 138, 142, 333, 403n23, 409n10. *See also* Jabrites
creation, 1, 3–4, 7–9, 21–22, 41, 44–45, 61–62, 89, 113, 142, 153–54, 158–59, 162, 168–69, 173–74, 177, 181, 186–88, 191, 194–95, 208, 215, 219–25, 231, 236, 246–47, 251, 271, 327–29, 344, 350–57, 386, 393, 399, 415n37
creed, 16, 75–76, 89, 103–5, 109, 113, 116, 120, 126, 128, 135, 137, 149, 182, 235, 270, 359, 406n23, 407n1
cross, 99,
Crucifixion of Christ, 87–92, 95, 102
Cyrene, 85

Dajjāl, 106
ḍalāla (deviation), 64, 108, 126, 151–52, 158–60, 318, 359, 364, 366, 372, 383, 394, 407n1, 418n2
Damascus, 140, 196, 226, 264, 325
Dao, 215–21
Day of Judgment, 23, 212, 300, 385, 417n21
Day of the Portent, 225–26
death, 5, 8, 93–94, 107–10, 141, 153–54, 158, 179, 200, 211–12, 219, 221, 236, 277, 308, 320, 342, 363, 397–99, 408n8; of Muḥammad, 14, 75, 372–75, 403n18
Deccan, 282
demons, 16, 111–12, 222–23, 299
dervish, 282, 286, 292
determination (*qadar*), 91, 107, 138, 141, 188, 325–26, 340, 361. *See also* Muʿtazilites; Qadarites; predetermination
determinism, 326. *See also* Qadarites; predeterminism
Devil, 92–95, 252, 257, 275, 299, 350, 414n10, 415n31. *See also* Iblīs; Satan
dhikr (remembering God), 13, 257, 348, 394
dissension (*fitna*), 46, 75, 228
divorce, 157, 376. *See also ẓihār*
Donatists (Christian sect), 128

eschatology, 13, 214, 226
ethics, 10, 215, 281, 315, 317, 339, 342, 368–69, 385, 392
Europeans, 359–62, 366–67
exegesis (*tafsīr*), 1, 19, 27, 37, 41, 47–51, 75, 145, 178–80, 204, 270, 300, 404n32. *See also* hermeneutics

faith (*īmān*), 6, 8, 11–13, 18–20, 30, 37, 42, 55, 70, 72, 76–79, 81, 102, 103–4, 111, 115–16, 124, 128, 131, 137, 141–46, 149, 162, 180, 183, 195, 200, 211, 216, 237, 240–41, 245, 250–52, 257, 265–66, 276, 287–89, 293, 318–22, 340–41, 344–45, 364, 376, 393, 396, 399, 414n16
fasting, 12–13, 97, 99, 126, 180, 200, 238, 331, 336, 410n26
Fātiḥa, 23, 28, 204
feasts, 106
Fire (*an-nār*), 10, 12–17, 56, 94, 139, 142–43, 310, 328, 352–53, 383, 408n9; *See also* hellfire
fitna. *See* dissension (*fitna*)
five prayers, 97, 253
Flood, 38, 353
forgiveness, 11, 20–23, 89, 149–50, 238, 255–58, 263, 265, 288, 315, 323–26, 355, 357, 395–97
freedom, 4, 9, 14, 75, 289, 315, 317, 327, 342, 391
free will, 140–41, 290
Friends of God, 19, 36–37, 152, 193, 229, 236, 243, 274, 304, 329, 350, 352–57, 414n15

garden (*janna*), 11, 13–18, 142–43, 211, 243, 285, 312, 328, 330, 352, 354, 376–78, 391

Gehenna, 107, 156–57
genre, 16, 24, 70, 75–77, 92, 103, 233, 235, 250, 259, 269–70, 292, 296, 315, 368, 380, 385, 404n33, 407n1
ghayba (of twelfth imam), 226–30, 412n32,34
God, attributes of (general), 31, 59, 64, 86, 88, 90–91, 103, 110–18, 135, 138–46, 151, 162, 184, 186, 191–199, 202–07, 215, 242–48, 264, 270–73, 276–77, 292–300, 307, 320, 353, 355–59, 393, 408n4
God, dominion of (*qadr*), 5, 13, 16, 246, 248, 288
God, essence of (*dhāt*), 31, 45, 90, 109–17, 138–45, 180, 182, 187, 194–95, 202–7, 273–76, 297, 302, 307, 357, 407n3, 411n22
God, guidance of, 6, 9–10, 23–24, 37–41, 45, 81, 115, 149, 229, 237, 241–42, 245–47, 273, 306, 318–19, 322–23, 327–28, 347, 381, 415n37
God, hiddenness of, 44, 294, 307
God, immanence of, 1, 4–5, 22
God, justice of, 11, 38, 40, 61–64, 82, 104–5, 112–13, 119–20, 140, 153, 162–63, 257, 315, 317–26, 330, 343–48, 353–55, 361, 381–82, 408n8
God, kindness of, 113, 120, 224, 240, 242, 271, 326, 329
God, mercy of, 5, 12, 15–16, 20–23, 29, 42, 68, 108, 111, 177, 184–85, 193, 195, 201, 212–13, 224, 271, 305, 321, 323, 330–31, 347, 354, 378–80, 384, 396
God, promises of, 11, 26, 42, 89, 112–13, 149, 163, 210, 331, 377–78, 396
God, providence of, 241, 245
God, sovereignty of, 4–5, 23, 111, 190, 315, 331, 353, 381, 397
God, speech of, 23, 40, 59, 62–64, 67, 99–101, 109, 112, 114, 118, 145, 186–87, 201–9, 276, 348
God, throne of, 4–6, 21, 28–32, 108, 110, 182, 186–88, 193, 240, 271–78
God, transcendent unity of (*tawḥīd*), 4, 13, 138–39, 181, 214, 233, 242, 250, 265–68, 271, 274, 417n9
God, voice of, 135, 195–201
God, will of, 10, 28, 45, 104–5, 108, 111, 115–16, 144, 187–91, 281, 310–11, 318, 327–28, 345, 352, 360, 391
God, wisdom of, 45, 60–65, 71, 94, 97–100, 111, 125, 139, 224, 272, 323, 345, 350–57, 362, 381, 404n32
God, wrath of, 21, 84, 212, 246, 306, 311, 346, 354, 356–357, 384, 410n3
God and divine beauty (*jamāl*), 22, 145, 181–85, 304
God and divine majesty (*jalāl*), 109–10, 145, 181–85, 204, 224, 259, 272, 293, 305, 358, 363
God and freedom, 4, 9, 117, 265–66, 301, 342, 353
God and knowledge, 4, 13, 28–30, 36, 40–41, 44–46, 61–62, 86, 105, 108, 111–19, 138, 140, 143–45, 150, 158–63, 180, 184–85, 190–95, 199, 203–8, 219, 239–49, 264, 267–74, 293–97, 320–21, 331, 340, 343, 353, 357, 379, 388, 408n4
God and love, 6, 22–23, 81, 95–96, 108, 162, 164, 180, 192, 195, 259, 273, 284–86, 290, 296, 303–7, 352, 354–57, 375, 377, 415n27
God and unity of Appearance, 122
God and unity of Being, 122, 208
God as creator (*khāliq*), 3, 5–6, 8–9, 21–22, 40–41, 62, 81, 86, 93, 95, 104–16, 120–25, 139–44, 153–54, 156, 161–63, 173, 177, 181–95, 199, 203, 207–9, 214–15, 218–25, 239–42, 250, 269–76, 288–93, 308, 319–20, 323, 326–32, 344–57, 382, 385, 397, 399, 416n8
God as master (*walī*), 23, 223, 237, 294, 345, 362
God as personal Lord (*rabb*), 250; power of, 4–5, 11, 31, 45, 61, 90, 93, 110–14, 117–18, 138–45, 162, 168, 173–74, 182, 184, 187–91, 203, 205, 208–09, 219–23, 243, 246–48, 268, 271, 274–75, 283, 288, 293, 315–18, 319, 326, 348, 352–53, 356–57, 358, 381, 384
God as the almighty (*qādir al-maqdir*), 8, 69, 80, 180, 194, 305, 308, 327, 334–39, 381–82, 385–88; alterity of, 4, 42
good and evil, 119, 138–141, 144, 224, 272, 289, 352, 386, 408n8
Gospel(s), 87–89, 95, 98–102, 112, 187, 229, 323

governance, 167, 315, 371, 380–82
ghulūw (excess), 145

Hadiths (traditions), 1, 3, 12–26, 32, 50, 53, 67, 87, 97, 100–1, 106, 131–32, 186–90, 200, 226, 229, 235, 251, 257, 291–92, 303, 305, 308–12, 351, 354–55, 372–74, 395
ḥajj. *See* pilgramage (*ḥajj*)
Ḥanbalites. *See* Ḥanbalī, school of jurisprudence
Ḥanafī, school of jurisprudence, 103, 332–33
Ḥanbalī, school of jurisprudence, 58, 92–93, 103–4, 151, 186, 196, 350
Heaven, 4–9, 21, 28–33, 37–38, 43–45, 50, 86–91, 108–112, 125, 153, 161, 178–79, 186–89, 193, 197, 200, 212–26, 240, 267, 275–76, 282, 295, 298, 300, 310, 320, 324, 326, 340–42, 376, 397, 411n20
Hell, 10–11, 16, 18, 105–9, 116, 193, 212, 240, 267, 278, 300, 319–20, 328, 349–350, 374
hellfire, 14, 162, 212–13, 322, 326, 343, 347, 350, 372, 383
heresiography, 76, 85, 137, 412n32
heresy, 86, 126, 193, 359
hermeneutics, 3, 7, 25–27, 46–47, 65, 68, 75, 79, 92, 392. *See also* exegesis (*tafsīr*)
history, 52, 69–72, 75–77, 214, 226, 309, 362, 365, 367, 371, 374
Holy Spirit, 86–89, 290, 397, 406n23
Ḥudaybīya, Battle of al-, 6, 404n28
human nature, 123–24, 182, 215, 221, 307, 385
Hurmiz, 81
hypocrisy, 41–42, 93, 131, 238, 254, 321, 359, 385, 391, 419n5

Ibāḍīs, 128, 146
idolatry/associationism (*shirk*), 55, 72, 97, 105, 107, 116, 122–23, 153, 182, 213, 246–47, 327, 332, 354, 393, 408n4
iḥsān, 13, 257,
imām, 23, 29–30, 37, 40, 106, 126, 145, 175–79, 197, 211, 214, 226–31, 236, 309, 326, 366, 369, 371–79, 404n32
imamate, 40, 117, 139, 175–76, 180, 229, 368, 371–79
India, 65, 119, 270, 279–83, 288
Indonesia, 192–93, 264
infidel. *See also* unbeliever (*mushrik*), 130–33, 144, 147, 149, 193–95, 241, 281, 285–89, 306
intellect, 31–35, 47, 165–67, 173, 180, 183, 190, 207, 240–43, 247–48, 260–63, 272–74, 286, 290, 293–97, 350, 356, 397–99, 409n20
intelligibility, 165–66, 190, 206–8
intercession, 18–19, 107, 116, 213–14, 237, 303, 382, 414n15, 417n21
Iraq, 82, 116, 262, 306, 333, 340

Jabrites, 138, 142, 409n10. *See also*: compulsionists
Jacobites (Christian sect), 88–92, 95
Jahmites, 109, 142
jalāl. *See* God and divine majesty
jamāl. *See* God and divine beauty
Javanese, 192
Jerusalem, 66, 85, 196
jihād, 67–68, 97, 106, 281, 352, 410n26
jinn, 8, 28, 48, 69–70, 97, 111–12, 239, 282, 319, 323, 328, 345, 348–351, 355
Judaism, 6, 15, 39–40, 56–58, 79, 81, 87, 92–99, 102, 145, 150, 340, 405n3. *See also* People of the Book
judgment, 11, 17, 33, 48, 89, 109, 115, 127–32, 146–150, 155, 158, 185, 218–220, 241, 248, 268, 275, 284, 295, 323, 340, 347, 370, 372, 375, 378–379, 404n32. *See also* Day of Judgment
Julianists (Christian sect), 88, 92
jurisprudence (*fiqh*), 104, 128, 161, 369
justice, 31, 97, 106, 112, 138–39, 161–64, 226, 292, 300, 321, 360–61, 364, 367, 370–73, 380–85. *See also* God, justice of

Kaʿba, 31, 97, 156, 276, 281, 286, 288, 290
kalām, 42, 135, 137, 151–60, 187–90, 201, 209, 270, 348, 368, 371
kalima (word, articulation), 103, 406n17
Karramites, 146
Khārijites (Ar.: Khawārij, "Seceders"), 128, 163, 325, 333, 373
knowledge: discursive (*ʿilm*), 235–39, 242, 244–45, 261, 273, 390, 416n38; experiential (*maʿrifa*), 139, 144–45, 233, 235–49,

knowledge: discursive (*'ilm*) (*continued*)
269, 271, 273, 276–77, 416n8. *See also* God and knowledge
Kufa, 147, 405n10, 413n38

language, 8–11, 32, 43, 76, 96–97, 100, 120, 125, 196, 215, 248, 251, 269, 287, 292, 320, 380, 404n32. *See also* Arabic; Javanese; Persian; Urdu
law (Muslim), 52, 54, 61–62, 67, 71–72, 89, 100, 129, 157–58, 177–80, 199, 215, 244–45, 292, 299, 301, 331–32, 340–343, 366–67, 384, 393–94, 406n26
Law (Torah). *See* Torah
legal theory. *See* law (Muslim)
li'ān, 54, 403n16
Light, Verse of, 5–7, 32–46,
literature, 41, 233
love, 53, 81, 88, 95–96, 192, 251, 257, 267, 273, 281–286, 288–292, 303–7, 352, 356, 381, 385. *See also* God and love

Macedonians (Christian sect), 88
madhhab (school of jurisprudence), 128, 146, 262, 390
Magi, 105, 138, 381–382
Mālikī, school of jurisprudence, 146
Mamlūk (Egypt), 51
Manichaeism, 79–80
ma'rifa. See knowledge: experiential (*ma'rifa)*
marriage, 89, 94, 267, 312, 377
martyrdom, 72
Marw (modern Merv, Iran), 142
Materialists, 154
matter, 36, 121–23, 165–68, 206–7, 351, 353, 399
Mazdians, 96. *See also* Zoroastrians
Mecca, 40, 49, 51, 56–57, 286, 290, 309, 335
Medina, 12, 28, 51, 67, 419n13
Melkites (Christian sect), 87–95
metaphor, 31–34, 41–42, 77, 88, 196, 396
miracle: prophetic (*mu'jiz*), 164, 167–68, 173
monasticism, 99, 286, 395
monotheism, 131–32, 173, 265, 405n4
Mother of the Qur'ān, 23
Munkar, 106, 115
Murji'ites (Postponers), 104, 141, 146–51, 163, 373–74
mushrik. See infidel; unbeliever (*mushrik*)
Mustadrika, 144
mutakallimūn, 135, 145, 153–54, 199, 205
Mu'tazilites, 30–31, 58, 63–64, 89–90, 103, 116, 138–146, 160, 193, 196, 206, 208, 211, 229, 240, 333, 342, 369, 372–74, 408n9, 409n10. *See also* determinism
mysticism, 192–94, 201, 233, 239, 246, 250, 265–67, 276, 287, 295, 385, 389, 416n8, 417n11, 419n4

nabīdh, 66
Najdīya, 373
Najjārīya, 144, 409n10
Nakīr, 107, 115
Naqshbandī, 201
nature, 113, 124, 143, 154, 217–18, 221, 224, 261, 272, 293, 297, 342, 359–60, 362, 366, 396
Nestorians (Christian sect), 87–91, 95, 102
non-Muslim, 5, 69, 75–76, 79, 85, 92

Ottoman, 201, 367

pagan, 79, 375
parable, 44–45, 81, 287, 296
Paradise, 14, 29, 40, 89, 106–9, 116, 213, 244, 285, 292, 310–12, 343–48, 391. *See also* garden
Paulicians (Christian sect), 88
Pen, the, 107, 188, 191–192, 346
People of the Book, 53, 55, 58, 95–98, 150, 323–24. *See also* Christianity, Judaism
People of the Qibla, 105–6, 132, 148, 150
People of Truth, 113–14, 202
Peripatetics, 206, 284
Persia, 270, 288, 363, 365, 381–82, 405n8
Persian (language), 120, 201, 215, 238–39, 259, 270, 277–78, 303, 380, 416n1
philosophers, 32–34, 87–90, 119, 140, 164, 177, 188–191, 195, 201, 206, 262–64, 284–85, 340, 362, 368, 386, 395, 408n5
philosophy, 32, 85, 137, 260–64, 284–85, 297, 367–68, 384, 395, 411n19
Photinians (Christian sect), 88
piety (*zuhd*), 13, 82, 96, 237, 256, 258, 295

pilgrimage (*ḥajj*), 97, 106, 159, 180, 334–35, 376, 401n2, 410n26; Farewell Pilgrimage, 127
pluralism, 75
poetry, 69–70, 169, 201, 233, 270, 287, 289, 292, 303, 385, 389, 404n33
polytheism, 130, 133, 162, 213, 265–68, 346. *See also* idolatry/associationism
poor, 11, 93, 252, 282, 299, 383, 418n4
poor tax, 97
prayer, 6, 12–13, 23, 26, 66, 80, 99–100, 126, 180, 184, 203, 247, 253–54, 282, 286, 306, 313, 322, 334, 372, 376, 398, 410n26. *See also* five prayers
predetermination, 14, 104–8, 111, 138, 141, 325, 408n8.
predeterminism, 140, 317
Preserved Table(t), the, 49, 107, 187, 194, 246
promise and threat, 48, 112–113, 139, 161, 163, 326, 331, 341–343
punishment, 11, 15, 30, 53–54, 89, 106–7, 113–17, 127, 139, 143, 157, 163, 185, 213, 237–38, 245, 258, 288, 299–301, 311, 318, 322–23, 329–31, 344–47, 361, 384, 391, 394

Qadarites, 138, *See also* determinism; Muʿtazilites
Qaḥṭān, 82, 405n9
Qāʾim, 230–31, 412n30, 34, 413n37
Qaraites, 145
qibla, 147, 149
Qūmis, 82, 405n8
Qurʾān: as Book [recording a person's deeds], 116; created/uncreated, 47, 58–59, 109, 112, 114, 139, 144, 146, 158–60; generality and specificity of meaning, 10, 52, 54–58; inimitability of, 7, 47, 68–73, 75; literary analysis of, 41; memorization of, 98, 100, 418n24
Quraysh, 106, 173, 373, 379

Rāfiḍī, 333
Ramaḍān, 13, 24, 97, 331
Rayy (modern Rey, Iran), 144
rebellion, political, 140, 384
recitation, 8, 23–26, 30, 49, 93, 100, 109, 112–14, 187, 204, 252–53, 257–58, 304, 326, 402n31
repentance (*tawba*), 13, 16, 20, 139, 142, 175, 183–85, 213, 322–23, 347, 354, 357
responsibility, human, 4, 11, 14, 20–21, 42, 75, 126, 138, 315–18, 326, 342, 358, 361, 366, 368, 380, 395
resurrection (*qiyāma*), 13, 16, 89, 115, 153–54, 173–80, 204, 209, 291, 299–300, 303, 307, 421n20;Day of Resurrection, 5, 18–21, 26, 40, 87, 107–9, 188, 197, 303–8, 312, 354
Return (*maʿād*), the, 117, 260, 326, 411n20
revelation, 1–4, 7–9, 22, 25, 48–60, 66, 69, 79, 86, 96, 119, 139, 158, 164–167, 177–180, 191, 242–246, 250–55, 263–266, 303, 324, 376–77, 381, 394, 417n12; context of (or circumstances of) (*asbāb an-nuzūl),* 24, 51–58, 75
Rustamid Imamate, 407n11

Sabaʾīya, 148–149
Sabellians (Christian sect), 88
Sacred Hadith, 1, 22, 305, 395, 417n15
Ṣaḥīḥ, 50, 188
scripture, alteration of (*taḥrīf*), 96–102
Shādhilī order, 287
Shāfiʿī, school of jurisprudence, 53–54, 103
schism, 147–151
Seat, 193
senses (five), 59–65, 113, 158, 160, 183, 199, 273–74, 298, 362,
shahāda (testimony), 103, 109, 142, 401n2, 410n26
sharʿ (divine ordinance), 145, 253
Sharia, 71–72, 89, 160–61, 256, 260, 263, 299, 343, 367, 384, 406n26
Shīʿa/Shīʿī, 1, 27, 29, 32, 37, 47, 68, 116, 126, 145–46, 164, 175, 181, 205, 211, 214, 226–31, 235, 259, 296, 309–12, 325, 369–71, 379–82, 403n18, 406n19, 408n9, 412n30, 420n3
shirk. See idolatry/associationism
skepticism, 77, 284
Ṣiffīn, battle of, 128, 325, 405n10, 408n9
slander, 54, 133, 238, 321
Sodom and Gommorah, 16
Sophists, 113, 361
spirits, 28, 35–37, 89, 219, 222–23, 268, 367, 397

spiritual master, 252
Stoics, 206
substances, 90–95, 110, 114, 180, 203, 225
substitution (within scriptures, *tabdīl*), 96–99
Sufi, 182–83, 192–93, 201–4, 235, 238–39, 244, 270, 286–87, 403n10, 407n3, 413n4, 416n8, 417n20
sultan, 201, 282–83, 367, 380, 383
Sunna, 56, 97–101, 104–6, 109, 129, 146, 152, 155–61, 188–90, 197–201, 210, 343, 362–64, 368, 373, 379, 407n1, 414n20
Sunnī, 42, 120, 229–30, 240, 244, 309–311, 333, 371, 375, 403n18, 413n38
suspending judgment, 109, 128–31, 147–50, 158, 407n10
Syria, 39, 92, 148, 288
Syriac, 202, 405n14

Tablet (archetypal scripture), 49, 187, 193–94, 209, 246
tajsīm, 199–200. *See also* anthropomorphism
taklīf, 143
Tamīm, tribe of, 186
taqṣīr, 145
tashbīya, 142. *See also* anthropomorphism
taʿṭīl (stripping the deity of attributes), 144–45, 192, 354
tawba. *See* repentance (*tawba*)
taʾwīl (deeper meaning of Scripture), 40, 46–49, 139, 145–46, 178–79
tawḥīd (unity). *See* God, transcendent unity of
Tawrāt, 202–4
Throne Verse, 4, 24, 27–32, 271
Tirmidh (modern Termez, Uzbekistan), 142
Torah, 15, 86, 93–94, 98–99, 112, 145, 156, 187, 229, 323
Traditionalists, 42, 58, 92, 104, 140–41, 145–46, 196, 350, 384, 408n6. *See also* Attributionists
transcendence, 145, 249–51, 293–94, 297, 393
Trinity (*ithbāt at-tathlīth*), 88, 91
Trumpet, the, 107, 421n20
truth, 8, 24, 37, 40, 44–47, 59–61, 69–72, 77–86, 89–91, 101, 105, 113, 118–19, 123–25, 133, 141, 149, 161–66, 179–80, 183–86, 196–206, 243–44, 249, 260–65, 273, 280, 285, 295, 298–305, 308, 318–19, 331, 343, 347, 360, 363, 367, 374–77, 406n16. *See also* People of Truth
Turks, 270, 380

Umayyad (dynasty), 128, 142, 325, 413n38
unbeliever (*mushrik*), 15, 37, 68, 75, 106, 109, 115–16, 125, 131–32, 139–42, 151, 159–63, 195, 199, 240–43, 286, 306, 322, 327, 335, 343–46, 407n1. *See also* infidel
universals, problem of, 34, 55–58, 117, 165, 167, 169, 183, 192, 203, 206–207
Urdu, 120, 270, 278

Verse of Light, 5, 32–46
virtues (*faḍāʾil*), 13, 37, 254–55, 376, 383
virtuous behavior (*adab*), 13, 256, 368, 370, 384,

war, 57, 69, 71–72, 101, 128, 180, 212, 282, 349, 367, 370
Wāṣilīya, 140–42
wisdom (*ḥikma*), 33, 40, 63, 94, 97, 99–100, 119, 124, 127, 176, 194, 205, 215, 224, 235–36, 264, 269–72, 286, 297, 301–2, 345, 350, 361, 386. *See also* God, wisdom of
women, 13, 29, 55, 105, 149, 291, 309–12, 364
Word (of God), 19, 58, 86–92, 101, 209, 323, 341, 349, 364

Yemen, 92, 186, 288
yin and yang, 216, 221

Ẓaʿafranīya, 144
Ẓāhirī, school of jurisprudence, 251, 384
ẓihār, 54, 56. *See also* divorce
Zoroastrians, 79–80. *See also* Mazdians

INDEX OF QUR'ANIC CITATIONS

Sura:verse	*Page*
Sura 1	204
1:4	308, 330
Sura 2	25, 168
2:2	3
2:7	241
2:23	404n31
2:26–27	318
2:28	397
2:30	205
2:41	324
2:62	300
2:80	94
2:81	393
2:81–82	11
2:87	399
2:89	207
2:106	65, 68
2:109	275
2:111	150
2:115	6
2:128–29	100
2:134	150, 379
2:136	9
2:140–41	150
2:141	150
2:142–45	66
2:151	97
2:156	365
2:186	6, 7
2:195	259
2:204	55
2:231	97, 99
2:235	258
2:253	150
2:255	4, 24, 27–28
2:256	231
2:258	397
2:259	210
2:270	213
2:281	50
2:284	20
2:286	11, 20, 124, 320, 323, 329, 344, 415n28
Sura 3	168
3:7	7, 46–47, 63, 208, 318, 349
3:14	294
3:26	381
3:27	258
3:31	303, 305
3:34	175
3:45	406n17
3:45–47	406n16
3:49	405n16
3:55	399, 406n17
3:59	208
3:61	191
3:70	324
3:97	334, 335
3:103	229
3:106	185
3:110	364, 368
3:121–29	417n19
3:128	306
3:134	12
3:164	99
3:173–74	363
3:178	320
3:179	351
3:181	93
3:183	156
3:188	53, 55
4:10	212
4:12	403n17
4:14	212
4:29–30	212
4:31	213
4:48	213
4:51	57
4:58	58
4:59	381
4:65	391
4:78	321
4:79	321
4:83	330
4:93	212

Sura:verse	*Page*
4:94	258
4:113	97, 99, 191
4:170	324
4:171	209, 324, 406n17
4:174	308
4:176	50, 403n17
5:4	304
5:9–10	11
5:10	405n16
5:15	209
5:16	110, 323
5:17	91, 308
5:18	95
5:24	72
5:38	55
5:49	56
5:54	375
5:57	304
5:64	6, 93, 185
5:65–66	323
5:70	180
5:72	91
5:73	88
5:93	53
5:119	378, 391
5:158	406n17
6:28	240
6:35	319, 327
6:61	397, 399, 421n18
6:75–79	153
6:76	246, 414n11
6:82	55
6:91	156, 239
6:102–35	
6:111	240, 327
6:122	239, 241
6:125	322, 327
6:145	53
6:152	11, 324
6:164	162, 346, 346
6:165	399
7:2–3	7
7:7	199
7:10	419n6
7:12	291
7:29	154
7:33	129
7:42	11
7:43	328
7:52	275
7:54	178, 187
7:96	324
7:138	93
7:143	118, 204, 210
7:144	196
7:145	208
7:155	328
7:179	300, 319, 349
7:186	246
7:188	260, 328
8:16	212
8:24	6
8:42	139
8:67	376
8:68	376
8:73	67
Sura 9	50
9:40	375
9:42	321, 335
9:43	325
9:61	148
9:71	149
9:94	148
9:126	347
9:128	50
10:1–2	3
10:3	187
10:10	210
10:23	327
10:27	210
10:31	404n31
10:35	229
10:44	343
10:99	319, 327
11:1	348
11:1–2	8
11:6	332
11:7	187
11:13	404n31
11:32	322
11:33	322
11:34	322
11:56	6
11:106–7	212
11:107	143, 144
11:108	213
Sura 12	3
12:1–2	8
13:1	8
13:2	4
13:11	11, 328
13:16	153, 327
13:17	341
13:26	332
13:27	318
13:29	294
14:1	8
14:4	10
14:11	183
14:27	149, 318
14:28	210
14:40	330
15:1	3
15:3	304
15:9	308
15:29	399
15:39	328
15:47	378
15:49–50	185
15:72	249
15:85	298
16:17	191
16:22	393
16:28	399
16:36–37	10

Sura:verse	Page
16:44	99
16:53	163
16:66	396
16:93	328
16:96–97	11
16:101–3	8
17:15	346
17:20	186
17:32	324
17:33	324
17:34	324
17:36	129
17:38	345, 415n27
17:48	334
17:82	201
17:84	306
17:85	399
17:88	48, 70, 100, 348, 404n31
17:88–93	8
Sura 18	318
18:6	319
18:17	10
18:28	241
18:64–82	418n4
18:65	321
18:67	330, 334, 338
18:72	330
18:75	330
18:82	321
18:101	330
19:16–21	406n16
19:17	91
19:29–33	406n16
19:59	322
20:4	275
20:5	31
20:12	196
20:15	346
20:39	6
20:50	415n37
20:51	150
20:52	150, 379
20:61	324
20:114	25, 191
20:121	16
20:122	352
21:2	348
21:22	152, 250
21:23	331
21:27	213
21:30	398
21:31	125
21:34	14
21:50	348
21:98	156
21:101	157, 329
21:103	276
21:104	154
21:105	186
21:107	305
22:39	68
22:47	149, 178
22:54	149
23:18–22	125
23:35	153
23:36	153
23:91	153
23:106	328
24:1	3
24:4	54
24:6–9	403n16
24:35	6, 32, 33, 36, 37
24:55	377
Sura 25	26
25:44	301
25:59	187
26:21	413n34
26:192–96	7
26:193–94	208
26:214	406n28
27:24	325
27:62–63	5
27:88	344
28:8	320
28:20	209
28:56	10
28:68	229
28:69	6
28:88	107
29:46	9
29:48	208
29:49	208
29:57	308
29:61	125
29:63	125
30:6	149
30:20–25	125
30:22–23	9
30:27	153, 354
30:40	332
30:41	329
30:45	330
30:46	125
30:47–53	9
30:48	125
31:13	55
32:4	5
32:7	344
32:11	397, 399
32:13	328
32:17	342
33:4	403n15
33:33	310
33:34	97, 100
33:37	348
33:40	83, 307
33:44	210
33:46	38, 39
33:53	376

Sura:verse	Page
33:59	376
33:72	419n6
35:3	327
35:45	329
36:12	155
36:69	348
36:78	153
36:79	153
36:80	154
37:96	327
37:165–66	294
38:27	325
38:47	150
38:75	185, 208, 309
38:82	245
39:5	125
39:7	346
39:18	323
39:22	241
39:23	348
39:33	375
39:42	397, 399
39:53	213
39:54	213
39:67	5
39:71	328
40:3	185
40:7	29
40:16	298
40:18	213
40:31	343, 345
40:85	322
41:37–38	9
41:43	48
41:46	11
41:53	294
42:11	63, 108, 155, 251, 349, 353
42:30	329
42:40	255, 415n27
42:51	191
42:51–53	9
43:57–58	157
43:58	173
45:3–5	9
45:20	9
45:23	10
46:9	180
46:12	348
46:17	54
46:41	324
47:19	149
48:2	396
48:10	6, 275
48:18	378
48:23	302
48:27	290
Sura 49	12
49:7	241
49:9	163
49:13	56, 373
49:14–15	12
49:17	12
50:3	153
50:16	108, 294
50:16–18	6
50:17–18	186
50:28	209
50:30	278
51:19	12
51:47	6
51:56	239, 345
51:56–57	349
52:34	404n31
55:1–5	191
55:26–27	6, 121
56:6	298
56:10–11	303
56:27–28	185
56:41–42	185
56:58–59	156
56:77–78	187
56:78–79	208
56:79	100
56:90–91	303
57:1–6	5
57:4	6, 108
57:10	375
57:21	324
57:27	395
58:1–4	403n15
58:7	7, 108
58:11	399
59:5	404n29
59:10	379
61:5	318
61:8	70
62:9	398
64:16	334, 335
65:7	11, 344
66:1	325
66:5	376
67:1–3	5
67:2	397
67:3	344
68:4	255
71:26	306
71:27	346

Sura:verse	*Page*
74:1	50
75:1	26
75:16	25
75:16–17	26
75:18	26
75:19	26
75:22	185, 304
75:22–23	7, 210
75:24	185
76:8–9	12
76:21	304
76:29–30	10
78:37	298
79:16	197
80:38–39	185
80:40–41	185
81:29	328
82:14–16	212
84:6	398
84:20	324
88:2–3	185
88:8–9	185
88:17	210
88:17–20	125
89:22	349
89:23	275
89:27–28	399
90:12–19	12
91:8	186
92:7	186
92:10	186
92:17–18	56
94:1	413n4, 417n10
95:4–5	412n28
96:1	49
96:1–5	191, 192
97:4	208
99:4–5	7
Sura 110	50
110:1	50
Sura 112	24, 31
112:1–4	354
112:4	155, 183